WRITING

༄ ༅

THE TRANSLATION OF MEMORY

Eve Shelnutt
Ohio University

Exercises
by Daniel Lowe
Indiana University of Pennsylvania

Macmillan Publishing Company
NEW YORK

Editor: *Diane Kraut*
Production: *Publication Services, Inc.*
Manufacturing Manager: *Nick Sklitsis*
Cover Designer: *Blake Logan*
Cover Art: *Study for* La Grande Jatte *by Georges Seurat*

This book was set in Galliard by Publication Services, Inc., and printed and bound by Halliday Lithograph. The cover was printed by Phoenix Color Corp.

Copyright © 1990 by Macmillan Publishing Company, a division of Macmillan, Inc.

Printed in the United States of America

All rights reserved. No part of this book may be reproduced or transmitted in any form or by any means, electronic or mechanical, including photocopying, recording, or any information storage and retrieval system, without permission in writing from the Publisher.

Macmillan Publishing Company
866 Third Avenue, New York, New York 10022

Collier Macmillan Canada, Inc.

Library of Congress Cataloging-in-Publication Data

Writing—the translation of memory / [edited by] Eve Shelnutt;
  introduction and exercises by Daniel Lowe.
    p. cm.
    ISBN 0-02-409820-5
    1. College readers. 2. English language—Rhetoric. I. Shelnutt, Eve, 1943–
PE1417.W737 1990   89-12773
808.0427—dc20   CIP

Preface

IN the first composition and creative writing courses I taught, I noticed that students undervalued their own experiences as sources of material. What was missing from their writing was a sense of the writer's authority, as if what they envisioned as their material was either too newly encountered to assess or too far in the past to be real. What they did not themselves believe turned into writing that was, if not unbelievable, less than convincing.

As I contemplated the problem, I realized that what the students failed to honor was their memories and the *distance* that memory provides. A person in the act of remembering is in two places at once: in the real place and time of the present and in the place and time recollected. The difference between the times and places produces a heightened awareness within the individual remembering; and from that awareness, a perspective emerges, a new way of seeing.

To develop that sense of perspective in my students, I began to assign them "memory exercises." A typical assignment might be this: "As quickly as possible, write everything you remember about the kitchen of your home on a Sunday morning in winter." I also required them to write stories and essays about the origins of other stories and essays they had written and to read the work of established writers who had written about the sources of their material. Each time the classes met, students talked about the experiences they had had while writing their "memories," and what they discovered was that the more they wrote, the deeper they went into memory. They began to appreciate the wealth that was stored there and to use it to seed their writing with details that brought it to life.

Writing essays about what they had written seemed to help students as much as the memory exercises I gave them. These essays forced students to ask themselves: What did I do in that particular piece of writing? What did I think of as I constructed it? How did I use memory in its formation? How did the writing develop and change as it took shape? How do I evaluate it now? The questions produced a tension or keen awareness of the difference between the original writer, then, and the evaluating writer, now. One piece of writing spawned another and another. As students completed their process analyses, they realized that the analyses themselves reflected another period in which the writer shaped material. The analyses in turn could be analyzed profitably and reconstructed. Students began to see the process of writing as fluid, as full of potential for revision, as a *continuing* piece of writing.

Ultimately, the students began to speak of all types of writing as *fictions*— as shaped material in which the conscious choice and arrangement of content creates an invention that is not so much factual as *suggestive* of a truth. This principle applies to the expository essay as well as to the short story.

In recognizing this similarity between fiction and essay, *Writing: The Translation of Memory* contains both short stories and essays. In both forms, the writers discuss their processes of shaping material. I believe you will be as fascinated as I am to follow the approach these writers take to both genres in seeding form with experience, to watch the demands of form *as* it evolves and points the writer one way instead of another, and to appreciate the quixotic nature of writing that many of these writers acknowledge in their process essays.

Because all but a few of the writers in the text wrote the process essays at my request specifically for this book or for my classes, I want to thank all of them for allowing us to enter their minds as writers and for participating wholeheartedly in the project of *Writing: The Translation of Memory*. They have made, among so many other writers I've been privileged to know as a teacher and writer, my teaching of writing perpetually exciting and fulfilling. I would also like to thank Anthony English of Macmillan for his faith in and support of this project; Diane Kraut for her fine editorial assistance; my former colleagues at the University of Pittsburgh for their encouragement, especially Dr. Alec Stuart, Dean of the Honors College for which the course "Autobiography and the Creative Impulse" was created, Dr. Phil Smith, Dr. Steve Carr, Dr. Paul Bové, Dr. Jim Knapp, Dr. Mariolina Salivatore, and Dr. Harry Mooney; my present colleagues at Ohio University for their enthusiasm; and my husband, Mark Shelton, for his abiding support in this and all of my writing and editing projects. And I would especially like to acknowledge the assistance of Daniel Lowe, whose superior work as a fiction writer, poet, teacher, and theorist in composition proved invaluable. He not only helped me assess the material in the text as it came in, but also wrote the apparatus accompanying the text: the questions and assignments in the text and the *Instructor's Manual*. He has brought unusually keen insight into the text. His views on it were never from a disinterested position, but were those of a writer and a thinker about writing whose passion is language and the intricate rewards and challenges of writing.

E.S.

Contents

Introduction	1

I. Rites of Passage

Kathleen George, **The Dance at St. Theresa's** *(fiction)*	7
Process Essay: **Truth**	15
Garnett Kilberg, **Thieves** *(fiction)*	22
Process Essay: **Composing "Thieves"**	32
Barbara H. Hudson, **My Father's Books** *(nonfiction)*	41
Process Essay: **Sources of "My Father's Books"**	46
Kevin Stemmler, **Branches** *(fiction)*	51
Process Essay: **Autobiographical Sources of "Branches"**	58
Sally Flecker, **Learning to Speak** *(nonfiction)*	63
Process Essay: **On the Importance of Washing a Priestly Foot**	71

II. Place and the Landscape of Memory

Mark L. Shelton, **White Castle: Sometimes Nothing Else Will Do** *(nonfiction)*	77
Version I	80
Version II	81
Process Essay: **Hamburger Journalism: An Essay on the Blending of Memory and Myth**	83
Kathryn M. Monahan, **God's Country** *(fiction)*	91
Process Essay: **Notes on Writing "God's Country"**	99
Jane McCafferty, **Eyes of Others** *(fiction)*	106
Process Essay: **The Sources of "Eyes of Others"**	118
Garnett Kilberg, **My Parents' First House** *(nonfiction)*	124
Process Essay: **Considerations When Writing "My Parents' First House"**	128

David Martin, **Sunday Morning** *(fiction)* — 136
  PROCESS ESSAY: "Sunday Morning": A Commotion of Memory and Place — 142

Daniel Lowe, **Heritage** *(fiction)* — 147
  PROCESS ESSAY: "Heritage": Autobiographical Sources — 157

III. Portraits

Karen Swenson, **My Aunt Elizabeth** *(nonfiction)* — 165
  PROCESS ESSAY: On Writing the Essay "My Aunt Elizabeth" — 170

Barbara Mellix, **When They Come** *(fiction)* — 176
  PROCESS ESSAY: The Sources of "When They Come" — 184

Kathleen A. Coppula, **Reason** *(fiction)* — 192
  PROCESS ESSAY: Sources for the Story, "Reason" — 201

Eleanor Bergholz, **Suspending Dread** *(nonfiction)* — 207
  PROCESS ESSAY: Sources for "Suspending Dread" — 210

Melissa Greene, **All the Hours of the Night** *(nonfiction)* — 215
  PROCESS ESSAY: Essay on Midwife Story — 225

Julianne Moore, **Vanishing** *(fiction)* — 232
  PROCESS ESSAY: Sources of "Vanishing" — 241

IV. Views: Position and Perspective

Mark L. Shelton, **Notes on the Writing of Medical Nonfiction** *(nonfiction)* — 249
  PROCESS ESSAY: The Usual Constraints — 256

Mark Collins, **Reporters Do Have a Heart** *(nonfiction)* — 263
  People Are Too Scared *(nonfiction)* — 264
  PROCESS ESSAY: Sources for "Reporters Do Have a Heart" and "People Are Too Scared" — 266

Eve Shelnutt, **Questions of Travel** *(fiction)* — 270
  PROCESS ESSAY: The Sources of "Questions of Travel" — 276

Daniel Lowe, **Elie Wiesel: A Response to Some of the Autobiographical Works** *(nonfiction)* — 286
  PROCESS ESSAY: The Wiesel Commentary: Sources — 289

Sally Flecker, **Feminine and Masculine Voices: The Beauty of the Countryside** *(nonfiction)* — 294
  PROCESS ESSAY: The Odd Couple — 299

Kathleen A. Coppula, **Not for Literary Reasons: The Fiction of Grace Paley** *(nonfiction)* — 303
PROCESS ESSAY: **Being Heard** — 311

V. *Culture in Experience*

Linda Mizejewski, **The Erotic Stripped Bare** *(nonfiction)* — 317
PROCESS ESSAY: **Sources of "The Erotic Stripped Bare"** — 326

Cynthia Kadohata, **South Springs** *(fiction)* — 335
PROCESS ESSAY: **Sources of "South Springs"** — 342

Catherine D. Miller, **The Use of Contemporary Culture in American Fiction: A Question of Mystery** *(nonfiction)* — 346
PROCESS ESSAY: **Getting Rid of the Audience: What I Have to Do Before I Write** — 352

Elwin Green, **Quest** *(fiction)* — 361
PROCESS ESSAY: **In Quest of "Quest"** — 370

James McCommons, **Michigan's "Peace Invasion"** *(nonfiction)* — 377
PROCESS ESSAY: **Sources for "Michigan's 'Peace Invasion'"** — 384

VI. *Language as the Shaper of Identity*

Barbara Mellix, **From Outside, In** *(nonfiction)* — 389
PROCESS ESSAY: **Sources for "From Outside, In"** — 398

Laura Lynn Brown, **Praying with a Pencil: The Writer's Journal as Religious Quest** *(nonfiction)* — 403
PROCESS ESSAY: **Towards the Mirage of Truth** — 413

Min-zhan Lu, **From Silence to Words: Writing as Struggle** *(nonfiction)* — 420
PROCESS ESSAY: **"Writing as Struggle": Conversions and Conversations** — 432

Kevin Stemmler, **Boo, Boot, Boots: Building Language** *(nonfiction)* — 438
PROCESS ESSAY: **Finding the Root** — 444

Ingrid Mundari, **Language as Image Maker** *(nonfiction)* — 450
PROCESS ESSAY: **Essay on "Language as Image Maker": The Shaper and the Shaped** — 455

Notes on Contributors — 461

Rhetorical Contents

I. Analogy/Metaphor

Laura Lynn Brown, **Praying with a Pencil: The Writer's Journal as Religious Quest** *(nonfiction)* — 403
PROCESS ESSAY: **Towards the Mirage of Truth** — 413

Kevin Stemmler, **Branches** *(fiction)* — 51
PROCESS ESSAY: **Autobiographical Sources of "Branches"** — 58

Sally Flecker, **Learning to Speak** *(nonfiction)* — 63
PROCESS ESSAY: **On the Importance of Washing a Priestly Foot** — 71

Mark Collins, **Reporters Do Have a Heart** *(nonfiction)* — 263
People Are Too Scared *(nonfiction)* — 264
PROCESS ESSAY: **Sources for "Reporters Do Have a Heart" and "People Are Too Scared"** — 266

II. Argument and Persuasion

Mark L. Shelton, **Notes on the Writing of Medical Nonfiction** *(nonfiction)* — 249
PROCESS ESSAY: **The Usual Constraints** — 256

Daniel Lowe, **Elie Wiesel: A Response to Some of the Autobiographical Works** *(nonfiction)* — 286
PROCESS ESSAY: **The Wiesel Commentary: Sources** — 289

Mark Collins, **Reporters Do Have a Heart** *(nonfiction)* — 263
People Are Too Scared *(nonfiction)* — 264
PROCESS ESSAY: **Sources for "Reporters Do Have a Heart" and "People Are Too Scared"** — 266

Catherine D. Miller, **The Use of Contemporary Culture in American Fiction: A Question of Mystery** *(nonfiction)* — 346
PROCESS ESSAY: **Getting Rid of the Audience: What I Have to Do Before I Write** — 352

Linda Mizejewski, **The Erotic Stripped Bare** *(nonfiction)*   317
   PROCESS ESSAY: **Sources of "The Erotic Stripped Bare"**   **326**

III. Cause and Effect

Barbara H. Hudson, **My Father's Books** *(nonfiction)*   41
   PROCESS ESSAY: **Sources of "My Father's Books"**   **46**

Cynthia Kadohata, **South Springs** *(fiction)*   335
   PROCESS ESSAY: **Sources of "South Springs"**   **342**

Karen Swenson, **My Aunt Elizabeth** *(nonfiction)*   165
   PROCESS ESSAY: **On Writing the Essay "My Aunt Elizabeth"**   **170**

Min-zhan Lu, **From Silence to Words: Writing as Struggle** *(nonfiction)*   420
   PROCESS ESSAY: **"Writing as Struggle": Conversions and Conversations**   **432**

Kathleen A. Coppula, **Reason** *(fiction)*   192
   PROCESS ESSAY: **Sources for the Story, "Reason"**   **201**

Ingrid Mundari, **Language as Image Maker** *(nonfiction)*   450
   PROCESS ESSAY: **Essay on "Language as Image Maker": The Shaper and the Shaped**   **455**

Elwin Green, **Quest** *(fiction)*   361
   PROCESS ESSAY: **In Quest of "Quest"**   **370**

IV. Illustration/Example

Melissa Greene, **All the Hours of the Night** *(nonfiction)*   215
   PROCESS ESSAY: **Essay on Midwife Story**   **225**

James McCommons, **Michigan's "Peace Invasion"** *(nonfiction)*   377
   PROCESS ESSAY: **Sources for "Michigan's 'Peace Invasion'"**   **384**

Garnett Kilberg, **My Parents' First House** *(nonfiction)*   124
   PROCESS ESSAY: **Considerations When Writing "My Parents' First House"**   **128**

Linda Mizejewski, **The Erotic Stripped Bare** *(nonfiction)*   317
   PROCESS ESSAY: **Sources of "The Erotic Stripped Bare"**   **326**

Sally Flecker, **Learning to Speak** *(nonfiction)*   63
   PROCESS ESSAY: **On the Importance of Washing a Priestly Foot**   **71**

Sally Flecker, **Feminine and Masculine Voices: The Beauty of the Countryside** *(nonfiction)*   294
   PROCESS ESSAY: **The Odd Couple**   **299**

Kathleen A. Coppula, **Not for Literary Reasons: The Fiction of Grace Paley** *(nonfiction)*   303
   PROCESS ESSAY: **Being Heard**   **311**

V. Narration

Garnett Kilberg, **Thieves** *(fiction)*	22
PROCESS ESSAY: Composing "Thieves"	32
Karen Swenson, **My Aunt Elizabeth** *(nonfiction)*	165
PROCESS ESSAY: On Writing the Essay "My Aunt Elizabeth"	170
Jane McCafferty, **Eyes of Others** *(fiction)*	106
PROCESS ESSAY: The Sources of "Eyes of Others"	118
Daniel Lowe, **Heritage** *(fiction)*	147
PROCESS ESSAY: "Heritage": Autobiographical Sources	157
Barbara Mellix, **When They Come** *(fiction)*	176
PROCESS ESSAY: The Sources of "When They Come"	184
Eve Shelnutt, **Questions of Travel** *(fiction)*	270
PROCESS ESSAY: The Sources of "Questions of Travel"	276
Julianne Moore, **Vanishing** *(fiction)*	232
PROCESS ESSAY: Sources of "Vanishing"	241

VI. Comparison/Contrast

Barbara Mellix, **From Outside, In** *(nonfiction)*	389
PROCESS ESSAY: Sources for "From Outside, In"	398
James McCommons, **Michigan's "Peace Invasion"** *(nonfiction)*	377
PROCESS ESSAY: Sources for "Michigan's 'Peace Invasion'"	384
Kathleen George, **The Dance at St. Theresa's** *(fiction)*	7
PROCESS ESSAY: Truth	15
Min-zhan Lu, **From Silence to Words: Writing as Struggle** *(nonfiction)*	420
PROCESS ESSAY: "Writing as Struggle": Conversions and Conversations	432
Linda Mizejewski, **The Erotic Stripped Bare** *(nonfiction)*	317
PROCESS ESSAY: Sources of "The Erotic Stripped Bare"	326
Garnett Kilberg, **My Parents' First House** *(nonfiction)*	124
PROCESS ESSAY: Considerations When Writing "My Parents' First House"	128
Sally Flecker, **Learning to Speak** *(nonfiction)*	63
PROCESS ESSAY: On the Importance of Washing a Priestly Foot	71
Catherine D. Miller, **The Use of Contemporary Culture in American Fiction: A Question of Mystery** *(nonfiction)*	346
PROCESS ESSAY: Getting Rid of the Audience: What I Have to Do Before I Write	352

Sally Flecker, **Feminine and Masculine Voices: The Beauty of the Countryside** *(nonfiction)* — 294
PROCESS ESSAY: **The Odd Couple** — 299

VII. Definition

Kevin Stemmler, **Boo, Boot, Boots: Building Language** *(nonfiction)* — 438
PROCESS ESSAY: **Finding the Root** — 444

James McCommons, **Michigan's "Peace Invasion"** *(nonfiction)* — 377
PROCESS ESSAY: **Sources for "Michigan's 'Peace Invasion'"** — 384

Ingrid Mundari, **Language as Image Maker** *(nonfiction)* — 450
PROCESS ESSAY: **Essay on "Language as Image Maker": The Shaper and the Shaped** — 455

Mark L. Shelton, **White Castle: Sometimes Nothing Else Will Do** *(nonfiction)* — 77
  Version I — 80
  Version II — 81
PROCESS ESSAY: **Hamburger Journalism: An Essay on the Blending of Memory and Myth** — 83

Sally Flecker, **Feminine and Masculine Voices: The Beauty of the Countryside** *(nonfiction)* — 294
PROCESS ESSAY: **The Odd Couple** — 299

Barbara H. Hudson, **My Father's Books** *(nonfiction)* — 41
PROCESS ESSAY: **Sources of "My Father's Books"** — 46

Catherine D. Miller, **The Use of Contemporary Culture in American Fiction: A Question of Mystery** *(nonfiction)* — 346
PROCESS ESSAY: **Getting Rid of the Audience: What I Have to Do Before I Write** — 352

Barbara Mellix, **From Outside, In** *(nonfiction)* — 389
PROCESS ESSAY: **Source for "From Outside, In"** — 398

VIII. Description

Mark L. Shelton, **Notes on the Writing of Medical Nonfiction** *(nonfiction)* — 249
PROCESS ESSAY: **The Usual Constraints** — 256

David Martin, **Sunday Morning** *(fiction)* — 136
PROCESS ESSAY: **"Sunday Morning": A Commotion of Memory and Place** — 142

Linda Mizejewski, **The Erotic Stripped Bare** *(nonfiction)* — 317
PROCESS ESSAY: **Sources of "The Erotic Stripped Bare"** — 326

Rhetorical Contents xiii

James McCommons, **Michigan's "Peace Invasion"** *(nonfiction)* 377
    PROCESS ESSAY: **Sources for "Michigan's 'Peace Invasion'"** **384**

Garnett Kilberg, **My Parents' First House** *(nonfiction)* 124
    PROCESS ESSAY: **Considerations When Writing "My Parents' First House"** **128**

Kathryn M. Monahan, **God's Country** *(fiction)* 91
    PROCESS ESSAY: **Notes on Writing "God's Country"** **99**

Eleanor Bergholz, **Suspending Dread** *(nonfiction)* 207
    PROCESS ESSAY: **Sources for "Suspending Dread"** **210**

IX. *Division and Classification*

Sally Flecker, **Feminine and Masculine Voices: The Beauty of the Countryside** *(nonfiction)* 294
    PROCESS ESSAY: **The Odd Couple** **279**

Kevin Stemmler, **Boo, Boot, Boots: Building Language** *(nonfiction)* 438
    PROCESS ESSAY: **Finding the Root** **444**

Barbara Mellix, **From Outside, In** *(nonfiction)* 389
    PROCESS ESSAY: **Sources for "From Outside, In"** **398**

Linda Mizejewski, **The Erotic Stripped Bare** *(nonfiction)* 317
    PROCESS ESSAY: **Sources of "The Erotic Stripped Bare"** **326**

X. *Process Analysis*

Laura L. Brown, **Praying with a Pencil: The Writer's Journal as Religious Quest** *(nonfiction)* 403
    PROCESS ESSAY: **Towards the Mirage of Truth** **413**

Daniel Lowe, **Elie Wiesel: A Response to Some of the Autobiographical Works** *(nonfiction)* 286
    PROCESS ESSAY: **The Wiesel Commentary: Sources** **289**

Mark L. Shelton, **White Castle: Sometimes Nothing Else Will Do** *(nonfiction)* 77
    Version I 80
    Version II 81
    PROCESS ESSAY: **Hamburger Journalism: An Essay on the Blending of Memory and Myth** **83**

Kevin Stemmler, **Boo, Boot, Boots: Building Language** *(nonfiction)*   438
    PROCESS ESSAY: **Finding the Root**   **444**

Kathleen A. Coppula, **Not for Literary Reasons: The Fiction of Grace Paley** *(nonfiction)*   303
    PROCESS ESSAY: **Being Heard**   **311**

Introduction

IN *Writing: The Translation of Memory*, you will find a collection of essays and short stories primarily by authors in the early stages of their writing careers. Each selection represents an interpretation of the writer's experience—a form in which the writer examines, adapts, and transforms a personal memory into a public expression. In these expressions of experience, the collection provides a field in which to examine the writer's molding of material, but it also includes a second level of experience: the writer's experience of the writing itself. Following each selection is a second work by the same author, an essay in which the author reconstructs the writing process by which he or she developed the preceding selection. In these *process essays*, the writers examine the circumstances that led them to write and review the process of the writing itself.

As you read this book, then, you will learn to read as a *writer*, a habit most of us neglect to develop. Almost always we read as *readers*. We take the final *product* of writing—the story, the editorial, the set of directions—and look no further than to be entertained, informed, or instructed. We rarely inquire into the construction of the characters in a piece of fiction, rarely imagine how the editorialist arrived at his opinion, and seldom consider what language has been excluded from directions to make them simple. For the reader, the product of writing is a sufficient end.

Writing: The Translation of Memory discloses the process that must precede the product. In the process essays that follow the selections, you will learn that none of the works was completed without false starts, multiple drafts, discarded ideas, and unexpected discoveries. You will sense that no selection emerged from the author's absolute certainty or confidence and will realize that much "writing" time was spent in staring at a blank sheet of paper. For these writers, and for all writers, the struggle to understand and use the writing process is as important as the idea behind the essay or story. Reading as a writer, you will begin to understand that the writing process is unending and that each writer develops a slightly different process. As you examine the processes these writers used and work with the questions and writing assignments following the selections, we hope you will develop a writing process of your own.

THE WRITERS OF THE ANTHOLOGY

The book includes 66 readings: 13 stories, 20 essays, and 33 process essays written by 26 different writers. Even if you've read exhaustively, there will be few, if any, writers whose names you will recognize. Most of the writers are still enrolled in or recently graduated from university. For a number of them, the essays and stories included here are their first publications. Others write for their local newspapers or magazines. A few have published books.

In their process essays, they reveal their awareness that they are still developing as writers. They recognize the progress they have made since the character they constructed several months ago and realize that a line of reasoning pursued last spring looks naive or incomplete now. But almost all the writers here vividly recall the sense of urgency that impelled them at the time. Imperfect as the work seems now, it was the best they could do in the conversion of memory and thought into written discourse. The work was essential because they learned from it how to begin to write the next essay, the next story. They knew they were acquiring craft, learning the process of thinking and seeing and imagining through writing.

The process itself can be frustrating, and it is rarely linear. You may write what you regard as a scintillating narrative essay on a memorable trip to the ocean that your audience finds tedious, predictable, and riddled with clichés. You may surprise yourself with the ease with which you complete a first paragraph, and then spend hours trying to construct a second. You might wad up three drafts of work and stuff them into the wastebasket, and then, hours later, find yourself uncrumpling them in order to learn how you phrased that certain sentence.

But over time, like the writers in this anthology, you'll find yourself acquiring craft as you learn the habits of thinking and reading as a writer. As you progress through the book, the essays and stories may begin to demand more time and consideration; the assignments and questions may require more thinking and a greater reliance on what you've learned thus far. The anthology is arranged thematically, and each successive theme embraces more abstract cultural and linguistic concepts.

ON WRITING AUTOBIOGRAPHICALLY

For the purposes of the textbook, you should not regard autobiography as the telling of one's life story. The autobiographical writing that appears here, particularly in the process essays, does not begin, "I was born in a wheat field in the heart of Kansas back in 1957, the daughter of two rugged farmers. A pretty child, I . . ." Few memories occurred to the writers in this book chronologically. Most say that memories, ideas, and characters often rose unbidden from unexpected sources, from recollections no others shared, from a kind of hodge-podge of fragmented experience with no sensible order.

If you read the sentence, "Think of your father," it is unlikely that the first image you recall will be your father cradling you in his arms, followed by his delight at watching you taking your first step, and so on. Such chronology may have little to do with the essence of your father or your estimation of and feelings for him. For writers in this anthology, the complexity of feeling and thinking that memory demands led them to write of fathers, mothers, siblings, friends, even books they have read. Writing was one way of defining those feelings, of giving them a context, of understanding them, of giving them a form.

Occasionally, you may be surprised at the personal revelations these writers make. You may more than hesitate, when responding to the assignments, before making similar revelations. But keep in mind that these essays and stories are not attempts at self-aggrandizement or confession. Instead, the writers use language to make meaning of their lives, of the ways they think as they live.

THE USE OF QUESTIONS

Most likely, you will not jot down answers to the questions that appear at the end of each process essay. The questions aren't designed for simple answers, and in some cases may have no answers at all. Instead, they're written to encourage you to reconsider the work you've just read, to push your thinking in directions you hadn't pursued in a first reading. No one can read even the simplest of essays or stories and retain everything it included. The questions can reveal larger or more subtle issues raised by the work that you may have missed initially.

Read the questions carefully. But at the same time, don't leave yourself at their mercy. If, when reading a textbook, you're in the habit of moving directly from the essay to the questions, you may want to change that habit. If you don't, you place yourself in the position of allowing the questions to mold your reading; you allow the textbook to limit questions instead of help you formulate your own.

Consider: you've just completed a story that moved and disturbed you. You're sitting at your desk, tapping your pencil on the pages, saying, "Hey now, there was something in that story that was missing in the others; when that little girl went into the basement with those two boys at the end, that *got* to me." But instead of looking for your own reasons rooted in your own experience for your response to the story, you look directly at the questions written by one or two other people who had different responses. Your tendency might be to say, "Ah, I see from that question that I was supposed to see a connection between the boy smoking the cigarette on page 223 and the girl dancing with the other boy at the end of the story. Maybe *that's* what I was missing, maybe that's what was bugging me about it." At this point, you've allowed someone else to structure your reading instead of structuring your own.

Allow yourself your own perspectives before entertaining those toward which the questions direct you. We are not asking you to ignore the questions; if we were, we wouldn't have asked them. Among the best tools for learning to read and write are the questions others ask and the readings others give. But don't revere the work of others to the point that you neglect your own.

RESPONDING TO THE ASSIGNMENTS

The writing assignments are placed under the heading "Possible Writing Topics" because they aren't the *only* ones that can be drawn from the stories and essays. Your teacher may want you to address other concerns; you may be interested in pursuing an idea the assignments can't anticipate. Leave yourself open to these opportunities.

For each story or essay and its process essay, there are two assignments. The first asks you to consider the ideas, issues, and concerns the writer develops in the initial work, and to write an essay that may deal with similar ideas and issues. The second asks you to write a process essay that describes some of the autobiographical sources for your first essay, and some of the decisions you made when working through it.

A question you may ask yourself before you begin writing is, "How much should I imitate the writers whose work I've just finished reading?" To some degree, it's likely you'll want to imitate a piece of writing you admire. The anthology you're reading is in part set up to encourage this. Imitation, of course, is one way to learn. If you played basketball while you were growing up, you probably tried to learn to throw an around-the-back pass after watching one of your heroes save a game that way. If you were involved in theater, you may have tried to take on the acting style of Meryl Streep or Jack Nicholson. Writing is no different. Already your writing has been shaped by what you've read, by the teachers who have had the most influence as you moved through school. If you admire the rhythm of a writer's sentences, if you admire the personality of the writer, or the ideas the writer articulates that somehow change your way of thinking, you'll want to work some of these into your own writing. Finally, you shouldn't resist this method of learning, as your writing will probably be strengthened by it.

But use imitation as a tool of learning, not as an end in itself. Remember, you admire another writer whose work is distinctive, fresh, unusual, or striking. Why would your own writing be fresh if you simply appropriate that person's writing style? Cultivate your own writer's voice that emerges from your own experience of the world. Allow other writers to inform your writing; do not allow them to commandeer it.

A FINAL NOTE ON THE ANTHOLOGY

As you read this book, you'll see that the anthology includes 13 stories—fiction—and that none of the assignments asks you to *write* fiction. Many of our very good readers had questions about our inclusion of stories in a textbook whose principal pedagogical concern is teaching essay writing. We considered these questions carefully.

But finally, we found the distinctions between writing fiction and writing nonfiction ill-defined, particularly as the writers here deal with them. Few, if any, would contend that writers can't learn from reading both. Some of the best stories in the anthology are nonfiction; some of the most honest and direct are fiction.

We believe this book can be an instrumental tool in your development of your writing process and in learning to write well. Writing well is among the most meaningful tasks you can undertake in terms of what it demands of you. If you respond to the demands, as have the writers in this anthology, you can discover a depth of insight that will make the effort of writing more than worthwhile.

I

RITES OF PASSAGE

Kathleen George

The Dance at St. Theresa's[1]

I was twelve, drying dishes, when my mother looked out the window to the house next door and said with a sigh of finality, "Well, that's it. Tomorrow's the day." She meant that my aunt and uncle would be moving in next door. She must have worried that we—in particular I—would come to know them better. Maybe she even sensed that we would grieve with them, that they brought a new sadness to our lives. I know a fall chill was in the air as it sometimes is at the end of August. In all likelihood I finished with the dishes at some point, looked out the screen door, shivered, and closed the solid kitchen door. And very probably I thought, looking at the row of houses across the alley—Dudash, Petrosky, Laslo, Laslo, Laslo, Hruneni, where my friends lived—that I was on the brink of a new period of my life.

When they moved in, I stood on our back porch with Muncie or Dolly or somebody. We leaned over the banister and watched Uncle Bart and his sons and some of the railroad men he worked with carry in a succession of chairs and tables and mattresses. Aunt Theresa stood on the sidewalk and gave directions, but so quietly that we couldn't hear them. She had on a house dress and slipper-like shoes called mules, but she stood as if she were dressed up. It wasn't a stiffness so much as a carefulness in her, a pride in the way she stood. I thought she was ever so much prettier than Bart was handsome and I thought how sad it was that one son should come out so plain—that was James—while the other—Paul—simply blasted you with handsomeness. I waved at them all and got a thrill when they waved back. From the house came the smell of bread my

---

[1] This work first appeared in the *Cimarron Review* and is reprinted here with permission of the Board of Regents for Oklahoma State University, holders of the copyright.

mother was baking for them. Probably no smell in the world says "the security of home" like bread does.

Over many fall evenings, before homework—I had just entered junior high school and the unstructured evenings of sixth grade were a thing of the past—I dried dishes and tried to pry information from my mother about our relatives next door. I sensed that my mother was brimming over with something and I worked on increasing the pressure until she couldn't contain it any longer. I found it was useful to mention that my Aunt Theresa was pretty. Sometimes I rambled about sad things—and that helped, too, to loosen my mother's tongue—illnesses, deformities, deaths in families I hardly knew. There was always somebody with reported gout or somebody's grandfather's hand had only one finger or somebody's sister had crossed eyes or somebody's parent died in their thirties. It was a small town we lived in and you didn't have to *know* people in your community to feel for them. We were all part of the same (and I didn't yet know how desperately I'd want to escape the crushing feeling of it), the families of tough, hard-working, deeply depressed immigrants, people determined to hang on through aching bones and the early deaths around them to American gold, determined to give their children something they couldn't even define. A new mentality. Fourth or fifth generation Protestant feelings of power.

A core of sadness about not really belonging could be tapped any day of the week in my mother as she washed dishes in scalding water I couldn't even touch. The rough red hands, the determination to be clean, was a part of our community identity, a part of what drew together Slavs, Italians, Poles, Croatians, Irish, Serbs, and Hungarians. My Uncle Bart had married a Hungarian woman and once I got my mother going by reporting that someone in my Guidance class had answered the teacher that Gypsies were Hungarian people. And the teacher, a Miss Devlin, who denied the richest part of her own heritage, had paused and replied that gypsies were also Serbs, too. She explained that even in the States, when they had means, Serbs preferred crates to furniture, alcohol to food. Roberta Fabish began crying and told Miss Devlin that that wasn't so; to which Miss Devlin replied that there might be one or two exceptions. But Roberta Fabish had to stay after school for talking back. I wondered at my own ability to stay silent when I surely had a heart as sensitive as Roberta Fabish's.

"There are no crates next door," my mother said. "And the house is solid. And the house they owned before this was solid."

"But why did they leave the other house?"

"To be closer to us. To have family around them." There was a lie in this, something that made my mother scrub at the stains which had already announced their permanence on our dishes. Just then we heard a knock at the door and my Uncle Bart's voice. He and my father often went for walks after dinner.

"We're going to make sure everything's okay on the block!" my father called as a joke.

"Be careful!" I called back to him, trying to joke in kind.

"Your uncle should have checked up a long time ago," my mother muttered. I knew she wanted me to *guess* what was wrong, to become her companion in suffering, but I was at a loss. "Is it a shorter drive to work for Uncle Bart?" I tried. He was a railroad man and went to work in blue stripes every morning before I was up but he came home about when I did.

"No," she said. "Not really. Actually it's longer." She began to scrub the ribs of the low-slung sink.

"Well, what about Aunt Theresa? Is it a shorter ride to McCrory's?" She took the streetcar, so it probably didn't matter. I'd see her at the end of the day if I was hanging around the sunparlor windows. She dressed in little suits with matching shoes or purses and she walked slowly. Somehow she always sensed my presence and waved at me, and, as I waved back, I thought she seemed nice.

"About the same, I would think."

"Well, it's hell and blazes farther for James to get to the college!" I exploded. I knew I shouldn't have said "hell" as soon as I said it.

"Where did you get that language?" she said, but I overlapped it with, "Do you want me to wipe off the stove?"

"I'll do it," she said.

"And Paul doesn't go anywhere important, except to the gym to practice boxing—" I wondered out loud.

Her back was turned to me. She wiped the stove which didn't need it, really, and volunteered the first real bit of information. It floated around her and I almost didn't catch it. "Your aunt has a weakness in her. . . She doesn't know right from wrong when it comes to men. She just needs to have people look out for her."

The kitchen was finished and I didn't know what else to say, not wanting to break the mood of confidence. I went into the sunparlor and rocked, looking out into the deepening dark of the evening for my father. He returned, as always, with a cheerful word—"We checked the whole neighborhood. Everything's 'kopasetic.'" Meaning *all right* in an antiseptic sort of way. I saw that these after dinner walks didn't restore him, but wore him out. He looked distracted from his good temper. He went into the kitchen and, in a tone like our priest used, asked my mother to be nice to Aunt Theresa.

For a succession of evenings, my mother, with a strained expression on her face, would invite my aunt over in the evenings for coffee or dessert. My aunt always accepted with an aloofness, and with displays of dignity and of perfect grooming from McCrory's products.

Our church—although we didn't attend often—was called St. Nicholas. Most of our neighbors went to a church just up the street on the edge of the woods called St. Theresa. "Do you think Aunt Theresa was named after the saint?" I asked. "And was I?"

"Oh, Helen," she sighed. "You were named after your grandmother. I've told you a million times."

"Well, I just wondered." I sat on the red stool and dried more slowly, reluctant to relinquish my mother's company for arithmetic and geography. "Did you know they're starting dances on Saturday nights at St. Theresa's?"

"That church sure knows how to make money."
"Muncie and Tootsie and Dolly are going."
"I don't believe it."
"They said so. So can I go too?"
"No," she said. "No, I don't think so. They're a year older than you."

I remember that I tried for months to get her to reverse her decision. I don't at this point remember for sure what the real first names of my friends were. They went so insistently and for so long by nicknames and last names—Tootsie Laslo, Muncie Dudash. While one foot dragged behind in the ethnic neighborhood, the other stepped out into a bouncy 1950's America. Where, underneath it all, I think so much must have been wrong.

It was the night before Thanksgiving on which my mother chose to tell me, as if I were much older than Dolly, Tootsie, and Muncie, and could understand such a thing, that my uncle had discovered an ongoing affair between my aunt and his own nephew (my cousin) Tony.

"You mean *Tony*?" I asked stupidly since she had already said so.

"Uncle Bart went home from work one day, early because he was sick, and there they were on the living room floor." I was silent. I hardly expected her to tell me more, but she did. I must have done quite a job of building up pressure. "All of her clothes were off and for a moment she looked at Bart as if she didn't recognize him. It was like a craziness. They admitted it. Tony made her crazy. He confessed that he covered her whole body with kisses."

I understood from her tone that she found the *whole* thing shocking, not just the fact that Tony was related to, younger than, and not married to my Aunt Theresa. "Confessed? You mean to a priest?" My voice was low to convince her that this was an ordinary question, something I might have asked of a friend—Dolly Hruneni, say—on the way to school.

"To your father. They confessed to him. Wrote it up and vowed never to do it again."

"Why did they bring Daddy into it?"

"I don't know," she said bitterly. "I don't know."

"Honestly," I said, "people are nuts." I couldn't imagine it. I shook as I tossed the dish towel and went to the dining room to delve into my homework. Lurid pictures passed before me. I wanted to cry and I wished my mother had won the battle between us and not told me. We would all sit in this very room tomorrow. I feared the knowledge would show on me.

The way my Aunt Theresa looked at her sons—I saw this at the Thanksgiving dinner and a month or two later when, because my aunt had persuaded my mother to let me work for her for a dollar a day, I spent a great deal of time next door—was like two versions of a curse. She would turn to James with a look of pity which said she couldn't do a thing for him, to Paul with a look of longing as if she wanted to catch onto his coat-tails and live life with the laughing freedom which was his trademark. Or at least, this is what I thought she was thinking.

"Would you say grace, Helen," my mother asked in a patient refined voice as if we always said it.

"Whoa, hold on," my father said to himself as he lowered his forkful of mashed potatoes back to his plate. "I forgot what a holy family we are." And then he winked at me.

I didn't know a proper grace, so I made one up as I went along. "Hail Mary, full of grace," I said. "Hail Joseph and Jesus about to be born of Mary"— and having located the holy family as they existed for me one month before Christmas—"bless our food and bless us all, let us always stick to our family, let us always know right from wrong. Amen."

"Thank you," my mother said. I don't think any more traditional grace could have made her happier.

"We came to Thanksgiving here once before," Paul said to me in a loud whisper as he leaned to pass me the mashed potatoes. "You were one year old."

"And a couple of months," my mother added.

"You sat right there," he pointed to a spot next to my mother. "And you threw mashed potatoes at me." His voice, because he was so close to me, gave me a shiver which made me shrug in defense. I turned to him, but he was just laughing at having flustered me. He had thick black hair and blue eyes and beautiful facial bones. My mother had told me people swooned over him all the time.

"And you said, in the clearest voice—I'll never forget this—" James went on, "Delicious."

"You did," my father said. "That's true." They were looking at me, probably much as they had then, but this time I felt babyish and awkward. My fingers grasped my fork too tightly. My mother had given me a red cardigan sweater to wear buttoned up the back with a red plaid skirt. I wondered if it looked right and felt acutely aware of my developing breasts.

"You wanted our attention," my Aunt Theresa said, not unkindly. "And you got it. Children are so themselves. Even at an early age. Like Paul who *hit* everything. And like James." She looked at him. And I did. We all did. He was only twenty, but his brown hair was thinning in imitation of his father's. Behind glasses, his brown eyes were further protected by heavy lids and darkish circles. "Even as a baby," she said, "James always looked as if he was thinking."

All in all, James had one of the kindest faces I ever saw. Still, when his mother looked at him even just to pass the salad, she looked sad, regretful. And somehow I understood her feeling.

"Do you ever work on the Stone Street train?" I asked my uncle. Dolly Hruneni and I used to sit on the wall after school sometimes and wave at the men in blue and white who sat jauntily in the caboose. Uncle Bart shook his head no.

When Aunt Theresa looked at Paul, something in her let go. "What a heart throb," my mother said of him. "People will go to see him box, just to see *him*," she had explained to me. I could understand why. Everything he did seemed fraught with a future—from the way he whispered to me about mashed potatoes to the way he popped out the door after dinner to go buy a pack of

Camels. Did I understand then, I wonder in retrospect, that there was a hint of something tragic in him, something not really happy under the freedom and independence. He came back hours later that Thanksgiving without explanation or apology. We were already eating leftovers. "Raiding the carcass," my dad said.

In between dinner and leftovers, the rest of us, the six of us, had gone for a walk. We formed couples—my aunt and uncle, my mother and father, me and my cousin James. I answered in a rote sort of way the questions James asked me about school. I liked it better when he fell silent and I could pretend we were on a date. And that he was his brother.

Up ahead, leading us up Corinne Street, down Harold, down Beatrice, and up Howard—three times, as if we didn't dare venture any farther from home—were my aunt and uncle. He slumped a bit, especially without his railroad togs. But she had the lines of a newspaper fashion drawing especially when she stopped for a moment—with stiff shoulders, and her head inclined over her shoulder, and her eyes averted. She wore a hat with a feather in it. The hat was placed at such an angle that you just had to notice it. I'd watched her touch up before we started the walk. She wore lipstick as red as her nail polish and used loose powder and creme rouge. My mother had mentioned often how wrong she thought it was that Aunt Theresa wore mascara every day of the week. It wasn't exactly a hard look, but it was far away and glamorous.

"Your mother is so pretty," I said to James.

He nodded agreement and smiled at me.

"And I like her name, the name of a saint. My name's a saint's name too."

"And my whole family," he said. "All of us." I thought over their names and saw that he was right. He really looked like one though. More than his father whom flesh had filled out a bit. James' small smile and the curve of circles under his eyes looked just like the holy pictures. Even though he had a kind look, I found I wasn't calm around him.

I thought of him in comparison with Paul and Tony whom I hadn't seen for a long time but who came to mind often that day, for reasons which are obvious. I was trying to work it out—what made James calm but not calming, what made Paul suggest deviltry in the slightest action.

"Your father is a wonderful lively man. Reminds me of Paul." James said as if reading my thoughts. "Fun to be around."

My father, when he was younger, according to the picture of him on my mother's bureau, looked quite a bit in the line of Paul and Tony. They got one set of family coloring and spirit; Bart and James got the other.

Just ahead of me my mother slipped her arm through my father's. His laugh floated back to us and I thought how lucky my mother was to have him instead of Uncle Bart. I called out to them, "Before I forget to ask—there's a dance this Saturday at St. Theresa's. Can I go?" My father was about to say yes when my mother said no.

"Why not?" he asked her.

"Not yet," she said.

It turned out that the Saturday after Thanksgiving was Paul's first boxing match and that a match on Easter Thursday was his last, the one that killed him.

My parents were planning to see his first one, they explained to me. And I was to stay home by myself or have a friend over. I could do homework, watch the television, listen to records, and if it was before nine o'clock go up to Wozjanovich's for a slice of pizza. I was actually uncertain about wanting to go to the dance (what if nobody danced with me?) but only permission to go to the boxing match would have stilled my complaints. To think I'd be missing the excitement. And for such ordinary alternatives.

Paul won his first match. "He was a sensation," my mother said. "People went wild for him."

I imagine I know what happened. I imagine money-hungry, greedy crooksters who come into my mind now like Gleason and Rooney from *Requiem for a Heavyweight*. I think they must have *bought* Paul and photographed him, pushed him and publicized him until he didn't know what he was doing. I think he probably liked it at first. And I guess from knowing him the little bit that I did that he became frightened and didn't like it so much after a while. Maybe they gave him the wrong sorts of opponents—people too tough for him.

I couldn't stand it that I wasn't allowed to go to the matches. I would hang around Aunt Theresa's house shining the faces of ceramic dolls and replacing them in a line on her mantlepiece in the hopes of catching a glimpse of Paul or a word from him or a word about him. Sometimes he hugged me, a sort of enveloping hug like in a boxing hold. I remember how nervous he looked on the afternoon of the night he got killed in the ring—only months after his stunning rise to our small town's version of fame. And I still find myself wondering what could have stopped the tragedy.

One March night, after pizza and television, my friend Dolly went home and I wandered around the house like a lost soul. I looked out the sunparlor window for signs of life, worried because my mother and father were coming home much later than I expected them. Finally I heard our car. I had to move up close to the windows to see anything because the panes of glass were tiny. Something was wrong in the way they walked and held onto each other, and eventually I discovered that they were crying. "I thought he'd get up," my mother said again and again. I know that what she said was true—that it had seemed like years while they waited for him to get up. Officials tried to revive him. And then failing, they carried him off. Some people left. Some people stayed. I think of the people who stayed as the good people who stood in silence as if they were in church. My aunt and uncle and James were allowed inside a door and my mother and father were allowed to stand outside it, a part of the larger crowd. Everybody thought, "These things don't happen. Once in a blue moon." Thoughts like that. A short time later, after what seemed like many hours, officials returned to explain that Paul was killed by a blow to the head at a peculiar once-in-a-lifetime blue moon angle.

Our lives went into slow motion.

My mother confided to me over dishes that my aunt blamed herself for her son's death. Her grief was such that she *admitted* this belief to my mother who clearly would offer her no rebuttal. Together, my mother and my aunt decided, for something with no easy explanation, that God had chosen Paul's death in the boxing ring to punish my aunt for her affair with Tony the year before.

I thought they must be right. I no longer wanted to work for my aunt; so I asked my mother to get me out of it, to say I had too much homework or something. I thought that this would have the effect of distancing me from my aunt, but it only caused her to pay more attention to me. She began to look at me with eyes I'd seen turned on James, with a look of pity and compassion. She began to bring me little gifts from McCrory's—hair barrettes, scarves, perfume, and makeup. I couldn't use them for they stirred up in me an agony of hatred. For whom, at what, I didn't know. Partly at Paul, I think, for falling into the arms of death.

A year later my aunt convinced my mother to let me go to a dance at St. Theresa's church hall. "We'll be there," I heard her saying, meaning her and Uncle Bart. I think it might have been their first time out to such a thing since the tragedy. James didn't do anything social and we were all worried about him. My mother preferred sewing to dancing and my father had begun to spend a lot of time at the bar he owned, playing poker, reporting to us that he was on a lucky streak and had to ride it. I took my homework or a novel I might be reading into the sunparlor and spent most of my time looking out the window and eavesdropping on conversations between my mother and my aunt in the kitchen. These were conversations I could just barely hear. To my surprise, my mother agreed to let me go to the dance. "Just watch out for her," she told my aunt.

On the evening of the dance, they came to pick me up. When they knocked at the door, I saw that my uncle wore a dark suit and my aunt wore a black dress. They looked to me much like they had at the funeral. Even though the church was a small distance away, we drove. I think now that they might have chosen to go for my sake.

The hall was huge and loosely hung with many colors of sagging crepe paper which had the look of being recycled from dance to dance. Up on a stage, a man sat in shadow, playing records. People of all ages were there—children of eight and nine years old and their parents and their grandparents as well as my friends and our teenage crowd. Across a steel-topped kitchen counter, women in aprons pushed plates of pierogi and cups of beer. The beer spilled a little there on the counter and more on the floor as people walked with two or three cups in their hands. The children skated in it. Some of the teenage boys were drinking beer. My uncle bought me a coke and then left me to my friends.

I stood stiffly in a full blue dress with puffed sleeves. I couldn't imagine that anyone would want to dance with me. My friends and I talked and pointed out boys we wanted to dance with whom we would consider asking on Ladies' Choice. As the evening wore on, women began to dance with women. Tootsie Laslo asked me to dance a polka which I didn't know how to do. She said it was easy and that she'd teach me. The spinning made me dizzy and I took a long slide on the beer on the floor. I never quite touched bottom but I felt embarrassed as if I'd fallen. I looked to my aunt and uncle, but they'd long since stopped watching me.

And then a man asked me to dance. He was about forty-five years old and he was very drunk. I was so taken by surprise I didn't know how to say no. He told me, breathing very close to my face, that he knew my father and was a good customer at the bar. It seemed important that I not be rude to him. His hand slid around my waist and then stopped for a moment feeling the seam of my dress. Suddenly he pulled me very tight. I tried to pull my head away to ask him his name, but he pressed his mouth into my temple until my hair was wet with his breathing. He pushed his whole body against mine and moaned. I thought I should spit in his face, but I didn't, couldn't, move. I hoped maybe someone would see and stop him, one of the overweight, undancing women who surrounded the floor on folding chairs. But they seemed to see nothing. From the corner of my eye, I saw my aunt and uncle dancing, so themselves, he sad, she beyond it all, having removed herself to a place where she was simply beautiful.

The drunk man held me so crushingly tight that my bones hurt. And I know he murmured something in the heavy wet breath that fell on my neck. I think it was "I'm sorry. I'm sorry." As he moved in my stiff arms I felt him lose himself—fall into me—and, as if he were as important to me as my father or Paul, I held him up until he righted himself.

Of course at the time I didn't think anything, confused and embarrassed as I was. I think though, if the memory of the feeling serves me correctly, that for a moment I was as lost as he was. And that after that, and again only for a moment, I floated up above it all in a state of temporary maturity. If you'd asked me, I would have known amazing things—that gypsy was a way of living with nothing, that God hadn't the time to notice minor sins, that children punished the sins of their parents and that's how the whole thing was run.

At the end of the song, I broke away and ran to my friends. The drunk man followed behind me trying to grab onto my dress. I couldn't have understood then how much of my life I'd spend going back and forth between my mother's house and my aunt's house. Then, in a brief infusion of spirit from my mother, somewhat to entertain my friends and more to cover the pounding of my heart, I turned and spit at him.

Truth

*W*HEN I tell somebody I write fiction, chances are they ask me, "Stories or novels?" I usually say, "Right now I'm working on stories." And they say, "What kind of stories? I mean, what do you write about?"

(I'm assuming that most people who write get into this conversation.) Sometimes I say "Stories about relationships among city people." Often this means nothing to my questioners who ask, "Romance or adventure?" And I say, "Well, no, more stories of psychological life." And sometimes—at least one time—I was asked, "You mean mind-benders?" I said no. But I wasn't sure. The few times I described stories to people they looked at me as if maybe the answer were yes.

At any rate, I got through and past this conversation with Bob, my Terminix man. Bob is about six foot three and very large-boned; he wears an enormous walrus mustache and large glasses. Bob has told me that he lives out in the country with his wife, far from other people. He couldn't stand to live any other way, he says. Bob is a self-made sort. He has taught himself cabinetry and computer programming. One day, Big Bob, guarding my house against little intruders, saw me typing and saw the stacks of paper all around me. We had the usual conversation. But Bob said, "Tell me one of your stories." And I did. Now we have a once-a-month ritual (which I find I look more and more forward to). He asks and I tell my latest story. He usually stops spraying to hear. And I read his face to see how he is reacting. I really like it when he stands there momentarily frozen with the spray can in hand. Or when he comes up from the basement and asks me a question about a character.

Several months ago, Bob began asking me, "Where do you get your ideas?" and more specifically, "the idea for that story." And I've found that I have ready answers to this question. Even when I try to hide from my sources I know what a great many of them are. It's a habit of mind, really—like the instant recall of and interpretation of dreams. Maybe it comes from analyzing plays for so many years. If I watch *Hill Street Blues* or *The Equalizer*, a part of my mind ticks off the fairy tale elements in them or what they're imitating or the template of personality types. I can't help it really. And frighteningly enough, I've sometimes found myself interpreting a dream *while* I'm having it. A voice (mine) is saying, "See, that means such and such, but that right there represents the umbilical cord, you see." It's as if I have a regular self which keeps a regular pace and an interpreter-self which like a wind-up toy picks up speed and bumps into everything in sight. It shows signs of wearing itself out (and I frankly hope it does).

Anyway, by the time Bob is spraying the baseboards near the front door, I'm usually telling him the eighteenth source for the story of the month. For instance, not too long ago, I told him "Tea Leaves." This is a story about a tea leaf reader who finally meets someone she can't read. She can't get any messages at all from the woman, a stranger, and her own fear of the blankness plunges her headlong into a deeper questioning about what she is doing. I explained to Bob that the story first sprung from my mother's report to me that a cousin-in-law of mine—a large, explosive woman who reads fortunes—laughs at her clients once they have gone. I was outraged by this and I tried to imagine what would stop her in her tracks. I explained to Bob that I combined the cousin with a Jamaican woman who manicured my nails a few times and who (I discovered in the process) listens to and counsels women on matters of love all day long. Another character—a client who couldn't leave a ne'er-do-well boyfriend—was a combination of a woman I'd heard in the manicurist's shop and a friend of mine who is in a troubled marriage. I told Bob that the client who upset the tea leaf reader was suggested to me by a student at Pitt who asked for an appointment with me, came late for it, and then had nothing but frivolous concerns—like how to get into theatre for social reasons, how to find a theatre company where there wasn't much rehearsal—all this on a day when I was very busy.

On and on. Bob and I talked about what the story meant. By this time he was half out the door, can and hose in hand. What I liked was that he had no trouble taking the tea leaf reader seriously. Sometimes she knew things, sometimes she didn't. He was right in tune with her skills and her ego problems. Bob and I discussed alternate endings: Should the reader lie to the blank woman or not? How much should she fight back?

What I didn't tell Bob—and what he may well have known intuitively—is that "Tea Leaves" is as much about me, the writer, dealing with plotting as it is about the reader making predictions on clients' futures. It's a story which works on the problem of how to know a character and of how well a writer can predict what happens to characters. The story is really in many ways about my own feeling of being stuck, my own growing disillusionment with my interpretor-self. The story plays out my own frustrations.

When Eve Shelnutt asked me to write an essay about the sources of "The Dance at St. Theresa's," I said, "Why, that's the story there is nothing to say about. It's virtually true." The character, Helen, is not my manicurist, my cousin-in-law, my neighbor, my secretary, or some interesting combination of the list. She is me. Eve said, "So? Write about that." My reaction was that I wanted to and I didn't want to.

The first thing I discovered when picking the story apart was that a great deal of it was actually *untrue* in the biographical sense. For instance—

My aunt and uncle never lived next door.

Next door to us on the right side if you stood at the front door of the house I grew up in were the Lehmans. (I can't help noting an interesting coincidence, if there are such things as coincidences: The family who now, this day, lives to my right reminds me in many respects of the Lehmans just as the family who lives to my left bears resemblances to my left-neighbors of years ago. Strange, isn't it?) To us, the Lehmans were peculiar because they raised their voices. They weren't well-respected in the neighborhood because their house was run-down and the kids didn't do well in school. Other kids used to taunt them and call them "the lame-brains." "Other kids" includes my sisters and my brother and me. People said that the Stifflers, who lived in the Lehmans' basement, were a great aunt and uncle of either Mr. or Mrs. Lehman and that they had once owned the house, but that the Lehmans just took it from them and banished them below. Until this moment, I had forgotten the Stifflers who are surely deserving of a story of their own....

I *think* perhaps Mr. Lehman worked for the railroad. My uncle did for sure.

But the railroad connection and the generally bad reputation of the Lehmans together probably made me put my aunt and uncle in that house. I do remember that for a short time we shared a phone line with these people. It was called a party-line. My mother once heard teenage Nancy Lehman talking with a boyfriend. Usually my mother picked up the phone several times before she interrupted with, "Excuse me, but you've been on for a long time and I have to make a call." But one day, my mother was too embarrassed to interrupt because what she had heard was Nancy saying in a husky voice—over and over—"I love *all* of you." My mother told me in some distress what she had heard. This sealed the wild reputation Nancy shared with her sister Peggy and her brother Francis.

In our largely Catholic neighborhood, the Lehmans were notable too as Holy Rollers. Nobody had actually been to their church, but everybody had strong ideas about how strange it was. And how Dionysian. My brother and I would play "Holy Rollers": He'd threaten me, I'd roll away from him shouting "Halleluja!" He'd roll after me, that sort of thing. (We also played "Oral Roberts." We especially liked to knock one another on the head with the heel of the hand—off a balcony, or a landing, or a piece of furniture if possible—shouting something like "Heal and make him whole! Oops!"

There was a way the Lehmans had of raising their voices to each other that reminded us of their freedom of expression in church. That usually freed us and started us in on one of the games.

My mother had an on-and-off-again relationship with these neighbors. It went from non-existent to surprisingly polite. One surprisingly polite summer (I would have been about twelve—miserable and awkward), my mother told me that June Lehman told her that I was going to grow into my looks, that she'd been watching me and seen great possibilities. I would have dignity and character, she told my mother. I would be interesting-looking. I didn't know whether to dislike June Lehman on my mother's general principles or to like her because she promised me a satisfactory future. Or in fact because she noticed me for the twelve-year-old that I was.

At any rate, I believe the Lehman family who lived in the house where I imagined Theresa and Bart informed the conflict between my family and the next-door relatives of my story.

The restless family that I put next door *did* exist although they never really lived near us and I didn't really know them well. I'd seen pictures of my cousin, the boxer, but he died before I was born. I was told—and definitely while drying dishes—that there had been a scandal just like the one I reported. I always imagined my father meeting with the people involved in a lawyer's office, a quiet room in which my father acted as part-lawyer, part-priest. For all I know I am imagining this correctly. My father must have seemed worldly enough to handle the truth and spiritual enough to engender guilt. I believe, but I am not certain, that sometime after the confession, the "Paul" character was killed. I do know that my aunt is supposed to have assumed it was in punishment of her.

Part of the feeling of truth of the story to me is that to the best of my knowledge I have captured the looks and behaviors of that family as I believe they existed. The "James" character I did know over a couple of years. He married an exuberant woman who made his life happy. Not long ago I heard from my mother (and I think perhaps many of my stories, not to mention the journal entry which suggested this story, are inspired by "things my mother told me") that James' wife was dying of a brain tumor and later that James had been, both through her illness and after her death, inconsolable. I think, in remembering him with his wife, I can understand that phrase, "losing someone who is a part of you." His wife represented his happy side, his will-to-live side just as his brother had stood for "beauty, self-expression, and getting out of the rut of daily life."

If that family never lived next door, and if I only think I knew them, then it is all the more surprising that I reported the story as true. It certainly seems to be only as true as other stories I have written—a mixture.

There are, however, other aspects of the story which make me feel that I am calling up a real past. For one, all of the tiny, tiny things—the view from the sunparlor, the supporting cast, are very real to me. I've broken the rules and crossed the barrier into magic by using the actual names of real people. They came to me and I used them like prayer or meditation to get me into the feeling and mood of the piece.

Miss Devlin, Muncie Dudash, Dolly Hruneni, Tootsie Laslo, and Roberta Fabish existed. Some of them are clearer to me than others. I can picture Muncie's face but that is probably because I have snapshots of us playing in my back yard. I can't recall what Miss Devlin looked like, but I can hear her. I can't hear Roberta Fabish's voice, but I think I can see her—of small stature, thin, and uniformly brownish in hair, eyes, and skin. I remember Roberta Fabish for two things: for taking on Miss Devlin, which I greatly admired, and for being the only student to beat me in spelling bees.

I loved these people once. And I still love their names, especially Dolly, Tootsie, and Muncie, for the burbling rhythm they create. When I use the real names and cross the danger line into intruding on their privacy, it's as if I'm calling a message to them—that I'm sorry I lost track of them and can't even picture their faces, that I hope they are well, and that I hope they remember me and our world. As soon as I wrote their names in my story, the world around them began to create itself. We were like peasant girls in a folk tale, generous toward each other, easily excited over a new blouse or skirt, competitive for each other's and everyone else's attention, desperate to be pretty, popular, and loved.

As I mentioned, I had been writing entries in a journal when I got the idea for "The Dance at St. Theresa's." In the journal, I wrote thoughts at random, letting one experience fold over into another. What fascinated me at first was the way something I'd remembered as morbid became funny and vice versa. I was particularly interested in this line between sad and funny because many of my favorite stories ride that line.

I recalled a specific scene in my journal, a very strong memory, of a time my mother told me of a family scandal. It seems to me now that she hoped to shield me from sexuality, but in fact she did the opposite; she made me curious. However, as I made the entry I thought that one day soon I would write the story of the scandalous aunt, a woman tortured by guilt and caught up in grief.

But what I actually put in the journal *immediately following* the memory of telling, over dishes, of my aunt's story was the memory of a dance at St. Theresa's (a real church in Johnstown, surrounded by woods in which I used to pick blackberries). I wrote in my journal, to my surprise, that in my guilt over what the drunk man did to me, I identified with my aunt.

Still, my small experience at the dance seemed to me just that, small, and too much about an uninteresting me to put into a story. I continued to think I would write the aunt's story. I considered the aunt's story for about two weeks before I actually began to write it. Could I modernize it? I asked myself. Or were the feelings more understandable set in the sensibilities of the 1950's? Should I place it after the son's death? A visit to the grave? Or before the son's death, including it? What would the occasion be?

While I was thinking this over, I happened to read William Trevor's story "Frau Messenger." It is a first-person narrative about the experience of an adolescent boy's infatuation with a romantic, terminally ill woman, a woman who influenced his whole inner romantic life. What caught my interest was the way Trevor's narrator speculated about what he must have felt back when events were happening. This speculation was interwoven with a search for the main facts of an important memory. I decided in very short order to steal the form. It seemed to me to provide just the purchase that I needed on the materials. The style of writing—the searching, thinking, recording—much resembled my journal entries which had more real energy than the story I thought I should write.

But then, what story was I actually telling?

The story of a girl wanting to grow up and not wanting to, of fighting for adult privileges because her mother was trying to keep her a child, of getting her way and then having a bad experience. The main energy of the story, though, seemed to come from the combination of and juxtaposition of two stories—the two sequential journal entries.

About a week after I wrote the story, it occurred to me that I'd written another version of the Demeter/Persephone myth. I'm glad it didn't occur to me as I was writing, because, in a sense, it's a useless piece of information to a writer. More useful was the feeling I had while writing of wanting to experience the story and not wanting to—which matched Helen's feelings of wanting and not wanting. I think all writing is just that—the writer's feelings while writing, about writing.

Now things have changed once more. In writing this essay, I have lost my connection with Helen. She is Helen and not me. At the moment I recognized the source of my identification with her, she went away. And I actually feel a little sad. A voice says to me that I also feel a little like Demeter having lost a daughter, in this case, to the process of fiction.

❧ QUESTIONS ❧

Kathleen George's "The Dance at St. Theresa's" and its process essay, "Truth"

1. While describing the nicknames and last names of her friends, the narrator in George's story says of them: "While one foot dragged behind in the ethnic neighborhood, the other stepped out into a bouncy 1950's America. Where, underneath it all, I think so much must have been wrong." How does George establish this tension between what is "right" on the surface and "wrong" underneath enforced throughout the story? Why is it so important for the adults in the story to maintain a sense of order and propriety when, "underneath it all," so much *is* wrong?

2. Look back through the story and note how many times Helen, the narrator, refers to or uses symbols from her experience with the Catholic church. How do these clash with her experience of the events in the story, particularly when she finds out about her aunt's affair and when she dances with the drunk in St. Theresa's?

3. How old do you think the narrator is at the time she tells the story? What advantage does this give her? How would you go about describing an event that took place years ago in your life?

4. In her process essay, George says of Helen, "She is me." What does she mean by this? If you were writing a letter to a friend, would you, after reading the letter, say "That is me?" What about a paper you wrote for the teacher of this class? Could you say of the person who's represented in that paper, "She is me"? And why does George change her mind at the essay's conclusion? How does writing about Helen separate her from George?

❧ Possible Writing Topics ❧

1. Write an essay about an event or series of events that changed your perspective on a particular family member. Describe as fully as possible each significant detail that led to this change of perspective. How did this change of perspective affect your perception of other family members? How did it change you?

2. After you've completed your essay, write about the "I" in your essay, the person who is putting down and describing the events. If that "I" were a character in a story like George's, what would you say about her? Would you say of this character or this person, "She is me"? If not, what are the differences? How does your identification of yourself when remembering the events, along with your role in them, differ from your identification of yourself in the essay you wrote?

Garnett Kilberg

Thieves

*T*HE trip was destined to be a disaster, Stuart thought as he looked at his older sister, Gail. She had lodged herself in the far corner of the Buick backseat. Her oval face was set in a scowl—all her features coming together in an ugly wrinkle. Her long legs, appearing even longer in tiny green shorts, were twisted around one another, entwined like rope. He knew she wasn't mad at him; they were closer than any of the brothers and sisters he knew. Being, at 12, both the oldest and wisest child in their neighborhood, Gail was a leader of sorts, an organizer, and she always made Stuart her second-in-command. But still her anger, her worry, was disconcerting. Something terrible had happened with their family, an incident that involved their Uncle Travis—Gail's favorite relative—something so horrible that instead of making their usual trip to their grandparents' summer house, they were going to a bungalow their uncle had rented on Lake Michigan. Gail was angry at their mother for not telling them what had happened, what was wrong.

To top it off, Stuart's parents were arguing. They had started on the porch, behind the morning glory covered lattice, and had edged their way toward the Buick. Now they were moving within earshot, the mother opening the car door between herself and her husband.

"He's my brother. I have to go to him," said Stuart's mother.

"Movie melodrama," said Gail, almost hissing under her breath.

"What about some loyalty to me? He's my brother-in-law. How do you think I feel?" said Stuart's father. "I'm the one who got him the job."

"I've already apologized for that. So has Travis. What do you want from us, blood?"

"Oh God," said Gail.

"Even your parents, *Travis's parents*, agree with me," said Stuart's father.

There was a silence. Stuart could see his father's shoes beneath the open door of the car. They were black and had designs, swirling little holes, on the toes as if they had once been soft and someone had decorated them with the tip of a toothpick. His briefcase was standing, crooked, next to them on the gravel driveway.

"So," Stuart's father finally said. "That's your final word. You're not going to change your mind?"

Stuart couldn't see his mother's head; it was above the car door opening.

"If I don't go now, we'll lose him forever. I can't change my mind."

The briefcase rose, disappearing behind the barrier of the door. Then Stuart's father's face appeared in the window, next to his mother's khaki clad hip.

"You kids have a nice vacation. Be good in the car and when you get to Uncle Travis's, do everything your mother says." Then, before they could reply, he was gone, his gray suited back walking away from the car, across the lawn, up the street toward the bus stop.

"Rob, are you going to phone?" Stuart's mother called after him. He didn't turn around, just shrugged his shoulders. Stuart's mother waited until his father had disappeared behind a cluster of tall shrubs, then got in the car, slamming the door.

"You mean we're not even going to talk to Daddy the *whole week?*" asked Gail, her face becoming even more distorted.

"Don't worry," said Stuart's mother, stretching her arm along the top of the front seat, looking over her shoulder to back out, "he'll call."

Despite the state of his family, Stuart was excited. This was his first vacation any place besides his grandparents' summer house. His mother had said the beach would be right in Travis's back yard and they could go swimming every day. There would be new places to explore, maybe a cave or a big gnarled tree where he could construct a fort. Even his premonition of disaster, his curiosity about Travis, was exhilarating. If only he could persuade Gail to share his excitement, everything would be fine.

Stuart stared at Gail, willing her to look at him, to speak. When she didn't respond, the rhythmic movement of the car began to make Stuart drowsy. He closed his eyes, yet didn't succumb completely to sleep, remained in the place between wakefulness and dreaming, thinking of Gail and Travis. He remembered when Travis and his new wife, Margie, had lived with them, for what seemed like a year, before Stuart's father had gotten him a position at his company. Stuart could recall Uncle Travis and Gail in the sun room, seated on wicker stools, leaning over the chess board. Travis was teaching the game's intricacies to Gail, her face as contorted in concentration then as it was now in anger. Her arms looked particularly slender in the big blue shirt she was wearing, the one Travis had given her with Chinese lettering on the back. Travis had pretended the letters read "kick me" in Chinese. Stuart could remember Travis, laughing, chasing Gail, also laughing, feigning attempts at kicking her. Then he imagined his father joining in the chase, his mother, Margie, the entire family running through the living room, waving in and out of chairs, trying to kick each other and he knew he was asleep.

When he woke up, Gail was reading a book, her features almost smooth again. Stuart's mother looked, the way she always did clutching the wheel, small and nervous. Stuart's neck felt stiff. He had been sleeping sitting straight up.

"Gail, do you want to play the license plate game?"

She gave him an annoyed glance. "Jesus Christ, you're almost nine. Why do you want to play that stupid baby game?" Stuart felt hurt, struck. He could almost envision, in his mind's eye, pink finger marks, remnants of a slap, embedded on his cheek.

"Gail, try to be pleasant," said Stuart's mother. "I'll play, Stuart. Do you want to start?"

Stuart could see nothing out his window except Indiana plates. He knew they had gone west from Columbus and were now headed north to Michigan.

"No, I guess I don't want to play. How long have we been in Indiana?"

"We've been out of Ohio for hours," said Gail.

There was no use trying to talk with her. As close as he and Gail were, Stuart knew she had dark moments, moods his father called them. Stuart was sorry this mood had extended to him, but she would get over it. She always did, coming into his room late at night, presenting her secret thoughts as peace offerings. Perhaps, Stuart thought, he could woo Gail by questioning their mother about Travis. He knew very little about the trouble. The only words from his parents' fights that had remained distinguishable, after traveling upstairs, were his father's shouts of "loser" and "liar." He knew his mother had argued with Grandmother over Travis, had even hung up on her, but no one had talked to him or Gail. Maybe, Stuart thought, if he began with innocent questions, he could carefully lead his mother to reveal the real trouble.

"Is Aunt Margie bringing the baby?" asked Stuart.

"No," said Stuart's mother without turning her head, offering no more.

"Is she leaving him with her parents?"

"Margie's not even coming, dummy," said Gail.

"*Gail*," said Stuart's mother. "Uncle Travis and Aunt Margie are having some problems. They're not any of our business so it's best we don't talk about them."

Gail was sucking her lower lip, as if considering whether or not to pursue the subject. Stuart felt guilty, ashamed; Gail's concern was obviously real, painful, while his had only been curiosity, a ploy.

"Hey," said Stuart's mother. "I bet you two are hungry. Stuart, do you want to reach up front in the cooler and get some sandwiches? There's some Orange Crush too."

Stuart shifted to his knees and leaned against the back of the front seat. He bent forward and flipped open the lid of the red and white cooler. There were six sandwiches wrapped in crinkled tin foil and six cans of Orange Crush sitting on a bed of ice.

"Do you want anything, Mom?"

"No, I'll wait until we stop."

"Gail?" he tried to make his voice sound casual, less urgent than he felt.

"No. . .well, just a sandwich."

Stuart selected two sandwiches and a can of soda, feeling icy in his palm, and reached forward to pull the lid closed. He slid back down, his leg brushing Gail's thigh as he handed her a sandwich. He moved back to his window and peeled the foil from his sandwich. It was egg salad: cold and a little wet. It tasted soggy. He smiled at Gail; he didn't want to wait for her nocturnal peace offering. He wanted Gail's comfort now. She didn't return the smile: She was no longer sucking her lip; instead she was staring at the back of their mother's head, the unwrapped sandwich on her lap.

"It'll be a cold day in hell before we see Margie again," said Gail.

There was a silence. Stuart couldn't believe it, but their mother was ignoring Gail's remark, pretending nothing had been said. Then, as if in slow motion, Stuart saw Gail's sandwich fly up. He didn't think she had aimed it, but the sandwich hit their mother's head over the right ear, then separated into individual slices of bread. One slice, spread with mayonnaise and a few clinging pieces of egg, landed in his lap. He felt the car swerve. Everything seemed to go colorless for a second, a blur, then the car was still on the shoulder of the road. His mother was screaming.

"*Out*. Gail, get out of this car."

Opening and slamming their doors, Gail and his mother slid out, moved around the car until they were facing one another. His mother leaned forward, hands on hips, lips moving fast, yellow and white flecks in her hair, her polo shirt collar flapping in the breeze created by the rush of traffic. The sound of passing cars obscured what they were saying, but when Gail climbed back inside, her eyes, looking as hard and clear as glass, had tears forming in their sharp corners.

Sullied darkness, like overlapping screens, was beginning to form as they reached Travis's neighborhood.

"I think this is the street," said Stuart's mother, stopping and balancing a sheet of directions on the steering wheel.

"Where's the beach? I thought Travis said it was in his back yard?" Gail asked.

Gail had been talking an hour back, submitting short challenging remarks, as if testing their mother.

"I'm sure it's close by. 'In the back yard' is just an expression."

Stuart's mother turned down the street. Sheltered by the trees were tens of little cottages, bungalows: pink, blue, green and yellow. There were pink flamingos, plastic, poised on single legs in most of the yards. Some of the lawns had posts holding silver balls. Stuart noticed a ceramic squirrel, affixed with wire, darting up a tree.

"This place is really tacky," said Gail.

"You know Travis is down on his luck. He can't afford beach frontal property."

"He should have tons of money."

Their mother stopped the car.

"What do you mean by that?" she said, looking over her shoulder, her raised eyebrows pushing her forehead into folds.

"Nothing," said Gail, glancing away.

"All right, Gail, but I'm warning you for the last time. This has got to stop." She turned her attention back to the road and began driving again, slowly, checking the house numbers. "Here it is: the green one with the big rock in front."

After they were in the driveway and began unpacking the trunk, Uncle Travis emerged from the house. He was a big man with a broad face. His cheeks ballooned even larger above his thick beard, as if a shave would release constricted flesh, swelling his face still more. Stuart imagined pricking a cheek with a pin, watching air seep out, then winced and ran his tongue along the soft lining of his own cheek.

"Meg," Travis called, spreading his arms wide. Stuart's mother ran from the car into his hug. Stuart and Gail followed, trailing their bags. When Travis freed their mother, he stood over them, beaming.

"So, how are my two favorite kids?"

"Where am I sleeping?" asked Gail.

Uncle Travis's face seemed to drop, his broad cheeks and smile melting into his beard. "You and Stuart are in the room to the right—the one with two cots."

Gail slung her bag over her shoulder, tossing both braids back and walked to the house. When she had disappeared inside, Stuart's mother and Travis looked at each other.

"Does she know?" asked Travis.

"Only things she may have overhead. She's confused right now, but she'll get over it."

"How about mom and pop? Are they over it yet?"

Stuart's mother looked down at him, smiling. "Stu, why don't you put your things in your room—explore the house."

"But I want to talk to Uncle Travis."

"We'll have plenty of time to catch up later, little buddy: a whole week," said Travis. "There's a garden house in the back. Why don't you check it out? Maybe you could make it into your own little fort."

"I don't do forts anymore," he answered, feeling acquiescence, now, would be a betrayal of Gail.

"*Stuart*, Uncle Travis and I want to talk. Go inside; we'll be along in a minute."

Stuart dragged his bag toward the concrete slab steps, intentionally going slowly, hoping to hear more.

The thin single mattress on Stuart's cot sank in the middle when he lay down, creating foam walls on either side of him. He felt trapped in the center. Their room was only slightly bigger than the storage pantry at home; there was an inch of water in the back yard and the entire house was wet and smelled of mildew. The evening had been awful. Gail had started a game of chess with him, but had gone into their room to read before they had even finished. She had said little to Uncle Travis, answering his questions with laconic utterances. And it was obvious his mother and Uncle Travis were just waiting for him to go to bed so they could talk. He could hear them talking now, only the clarity of their words muffled by the flimsy walls.

When Stuart had come to bed, Gail had pretended to be asleep, but he knew she was awake, even now. Her steady breathing gave her away. He wished she'd come sit on the edge of his bed, talk, mend the unpleasantness that had occurred between them earlier in the car.

"Gail," he said toward the dark space dividing their cots. "What do you think Uncle Travis did to make everyone so mad at him? Do you know?"

He wanted to sound sincere, transform his curiosity into a concern as real as hers. But there was a short silence before she spoke and when she did, her answer was perfunctory, just a string of words not completely reflective, Stuart felt, of her thoughts.

"No," she said. "I heard Daddy say what he did; the word was something like 'imbecile,' only longer. It has something to do with money and Daddy's office."

"Maybe Travis acted like an imbecile at work, embarrassed Daddy." He was happy to be conversing with her, offering a suggestion.

"No, the word wasn't 'imbecile'—something longer."

"Maybe. . ."

"Shh," she breathed. "They're saying it now."

Stuart heard the flutter of Gail's sheet as she tossed it back and rose from her bed. Stuart sat up. He watched her dark form move to sit, cross legged by the glowing yellow crack beneath the door. In the faint light, he could see the space between her pajama top and bottom, the way her elastic waist band dipped, exposing the curvature of her backbone. He sat very still until, finally, she stood and returned to bed.

"The word is 'embezzlement,'" she said, almost as if she were thinking aloud, talking to herself. "He took thousands and thousands of dollars from Daddy's work and kept them in the bottom drawer of Margie's dresser."

A thief? Uncle Travis was a thief.

"Did Margie know?"

"She had to," said Gail. "The money was in her dresser."

"Why did he do it?"

"Because everyone at Daddy's work was stupid. Travis said everyone, *even Daddy,* was unfair."

"What did Mother say?"

"Just that Travis should have waited. Everyone liked him—everyone always likes him—he would have gotten a promotion eventually." There was an odd toneless quality to her voice. "She said he wouldn't have been a clerk, doling out expense money, forever."

Stuart felt her interest slipping, receding into her thoughts. He wanted to prolong the conversation.

"Did Travis. . ."

"Stu," she said. "Let's just go to sleep."

When he finally slept, he dreamed of an enormous bureau drawer filled with dollar bills, a confusion of green paper surrounding stacks of neatly folded blue shirts with Chinese symbols on the backs.

Stuart was the last one up. The bungalow's main room was divided into a kitchenette side and a living room. Stuart's mother was standing at the sink in the kitchenette side, washing dishes. When she saw him, she removed a hand from the water to pass him a yellow plastic plate with toast and two wrinkled strands of bacon.

"Where is everyone?" asked Stuart.

"Uncle Travis went to see if he could buy you and Gail some rafts."

Would he steal the rafts? Stuart imagined Travis running from a store, two huge inflated rafts tucked under his arm. Later at the beach, policemen would arrive to retrieve the rafts. Stuart envisioned himself, floating, saw the darkened trousers of the police as they waded in after him.

"He didn't have to do that."

"He wanted to do something special for you and Gail."

"Where's Gail?"

"Outside," said his mother, indicating the window with a tilt of her head. "Look, she's already found a friend."

Stuart took a bite of bacon, the tip crumbling on his tongue, sending a little tremor through his system, and looked out the window. Gail was sitting on the big rock at the driveway's end, wearing her yellow terry cloth bathing suit cover, gathered at the waist with white spaghetti shoulder straps. A fat boy in a T-shirt and bathing trunks was standing next to her, talking.

"Who's he?" asked Stuart, knowing immediately he didn't like him.

"He lives down the street. He said he'd take you and Gail to the beach."

"Why does *he* have to take us? He's no older than Gail," said Stuart. He wanted to be alone with Gail to talk about Travis.

Stuart's mother turned around, wedging her soapy palms behind her on the counter. Her eyes were swollen as if she'd been crying or hadn't gotten much sleep. "You're not going to start giving me problems too, are you? He's not really taking you—just showing you how to get there. Uncle Travis and I will meet you there in a little while." She paused. "Now finish your bacon and go get into your suit."

After Stuart had changed and started outside with the towels, he noticed the boy was even fatter than he'd appeared from the window. His T-shirt rode up over his belly creating an expanse of flesh shaped like a gigantic eye, his navel a blinking pupil.

"This your kid brother?" the boy asked. His eyes were small and moist like fish eyes.

"Uh-huh," said Gail. "Stuart, this is Chuckie. You ready?"

"Yeah."

"Okay," said Gail. "Let's go."

Stuart walked down the road two paces behind them. Gail always managed to do this: find friends who would do as she wanted. But usually they were not fat kids like Chuckie and usually she let Stuart share her power. He didn't think her slight now was intentional, only a result of her preoccupation with Travis.

"Look at this crap everyone has in their yards," she said as they passed a lawn with a flock of pink flamingos.

"My parents have some Dutch people and a windmill," said Chuckie.

"Well," said Gail, sucking her lip as she paused to retie a strap on her freckled shoulder. "That's different. A windmill is different."

They walked along the water; tiny waves lapped the edge, leaving dark imprints that quickly faded, absorbed by the sand, only to be replaced with another imprint. Stuart attempted conversation, but found his uncompleted sentences left hanging, ignored. Gail was too possessed with Travis, Stuart assumed, to answer. Chuckie was too occupied with Gail, probing clumps of seaweed with a stick, reciting legends of the beach—a ring he'd found when diving, his school friend who'd died after walking out on the ice last winter— barely suppressing his glee at the slightest response from Gail. Chuckie would have gone mad, absolutely crazy, Stuart thought, if he had met Gail at her sharpest, when she wasn't preoccupied.

When their mother and Travis arrived, Stuart abandoned his efforts at conversation to join them on the towels, lending, with some relief, his new raft to Chuckie. His mother and uncle helped Stuart build a sandcastle with a drawbridge, little shells as windows and dried seaweed for hedges. Gail and Chuckie, dragging their rafts, staged three walks in front of the castle. Each time, Stuart felt less enchanted with the sand, the drying seaweed. He wondered if Gail had confided to Chuckie about Uncle Travis. Later, when they started home, Stuart wasn't surprised to see Gail's mood had changed from detachment to darkness. Her features amassed, again, in the center of her face, her shoulders hunched forward as she walked. Stuart tried to stay between his mother and

Gail, prevent a dispute. Yet as soon as Chuckie left their group, Gail accused their mother of being rude to him, creating little dust clouds as she stamped her foot in the road. The argument was inevitable. But Stuart was surprised that his mother's punishment—not allowing Gail to go out to dinner with them—was so harsh. He was even more surprised that Travis remained silent, didn't try to intercede on Gail's behalf, the way he always had when he had lived with them. Stuart felt worse than he had in the car the day before, even worse than he had when he was alone with Gail and Chuckie. At the restaurant, he stole mints from the cashier's station, planning to give them to Gail to cheer her. But when they got home, his mother announced that Gail was already asleep. "Probably for the best," said Uncle Travis.

Stuart woke to darkness. He knew he wouldn't be able to return to sleep. Everything in the room seemed damp: the foam mattress, the walls, his hands. He felt sick recalling the day's events. But at least now, he thought, Gail will see that Uncle Travis isn't so special. After seeing him not stick up for her, she'll know not to worry about him. Stuart reached beneath his pillow for the mints and rose from the cot. The concrete floor felt wet and slick beneath his feet.

"Gail," he whispered, sitting next to her on the cot. She didn't answer; but her silent breathing indicated she was asleep. "Gail," he said again, "wake up." He pulled back the sheet and felt for her shoulder, but found a wad of cloth. Gail was gone! Only a pile of clothing, arranged like a body, remained. Stuart's throat seemed to drop, slip through his chest as he went to the open window. The moonlit back yard was empty except for the garden house: wet and empty, a long lake, short shoots of grass protruding like weeds in a pond. The mints slipped from his hand. Stuart's throat felt constricted, pulled tightly shut. He wanted to cry out, but he couldn't. He wanted to get his mother, but he couldn't. If he told now, he would lose Gail forever. But what if Gail was gone for good? He started for the door, then heard a noise, a soft creaking, in the yard and turned back to the window. The garden house door was opening. Gail and Chuckie came out, their bare feet sunk ankle deep in the watery grass. Stuart watched as Chuckie kissed his sister, his fat stomach pressing her against the garden house wall. Stuart walked backwards to the bed, sitting down, watching the window, waiting. No more than a minute could have passed before Gail appeared on the window ledge, crouching, her long legs, silhouetted against the moonlight, making her appear like some type of monstrous insect.

"Gail," Stuart said, surprised by the breathy quality of his voice.

"Stuart! What are you doing up?" she said, seeming to spring to the floor.

"Waiting for you. Where did you go?"

"You're not going to tell, are you?"

"Tell? No, I won't tell. Where were you?"

She sat next to him on the bed, still wearing her yellow bathing suit cover. Her slender shoulders looked especially fragile in the pale light.

"I was just mad so I went out for a while. Nothing seemed fair. But I'm all right now. Are you mad at me?"

"No." He thought he should leave, but felt too shaky to stand.
"We'd better go to bed now before Mother or Travis hears us," she said.
"Okay," he said, rising carefully, his knees still feeble.
"Stuart," she said as his leg touched his cot.
He looked back. Her oval face was half shadowed. The eye on the illuminated side seemed larger and brighter than it ever had before. "You're not going to tell."
"No," he said.

Early in the morning their father called. When Gail came out of the bedroom to talk, Stuart was surprised to see she was wearing her blue shirt with the Chinese symbol. As Gail took the phone, Stuart watched Uncle Travis to see if he would notice. Travis took a sip of coffee, a few drops clinging to his whiskers. Then he smiled. He waited until Gail was off the phone, then, as she passed his chair, he kicked her, tentatively, from behind. Gail giggled. Her face looked guileless, as if there had been no estrangement between her and Travis.

The four of them, with Gail and Stuart balancing rafts on their heads, started for the beach early, before the neighborhood showed signs of movement. Stuart's mother lifted her shoulders and sighed as they left the driveway, still happy from talking with his father.

"Even the street seems prettier," she said, looping her arm through Travis's.

Stuart looked down the street. Yes, it did look prettier, woodsier. Then something caught his eye, the *only* trace of bright color, a yellow and white windmill. The raft slid from his head to the road as he stood, staring.

"I've got to go back," said Stuart.

"What?" asked his mother.

"I've forgotten something. Just go ahead. I'll catch up."

He left the raft in the road and walked quickly up the driveway, around and behind the bungalow, his feet squishing the saturated grass, to the garden house. He pressed his thumb beneath the rusted hook lock and jarred it loose. The door fell open, casting a shaft of sunlight across the only room of the house. There was a confusion of color: pink flamingos stacked against one another, on top of each other, ceramic squirrels and silver balls piled at their feet. He only looked for a moment before closing the door, relocking it. But as he gazed at the bubbled and peeling paint on the door, he realized his mind's eye had registered details—the scratches on a silver ball, the tip of a flamingo's crooked beak, black as if dipped in paint, and the solitary eye of a ceramic squirrel, looking up at him. His lungs felt heavy with the water that had warped the door and clung to everything else, as he remembered his sister's eye—so bright in last night's moonlight. He started back across the yard, slowly at first, then began to trot, run, his toes slipping backwards in the water, as if he might not be able to catch up—as if he had already lost her.

Composing "Thieves"

*L*IKE most stories of mine (and, from what I'm told, of most writers), "Thieves" grew from a single mental picture, an image that had appeared countless times in my mind's eye before ever being transferred to paper. Other images—as well as characters, language, and events—in the story came from a variety of places: the time when the impetuous image originally occurred, subsequent times, sources I'm unaware of, stray remarks and scenes I encountered while engaged in writing the story, and from my imagination. Since many of the sources and the ways in which they evolved can be traced, writing about them, at first, seems an easy task. Yet I think I join the ranks of many writers (certainly several of my former teachers) when I say that the way in which one image begets another image, and one event begets another, is an elusive process, one that few people (if any) are conscious enough of to re-create completely. The difficulty is exacerbated by the fact that some of the sources are so personal that they're painful to discuss, while others—often the most powerful in print—are embarrassingly banal. Talking about "Thieves," in particular, is further muddled because in both structure and content, the story closely parallels a real chain of events in my life, from which, paradoxically, I feel more emotional detachment than I do from stories of mine that are more rooted in invention. This close resemblance to reality, combined with the emotional detachment from it, is so unlike what usually happens in my work that it seems misrepresentational to discuss it. However, after consideration, I've decided that since every story is atypical in one way or another, I'll go ahead and undertake the telling of the story's composition, hoping that this paragraph—though it offers no revelations—serves as an adequate disclaimer for the things I can't cover, reconstruct or explain. Perhaps the best way to proceed is to break the story into components, beginning with the image that acted as an impetus for the story's conception.

The image from which the rest of the story evolved is Stuart's view into the garden house—the "confusion of color: pink flamingos stacked against one another, [and] on top of each other." To me, an image is a little like my baptismal cup, a piece of silver that was once shiny, but has become increasingly dark and tarnished after years of being carried around in boxes without being polished. Polishing it would be akin to putting a mental image into print. When I began "Thieves," the image of the flamingos was particularly murky. I had first seen the image's source approximately 18 years before I wrote the story. While sharing a bedroom with my sister in a rented cottage in Cape Cod, I opened our closet door to be confronted by a sight similar to the one Stuart encountered behind the garden house door in "Thieves." My older sister and a boyfriend—a long-time friend of the family, not the least bit plump, now deceased, who, along with his mother and sisters, was sharing the cottage with us—had raided the neighborhood, relieving it of all the pink flamingos. (Unlike in my story, my sister and David took no other yard ornaments that I can recall.) I remember how stunned I was, not only by the gaudy beauty of the birds crammed in a small space, but also by the fact that my sister had accomplished such a feat without my knowledge. The stolen birds represented both her rebelliousness and her secret life, a life from which I was excluded. Had anyone asked me the image's origin while I was writing the essay, without hesitation I would have been able to say, "It came from the time my sister and David stole the birds." Yet while engaged in the writing process I doubt I ever seriously pondered the source or its meaning; and, even though "Thieves" revolves around the relationship between two siblings, I never consciously wondered whether my persistent memory of the image suggested anything about my relationship with my sister. In fact, I so completely forgot about my sister's connection that it wasn't until after the story had been accepted for publication that, with some trepidation, I mentioned the matter to her. My worry was unwarranted. To my astonishment, my sister didn't even remember stealing the birds! This shouldn't have surprised me since I can think of one long-time friend who, upon seeing me for the first time in several years, proceeded to tell her memories of our years together. None of them were familiar to me. When it came my turn to reminisce, I discovered that although we'd spent an important part of our lives together, we had practically no memories in common. Such is the nature of memory and also, it seems, the nature of the creation of a story. What may mean an enormous amount to one person, enough to be transformed into a piece of fiction, may be of no consequence to someone else.

    I had the image, but wasn't sure what to do with it. I wanted to write a story in which the main character stole the birds; I wanted to be right there with the character, plucking the creatures from the moonlit yards, running to hide in the bushes at the onslaught of car headlights. But how would I get to that spot? I decided to begin with the beginning of our actual trip to Cape Cod, working my way towards the image which I expected to be the last in the story.

    Since I didn't remember the departure, itself, I created one, a composite of many departures. The setting I chose—the house with a "porch behind a morning glory covered lattice"—was not a place I ever lived. Rather, it was a house I often passed on walks around the time I wrote the story. The only difference was that the lattice I passed was rickety and old, covered with chipped paint and decorated by no more than a handful of sky-blue morning glories. On my walks, I always pretended I'd purchased the house and was free to do with it as I wished. I planned to strip and paint the lattice, then drape it with a blanket of morning glories. So, in my story, I did just that.

    In an early handwritten draft of the story, I believe—though the draft has long since vanished and I can't be sure—that Stuart was a female. However, I think the female version of Stuart so closely resembled me that in order to avoid simply recounting my vacation, I needed to do something drastic. Such a shift isn't difficult. I frequently write about young boys, drawing on my son and his friends as sources. But even without this reservoir, I don't think it takes any special adroitness to write from the point-of-view of a child of the opposite sex—at least not any more than it takes to write from the point-of-view of a child of one's own sex. If Stuart's name—along with a few other words and pronouns—were changed to Mary, I doubt readers would find her any more masculine than they now find Stuart feminine. As groups, boys and girls may have general differences, but as individuals they are all idiosyncratically different from every other person, regardless of sex, which means, of course, that one doesn't need to do anything to them to make them appear more like boys than girls or vice versa.

Stuart's character's name went through several changes. Often I begin writing about a character under one name and then switch names as the character develops and no longer suits his or her name. Stuart, the name of my grandfather (spelled differently) and of a former teacher, is a name I admire for its ability to be serious and kind and intelligent all at the same time.

"Gail"—the name of the first girl who ever asked me to play at first grade recess, a request that so startled me that I told her I had other plans and hid for the remainder of the recess—is suitable only by its close association (in my mind) to childhood and its ability to tap some usually suppressed emotion. The image of Gail, pulled tightly in the corner of the backseat, is derived solely from my sister. I remember many a family trip where she remained wrenched on her side of the imaginary line she had drawn for us, while my brother and I remained on the other side. (The first draft, I think, also included a third child. But, again, three children too closely mimicked my own family. And, more important, the third child was superfluous, didn't contribute to the story, simply became another name for readers to assimilate.) My sister was a resourceful girl, always sewing, reading, weaving, or embroidering. I envied her large array of skills and interests. My poor eyesight, coupled with a predisposition towards car-sickness, prevented me from doing much of anything during a journey. So I watched her. On that particular trip to Cape Code, my sister was angry; I'm not sure why, probably because she had to leave a boyfriend behind to go on a trip with us (unlike 12-year-old Gail, my sister was closer to 15). When I wrote the description of Gail, I was in the upstairs office of a large old house we owned in Pennsylvania. I remember trying to make her physical appearance seem tight, wrapped up in herself, her legs twisted. I wrote several similes, none of them (including the "entwined like rope" which seemed too sinuous) were satisfactory. I remember going to the top of the stairs and calling to my husband and son, asking for suggestions. They both gave me several which I scoffed at (poor souls, my husband and son) and went back to my office where I decided, for lack of anything better, to keep the rope image.

The parents, I'm ashamed to say, are quite generic. But at least they're *my* version of generic parents. While some people's generic father might wear a cashmere sweater and golf slacks or an olive green factory uniform, my generic father wears a gray suit, carries a briefcase, is always going to work, and wears wonderful wing tip shoes. To me, the shoes are the most lucid part of his description. As a girl, I was paid to polish my father's shoes. I can clearly recall my absorption in the dark chocolate-colored leather and the curious design of little holes, the only decorative part of my father's dress, aside from his tie. I didn't know the character's name until the mother in the story called, "Rob, are you going to phone?" And the mother's name, I don't recall now (though I will look it up before I finish writing this).

The argument between the parents in the first scene never occurred in any form between my parents. Except for an occasional disagreement about something small—a book, a date of an event, someone's last name—I doubt I ever saw them argue. But snatches of the dialogue are taken from autobiographical moments. For example, I've heard my son say things like "movie melodrama." And although the line, "What about some loyalty to me?" seems ubiquitous enough, probably muttered by hundreds of husbands a year, it is a combination of words that so clearly evokes an image of my first husband that just typing it makes me shiver. Still, even without a fight, there was something mysterious about that trip to Cape Code. To begin with, my father didn't go; nor did the father of David, the boy who assisted my sister in stealing the flamingos. Also, my mother and David's mother seemed to spend more time away from the children; we were on our own quite a bit. I think that David's mother was having marital problems (she later got divorced) and was meeting my mother to discuss the situation. So when I first began writing "Thieves," I considered having the mother on her way to meet a friend who was contemplating a divorce; the father's anger, I reasoned, could be a result of being deserted, or of disapproval over the mother's involvement in another couple's problems. Later, I mentally changed the friend to a man, the mother's brother. And, finally, I decided that in spite of the fact that a divorce was an infamous deed of some magnitude at the time we went to Cape Cod, it was too commonplace at the time I was writing the story to constitute an adult secret of any weight. So, to find the source of the parents' anger and secrecy, I mentally listed and played with various crimes, problems, and passions of people I've known. Travis, the embezzler, was the result.

I'm surprised, as I write this, to discover how many sources contributed to the creation of Travis. His character—or personality—is a combination of two people whom I know well, and, understandably, don't wish to reveal or discuss. His crime comes from a third person. And the image of the dollar bills in a dresser drawer from a fourth person. (I was once told of a person who made a great deal of under-the-table cash, and, to avoid drawing attention to the money kept it in a dresser drawer rather than a bank. Whenever I hear of that person, I imagine the dresser drawer.) Travis's ability to play chess comes from yet another person, my grandfather, the only person with whom I've ever played chess. The challenge and intellectual nature of the game is such that it creates a bond between the opponents. Alluding to Travis and Gail's chess matches (as well as the shirt Travis gave her) seemed a way to establish their relationship as something special, different from the typical relationship between an uncle and a niece, but not suspiciously different. Probably the car trip to reach Uncle Travis took too long, what I've heard deemed "driving to the story." But it gave me time—though I'm not sure I needed it—to fully imagine Travis in my mind's eye before he ever appeared on the page.

I believe the only allusion to the actual route of the trip occurs when Stuart asks, "How long have we been in Indiana?" and Gail replies, "We've been out of Ohio for hours." I imagined them to be driving from Cincinnati to a small town along Lake Michigan. To readers, such a detail may seem unimportant, but it's crucial to me to have some sense of place while I'm writing, even if that place is in transit. I couldn't use the actual route to Cape Cod since I had no memory of what passed by outside the windows, so I chose a route I've traveled frequently enough to recall the scenery. Conversely, the fight between the mother and Gail was inspired by an actual fight between my mother and sister along the highway to Cape Cod. Only the real fight was much more violent and dramatic than the one relayed in "Thieves." I don't feel comfortable presenting what provoked the real fight—there was no egg salad sandwich thrown, the image of specks of eggs all over someone comes from a different situation—but think it's safe to mention that it ended with my mother trying to force a $10 bill on my sister, insisting that she catch a bus home. The landscape as a whole is lost to me, but I clearly recall my sister's face, and the way the swish of passing cars rocked our car, my brother and I waiting guiltily (for we'd had some part in the ordeal) in the backseat.

By the time the characters reached their destination, I knew them well enough to realize that I wasn't going to have my way with the story. Stuart, who is clearly the character from whose point-of-view the story is being seen, was far too timid to disappear into the night to collect flamingos. I was sentenced to be an onlooker, seeing the birds the same way I'd seen them in my own childhood. But still, I wasn't quite sure how to reach that image, the one of the flamingos crammed in a small place. As is best in a story, I didn't worry about it; instead I concentrated on the place to which they'd just arrived and on the characters.

Like many of the entities in the story, the rented cottage is a combination of places. The bedroom I envision is from the Cape Cod house. But the house, itself, seems to be drawn more from a place where my son and I lived when he was about 5 years old. The house was cottage-like with an all-pine interior, a small barn in the back, and a lake to the left of the driveway. And it was damp. I remember the silver fish shooting across the floor and the way my lungs sometimes felt "heavy with the water that. . .clung. . .to everything." Originally Stuart and Gail had separate bedrooms, but it was suggested to me in a workshop (I was in the M.F.A. program at the University of Pittsburgh at the time I wrote the story) that the story would be tighter if the two shared a room. (It was a good suggestion since it eliminated a lot of logistical moves to set up the conversation of the first night.) I invented the conversation through a play of chatter, both verbal and on the page, in which I discovered the sound similarities between "embezzlement" and "imbecile," resulting in Gail's statement, "I heard daddy say what [Travis] did; the word was something like 'imbecile,' only longer."

I met Chuckie for the first time when Stuart did. Although I knew there'd be another boy—an accomplice—I had no idea he would be fat—or that Gail would be wearing an outfit like one my sister had when she was 10 or so, with spaghetti shoulder straps—until, through Stuart's eyes, I glanced out the window. And there he was, the little fat boy from our street in Cincinnati, the boy who had, with all his pranks, evoked my suspicion (I'm sure he's the one who lifted my son's coin collection) the way he was now evoking Stuart's. I mitigated my dislike for him my naming him Chuckie after a next-door neighbor boy from my childhood whom I had a crush on. But regardless, I was almost as miffed as Stuart that he had to come along to the beach (a scene which, like the walk back from the beach, seems too quickly told).

The way the waves lap the shore, "leaving dark imprints that quickly faded," was taken from another story of mine that I'd written several years previously. Most of the other images in "Thieves" occurred unexpectedly as I reached points in the story where they seemed to fit. For example, the shirt with the Chinese symbol on the back had been my most beloved item of clothing when I was about 8 years old. My father, like Uncle Travis, kicked me every time I wore it. In my mind, I can see it both in color—a sapphire blue—and in an old black-and-white photo of me, sitting on the edge of a crater-like hole in our backyard, wearing the shirt, my back to the lens, and a partial view of my face, caught, as I turned, squinting into the sun, to have my picture taken. I also have a photograph of the "sandcastle with a drawbridge, little shells as windows and dried seaweed for hedges" which was built in North Carolina by me, with the help of my stepsons and some friends. The fact that I saw Orange Crush, instead of Seven-Up or Diet Pepsi, in the cooler on the front seat is undoubtedly because it was one of the few types of soda that I can remember being allowed to have as a child. When I was little, we went twice to Mexico for close to a month in the winter; in the afternoon on those trips we were allowed to get an Orange Crush from the canteen at the Hacienda. I remember those bottles—which somehow were transformed into cans in the writing—better than other whole vacations. Stuart's affinity for building forts came from a stage my son and other neighborhood boys went through, turning every spare piece of wood, along with old boxes and shingles, into forts. I think the ceramic squirrels came from a yard ornament shop perched along the road I traveled, between Butler, Pennsylvania and Pittsburgh, several times a week during the period in which I wrote the story. But the story does have some contrived events and images. Once I had some general idea of what the story was about, I added Stuart's theft of the mints and his daydream about Travis stealing the rafts. They seemed needed.

My favorite scene in "Thieves" is when Stuart witnesses Chuckie kissing Gail, "his fat stomach pressing her against the garden house wall," and a moment later sees Gail "on the window ledge, crouching, her long legs, silhouetted against the moonlight, making her appear like some type of monstrous insect." Although I did not, during that specific trip, see my sister return from her night heist, I knew a lot about using windows as doors. For about a year during high school, my sister and I frequently waited until we thought our parents were asleep, then vanished out the windows on separate excursions with friends. It was easy on the nights we were allowed to sleep on the ground floor. On other nights we had to climb from my window to a lower roof, then drop to the ground. On one occasion when I got caught (my sister was much more practiced and adept than I) I remember feeling like a huge insect squatting on the window ledge as I saw my mother's form in the darkness. I never saw anyone like Chuckie kiss my sister, but I did see it as I wrote the story with no more difficulty than I saw the things which really occurred. When writing the first draft, I had expected the story to end at about the point where the kiss occurred. But I ran into a logistics problem. To have Stuart see Gail and Chuckie carry the birds into the garden house (which, incidentally, was the first name for the story) would eliminate any element of surprise when he later saw the birds crammed together, perhaps even eliminate the image entirely. And if he didn't see them take anything into the garden house, why on earth would he climb out the window and go look in it? So instead of forcing it, I placed the image on reserve and concentrated on Stuart's encounter with Gail and their ensuing conversation. The sister's eye, appearing "larger and brighter than it ever had before" was taken from my son who has enormous hooded eyes. I had no idea that it was serving as a foreshadow for the eye of a ceramic squirrel. When the conversation ended, I had no choice but to put the characters to bed and hope that a way into the garden house would surface in the next fictional day.

I, of course, knew what Gail had done, which explains her wearing the shirt with the Chinese symbol on the back and her changed mood in the morning. But it wasn't until (at least I think it wasn't) the characters were out in the road that the absence of yard ornaments in the neighborhood provided me with a strategy for getting Stuart to the garden house and the image. As soon as Stuart's mother mentioned that the street seemed "prettier," woodsier to Stuart's mind, Stuart had some idea of what had happened; he thought his sister was behind the removal of all the artificial scenery. So, there we were, Stuart and I, racing back through the saturated grass; he to prove his theory, and me to reclaim my image. Delighted as I was to have found the means for reaching this image, I felt nearly as breathless as Stuart must have been when the door fell open, exposing the once murky image to a "shaft of sunlight."

It's odd, but now that I've finished writing this essay, I realize that "Thieves" doesn't parallel one singular chain of events in my life nearly as closely as I thought when I began the essay. Rather—although the trip to Cape Cod does serve as a focal point—the story reflects a contribution from many forgotten sources, some autobiographical, some not. And, to my surprise, I find I'm not as devoid of sentiment for those sources, and the story they produced, as I originally thought. Just thinking about them has generated a surge of suppressed longings and sentiments. If this essay were a piece of fiction, I think I would go back and change the opening paragraph to coincide with what I'm saying here, to better prepare the readers for my inevitable conclusion. But since this is an essay in which I'm trying to unmask some truths about composing fiction, and writing in general, perhaps it's best that I leave things as they are. Maybe, that way, this essay can serve as more of a record of what I, as a writer, sometimes think when I begin a story in contrast to what I've discovered by the time I've finished.

QUESTIONS

Garnett Kilberg's story, "Thieves," and its process essay, "Composing 'Thieves'"

1. What advantage does Kilberg gain from telling the story from Stuart's perspective? Why choose this third-person perspective, rather than telling the story from the first person, as Kathleen George does? How would the story be changed if it were in the first person, told by an adult Stuart looking back on his childhood?

2. What has Stuart learned about himself at the story's end? How has his perspective been changed? How has his life been altered? How do you imagine his relationship with his sister will be changed from this point?

3. In her process essay Kilberg writes, "By the time the characters reached their destination, I knew them well enough to realize that I wasn't going to have my way with the story." Does this mean that at that point she'd lost control of the story? How can the writing process produce a story or essay that is markedly different from the writer's initial intentions?

4. Consider, for a moment, the "single mental picture" Kilberg mentions in the opening sentence of her process essay. Do such pictures cross your mind as well under different circumstances? What other images attach themselves when you study that mental picture?

Possible Writing Topics

1. Write about an event from your childhood, where you begin by focusing on a "single mental picture" that for some reason you've found yourself preoccupied with over time. This time, try writing the essay from the third person, as if you were looking at yourself as a he or she rather than an I. Before you begin, you may want to go back to an essay you've written in the

past in the first person, and change it to the third, and see what effect that produces. And prior to writing your first draft, jot down some of your ideas, some of the ways you plan to write the essay, some of the things you want to be sure to mention.

2. After completing the essay, write a second essay about how the initial ideas and plans you made for writing were changed by the process of writing. How close is the final copy to the ideas that floated around in your head? Is that final copy stronger or weaker than you thought it would be? Are you pleased, or disappointed, with how your imagined draft matches your actual draft?

Barbara H. Hudson

My Father's Books

WHEN I was in elementary school, my father often rose from his chair after supper, walked back to his study and returned with a book. "I'd like to read you something," he'd say, and the five of us seated at the table (my mother, myself and three sisters) would stop talking—I was usually listening anyway—and turn our heads toward him as he sat down again and opened the book with long slender fingers. We'd squirm a bit, maybe one sister would glance at another, and he would begin to read, peering through the bottom lens of his bifocals and into a hardback library book or one that he'd bought at a used-book store.

Sometimes he'd introduce the passage by saying, "I read this this afternoon," but more often he didn't. He simply read, and we would listen, because my father kept his thoughts to himself and in many ways he was a stranger, and we were polite to strangers. Often he read a poem with strange, archaic language or a story with frightening imagery: I remember "watching" a beggar die outside a peasant's door.

At other times, he'd read from an essay or something equally hard to understand. Then he'd stop and the uncomfortable silence would follow.

Sometimes my mother would grimace and say, "Why did you read that?" He would smile and turn red. Or she might ask, "What do you think of what you've read?" and he would reply, "I thought it was interesting." Occasionally one of the daughters would have grasped enough to say, "I liked the part about the nightingale," and a small chorus of yeses would follow.

Then he'd get up from the table and we'd all say thank you, but even as he walked back to his study, one of my sisters would have begun to talk, as though his reading were only a pause in the conversation.

During those elementary school days, I usually listened in distress because my father was reading something that I didn't understand, that none of us did. He expected us to. Why else would he read it and not explain what it meant? We were letting him down somehow.

In high school the humiliation became resentment. Why was he doing this to us? His readings never had anything to do with what we were talking about, and then we had to endure that awful silence. Couldn't he see that we didn't enjoy it? I was amazed that his pride wouldn't keep him from opening the book.

Not until I was in my twenties did I begin to understand something of what my father was trying to do and why he was doing it, and in the midst of that process, I began to discover something about myself and why I write.

At eighteen I left my father and his books in El Paso, Texas, and went away to college in Nashville, Tennessee. I didn't know it then, but never again would I go home to live. Perhaps I needed the distance to begin to make sense of my childhood.

At twenty-five, I went back to college for the second time. I had been a biology major and a secretary and I had spent a year in nursing school, but finally I decided to major in English because I wanted to write. I didn't know why exactly, except that I had found a certain satisfaction in writing that I hadn't found with anything else, and I hoped that writing could integrate the paths I'd tried or wanted to try. "I'm interested in too many things," I'd say to people who asked.

So six years after my last college-level English course, I took a fiction writing class with Dr. James C. Robison, a writer of short stories, who, as another professor told me, would scrutinize every word, every line, every sentence. After the first class I desperately wanted to drop, because as I sat listening to Dr. Robison talk about writing short stories, I suddenly realized that I had no concept of what it meant to write one. Apart from academic writing and letters, I'd written only poetry. I wasn't even sure I knew how a short story worked. How could I write something I didn't know?

But I stayed in the class—the "why" is another story—and decided to hold myself to what felt like a long hike up a steep hill with no certain destination.

Dr. Robison asked us to begin with a character sketch of a person who interested us, real or imagined, and after struggling to think of someone, I chose my father because it was Sunday afternoon and the sketch was due on Monday and he was an interesting person whom I could easily see in his small study, surrounded by books on cryptography and genetics and the meaning of dreams, anthologies of short fiction and essays, old family Bibles that didn't belong to our family, dictionaries of foreign languages and famous quotations. I spent a happy afternoon re-creating him and his books.

The next step was to put the character into a story, and mine was a story of description, detail after well-wrought detail: about a man who could walk into a room with thousands of books, pause momentarily, then walk straight to the one he wanted; a man who took long walks in the desert, who didn't speak much, whose wife spoke to his children for him.

One afternoon after I'd turned it in, pleased with my details, Dr. Robison invited me to sit on the porch of one of the dorms, each of us in a rocking chair looking out onto the Southern lawn. He began by saying that the reader needed some insight into my character, some understanding of his motivations and his history. As the story stood, there was nothing to explain why this character didn't talk. What happened to him? His reserve is so extreme.

I didn't know. And suddenly I saw my father from the perspective of someone outside the family. Why didn't he talk and why didn't I know him any better than I did? I was embarrassed: it wouldn't take much for Dr. Robison to figure out that this was my father. In fact, I realized, he probably knew already. And then I was grateful that we were talking about my father with the same distance I had used to make him into a character, a distance that protected me sitting there with my professor, but one which enabled me later to look at him again, as a person, a man with thoughts I didn't know. Why didn't I know them? I wondered. Was it just because he didn't say, "This is what I think"?

And why were his books so significant?

At Dr. Robison's suggestion, I rewrote the story from another point of view, choosing the perspective of a teenage daughter, and what had taken hours spread over days to write before took little more than a morning and an afternoon. I was amazed at what I'd written: something that I couldn't have said any other way, that I *wouldn't* have said any other way.

It was as though the words had been hidden somewhere, in a room in the back of the house or in the basement, and when I'd gone searching for words because I needed to write a story for a deadline, when the doors I usually opened for writing weren't appropriate, and when my sense of urgency kept me trying, I finally came to this door. In my relief to find one that opened easily (that seemed, in fact, to push itself open), I hadn't checked the words like I usually did, and there they were in my story. There was my father, trying to say something he hadn't said in the first version. What was it? And there I was, the daughter, trying to say something I'd never said before.

The answers didn't come with that story, but since then I've begun to make some connections. I've begun to realize that my father was trying to speak to us when he read after supper. He was trying to say something he couldn't form into his own words; and somehow the words of his books were more familiar, more safe, more rich and complex, more intriguing, more precise than his own. He needed to say things and he used his books to say them for him: a covert self-expression worth the discomfort it brought him and the rest of the family.

As I've continued to look at my father and the way he used (and still uses) books, I've begun to find words to construct a meaning for my writing—one that was forming even as I wrote my first story. It goes something like this: I write because the world within pushes to get out, and I can't seem to get it out any other way.

As I look back now on that first character sketch, I see the process differently. Then I felt as though my choosing to write about my father was rather arbitrary. Now I believe that it wasn't. Instead, the father who lived (and still does) within my subconscious mind—the one I'd taken with me when I left El Paso—was pushing to get out, where my conscious mind could make sense of him.

My childhood assumption of this quiet man had been that he didn't want to tell us what he thought, not that it was hard for him. But when I began to write him into the revisions of my first story, and later when I wrote a play about a father and a daughter, I found myself able to write both sides—the father who feared intimacy more than he wanted it and the daughter who wanted it more than she feared it. And in a strange way, I found myself siding with the father. I find it hard to communicate too, I wanted to tell him.

As I've suggested, I believe that my father reads aloud from his books because communication for him is complicated, and not just a matter of saying what's on his mind. Or maybe it is: because his mind is such a complicated and complex place. In the same way, I write because communication is difficult for me, and even as I write those words, I can't help but hear the question I've heard all my life: "Why are you so quiet?" Now I can see the irony of asking a reserved person to account for her reserve, but I also remember the pain of not knowing why and feeling that I should. I couldn't remember being any other way, but I knew that it made me different—the world outside was a noisy place. I spoke when I had to, and sometimes I wanted to, but more often I swallowed my words, not knowing that one can only swallow so many words before they begin to leak out, or burst through a door somewhere.

My father's bursting from his door was my first significant realization of the world within that was pushing to get out. I don't like to say that I would go crazy if I didn't write, if I didn't keep opening those doors, but I don't want to risk it: the house might explode. My house anyway.

It's quite a house too. During the time that I was so shy, I took in pages and pages of images and the meanings they suggested, more than I wanted most of the time, certainly more than I could make sense of.

My family provided the most: my silent father who was born in el Paso, who decided not to be an electrical engineer after he graduated from college but went instead to medical school, to become an ophthalmologist; my gregarious mother, who grew up in North Carolina and abandoned her graduate work in English to marry my father and leave the South. My sisters and I grew up in a house that valued learning, with a father who knew math as well as eyes as well as many other things and a mother who could not help but be Southern in a place where dust storms and not rhododendron bloomed in the spring. It was an upbringing that gave me an internal houseful of images and a lens through which to see them. My father reading at the table is one: a complex image that gathered meaning with time and repetition. Other images stuck because of their singularity.

For example, one summer when I was six, we took the train from El Paso to North Carolina to see my maternal grandmother and my mother's three brothers, their wives and children. It was a biennial trip my mother had begun before I was born and one which we would make every other summer until I was in college; even then I would travel from Nashville to Boone to see my grandmother.

On this particular trip we had to change trains in the middle of the night when we got to Little Rock, Arkansas. We had to change trains on other occasions as well, but the transition wasn't significant, and for those trips, I would remember other things.

We had left El Paso the night before, and I remember waking up in our sleeping compartment and thinking of how the big black porter had changed the chairs and sofa into beds, as though with magic. We ate breakfast in the dining car, swaying as we lifted forkfuls of scrambled eggs. I didn't eat much. It was too strange: all the movement. Then we found our seats in the coach car and spent a long day listening to the rattle of the wheels on the tracks, watching the desert change into grass and trees, before falling asleep again, upright this time, our heads in funny positions.

As we drew near Little Rock, my mother and father roused us: four daughters, the youngest a baby. It's time to get up, sweetie, my mother said.

I woke to a sense of urgency and the fear that I would be forgotten and left asleep on the train, realizing even as I woke that my mother had not forgotten me, but the feeling wasn't gone: I was still afraid of being lost in the shuffle. I don't know what my father was doing. Sometimes he had a way of disappearing.

When the train stopped, we all got off somehow and made our way to the station. It was late June or early July, and the air was warm and heavy, so different from the cool dry air of El Paso when the sun went down or the cool damp air of the mountains where my grandmother lived. I didn't like it.

Once inside the station, we sat down near a woman dressed in black: not a dowdy woman, plump and motherly, on her way to see grown children, but a strange woman. Her eyes were dark and sunken, and her face was thin. She wore deep red lipstick.

My mother, who will talk with almost anyone, began a conversation, and we all found out that the woman was waiting for her dead husband. His coffin would be on the train we were waiting for. I'm so sorry, my mother said.

The woman went on to tell us that he had died somewhere outside of Arkansas and was coming home to be buried. I don't think I'd ever heard such language: "coming home to be buried." It was stranger than the woman, and as she talked, I saw a wooden coffin, swaying with the train, moving slowly toward the room where we sat, with a man who had once been alive now enclosed in something dark and stifling.

My mother wasn't disturbed. She spoke with empathy and concern, but I heard the distance in her voice as well: This woman's life is not ours. I was confused. My life seemed permeated with the woman and her dead husband. He swayed in his coffin as I had swayed that morning in the dining car, and in some scary way I sensed that my world had changed forever, now that I knew that such things existed.

And that knowledge would have been enough for me, significant as it was on that warm Southern night when I was afraid of being separated from my family. I might have forgotten the woman and her husband, as I grew older and death became more familiar.

But I didn't forget. When the train arrived, the coffin wasn't on it. I don't remember exactly how we found out, whether we were with the woman when she was told (by whom I'm not sure), or whether she went away and came back. What I do remember is her response: she was hysterical with rage, transformed from a woman who was strange into one who was terrifying, her face contorted and her voice a screech.

The world that had widened for me only minutes ago exploded. If the coffin wasn't on the train, where was it? I was quiet on the outside, but inside I was out of control and reeling through space, in limbo with the coffin. And I took that feeling with me as we left the woman to climb the steps to the train, to walk through the narrow door and find our seats, the smell of upholstery and stale air making me nauseous, as it always did when I first smelled it. Slowly the wheels began to turn, until they were a clatter against the tracks and the lights of Little Rock were gone.

We were a family well-schooled in silence when it came to disturbing situations, and so it was with this one. We never talked about it. It became a part of the wealth and burden of memory, eventually pushing itself onto the page.

And as the words came out, I tested them again and again for their meaning and their sound. Is this what I sense in that nebulous part of my brain? Does the external language do justice to the internal?

In this essay, I've tried hard to be accurate: My father never explained what he read; my mother was the one who spoke to the woman in black; I felt this way. Were I writing a story, who knows what would happen. Maybe the father would read the same story for a week and each time make up a different ending. Maybe the mother would refuse to speak to the woman, and it would be one of the daughters who asked the questions, different questions. The transformation of memory by experience and imagination is fascinating: how the internal and the external worlds interact to provide the material for essays and stories.

And for me, the memories are there, ready to be transformed, demanding at times to be accounted for. So I work with them: to hear what they have to say in the best way I can say it.

Sources of "My Father's Books"

I began working on this essay when I was a first-year graduate student in the English Department at the University of Pittsburgh. The essay was to be the major project of a teaching seminar I was enrolled in, one designed for graduate students who were teaching a particular undergraduate composition course for the first time. I was a new MFA student in the fiction-writing program and was much more comfortable thinking about my own development as a writer than anything that had to do with teaching.

Actually the essay began even earlier, before I ever entered the classroom. In order to prepare for teaching composition, the new graduate students were sent a copy of the text during the summer. We were encouraged to read the essays and write our own responses to the questions, as though we were the students. One assignment asked the reader to write about an event that she or he had perceived in one way when it happened but now perceived differently, or could imagine perceiving differently. I thought of my father and his readings after supper and the change in my understanding of what he did and why. It was an assignment I could respond to narratively, with a story, and I enjoyed doing it.

Later in the semester, when I was teaching, the time came for me to begin thinking in earnest about my project. One of my seminar professors had suggested that some of us write personal essays about writing and teaching. The last we want to do, he said, is send you to the library. So I brought out the short essay I'd written during the summer (actually I brought it up on my MacIntosh computer) and began to work on it.

I read over what I'd written and made some changes: a word didn't sound right, the rhythm of a sentence was off, there was something else that needed to be said, or maybe I'd said too much and something needed to be taken out. When I had revised what was there, I began asking myself how this business with my father figured into my own writing, and as one sentence followed the other (sometimes with great struggle) I made some connections I'd never made before. I don't think I put a word in about teaching, only writing.

Part of the process of completing the paper involved turning in a rough draft several weeks before the final was due, an obligatory chance to give ourselves another reader. In my professor's written response, he asked me how I would approach reading differently from my father and how that might connect with teaching. It was a wonderful question: he gave me a way to talk about teaching that I hadn't thought of before, and I was grateful. It was a class for teachers after all.

You may be wondering where all that material is, given there's not a word about teaching in my current essay. The original paper is on another computer disc, labeled PROJECT.

Several weeks ago (I am now in my second year of the MFA program), Eve Shelnutt asked me to write something for a book she was putting together. I happened to think of my seminar project (something already written) and gave her a copy to read. The following week, she drew me aside and said, I'm sure you're a wonderful teacher, but I like the first half best—the part about your father and your writing. Can you take out the part on teaching and write more about writing?

Sure, I said, not wanting to miss an opportunity to be in a book. Besides, that's the part I enjoyed working on the most.

So I sat down at my MacIntosh again, and did what I'd done before with my short essay. I began with the first sentence: "When I was in elementary school, my father often rose from his chair after supper, walked back to his study and returned with a book." I asked myself if this was the way I wanted the sentence to read. Did every word fit? Was the rhythm right? Did the external sense still match the internal? Yes, I could say.

And so I continued: sentence after sentence. Many I left the way they were, but some I changed because I had changed over the past year and was now a different reader of my own work.

Finally I came to the point where I moved from looking at my writing to looking at my reading in the original project. From there I would move to teaching. The transition went like this, beginning with a section I hope you will recognize, even as you realize that it's slightly different from its counterpart in this book:

> I write because I don't talk much. Why not? I can't help but hear the question. I've heard, "Why are you so quiet?" since I began to play with children other than my sisters, who never asked. I remember the discomfort of not knowing why: I couldn't remember being any other way, but I knew that it made me different—the world outside was a noisy place. And sometimes I rose to the occasion, to speak a few words, but more often I swallowed them to keep my peace, not knowing that one can only swallow so many words before they begin to leak out, or burst from a door somewhere.
>
> So I write because my world within pushes to get out; my father reads for the same reason, voraciously. Writing and reading, then, have come to mean more to me than taking notes in a class or flipping through a magazine, though I still do both.

What you have goes like this:

> . . . I write because communication is difficult for me, and even as I write those words, I can't help but hear the question I've heard all my life: "Why are you so quiet?" Now I can see the irony of asking a reserved person to account for her reserve, but I also remember the pain of not knowing why and feeling that I should. I couldn't remember being any other way, but I knew that it made me different—the world outside was a noisy place. I spoke when I had to, and sometimes I wanted to, but more often I swallowed my words, not knowing that one can only swallow so many words before they begin to leak out, or burst through a door somewhere.
>
> My father's bursting from his door was my first significant realization of the world within that was pushing to get out. I don't like to say that I would go crazy if I didn't write, if I didn't keep opening those doors, but I don't want to risk it: the house might explode. My house anyway.

I'll leave it to you to try to account for those differences that interest you, except for one: "And sometimes I rose to the occasion" in contrast to "I spoke when I had to, and sometimes I wanted to."

Rising to the occasion was the theme of my first semester as a teacher and a graduate student. As a quiet person, I felt that I had farther to rise than most people to get up in front of a class and behave as though I had been quick-witted and assertive all my life, when in fact, as a student, I had always been among those who said the least. I often felt that one more occasion would do me in: the house would explode.

So as I worked on my project during that stressful semester, the phrase "sometimes I rose to the occasion" was rich with meaning. You couldn't have paid me to take it out. It was a memorial to my suffering. But when I read it a few weeks ago, I thought it was a little melodramatic and changed it. I'm not suffering in the same way.

As far as the rest of the essay goes—how I came up with something more to say about my writing—it grew out of my desire to write about the train trip, an event that was pushing itself into my consciousness. Even as I sat in front of the computer writing about my father's and my mother's histories, I began to think about that night in Little Rock, and writing about the event became a current way to illustrate the process I had been talking about: how the images of memory work themselves onto a page and ask to be made sense of. I didn't know exactly what I was going to say until I began to write, and even then I had to work at it: I had to concentrate on what I saw and smelled and heard, and remember how it all felt and why it was so significant.

I'm not finished with that train trip yet, as I wasn't finished with my father and his books after writing my first essay. That essay ended this way:

> Not until I was in my twenties and had gone back to college as an English major did I begin to understand what my father was trying to do. Here was a quiet, reserved man who spent most of his free time reading in his study, who had a wife who loved him but didn't understand him (her responses to his readings were much the same as ours though the words were different), and who had five daughters (another one had come along) who must have seemed to him at times like Martians.
>
> When he announced his intentions to read, he was making a space for himself amidst the clutter of a family meal. He was saying, "This is important to me." His readings were a gift and even then I sensed that we received them like a hostess who takes the present and sets it aside to open when the guests are gone, and perhaps she forgets. I knew that we were failing him somehow, but not until later did I realize that he wasn't positioning us to fail him. He was a very self-protective man, trying to be a father to his daughters by telling them who he was in the safest way possible—through the writings of others. He *hoped* we would understand.

Perhaps it's fair now to say that writing my essay was a process: a process that I found very worthwhile.

❧ QUESTIONS ❧

Barbara Hudson's "My Father's Books," and its process essay, "Sources for 'My Father's Books'"

1. Re-read the paragraph in which Hudson says, "I write because communication is difficult for me...." How is it difficult? Is it simply Hudson's reticence that pushes her to write? Consider the advantages with regard to communication that writing can give you over speaking. What are some of the disadvantages?

2. In the final paragraph of "My Father's Books" Hudson writes, "And for me, the memories are there, ready to be transformed, demanding at times to be accounted for." As you read through the essay again, how do memories "demand to be accounted for"? Does Hudson control which memories make that demand. Do you have memories whose significance seems inexplicable?

3. Read the two parts of the drafts of "My Father's Books" that appear in the process essay. Which to you seems stronger? What makes it so?

4. Hudson says of the first draft that for a long time, "you couldn't have paid me" to take out the phrase "sometimes I rose to the occasion. " She calls it a memorial to her suffering. And yet, in the end, she cuts it because, she says, "I'm not suffering in the same way. " Find an essay or a journal or a paper that you've written in the past and reread it. How do you respond now to what you wrote then? Are there phases you'd like to change that now don't seem completely honest, completely on target?

❧ Possible Topics for Writing ❧

1. Hudson says that while discussing her story with her professor, "I was grateful that we were talking about my father with the same distance I had used to make him into a character, a distance...which enabled me later to look at him again, as a person, a man with thoughts I didn't know." Write an essay about a friend or family member from the perspective of someone watching at a distance. For instance, write an essay about a sister you know well from the perspective of a neighbor who lives across the street, but does not know her well.

2. After completing the essay, write a process essay that addresses the difficulty you had in gaining this perspective. Was it easy? What did you have to intentionally forget? What did you have to remember that normally you would take for granted? Was it possible to gain the objectivity necessary to write an essay that was honest, true to the perspective you tried to gain?

Kevin Stemmler

Branches

UNLIKE other children, Sandy and I were never allowed to sleep in church, or whisper, or giggle, or remain seated when everyone else was kneeling. Other parents let their children stretch right out on the pews, but not us. While the grown-ups recited Latin, Sandy and I were trained to leaf through a series of "Books for Little Catholics" that were sold in the damp church basement. And we had, between the two of us, the entire series.

If I had to pick a favorite, I suppose *My Book of God* would be my choice. Sure, it didn't have the plot of a Bobbsey Twins story, but it did have interesting pictures of people who were eternally blissful because God loved them and they Him, people who were happy because they did "what God told them," people who were strong because "with God's help" they could do anything.

But my favorite part of the book was the center that always fell open to expose the rusting staples that bound the pages together. Here, at the core of the book, was God the Son. Underneath a drawing of Jesus surrounded by children who were attached to him by vines, was the line: "We are like branches growing out of Jesus." Mesmerized, I memorized the line, and on Palm Sunday of 1963 when Johnny Kolchek's altarboy gown caught on fire while he reached to light the top row of candles, I turned to Sandy and spouted: "We are all branches growing out of Jesus."

When the ushers, rather immediately, had clapped out the flames of the ignited Johnny, Sandy turned to me and, on cue, responded as the model Catholic child, "As long as we grow out of Jesus we will yield good fruit."

My father gave me a peach rub for speaking in church; Sandy's arm was lightly pinched by mother, her way of saying "Act like a lady," without having to speak in God's house in anything short of Latin.

Although St. Anne's was probably the last church in the whole world to give up the Latin mass and switch to English, eventually we came to a point where Sandy and I could read along with the mass. We gave up, for good, our

Books for Little Catholics and watched, through the years, the development of Johnny Kolchek into a model, priestly man. While Johnny never duplicated his Palm Sunday of 1963 performance, Sandy and I would turn to each other on every Palm Sunday after and deliver our lines of branches and good fruit. And after a while, we could do this without reprimand—peach rubs or pinches—because we were too old for all of that. And my hair, already, was becoming too thin to risk a harsh rub.

By the time I reached the age of twelve, God's master plan for my future was already in full gear. Before I could grow into my funnel shaped body, I had to survive a year-long test of will. On my eleventh birthday, out of the clear blue, the angel of God appeared before me and presented me with fifty extra pounds that my body's frame was too weak to hold. But because Mary did not reject God's gift sent from an angel, and because I wanted to be happy with God, I did what he commanded. With His help, my weak body was able to carry the extra fifty pounds of fat, and I became a strong person, able to carry my excess weight through even the biggest throng of foes.

Six months before my twelfth birthday I decided to do something about my heavenly weight. We were across the street, at Uncle Arnie and Aunt Emily's, for a fourth of July cookout. Uncle Arnie was stretched out in a lounge chair, his right arm raised above his head exposing a white mass of deodorant that looked like he had tucked a cupcake in his armpit. I was eating my third hot dog when Uncle Arnie, observing me from behind the dark lens of Aunt Emily's cateyed sunglasses that he frequently wore, rubbed the large mass that rose from his ribbed tank-top and said: "You got a stomach like mine, Timmy." I wanted to cry, but I just stared at the butt of my hotdog and shrugged my shoulders. Being compared to Uncle Arnie was more than I could bear. Sandy and I had always agreed that Arnie was one of the most repulsive people we had the unfortunate luck of being related to. Sandy rushed to my defense, though, and commented, "Those sure are nice glasses you got on there, Uncle Arnie. I wish they made those kind for girls, cause I'd be sure and get me a pair." Sandy's delivery was so sincerely convincing that Uncle Arnie not only thanked her put pointed out that they were actually Aunt Emily's sunglasses: "Ain't that the damnedest."

Later, while the grownups listened to the double header on the Panasonic transistor, Sandy said, "Don't feel bad about it."

"Feel bad about what?" I asked, pretending that Uncle Arnie's comment was the furthest thing from my mind.

"About Uncle Arnie telling you you're fat."

"Oh, that. It don't bother me," I lied.

"I heard about this diet on the radio talk show. They say if you drink lots of water before every meal, you'll lose weight. Maybe you could try that."

I looked at Sandy with a wounded expression. It was the first she'd acknowledged the issue of my weight.

"You're not *fat*," she went on to explain, "but if you don't watch it, you're gonna be."

Thanks to Sandy's diet tips, I had slimmed down considerably by my twelfth birthday. I don't honestly know how much of my success was due to the water diet, or how much was due to God and his plan. For somewhere in those six months, I managed to grow a few more inches, which I wouldn't have noticed except that my church pants were looser at the waist and the hem no longer bunched at my shoes, but hung loose at the top of my socks.

Although I shed my fruitful pounds, my looks did not improve. In fact, I started to look worse. If indeed I was a branch growing out of Jesus, I was certain I was a thorn in His side. It did not seem possible or likely that I could yield anything good.

"Hey four-eyes!" Uncle Arnie called across the street.

I fought the urge to tell him what I really wanted to tell him and hollered back, "What?"

"Tell your parents that we're having a pinochle party on Saturday. And tell your old man that maybe he should borrow your glasses for the night!"

Aunt Emily emerged from the front door just in time to stop me from informing Uncle Arnie that he was the biggest jackass in the whole county. "You quit picking on him, Arnie," she yelled, then to me: "Don't you pay him any attention, Timmy. You look handsome in your glasses." I smiled at Aunt Emily and turned around to whisper, "Jesus." By the time I walked into the kitchen, I was beginning to cry. "What is it? What's wrong?" my mother asked.

"Uncle Arnie says you're playing pinochle there on Saturday night—" And I started to cry at full speed.

"*Now* what did he say to you?" I should have played my cards right, now that I had my mother's sympathetic ear in my favor, and played Arnie up as the worst person in the whole world and couldn't we *please* move far far away from him; but instead, I reneged on my hand.

Filled with the spirit of anger and hate, I gave a full-fledged wail of "Jesus Christ I hate that man."

My mother, the branch grown full straight from Jesus' side, ran the limb of her arm smack into the center of my mouth. "We don't talk like that in this house, young man, no matter how angry or hurt we are. I never want to hear that come out of your mouth again."

Instead of calming or shocking me, my mother's gesture served to stir up the holy spirit even more inside me and I pushed my way back out the kitchen door and, mail still in hand, I galloped across the backyard, bucking my head and wailing the news of the holy spirit. "Jesus Christ," I sirened, "Jesus Goddamned Christ Almighty! Jesus Jesus Jesus Christ!" I might have run wildly for the rest of my life if Sandy hadn't stepped in to lasso my body with the stiffest right punch that was every thrown. I remember nothing of falling to the ground, of being dragged back into the house. I woke later that afternoon with a swollen face and sore mouth. At dinner, my father's question "What happened to you?" gave me reason to believe that not a word of the day's activities had been repeated. "I fell," I answered. And it was to be my first fall into acceptance of who and what God had made in me.

By the time I was in High School, I had the broadest shoulders of any other kid in the school, or so it seemed at any rate, probably because in proportion to my waist size—a mere twenty-eight inches—my shoulders looked huge. Uncle Arnie, of course, would say, "It looks like your shirts are still on the hangers!" God, what an ass.

Johnny Kolchek was a senior that year and quarterback of the Warriors. Rumor had it that Johnny made the entire team join in a group prayer before every game, and that he was also responsible for the prayer chain letters that showed up in everybody's locker. This wasn't the run of the mill prayer chain letter; this one promised the direst doom, nothing short of the fires of hell if you didn't pass it on to five other people. Johnny Kolchek was a likely candidate for pinning the rap on, but I still had my doubts that Johnny had it in him to fill a page with such ugly prophecy. See, some people, like Aunt Emily, believed that when Johnny had his near-fatal brush with fire on Palm Sunday in 1963, that Johnny was given a message from God that meant he was special. Because of the weave of the altarboy gowns, fire should have consumed it immediately, which would have possibly made Johnny a likely candidate for sainthood and a definite threat to Saint Joan of Arc's secure position.

Aunt Emily entertained this notion with some degree of seriousness. "It's just as well he didn't burn," she'd say, "cause chances are they'd just pluck his sainthood from him someday, the way they did poor Christopher."

Anyway, it was hard to imagine that someone as close to sainthood as Johnny Kolchek could be the mastermind behind the fear and wrath that filled the chain letters.

"Johnny's probably never even touched himself below the waist," Sandy would say in a low whisper when Aunt Emily would launch into her Lives of the Near-Sainted speech. And it was truly difficult to imagine that Johnny was capable of any thought or deed that would be impure.

I sometimes felt myself projecting into Johnny's life, mainly because he was handsome and popular and because he was always turning up where I was—school, church, even the same places my friends cruised on the weekends. What was more odd was that my appearance, from the back, must have resembled Johnny's, for people would often come running up from behind to tap me on the shoulder; "Johnny—" they'd say, then, "Oh, I'm sorry, I thought you were Johnny." On Sundays when I received communion, I studied the expression on his face. He had eyes like the artist's rendition of Jesus in *My Book of God*, the drawing that preceded the passage: "No one can pretend to know what God really looks like." His eyes were crystal blue and clear, trite as it sounds. Thanks to God, Dad had finally gotten Health Benefits at work and we were able to afford contact lenses for me, which were tinted a blue that unnaturally matched Johnny's eyes. As far as I knew, the similarities—shoulders and eyes—ended there. But when the Warriors were victorious thanks to Johnny's skills—and prayers—I found myself wanting to identify more with Johnny.

When I found my letter of doom wedged in my locker, I folded it neatly and stuck it inside my pants pocket. Later, at home, I addressed an envelope to Uncle Arnie and mailed it to him. I knew it would throw Arnie for a loop, but I never imagined it could have the impact on him that it did.

The night before the Warriors' final game for the State Conference, there was a huge bonfire planned at the school to incite the student body to support the team's spirit.

I had been in the bathroom, studying my face in the mirror of the medicine chest, trying to find a way to suck my lower lip under my upper to make the line of my mouth smaller, my lips smoother like the angelic mouth of Johnny Kolchek. I had been more conscious of other body flaws now that I had gotten rid of my glasses, and I had recently been obsessed with the way my lower lip widened and spread out as though it had been pressed against a pane of glass.

I didn't hear Sandy push open the bathroom door—the lock hadn't worked for as long as I could remember—but before long, in spite of my trance-like focus on my mouth, I could feel that I was being watched. How many times Sandy had seen me rearrange and swallow my bottom lip, I could not say. But she had been there long enough to realize I was obsessed with something in my reflection there.

"Trying to count the hairs on your face?" she finally asked.

I was too embarrassed to yell at her for intruding. So I simply looked at her with blank eyes that suggested that she wasn't really there, that I had heard nothing.

Sandy always hated it when anyone ignored her. I think she saw herself as one of the four elements that allowed the world to exist. Pretending that Sandy didn't exist was the easiest way to fight back. And it worked like a charm, at least that time, for Sandy reconsidered her posture, pulled her hands from her hips and let them sway at her sides. Her face softened, her taunting grimace relaxed into a softer expression. From these new lips—thin and smooth—came words, soft, "Whatcha doing?"

"Nothing," I answered, staring back at the mirror.

"Sorry to bother you but I need to get ready for the bonfire, too," she explained. "How much longer will you be?"

"I don't know," I said, shrugging Johnny Kolchek's shoulders. And I continued to stare into the mirror. Sandy moved her body closer, wedged her way in front of me and she, too, stared at our mutual reflection. From the angle it looked as though her forehead brushed my left cheek, though from our side of the mirror I couldn't imagine we were really that close.

I was no longer watching my own image; I stared at Sandy, lost in her own gaze. "Don't stare too long," I whispered, "or you lose sight of yourself."

Sandy blinked, her eyes met mine in the mirror with a stunned confusion, then she smiled.

"We are branches growing out of Jesus."

"And we will yield good fruit."

I have this theory about God.

Just when you think you've got a handle on the mystery of existence, God will throw a curve ball to remind you that it's not your ball game to bet on.

Someone else had a theory about God, once, that Aunt Emily espouses: The Lord works in mysterious ways. Of course, that seems to reduce life to a maxim, but take it for what it's worth.

The night of the big bonfire proved to be a cool autumn night. Large sparks would rise from the large mass of wood and threaten to land in the dry patches of leaves that covered the nearby fields. As Johnny Kolchek led the rally in a group prayer, to conclude the evening's festivities, a green log on the fire let out a hissing, spitting small bunches of flames onto the platform where Johnny stood spewing the Our Father. It was really a beautiful moment. Johnny kept right on praying, ". . . forgive us our trespasses as we forgive those who trespass against us and lead us not into temptation. . . " while members of the team raced around trying to stomp out the small bursts of flame. I looked across the crowd to find Sandy's face, which wasn't difficult since she had already spotted mine and was waving an arm in the air to get my attention. I smiled back at her and on the way home, in Dad's Rambler, we laughed ourselves silly over the coincidences of the bonfire and Palm Sunday 1963.

Closer to our house, though, we stopped laughing. From a good mile away we could see the flames shooting high into the black sky, bursts of flames that were far more threatening than what we'd witnessed at the bonfire. "Do you think—" Sandy started to ask, but I interrupted, "No, it's on the wrong side to be our house." Closer, we realized that the source of the shooting fire was directly across the street from our house. We drove as close to the fire as we possibly could and parked the car on the berm of the road. I ran a wild pace to see my parents standing next to Aunt Emily who was in a state of complete frenzy. "What is it?" I screamed to my father, over the roar of the blaze.

"It's Uncle Arnie. He went back in the house and hasn't come back out yet."

"Didn't anyone stop him?"

"No, he snuck around the side."

I don't know what obsessed me, but I sprinted past the group of neighbors who had gathered to watch the firemen battle the blaze. So far, only one truck had shown up, although more sirens could be heard approaching from the other end of town. I ran to the side door that opened onto the basement stairs and yelled for Uncle Arnie. While I was tempted to flee, I was tempted to pursue this bizarre act that I had somehow undertaken. I went up the stairs and into the kitchen. I could see how the flames were beginning to spread down the walls of the livingroom and realized the fire was contained in the upstairs of the house. And there, on the stairway to the bedrooms, was Uncle Arnie's large body, crawling down the steps like a wounded animal.

I don't know how I managed it, but I half-dragged, half-carried the mass of Uncle Arnie through the kitchen and out the side door. As soon as we came out, there were people pulling us further from the house and they all seemed to be in a state of panic, now that Arnie was outside again. I didn't really let go of Arnie's body, I left my arms cupped under the armpits of his spread arms. He started to mumble something stupid about a letter, but I kept saying "It's okay, never mind."

"No," he said, "you don't understand. It's my fault—it's the letter!"

"What?" I asked, and then I noticed the crumpled paper in Arnie's hand, recognized against the light of the brilliantly lit sky the handwriting of the chain letter that I had addressed to Arnie. I let his body drop to the ground and left him to the attention of the neighbors and Aunt Emily.

"Jesus Christ!" I was screaming, prancing my way to Sandy's side, "Jesus Christ! He thinks the fire's because of that goddamned letter I sent him!"

Sandy looked at me with the eyes of wisdom and reached out to touch my arm. "Calm down," she said, her voice steady. "Just calm down."

"But what if I caused this to happen? What if the letter is really *real*?"

"Jesus, Tim, that's so damn stupid I can't believe you even said it. If you really believe that Uncle Arnie's house caught on fire because he didn't write a letter to five people to escape the curse, then you're crazy."

"But what if it's true?"

"It isn't. Okay? It isn't true."

We stood facing the burning house, Sandy's arm half-way across my shoulders. The trees in the front of the house were now just black shadows of branches, their dried leaves having been torched.

The next day the newspapers were full of predictions of the Warriors' night game and on the front page was featured of photograph of Johnny Kolchek praying. On the bottom of the page was a picture of Aunt Emily and Uncle Arnie's burning house. The caption pointed out that in the fuzzy shadows to the left of the house was the body of Uncle Arnie, clutched in the strong arms of his nephew, Tim, who saved his life. "Thank God for Timmy," Aunt Emily was quoted as saying.

As fate would have it, Aunt Emily and Uncle Arnie lived with us for the months it took to salvage and reconstruct their home. The entire day after the fire Uncle Arnie spent writing letters and addressing envelopes to people, explaining his recent misfortune for not having answered the original request immediately. And anytime I entered the room, he stopped to smile at me, treating me as the hero that the newspaper reported me to be.

As fate would have it, the Warriors not only lost their big game that night, the game that would launch them into State fame, but Johnny Kolchek suffered a broken collarbone in the third quarter. "It's a pity, really," my father said when we came home from church on Sunday.

"It sure is," my mother agreed. "But you gotta give the boy credit, I mean, there he is up there on the altar before mass, lighting the candles. Never see him shirk his duty. He's a good boy."

"God certainly does shine himself in odd ways," Aunt Emily added. "That boy, he's going to make some lucky woman a good husband someday. He'll be a good catholic father."

"Are you interested?" I asked Sandy.

"Sure," she said, "I'll marry him and yield his fruit." I no longer remember the laugh that followed Sandy's remark, even though I think I remember seeing her face light up. *My Book of God* was right: there are things we cannot see with our eyes. Even in the past we cannot always see the future as clearly as we want.

Autobiographical Sources of "Branches"

*T*RYING to uncover the autobiographical sources that influenced the writing of "Branches" is difficult, mainly because it is not easy to separate fact from fiction in the story. Memory has a way, I guess, of making the factual seem fictional and the fictional seem true. I do know that the kernel of the story rests on the memory of Johnny Kolchek's altarboy gown catching on fire somewhere around 1963. While I invented Johnny Kolchek's character, the event is true. It happened on Palm Sunday in what must have been 1963 since I was only four or five at the time and the old Saint Rose Church was still standing. On both sides of the altar were large risers that displayed a large variety of statues of the saints. A double row of candles fenced in the statues that, since it was Palm Sunday, were hidden under purple cloths. Before mass started an altarboy came out to light the candles and instead of lighting the top row first, he lit the bottom candles. In reaching over to light the top row, one of the flames made contact with the wide, loose sleeves of his gown and instantly went up in flames. There was a brief period of confused shouts as someone in the front pew rushed to clap the flames in his hands. It was an even I will never forget.

Unfortunately, this memory is not an important memory for my family since no one else seems to remember the event. This past Palm Sunday I was reminded of that day and I happened to ask my family if they remembered the time the altarboy caught on fire. Everyone denied any recollection of such an event, except for my sister who said that while she honestly could not recall the event, at the same time it did not sound totally unfamiliar. It was this reaction that led me to write "Branches," for I became instantly fascinated by the fact that a shared event could be forgotten by some while it left a distinct impression on another person. What this says is that memory affects people in different ways. It is tempting then to suggest that those who write have a way of making what may become trivial or forgotten events to some people important memories to rely on in fiction.

Originally the story opened with a long, tongue-in-cheek narrative espousing the narrator's theory about God. After typing the first draft, I realized that this was not necessary to the real story, although it was necessary to get me to the point where the story really began. This discussion of God was what took me to my first scene, which is now the beginning of the story. While this prewriting exercise got me to the opening of the story, it also made me realize what was feeding the story. Although it was less obvious as I wrote the story, I can see now that the impulse for the story was based on my religious upbringing and all the events surrounding it.

Like Timmy and Sandy in the story, I was raised on a series of books designed to familiarize Catholic children with their faith. As a child, I read these books with extreme fascination, mainly because of the element of mystery involved. It was not until recently, when I rediscovered these books in my parents' basement, that I realized what really attracted me was not so much mystery but irony. As mentioned in "Branches," the books really did have illustrations of God and Jesus followed by lines such as "No one can pretend to know what God really looks like." I imagine such irony played an important role in the decisions I made as I created my characters and plot.

I had planned on writing a story from a third-person point of view with the narration attached to Johnny Kolchek's character. Instead, the narrative that has been edited led me to a first-person narrator who witnessed the event. By the time I introduced Johnny into the story, I sensed that it was more important to write about someone who was intrigued by the event instead of a character who experienced it first hand. In so doing, I had to find a way of making Timmy examine Johnny in relationship to himself. Since I did not want the story to depend entirely on Timmy's sense of self, I needed a device to provide an outsider's point of view. Thus, Uncle Arnie ended up in the story as the antagonist.

While Uncle Arnie has nothing in common with any of my real uncles, his character was created out of a comment made to me by an uncle at a family gathering. Sometime around my twelfth birthday I developed a body that matches Timmy's in the story. This event did not take place on the fourth of July but on the occasion of my grandparents' fiftieth wedding anniversary. Because this was a painful moment in viewing myself through another's eyes, I cannot forget the memory. I was wearing blue shorts and a green and blue striped tank top, standing on my uncle's porch eating a hot dog. My uncle stopped beside me, put a hand on my large stomach and remarked, "You sure are *growing!*" I felt, for the first time, my physical unattractiveness and knew my uncle was right. I was fat. For many years I felt a sense of repulsion at that memory and repulsion toward my own self-image. When it came time to create Uncle Arnie, I fueled him with all the negative feelings I had from the memory of my grandparents' anniversary party. I realize now that making Uncle Arnie all-around repulsive made it easier to present and identify with Timmy's feelings about his own image. Perhaps the reason Timmy does not respond to Uncle Arnie's comment, "You got a stomach like mine, Timmy," is because I could not respond to my uncle's observation. The reason Sandy comes to Timmy's defense, to speak when he is unable to speak, is because I wanted to make Timmy vulnerable somehow. By not allowing him to articulate his feelings at the time, I hoped the delayed recounting of events would make his character more trusting, or at the very least, more sympathetic.

I am tempted to say that nothing else in the story is autobiographical in any manner. Certainly the prayer letter, the bonfire, and the house fire are all fictional devices that enhance what I felt were ironies in the characters' lives. Since I am trying my best to be honest here, I must add that while the other details in the story are mostly imagined, they are still products of my sensibility. Timmy's sense of self—particularly the scene with Sandy at his side, staring in the bathroom mirror—is too factual to label as fictional. This scene evolves out of a memory I have of getting ready for the Junior High Christmas Dance, which was, I might add, the occasion of my first slow dance and the night I got the stem of my glasses tangled in my sister's girlfriend's earring as we danced. I was in the eighth grade, my sister in ninth grade. As she dabbed more Musk Oil on, I reapplied my English Leather cologne, then stepped forward to examine the shape of my mouth in the mirror. Like Timmy, I was trying to suck in my lower lip which seemed entirely too wide for my face. In the middle of this trance-like stare, I felt my sister watching me, only when our eyes met in the mirror I didn't try to hide my feelings. "I'm ugly," I said to my sister's gaze—a statement Timmy could never make to Sandy.

In their proper perspective, all the autobiographical events I have just related are rather trivial, despite the fact that many of them are still quite painful to recall. It is this pain that limits what I choose to relate as autobiographical in the story. It is also the embarrassment of these memories that keeps me from exposing more. This, too, is what keeps "Branches" from being strictly an autobiographical story. I imagine every writer wants to share parts of his or her life with a reader, yet at the same time he or she wishes to keep some things sacred and private. This probably accounts for the fact that I said the kernel of the story rests on the memory of Palm Sunday in 1963. By focusing on this as the event of the story, the autobiographical elements seem more subtle. Finally, this memory, combined with all the fragmented memories I have of my Catholic rearing and the ironies I see in these events, forms the overall memory that influences the story. In short, the ironies become the memory.

Since no one I knew who experienced the events of Palm Sunday 1963 seemed to clearly remember the event, I began to think that maybe what I was convinced was factual really was a fictional invention after all. Regardless, this idea at least provided me a purpose for writing the story and since no one could challenge the truth of the event, it gave me certain liberties to create it as I wanted it to be. Thus, I did not feel constrained by my material, nor did I feel obligated to present the real events in a truthful, factual manner. Because the altarboy's catching on fire was a significant memory for me, I assumed others who shared the event would find it significant as well. Since my family failed to find it significant, I decided to create a story where the event was not only a shared experience but significant to the entire community of the story.

Johnny's representing, at first, the extreme opposite of Timmy's character creates an irony for Timmy who finds humor in Johnny's actions yet envies him at the same time. Not only does Timmy find himself mistaken for Johnny as he gets older, but he ends up replacing Johnny's heroic position through an event with similar elements. Timmy's rescue of Uncle Arnie from the burning house is ironic, too, since Timmy finds Uncle Arnie such a repulsive man, and it is equally ironic that this event takes place the night before Johnny's injury brings his heroism to a human level.

The fate that the narrator comments on at the end of the story refers to the influence of the religious ideology in the story. This is the note the story ends on, mainly through subtle implications that Sandy will one day marry Johnny Kolchek. I cannot say exactly why this sense of fate fascinates me, except to draw again on those books from my Catholic childhood and to say that such ironies do have their sources in my own experiences. While Sandy's implied marriage to Johnny may seen too contrived or forced, I can only draw on my own life to defend the decision to include that information. My sister married a man whom I met the year before they started dating. At the time he approached me and told me how much he admired my sister. I turned to my brother, who was standing next to me, and said, "Why doesn't someone tell him he has a snowball's chance in hell." Two years later they were married. I still find that incredible at times, but I offer it now as proof that Timmy's stance is adequate, that even in reviewing the past the future seems unlikely. Here, again, memory has a way of making the factual seem fictional, the fictional seem true.

~ QUESTIONS ~

Kevin Stemmler's story "Branches" and its process essay, "Sources for 'Branches'"

1. How frequently and with what devices does Stemmler reinforce throughout the story the theme announced in the title? What advantage does this reinforcement lend his writing?

2. What becomes of Timmy's desire to emulate Johnny Kolchek? How is he changed by the ironies throughout the story, particularly at the end? Was there too much that was coincidental in the story? If you would argue yes, then what do you make of the narrator's comments about fate and about coincidence, and how they resonate in the last line of the story?

3. In his process essay, Stemmler says that "memory has a way of making the factual seem fictional, the fictional seem true." Can you recall incidents from your own childhood whose details you're not sure are real or fictitious? Can you remember arguments between people who disagreed about the details of a shared experience? When writing about a memory, is it always necessary that you be sure that your memory is accurate?

4. Both Stemmler and Kilberg, in another essay, make the point that many of the events of their lives they remember as important were forgotten by those who experienced the events with them. How do you explain this? And as you write about past experiences, what does it say about your perspective on that experience and all that you have to offer while writing?

Possible Writing Topics

1. Write a brief essay about a time when you achieved something for which you received admiration and respect from others. Then try to write the same essay from the perspective of someone who may have been watching you while you achieved this. Try to describe the same series of events while using the first person, but do it from the two perspectives of a person participating and a person watching.

2. After you've completed the above essay, write a process essay on what the shift in perspective on your experience does to the description of it. Can you now imagine an event for which two different people would have entirely different memories? What would happen if you combined pieces of both of the essays to give a third-person description of the event? Would you argue that this would be the most accurate description?

Sally Flecker

Learning to Speak

My four-year-old niece makes good use of her time. She has been to my house before and knows where things are. To her brother, who is only a little over a year old and who has also visited here before, the house is neither familiar nor strange. Danny looks out unwaveringly at the world through clear blue eyes—the eyes, it often seems, of an old, slow man. He stands, planted in the spot where his mother put him, and he looks around, patiently waiting for something, but not yet knowing what. He'll know it when he sees it, and in the meantime he'll stand, leaning slightly forward the way babies in diapers seem to do.

My gray cat tries to slide, unnoticed, around the edges of the room. Danny, of course, sees him and calls out excitedly something that sounds like "Duck, duck." Croque is startled like a cartoon cat with his body arching sideways in a boomerang kind of curve. He scurries faster than Danny to a corner of the room from which he can appraise the situation. Life, for Danny, offers lots of pleasant surprises, and the happy introduction of the cat into the scene is one of them. The world is something that happens for his pleasure. He runs in his heavy-footed, straight-kneed way toward Croque: "Duck, duck, duck." The sound pleases him in the way it is shaped by his tongue, lips, and teeth; for the control and mastery he feels as he is able to say it once, then again; for his nascent sense that this sound represents something. But categories blur. Danny lives on a farm. When he is in the barnyard, he chases after the ducks: "Duck, duck." He uses the same word to call to the dogs, too.

While Danny is busy with the cat and his mother and I talk, Katie walks once around the first floor of my house—just in case she might find something to play with. She doesn't, and she really didn't expect to. Matter-of-factly, she arranges her bag of toys on a corner of the couch and gets on with her life.

Katie has brought Barbie with her. She dresses her in a tangerine-colored tulle party dress which fits tightly through the torso to show off Barbie's world-famous breasts. Katie asks me to pull the doll's blonde hair into a pony tail.

Barbie's bangs ruffle across her forehead. Her hair, though, is starting to hang in long hanks. It is a universal fact that on all Barbie dolls the hair becomes annoying after a while and one simply cannot do a thing with it. But Katie doesn't know this yet. This is her first Barbie. She doesn't know that all Barbies go bad in the end and that the wardrobe, once wondrous, will come to seem flat and limited. It takes an act of great will to rescue a Barbie.

After Barbie is ready, Katie brings out an already-dressed Ken.

"Oh, Honey, you look beautiful," he says to Barbie. "Let's get married, okay?"

"Okay." Katie does both voices in the same monotone. She brings the two dolls together face to face and makes smooching sounds.

They finish their kiss.

"Oh, Honey, I'm going to die." In Barbie's voice you can hear a regretful acceptance, the placidity of martyrdom.

"Oh." Ken's voice merely records the fact. "She died."

Later, my sister-in-law wriggles Danny into his coat. She tells me that Katie woke from a bad dream the other night. The Chipmunks had been killed by G.I. Joe. In the car when Danny gets cranky, Katie tickles him efficiently as though it is part of the terrain, her work, as though in keeping him happy, her life will be smoother, less complicated.

At four years of age Katie has her themes—sex, marriage, love, motherhood, and death. I'm not surprised to find these are her themes. Her young world is focused on the home and its definitions. What does surprise me is the mirror she offers me. I look into Katie's young face and I see my own round cheeks and the bags I get at the top of my cheekbones when I am tired. But now the resemblance I see supercedes the physical. I see the issues that I am struggling with, at age 34, to resolve. And I see they haven't changed in their essence since I was her age. Katie's drama—You look beautiful, Let's get married, Kiss, and Die—is admirably succinct and not far off the mark, although the nature of the death I am only now learning to name.

I have to confess here that I have never had a Barbie doll. I grew up with a Shirley Temple doll who was decidedly not "that kind" of doll. She was half again as tall as Barbie, a chunky-legged doll with red apple cheeks and the straight up and down torso of a ten-year-old child. Her mouth was fixed in a friendly, wide smile with the trademark dimples and I loved her dearly. Shirley Temple was the cherished child, and rather than envy her or wish that I was loved as she was, I believe I grew up appreciating the fact that this was a world in which Shirley Temples could exist. Shirley Temple was a child's child, an optimist's doll, a political statement in a world where people still believed in the impact an individual could have.

My grandmother made clothes for my Shirley Temple doll of scraps left over from the pretty dresses she had made for me and my sister. I had three store-bought outfits for her as well, carefully chosen on birthday excursions downtown. I never grew disenchanted with Shirley's wardrobe. I remember I had for her a shiny pink birthday party dress that came with a white nylon picture hat. Party outfits were standard fare for dolls. You bought a party dress before you even considered any of the other ensembles. But the next item of clothing I chose for her was a raincoat, a sensible, sized-down version of an adult trench coat. The rain hat that accompanied it was flat-topped like a Gloucester fisherman might wear. As I look back on this, it seems to me that the juxtaposition of outfits allowed for a more complex statement than Barbie's come-hither clothes could—a statement about who Shirley could become—a grown-up person with some down-to-earth goodness, common sense, and dignity. Barbie, simply, unfortunately, with her role as doll definitively outlined at the expense of the child's opportunity to imagine, becomes eventually like the mother of one of my childhood playmates, a woman who I could notice even at age 11 wore too much mascara, spoke in a cigarette-husky voice, and whose hair was always stiff with hair spray. Barbie is perpetually suggestive, but because she is not permitted to grow up, the suggestiveness becomes, at some point, an embarrassment.

Although I never possessed a Barbie, I did own what I consider to be a precursor of the Barbie doll—Miss Revlon. Though my attachment to her never elicited the same intimacy with which I loved Shirley Temple, Miss Revlon fascinated me. She was more quietly shapely than Barbie. Her feet, I thought, were wonderful—dainty and in a permanently arched position so that she could accommodate what we call now when Barbie wears them—fuck-me pumps. In her earlobes were two miniature pearl earrings. One day I discovered these were simply two straight pins stuck into her empty head. I was impressed then by illusion, by the way something can be other than what it seems.

Miss Revlon was a "lady." She didn't have a first name—that would have been too familiar. Perhaps what I cherished in her was her self-containment, neatness, and poise—all things that I, at 11 awkward years of age, had no hope of having and which, as I get older, believe more and more to be qualities you never see in yourself although others may see them in you. It's as though the "Emperor Has No Clothes" story has been twisted and only the sovereign herself is acutely aware that she is not covered as well as she would like to be.

I have always daydreamed while I washed dishes. I wonder now if it is purely coincidence that the years when I encountered my personal wasteland and felt the most defeated by the direction my life was moving in were the years that I had a dishwasher. When I was young my first real responsibility was to wash the dinner dishes. My childhood house was built on a hill and, instead of looking into a neighbor's back yard, I looked into the boughs of a huge oak tree. Through the leaves you could see the hills of Castle Shannon, a community some three miles away. The view allowed me a chance to watch the play of nature and experience openness, distance, and possibility. It is no wonder to me that it was here that I waited as a young girl for my "visitation."

The nuns at school had told us that God would some day call us for a vocation. Literally, I awaited the call. I didn't really expect to *see* God or actually hear His voice. I expected, I think, a flash of sunlight through the oak leaves, a beam that would ricochet off the aluminum awning of the back porch and strike me with the sudden knowledge of what He expected me to become. There were only two options—to become a nun or a mother. I was nervous about hearing from God on this matter, but the tension of waiting to find out was unnerving as well. Night after night, sweating with steam from the sink, I prayed and scrubbed, scouring the sticky, crusty bottoms of pans, promising God that, like a good girl, I would enter the convent if He told me to. I would sentence myself to the shining, sterile linoleum corridors, to the tiny, immaculate room with the single cot, images I head gleaned with stealthy sideways glances on Wednesday afternoons as I trailed shyly behind Sister Mary Caroline, my piano teacher. In my heart, though, wordlessly I pleaded for a crack at the more familiar, messy, hearty, raucous motherhood. What I fully expected was that I would be expected to do the very thing I imagine I am least fit or equipped to do—that God would demand that I live the life I dreaded most. After all, that is the stuff from which martyrs are made and I knew all about martyrs, having spent several years in Catholic schools and being a direct descendent of several generations of "Christian Mothers." But God did not come and tap me on the shoulder, and over the years I lost that heightened feeling of expectancy. Now I am able to wash dishes without looking over my shoulder for God. I do still let my thoughts drift, though, and it seems that this year I have spent looking through the soapsuds, trying to piece together what went wrong in a relationship with a man I loved. In many ways, I have once again been waiting for a particular and silent male voice to reclaim me, to make itself heard.

The problem is that this man whom I haven't yet scrubbed out of my thoughts does not have much practice in speaking about what he holds close. On firmer ground he is when he maps out ideas, those more distant shores. I think he would like to bring out into the open the choices he has made about our relationship, the choices we have each made about the other, but instead he mumbles and looks down at his feet. I understand, I think, the problem. I've put in my own time studying what makes concrete glimmer when you squint at it long enough. I know what he is looking at, and what jams his voice. He doesn't have practice at naming, for others to hear and heed or not, what he wants. Naming, laying out boundaries, taking a stand, is risky business. Regardless of how little energy he is willing to put into his grasp, he is terrified of the free fall, of having empty space all around him, afraid he'll be left without choices. What he doesn't know yet is the difference between having true choices and having the illusion of choice. So he's stuck in the quicksand of not being able to structure his world any more than my nephew Danny. The world is something that happens *to* him, though, rather than happily *for* him because, unlike Danny, he has a sophisticated memory. Danny, on the brink of discovering the ordering nature of language, can be pleased with what appears in his narrow field of vision, while innocent of and unburdened by the power to summon or choose, haunted rarely by the image of what is missing, let alone paralyzed by potential regret.

He wants me to put words in his mouth. "Ask me questions," he has begged me at times because he can't begin to ask himself. I would line the words up, stack them carefully like the dishes in my drainer, offer suggestions for what he feels, but of course, there's no use to that. You have to fight to own your words. This finally is the lesson of my growing up.

If I went back to my first-grade classroom I would be struck by how miniature it is—the desks, the bookshelves, the windows, the low ceiling. But of course it was not small to me when I was six years old. I was an earnest child, I think, and although I sat in the back of the classroom and felt largely invisible, I had no desire to do anything my teacher would be displeased with. We had different prayers and songs for different times of the day and I knew them all back then, knew every word. We pledged allegiance only at the beginning of the school day. But we said prayers before class, at the end of the morning, after lunch, and before going home. One day as we said the "Our Father" after lunch, I was pounced on by Sister John Joseph for not saying my prayers. I didn't see her coming because I was standing beside my small desk, hands held with palms together and fingers matched and pointed toward heaven, my eyes tightly closed. "But, Sister," I protested when she yelled at me, "I was saying them to myself." She would have none of my explanations and humiliated me further by forcing me to say "Out Father" out loud, solo, while the other children sat in their seats and watched and gave a silent prayer of thanks they were not me. I had seen my mother one day not saying her prayers out loud and when I asked she told me that it was okay to say them in your head. I was so impressed by the idea of words spoken only in my head reaching God that I wanted to experiment.

The lesson in this, for me, was an awareness, I think, of appearance versus a sense of what I could experience and hide simultaneously. I stumbled through the prayer, faltering only in a few places, but the experience of fear—the fear that the words might not come when I needed them—shadowed me, and perhaps in a strange way guarded me like the Guardian Angel we were told we had. I believe that this was my first understanding of complexity. Because of this moment, I knew myself in a different way as someone who had an inside and an outside life that were not the same. And I think that rather than feel angry at being treated unfairly and ungenerously by Sister John Joseph, I understood that I knew something she, a woman forced to take on not only a new name but a man's name as well, did not or could not afford to know. This was my first experience with the power of the spoken word. But the power here was merely lip service, and if I chose to avoid trouble for the rest of my school years by always saying my prayers aloud, I knew then that it was a choice *I* was making and that there were other ways to choose to do it as well. My acquiescence was also my defiance. I lived my life in two places, and this is how I balanced, how I survived. When one was too difficult, I sustained myself through the other.

About the same time that I was waiting for my career-counseling visit from God, my father made a friend in the new parish priest, Father DeLuca. They played golf together every Wednesday and my father called him by his first name. Once a month the fourth grade was walked over to church for confession—an ordeal I alternately loved and hated. I loved it because the nuns distributed books—illustrated Old Testament stories and Lives of the Saints. I loved the Lives of the Saints and was particularly thoughtful over the story of the young Christian boy who was chased by the pagans as he carried the host for communion to the others who had to hide in the caves because of their faith. He was beaten to death, of course, because he refused to relinquish his holy package. When his body was found, there was not a bruise on it. His face bore a saintly smile. I don't think I thought he was particularly wise to die so young, but I believed absolutely in this boy's innocence and purity—the halo effect—which I could not hope to gain myself.

The reason that I hated to go to confession was two-fold. I was nervous in the confessional box. For one thing, you couldn't see. There was no way for the light to leak in. Your ears had to act as your eyes as you waited for the priest to slide open the screened window between your box and his. There were too many opportunities for miscues. I was always afraid that I would mistake his closing the window on his other side for the opening of mine and I would begin my "Bless me, Father" too early. On the other hand, what if I failed to hear him close the first window and continued to kneel silently while he waited impatiently for me to begin? It was on the logistics and correct interpretation that I concentrated my attention and nervousness so that I would not have to address my other source of anxiety.

The problem was, when I was 11, I was a "good" kid. There I was, once a month in the confessional, having to give away secrets. I had secrets, a side that was private, but that's not really what we were there to discuss. What I was supposed to talk about was what I had done wrong, how I had been bad. I made up things to tell—innocuous venial sins, weighed for plausibility the way a stomach ache or ear ache were vague enough illnesses to avoid absolute confirmation when you were troubled and needed a dodge. "I told two lies and was disobedient to my mother three times," I told the priest. But if he had asked me how I was disobedient to my mother I'm not sure I could have made up a story to tell him. I did the things my mother told me to do, or I argued with her, but I truly don't believe I knew how to be willfully disobedient. So confession became the lie I told, a complicated and ironic tangle. The situation was heightened further by my father's association with Father DeLuca and the priest's corresponding recognition of me. I was no longer just another sixth-grader. I was afraid that Father DeLuca could recognize my voice in the confessional. "You've made the same confession three weeks in a row," I could hear him shout. "You're lying about lying." It would be an exposure like the one in first grade, but of larger proportion and more fearful because this time I was waiting for it to happen.

Something did happen in the dark confessional box. It was more quiet and private, but it still marks me. I told my lie, was given a penance—say three "Hail Marys" and two "Our Fathers" and resolve not to sin again, which I, of course, would have to do in order to have something to say the next month in confession. Then it was time to say the "Act of Contrition." Saying the "Act of Contrition" is like playing a Bach Invention on the piano. If you stop anywhere, it's impossible to pick it back up. You have to go back to the beginning. About three lines into the "Act of Contrition," I stumbled. I tried to start again but got tangled up in the second line this time. By now Father DeLuca tried to help by mumbling the words where I stumbled, but that only confused me further because he was on one part and I was on another. The words to the prayer faded like the Cheshire Cat's grin; I knew less of it each time I tried. Father DeLuca finally lost patience with me and sent me on my way. I heard contempt in his voice. I emerged from the darkness feeling stripped and pruny, the way you do when you've been in the bath too long. I thought the person who had been waiting for her turn looked at me as if I had leprosy.

After that I mumbled and looked down at the ground whenever Father DeLuca was around. I was sure he knew that I was the girl who didn't know her prayers and I was terrified that he would expose me as a sham. I bear the burden of that encounter to this day, as if it were a curse that had been placed on my head. I can't recite the words to anything without mixing them up. If I'm singing, I have to make up words to half the song. And I bungle cliches like Archie Bunker. On a family vacation recently, Katie asked me to say prayers with her at bedtime. I knelt down with her at her cot and listened as she said a simple child's prayer, asking for the health and safety of family members, including me. I was touched to be named in her prayer, but then she asked me to say the "Our Father" with her. I could not and I felt as lost and flustered as I had when I was 11 years old in Father DeLuca's confessional.

After Katie was tucked in, I sat outside by myself and watched the stars and thought about the power of language and what it has to do with me. I tell this story because I understand how I lost, back then, the comfort that my nephew Danny will soon have with words—the comfort and power of *knowing* words, having them at your command, being able to point to a duck and say its name, being able to point to a cat and know that it won't work to call it a duck, having the comfort and power of making distinctions with language. What I learned that day in the confessional was not to take that comfort for granted. I learned that words I can recite without thinking are fickle and when they're elusive it means that I have to begin again to figure out what I want to say and to find a new way to say it. To speak truly is sometimes to acknowledge that words, thoughts, ideas, don't have to be sure and rightful, immovably fixed in place. I have to look *through* an idea to figure out what it means and where it belongs and live with the absence of comfort—there are times when I simply *can't* figure out what something means or how it fits in.

❧ ☙

These are a few of my stories. They are important stories for me as a woman learning the place of speech in taking on a real place in the "real" world. Keeping my voice inside, cloistered, for so many years, gave me a chance to focus that voice, to hear it clearly, the way you might hear the sound of your footsteps if you were walking alone through snowy, nighttime streets. I knew my voice and I have believed in it and learned to listen to it when I am troubled or confused. But keeping my own counsel was wise only to a point. Until I began to also speak aloud, learned to recognize my voice in a roomful of noise, could I be the person I needed to be—a person who makes choices in the "real world" instead of having choices made for her, or sometimes only choices slipped to her like table scraps. Learning to have a voice means learning to use the power to choose. It also means not settling for crumbs.

But it also means learning how not to speak for others, how not to understand or be understanding. I was so busy understanding why the man I was in love with didn't continue to love me, why he had to fix what had been making him hurt, that I forgot to take care of myself. Instead I adjusted myself, steeled myself for the ways he would hurt me.

Speaking for him when he could not speak, giving him the questions, was in a way like praying silently. But neither God nor this man can answer, *should* answer, because I should have been asking for myself. I will continue to wash dishes, but the voice I listen for will be my own.

Katie's drama concerns me. Women have been coming to see the way we have been kept isolated and disarmed by the myths of beauty and youth, by the idealization of marriage and motherhood. I hope the world Katie comes of age in offers more than the "Honey, you look beautiful—Let's get married" casual relationship. But perhaps I am even more disturbed by the fact that it is Ken who gets all the lines. All Barbie knows to do is agree ("Okay" to his proposal) and to remove herself (very humbly—"Oh Honey, I'm going to die"). Barbie doesn't know yet that there are other lines she might speak, however silly or profound they might be.

Danny, who can't talk yet, is stuck in a world that plays itself out before him. The good news for him is that unless his development is arrested, he'll grow to act upon the world in ways he cannot yet imagine. He'll learn the rightful use of speech. To imagine a grown person who can only react happily when the cat appears and sadly, perhaps, when the cat is out of sight (with maybe only a vague, undifferentiated sense of loss or absence) is to imagine something is wrong. Yet that's how I've been and I believe my experience is not so unique, that variations on this theme have been played out in women's lives. I want a doll for Katie and Danny to play with, to imagine with, who is neither Shirley Temple, nor Barbie, nor Miss Revlon, but who is parts of all of them and others besides. I want the doll that I have not yet imagined. So I think I'll wash a few more dishes and have Katie and Danny help, and we'll make a huge, soapy, watery mess and soak our clothes in the doing and blow soap bubbles into the air and talk about what we haven't yet imagined and all the things in the world that we know are not ducks.

On the Importance of Washing a Priestly Foot

*T*HE Lenten season several years ago in my city was marked by a controversy that seemed silly to some, aboriginal to others, and deadly serious to yet a third group. The bishop of the Catholic diocese that year decided, I suppose, that things had gotten out of hand in terms of letting women have a place on the altar (although they were still certainly not in the sacristy) and allowing them to participate in certain of the liturgical rituals. He put his foot down (it having already been thoroughly scrubbed, I suppose) and forbade women to wash the feet of priests in the traditional Holy Thursday service. His decree was based on a formal and narrow sense of the relationship between the New Testament event and the meaning of its enactment. There were no women present at the last supper, he said. No woman washed Christ's foot that night, so no woman should wash the foot of the priest, as the stand-in for Christ, now. It would, he said, be false.

I followed the news coverage, amused and not thoroughly surprised. I had breathed in the air of inequality all those years in grade school. I knew that the presence of one priest in the school cafeteria had the chilling, silencing effect of the giant's presence in fairy tales. God help you if he discovered, when you went to empty your lunch tray, that you had hidden the unfinished strands of canned spaghetti in your milk carton. Nuns struck their own brand of fear, but it was limited to the classroom. Instinctively, we countered the power they wielded over us by laughing, after the moment of confrontation passed, about the way we had been able to make them glower at us. The delicate clink of their famous rosary beads might give us pause for a moment; we would stash our comic books, stick our gum under the seat—minor scurrying. Their presence was not strong enough to summon forth the absolute, heart-stopping terror we could feel in the presence of a priest.

On the other hand, it was the magnanimous priest who stopped in occasionally during religion classes. For him, we would perform the Baltimore Catechism:

"Who made you?"
"God, made me, Father."
"How did God make you?"
"In His image and likeness, Father."

Also it was the "benevolent" father, with Santa Clausian good humor, who gave out the biggest Hershey's chocolate bars we had ever seen every Christmas on the last day of class. Our homeroom sisters distributed small plastic statues of the Blessed Mother or holy medals with the Pope's image stamped on. Astute readers of the text, we Catholic children were. It was not lost on us that the priests got to be fathers, while the nuns were only sisters, clearly less powerful.

So I was not surprised when the bishop decided that the sisters and lay women were not fit to wash the feet of men. Nor did I feel particularly threatened as a woman. I had long ago wriggled away from the tight grasp of Catholicism. I viewed the proceedings from a pleasant distance and thought with a safe sense of irony that if the bishop really thought a strict interpretation was appropriate, the priests whose feet were to be washed would have to be Jewish.

That comfortability changed, though, on Easter Saturday night. Gathering early for the holiday, the adults sprawled out in the living room and talked about inconsequential matters, relishing the moments of relaxation after having gotten the children bathed and to bed, enjoying the familiarity of our childhood home, slipping back into old roles and patterns as though none of us had changed. We talked about whether Katie would find her Easter basket if we hid it behind the chair. Would we remember how many eggs we hid under the cushions of the couch and chairs so that we wouldn't be surprised to find one months later nestled in the crack between the back and the seat? Into this conversation, my mother brought up the controversy of the bishop's decree.

Actually she didn't bring up the controversy of the bishop's decree. I misrepresent her. What she brought up was her opinion that the women who were picketing the diocesan offices because of the decree were ridiculous. "Don't those women have anything better to do than to make a fuss over washing someone's foot?" she said.

Now my mother hates a fuss. And I bristle when she dismisses someone else's feelings or point of view as—silly. My first reaction to defend the picketers was reflexive more than philosophical. My sister and sister-in-law jumped into the discussion, however. Both usually hold a more traditional perspective than my own. Both are less quick to take a side in an argument. Both, this time, agreed with me that something critically important was at stake here. As I argued this, I also saw how this specific issue connected to the same habit of mind that kept women in marginalized positions in society.

I tried to spell out that connection, make it visible so that my mother could see what I saw. I tried to show her how that narrow view of a woman's rightful place in the church also had something to do with the fact that as a middle-aged woman, her keen eye, analytical mind, and sense of pride that refuses to give any task less than her best earns her a job for which she is paid a salary that hovers around the poverty level.

What I didn't have were the words to show my mother how it worked together. How I could see that the feminization of poverty—that after years of working hard at raising a family and later low-paying, high stress jobs, the best she might hope for as she grows older is to live off of pitiful social security checks—was all part of the same package that the sister/father inequality and the father knows best daddy who goes off to work so he can "provide" for the wife and kids are part of. I wanted to show her how hidden it can be, how something as unattractive even as the issue of washing the feet of priests can cover powerful assumptions that make her life, in the long run, more difficult and unfair.

But I didn't have the words.

I didn't have the words to make my point to my *mother*. I could have had a conversation about the issues with women who are my colleagues. I have the language to discuss it with those who already agree, who share my assumptions. And while I don't discount this, in certain ways it's much more important that I communicate my beliefs about the rightful place of women in the world to those who would disagree with me, to those who would dismiss me. I have to learn to talk ably enough that my mother will hear me.

So that's why I write. To get better at getting my ideas articulated and my visions more precise. I write for myself so that I can write to my mother.

Which is to address the general question of why I write the kinds of essays I write. Which is to provide a sense of where I am coming from. Which hasn't yet addressed the act of writing this particular essay.

I teach composition courses to college freshmen. We spent a class recently trying to pull apart a definition of education which suggested that education was truly a result of three lines colliding: one's place, one's experience, and one's history. In their initial reading of this text, the class approached the line as though the writer was merely reiterating, perhaps emphasizing, the same point. The closer reading was more useful, though, and I found myself thinking about these three paths, about the precision and uniqueness of a moment that they suggested. My essay, "Learning to Speak," built up momentum along the trajectory of my experience. I began the essay by recounting Katie's visit to my home. Danny, in the beginning, was there, it seemed, to provide context, background, to Katie's sober play with Barbie and Ken dolls. I didn't start out to write an essay, though. I just started out writing because there was something compelling about that moment; it was a story I had to write. In fact, it was a story that woke me up. Katie's visit had happened on Sunday. On Thursday, I came home from work exhausted and decided to take a nap. I didn't sleep for very long, though, and what woke me up was the memory of Katie playing with Barbie. I hadn't really thought much about it at the time, or in the ensuing days. And then all of a sudden it was there, nudging me, shaking me awake, a voice inside my head saying, "My four-year-old niece makes good use of her time," demanding to be written down. When I wrote three pages describing the visit and her play, I found myself explaining in writing how surprised I was that some of the same issues I heard Katie working on were my own. I said that they weren't far off the mark. I also said I wasn't sure what mark they weren't far off of, that I wasn't sure what I had meant. I wrote the essay to find out.

It is a recursive essay. One memory pulled in another and another and I wrote them all down as though I were a scribe, recording, taking dictation. I didn't know for a long time why these stories were there, what washing dinner dishes had to do with my embarrassment in a confessional box, what Danny had to do with any of it. In some ways, I think they don't have anything to do with one another until *I* make them connect, that it is a willful choice on my part that I look at some of my recent experiences in light of some of my childhood experiences. Through it all I worried that my choice to write into the essay material about a relationship that I was no longer involved in was purely cathartic. Would it make sense or matter to anyone but myself?

But it was very much the ground upon which I was standing as I began to write. My place. In some ways, the writing of this essay became, as I worked issues out, a definition of that place. If, in some ways, this essay is an elegy for a love affair, it is also a fanfare. In locating my experiences as a woman who has been acted upon, I also begin to define my place as a woman with responsibilities to act. As I connected the ideas of acting with choice and speech, I began to see why Danny truly belonged in the essay. He gave me a way to open the essay up. While I believe that, as a class, women have been oppressed, I also see the ways that men, in general as the oppressors, also limit themselves. It all makes me sad.

While that sadness stays with me, it doesn't have such an upper hand. I haven't talked yet about the line of history explicitly, although I think it's fairly obvious that the history of which I am a product is the history of a patriarchal culture at a time when it is being challenged by those it has marginalized. When I was a student in college, we all thought we were the generation that could change the world, that *would* change the world. It's popular to look back on those times now and laugh about how idealistic we were, how naive we were. A friend who read my essay laughed when she read how I described Katie's matter-of-factness, said that she would have described me in the same, get-on-with-it and do-what-you-have-to-do way. I'm not idealistic anymore. Or at least in the same way. I'm more reasonable about what I want my writing to do. I want my writing to start a conversation somewhere in the world, with me, with yourself, with someone else, and finally, with my mother. I forgot to ask my mother, that Easter Saturday night, what she thinks. Or maybe even worse, I failed to imagine that she had something to say, a way of seeing that I might try out. So I'm going to give her these essays. And ask her to speak.

QUESTIONS

Sally Flecker's "Learning to Speak" and its process essay, "On the Importance of Washing a Priestly Foot"

1. In her essay, Flecker writes "You have to fight to own your words. This finally is the lesson of my growing up." As you reread the essay, where and in how many ways do you see this fight, this struggle taking place? What does it mean to "own your words"? Who or what would take them from you, or see to it that you lost the fight to own them?

2. Reread the conclusion of Flecker's essay. Would you describe it as a neat summary of all that's proceeded it? Where does she leave you as the reader of the essay? If she has not reached the point where she can define succinctly what "Learning to Speak" means to her, what then has she learned?

3. In her process essay, Flecker draws sharp distinctions between the power a priest has and the power a nun has. Can you think of other illustrations of institutional differences between the sexes that we often accept without question? Why do we fail to question such differences?

4. Flecker says that she didn't have the words to say to her mother what she could have easily said to her colleagues. Why doesn't she have them? What makes for the difference? And how is your reading of this influenced by Flecker's discussion of her interaction with priests, nuns, the man she loved, herself?

Possible Writing Topics

1. In her process essay Flecker says that stories and memories she uses in "Learning to Speak" "don't have anything to do with one another until *I* make them connect, that it is a willful choice on my part that I look at some of my recent experiences in light of some of my childhood experiences." Write an essay about a recent experience that was heavily influenced by experiences you had as a child. You may have to deliberately make connections of which Flecker speaks; the key here is in not making deliberately false ones. Focus on those that seem the most honest.

2. After you've completed the essay, write a letter to one of the people who appear in your essay, whether it is a parent, a teacher, or a friend. Explain to the person that you are sending an essay you wrote in class, and tell him or her why it was important that he or she read the essay. Tell this person what it means to you to have him or her read it.

II

PLACE AND THE LANDSCAPE OF MEMORY

Mark L. Shelton

White Castle: Sometimes Nothing Else Will Do

FINAL VERSION

*T*HE last time I drove from Pittsburgh, Pennsylvania to the Arcadia-High White Castle in Columbus, my wife consented to go with me. She is not particularly big on eating White Castle hamburgers, though she is willing to eat two or three; she came along on the four-hour drive to soak up some of the ambiance I had been telling her about, ever since I had begun the practice of driving casually to Columbus, buying a sack or two of hamburgers, sitting on one of the stainless steel benches and munching a few, and then driving casually back to Pittsburgh.

"There are other places to eat in Columbus, you know," she said hopefully, as I merged onto I-70.

"Sure, sure, I know," I replied, "they have Burger King, I think, and I'm sure there's a McDonald's on High Street."

"They have those in Pittsburgh."

"Exactly. That's why we'll go to White Castle."

On the way, I reminisced about growing up on Chicago's South Side, where there was a White Castle about three blocks from the house, and no fewer than eight between the house and Comiskey Park, where the White Sox played.

"We used to stop on the way to the ballpark and buy a sack—that's twelve—and then stop again on the way home for a nightcap; I usually got cheeseburgers on the way."

She is seldom impressed by my gastronomic history, but this seemed to have some impact. "Didn't you feel sick?"

"Nope. Moderation is the secret. Most people think they don't like White Castles because they try to eat too many; I tend to think of them as oysters—a dozen a sitting."

I went on to tell her how they carefully monitor all the ingredients, beginning almost at the farm. I even recited from an old *White Castle House Organ*: "A griddle covered with White Castle hamburgers is indeed a delight—to the sense of sight, to the sense of smell, to the sense of taste. Such an end result is the fruit of labors of many, from the farmer who tills the soil and the cowboy who keeps his lonely vigil over the herd, to the skilled operator who takes buns, beef patties, pickle and onion, and fashions them into the final product: the White Castle hamburger."

"Where did you hear that?"

"They publish a magazine," I began, but she just shook her head and looked down at the map; she is not one for hero worship.

But I *do* worship the White Castle hamburger. Even when I was small, they held a mystique, a vagary, that still satisfies. The White Castle chain, formed in Wichita, Kansas in 1921, is still operated as a private concern by the son and grandson of the founder, Edgar Ingram—there are no franchises, no outside management in restaurant operations. From the lonely cowboy to the skilled operator, it's still a family business, a model of homespun integrity and devotion to quality that brings a lump to my throat.

"Make sure you pick up a copy of *The White Castle Code*," I tell her, trying to keep her interest up. "That will make it seem more like a pilgrimage. The code is a . . ."

"I know, I know," she said, "it's a model of homespun integrity that brings a lump to your throat. I am getting hungry, though."

We drove on in silence for a while. I had begun making little excursions to Columbus shortly after I moved to Pittsburgh, breaking a vow I had made when I was younger to never live in a city that didn't have White Castles. A college roommate of mine had even gone so far as to specify to the placement service the ten metropolitan areas in which he was willing to consider employment, the little list on the side of the carton reading like an honor roll: Chicago, St. Louis, Detroit, Indianapolis, Columbus, Cincinnati, Louisville, Minneapolis–St. Paul, New York and New Jersey, though in the past few years they have opened restaurants in areas like Ann Arbor, Michigan, Lexington, Kentucky, and Dayton, which makes driving through Ohio a pleasure unequaled by any other area in the country: no fewer than thirty-four White Castles occupy the stretch beginning in Covington and ending in the eastern suburbs of Columbus, a veritable bite-sized burger belt, an onion-paved heaven.

But the drive from Pittsburgh is good for the anticipatory sense; the excitement begins to build when you eschew I-270 and plunge straight into the city . . . well, it's an experience in itself.

She, though, is cautious. "Aren't there some on the outskirts, someplace?" It is near midnight, and the boarded-up buildings that line portions of I-71 do look a bit ominous.

"Sure there are, but this is a *real* one, not suburbanized or anything—it even has a jukebox."

My wife, who likes jukeboxes, is not convinced. "I'd rather skip the jukebox."

We exit the expressway, and cruise slowly up High Street. She locks the doors. But then she spots it at the same time I do, the harsh fluorescence giving it a kind of stark beauty, like a monochromatic photograph. "It's not as big as the one in Chicago," she says, getting into the spirit of the thing, "but it is . . . " she surveys the parking lot " . . . *authentic*."

I park, and we get out and stretch, and I look at my watch. "Not bad," I say. "About three hours and forty-five minutes."

We enter, as though into a shrine. There is something on the menu that I have never seen before, and she points it out to me.

"What are onion chips?" she asks me, holding onto my arm.

"I don't know, but we'll try them. How many do you want?"

"Onion chips?"

"Hamburgers."

"Um, I'll take two, and some onion chips, and a Coke."

The woman at the counter calls me "Shemp." I order, smiling at the woman, who looks at me as though my name *were* Shemp. "We'd like forty, and two large onion chips, and three Cokes, large, to go."

Such an order doesn't even raise an eyebrow. When I worked as a stock clerk in a liquor store in Chicago, we routinely ordered one hundred or so, on Saturday afternoons when the boss left early. Then the five of us would sit in the back, silent except for the sound of the empty paper cartons hitting the tile floor.

An unrecognizable song emotes from the jukebox, alternately high and tinny, and then a few seconds of stool-rattling bass; it sounds as though something is wrong with the speaker. We stand at the window, watching the woman expertly fill forty little cartons. "An experienced server can prepare six hundred hamburgers an *hour*," I say.

When the order is bagged and placed on the counter, we leave, and on the way to the car, I open a bag and pull out two, handing one to my wife. "I think I'll wait," she says, "until we're in the car."

We sit for a little while in the parking lot, eating and watching people come and go; a man in a three-piece suit, three teenagers, one carrying a huge radio, two women in nurses' uniforms, a cab driver. The onion chips are not very good; they seem to be made from the skin of the onion, and when she holds up one with the stem trailing from it, battered and nicely browned, I can only shrug. "It's something new," I say. "Give 'em a few years to perfect it, and then try; it's just like the White Castles in the suburbs—it will take a little while to work out the kinks in the system."

She is just starting her third hamburger, at my urging, when I start the car and begin to move out. "We want to be home by sunrise, don't we?" I ask, and she groans.

"I forgot how late it was," she says, "but we have plenty of food to last us the trip home; I'm not worried."

As I merge back onto the interstate, she asks, "Why did that woman call you Shemp?"

I shrug. "Maybe she calls *everybody* Shemp."

But that is too easy an answer, I know, too pat. Perhaps she senses something she has learned in her twenty-seven years behind the counter, that makes her conscious of the presence of a true aficionado, of someone who drives for hours for a White Castle hamburger, something, perhaps, akin to what twins feel, when one feels great joy, or a sharp pain. I voice this, half to myself, and she looks at me.

"I think that's going a bit too far."

I shrug again. "Next time, we'll try an experiment; you go in and order, and see if she calls *you* Shemp."

"Next time?"

Next time, I think, *perhaps in a couple of weeks.*

VERSION I

The corporate mail bag of the White Castle System, headquartered in Columbus, sprouts letters of at least three distinct types: First are the requests for franchise information, often from life-long customers who have dreamed since childhood about someday owning their *own* White Castle; second are requests that the company open up an outlet in their neighborhood/town/city/state/country, one that is not currently served by a little porcelain restaurant; and finally, letters from indignant customers when the company remodels, or, ineffable horror, *closes* their favorite White Castle, and replaces it with a shiny new restaurant in another location.

Such was the fate of the White Castle at 5th Avenue and Northwest Blvd. in downtown Columbus. "The building was, unfortunately, just worn out," says Gail Turley, director of advertising and public relations for White Castle. "We'd remodeled and patched and repaired the building for years, until finally there wasn't anything more that could be done," so the building was razed, a victim of its own success.

And of the changing times, as well, Turley recalls. "When we still had curb service at the 5th Avenue store, it did very very well, but after curb service was discontinued, business dropped off—our policy isn't to actually *close* an outlet; what we try to do is *replace* them with new outlets in other locations."

So there are new White Castles appearing all the time, a "deliberately moderate but steady expansion plan," says the letter that is sent to the legions that have inquired about a franchise, a plan "with new units financed from current revenues."

The units, which now number 170 in ten metropolitan areas, are not as cramped by such moss-backed attitudes as one might at first think. For instance, the company opened its first non-freestanding restaurant earlier this year at 30 N. High Street in downtown Columbus. Geared for the downtown shopping and business trade, it has the capacity to produce 4,000 hamburgers an hour. And, in an enterprise that serves as a sort of memorial to the almost forgotten curb service, the company is building three test units that offer drive-thru service, one in Hamilton, Ohio.

"We studied the drive-thru idea for quite a while," says Turley, "so the new locations will have several things not ordinarily found in the drive-thru restaurant. First, we're experimenting with the use of a two-way television monitor, rather than just a microphone—instead of just hearing a voice, customers will *see* who they're talking to. Also, we'll have two windows, not just one—at the first window, the order will be checked, and the monetary transaction made; at the second window, the food will be picked up. This allows us, really, to serve two customers, one at each window, rather than just one."

Turley is, as most longtime members of the "family" (the word "employee" is seldom heard around White Castle) are, quick to tell an anecdote about White Castle devotees. In his 32 years, he's heard and told thousands of such stories, and lately he's found an outlet for them, in the form of television commercials. "We've just finished producing our second series of 'True Facts' commercials for the Chicago area, in which we tell stories brought to us by customers about the lengths to which they'll go for a White Castle hamburger."

The current series features a story about a wedding reception in Colorado that featured 200 White Castle hamburgers. One of the most telling stories in Turley's repertoire, though, is that of gourmand and publisher William M. Gaines, founder of *Mad* magazine. A member of several international culinary and gourmet societies, Gaines found a place in the hearts of White Castle devotees by including the White Castle hamburger (along with other such delicacies as white truffles, white caviar, fresh *foie gras*, and Scotch salmon) on his list of "Ten Foods Better than Sex" for the *Book of Sex Lists*.

"It's amazing," says Turley, "the number of chefs and gourmets who, after an evening of preparing delicacies, stop off at a White Castle on the way home for a sack of hamburgers."

VERSION II

Shemp has a fantasy: he is rich, see, but rich in a world where the common denominator is the White Castle hamburger.

As a child, he imagined owning a Rolls-Royce, and driving the Rolls-Royce right up to the White Castle on Ludlow Avenue, sliding quietly to a stop in front and leaving the car, four-way flashers blinking, round and yellow, whilst he went in and ordered 24 to go, and a large Coke. Traffic weaves around the big car, but the fantasy was always silent, except for the order, and the sound of the little white cartons sliding into the bag, two cartons per layer, six layers per bag, two bags make *twenty-four, and a large Coke*, the woman says, and the scratch of her voice wakes Shemp out of a reverie in right field, or history class, and he would smell *onions*.

Now, Shemp sits behind a desk somewhere, with the suspicion that he should be doing *something*, but instead he is thinking White Castles. Shemp works for a large company, large enough for him to while a moment or two away thinking his thoughts: *Willoughby, the district manager, comes in with six sacks of cheeseburgers; Willoughby asks Shemp to come along with a client for lunch, and they steer into the lot of the White Castle at Broadway and Sixth, the client saying he'll just hop out and run in, they can eat them in the car; Willoughby asks Shemp to go out for a couple after work, and they pull into the lot of the White Castle on Vine, where a painted sign in the window says, "Happy Hour, 4–7 pm—Two for One."*

Shemp doodles on his scratch pad, drawing the White Castle "Goose and Golden Egg;" he remembers an image from his college days, one time when he and Wrench and Leo and Spoon have driven the four hours from Charleston, West Virginia to Columbus, to the White Castle on Ohio 317, in the suburbs.

The four boys sit against the hood of Shemp's old Mercury Meteor and eat, the little cartons skidding around the hood in the breeze. It is late, maybe 2 a.m. There is a panhandler, one of those bums with a knapsack on his back and a long walking stick made from the leg of an ironing board, and he is asking people as they came out of the White Castle for their change. He is having little success, and a few people even shove him out of their way, guarding the white sacks in their arms like a stream of halfbacks. The panhandler isn't having any luck.

And then, a well-dressed man comes out through the swinging doors and pauses a minute, as though disoriented—sometimes one can forget which door one enters, what with the four gleaming walls of exactly the same length.

So the gentleman pauses a little, and looks around, looks directly at the panhandler. Perhaps the panhandler says something, perhaps he just extends his hand in one of those hopeless gestures, when there is only the spirit guiding. But the gentleman speaks back, reaching into one of his sacks as he speaks, and pulls out four cartons, holding them out toward the man on the sidewalk. Shemp stares, transfixed. *He just gave that guy four Whiteys*, he wanted to say, but his amazement holds him, holds him long after the gentleman has driven off, long after the tramp has wandered off and left the four empty cartons tilting in the breeze.

At his desk, Shemp reaches the fruition of that moment again. *Shemp in line at Traffic Court, paying his fine with a sack of cheeseburgers; Shemp buying two large onion rings worth of gas; Shemp tying the last knot in the string that surrounds the insulated packing crate, addressed to the IRS in Kansas City; Shemp at the 24-hour banking machine, filling his arms with the little cartons and recording the transaction in his checkbook . . .*

It is Friday, and Shemp lingers a little longer before clearing his desk; Willoughby is winding his way through the desks, stopping occasionally to chat: payday. As he nears Shemp's desk, there is the faintest change in the air, the humidity, and Shemp looks up from the neat desk, the uncluttered stacks of paper, as Willoughby makes his way to Shemp, carrying a large carton, and from the top of the carton, bags are visible, white bags, and in each—Shemp knows this with conviction—are two cartons per layer, six layers per bag, six bags in each white pasteboard carton, and from Willougby's smile, Shemp knows that this month there is a little something extra in the pay envelope, a cheeseburger perhaps, something like an honorarium for loyalty.

Hamburger Journalism: An Essay on the Blending of Memory and Myth

*T*HE changes that the short personal essay "White Castle" went through on its way to becoming the finished piece that appeared in *Ohio* magazine as my first "nonfiction" (I place quotation marks around "nonfiction" for reasons I will detail in a moment) publication are many and varied, but the only important change was the change that in fact presaged the movement of the piece from a truly dreadful and simply declarative exposition, through a rather more interesting fantasy piece, to an essay that still captures, for me, the essence of personal writing. The change I refer to is the change in what I refer to as "voice," and I submit that the success of a given piece of writing is almost totally dependent on finding the appropriate voice that will permit the use of the writer's informational resources—memory, interpretation and fact. A voice that limits access to these resources is a voice inappropriate, and nothing is so difficult to embrace as a piece of writing in which the method by which information is transmitted is at odds with that information.

Writing teachers appear to know this instinctively, although nothing could be further from the truth; they know this because they have read thousands of pages of student writing in which an inappropriate voice has been chosen, usually through the passive act of not choosing any voice at all, or where voice has been chosen for all of the wrong reasons, as Version I of the White Castle piece aptly demonstrates. Before discussing the three versions of the essay, it would be instructive to talk first about the genesis of the article, my understanding of what "nonfiction" is—or can be—and why this particular essay is to me an interesting example of the relationship between memory and the essay.

I grew up in Chicago, in a family that enjoyed its White Castle hamburgers; whether we enjoyed them inordinately more than other families in the era before McDonald's, before cholesterol was a suitable topic for discussion, before nouvelle cuisine I cannot say for sure (although I rather suspect we did); we did, at any rate, eat them on a somewhat regular basis, generally on Saturday evenings when my father was working the day shift and thus arrived home about 4:40 p.m., or the night shift, when he would arise from his sleep at about the same time to eat dinner, watch the news, and then return to bed for a nap before leaving for work at 10:55 p.m. I can clearly remember my mother saying to my father as we sat at the breakfast table those day shift mornings, "Why don't you bring home a sack of hamburgers for dinner this evening?"

To the uninitiated—that is, to those who have not grown up in a metropolitan area where White Castle restaurants are entrenched—some glossing is in order. The White Castle hamburger is a patty of hamburger meat about the thickness of a slice of Kraft American Cheese, and somewhat smaller in area; it is cooked on a stainless steel griddle on a bed of chopped onions; it is served in a very soft, dome-shaped bun with two pickle slices, packed into a white cardboard box shaped like, well, a little castle, and sold, when I was in my formative years, for 12 or 13 cents; by the time I left for college, the price was up to I believe 22 or 23 cents, and they are now probably more like 30 cents—still, however, representing good value to those who like them. The "stands" themselves (I said "restaurants" earlier to sort of ease you into this) were constructed almost entirely of white enameled steel embossed to look like castle masonry, stainless steel, glass and white tile; they are brightly lit as operating rooms, and about as comfortable. The castle motif is evident in the ramparts around the roof. White Castle hamburger stands are open 24 hours a day, 364 days a year, closing at midnight on Christmas Eve and reopening at midnight on Christmas Day; further, it takes a great deal to close a White Castle hamburger stand. I· remember, for example, that when a tornado ripped through the South Side of Chicago when I was nine years old, my family ate White Castles by candlelight that evening; although the devastation in the immediate area was often dramatic, the White Castle at 95th Street and Cicero Avenue was miraculously unscathed, and I expect that many South Side families dined similarly that night. Further arcana necessary to appreciating the White Castle is that they are colloquially sold by what is termed a "sack"—that is, 12 to a white paper bag—and that if one wants catsup and mustard on one's White Castles (the "hamburger" is implied), one might be surprised to see the counter woman squirt a grayish liquid from a squeeze bottle, which is catsup and mustard mixed together. One begins to get a sense not only of the efficiency of the whole operation, but of the surreal as well.

Because it is, as many of the best experiences are, somewhat surreal; those shiny white buildings are iconic to Midwesterners in particular, in the way that many people eat at the prominent fast-food franchises nowadays—one doesn't necessarily get much, but what one gets is astonishingly consistent. The White Castle stand was an anchor of familiarity in a changing world, and thus inspired a loyalty that has them appearing at weddings, funerals, family reunions, prom nights—they were a habit without one being particularly mindful of them as such.

Little of this, of course, is reflected in the first version of the essay. I had been waxing eloquent about White Castles with an acquaintance of mine who happened to be an editor at *Ohio* magazine. I was in graduate school at the time, working on a degree in fiction writing, and my journalism experience had been limited to the kinds of things that one who loves writing finds himself doing—school newspapers, suburban weeklies, pasting up senior citizens' throwaways. "We have the restaurant issue coming up soon; why don't you give me 750 words on White Castle?" he said to me. Nothing, it would seem, could be easier. "How do I do it?" was my first question, and he gave me a few off-the-cuff pointers, one of which almost shipwrecked my career before it began. "We (the editorial "we") are not fond of first person," he told me. So I began trying to write about what was in a way intensely personal material in third person, and the result still embarrasses me: Version I is boring, it is breathtakingly inane (I can say all of this now, though at the time, the sheer labor by which I wrenched those words together was harrowing work, and left me irritable for days), and most of all, it doesn't capture the essence of what made me, in the editor's mind anyway, the right person for the job—*anyone* could have written version I, which almost automatically means that no one should have. The peculiar constraints of nonfiction writing compound this; if I were writing a short story, say, where the events took place in or around the White Castle of my childhood (or, for that matter, in or around the family of my childhood), one could invent Gail Turley, if one needed him, put words in his mouth, invent the stories he tells; if one is aspiring to objective journalism, however, this would not be cricket. Besides, Mr. Turley might not like it. Objective journalism is uniquely suited to reporting on the events of the day; the less immediate the story becomes, the less objective the reportage almost automatically becomes; the *New York Times* "Week in Review" section is a perfect example of this. Almost all of the stories covered in "Week" were covered as news in the daily editions, heavy on who, what, where, etc. "Week," however, is more interpretive, more analytical than anything that resembles straight reportage. The string thus extends to the restaurant guide of a Midwestern magazine, where there is no such thing as a scoop, unless it is mashed potatoes.

So initially struggling with form, I tried to write objectively about something that I am not objective about, and failed. All of the material was culled from a phone interview with Mr. Turley, and the piece is heavy on "information"—number of restaurants, new trends in service, the latest commercials. All of it, however, nothing that anyone is dying to know. Rereading the piece now, I remember vividly the struggle I had in writing that first version, the job I did on myself in suggesting that something done by the publisher of *Mad* magazine could be of the slightest interest to anyone, the stretching to approach 750 words (on my typescript, I see in the corner the notation "710 words," indicating that even *that* was a failure). And the voice? The piece is all but voiceless, written in a style immediately recognizable to teachers of freshman composition as what can be charitably described as "dutiful."

My only defense is that I recognized that this was a truly terrible piece, and that I needed to try again. Still sticking honorably to the notion of third person, I wrote Version II, which is a fantasy of sorts, but one that at least begins to capture something of what I knew about White Castle, begins to use what was my best resource—memory—as material. If version I was far too stilted and factsy, version II errs perhaps in the opposite direction; to stay in third person, I created a persona, a worshipper only slightly exaggerated from what I saw so frequently that it was not immediately apparent that such worship was unusual; for example, it was not particularly campy for wedding parties to have White Castles served as a sort of midnight supper at the reception—Northsiders and out-of-towners might have thought so, but we did not; prom night meant a stop at White Castle (the harsh klieg-lighted atmosphere made the ladies' dresses show up particularly well), as did the return to the city from some excursion to the northern suburbs or from a vacation in Wisconsin. White Castle was always open, the menu so limited that there was seldom a wait (an experienced server *can* make 600 hamburgers in an hour), the taste so distinctive as to be an acquired one, as for blackened redfish or gelatto. As a stock boy at Caravetta Liquors on 95th Street, we routinely converted our paychecks into mock White Castle currency—I dimly remember having takehome pay of about sixty dollars a week, which would be roughly three hundred a week in hamburgers (I think now that customers hearing us discuss our salaries must have thought we were the most extravagantly paid bottle-dusters in the world), and around Christmas, the busiest time of year in the liquor business, a thousand-hamburger salary was not impossible. We of course did not spend it all on White Castle hamburgers, but the idea, the worship, was there.

The "factual" events of version II—the Rolls-Royce, the panhandler— were in fact scenes I had witnessed at White Castle, and it was remembering the panhandler that brought to me the idea of a barter economy based on White Castle hamburgers; the gesture of giving, rather than small change, four hamburgers was at the time a symbol of their universality, though I acknowledge the impracticality of the system. I had, remembering that scene, the essence of the article; what was then needed was voice.

I was called "Shemp" in those days, for no reason that I can divine except that one good friend was called "Curly," and his girlfriend, who lived across the alley from me, was named Maureen and hence called "Mo." Her brother, who worked with us at the liquor store, was called "Moon," although the reason for that escapes me. This was before the recent Three Stooges renaissance that gripped certain parts of the nation—at the time, I am sure that the Three Stooges were in fact in general disfavor. Our letter jackets (the liquor store crew was primarily members of my high school swim team) bore these names in script, and the bright red Caravetta Liquors t-shirts that we wore to work had our names or nicknames across the back in large block letters, so that I was called "Shemp" was no secret from the women, generally middle-aged, generally with long years of service to the firm, who worked at the 95th Street White Castle (in fact, someone sent me a clipping several years ago about four of these ladies, who had each had thirty years of service at that particular stand, at the time a company record for concentrated longevity at one location); they knew us as well as our own families, too, because we ate there frequently, perhaps two or three times a week. And although none of these women ever called me "Shemp," it is conceivable that one of them *could* have, and from that conception came the voice of a White Castle aficionado, an older, more established Shemp, but one who retains the special relationship that it was common to have with those little sandwiches.

While version II is certainly more interesting to read and contemplate, it has several problems, two of them major; first, it has too much of the flavor of the insider, of the familiarity that I certainly had, but as I grew older, found was not universally shared—many of those with whom I went to college, for example, were disdainful of White Castle hamburgers, generally for what one might call class reasons—as an undergraduate, I attended a state university in Michigan, where perhaps 35 or 40 percent of the students were from the middle and upper middle class suburbs of Detroit, and they associated White Castles with Hamtramck and River Rouge, the solidly blue-collar and industrial parts of the city. In graduate school, too, I encountered an attitude toward White Castles that bordered on outright derision, much of it based on the erroneous assumption that White Castles were the same as White Towers, which they bear no resemblance to, save some rudiments of the architecture; the hamburgers themselves were no more like one another in appearance and taste than frog legs resemble chicken. But there was an attitude problem of sorts created by implying that the world should be as Shemp would like it to be.

The second problem I saw with the piece was a bit more journalistic; if version I went too far in supplying unwanted information, version II went overboard in the direction of the idiosyncratic—I *still* love the paragraph where Shemp pays his traffic fine and his tax bill in Hamburgers, and makes a withdrawal from a 24-hour banking machine, but in letting on that I think this way, I probably expose more about the way my mind works than one should be willing to admit. And the voice of version II is for me one of the voices of fiction, an attached narration of sorts, which is not particularly appropriate for a restaurant guide. However unsuccessful Version II is as a magazine piece, however, it was certainly successful in cultivating the material I eventually used in Version III; the information in Version II is personal information, personal in the sense that I had either experienced it or imagined it: Version II began to define for me what my relationship to writing the piece could be.

The obvious bridge between II and III, of course, is the scene where Shemp and "Wrench and Leo and Spoon have driven the four hours from Charleston, West Virginia to Columbus, to the White Castle on Ohio 317, in the suburbs." The less obvious bridge I alluded to earlier, when referring to the curious sense of worship White Castle fans have for the food, the buildings, the ambiance. My wife, reading Version II, made an offhanded comment about how White Castle hamburgers seemed hardly to be worship material. As she said that, the question for me as a writer became, "How can I explain it? How can you explain a devotion to something as inconsequential as a fast food restaurant?" The framework of version III does not answer those questions explicitly, but rather implies that while it may finally be inexplicable, it is in fact the case that such devotion can and does exist. This point became the center of the article.

The voice in version III, while first person, is not strictly my own, because it suggests a certain distance, a certain fascination that borders on camp. The reverential voice is more tongue-in-cheek than sincere, I think, even while ostensibly documenting the reverence the persona of the essay claims to have for White Castle. The actual facts of my long-distance relationship are somewhat more muddied than version III suggests; when I attended school in Kalamazoo, Michigan, I did on perhaps a dozen occasions drive west to the White Castle on the outskirts of Gary, Indiana, eat, and return; I never let a college friend go to Chicago for the weekend without bringing me a sack or two back, and one weekend, when I visited a friend in Carbondale, Illinois, we drove something like four hours to St. Louis to buy White Castle hamburgers. Also, on any trip through the Midwest, I would detour to allow a stop, or maybe two, at White Castles whose locations I had plotted on a map. Version III is thus not strictly factual, although it is rather more factual than not; while my wife and I did not make the specific trip described in the piece, we had made similar excursions, had indeed ended up very late one night at the White Castle at Arcadia and High in downtown Columbus, although we were en route from Pittsburgh to Cincinnati at the time; the jukebox was real, the onion chips were real. The piece is, as I think most interpretive or experiential (what the anthologies call "new") journalism, an amalgam of what Nero Wolfe calls "intelligence guided by experience." If I were called upon to do a more fact-oriented piece about White Castle, say about the decision to open those drive-thru windows, I would never dream of stratifying information in the way I do in version III. But certain avenues of expression, of which the personal essay is one, permit, I think, somewhat more freedom than we would allow a newspaper reporter covering, say, a fire at a White Castle. The flashier "journalists," writers such as Norman Mailer, Tom Wolfe and Hunter S. Thompson, at times so completely blend fact, fantasy, personal experience and interpretation that they practice, for all practical purposes, in a new genre; for them, the lines have blurred completely, and "nonfiction" often comes to mean "based on a series of events; some of which actually happened."

This is not all bad, as long as the reader is not misled by what he is promised as opposed to what he gets. The personal essay is a uniquely self-reflective form, different from objective journalism, different from fiction in that the personal essay is almost a bridge between facts about the human experience and interpretation of it. Classic American essays—one thinks of E. B. White's "Once More to the Lake," or Calvin Trillin's paens to American cooking—are not so much, finally, about a specific trip or a specific restaurant so much as they are about the linkage the essayist has made between an event or several events and his own perceptions of the world he or she lives in.

This may seem a digression; however, it is interesting for me to consider this relationship in the context of the three essays about White Castle; if the facts in version I were inaccurate or fraudulent or made up, I would have expected censure; the "facts" in version II, although line for line there are probably more fact-based sentences than in version I, are framed in such a way as to make the question irrelevant—if the piece began, say, "Mark 'Shemp' Shelton, formerly of Chicago, has a fantasy about White Castle hamburgers...," I would have established for the reader a different opportunity for expectations about facts; version III, while on the surface factual (and indeed, containing, part by part, far more "facts" than either of the other versions), is framed, I think, in such a way that transmittal of information, of facts, is not the primary expectation of the reader; on the contrary, what I think a reader expects from the personal essay is a perspective, a voice, a way of seeing a particular set of circumstances or events which become meaningful only in the context of the writer's skill at transmitting something more personal and more idiosyncratic than information.

I think now that much of the reverence that suffuses the piece— all of the three, really—is in fact a reverence for the bonhomie and sense of community that regions of Chicago's South Side still had when I was growing up there, and a reverence that I still have for the steelworkers, butchers, glassmakers and stationary engineers that made up much of the blue-collar South Side; the White Castle is symbolic in a way, an anchor in a community; a chain of hamburger stands, clownless, gimmickless, severely austere in decor and with the minimum number of amenities, a menu limited to what one fellow grad student once denigratingly referred to as "prole food." As I reread version III, which eventually appeared in the magazine, I hear a voice trying to explain, in 750 words, that there is something more to it than hamburgers, which is the voice that seems to me to fit the task at hand.

That version III is successful because it is cohesive and coherent is only part of what makes it for me a better essay. It also melds the relationship between time and event and memory that makes things worthy subjects for essays, a melding that allows a certain level of satisfaction for having provided information, but also a satisfaction that comes from having provided a perspective on a subject that the writer is uniquely suited to provide. That version III breaks rules one associates with nonfiction is unavoidable: it is in first person, it aims for a mood rather than analysis, it is a scene, rather than an entire story. The trade-off, though, is that it allows the writer to use a sense of the story developed over time and reflection, rather than being limited to information universally available.

QUESTIONS

Mark L. Shelton's "White Castle: Sometimes Nothing Else Will Do" and its process essay, "Hamburger Journalism: An Essay on the Blending of Memory and Myth"

1. Do you agree with Shelton's assessment that version III (the final version) is the strongest? Which did you find most informative? most interesting? most enjoyable to read? most personal? What elements of the process essay might you describe, in Shelton's terms, as "personal"?

2. What parts of the first two versions are integrated into the third? What parts are lost? What *sense* of the first two versions is captured in the third, even though the actual words of the first two are not written into the third? How does Shelton achieve this?

3. In his process essay, Shelton writes, "I tried to write objectively about something that I am not objective about." Write a paragraph where you try to describe objectively a place that you know well and care about. What is lost? Does the fact that you aren't physically present in your description inhibit your ability to describe what the place means to you?

4. Shelton writes that the third version is not "strictly factual," that his description of the event of the third essay did not actually occur. Does this change your reading of the essay? Does it seem legitimate to you as a writer to enhance certain descriptions of your experience of a place in order to produce an effect for your reader? Does the third version, despite not being "strictly factual," communicate what Shelton has treasured about White Castles in memory?

Possible Writing Topics

1. Consider a place you're particularly fond of, and write two drafts of an essay. In the first, describe what goes on in the place, as if you were sitting there for the first time and describing what events unfold as you watch. In the second draft, describe some of the memories—the events in which you were personally involved—that you have of the place that distinguishes it from other places. Feel free to enhance certain information as Shelton does, but try not to strain credibility.

2. Write an essay where you evaluate and criticize the two versions of the essay you wrote, comparing the strengths and weaknesses of each. Which was more interesting to write? Which more difficult? If you were to choose one version of the essay to show to a person who had never been to the place you describe, which would you select? Why?

Kathryn M. Monahan

God's Country

*I*N July, the trees of the Appalachian Mountains drip green over the exposed bed of a rusted red pickup truck traveling down the twisty one lane road toward the river. Noise of the lush growth is lost to the sound of water over rock at great speed just as the river is lost to sight down to its very edge. It is a wonder that a road could ever push its way through such a tangle. Exposed roots of the trees form a set of guardrails, holding back dusty earth on one side, keeping muddy yellow clay loosely in place on the other. Their ancient pervasive strength now directs them into the road, hooving up the pavement and displacing red dog chips into the mud. Each bumpy heave of the truck bed testifies to this, sending the passengers upward toward the spilling green.

If there have been enough hard summer rains, the trees in September explode toward the sky in a mad profusion of oranges, red, and golds, as if the tangerine of the sun itself were born and fired into its orbit from those very mountains. There is no downward glance of tree toward road and river, and the passengers bumping along in the back of the truck look painfully upward at the golden juice trickling through the leaves. It is impossible to say whether it is the streaky sunlight or the violence of colors which causes them to shade their eyes. They travel upward this time, in accordance with the sun and the mountains.

Her husband is unimpressed. "Sounds like God wrote this stuff," he mutters.

"I was only in high school," she protests. "But this is exactly how I remember it looking. Exactly." She continues.

By November the trees are either bare or dead brown, most of the leaves washed by rain to the floor of the forest, forming a thick, slippery matting of silent decay. The clean chill of the air seeps inside the trees, whitening their outsides. Rigid pointy branches like too thin arms poke blindly outward. It is too cold now for the open bed of the truck; people enter the woods on foot, in groups of no more than three, as if to prevent the bright plaids and oranges of their winter clothing from disturbing the grey-white balance. Travel is across the top of the mountain, a short walk to an edge where sky meets the rocky faces now exposed between the trees. Slabs of dark, thunder grey stones unevenly terrace down to the river, where low and quiet water shows the continuation of rocky steps into its bed, yellow boulders becoming ordinary tan pebbles.

    Like flipping through the pages of an old calendar, she thinks. "It just isn't right," she says aloud.
    "It's awful," her husband agrees, then seeing her face adds, "but it's good description." He grins. "Your teacher certainly liked it. Notes and exclamation points all over the place."
    She sighs. "Excellent!" written in red with a cheerful flourish slants across the top of the page. It had seemed encouraging initially, definite support of her vague idea to read the old papers again. Now the word screams, garish, like some bad headline. "This is all I want to remember," she tells him sadly, nodding her head toward the pages.
    "You don't want to go back," he counters calmly.
    I know, she thinks, I know. But when she closes the notebook she shuts her eyes, trying to concentrate on the details of a green and white winter, and of icy Aprils with patches of depressing snow prayed into thaw. "Just this," she murmurs.
    "Carolyn, your grandmother died. It's only natural . . . "
    "Don't," she interrupts him. "I know." But she doesn't really, not after five years away. Not one bit more about how to make this trip back than . . .
    Her husband taps the notebook. "There aren't any people in here." He continues doggedly, "You aren't in here."
    "Soon enough," she says fiercely, "I'll be there soon enough." Her words carry the sound of uneasy hope, and fear. "*Not just this*," whispers her heartbeat.

    Seeing the strain on her face as she bends over the open suitcases, her husband reads the complaint of an aching spine and moves toward her, to tend it.
    "Jim, where's the map?" She hears the irritable note in her voice, the almost beginning of a whine, and is both grateful and annoyed for the hands kneading her shoulders.
    "I don't know, honey. Do you want me to look for it?" Answering his own question, his hands lift from her back to sift through the collage of material divided into piles between the suitcases.

    Always the suggestion that you have made a mistake in leaving, she thinks, and remembers the jealousy of the mountain, and her resentment.

"Protecting," her neighbors had said, "sheltering." But the invisible harm those hills had protected against had become for her the palpable sensation that she would smother in all that beauty, and fear that the trees would some day paint away the road and the rusty truck.

"Eternal," they said in the church, "ageless." But they trivialized the possibility of any other geographies as thin and dismissible, mere lines and dotted tracings on an ill-folded map.

"Ain't never goin' that far away," Wade had said. Better to tuck the map away again, in whatever forgotten place it had come from.

Straightening suddenly, Carolyn puts her hand to the back of her neck, as if to catch a sharp pain crossing there. But the pain is only memory, and she begins rapidly loading the piles into the luggage, hurried now, and finished before her husband can realize what has happened. The two light brown suitcases sit neatly atop the bedspread, their grainy plastic surface ugly against the smooth cotton.

"Never mind," she says quietly, raking her nails against the texture, "I won't need it."

She zips them closed, making noise over something he is trying to say, some faint protest that can't possibly matter. He is flattening and thinning as if she were already driving the car away, seeing his disappearing reflection wave good-bye in the rearview mirror.

Turning to him, she checks his eyes for distance too, almost expecting to see a tiny shrinking shape moving across the iris, disappearing at length into a black pupil. But the fanfolds of the blue irises, still round and immediate, widen slightly instead, coming closer as if to absorb but not shrink her. The black pupil enlarges slightly as it meets her own in a kiss.

By the time her car reaches old 19 South, the mountains are beginning to appear. Not the intimately known hills surrounding a place once called home, but neighboring mountains with cheerful valleys like those on postcards, showing them with a white rail fence paralleling the yellow line of a falsely charming country road. "Pleasant Valley" they are titled, or worse, "Mt. Hope."

But the movement of slow sun across the valley does not lull her, and the postcard fades. The sound of the car on the highway fades too, replaced by the cheap twang of a guitar, and a woman's high nasal voice singing of the everlasting and abiding love of Jesus.

Carolyn tries to laugh at Jesus, standing on a beach in Florida with too many clothes on and an improbable halo behind him, but she cannot, because shining through Jesus is the glossy black polish of Wade's hair. Sweat from the stifled air of the hot church makes a shadowy trickle of grey down the sides of his face, stopping when it meets the dark stubs of his beard. It does no good for her to move away from the tense black and white of his uncreased neck, no good for her to move to sit behind Brother Crouch instead: his arm still comes out, reaching around her to find her fifteen-year-old breasts, advertised as older by the thin slick orange material of the dress, and its clear plastic buttons following the line of those breasts down to her waist. Her arms cannot still their trembling by moving as Wade moves, with the green and yellow leaves above them in the truck. Later he tells Jody about her trembling, and Jody repeats the mocking version to her.

The sun is high enough now to demand that she roll down her window. She glances once at the scenery, then concentrates on the steepening road.

This arrival is not notably different from that of any other visit except that Mother cries at the outset, and that the kitchen is filled with food gifts—hams, and coffee, and pyrex dishes of squash and zucchini casseroles. The neighbors have been thoughtful.

She checks each of the small rooms for changes, her mother trailing, offering sporadic comments. When they reach the bedroom, Mother watches as she unpacks the suitcases, approving the tidy efficiency which barely disturbs the neat bedspread.

"Honey, what is this?" she asks, picking the sea nut up from the dresser.

"Oh. Something Jim brought me once from the Florida Keys."

"You always like to bring some little thing from your place, don't you honey?" This last said as a phrase.

"Something to ward off—" she tries to joke, but Mother senses her tension, and her mouth begins to shape a sad and worried "O." Seeing this, Carolyn emends, ". . . it's just real pretty . . ."

"Carolyn, don't be uneasy." Then, "Why don't you take a nap? We'll be busy later, and up most the night with all the people, I expect."

As her mother's voice continues its litany of all that must be done, of dust and wills and money, she tires too, hearing the questions ahead.

"Planning to stay for a while this time?" "Coming back?"

"You'll be back, they always come back." Fat and florid faces nod assurance, claiming petty wisdom.

"Can't know what you see up there. Can't be anything as nice as this place."

"Ain't they a lot of crime up there? Ain't you scared?"

Her unspoken responses, all the choices of answers repressed, begin an angry hum in her head.

"I'll sleep," she says to Mother.

She likes the contrast of her red shoes against the lavender carpet of Toomey's funeral parlor and the mahogany of the sea nut rubbing in the pocket of her skirt. The red shoes feel good too, moving with slippery steps over the nylon surface.

At her first funeral—a young cousin killed in a mining accident—they had been young enough to skate across the carpet, sneaking up to the adults and giving them little static shocks. They were sent out of the viewing room to misbehave, but the wailing of Aunt Mary followed them into the hall, meeting them at the water fountain, and even at the doorway. There they could look outside and discuss who owned what car, and which one cost the most, and whether or not they would go into the mines. She couldn't go, of course, she was a girl. But she knew she could never grieve like Aunt Mary either, pounding on her son's chest, and testifying to Jesus about her faith. In between running out to the parking lot and getting drinks at the water fountain, they crept back in to watch Aunt Mary. After a while they had pulled her away from the coffin. At the end of the night everybody sang "Amazing Grace."

"There you are! We bin lookin' for you, your momma's ready to go." Her aunt's still-young face, pretty in the way they called "right smart," swam in front of her.

"Mary?" she questions, confused.

"I kin see you're tirert," the woman says softly, "and your momma's wore out too."

"Why child, don't cry! I thought you'd be glad to see me." Aunt Mary's voice soothes like the warm brown of the sea nut.

"Momma, why wasn't Mrs. Harmon at the funeral home last night?" The effect of Aunt Mary's words has not worn off. She relaxes her face over the steam of the coffee cup, wondering what its color should be called, and whether the tinkly silver of the spoon makes a difference.

"Carolyn, quit playin' with that. You're making me nervous."

The sharp comment translates Mother's unease. Raising her face from the cup, and seeing Mother's, she quickly urges, "What happened to her? I know she's old—Just tell me."

The urgent calm of her voice becomes the shrill screech of the spoon dragged across the table top.

The note at the bottom of her paper had read, "... it is the differences among us ... you do fine work ... keeps us teaching, and learning." But she can only see the teacher's lips, thick and ugly and covered in purple, reading the note to herself, no sound coming out. Carolyn leans forward in the kitchen chair, straining to hear the slow thick speech reading aloud of Antonio's despair, but the lips only tremble with age, as the others in the class imitate the clicking of her dentures, a nasty rasping noise that only the church women with their ratty teased hair can cover with the guitar hymns. But Mrs. Harmon doesn't know the words to "Unseen Hand," and she continues to tremble, and her grey eyes fill with tears as she hears the others clicking and the women testifying and shouting.

"Happened, oh, about two months ago," her mother is saying. "They say Wade did it. He's in jail right now." "Awful thing is," Mother continues, shaking her head, "they didn't bury her. Cremated, and had to go clear to Charleston to do it." After a pause, she adds, "Carolyn, be glad. Be glad your grandmother died peaceably, and that we can plant her in the ground that way." Mother nods her head, certain of her rightness.

The maples of Highlawn Memorial Park shush that there is nothing to be disturbed about. The preacher reads from Isaiah: "All flesh is grass and the goodliness thereof is as the flower of the field: the grass withereth, the flower fadeth, because the spirit of the Lord bloweth upon it: surely the people is grass. The grass withereth, the flower fadeth: but the word of our God shall stand for ever."

She imagines the wheatfield of a midwestern farm, sun beginning in one corner and traveling across it, bleaching the wheat at first; then as it moves, bleaching and bleaching until it burns the wheat. There is no wheat in this part of the country: only the mountain recording a tiny red truck as it moves downward, disappearing.

The sneezing sound of the shovel in ordinary garden dirt denies the yellow clay and the red dog road.

Jesus and Grandma and Mrs. Harmon face away from the sun on an ocean shore; Grandma bends to touch the soft, fragile braid of the sea oats, marvelling that there *is* something new under the sun. But Jesus and Mrs. Harmon watch them, the frail ceremony of the living, and both tremble.

The neighbors murmur about the goodness of God and Grandma, the leaves of the maples waving with their words. The dirt sneezes quietly on the metal lid of the coffin. Nothing to be disturbed about, it shushes.

"Carolyn, you awake? Jim called. I told him I'd have you call back as soon as you woke up." Mother stands, waiting. "He said something about finding the map." Her bare feet trace the rippled brown and white pattern of the linoleum.

She watches Mother's feet, trying to think about the lines and dots of a map that includes Jim, wondering how they will thicken again. The white rail of a fence traveling with the yellow line of a two lane highway becomes four lanes, then bridges; warehouses surrounded by chain link fences. Finally, the black exhaust of a city bus.

That must have been what he was trying to tell me about, she realizes. When I was packing. She waits, checking memory for sound; but still she cannot hear him.

"Mother. Does that television have to go day and night?" She snaps irritably, covering her distress, hoping the words will command her attention.

"It keeps me company," her mother sadly replies, moving out of the room.

"Maybe I'll call Jim." She tests slowly, shaping the words as clearly as she can inside her head.

"Honey, do you have anything you want washed? I'm about to do laundry," Mother calls.

As if television could ever be the reason. She shakes her head, sighs. "Maybe I'll go for a walk," she calls to Mother.

One winter morning she had walked over to his house, hoping to get a ride to school, and some kissing. It was cold, but she had wanted to take her coat off anyway, and neck outside against the wall of the house. She wanted to feel the gritty surface of the grey green tiles against her sweater, and his hands warm against the sides of her neck as she looked up at the red wave of the sheet metal roof.

Instead, she found Wade bent under the raised hood of the truck, picking out pieces of fur and gut and tiny animal parts.

"Hit was a kitten," he explained with a happy smile. "Must of crawled under here to git warm. I didn't know hit when I started the truck."

The smile confused her. Before she could respond, Wade said, "Here. Looky here."

She looked. In the palm of his hand sat the grey unbloodied paw, perfect. Then she looked up into his face. It was still smiling, exposing the strong teeth that would surely snap her in two.

"Ain't found the head yet," he continued, bending under the hood again.

Later, his hands had been cold, not warm.

She had wanted to be sick then, and now, facing the edge of the sky on the rocky strip of mountain, she wants to be sick again. But all she can do is try to breathe against the scene, and the expanding and contracting of her stomach. She sits, her arms wrapped around her legs, forehead resting on her knees, and rocks.

"Oh God," she repeats, squeezing her legs as she rocks, "Oh, God."

After a while she feels the cold ground beneath her, and rises to walk back to the house, turning her back to the mountain. She ignores the view around her, keeping her eyes to the ground just ahead of her, relieved when the sharp red dog chips give way to the grey black asphalt.

Coming around the last bend in the road, she looks up to see a truck parked across the end of the driveway. Her shoes disturb the gravel as she approaches its front, the motor still warm against her hand and the cool breeze of the air. And before she can make it up the last step of the porch, he is there, holding open the screen door, saying, "Heared your mammaw passed on. Come on in." Then, smiling, "Yore mommy ain't too pleased to see me."

The slam of her mother in the next room, and the white streak left by her rude absence testify to fury. Carolyn is the cause of all this.

"How did you get out?" She is angry too. She spits the words against his smile.

He was not expecting this, at least not right away. His green eyes darken and the lids narrow slightly. But his voice remains cheerful and even, saying, "Mommy. She took out a loan."

She nods. Of course.

They stand near the open door, close enough that the light augments the orange flecks dancing in his green eyes. The thick black hair shines, stopping inches above the blue collar to show the white neck. The cheap cologne used to cover the smell of the liquor is the same, and the smell of the liquor is the same. She seats herself in the armchair next to the door.

Wade moves in front of her to the couch, where a girl with yellow hair sits, skinny and stringy like she ought to have been nervous. Seeing her notice, he says, "This here's my wife, Lorry."

"Hey Lorry," she says, hoping her face is pleasant. The girl answers.

Not a day over seventeen, she thinks. She pictures Wade and his mommy and Lorry in the courtroom.

"How long you two been married?"

"'Bout two, three months. Wade 'n me run off the week 'for he's picked up. Spent three whole days in Virginia. Wade wouldn't drive to the beach though."

Not a bit nervous, she thinks, not even high strung. Bold.

"Pregnant." She lets the word slip out, a statement, not a question, completing the courtroom scene.

"No sir," Wade reacts, "I know how to use them rubbers." He is angry at her mistake.

That's right, she thinks. "Pregnant" not to be directly mentioned unless said in a sugary twang pretending hopeful inquiry.

"'Course you ain't wanted to lately," the girl interjects with a giggle. "Too lazy."

"Shut up." He leans his face too close to the girl. Then, relaxing, he tilts his chin toward the television. A church trio accompanied by an upright piano sings about flying to the glory.

"Mommy kin play that on the guitar," he says proudly. "Plays it up to the holiness church all the time."

Your mommy and half the country, she thinks tiredly. Even I remember those words. She leans back in the chair, closing her eyes. Lorry begins to croon with the singers.

Mrs. Harmon's worried face floats before her. Don't worry, she assures the face, he can't hurt anybody else for a while. And he knows that.

"What is this?"

She opens her eyes. Wade sits at the edge of the couch, arm extended over the coffee table toward her. The sea nut sits in the middle of his open palm, wobbling slightly.

God damn it! He must have already questioned Mother about it. She stops herself from reaching forward to grab it.

"That's mine, Wade. Give it to me."

The fleshy part of his thumb nudges the sea nut, making it jump.

"Looks about like a buckeye, don't hit?" He pauses, studying it between thumb and forefinger now.

"Or like one of them worry beads, from up to the ten cent store." Looking up at her, he grins, taunting. "That what you use it for?" He waits for her reaction.

Seeing none, his eyes narrow again. He considers. Then he smiles, and bends his head over the sea nut, examining it a moment more. Shrugging, he drops it casually in the pocket of his flannel shirt, as if she has given him some inexplicable gift.

"You always did like blue," she says, forcing the words. She is afraid she will be sick forever. "Your shirt . . ."

"And you always was a funny turned person. Did you know that?" He rises slowly, stretching deliberately, as if they have been there for a long time.

"We're goin'. Got to pick Mommy up from work." More sharply he says, "Lorry, finish that singin' in the truck." The yellow haired girl exits between them, waiting on the porch.

"You take care of yoreself up in that big city," he says softly. "And tell yore mommy I said 'bye." The green eyes are solemn now, the orange flecks stilled.

She stands at the screen door, watching them repeat her crunching steps across the driveway. She continues watching as he starts the truck, knowing he will check to see that she is still there before pulling away.

She is. She wonders how many trucks there have been over the years, and what colors. She wonders how it would have been to turn his open palm over to hers, catching the sea nut between their hands.

The silver truck has moved only two or three houses away before his arm comes out of the window. The small object rises in a strong smooth arc over the rust and brown and green of the weeds growing beside the road, then drops from sight. Moments later, the truck disappears too.

She nods. "Well," she says finally.

After the door is shut, she bends to snap the television off. In the next room, her mother is crying.

Notes on Writing "God's Country"

*T*HE story "God's Country" is my first attempt at fiction. Consequently, the experience has been of a dual nature: how to write *a* story, and how to write this particular story. I had hoped to have an understanding of the general process (Let's Plot!) before beginning the specific, but they happened simultaneously, with a good bit of trouble. It is much easier to learn how to swim, or to drive a stick shift.

As I began writing, my first problems were with form: I didn't (and still don't) know many of the rules. Where do the quotation marks go? Must they follow each line of thought around? In print, that looked too much like spoken dialogue. Yet was it clear when the main character, Carolyn, was simply rummaging around in her head, and when she was actually conscious of articulating an internal dialogue? My conviction is that single quotes should go for internal dialogue, doubles for spoken words, and nothing for thoughts—with some liberty permitted. However, I was pretty clear that this system would violate the limits of acceptable student writing.

Even the rules I thought I knew became troublesome. Where do you indent? Each time someone speaks, or finishes speaking? Or is it more a case of paragraphing by ear? Does action following narration or dialogue get its own new paragraph? Always? What are the limits of short story form?

Flannery O'Connor tried to help: a short story is a complete dramatic action. Class instructions: write a traditional story, and include all traditional elements (i.e., resolution). Immediately, I spotted—or created—a problem. Modern life isn't dramatic except one or twice in a lifetime. Most of it seems to be drama through psychology, and unresolved psych at that. The information that modern resolution is best rendered through personality didn't help a bit. I like black and white answers, but, like drama, in my life they are hardly ever available. We mostly walk around, irresolute. My character had to. That was the truth of her story.

Still, I chose to "write about West Virginia," as I did think I was doing initially, because it offers drama. It is a place more weird and complex and extraordinary than any city I have ever lived in, and its influence on me has been profound. In some ways, the hills share common ground with the deeper South we have been reading about in class. I was struck by, and a little angry with, the obvious love these authors have for the place, even while describing the insanity and unhappiness the South seems to breed. My own strong feelings, and the fact that I have never before written a word about living in West Virginia, revealed to me that there was probably a story here.

Bad move. The story originally began with a character in the library, on her way home to discover that the daughter of one of her friends has married a very bad man. Unfortunately, in order to hear the news, the character had to walk down Main St. to meet a friend driving her home. The three of us got stuck on Main St. because I decided to go on and on about the ugliness of the town as contrasted with the overwhelming beauty of the mountains. Notice there is no longer a character. Just "I."

Also, the story of the marriage was a hair too close to autobiography. When I was in high school, a friend of mine did marry someone certifiably crazy. She was the first in our group to marry, and while I knew there would be more of this happening soon, her marriage, in particular, was a shock. The man she married does remain in the story as the character Wade, in part, but also in combination with another man I knew by virtue of my friendship with his wife and children while he was in jail. The composite of these two men represent for me a certain type of West Virginia character, one which appalled but fascinated me during the years I spent there. Revulsion ultimately won out, to my mother's great relief, but there is still a part of me very much interested in the extremes of human characteristics.

At any rate, I hadn't combined anyone with anyone yet. I was still stuck on Main St. with my friend, flunking my class. I decided to abandon the story, and simply write, as if for a journal entry, where the writing can be as dreadful and untruthful (or vice versa) as it comes out. That is where the red truck of the story enters, and the description of the mountains. I have been in the back of that truck a hundred times, and down that twisty one lane road a hundred more. I remain impressed by the knowing of those shades of green, so many that no human could possibly ever name them all.

The disparity between my geographical description and Wade's character seemed significant. I was no longer stuck on Main St., but neither would anyone ever know that real people were in that red truck. I had gone too far in the other direction. But the disparity in language between the two segments interested me. How is it that we remember? Why do we remember in such different ways? I had a beginning. A character remembering, trying to pick and choose her way through image, sensation, and time. Carolyn was similar enough to me to have my memories, and yet she could be made different enough to have her own style and experiences. Sure. How?

I decided on more free writing, in order to gather more memories, and to generate some odds and ends that I hoped would provide a sort of list from which I could select and recombine events. My high school English teacher came up, and the funeral of a good friend of mine last year, and my grandmother, who was courteous enough to bring along Aunt Mary. No odds and ends yet, but certainly some material to transform.

I thought about why Carolyn might remember any of this, and came up with the idea that she was going back for a visit. But if, like me, she remembers West Virginia with not much pleasure, she must be going home only for something important, like a death in the family. So Grandma had to die (my mother would have a fit; Grandma is actually alive) because she was the only logical person to do so. A mother's death would be a very different story, and my friend Leah's death was also too important—I was afraid I'd end up right back on Main St., only mourning.

As Carolyn makes the trip back to West Virginia, her memories become more intimate, probably because that is what happens to me every time I go home. But in rereading the story, it seems abruptly revealed and weakly developed in her conversations with her husband, and almost dismissed when she turns her back to the mountains at home. While I think there is a certain general truth to the idea, I think it could have been differently handled, with less of me intruding. Why couldn't Carolyn have mused over this all at home? The geographical description could have been much better dispersed that way. I simply didn't think of transforming that particular element.

I caught myself over and over trying to write my own viewpoint, instead of Carolyn's. Originally, the wake scene included the bit about the neighbors' irritating questions and assumptions. But the diatribe went on too long, and the grandmother started to have too much space. I considered removing that scene, but wakes are really where the excitement is, in my experience anyway. The grandmother's wake became replaced by the very real memory and the very real death of Aunt Mary's son. I hoped that this would also serve to reveal something about Carolyn's character: her refusal to cope with painful situations until shoved into confrontation. I felt I had to choose one of my own real memories, because Carolyn and I are very different in this respect, and I was having trouble handling her. When my grandmother dies, she will have all my attention. And for me, the more painful something is, the more I need to poke at it, although I can lie about it as well as the next guy.

Once there, Aunt Mary served as the one nice character in the story, which my own sense of truthfulness about the place seemed to demand. And Aunt Mary serves also to put Carolyn off guard before she learns of the murder of Mrs. Harmon. This is also true to place. The outlandish can be depended upon to interrupt the ordinary, with rude regularity.

Mrs. Harmon is my high school English teacher, and I am very sorry that she is dead (of natural causes). But because Wade is the character he is, I thought I would hang her death on him, establishing his capacity. I did not want the murder to be much described; like a mother's death, that would be a different story. Also, had the murder happened in reality, it would have been as I described: questionable, and overwhelmed by both the force of the setting and the characters. Action simply means so much less down there, especially with the added influence of fundamentalism. The focus never seems to be on what is really happening at the moment, but on another time or another life. I think this is what I tried to give Carolyn.

If the murder was too large an action for the story, what would serve to reveal Wade's essence? The kitten story was one of those odds and ends I had hoped for, although it did not come to me during that initial free writing session. I did not witness this event, but the story was told to me about one of the men who is Wade. It is a strong memory for Carolyn, strong enough to distract her from the mountains, and I hoped strong enough to carry the transition from memory to actual event.

I had no idea what would happen when Wade and Carolyn met. My interactions with the two men who comprise Wade were nothing like their meeting. They were men I argued with, watched, and came to avoid, but I never liked either of them, nor was I ever sexually involved with either. Yet if any part of this story satisfies me, it is those last few pages. They are not biographically true, and yet they are true, in a way I don't fully understand. Perhaps those last pages most convey what I wished to say. I know they convey a part of my belief about the interactions between people, and that they do explain something about small town life in a mountain country.

I don't know how the sea nut came to play in their meeting. I was outside my apartment one night waiting for a cab, and the idea of Wade taking the sea nut simply came. At the time it seemed like a combination of inspiration and deliverance, because I was afraid of getting stuck again. I was so relieved to have it that I did not question its use in the story. But I do now. Why a sea nut? I do have one, but I wonder if a reader might not be distracted by wondering what the hell it is, and what it "means" in the story. For a woman as interested with color and touch as Carolyn is, it is not well described, nor is its use well explained by the author. A case of forgetting the all important question of *why*.

Other choices I made can be better explained. Jesus and an undercurrent of sex figure in any story of southern life. Trucks and television figure in most rural and small town stories. Roads are explained by the isolation that West Virginia geography and sociology provides. And because I lived there, these are significant personal themes as well. Other choices, like colors, and eyes, and touch, are simply facets of me, made for reasons as varied as my nearsightedness, the way I dress now, and the way I used to dress, and my job as a nurse.

With the basics of the story in place, questions of form rose again. When I reread the first two typed pages of the story, I realized that it simply is not plausible that anyone remembers in such elaborate terms, even though they remain pretty much as I wrote them when I was remembering the mountains. So I chose to have Carolyn reading a description from an old high school notebook, which I hoped would also tie in with the teacher, Mrs. Harmon. Thin, I admit. But it was at this point that I learned something of the truth that altering one point, or even one word, changes the story. Originally, Carolyn was named only as "the woman," and the narrator was telling the story with interruptions from her memory. Having her read off the page, and explaining that, however, made her too real. All of a sudden she needed a name and a husband to talk to. This was somewhat of a technical help, because most of the dialogue in the story is between women, and all those hers and shes became very confusing. Yet it was a technical hindrance also. Here is where my narrator and character began sliding into one another. Carolyn would jump in and speak where the narrator could have provided the information, and the whole business started to be a mess. Initially, I did not mind this so much. It seemed in keeping with the notion that it is very difficult to tell what we consciously and unconsciously retain and divulge, and with my own feeling of uncertainty about how much control we have (or ought to have) with the process. At some point I decided that this might simply be self-indulgence, an excuse for sloppiness because it was easier to write, and because it was what I wanted to write. By now I knew that what I wanted to write was not the same thing as the story, and I tried to neaten things up, with only moderate success—as in the packing scene, where "the woman" slips in again.

Unfortunately, this did not help my beginning. I knew it seemed too long, and made the balance of the story topheavy. I knew vaguely that it delayed the entrance of my character. And I suspected that a reader might assume the remainder of the story would follow in a similar style, and refuse to put up with it. As a defense, I can only say that I ran out of revising time, and that getting from point A to point C in even a linear fashion seemed more than enough to manage.

I am still left with many questions. How bad a choice was my use of the present tense? I chose it in order to make a past tense type of action (remembering) seem more immediate and real. Now all those "s" sounds seem ungainly to the ear, awkward. How are transitions accomplished? I recognize some of the methods in close reading of other authors' texts, but how do I make them appear in my own writing? Is it really true that point of view must never wander? I had no idea of this; only that it must remain consistent with the scope and language of the characters. What am I allowed to decide about form?

Attempting fiction is harder than learning to swim, and it takes more time and concentration and commitment. But its amazing complexities are a pleasure, and even so slight a beginning as this first story has been an exciting attempt to personalize the process.

❧ QUESTIONS ☙

Kathryn M. Monahan's "God's Country," and its process essay, "Notes on Writing 'God's Country'"

1. Of the initial long description that opens the story, Carolyn says, "But this is exactly how I remember it looking. Exactly." How do the shorter, less formal descriptions of place offset or counterbalance not only this initial description, but also Carolyn's statement? Finally, is her memory accurate? Is it complete?

2. What is your response to the different characters in the story, particularly those Carolyn encounters when she comes home? How do the characters give a different sense of place than the one described in the opening paragraphs? How is the psychological or emotional sense of place tied to the physical sense of place?

3. In her process essay, Monahan says of West Virginia that "it is a place more weird and complex and extraordinary than any city I have ever lived in, and its influence on me has been profound." How is this statement supported in her story and essay? And to what degree can this be said of any place you

might have come from? To what degree does familiarity with a place give rise to its complexity?

4. Monahan asks, "How is it that we remember? Why do we remember in such different ways?" Can you speculate as to the answers for these questions? Does Monahan answer them, in part, for herself?

Possible Writing Topics

1. In the story, Carolyn's husband says of her description, "There aren't any people in here. You aren't in here." Write an essay about a place with which you are familiar where you describe as carefully as you possibly can the details, the landscape, the structures that make the place meaningful to you. But don't insert yourself physically into the description. Try not to recall specific, personal memories in the writing.

2. After completing the essay, write a second one where you discuss whether the essay you've written evokes the place as it exists in your memory. Were you hindered by the restriction of not recalling personal memories? Would you call your description objective, or are your feelings for the place revealed in your descriptions? If you call your work objective, how is that objectivity evoked? And if your feelings are revealed, how did you communicate this through your writing? Which phrases and sentences are objective, which revelatory?

Jane McCafferty

Eyes of Others

FRANK said, glancing at the children in the rearview, "I don't need no backseat drivers, and that means you." Corrine, his wife, said, "How 'bout another front seat driver?" She was trying to make a joke and smiled over at him, her face already lined deeply, worn looking, though she was a mere thirty-nine. Her hair, newly dyed a color that lingered somewhere between orange and auburn, was cut in a bowl shape, and she'd tried to curl it back to make a frame for her face like the rolled back brim on the sort of hats she'd always felt looked good on her. Frank peered ahead, peering at the road in a sort of concentrated boredom, as if there would be no surprises, no turns or swerves. And yet the road itself was one long swerving turn, one snake-like curving narrow surprise of a mountain road, and Corrine thought, "Should I be scared? Shouldn't I feel my heart leap, maybe in protest or fear when our car gets too close to the cliff and Frank doesn't seem to notice a bit?" She was aware of something inside of her trusting Frank, trusting wholly and heavily, and also aware lately that this trust sprung from a deep passivity, a resignation she'd made—when?—she didn't know. But she had a growing suspicion that it was wrong to trust because you were too tired not to, to trust because you didn't have the energy to sit on the edge of your seat, alert and admitting that possibilities plagued every moment of time, made each second a precarious beginning of sorts.

She stared out of her window and saw the clawing trees, black in the dusk, stuck firmly in the month of February, in the cold dead ground of Virginia, and something cruel in her personified those trees, just so she could laugh at them inwardly, just so she could think: you trees are stuck and I'm in a moving vehicle, headed somewhere.

"Look at the sky," she said to everyone. A color deep as beets stained the stark blue horizon, and flames of orange light rose through the red like a fan. Moving. Motion. Sometimes she felt that simply being a passenger was the most interesting privilege the world afforded, and the only thing that felt right. She loved staring out the window of a car. Passing things by was like getting them over with.

The children in the back who Frank had warned not to backseat drive were both nine years old. The boy was Corrine's and the girl was Frank's, and yet they looked strangely related, both of them wiry, dark-eyed, dark-haired, and pale. And the expressions that passed heavily through their eyes—now astonishment, now sadness, now a look that seemed almost accusatory—sometimes seemed like expressions they'd planned, a conspiratorial symmetry, a symmetry that had, in the beginning, seemed to Corrine like one more reason she and Frank should be together.

"Figure we're all hungry," Frank said. They were heading toward a tunnel.

"I am," Corrine said. "Kids?"

"Huh?"

"You kids ready to eat somethin'?"

She looked back at them; they shook their heads sleepily. "Yes," one of them said, though Corrine was unsure which one. As they entered the tunnel the car filled up with light, and the sudden, contained sound of engines and their echoes. The children sat up, their hands clutching the back of the front seat.

"Are we really under a mountain now?" the girl, Helen, asked, her mouth an inch or two from her father's neck.

Frank said, "We sure as hell are. A big old four thousand foot mountain is restin' right on top of our heads."

The boy, Kyle John, tried to whistle in appreciation, an imitation of a man, but the sound that emerged was more like the sound of wind in a room when a door to the outside is opened for a second. He gave up trying, and instead said, "If the mountain falls on us, we'll all be crushed out dead and we'll leak out of our bodies and be our *souls*. And then we'll all fly on up to Heaven and Michael Archangel will say to us we have been good."

"Honey," Corrine said. "Michael *knows*. He won't have to ask. He'll be there at the gate with his book and he'll say, "Let's see. This must be Kyle John Harley from 909 Clampers Lane in Bear, Delaware. Kyle John, it looks like you been a bad boy. I count twenty venial sins in one week." Corrine said this looking at the profile of Frank, knowing that the tunnel light would soon be gone, that when they got out the dusk would have lowered further, and Frank would be even harder to see.

"That's all shit and you know it," Frank said. Kyle John sat back.

"It's a matter of stories to teach your children *faith*, Frank, and *you* know it."

"Scarin' that boy to death as if he don't have enough to be scared of right here on Planet Earth."

Frank was always calling the world "Planet Earth." It made him sound like a man who'd traveled in space, a man who compared this world to the last one he'd seen. Suddenly Corrine wanted to please him. Moments like this would grip her, and she'd believe that if she didn't please Frank, somehow, everything would start ending.

"Honey? Kyle John? You know Michael Archangel's just a little story, don't you? And heaven, you know heaven's a *state* of *mind*."

"Yep," came the sturdy voice of the boy, whose arms were crossed and who closed the lids down over his round, dark eyes when Corrine, wishing to barter smiles with him, turned around to the back seat.

"Heaven is the absence of all worries," she added, and smiled at Helen, who smiled back.

"Heaven's where you get to see the soul of your dog if he died," Helen said, and hugged her small self, her eyes shifting to her own window. Last week, the dog she'd had since she'd been two had been struck down by a car. She'd laid on top of the animal as the last seconds of life whimpered out of him, and screamed when they'd tried to lift her off the dead body.

The tunnel ended abruptly, the way every tunnel does, darkness instantly flooding the car, a new and deeper silence, the sky overhead again, nothing protective about it.

"That's true, honey. You'll be with his soul," Corrine said to Helen, and she saw Frank roll his eyes. She could imagine his thoughts: a soul can't play fetch; a soul can't roll over; a soul can't curl up at your feet when it's cold. A soul ain't shit.

"I can feel Warren lookin' down at us all *right* now," Helen said. Why Frank had named the dog Warren, nobody knew. When Helen asked once he'd said, "It's a name, ain't it?"

Corrine turned in her seat to stare out the back. She could still see the lit mouth of the tunnel. "We'll get off of this road and hit the pike," Frank announced. "There's gotta be a Ho Jo's or some such place." Corrine opened the glove compartment and peered into the clutter, watching as if it might begin to swirl or entertain her. Then she slammed it shut hard and stared out the window again.

"The cutest boy . . . the cutest boy . . .

I Ever saw . . . I ever saw . . .

Was sippin' ci . . . der through a straw, der through a straw," sang Helen, her voice like something you hear when you press a glass to a wall, something coming from the room you happen to live next to.

She was so unlike Frank, Corrine thought, and turned to look at the girl. Helen, still singing, smiled at Corrine, washed by headlights of a passing car in these moments. Her eyes, large and almost black, were certainly not Frank's eyes. Corrine once again tried to picture what Helen's mother must've looked like. An older Helen? That pretty? Frank's eyes were small and blue, cloudy behind his glasses. Does Frank ever look at Kyle John and think the same thing? That he must get his wiry strength, his strong jaw, from his father?

With her thumb and index finger she massaged her eyes and thought of her ex-husband hauling freight, looking forward to heading home to his new wife. One time Corrine had said to Frank, "My life has too many *sections*." And when she tried to explain just what she meant by this, and couldn't, she'd felt another *section* cut itself into her life.

"Now forty-nine kids, now forty-nine kids
All call me Ma, All call me Ma
From sippin' ci . . . der through a straw . . . ," sang Helen, suddenly singing loud and very clearly, her voice pretty and so young. Frank and Corrine looked over at each other. "She can sing," Corrine told him, and one side of his mouth shot up, like something had hooked into it and tugged; this was only one of his smiles, a secret smile in which the mouth acknowledged something while the rest of the face remained in some private dark that Corrine felt she could enter if she was patient, if she gave it time and learned to understand more and more that Frank was a special sort of man. A deep, private man.

In Howard Johnson's they sat in a booth—Frank and Helen on one side, Corrine and Kyle John on the other. Kyle John was reading aloud from the dessert menu, stumbling over words that Corrine felt he should know. "Sigh-rup" is how he read the word syrup, and Corrine said, "For Christ sake Kyle John, the word's syrup; you've only had it on your ice cream a thousand times."

"A thousand?" said the boy. "No way." Then he kept reading aloud and the three of them pretended to listen as if it were a tale with suspense in it.

"What can I get y'all this evening?" asked a waitress, stocky in her aqua and white checked uniform. She looked to be about sixty, and she didn't have any eyebrows. Her hair was bleached blond, yet the rest of her was plain as possible, not a trace of make-up or jewelry, the face lined and proud and nodding efficiently to Corrine, who smiled at her, admiring her somehow.

"These two want the spaghetti special," Frank told her. "And the lady will have the fish, and green beans for the vegetable if you have it. And I'll have the Salisbury steak and whatever comes with it."

"Fried or mashed?"

"Mashed," Frank said. "No, make it fried."

Corrine smiled. His moments of indecision were so rare that when they came about, even in exchanges this simple and impersonal, they made him look vulnerable. And vulnerability, to Corrine, was a sign of hope.

"I decided we ain't gonna knock on the door when we get there," Frank said. They were eating now, the children involved in trying to twirl their spaghetti.

"Oh, Frank, why not? My friend Lydia Merris told me a story about doin' the same thing, goin' back to her old house in Wilmington and knockin' and sayin', 'Hello, I'm Lydia Merris. I used to live here. I was wonderin' if I could come in? Just to see my old house?'

"And the people said, 'Sure, you come right *in*.' And they showed her around. She wanted to look way back in one of the hall closets where as a girl she'd written something. She had this memory of writing something on the wall back there and couldn't remember what it was. So she told the people: 'Can I look back in that closet?' And they said: 'Why not?' And ya know what she found? Her own handwriting, twenty years younger and it said: 'Blue blue, my world is blue/Blue is my world when I'm without you.'" Corrine laughed. "That was the words to her favorite song back then." Corrine shook her head, laughed again.

"Well, I just don't think I'm the sort to go knockin' on a stranger's door," Frank said. "Funny how the closer we get, the more sure I am that I just wanna look at the outside of it, look *hard*, fix it firm in my mind for good, then drive away."

"We came three and a half, no, *four* and a half hours just for the outside view?" Corrine said, smearing a dollop of tartar sauce over her dry, fried fish.

"Are we enjoyin' ourselves? Are you gettin' a nice dinner and some scenery out of the deal?"

"Oh sure, Frank. I think it's fine either way. I'm just sayin' if it was *me*, I'd be goin' *inside*. I'd be wantin' to see the rooms."

"Different strokes," Frank said.

A baby, stranded in his high-chair at the foot of a table of young adults, looked over at Corrine just as she'd looked over at him. He was well-fed looking, still bald, and seemed determined not to smile. She'd noticed before that the babies of today seemed very serious. She'd mentioned this to her sister who told her a theory that the babies of today *had* to be serious, since they were the babies that would have to deal with the nuclear war when they grew up.

"Can we sometime go back and see *our* old house, Mom?" Kyle John asked, his mouth packed with spaghetti and circled with sauce.

"You can do that when you're grown. We're goin' to see where Frank was a *boy*, where he lived a long, long time ago, not where he lived a few years back. When you're a man you can take your wife and kids to the house we live in now and you can tell 'em all about us." Corrine laughed, imagining this, a picture of Kyle John in her mind, looking the same only stretched out into six feet tall and behind the wheel of a car, pointing, a pretty wife beside him saying, "Really? You're kidding!"

"I ain't gettin' a wife," Kyle John said. "I'm gonna be a bachelorhood,"

"*Bachelor*," Frank said, smiling his full-smile, his whole face transformed for two or three seconds.

"Bachelor," Kyle John said through his spaghetti.

After a pause Frank said, "Food's good."

"You can always get somethin' decent here," Corrine said.

"You could marry *me*, Kyle John," Helen said, and laughed until her face was red and she nearly choked on her food so that Frank had to pat her on her skinny back, his hand looking dark and heavy and strange on her pink and white striped blouse. For a second or two, watching his hand pat the narrow pink and white back, Corrine thought: What is that? What is that patting that back? And then, relieved, she'd answered herself. "A hand. It's Frank's *hand*."

Sometimes you could think about something or stare at something and instead of knowing it better, it would vanish; the meaning of it seemed to leak out and leave a hollow strangeness in its place. Corrine, the first night she'd met Frank in a bar called "Your Home," had told him this had happened to her as a girl; she'd look at a table for ten seconds or more thinking: Table. What's a *table*? Later, drunk on vodka and cranberry juice, she'd looked at Frank and said: "Man. Man. What's a man?" Then she laughed until she cried.

The car was an old 67 Malibu in excellent shape. The inside of it was spacious, the seats blue and white plaid, untorn, the outside a sleek shade of navy that looked black in the night. It was Corrine's car, the one her ex-husband had bought for 600 dollars. He'd always known how to find deals. Frank thought of it as a clunker, as an embarrassment, and yet it ran better than his Impala which was only two years old. They were back on the mountain road now, and Corrine pointed out the stars to the children.

"I bet you didn't know there were so many," she said. "More stars than there is sky."

"It's the prettiest thing we ever saw," Helen said. Even Frank looked up every other minute or so in a sort of awe. Some of the stars were so low it looked like they were headed right into them, like they could drive through one and swerve around another.

"When I was small I'd sleep outside and stare up at this kinda sky for hours and hours, happy as a pig in shit," Frank said.

"You used to sleep outside?" Helen said, sitting up, one of her hands patting the hair that fell shaggily onto her father's thick neck.

"Sure, I did. We all slept out. Weren't so many maniacs on the loose back then."

"Can I sleep out sometime—Me-n-Kyle John?" Helen asked him.

He laughed. "Yeah, right in the back yard on that nice slab of concrete. Right next to Hogan's fence so the killer dog can sniff ya all night and keep away the crazy asses."

"Daddy!" Helen said, and tried to laugh. The stars kept getting brighter, more plentiful as they rose.

Corrine said, "Who can see all this and not believe in our Creator?"

Frank said, "Me."

They were on a small, dirt road now. Pebbles shot up under the car and clinked. No one spoke. Trees on either side of the road twisted into the bright night air, their bare selves almost hard to look at. Corrine lit a cigarette and cracked her window. As the road came to an end and Frank steered the car onto a similar road, he said, "That road we just left was known as *Bonnie* Road. That single house we passed with the porch was where a deaf girl lived, a deaf girl named Bonnie who'd sit out on the porch and wave. A real, real pretty girl. It was a shame. Bonnie Travels was the full name."

"Did she die?" Kyle John said.

"Hell, who knows. Do the deaf die young? I don't know." Frank said. "But she was the prettiest thing. When we drove past there a minute ago it was almost like she was there on the porch, a little golden girl, watchin' and wavin', day or night . . . this is *my* road by the way. We're comin' up on my house. You'll see it soon."

The house, at the very dead end of the road, faced the car as it approached like an official telling them to stop. "Holy shit," Frank said, cutting the engine. "Holy Mother of Shit." He turned on the highbeams. The children were utterly silent. What could you say about a bright aqua house with shutters like slabs of milk chocolate, and a huge statue of Jesus standing on the flat, black front yard, his white robed arms outstretched into the dark? There was one light on in the house, an upstairs light filling the central oblong window with a flat orange color.

"Oh, Frank, I'm sorry," Corrine said, seeing the pained look that replaced his shock.

"This is it?" Helen said.

A dark human shape passed before the window, then appeared again, stopped and stared out.

"This is it?" Helen said again.

"Of course this is it," Frank snapped. "Why the hell else do I have my highbeams on?"

The person in the window was a man, and now he was opening the window, leaning out. Frank got out of the car and Corrine rolled her window down. The man called out, "Is there car trouble?"

"No, sir," Frank said. And Corrine knew he was thinking: "There's *house* trouble, that's what there is."

"Do you need a telephone?" the man called down. His voice was aged; it fell down through the dark slowly, each word enunciated and separate as a jagged stone.

"No, sir," Frank said. "I don't need . . . I used to live here. It's where I grew up, this house."

"Well! And what is the family name?"

"Luzay. My father was George J. Luzay of Luzay's Tavern."

"I believe I used to stop there myself," the man said.

"Good," said Frank. "I have to go now." He came and got into the car. "Shit," he said. He started up the engine and looked once more at the house, the man gone now from the window. On the front porch an assortment of statues of God knew who stood around in a huddle.

"This ain't it, Helen," Frank said. "I lied. I never lived here."

As he backed the car up to turn, the man appeared on the steps of the porch, waving them in. Soon he was out on the front lawn, a thin man in overalls, a white beard, and no coat, dwarfed by his own looming Christ statue. Corrine rolled her window back down.

"Please stop! Please come on in! I'll fix you something *hot*."

"Crazy sonofabitch," Frank said, the car turned away from the house now. He laid his foot on the gas and drove away, dirt clouds rising in the dark behind them, both children kneeling to look out the back window. Corrine turned, looking that way, too.

"Frank, this is a crime. He's chasin' us now; we gotta go back," she said. "He's lonely Frank. We gotta go back. Frank!"

Frank would not slow down. Helen began to cry. "I wanna go back and talk to that old, old man," she said. But the old man was out of sight now. Trust, that had been so thorough on the way up, crumbled on the way down, though the actual driving had improved, and Frank seemed to anxiously take note each time the road got smaller or curved.

Every family outing they tried to take seemed to fail. They'd gone to Great Adventure last spring and when they'd toured the Safari Section, baboons had jumped onto Frank's car, terrifying them all and enraging Frank, who liked to keep his car perfect. They'd gone to Manuel's, a Mexican restaurant in lower Dover, and Helen had thrown up right onto the table. Even Rehoboth Beach in early October, when they'd nearly had the entire beach to themselves, proved a failure. Corrine had imagined she and Frank would sit in chairs, soaking up sun, their feet lost in sand, watching the children swim, chatting or flipping through magazines, then eating the lunch she'd packed.

Corrine stared at the brilliant stars and remembered everything about that lunch—the fried chicken, celery stalks with cream cheese and paprika, grape juice, banana cake, the six of beer. She could picture it all wrapped, the perfect way she had fit everything snuggly into the cooler. But Frank that day, after drinking half of the beer before noon, had told her, "Think I'll go for a little stroll," and kissed the part in her hair before walking off. She could remember smiling up at him, him smiling down at her, the memory of desire still in both of their eyes. She could remember the way she believed those smiles meant love that day.

"I'll stay here and watch the kids," she'd told him, as if there'd been a choice. She'd turned to watch him walk down the boardwalk, most of the shops closed up, hardly any people around. And four hours later, after an hour of searching, she and the children had found him drunk in a bar, watching a Phillies game, flocked by other men. She could still see the look on his face when she walked up behind him and tapped his back. She remembered how tight her skin felt, how she'd felt ugly, her hair sandy and tangled, her nose greased with sun screen, her lips chapped. He'd looked at her like she was such a perfect stranger, she nearly became one.

"I think from now on I just wanna stay home," she said, when they were almost off the mountain. She sighed. "I think we're not meant to go taking stupid day-trips like we do." Frank didn't reply. She looked into the backseat where the children had fallen asleep, each of their heads against a door.

"It's terrible," she added.

"Oh, come on, Corrine. It's no tragic thing," Frank said. "It was my idea, and I take the blame. The next time we take a day trip, it'll be to someplace normal, some place that has to do with the *present*. You can't drive up to your old boyhood home and expect to come off the mountain happy. It's not normal. I shoulda known."

"No, it's not just today. It's everytime we go somewhere. Something always goes wrong. I wanna get on home and never leave again."

"Corrine, you're soundin' like a little child," he said. And then he said — for some reason she couldn't follow, "I'm a realist. I'm as realistic as they come, and that's all I know."

She didn't speak anymore for almost an hour. They were on the freeway and she kept thinking of that man, that old man in the bitter mountain dark, tearing out of his house in his overalls, pathetic, begging them to come back. Frank had turned the radio on, a station with no commercials, just canned music, elevator music as her sister called it. We might as well all *be* in an elevator, she thought, and wasn't sure why.

"Frank?" she finally said.

"Hmmmm?" The way he answered let her know that he'd been off in his own thoughts. His tone seemed to say he hadn't even noticed the long thick silence that had settled between them.

"Frank, I'm so hungry. Could we get dessert? The dessert we never had after dinner?" All of a sudden she knew she didn't want to go straight home. She wanted one last chance to redeem this outing, to make things right.

"Sure. It's only ten. We'll stop in the next place we see. You can get anything your little heart desires," he said, and reaching over, patted her on the leg. She took both of her hands and grabbed his and held it there, squeezed it, the tears in her eyes sudden and blurring the lights of the car in front of them. She bit down hard on her lip, not wanting to cry, not wanting to make a noise.

"Sound ok with you?" Frank said, his captured hand beginning to stir for release.

"Ok," she said and let go.

"Wake up! Kyle John? Helen? Time to wake up, kids. We're about to have banana splits or anything else your little hearts desire," she told them. Frank was out of the car already, in the parking lot stretching under the harsh lights that gave the air a metallic, greenish tint. In his blue unzipped parka, his flannel shirt and jeans, he looked like so many men, she thought. "Why him?"

"I'm not hungry," Helen said, in a voice that was almost a whisper, a voice that seemed to come out of a dream she was having. Kyle John pouted and blinked and stared at her as if trying to remember where and who he was. Waking people up had been something that had saddened Corrine throughout her life; how solitary and difficult life looked on the faces of those who were fighting their way out of sleep. Tonight, these children in the parking-lot light seemed so far away, she had to fight back tears once again. And then she grew suddenly angry with them for taking so long to change gears.

"Come on," she snapped. "I said it's dessert time and I meant it. Now both of ya out of the car and have some fun. You all can sleep when you're dead."

The children each opened their door and nearly fell out of the car. In the lot they stood and groaned about the cold and Frank called over that he didn't want to hear it.

"Don't complain. Don't explain," he hollered. It was one of his favorite sayings. He walked up to the door of the new-looking Howard Johnson's and the three of them followed suit, quietly. Frank held the door for them, his eyes straight ahead as they passed by and entered the restaurant. There was no aqua and orange in this Ho Jo's. It was spanking new and attempting to be rustic. Everything was brown and rust-colored, and the fake wood gleamed.

"Four of you together?" asked the hostess.

"Are we together?" Frank joked, looking at Corrine who laughed too loudly.

The children looked startlingly awake now. That was the way it was with children. They looked both more asleep and more awake, as if the border between these two states shrunk with age.

Helen ordered a dish of chocolate ice cream and Frank told her that was the most boring order he'd ever heard. She laughed. "So," she said. "Big deal if it is." And then she laughed again. Kyle John got the clown sundae; it arrived on a long metal plate. The clown's face was done with M&Ms and a sugar cone made his hat.

"That's cute," Corrine said. Weight conscious, she'd ordered a cup of vegetable soup. "Excuse me. I have to go to the Ladies," she said, before taking a spoonful.

In the blue-tiled bathroom, another woman was at the sink washing her hands. Corrine went into a stall and waited for the woman to leave. She wanted to reapply her make-up, but needed privacy. How some women could stand in public, encountering themselves in the mirror while others watched, Corrine would never know.

When the woman was gone, Corrine slipped out of the stall. She stood right next to the mirror, and dug up foundation, lipstick and mascara from her purse. She applied only the foundation; she didn't want this to be too obvious. She blended it in until her skin looked younger, more even-toned. Then she smiled brightly, her eyes colliding with themselves. "Soup time," she said and walked out.

Back at the table Frank said, "Corrine, this was a great idea. Sometimes you have the best ideas of anyone I know."

A part of her that had sunk inside now fought its way up to the surface, and she smiled what she knew to be her prettiest smile. Frank winked and went back to his sundae.

There was a woman across from them alone in a deuce-booth, eating a full course meal. She wore a very outdated paisley dress—the colors were harsh greens and blues. She was hunched over her food so that her thin black hair fell into it. Corrine got a glance at her legs under the table—skinny in dark nylons. Old, red, outdated shoes. Corrine's heart lurched forward. No matter how absorbed or comfortable people looked, it was never nice to see them eating in public, alone.

"Did I ever see a real clown, Mom?" Kyle John said.

"You did," she said. "You went to the circus. Don't you remember?"

"Sort of."

"You had a great time, Kyle John. You loved it."

"I did?"

"You did."

"Did I ever see a real clown, Dad?" Helen said.

Corrine watched the woman's sharp snow-white elbow jutting out as the woman cut into her food. The woman paused suddenly, put down her fork and pushed her dark, straight hair behind her ear—a curtain pulled back for Corrine. Corrine stared at the profile, the full lips, the skin like stale sheets, the unblinking eyes set low in the face and staring ahead as if recalling something, as if in a daze. Then the woman sucked in her cheeks and arched her neck up and stared smack at the ceiling. She sat there in this odd position for nearly a minute, Corrine holding her in her peripheral vision, fascinated by this stranger.

Frank was in the middle of a story about what happened to Helen the day she'd been to the circus—she'd gotten lost and ended up in the wrong section with an old lady and her retarded son. "I was nearly crazy thinkin' you were gone for good and when I found you, you smiled and said, 'Hi, Daddy!'"

"No!" Helen said and began to laugh her side-splitting laugh.

"Four years old and lost with a big retard and his mother at a circus and you thought you were in heaven."

Helen, through her uproarious laughter, spit some chocolate ice cream out and some of it landed on Kyle John's clown.

"You gross pig!" he said, but then he was laughing as hard as Helen.

A man stood in front of the woman in the deuce-booth now. The back of him was tall, straight-legged and broad-shouldered in a black wind-breaker. He was blocking Corrine's view of the woman's face.

Then the man bent down and kissed the woman on the cheek, then on the lips, and slid into the seat across from her.

"I got lost once but really I ran away," Kyle John was saying. "'member, Mom? 'member I ran away that time?"

"Yes," she said. Though she didn't turn and stare directly at the couple, she could see them from the corner of her eyes perfectly. They weren't saying a thing. They simply stared at each other. "Tell that story, Kyle John," Corrine said, and as he spoke, she found a way to look over at them without it seeming rude; she pretended to be looking slightly above them.

The man had longish brown straight hair and a nice looking face. He was somewhere in his thirties. His eyes and the woman's eyes were perfectly locked together, their smiles small and intensely private. Corrine could not look away now. Kyle John must've said something funny, for even Frank had exploded into laughter. The couple would not look away from each other. They held the refuge of the deep gaze without even blinking. Their subtle smiles seemed to contain every important thing this world could ever offer. How did they know each other? Where did they meet? How long had this been going on?

"It's true, right, Mom?" Kyle John said.

"Every word," Corrine answered, to what she didn't know.

The woman finished her meal, still looking at the man as she ate. Why didn't they speak? Why did they feel they didn't need a single word?

They rose to go. The woman's coat was as strange as her dress—a flowered coat like you'd wear at Easter time in 1950. Even as she slipped into it, her eyes did not leave his.

Only when they walked up to the register to pay did they stand side by side, both of them looking at the cashier. Corrine could not let them go. "I need some gum," she announced, and got out of the booth and headed toward the couple. She stood in back of them as they paid, breathing in their smell, a strange, mysterious, perfect smell like the smell of a house in which the same people have lived for a long time. She looked into her purse, pretending to search for coins. She looked up just a few inches from the billowing flowers on the long narrow back of the flowered Easter coat. And then the sound of the register slamming, the cashier saying, "Thank you. Goodnight," the couple turning and walking out the door, and Corrine following behind them, far enough away to be inconspicuous, close enough to hear what they might say to each other. But they didn't speak or even hold hands, just kept walking in their silence, heading to their gray car.

"Excuse me!" Corrine yelled. The words had escaped her, surprised her. The couple turned and faced her. They stared at her, first blankly, then questioning. Corrine stood a few yards away and could not think of what to ask them.

"You dropped this," she finally said, and dug frantically into her purse for some money. She brought out a limp, five-dollar bill, one corner of it streaked with orange lipstick.

The man stepped up and took it from her, nodding, and then his voice—deep and straightforward—thanked her.

"It was nice of you to follow us out here in this cold," the woman called, her strange, pale face breaking into a smile before she got into the car and shut the door.

"Mom!" came the voice of Kyle John, ringing in the air behind her. "Frank wants to know what you're doin' outside!"

The Sources of "Eyes of Others"

I happened to write the first sentence of this story one morning as soon as I woke up. I have no idea where the sentence came from; I had not to my knowledge dreamed it or thought of it before I sat down to write, but there it was, "Frank said, glancing at the children in the rearview, 'I don't need no backseat drivers, and that means you.'"

The sentence gave me the seeds of Frank's character, the children in the back whom I imagined he had spoken to, and most importantly, it gave me a sense of *place*.

When I feel my characters rooted in a particular place, I immediately know a lot about them. In this story, place happens to be the inside of a car, which is not a place normally associated with rootedness. But it is a specific place, and one that I have strong feelings about. Car interiors have an intimacy no matter what the characters inside them are like. In cars, people are trapped together in a small space, sharing both the fact that they are headed in the same direction, and the unspoken solidarity resulting from relinquishing control to a driver, a trust that is profound. Immediately, then, I knew that the characters in this story understood at some level of consciousness that if they were to crash, they would crash together.

This intimacy of place is deepened by the fact that through the windows of a moving car, the world is immense and detached, as framed as a film, and yet very much the world that contains and affects the inside of the car; the world outside gives the car interior its essence. The car is pitted against infinite space, and so the space within, by contrast and opposition, becomes intimate. One could say this about a house too, or any shelter, but while a house is rooted and brimming with images of the illusion of stability, it is this illusion that car-travel denies, these houses that cars pass by.

In spite of this forced intimacy of place, I also sensed the characters were experiencing their solitudes in a way that riding in a car catalyzes. Each character has a different window view in the story, which means they are observing different worlds tear by at high speed, and having to bear at the very least their own thoughts about those worlds, about those landscapes that do not include them. It is the tension between isolation and intimacy that I felt immediately as a large part of this story, or at least a part of the knowledge that helped me to write it.

I owe some of my feeling about car interiors to memories of driving around with my father, a man who seemed more at home in a car than in a house. When he had spare time, he went for a drive. It was interesting to ride around with him because he drove as if looking for something without knowing what that something might be. Anything in the landscape was potential for him to suddenly "discover," whether it be the wall of an old church we passed by every day, a billboard, or something exotic like a field of cows on a backroad. Often he would stop the car and nod his head in the direction of whatever he had singled out, and no matter how mundane the sight was, it emerged with a certain power simply because he had chosen it as something to notice.

I am comfortable with characters in cars, then, because I was so often in them as a child, and because of the way my father drove—dependent on the mystery of an unkown destination, and the anticipation of finding it out. That is similar to the way I write, even when my characters are rooted to particular plots of land. Like my father got behind the wheel of the car, not knowing where he was going and what he would find along the way, I sit down at the typewriter and write a first sentence, which can be likened, I hope, without stretching the metaphor too far, to backing out of a driveway. So a car moving through a story feels very natural to me, the action of it mirroring a basic impulse behind the writing.

Another impulse behind all writing is to stop time—to use language to shape the fluid into the stable. It follows, then, that memory housed in moving cars would intensify that impulse. While most memories are motionless, and seem stronger the more securely they are fixed in particular space, the memory of car travel contains both the static images of the people sitting inside of the car, and the images and sensation of *motion* that feels antithetical to the nature of memory itself. This may explain why unlike any other story I have written, this story spilled out of me in one day. Perhaps as I wrote I was racing my own memory of motion.

Besides the car, the first sentence of this story gave me the name *Frank*. My next door neighbor in early childhood happened to have been named Frank, and it was his image that surprisingly came into my mind. This lead me in the next sentence to imagine his wife Lottie, who turned into Corrine somewhere in the fourth paragraph when I could no longer tolerate the name Lottie. While I had more exposure as a child to Lottie than I had to Frank, her face refused to clarify itself in my mind before it faded away completely, its residue a blurred sadness. The character of Corrine, as a result, was sad from the beginning.

In remembering the faces of adults from my childhood, I often confront myself with possible sources for fiction, those faces always being embodiments of worlds I could not comprehend, images composed of old perceptions grown dream-like. And because the old perceptions were incomplete, devoid as they were of supplementary understanding needed to begin imagining what they meant in the context of an adult life, the remembered images born of those old perceptions seem to call for language, for understanding that might complete them.

The characters of Helen and Kyle John were also written into the first sentence, though both of their characters waited to emerge until the third paragraph when Corrine's character was fairly well established. I think that I needed to wait in order that they be the right children for Corrine, or rather the wrong children; since this story focuses on Corrine's isolation, the children needed to be young and sweet, incapable of understanding her position. I didn't consciously decide this, but in retrospect I can see that they do add to rather than alleviate her isolation. A few years older, and one of them might have had more potential to communicate with her. A few years younger, and one of them might have been on her lap, providing at least physical contact. So, in a sense, the source of the children is derived from the character of their mother. They are not based on any particular children, certainly not on my neighbor's children or myself as a child, though my childhood memories of how mysterious it felt riding in the backseat of a car at night on the freeway helped my imagination to attach itself to both children. From memory I know very well how Helen felt leaning forward to ask her father a question as he drove. And the song that Helen sings about sipping cider is one that I remember hearing twenty-one years ago headed to kindergarten in a car packed with children I did not know. One of the little boys in the back of the car happened to suddenly belt this song out and sing it solo all the way through, while the rest of us fell silent and listened. It was a stunning and obviously unforgettable rendition. I gave to Corrine both the admiration and isolation I felt listening in a car full of strangers that day, and Helen sings as loudly and clearly as memory tells me that boy sang it in the early autumn of 1965.

Kyle John seems to embody the quality of earnestness that I have seen in various children his age. Memories of one of my younger brothers might have helped me develop him somehow, though the influence was not consciously felt.

Like the characters Frank and Corrine, my neighbors Frank and Lottie were both on their second marriage, and the children which each of them brought to the marriage clashed. Frank's children were older. In my memory they are sitting on the front stoop, smoking and staring unhappily into the street, while Lottie's wild little boys ran around in cowboy hats and football helmets. The family seemed more like a group of people that just happened to have ended up living under the same roof together. I have a fairly clear memory of my mother in our old kitchen explaining to me that Frank was not the *real* father of my friend, Lottie's youngest son. The whole notion of the possibility of families severing astonished me. I was only three or four at the time, and memory tells me that learning this had a big effect on me, big enough so that I began to pray regularly that my own family wouldn't break apart. Corrine certainly doesn't feel that she is in the midst of a solidly unified group. I have given her some early fears of my own, anxieties inspired by my neighbors and cultivated by my imagination at a very early age.

While the *inception* of the characters Frank and Corrine can be traced to my memory of my neighbors, Frank and Lottie, the developed characters are not based on those neighbors, whom I have not seen since I was five. I had never even considered that they would enter into my fiction until that morning when I happened to sit down and write that sentence.

I had, however, considered writing about the people who inspired the couple at the end of the story who Corrine follows outside. The fictional couple is based on people I saw three years ago in a Philadelphia Burger King. They are by far the least transformed material I have ever included in a story. I saw them one dark, drizzling February day when I had been out looking for a job. I was taking an extended coffee break, sitting in a booth in Burger King with a window view of a city street at lunch rush-hour. A woman sat in the booth in front of me, facing me. She was strangely attired in a long polyester flowered dress with a long-stemmed plastic rose pinned in her black hair. Her pale face had a drawn, pinched, defensive look and she seemed vulnerable, sad, and utterly anxious.

After a while, a man entered and sat down across from her. Her eyes met his and locked. Her expression was completely transformed; anxiety and defensiveness vanished, replaced by a radiant, perfectly relaxed honesty. They stared at each other in a silence that seemed a palpable protection, as if a glass room had been suddenly formed around their booth. It seemed as though they had not seen each other for a long time (or so I began to imagine) and that their lives were so intertwined, their souls so full of knowledge of each other, that they did not need words, that words in fact would not have touched on the depth of this reunion.

They were a startling contrast to everything around them: the canned music of Burger King, the loud conversation coming from the other booths, the lingering gloom of a low winter sky, the scattered crowd rushing down the sidewalk, and myself, attempting to muster up the ambition to get out of the booth and continue the job-hunt. Because the couple had a powerful connection that I felt I lacked at the time, they were riveting. They sat there looking at each other for quite some time. Then, without speaking, the two left in unison.

My coffee gone, I exited a few seconds later, and ended up walking behind them on the sidewalk for a block or so until our paths diverged. I gave up looking for a job that day and went back to my room so that I could write a story about the couple. It failed miserably. I was too nervous about not having a job to concentrate, and I doubt I had enough distance from them that day to shape their significance into fiction.

Three years later, in this story, when I heard Corrine mention to Frank that she wanted to stop for dessert, I suddenly knew that I would give her the opportunity to see this couple. I felt a lot of resistance to writing the end of the story, for it was the first time in the story that I knew I wanted something to happen before I was writing it. I feared that the couple didn't belong in this story, even though I wanted them to. I was afraid Corrine would see the couple and refuse somehow to acknowledge their power. For this reason I was relieved when she finally followed them out into the parking lot and cried "Excuse me!" She has reached, at the end of the story, a state of isolation that will demand she change.

"Eyes of Others" draws its source from memories of mine that range over a span of twenty-two years. I could have never predicted these memories would find a home within the same story, and yet, after the story was written, I felt that what had happened in it was inevitable. It is paradoxical to end up feeling this way when the writing itself seems to depend on chance—the chance of waking up and writing the first sentence with the name *Frank* in it, the chance that Frank was in a car, the chance of remembering the faces of old neighbors, and so on.

Source, then, seems inextricably tied up with seemingly disparate memories connecting somehow, through language. Most memories seem to acquire a deeper significance through their interaction with each other.

∾ QUESTIONS ∾

Jane McCafferty's story "Eyes of Others," and its process essay, "The Sources of 'Eyes of Others'"

1. McCafferty describes Corrine's thinking: "Moving. Motion. Sometimes she felt that simply being a passenger was the most interesting privilege the world afforded, and the only thing that felt right." On long car or bus trips, have you had the same sense? And on reaching your destination, how does this change? How does Corrine's love of car rides underscore the crisis she's facing? When she and Frank and the children stop at different places throughout the story, how does Corrine's situation change?

2. Corrine asks of the couple she encounters at the end of the story: "How did they know each other? Where did they meet? How long had this been going on?" What does this couple possess that Corrine has no access to, and how does McCafferty establish the contrast between this man and woman and all that Corrine has experienced in the story?

3. In her process essay, McCafferty writes, "Car interiors have an intimacy no matter what the characters inside them are like." Has this been your experience? Can you recall trips you've taken with others where this intimacy has made you uncomfortable, where the trust McCafferty speaks of has been tenuous at best? Would Corrine have encountered all that she did in the story had she not been riding in the car for a long time?

4. McCafferty writes of her experience of driving with her father, "Often he would stop the car and nod his head in the direction of whatever he had

singled out, and no matter how mundane the sight was, it emerged with a certain power simply because he had chosen it as something to notice." In the story, does Frank possess the power McCafferty speaks of? How much of this can be attributed to the trust that, as McCafferty points out, we must give to the driver of the car? In your own experience, do the driver's observations gain more power and notice because he is in control of the vehicle?

Possible Writing Topics

1. The sense of place McCafferty describes—the interior of a car passing through *places*—is markedly different from the sense of place that appears in Shelton's essays and Monahan's story and essay. Recall a trip you took in a car or bus that for whatever reason is particularly memorable, and write an essay where you tell your audience the story of that trip. You'll need to write about the places you traveled through, the places you stopped, the conversations you had with those who traveled with you.

2. After completing the essay, write a second one where you describe how you remembered the details of the trip, which memory triggered another, which you decided to include, and which you eliminated. Does your essay end with your arrival at your destination? Is there another way it could end? How difficult was it to give this essay direction, a purpose aside from the trip itself?

Garnett Kilberg

My Parents' First House

SINCE I was only 2 years old when my family moved into the first house my parents owned, I don't remember the event, but I do know that there wasn't any grass in the yard, only dirt and mud. I know this because of old black and white photographs: one of me balanced on the rim of a huge crater-like hole in the back yard, and another of me, filthy, my face and arms streaked with dried mud, sitting on a newly trowelled sidewalk—the swirls in the concrete reminiscent of cumulus clouds—bordered on either side by dirt and mud. When I think of the photo, I can recall the feel of mud patties, the consistency of thick pudding, in my hands. (There was a time, I've been told, when my sister and I were punished for scrubbing our neighbor's windows with mud.) I imagine the entire neighborhood looked like a freshly roto-tilled field, where dirt and huge chunks of earth had been overturned to make way for one of those ubiquitous housing developments of the 1950's.

But my first real memory is after the grass had been planted, and grown, and been mowed countless times. Tens of similar red or yellow brick houses—most with a large plate glass picture window, three bedrooms, a single car garage, and one struggling dogwood held in place on the lawn by string and three stakes—stretched as far as I could see. The houses were so alike that I remember one evening when we were sitting in the living room, and a strange little boy walked in the front door. He took one look at us and burst into tears. It turned out that he was visiting his aunt and uncle, our neighbors, but when the streetlights had come on (the universal signal for going inside) he had become confused and didn't know which house was theirs.

Our address was 5204 Strawberry Lane. The numbers rose in a graduated line over the mailbox.

When you walked in the front door, there was no real foyer, only a small entry way, a patch of linoleum that sidled the living room carpet. Even though the house had been brand new when my parents purchased it, from my earliest memory the carpet was thin. Like a campsite, a small circle was worn in the center of the room with paths emerging from it in the most traveled directions, off to the hallway that led to the bedrooms, and toward the kitchen (of course, there was no dining room). There wasn't much furniture in the living room: a small desk in the farthest corner (which later became mine, then my son's), two sofa sections separated by a round wicker table, a chair, an antique pie chest with two wooden doors containing wonderfully decorated tin panes, a television, and two book shelves (which, many coats of paint later, I now own). The center of the room was where we lay on our stomachs to read, draw, play games, watch television, or occasionally drag out the wicker table to serve as a frame for a tent.

If you followed the path that led to the kitchen, you saw what, at first, appeared to be a plain square room: the refrigerator was against one wall (though we always called it an ice box), then a counter, containing both the sink and the stove, wrapped around the two walls to the refrigerator's left. The fourth wall was what set the kitchen apart from the other kitchens on Strawberry Lane. Above the redwood picnic table and bench, which we used instead of more conventional seating, was a magnificent picture of a window painted on the wall by my mother. She had painted it complete with louvered shutters and, I think, a flower box filled with geraniums. I can't recall the scene outside the window, but I know it was of some distant land, perhaps Mexico since my mother's parents took our family to Taxco during two or three winters for extended holidays. There was, I think, a cobblestone courtyard in the painting, with lots of colorfully dressed people milling around a central fountain, and it seemed like there was a hill sloping off in the distance. Usually I didn't pay particular attention to the window—it was simply part of my house, like the stove or the pie chest. But I can remember, on other occasions, being fascinated by it. I'd sit on the picnic table bench and stare at the mural, alternately trying to convince myself that the window, and the scene depicted outside it, was real and I could climb through it into another world, and astonishing myself that it was merely an illustration that my own mother had created.

My mother, the daughter of a journalist who became a major newspaper editor, had wanted to be an artist, but her parents had persuaded her to go to Oberlin College and major in English Literature, an area they felt was more acceptable. My father, an athlete and a brilliant student (I recently learned he won a statewide high school Latin competition), had attended Oberlin on scholarship. He had wanted, like his father and his aunts, to become an attorney. But because of his marriage and the birth of my older sister, he had dropped out of law school. His father was deceased and had, I believe, lost what money he did have in the Depression. So both my parents were products of interesting homes, and of their own thwarted ambitions. What did they think as they stood in that dirt yard with their two small children, a third child on the way, looking at the square brick house that they were about to buy? Were they sad about what they had relinquished in order to be able to purchase such a place? Were they excited about the prospect of acquiring their first home? Or did they shrug, and say, "Oh well, it'll only be a few years—a start so that we can buy something else." Because, indeed, it was what the advertisements always refer to as "a nice starter home."

Once we had lived in the house for a while, there were signs that they weren't as happy there as they could be; the most obvious sign was the amount of time they slept. My father took naps on the couch or the living room floor, usually with a book or a newspaper open across his chest. Once I remember him waking up, furious to find the three of us children with our heads pressed to his stomach, listening. My mother, a person with almost limitless energy now, seemed to spend a great deal of her time conniving to find time to sleep. In the summer she liked to take a nap during the most boring part of the day—mid afternoon—when it was too warm in the unshaded neighborhood to play outside, and nothing was on television except adult programs. I remember my mother lying face down on her spread, lost in the type of sleep that made her seem a part of her bed, while the three of us stood in the narrow space between the bed and the dresser, nudging her, whining, "Get up, get up, there's nothing to do." Without lifting her head or opening her eyes, she would answer, "Why don't you read a book or draw a picture." But we were relentless, seldom leaving for more than a few minutes. Only after I grew up did I realize how depressing it must have been for her in that little master bedroom, the main window so high and squat that it looked like a basement window (they made them that way in the front bedrooms for the sake of privacy), surrounded by three small children, on a street where her neighbors, though cordial, ridiculed her love of art and classical music, thinking she was putting on airs. She and my father were stuck in that house for a total of eight years. Even though they had managed, after their first five years, to put the house up for sale, a recession, and a multitude of similar houses, caused it to sit on the market for another three.

I knew, of course, that there were more interesting places to live. Several times a year, we went to my mother's parents' home, a beautiful house with its own small library, a long dining room table with buzzers at each place for the maid, silk wing chairs, a grand piano, and gardens so exquisite that they once were photographed for a magazine. We were walked through cocktail parties on their brick patio where we were introduced to distinguished journalists. (Once I was told I was meeting Dick Tracy's father; I think he was the man who wrote the script.) I sometimes fantasized about living in my grandparents' house. But this is not to say that I realized my parents' house was as stark as it certainly must have been.

A child, I believe, is able to both penetrate and pull from a place in ways an adult never can. I can honestly say that as a girl I saw almost as much mystery in the crevices of one of the red bricks that made up my parents' home as I now sometimes see in an entire city. The house and the neighborhood were a complete world to me. A trip to Woolworth's, located in the plaza that was separated from the development by an apartment house, was as big an adventure as a cross country junket. If we chose to return home through the backyards instead of by the front sidewalks, each property line constituted a pernicious border to be crossed, each yard a country in itself. Most yards were simply green squares of grass like our own, but others were wonderlands occupied by topiary-like shrubbery, fake pools or little patios; while others were clearly dangerous territories, yards cluttered with weeds or broken trash, inhabited by angry adults or dirty children who would yell at us to get off their property.

My sister had a way of making even the simplest things seem dangerously complicated. For instance, the little boy who wandered into our house had not done so by accident. He had correctly gone into his aunt's house, only to wind up inside our house: a phenomenon as strange as an episode of *Twilight Zone*. Perhaps someday we would open our parents' door and find ourselves in another house, but maybe we wouldn't be so lucky as to have the place we wound up be right on Strawberry Lane.

I shared a room with my sister. Like the rest of the house, it was square. There were two windows, one that looked on the backyard, and a second one that looked on a house owned by an older couple with two Siamese cats they treated like children. Our bunkbed was pushed against the second window so that just a corner of it cut into the compartment created by the lower bunk, which was mine. I sat there so often at night, watching for something to happen, that when I envision the room, the focus is the corner of that window. I can see the murky darkness coalescing outside; I can see the pattern of the wallpaper that skirted the window—little squares with bursts of foliage inside; I can see the smooth pale oak of the bed post I held. But I can't remember the other side of the room. Nor can I see the top bunk where my sister slept. I think I only *did* see it once or twice. It was a mysterious place where she would not allow me to look.

The house also contained a small bedroom—a half square—that belonged to my brother, a tiny square bathroom with a frosted glass window, and a short hallway. There may have been a crawlspace upstairs, but certainly no attic. There was, however, a large—at least it seemed that way to me—basement with a concrete floor and painted cinder block walls. We children had the run of the basement. My sister and I turned a good portion of the floor into a miniature city (a project that lasted several years). We taped down intricate cardboard houses with wax paper windows so that they wouldn't topple. With a squeaky black magic marker, we drew roads right on the floor. My mother did not mind. We built and built, and decorated and decorated, with no interference. My sister could make almost any tiny accessory with her hands. It still amazes me to recall the tiny baskets she wove from the long grass that grew across the back edge of our yard. We could do almost anything we wanted, free to lose ourselves in invention. To an extent, that was also true of the rest of our house and my mother. I remember coming home one day to find an enormous nude snow sculpture my mother had constructed in the front yard, and on another to find that she had painted most of the living room furniture, including the television, green. They did not care much about what the neighbors thought.

My parents have moved many times since that house. They have lived in four states. They seem happier than many young couples; they still hold hands. My mother got her M.F.A., and now has her own small studio in which to work. Though she did sometimes continue to paint on the walls (I remember a vase she painted for a vine that had pushed its way through a crack in the wall, mice painted in corners, and shelves painted above a window), her work has become more abstract and is usually on canvases, while her houses have grown more like my grandparents' house. (Some of the furniture is literally the same, since my mother inherited several of their antiques.) Recently my mother and father moved back to Oberlin where they met and always wanted to return. While renovations were being done to their house, they stayed in a condominium in a suburb of Cleveland not far from Strawberry Lane. During a visit to my mother, she asked if I wanted to run by the old house. It had been almost twenty-five years since we'd lived there. The tiny trees were mature, thick and leafy. The houses, though still brick and solid, looked a little old and run-down. My mother chatted happily as she pulled over to the side, "Can you believe that some of these sell for thirty or forty thousand now; when we left they were about sixteen."

"Which one is ours?" I asked.

"Come on, you recognize it," she said, sounding exasperated. "It's right here."

I looked again, and, sure enough, it was 5204 Strawberry Lane. But it wasn't the way I remembered it. And as I sat there considering it, I began to feel embarrassed to see it revealed this way—indistinguishable from all the other houses we had passed.

Considerations When Writing "My Parents' First House"

*E*ARLIER this year, I wrote an essay discussing how I composed a short story called "Thieves." Done in a growing tradition, the essay focused on the transformation of autobiographical material into fictional artifact. As most writers who have engaged in this process are aware, memories are often actually memories of memories; but when the idea is to create fiction, it doesn't matter— ultimately, at least—how much the factual source is altered. With a personal essay, it does matter, which is why discussing the sources at length bothers me—

such a discourse almost seems akin to relaying how I transformed fiction into fact.

This is not to imply that the information isn't true. As the cliche goes, I'm sure it's true, but not always sure it's accurate. Because, of course, another truth the process reveals is that not only are memories tainted with subsequently acquired knowledge, but also subject to interference as one grows and matures and one's physical and intellectual point of view changes. For example, I know I can envision the desk that was in my parents' living room since it was passed along to me and sat in my son's room until about a year ago. Yet the desk in my memory was large and imposing, a place of honor to work, while the same desk, the one in my son's room, was cheaply made and dated, an eyesore that could have been destroyed with a few swift kicks. So instead of concentrating on sources, this essay will focus on organization, the choices involved while writing "My Parents' First House," as well as the value of such a piece, and the distinction between long-held memories and newly acquired memories.

I'm not conscious of trying to conceive images to use in the beginning of "My Parents' First House"; certainly I never went through a logical process of selection. If anything, it was a process of elimination. Whenever possible, I begin with what seems most striking, and hope that what follows will be more striking. If writing is organic, it seems absurd to save the best for last. It's like not planting the seed because you believe it to be more perfect than any fruit it might produce. Yet there are things I find powerful (the window on the kitchen wall, for instance) that I knew I was going to use but wished to postpone; however, the deferment was for logistical considerations rather than an attempt to conserve material.

My most vivid memory of Strawberry Lane is the photograph of me on the sidewalk. I don't remember the moment the photo was snapped, but I remember staring at the photograph, wondering why it had been taken. And recalling this remembering as I wrote served to evoke many long buried sensory images—playing in the fresh earth, trips to the outside steel faucet, the silvery coldness of the braid of water as it rejuvenated the clump in my hand, and, most delightful of all, the plasticity of the mud patties. To me, these memories are important and striking. These were not memories of memories, but, rather, recollections prompted by thinking and writing about the photograph. All this reflection led me to wonder about the neighborhood, whether it was, indeed, like a "roto-tilled field." Yet few of my memories, particularly newly acquired ones, occur in panoramas, and I had no photographs in my possession, so I kept the mention of the field as conjecture. On the other hand, the opening of the essay did contain some less fresh memories. The scrawny dogwood, for example, was most definitely a memory of a memory; as a matter of fact, I used an almost identical description of it in an entirely different essay that I wrote about ten years earlier. But I knew that it was a fitting image. It worked because it conveyed a sense of starkness, and—along with the single car garage and the plate glass windows—forced readers to rely on their own encounters with such neighborhoods. I wasn't actually thinking of readers in the sense of an audience, but in a much more general sense, attempting to shape what I was saying so that I saw an overview of the neighborhood, not unlike the cinematographic device of providing a distant view before zooming in on a small area.

I wrote the first few pages (through the section describing the window on the kitchen wall) during several different train trips into Chicago to teach. There are few places as agreeable for writing as the train: the phone doesn't ring; there is no way to get up and pace; talking to one's self must be kept to a minimum; and it's impossible to let guilt about neglected chores get the better of the situation. While surrounded by people quietly reading the morning newspaper, I was lulled by my thoughts, able to completely submerge myself in the past. This was when I was able to recall things I hadn't consciously considered since my childhood: the mud patties, the linoleum entry way, the round wicker table, and the camp-site-like spot on the carpeting. There was a certain absolution in being able to write an honest account of such ugliness, but prospecting for long lost images was even more exciting. For the first time in over twenty-five years, I saw the thin lines of my mother's paint brush strokes against the smooth pebbled plaster of the kitchen wall. But even this wealth of memories created problems. There was a danger that each new memory might take the essay off track, trigger a new course. And some of the memories, though significant to me, were actually quite trivial. Who, but me, cares that I was able to recall the circular brass door clasps, pressed into the wood like miniature pie tins, used to pull open the sliding closet doors that were so common in the 50's?

But throughout the essay, the narrative did change course more than once. Part of writing *is* triggering new paths. The first time was expected. I knew that I had to bring the readers inside the house, but every way I considered seemed abrupt, so I simply decided that the transition *had* to be abrupt. That's when I presented the address—5204 Strawberry Lane—and switched to second person. I debated over the change to "you," because such usage can appear both self-conscious and presumptuous. Yet in the situation at hand, second person seemed appropriate because I *was* extremely conscious of the reader, and actually wanted the sense of walking an imaginary "you" through the house. The ensuing places where the essay found new directions seemed less abrupt, more organic, which means that although I hadn't planned to discuss them, when they appeared in the essay they seemed inevitable. In other words, the paths the essay was taking were helping me to discover what the essay was about.

For example, after talking about the window my mother painted, it was natural that the subject shift to my parents. I learned that, in part, I wanted the essay to be a tribute to them, an acknowledgment that they had relinquished something in order to raise their children. (Though I guess the title should have told me that.) Then, while writing about my mother's naps, I began to consider how much more a child is able to extract from a place than an adult. Because I didn't want to lose this idea, I stopped right in the middle of talking about my mother—feeling I knew so clearly what I wanted to say about her that I could finish it when I had the final draft in the typewriter—and began on the new idea. I had undoubtedly considered the idea before, but never so completely as when I remembered what I imagined as I peered into the crevices of those red bricks. I remembered the way I had marveled at the possibility that there could be entire villages, like the small Swiss burgs contained in glass snow balls, built along ridges inside the crevices. How could an adult ever get that from a brick? But I knew that I needed a transition between a child's point of view and my parents' discontent, so I again interrupted the course and began writing about my grandparents' house, a perfect comparison to a place that is ostensibly bland but has hidden treasures, because my grandparents' house was so overtly grand. The comparison also seemed apt because it provided some illumination into my mother's background, while showing that the scenery in my childhood was not always as desolate as my essay was beginning to make it sound. After writing this transition, I returned to the section about a child's ability to "penetrate and pull," where I recalled how at the onset of the essay I'd envisioned the backyards as countries. I had considered including this image in my initial panorama view of the neighborhood but had dismissed it because I didn't want to spend too much time on the neighborhood before getting inside the house. But here, when talking about how much a child is able to pull from a place, the idea of yards seen as countries seemed to work well. Then I was presented with a natural, though again unforeseen, opening to talk about my sister.

She was germane to the essay because of the impact she had on my point of view as a child, and the essay, I was beginning to see, was not only about my house and my parents, but my childhood—an abbreviated account, but nevertheless, an account. In addition to wanting to show her influence on me, I wanted to show her creativity, what I considered her most interesting quality. I hadn't intended to mention the boy who wandered into our house again, but was delighted when, like a view coming into focus through a microscope, I saw my sister in the short dim hallway, explaining in urgent whispers how the boy had appeared in our house. My delight quickly turned to distrust when I considered the fact that although I'd often, fleetingly, thought of the boy in tears, this was the first I had recollected my sister discussing it with me. And while I was accustomed to forgotten images returning, I was not used to entire scenes materializing. Could it be that I had invented this memory, and with this type of doubt was it fair that I include the section in my essay? Yes, I decided, because, first of all, it was clear in my mind's eye, and, second, it was certainly something my sister would have done.

This passage about my sister led me to the room we shared, where I was surprised to find so much of the room lost to me. I had expected that when my room came, it would be a grand finale of sorts. But here it was and the only thing that stood out was the window. At first I was disturbed by this, but, after some reasoning, decided that since the bedroom window and the bunkbed were all that I recalled about the room, it was best that I simply focus on them rather than attempt to unearth other details that might work to dilute the power of these central images. After all, the window had been the focus of the room for me as a child. Also, it seemed to create a nice parallel with the imaginary window on the kitchen wall, subtle because of the fact that it wasn't planned. Then, even though I had envisioned the essay ending with my room, when I finished with it, it seemed important to at least sketch in the rest of the house before moving to the drive I'd taken past the house with my mother, the place I'd thought would probably serve as the conclusion.

I paused for longer than usual when writing about my brother's room, thinking that since he was part of my family he deserved more attention than I was giving him. But a piece of writing tells as much by what it omits as by what it states, and, regardless of the amount of affection I have for my brother, he was not a huge part of my childhood. In many ways we were a typically sexually segregated family of the 50's; my brother played baseball, cut the lawn, visited the barber with my father; my sister and I played dolls, embroidered, and did things with my mother. Even when the neighborhood children got together and played—*Combat*, after the television series, was a favorite—the boys were soldiers out in the yards, while the girls were nurses in the driveways.

Again, when my essay reached the basement, I reconsidered. This wasn't a place that I could sketch in; we had spent too much time there. I could have told several different stories about the basement, and although I'm tempted to relay a few of them here, I realize now, as I did when writing "My Parents' First House," that the memory of the miniature city is the strongest, and works best when unaccompanied. Somehow, it, with the idea of all the little buildings, brings the essay full circle, back to the neighborhood. The panorama I had envisioned had materialized.

I want conclusions in essays I write, like resolutions in short stories, to come as surprises whenever possible. But as I mentioned earlier, I was aware from the start that unless something better presented itself, "My Parents' First House" would end with my most recent trip past it with my mother. Yet, despite the fact that the ending was anticipated, I was still startled by the last line because it wasn't until the moment I wrote it that I truly explored what I had felt at the time we viewed the house, or fully understood the implications of my essay. Yes, my family had been special, and I had, with my writing, been able to convey some of that specialness, but, still, the specialness was probably, in some ways, "indistinguishable" from all the other special childhoods there. It wasn't exactly the conclusion I would have chosen, but I wondered how I hadn't foreseen its inevitability considering I was writing about a look-alike house in a look-alike neighborhood during a look-alike phase of American history.

Now that I'm nearing the close of this essay, I feel that I should talk some about drafting and revising. But "My Parents' First House" only required two drafts, the one I began on the train and the final typed version. This is not to say that the process was quick and easy. The first draft took me several train trips and one session at home (on the train I often paused to think, while at home I sometimes paused to sleep—two or three sentences can sometimes exhaust me), and from looking at the first draft I see that many words are slashed out and replaced. Insertions are made in the margins. There are a few false starts at different places in the essay. I even called my mother and read a few passages to her in order to verify accuracy, a call which resulted in three factual changes—my age when we moved to Strawberry Lane, the subject of her degree, and the amount of time my sister and I labored over the city in the basement. But, overall, the gist of the drafts is the same. Drafting, of course, can be important, but it was not of particular importance in this essay. Rather what was of importance—at least it's what keeps coming back to me—is the idea of truth.

As essential as the idea of truth should be to a writer—and has always been to me—I feel uncomfortable and pretentious addressing such a subject. In part, my trepidation is caused by the fact that the entity has been discussed so much that I assume that my thoughts—like in the opening when I discuss truth and accuracy—will wind up sounding like a cliche. Or that they'll sound puerile. What more could I add to a discourse that has been covered so thoroughly? Yet the idea of truth is what I find my mind continuously returning to as I write this essay, and I wonder how I can ignore the subject when I won't allow my students to escape with a shrug and the claim that there's no more to say, it's all been said, their voices are powerless. After all, the need for truth and understanding—as pretentious as it may sound—is what makes many writers write, certainly it's a big part of what makes me write, and what has always made me prefer fiction over journalism and other forms of nonfiction.

I'm aware that in some ways that sounds like a contradiction. I remember once mentioning that I thought an acquaintance, a fiction writer, was prone to fibbing. The person with whom I was talking, another fiction writer, lifted his eyebrows in mock surprise and exclaimed, "How strange—a fiction writer who lies." As obvious as his statement should have been, I was taken aback; because of my own obsession with truth, it had never occurred to me, in *that* way, that some might see my profession as the making of lies. In what is undoubtedly slightly eccentric behavior, I'm obsessed with knowing where I've been, what I've done, and understanding it all. I save ticket stubs, restaurant cocktail napkins, date books; I write down notes, take photographs, and study and compare them.

Yet I know that in the unlikely event that I'm ever called upon to recount the whole truth, none of this evidence will matter much, because in reality, the whole truth is elusive, and there will always be some missing piece of evidence. Besides, I know that my careful reconstructions of the truth have sometimes aroused more suspicion than a less careful lie might have. Yet with fiction, to my mind anyway, it is impossible to tell a lie because not only has the word "fiction" absolved the writer, but the writer is creating a new truth, her own truth, in both the story and whatever underlying meaning unexpectedly emerges, the overriding metaphor. I'm not saying anything new here. I doubt I've ever heard of a fiction writer talking about his or her work without mentioning the need or search for truth. But how does that translate to nonfiction?

It has always seemed to me that truth in nonfiction is close to impossible because to achieve it, *every*thing would have to be relayed, and it would all need to be accurate. Yet comparing writing "My Parents' First House" with my most successful works of fiction has helped me realize that the types of truth that appear in fiction aren't exclusive to fiction. As many writers note, in fiction, a description (or sense) of place often serves as a point of departure, an impetus from which one's own truth in the form of fiction grows. In a personal essay, place can still be a point of departure, only the direction is different; instead of moving outward—like a plant opening to the sun—the process is inverted—like the roots digging deep beneath the ground—in a search for what created and secured the place in the writer's mind.

In "My Parents' First House," I was not attempting to invent things from something present, but, rather, attempting to use something present in my mind to find things lost or unconsidered—a new truth that could emerge from my view of the past. And many things I had forgotten did reappear to me, sometimes creating new dilemmas. For example, although it may sound like I was easily able to include the passage about my sister's explanation of the boy wandering into our house, it was only after much consideration that I was able to liberate myself from the need for accuracy and realize that though many forms of writing are wrought with contradictions and inaccuracies, they are often, as the cliche says, looking for a truth that can't be found in accuracy, but can only be surmised by examining and re-examining. And still, after all my consideration and justification, the vision of my sister in the hallway nags me. If the same scene had occurred to me in the same way in a piece of fiction, it would have been a moment—albeit a small moment—of glory. But in a piece of nonfiction, the manner in which the vision appeared bothers me and I can't help but wonder if, at that moment, my recollection was beginning to turn into a work of fiction, and if I had gone one step further in following that scene with my sister, I may, indeed, have discovered a new and perhaps greater truth, but not one that resembles the actual physicality of my childhood as much as the one I've presented.

∾ QUESTIONS ∾

Garnett Kilberg's essay, "My Parents' First House," and its process essay, "Considerations When Writing 'My Parent's First House'"

1. Kilberg writes: "I can honestly say that as a girl I saw almost as much mystery in the crevices of one of the red bricks that made up my parents'

home as I now sometimes see in an entire city." How does she support this throughout the essay? What particular images does she choose that evoke the most memory? Do you agree with her perception of childhood? Do you remember what Kilberg calls "the mystery" of day-to-day life as a child as a thing more provocative than day-to-day life as an adult?

2. What sort of statement is Kilberg trying to make at the essay's conclusion? What is the source of her disappointment? Recall trips you've taken to places you hadn't visited for a long time. Were you, like Kilberg, disappointed? Were you nostalgic? Did seeing that place trigger memories, or did the place seem somehow "indistinguishable" from others?

3. Kilberg writes that she selected certain images from her old neighborhood because they "forced readers to rely on their own encounters with such neighborhoods." To what degree must a writer rely on a reader's experience when he or she writes? How much can you, as a writer, count on your reader knowing? How does Kilberg create a tension between what you as a reader may recognize and her own experience of the intimacy and unusualness of her home?

4. Kilberg writes, "Yet I know that in the unlikely event that I'm ever called upon to recount the whole truth, none of this evidence will matter much, because in reality, the whole truth is elusive, and there will always be some missing piece of evidence." For Kilberg, the story of the lost boy and her sister is that "missing piece of evidence." In your own writing, to what degree is it important that all the evidence be accurate? If memory is not accurate, as Kilberg suggests, is the sense of truth in a particular memory enough to include it as a fact? How does Kilberg's sense of truth and accuracy jibe with Mark Shelton's *White Castle* essays?

ೞ Possible Writing Topics ೫

1. Draw a detailed map of a place you knew well when you were younger and label each structure or thing you include. As you draw the map, on a separate sheet of paper jot down specific memories that you recall as you work.

2. Write an essay describing a place based on the map you've drawn. Don't limit yourself to the things you've included in the map should you think of others as you write. Did the act of writing trigger certain memories that the map did not? How do you account for their recollection? How is the completed essay different from the way you envisioned it as you consulted your map before writing?

David Martin

Sunday Morning

ALL morning, from the boy's window, the sounds, as if he'd been awake. Wild birds cawing, parrots, wonderful songs, questions, demands—some made him want to hum, others say *I'm sorry, I'm sorry*. Car horns too. This one just now, three short blasts, and then the engine roar, brakes whining, and then the horn again. The boy stood on his mattress to see. In the street, rolling slowly to a halt, a yellow school bus (converted by a layman to read *First Baptist Church*) bursting with dark-haired children, their arms and heads sticking out the windows. "C'mon," their voices called, *rápidamente*. He leaned further out his own window. He felt an urge to join them. There was time, the bus moved slowly enough. It was as big as the street.

Rickie climbed down from his mattress. He left the room and knocked on his parents' door. He heard a whisper. Come in, Esmeralda says. What do you want, little bird? Rickie tells about the bus. They're honking. I want to go. From his side of the bed he can see his father roll over. Es shrugs Richard's shoulder. She buries her face there, whispering, giggling, her feet creeping below the sheet. Get some clothes on, he hears his father say into the pillow, and ask them where they're going. And make sure they bring you back.

Rickie stands there waiting. He wants to be held.

Get your clothes on, Es says, then come back. I'll give you a quarter for the Offering.

And I'll comb your hair. Now hurry. Vamoose, his father says, his arm raised as if he'll slap Rickie lightly on the butt. Or you'll miss it.

Out the door, Rickie runs across the grass chasing the bus. Further down the road it has stopped, its horn honking and the children looking back at him. The girls, he can see, are all dressed in pink and yellow dresses. "Here comes one," they shout. *Venga, venga*, "we'll be late." He runs to the bus door and up the three rubber matted steps. The driver smiles under wraparound sunglasses. "C'mon, hurry, little one."

Nervous, Rickie asks him the questions his father has instructed him to ask. *Sí, sí,* the man says, *vamanos.* The door shuts and the bus moves. The children elbow each other, laugh and point and beckon him to sit on their seats. He plops down beside a boy who looks his age and they immediately talk about their feet, his dirty already.

Such a little *pájaro,* Es says, combing her hair. Were you like that when you were a little man? Richard lies flat on his side, his head propped on his hand, pillow doubled. A little bird? No, a tiger. He snuck through the grass, climbed trees, waited on a branch until they passed beneath: then *swoop,* surprise. But nothing ever passed. So he'd sit and whistle and like a monkey climb higher and shake leafy branches.

In her robe Es sits on the patio wall watching the street. She holds her head high, the breeze lifting her hair from her neck. It's a wonderful feeling. The sun, bright and warm, makes her squint, seeing pink and orange. Only in the shade can she focus on anything. The sound of leaves rippling, grass bending.

Richard places a breakfast tray before her. Pancakes, he says. And coffee. No cream. We'll get some when Rickie and I go to the store.

He too sits on the wall and faces Es.

She sighs. Aren't you eating?

No, he has work to do.

But you should eat. You'll be working tomorrow. You need your strength. Did you call Mr. Shelton?

No change. I'll get some later, take Rickie to the store.

Feeling the patio tiles cool against her feet, Es shuts her eyes while she chews. In her mind she retraces her way through each room of the house, now, as it is, and before, when they first saw it, last night. Three concrete steps to the patio, red and yellow diamond-shaped tiles; the oak door; the living room, large, dark, and cool, white stucco walls tall and wide; enough room to dance on the maple stripped floor, glazed, freshly waxed. It all *smelled* so new, this home of theirs. And the kitchen, clean, with so many cupboards and a new refrigerator, white, the stove too, and a double porcelain sink soft in the evening shadow from the windows above. Look at this, Richard said, just look at this. Es followed his voice echoing throughout the house and down a dark hall. She entered the first of many doors. Another room. White. This one almost as big as the living room. And a closet, Richard said, will you look at this? and she followed his voice closer behind a door. He grabbed her. Guess there's plenty of room for your clothes *here,* he said. We'll buy more so you can fill it. Es stared at her feet, embarrassed. We could put Rickie here, she said. He needs his *own* room.

Ah then, you haven't noticed, he'd said. He took her by the hand and pulled her back through the room. Bed here. Your dresser there, he pointed, never stopping but leading her out into the hall again. He opened another door. Bathroom. See? Big enough. Es put her hand on the counter and tried to take it all in. It was getting darker outside, the window there at the end of the room with venetian blinds. Feel how deep this tub is, Richard said, and as she was passing her palm against the cool curves he pulled her back to her feet. Now. See. Another room. *Voilà!* Richard swung the door open, his voice booming now off the high walls and the empty place. For Rickie, he said. Es felt herself droop. The walls dark, only a little light entering the double window. All around her as she swirled about first on one foot, then the other, her dress clinging to her knees and above (*Pirouette*, Richard thought), a pattern of birds: sparrows perched on twigs, barn swallows, stoic robins staring off into the room's space. Our little man needs a room of his own these days, Richard said, and Es followed him back to *their* room, where she stood as the evening closed in shadows around her, hiding in its darkness all of the newly found space, leaning against the door, listening to her own breathing. Later she would hear Richard unlocking the station wagon and she would begin the task of unpacking.

    Rickie stood on the sidewalk, a safe distance from the house, holding his flashlight. Whose house was it, anyway? And why were all of their boxes scattered on the lawn? *He* couldn't find *any*thing. The window from the kitchen opened. He saw his mother there holding a candle and banging pans, running water. She is singing. She is cooking. Seems to know something about all this. He looked again at the dark brick house. Behind him, in the street, someone yelled *yeeehaaaaaaah!*, like the Indians do when they're about to let the tomahawk rip. He turned to see a car swerving up over the curb opposite him and then swing back into the street, like a toy he'd seen once, the batteries low, the car meandering down the wide street drunkenly. Smooth asphalt. There is danger here. There is danger here and they don't even know. He turned on his flashlight. He would keep watch.
    Hey Rickie, lend a hand, will 'ya?
    He looked at their car. In the yellow oblong circle of light he saw the station wagon tilted at the back.
    Shine that light over here.
    Under the tire he could see his father taking off the wheel. They had driven the last half mile with it flat. That, he thought, had been great fun. Es had cried, almost, telling Richard to stop, they'd never make it, they'd ruin the car, and then, and *then* where would they be? In the dim light Rickie looked at the car's back windows, the streaked dust and the outlines of faces and stickmen he'd traced during the long hot drive.
    Shine that light a little more down, son. I got to find a lug nut.
    Es loves the feeling of the tile and the wooden floors against her feet. They made a slapping sound, even as the rooms began to fill, and it made her feel

young. There is room for Cecilía, and Rosita, and Charles, and Mamá and Papá. They could all move here too and it would be like a hotel with a grand lobby. Cecilía must be the first to come. They could go to the market and buy lemons and peppers and sweet Roma tomatoes. Yes, Cecilía must see. She, too, would fall in love with the patio and the sunlight and she could make drapes (with Es's guidance). If only their mother and father would leave that trailer, they, too, could sit here and drink hot black coffee in the morning, and in the evening, for Papa loved to hold the mug in his hands, and laughing, Come here, Mamá, sit on my wide lap. Sit here and I'll whisper in your ear, and Es would blush and Rosita—Let's take a walk.

Rickie runs back over the grass and hops up the steps. I'm home. It was fun. I'm going next Sunday and they're going to pick me up right outside the house.
Es brushes back the boy's thin hair. Did you say your prayers?
He nods. Where's Dad?
Inside. You hungry?
He nods again.
Come. I'll make you something. We don't have any milk, but there's some lemonade left.

My little *pájaro*, Es says.
You think we should keep him, Richard asks.
She drops her brush to the floor. It lands bristles down, bounces, the handle clattering. Her hair is pulled to one side, hiding one smooth brown shoulder. Keep him?
Richard laughs and rolls onto his back. He faces the white plaster ceiling and follows its sworls with his finger. We could sell him. Child labor down here, don't you know. Make a damned good houseboy.
Es stamps her foot. Stop that.
Make a pretty good piece of change, too. All off the top.
She picks up the brush and rears it back.
Out of the corner of his eye he watches, waits, moves his arm swiftly to knock the brush down beside him on the bed. I don't know. It's not a *bad* idea.
In her mind she can see her son dressed in a white long-sleeved shirt, square cut almost to his knees. He carries a tray to a man seated at a long mahogany table glistening in a cool room. There is a ceiling fan and high-topped wicker chairs sit in every corner. The man smokes long white cigarettes and mutters to himself, his black hair moist and pulled straight back along his skull. No, Es says, never.

Richard takes her arm and holds it, poised, then resisting, then limp, away from him. He laughs. Her eyes are black. She's ready to spit, her lips pursed tight. Like a snake rearing its head. Easy, *chicita*. Easy. You'll bite me.

Es growls. I'll rake your eyes out.

Try it, he says, a smirk on his face.

In an instant she frees her hands, rises, strikes. Too late. As she falls toward him he has lifted his leg and safely enveloped her. Her arms flail out at his face, menacing, she realizes, only herself. Leave me be, she says. I'll scream. Worthless. He just lies there, grinning, the monkey and the tiger propped against the pillows.

Breakfast over, Richard and the boy climb into the car. The sun is hot now and they both have to roll their windows down quickly. Rickie kneels on his seat and holds his head out. The slow warm wind whips his hair back.

Together they drive through the neighborhood, pulling in at every corner store. Is it open?

Rickie scans the windows plastered with paper signs. Nope.

They drive on.

Sure is dead around here.

Yep, sure is dead.

The streets are almost empty of traffic. Cars lined on both sides, and driveways, too, like neat trains. On porches they see old men in clean undershirts sitting just beneath the shade, some with newspapers spread over their laps and others with hats tilted, further shading their eyes. Richard waves to a few of them. Rickie does too as they pass by. Some of the old men respond. Most stare.

They drive on in silence down the broad road. Follow the main streets, Richard says, bound to take you *some*place. And it does take them. Past stretches lined with tall spindly pines, boulevards with islands of thick aloes and cacti. Bent palm trees. The roads gets hotter, wider, and they pass by shops painted white and yellow. The buildings get newer, bigger. Richard pulls the car into a huge asphalt parking lot where the heat passes through the station wagon floor and Rickie can feel it through his sandals. They stop with the rest of the cars, chrome gleaming.

Here's what we're looking for, Richard says, and he shuts the motor off.

It's a supermarket, bigger and newer than any Rickie has seen before. They walk up to the door, Rickie jumps on the rubber mat and the glass door slides open. Both of them are relieved by the cold air. Together they grab a cart. They take their time and examine everything they see with their hands and eyes. They sort through each aisle. They find candles, light bulbs, and a mixing bowl (for theirs had broken on the trip), an extension cord, potatoes, lettuce, grapefruit, ice, melons, beer and milk in bottles sweating under the flourescent light, until their car is full.

You need anything?

The boy claps his hands together and thinks, like Es when asked the same. A knife, he says, his eyes growing wide.

They go back through the aisles until they find a case full. Richard pulls out a Barlow, opens the blade, eyeballs it at arm's length. You like this?

The boy takes the knife in his hand and makes the same inspection. Yes, he says, it'll do.

When they arrive back at their house Es greets them out on the lawn, their arms full with brown sacks. I wish you two would've let *me* go too. I didn't know you were buying out the whole town.

We needed some things, Richard says.

In the evening Es, Richard, and the boy sit on the patio wall eating melon slices. Es pours salt on hers. Richard spits his seeds out onto the grass. Good place for a garden.

Rickie tries to spit too. His seeds dribble out over his lips.

I called Mr. Shelton, Richard says. He wants me at the shop at nine sharp.

Did you ask about the lights?

Yes. Should be on by tomorrow noon. First month's rent due then too.

At night, lying on his mattress in his room, empty save for the upended crates he's made into shelves for his clothes, his tattered books and his knife, Rickie leans his head on his hand. He is looking at the dark shadows of the birds. He can hear the strange sounds again, as in the morning, something like an owl's screech. And the cicada roar. He can also hear his parents' footsteps. He can hear their whispers, Es hanging up and smoothing Richard's shirt and trousers for tomorrow. There's a knock at his door, very close, and yet, in the dark, miles away. The door opens and the flashlight pours onto the floor.

You asleep? I want to show you something.

Rickie takes his father's hand and follows the strong arm and the dim light across the hall floor. Together they approach the door at the end of the hall. Richard grabs the knob and pushes the door open. Inside, they walk through the darkness, bare feet scraping against the wood. It's the smallest and coolest room in the house.

I wanted to show you this, his father says, switching the flashlight off.

Behind he could hear his mother approaching. She stopped and leaned against the door jamb.

This, here, Rickie, is going to be your sister's room.

The boy looks up at the outline of his father.

From behind he can feel the nearness of his mother's hand. It lands softly on his shoulder and rests there before she pulls him close and he feels her soft cotton dress against his nose. Outside the last cicadas roar and a flutter of wings rises in his ears.

This is all good.

"Sunday Morning": A Commotion of Memory and Place

> By the time a writer has reached the end of a story, he has lived it at least three times over—first in the series of actual events that, directly or indirectly, have combined to set up that commotion in his mind and senses that causes him to write the story; second, in memory; and third, in recreation of this chaotic stuff. —*Katherine Anne Porter, "Noon Wine": The Sources*

I give myself to memory.

During the summer of 1980, the peak of sunbelt fever, my wife and I moved to Houston. I needed to find who I was and what I could be, and to do this meant escaping Kalamazoo and my past. I needed to exile myself so I could concentrate without interruption, so I could think and see clearly. Yet every evening as I sat at my desk and looked out at the violet sky, I thought about Michigan. I tried to make sense of the new world we were discovering, the maze of sounds and colors, ideas and textures, yet memories of people and places rose within me unchecked, bringing with them disturbing emotions I thought I'd buried. I lost sense of who I was. I lost the protection identity gives us from the world. I stumbled through a labyrinth of confusion as I lived and wrote.

I thought it was important to write about my experience, that constant collage of old and new, and I relied on intuition, rather than craft, to help me sort my way. Now, seven years later, as I recall how I wrote "Sunday Morning," I know I can't completely unravel the creative process. That time of my life was too chaotic, and the memories too slippery and winding. All I can say is I invested my interest in form. I let intuition and memory take over. Seven years later, I now know that writing "Sunday Morning" provided me a new identity in the face of confusion.

My chief interests in any story are images of character and place. For me, a vision of place and a character's action is enough to begin. I found the name *Esmeralda* on our drive south. A blue Nova shot past us, its rear window covered with large silver letters: E-S-M-E-R-A-L-D-A. As the sun shot off their glitter, those letters squirmed and danced before me. It was such an immediate and typical slice of Texas life, a gaudy proclamation, that I fell in love with that image. Half a year later, when starting a story that preceded "Sunday Morning,"

I wrote the words *Esmeralda hovering over her mother's recipe* at the top of a page. This phrase provided a character, a name I was in love with, and an image of a place, for those words signified upper Michigan to me. My view widened. I recalled details: orchards, sandy soil, rivers I had canoed, the smell of Lake Michigan, the *feel* of the land. I saw a woman with long black hair standing in a kitchen inside a summer cabin, near Traverse City and Petoskey. Memory and desire swelled as I wrote that phrase:

> I was in Southern Michigan, in Keeler, and I was ten. I'd been dropped off at a migrant worker's camp. It was near sunset, the sky at the horizon stretched long and blue and pink. The grass was already wet with dew. I passed tiny dirt-floored sheds and entered a circle of running, screaming children playing volleyball at a badminton net. I joined in and quickly learned there were no rules, just energy and noise. The children shouted loud and rapid Spanish. A barefoot girl with black hair handed me the ball and smiled, chittering something I couldn't understand, and then she danced around me. Later, I saw her between the sheds chasing lightning bugs. Behind the open doors I saw mothers preparing dinner on portable stoves by lantern light. The fathers sat outside, smoking in the dirt, their faces stern and empty from the day's heat. . . .

Where had this come from? And where had it been hiding? As I stared at that girl, I knew that I was in love—I was at the core of something intimate and vital, something real. Esmeralda must be that girl grown older.

That vision of place lured me to explore more of the memories rising within me, memories I didn't understand. Eventually I had series of scenes, a sequence of rhythms and images and associations that I shaped into a story called "Esmeralda."

Still, I felt the commotion of memory. "Esmeralda" represented only one path of the labyrinth. All of the internal stirring, the move south, losing myself in my work, this preternatural memory, was too strong to ignore. Two weeks later I started a story about a boy who had just moved to Houston and who was suffering from the shock of this new environment. During our first months in Houston I was always seeing people I recognized; I would speak up or reach out before I realized I had tricked myself. I had only recognized a familiar quality or fragment, a certain posture, a silhouette, a turn of phrase. I also experienced déjà vu and relived conversations. Dreams, at times, were so vivid that they seemed inseparable from waking life. And yet, as if to mock us, the lush, vibrant Texas reality surrounded us. These disjunctions promised madness.

I planned to have the boy in "Sunday Morning" waken much as he does now, to the sounds of birds outside his window. This noise was meant to reflect internal disturbance, the beginning of a breakdown. Two sentences into the story, however, I heard a horn. I looked out and saw an old school bus, teeming with Hispanic children, honking as it stopped and started down our street. I remembered riding such a bus in upper Michigan to attend a Catholic mass during summer camp . . .

> The bus stopped at the intersection of two one lane state highways. We walked onto a field behind a whitewashed billboard. A Mexican priest wearing wraparound sunglasses had already emptied the folding chairs from his pickup and set them up in semicircle rows around the back of his truck. Migrant families quietly arrived and filled the seats. The priest, now in his white vestment and still in his sunglasses, stood beside the altar on the tailgate and began. The service was in Latin. I, a protestant, fumbled through the service, unable to make sense of the cardboard missal, and kneeling and standing, the chants and responses, the melodic voices surrounding me under the noon sun, the dragonflies buzzing around us in the mown grass.

On our way through Indiana and Mississippi we had witnessed dozens of similar buses, each belonging to some hybrid sect or traveling choir. As the bus outside our window continued to honk, I heard the children's gathering voices and felt as I did when I was a child—I wanted to join. They were on their way to glory; I knew I must get that boy on that bus. Suddenly, I saw Esmeralda waiting on the other side of his bedroom door. "Sunday Morning" wasn't a story about a boy going mad—it was another story about Esmeralda and her family in that new setting. The story lifted itself from the boy's shoulders and settled around his new home.

Birds were still important to me, so I let them enter the story as they wished. I pushed through a first draft, creating a string of scenes based on association and intuition and memory. But I had no final scene. I stopped short when Richard and his son returned from the supermarket. Much of the expansive feeling in that shopping trip I borrowed from Saturday mornings when I rode to the lumberyard and hardware store with my father. Later I remembered how on the hottest July and August evenings my family ate watermelon on our porch in a silent, seed-spitting ritual, offering small talk only when the heat faded with the first evening breeze.

I don't know where I *got* the material for the final scene. I felt fairly secure with Richard walking in on the boy before he was asleep Sunday evening. Richard had something on his mind—I didn't know quite what—he's the kind of man who can't restrain himself once he gets an idea. I was trying to find a timing. I had to somehow complete the arrangement of that "chaotic stuff" of memory. My strongest device was a narrator. I had no dominant character. I had no crisis, either, only fear and wonder. Their move had been somewhat desperate and they were still recovering and settling in. Their fears were private. They needed sanctuary, a moment of wholeness, an affirmation of what they know to be right. Timing was all I could rely on to finish the story.

My mind was full of colors and sounds. As I listened to the quiet inside the boy's room, I discovered Richard with a flashlight. I pictured how that light must look on the wooden floor. I knew that Richard must lead his son away from the birds and into the hall. I was full of the enchantment moving brings, how we break from habit and rediscover ourselves. We lose the protection of familiarity. Our lives spill into disorder. We live by candle and shadow, eat pork and beans from the can.

Everything is anticipation, I remember thinking, and that, I knew, was what "Sunday Morning" must be about.

My interest in Richard and the boy had grown from my love with Esmeralda, that little girl in the migrant workers' camp grown up. I trusted her attraction and complexity, her love and fear, and as soon as I felt her presence behind the door, Richard was telling his son, even before *I* knew it, that his mother was pregnant. *That* gave all the chaotic stuff a form. It was a spontaneous moment for me and the characters. They draw near each other in an unspeakable moment, a suspension of love and fear and mystery.

Richard and Esmeralda aren't based on any real people, but their lives hold marvelous similarities to many people I know. They attracted me. Their situation, moving south, was similar to mine. I also must have been thinking about my first years in college, when I shared a flat with a married couple and their parakeet, a situation that allowed me to observe intimacy. Perhaps I recalled the visit to the migrant workers' camp because we lived in a Hispanic neighborhood, submerged within a cacophony of noises and converging cultures. We often visited the zoo and were struck by the flamboyant birds and their embarrassingly erotic whistles. They signalled shame and guilt. We laughed and cried. We had escaped the Midwest. We had a future.

I called the story "Sunday Morning" because that, for me, was the story's emotional center. And while I wrote the first ten drafts I listened to Miles Davis' *Sketches of Spain*.

⋙ QUESTIONS ⋘

David Martin's story, "Sunday Morning," and its process essay, "'Sunday Morning': A Commotion of Memory and Place"

1. Read through the story again and find passages where Martin evokes place through description and narration. Does this description contain a sense of the new, a sense of the strange, as Martin argues in his process essay? What most effectively communicates this? Has your own experience of change felt similar? How does it differ?

2. Notice that Martin doesn't use quotation marks to set off dialogue in this story. Why do you think he employs this strategy? Is this a strategy you would use for a paper you would hand in for this or another class? What are the risks in using a device that is deliberately unconventional?

3. In his process essay Martin writes, "Seven years later, I now know that writing 'Sunday Morning' provided me a new identity in the face of confusion." Can you conceive of a way that the writing process could shape an identity that you would not have without that process? Have you ever written something— whether it was a paper for a class or an entry in a diary—that gave you a perspective you wouldn't have had if you hadn't written?

4. Martin writes of his characters, "Their fears were private. They needed sanctuary, a moment of wholeness, an affirmation of what they know to be right. Timing was all I could rely on to finish the story." Can you get a sense of what Martin means by "timing"? Is *when* something is placed in an essay or story as important as *what* is placed and *where* it is placed? Look back on other essays you've written. When you shift certain events around in the essay, in what ways is the essay changed?

❧ Possible Writing Topics ❧

1. Write an essay about your first experiences with visiting a place you had never been to or seen. Try to recall your first impressions, how the things and people you saw affected you initially, what your fears were, what your hopes were at that time. Select a place that had some consequence for you, a place you visited for more than a few hours, or, if the visit lasted only a few hours, be sure that it is a place that left a distinct impression.

2. After writing the essay, write a second one on the same place that the perspective of time has given you. How accurate were your initial impressions? How has time or familiarity changed experience of the place? How important is Martin's sense of "timing" in your recollection of this place? In other words, had you encountered the place at a different time of your life, how would your impression of it have changed?

Daniel Lowe

Heritage

IT descended on the Volkswagen as surely as the heat, large and broad as Indiana seemed then, narrowing as it found and enveloped the three passengers. It centered around the woman, who sat opposite the driver, her hands resting on her full belly. But each of them felt it as something cool between the shoulders; and since for the three of them it could not be intimacy, it was at least a protectiveness.

The woman hardly recognized it, saying only, once more, and as softly as she could, "It's so hot." The man in the back seat merely shifted his feet and continued to stare out the window. But the driver, the woman's husband, felt it more strongly, since he had travelled so much, too much, really, and he felt it as a memory of something his father once said.

The father had told the driver, whose name was Joseph Potter, "Like any child, son, it's your responsibility to outlive your parents; that is a parent's comfort and legacy on his deathbed, and at his funeral, and any violation of that is an unnatural act, Joseph, like being born without eyes or a full set of fingers." The memory frightened Joseph, and he turned to the woman, whose name was Emily, and said, "Are you okay? Comfortable?"

The woman nodded.

"Will the car make it, Joey?"

"I'll *make* it make it."

For the first time since they'd left Chicago, the young man in the back seat, Michael Potter, shifted his weight so that his damp uniform squeaked on the vinyl covering. This, whether he realized it or not, was a comment; but as of now, he *would* help if the car did break down, instead of hitchhiking further down the highway. He continued to look out the window, observing the symmetry of the corn rows, the fit of the trees into the ground, and the angle of the roofs as they met barn walls.

Joseph listened closely for anything Michael might say, then whistled a friendly, unknown tune. The brothers did not love one another. Michael wouldn't admit to taking leave to celebrate the impending birth of Joseph's first child.

He hadn't volunteered to stack the boxes of blue and pink sweaters and trousers in the trunk of the Volkswagen upon departure. But he sat in the back seat in order to save himself the bus fare back to the coast, where his ship was docked, and Joseph, who felt his family obligation far more than his brother would, hadn't refused him the space.

The thing that bound them together was now unrecognizable from who they were: Joseph fretting over the child, Emily sitting very still, her hair blown back by the hot wind that passed through the windows, her face red and puffy. She wasn't thinking of anything, but there had been that quiet look of contentedness, her mouth upturned at the corners, ever since she'd told Joseph of the baby, and Joseph mistook it for a knowledge he could never possess. He sometimes regarded her jealously.

"Are you sure you're all right?"

Emily smiled at him and nodded.

"The skin on her neck's raised a little," said Michael, and the sound of his voice startled them both. Michael wouldn't allow tenderness, but the observation was made with concern because it didn't fit in with what little he knew of Emily's body.

"Maybe if we could stop in a while and get something cold to drink," said Emily.

"First place I see, we'll stop. I could use something to pour down my gullet myself." Michael offered a one-syllable response that Joseph couldn't discern, but he let it go by as he hadn't in the past: if something *did* happen to the car, he'd need Michael's help. Joseph glanced out the window and tried to appear casual, the effort itself needless, because it was too hot for thought or notice, and the other two ignored him. Joseph was momentarily taken by the flatness of the land, its stability, the cornstalks almost gray under the covering of dust, and the largeness of the sky, inscrutably blue as his brother's eyes. This startled him, and he looked over his shoulder. He was born here; both of them were, and that they should be so different was somehow a cheat of the land; it was *not*, after all, stable.

Joseph thought of the baby and remembered his father's words. For a moment he felt his foot dissolve, and pressed it more heavily to the accelerator, as if he could outrun the memory, as if it pursued him. The baby had begun to move inside Emily's belly, and at nights when she and Joseph lay in bed, he watched what he imagined was a knee or elbow trace its inside, Emily saying sometimes it was so tight that she swore she could feel a footprint. But it wasn't Joseph's fear that the baby would be born unwhole that disturbed him when he thought of his father (and his father's wish had been fulfilled, since he had been dead three years), rather that the words had caught Joseph now, with his own child alive and waiting: for a moment he feared for its life as if it were his own.

Emily had told him, "Sometimes at night when I'm sleeping I can feel him curled up right here, to be close to you."

"Generator light's on." Michael said this with such evenness that it sounded as if it were a comment on the weather. Joseph didn't hear the words.

"Your generator light's on, for Christ's sake," Michael repeated, but with the same evenness. This time Joseph *did* hear, and his heart flew up and choked him, as if the road had given out and they were now sailing through space.

"What should I do?"

"I can't tell what's wrong from the color of the seat," said Michael. "Pull over."

When Joseph braked too hard, he saw peripherally the tightness around Emily's lips that she tried not to show, and he squeezed her hand.

"It'll be all right."

A dust cloud rose from the shoulder of the road and covered the Volkswagen, so when he opened the door and got out, Joseph coughed as his skin was coated. Michael had already released the latch to the engine compartment, his white uniform blazing like something come down from the sky, and there was a steady energy that showed about his face and the movement of his arms. He spat once into the dust.

"Belt's broken."

Joseph saw the frayed cords lying about the engine parts.

"You'll make it a few miles down the road, then the battery gives out."

Joseph felt only the immensity of the heat, then he unwillingly remembered a blue music box he'd once seen near the bed of a woman he had slept with who was not Emily, and nothing would be cooler than that now.

"Shit," Joseph said, and flung his hand at the sun. Inside the car, Emily still sat with her hands on her belly; the placid disconcern and thoughtlessness had returned to her face, tinted blue by the windshield.

"You sure we can't make it all the way home?" said Joseph.

"Home to Fort Wayne. Then you can wave your hands all you want, but that baby will be born here sure as you're standing for all this car will do after that."

That his child could be born where he and his brother had grown up struck him as panic: there were grease stains on the sleeves of Michael's white shirt. His father had said of Michael, when they were young, "When I ask him for a monkey wrench, that's what he gets, even if he hasn't seen one before; that's a skill you can't learn." The words, like most of what Joseph's father had told him, unlike those Joseph had remembered earlier, appeared in his consciousness as written on a sheet of paper that was instantly consumed by flames.

"How many miles down the road?"

"Depends on how much juice is in the battery."

They had been travelling down a seldom-used highway, and only one truck had passed since they stopped, raising the dust again and fanning the warm air.

Michael said, "If I had the tools to get at it and a spare belt, I could have it done in half an hour."

Joseph stared along the flat land until it disappeared into the sky, then glanced back at Emily, who lay with her head against the seat, eyes closed. Her isolation softened the surprise of his brother's concern for her.

"What are the chances of finding a filling station around here?"

"Not good. And besides, it isn't a filling station you want, it's a service station."

Michael spat into the dust again.

"But I don't see as we have any other choice right here, and it isn't getting any cooler standing around. So let's go."

Once back in the car, when Joseph had turned the key, Emily's eyes opened, and she smiled at him, her lips not parting.

"Everything okay?"

"We'll have to stop somewhere to get the car fixed, but it shouldn't take long. Go back to sleep."

He'd said this meaning to reassure her, but she would not close her eyes again. Joseph had married her less than a year ago, and had he struggled he wouldn't have been able to recall the events that led up to that, only remnants, such as a meal they'd once eaten at a restaurant or his arm around her shoulder at a movie. Her condition now, as uncomplaining as she'd been since it began, had attained a constancy that seemed to draw all the time before inside it, and he'd never known her as anything else.

"There. Up on the right." Joseph saw Michael's hand near his face, its finger pointing towards a one-story brick building cut out of a corn field, a single gas pump in front. Each of them had the impression that the station had been closed for years, until they pulled into the lot and saw that it wasn't so much an old building as one that was once new made to look old.

The woman inside the station sat with her husband in the repair room, their two children lying on their beds in the adjacent rooms; and when she saw the Volkswagen she knew with increasing certainty, before the figures inside were quite discernable, that the woman in the passenger seat would soon have a child. It frightened her into saying, and she didn't speak often, "Arnold, a pregnant woman's coming here."

The man didn't watch her as she went out the door to greet them, but continued to polish the wrenches that he hadn't used for days, stacking them with such precision in the tool chest that they looked like a single piece of metal. In from the cornfields early since there was little to do in the long days of July (he had never seen the man for whom he worked), he cared for his tools as if they were his children's teeth.

Immediately Joseph was repulsed by him, though there was nothing in the man's face, which was quite handsome, to warrant his reaction. But had it not been for Emily, and the kindness of the woman, he'd have turned without speaking, stepped into the car, and driven until the battery died, and left it and his brother along the road. Michael blinked twice to adjust his eyes to the darkness, then stared at the tools that still managed to shine.

"And we have some grape pop in the machine," the woman was saying. She had her arm as far around Emily as it would go. "It's not cold, but it'll still cool you off, especially if you just stay out of the sun for a while, sit and relax while Arnold takes care of your car."

She touched her hand to Emily's cheek.

"Arnold, these people have something wrong with their car."

He did not react, but closed the lid of his tool chest and locked the clip; the woman led Emily into another room, where she sat down in a wooden chair in front of the pop machine. The red letters of Coca-Cola had faded and bled into the white.

Michael moved his eyes from the tool box to Arnold's face.

"You give me a screwdriver, a wrench, and the belt and I'll fix it myself." But the fierceness in his voice was noticed only by Joseph.

The man rubbed an invisible grease spot from his hand.

"Is that your baby?" he said to Michael.

"You think I'd be out here in a Navy uniform if it was?"

The man stared back at him.

"Well if he managed without you in making that baby, I guess I can fix that car without you, too."

"Listen," said Joseph. "We'd like a quick fix. And if you can't do anything besides sit there, I'll just take it further down the road."

The mechanic smiled, a smile that on a younger child some might regard as pretty, had it not been for the solitary motion of his mouth; the rest of his face seemed separate from it, immobile, his eyes polished as silver.

"That'll be about fifty miles," the mechanic said. "And by the looks of the three of you and that car, I wouldn't try it. So go on out and pull it into the garage. Mind you, I don't like fixing cars, mostly because a horse and buggy will serve you fine. And if you'll take my advice, that's what you'll get next time, after this thing breaks down for good, and by the way that won't be long."

The mechanic sat with his hand on the tool box, his mouth suddenly closed and his eyelids lowered; the expulsion of words, he seemed to be saying, was an accident, one that his wife, who only half-listened to them as she watched Emily resting with the soda bottle nearly balanced on her belly, had grown used to and worried over almost by habit.

"Arnold," she called to the mechanic. "Maybe Gloria should come see Emily here. She's never seen a pregnant woman, except when she was too young for it to make any difference. Emily's her name. Emily Potter."

But Joseph didn't hear this; he had gone out to the car and then hesitated before climbing in and turning the key. He could not suppress his preoccupation with the land, the rows of corn that stretched on and on on either side of the highway, disappearing into the haze of the sky to the north, and reaching a dwarfed barn and farmhouse to the south. Joseph would not think, not even consider driving off alone now, leaving Emily, Michael, and the baby behind, but the sense he had now of all the fields and rows somehow pointing towards him, lifting him out and leaving him in isolation, was that urge itself, though he didn't recognize it, couldn't recognize it. His father had said of him, even written in letters to Joseph's mother when he was away from home (letters that she had later burned for fear the children would find them): "In Joseph, there's his intelligence, yes, and I'm proud of that, but what worries me sometimes is that kind of hateful oddity, or more likely an oddity of hatefulness that I've never put my finger on. And most likely neither will he, because the boy's so responsible."

But it wasn't responsibility that insulated Joseph now, though that was how he felt it. He steered the car towards the garage, thinking only once or twice of the many long trips he'd taken, first to see the woman with the blue music box, who said "Do you think you have to go away to school to be smart?" and then to see Emily, before they were married, driving hundreds of miles on the weekends during the summers he worked out of state though there were jobs available in his hometown.

Michael raised the garage door as Joseph pulled up.

The mechanic had reopened his tool box, and laid the wrenches side by side on a white scrap of bedsheet. Joseph saw that a young girl, no more than fourteen, had joined Emily and the woman, and was now drinking grape soda as she stared at Emily's belly. Her name was Gloria, and she had come from her room and crossed the garage floor while Joseph was outside. She had glanced twice at Michael, then a third time before her hand was taken by her mother, who told her, "This woman's going to have a baby, just like I had Jerome, but you were too young to remember," Michael barely acknowledged the girl's entrance, more fascinated than angry now by the mechanic and his precision with the care of his tools. Joseph watched Gloria's hand twitch, and it looked to him that she wanted to lay it across Emily.

"I hope you don't mind that," the mechanic said to Joseph, but without concern or deference, with the same polished eyes, the same detached movement of his mouth. "She's never seen a pregnant woman before, and I suppose she ought to learn."

"I take it you don't get much business," Joseph said.

"I don't look for it. You don't see many signs or gas prices hanging out over the road, do you? But my wife, she thinks the boy and girl ought to see the customers. We don't send them to school; teach them ourselves." Then his eyelids and mouth closed again suddenly, inviting no response.

"Can we get to this?" Michael said, only impatient now for the work to begin because it was something not started and not finished.

The mechanic picked up the wrench without comment, and it fit into his hand as if his palm had been slotted for the handle. But instead of approaching the hood of the Volkswagen, he slammed the end of the wrench into the nearest wall, even Michael flinching as the sound vibrated along the garage. After a minute, a boy walked out from behind the corner and stood with his overly large hands at his sides.

He stared at Joseph, as if he knew beforehand that the car was his trouble, the boy's eyes pinched too closely toward his nose, and Joseph assumed he was waiting for him to say something.

"Your father's going to fix my car," he said, knowing that the statement was ridiculously obvious, but the boy continued to stare at him, and Joseph gradually saw more of the mother's face in the boy's rather than the father's.

"He can't hear you," the mechanic said. "He just felt the vibrations on the wall where I hit it. He was born deaf. That was because we lived in the city then; I knew it before he ever came out of my wife. That's why we moved out here, and I'll be damned if I'll let either of them kids so much as visit the city, I don't care if they die in this very building."

"Arnold." This was the mechanic's wife, out from the refreshment room. "I don't think these people need to hear all that, and especially not around Jerome." She stood with her arm still around Emily, Gloria behind her, who glanced almost anxiously from her father to Emily. The mechanic closed his eyes a moment.

"Jerome can't hear any of it anyway, Amelia. And this man is about to have a baby, and he ought to know."

"Just the same," said the woman. "Mr. Potter, we'll be out back on the porch swing if you want to join us."

"Daddy, she's pretty, isn't she?" said Gloria. "Emily, I mean. She's really pretty, isn't she?"

But the mechanic had turned back to the car as the three women walked out the door in the back of the garage. The deaf boy hadn't moved, hadn't even seen his mother or sister, but continued to stare at Joseph. Joseph was now uncertain that the boy even saw him, and that he was instead looking at the car as if Joseph were transparent. But the boy would not turn away; his eyes, like his father's, held no curiosity.

"You ought to stay right here, Mr. Potter," the mechanic was saying, "and learn something about how to change a generator belt, like your brother *says* he knows."

"Look," said Michael. "We don't need lessons. Christ, I could have this thing done by now and be half way back to the coast. And that woman's gonna be hitch-hiking to the hospital, Mister, to have that damn baby."

The mechanic smiled again.

"Truth is, it's not near her time yet," he said. "But even if you *can* fix that car, there's things you ought to learn, too." He walked over to the boy and passed the wrench in front of his eyes. Jerome caught it before it left the field of his vision and his father turned his shoulders and rested his hands on the sides of the boy's face. When he spoke he exaggerated the movement of his mouth.

"Fan belt," he said.

The boy walked over to the car and opened the hood, and when he began to work on the engine, Joseph would have thought he himself was deaf for all the noise the boy made while he loosened bolts and set them carefully down alongside the tires.

"And it's not just cars he can do that with," said the mechanic, without pride, as a statement of fact. "The man I farm for, Jerome can fix his tractors, or ready up his plough in the springtime. And he always does it the same way; you can't hear the wrenches moving any more than you can hear his arm muscles."

The boy worked slowly, but with a steady precision that didn't waver.

Michael regarded him with a thin film on his eyes that was jealousy, but behind that an appreciation for the boy's efficiency, an admiration for a job done where even the sound wasn't wasted.

"He works well," said Michael, not so much to the mechanic as to Joseph, but his words so close in tone to the other's that Joseph wanted to say, "I wish you'd fix the car; I wish you'd fixed it out on the road before we ever had to pull in here." He was not frightened by the boy or his father, and he did not feel any sense of danger. But he knew now that had the deaf boy been in his own family—and he was convinced he could have been, could even see his picture now, squared neatly by his mother next to his brother's and his own—that Michael never ever could have done a thing with his hands that the deaf boy couldn't do better, and that position in the family filled, he and Michael would have grown up much more alike, much closer than the mere obligation of their blood made them now. And this possibility did frighten him.

"I taught him most of that, it's true," the mechanic said. "But there are some things he picked up himself, I don't know where from. Just watch here. He's got this little dance he does when he's about ready to take out what's left of that belt. Any time now."

With a sudden shift of his feet, the boy whirled away from the engine compartment and tossed the wrench two or three feet above his head, and as it came down he caught it as a baton twirler might, and held the handle end out to Joseph.

"He wants you to help," said the mechanic. "I don't know why he does that little circus act, and I tried to stop him for a while, but he wouldn't stop. It's not bad, anyway."

Joseph couldn't keep himself from taking a step away from the boy.

"See, he just wants you to help because he knows it's your car."

"I don't know a thing about cars," Joseph said. "I'd be useless."

"Of course you would," said the mechanic, "but he just wants you to make one turn of the wrench on that last bolt, then he'll put the new belt on and you'll be out of here. It won't cost you any less money, though, so don't be looking for a break."

Joseph no longer attended to what he was saying, but only felt the necessity of avoiding the boy.

"Michael can help him," he said. "At least he'll know what he's doing."

"But it's not his car, Mr. Potter. Jesus, the boy isn't but twelve years old and he's just trying to learn a little responsibility."

"Would you do it, for Christ's sake?" said Michael, who had already begun to see his shipmates readying themselves to leave port. "I don't plan on taking a vacation in this joint, and it sure as hell isn't going to hurt you to learn something about how this thing operates."

Joseph bit his lower lip as he took the wrench from the boy's hand, though he wasn't thinking of what Michael had said or the mechanic's chastising him for his hesitancy. Once under the hood of the car, the boy took hold of Joseph's hand, his fingers sliding over it once because of the grease, and guided it to the remaining bolt.

"Jerome can work with his hands," the mechanic was saying to Michael, "and a man that can work with his hands has a job anywhere any time." But Joseph heard this only peripherally, as the boy held his hand and turned the wrench with him; instead he was thinking of Emily and the baby, the woman and her daughter Gloria all sitting in the swing in back of the garage, and though he could neither see nor hear them, if someone had asked him later, he wouldn't remember correctly if he had gone out to see them or not.

The swing rocked slowly under their weight, and they faced a small patch of yard that for the most part supported chicory, the small blue flowers waving in the occasional breeze that cooled the skin of the women. Gloria was almost resting her head on Emily's shoulder now, her lips tinted purple from the grape soda so that she looked as if she were cold. The woman sat with her arm extended along the back of the swing.

"Are you resting okay?" she asked.

Emily continued to rock with her eyes closed; the woman couldn't be certain that she was awake and listening, but she went on talking anyway.

"Having a baby's a nice thing," she said. "Real nice, but probably everyone has told you that. When we had Gloria we were so proud, because she could scream so loud and healthy, and learned to walk and talk faster than a lot of babies."

Gloria buried her head more deeply into Emily's shoulder. The woman sighed once.

"But when Jerome was born, of course, he couldn't hear any more than them flowers, not even the doctor's slap, and Arnold moved us out of the city because he said it was at fault. But I don't think he was right. I've watched him some times, Jerome, I mean, when he sits out here with me or even all by himself. One of those big trucks comes by and he doesn't even flinch, doesn't move an inch, just looks out at the cornfields and the sky. And see, if we lived in the city, he'd see all the buildings and the people, even something as bad as a car crash or an ambulance siren, and it wouldn't be no different, say, than a stalk of chicory or a luna moth to him, and I think that must be peaceful, maybe even beautiful. So I stopped feeling sorry for him."

Emily hadn't moved, and even Gloria's eyes were closed now.

"So it's good if they come out right, but if they come out wrong, it's okay, and you can thank God any way."

She heard the car engine start, and Emily opened her eyes.

"Sounds like they got your car fixed," the woman said.

When the three of them returned to the garage, they saw the boy wiping the grease from the wrenches as carefully as his father had. And because the imitation was so close, and perhaps more so than if the boy had not touched his hand, Joseph watched him and hated it.

"I got one thing to ask of you," the mechanic was saying to Joseph. "Now this is going to cost you thirty-five dollars, see, but Jerome needs to know that it's his work that got us the money. So I'd appreciate it if you'd drive the car out of here so he knows it runs right, and then I'll send him out after you."

"I'd rather give the money to you," said Joseph, not looking at the mechanic, but from Emily back to the boy.

"But I didn't fix your car, Mr. Potter."

Joseph got into the Volkswagen and pulled it out into the heat, parked it, and stood waiting outside as the deaf boy walked towards him. Joseph watched him closely, but did not actually see him, and was instead thinking of another child, only much younger, a baby a few months old that he gradually realized was his own. It was sitting in an immense field, endlessly flat, that had grown over into weeds and wild flowers, the sky perfectly blue and cloudless, the wind blowing in the child's hair, only there was no one there to see it, no one for miles and miles, and the child not even crying, not even moving, its face expressionless, staring into the evening sun as if it would hang there until it burnt out.

At length, Joseph saw the boy standing in front of him, and shook himself awake, not startling the boy, who was simply waiting. Then his wallet was in his hand and he tore all the bills from its pocket and crumpled them into the boy's palm and wrapped his fingers around them.

"Look," he said. "I don't know how much is there, but more than thirty-five dollars. Look, just take it and get out of here, away from this place; I don't know, Christ, anywhere, there might be a truck coming, but just don't tell your father, take the money and run away; run now, even, run now."

But the boy did not, and he opened his hands and looked at the money, his face showing excitement for the first time since Joseph had seen him. His eyes widened and his mouth tightened up and he let out a loud whistle that Joseph hadn't heard since a night in Canada when the loons flew overhead, bringing him upright from sleep, and his own father pulling him back down, saying only, "It's their time," and Joseph not knowing until years later what he meant.

But that thought, too, had burned and disappeared from his consciousness long before the boy had run back to the mechanic, nearly jumping up and down when he put the money in his hands, and the mechanic had walked slowly back out to the car, smiling all the way with the money held out in front of him.

"Here, Mr. Potter," he said. "I took out what you owed us; you'll be needing the rest of that for gas, and maybe even another repair." But then the mechanic brought his face close, his eyes no longer polished, his breath whistling through his teeth.

"I saw what you did there with Jerome. But it doesn't matter. See, maybe the one thing you can do right is take the only thing God gave you and put it in the necessary spot and have all them kids. And I don't want you for a neighbor, but maybe before they're grown you should move them out here about twenty miles down the road, and you'll see what I mean when I say at least Jerome's safe."

Then the mechanic walked away, and Joseph said, barely audibly with his face hot, "You can't know that. You can't even make that guess."

But he didn't have time to even wait for the mechanic's voice to die out in his ears, since the woman, Gloria, Emily, and Michael were all walking towards him. Joseph opened the door for Emily, and Michael climbed in back, assuming the same position he had before the car broke down. The woman rested her arm on the roof of the car and wiped her face with her hand.

"You take good care of that baby. I'm sure it'll be beautiful."

And she and Gloria waved as they drove off, Joseph knowing that the girl continued to wave long after the car disappeared.

But this knowledge, which he believed he'd had for a long time, was fading as surely as the sun now, the sky darkening in the east, fading in each of them. They felt it as a thing receding, backing out through them, then above the roof of the car and gone into the evening, though this time each marked its passing. Michael said, "If the weather and the car holds, it'll be an easy ride home." Then he thought only of the waves lapping with soothing regularity against the sides of the ship that lay waiting for him. Emily nodded and smiled, saying nothing, but closing her eyes as she saw five tiny fingers close round her thumb.

But Joseph clung desperately to what he now knew could not stay, even tensing his arms against the steering wheel and rising a little out of his seat as if to pursue what he had already lost, saying over and over again, "I will love this child, I will love this child," the last time audibly, so Emily reached over and squeezed his hand.

But in the reddened moon that rose over the fields, he could see the smiling face of the mechanic, and he could hear his baby laughing at him, laughing even now in Emily's belly, laughing as it was born, laughing long after he'd closed his hand over its mouth, its laughter rising higher and higher in pitch as it echoed off the moon forever.

"Heritage": Autobiographical Sources

THERE is a point of inception for every story. That point may occur years before the story is written, years before the writer knows he will write stories or anything else. I have friends who tell me they sit down at the typewriter with nothing in mind but the intent to write, and intention itself loosens memory and the story is begun. Others sit down with a phrase they have written or read, captivated by its message or rhythm, and through faith in that rhythm—which it seems to me they must somehow recognize—a first paragraph is constructed. I mention these only because they are methods by which writers *call forth* inception, and because they differ from mine. More often than not, I will think of a last line and work toward it (a last line that usually changes through the process of writing the story), rather than thinking of a first line and working from it. But the most important thing is that writers cultivate memory, experience in its immediacy, and most practically, *time;* otherwise there will be no beginnings, ends, or middles, nothing but the romantic label of writer (which through practice loses its romanticism quickly enough) and the self-indulgence of writer's block.

I also want to mention that good readers might at least question any writer who writes of the sources of a story after the story's completion. I wonder as I write this if "Heritage" now shapes my memory rather than the other way around. And remember this is one story and one writer; do not seek instruction or example here. This is a rendering and thoughts on that rendering.

Four years ago, I was driving through Indiana towards Fort Wayne, my wife—seven months pregnant—in the passenger seat. I had just left my sister's wedding and was now headed for my grandparents' house and a baby shower held for us. The trip out from Pittsburgh, where I had just finished school, was the stuff that two-star slapstick comedies are made of, if it had not been so insufferably hot. I was driving an old Volkswagen that stalled at every stop, and with the starter jammed because of the heat, I had to crawl under the car and smack it with a wrench at each intersection. After stopping to try and correct the problem, I was late for my sister's wedding, and driving seventy miles an hour towards her home, when the generator light came on. It may as well have been the headlights for all I knew about cars. We limped into her driveway just as the minister was threatening to leave; the wedding came off, the generator belt was fixed at a busy local service station, and we were on our way again. My wife had held up marvelously well under the conditions, even as she was now sleeping, sweat beading on her upper lip.

It was then I began to feel the foolishness of my situation, its lack of dignity, its ridiculousness. Note that I didn't feel foolish or undignified, but that the situation seemed so. I was already once removed from the experience in which I was involved, as if looking in on my own life. This becomes, I believe, second nature for those who comb their lives searching for something to write about. And in that state, I felt the pathos of an unborn child laughing at its father in his helplessness. And I knew I had an image for a story.

But you see, all this is somewhat embarrassing, and all that follows may be the same. I do not want to laud the details of my life as worthy of story or art; they are not. Do not confuse me with Joseph Potter. Writers who make a habit of confusing themselves with their characters succumb to melodrama and may eventually be ashamed of their prose. But I do believe when immersed in the writing act that one must drop some of one's humility and self-consciousness in order to perform, if indeed writing can be viewed as performance.

It was a long time before I had the opportunity to begin writing "Heritage." I have never "seized the moment" of a story effectively; any time I've tried, I have ended up destroying my efforts almost before they're completed. Emotion, the source of so many of my earlier efforts at writing, must be tempered by time and intellect. I did not trust my emotional reaction to that original image, but as I turned it over in time and it collected other artifacts from my experience, it became more legitimate and significant.

In the interim before I began writing, my first son was born. I do not need to speak here of the radical shift that this gives to one's perspective of one's own father. And I began to recall things he had said—and my father is still alive—most significantly that it was unnatural for a child to die before its parent, that this was the most horrible thing. I feared this already, as I had feared my own unborn child's deformity (even as I've always been fascinated and disturbed by deformity) though he was born completely healthy. Both of these things made their way into the story, the first not at all literally, since I changed the memory to suit the needs of Joseph (as if he literally needed anything), the second in the form of the deaf child, Jerome. And as I continued to consider fatherhood in all its apparitions (because they seem ghostly and ephemeral to me), the character of the mechanic rose from the darker ones. He was among the easiest to put together because of his limitedness. And I must stress that he was nothing like the mechanic who fixed the generator belt in *my* car; that one was young and cordial.

The other characters I also had in place before I began writing, though these I needed primarily for effect or for a single scene: Michael to pressure the forced intimacy of a long car ride and the obligatory intimacy of family; the mechanic's wife because otherwise there was so little natural kindness in the story, and for the scene on the porch swing; and Gloria to perpetuate the healthy memory and impact of Emily's pregnancy beyond the lives of the adults in the story. The names of all the characters were chosen because they meant something to me; this helps me to care more for those characters. Joseph is a name I've used for characters in other stories. Potter is the last name of a boy I knew when I was growing up. Michael is my brother's, who, coincidentally, joined the navy two years after I finished the story, and I now have a picture of him in a white uniform. (But again, he is nothing like the Michael of the story.) And I should mention, too, that I know the faces of my characters even though I rarely describe them. The mechanic's I took from a man driving a garbage truck waiting for a traffic light to change. I do not think detailed physical descriptions are necessary as long as the writer gives the sense that he knows what his characters look like, what they wear.

The most difficult thing about finally writing the story was discovering the point-of-view through which these characters could complete their journeys. (And in a sense, I mean *their* journeys. Once I begin writing, it seems I'm a guide.) After all, the writer determines this decision by the time the first sentence is completed, and unless he wants his reader to distrust him, he must remain constant to it. For this and other more nitpicking reasons, I will tinker and tinker and tinker with the beginning of a story, rejecting one opening, revising another, as I rarely do with an essay. Even this essay began at point A and will move fairly linearly to point Z. Perhaps I demand more from my stories than I do my essays, I may care more. But the process of writing them is entirely different.

I originally opened the story with some version of the lines that now appear in the third paragraph: "The father had told the driver, whose name was Joseph Potter, 'Like any child, son, it's your responsibility to outlive your parents. . . .'" I tried this several ways, but each time I'd written two paragraphs into the story, I was dissatisfied. The narration was too closely attached to Joseph (even though it was his story), whose perspectives were not entirely trustworthy, considering his state. And I wanted to communicate a nurturance that I had felt—and it seemed to me others had felt—whenever in the presence of my wife, a nurturance that always seemed just beyond human articulation. And the effect of the end of the story—the laughter of the unborn child—was to be in part that nurturance stripped away. That was when I remembered a favorite Paul Bowles story, "The Circular Valley."

That story does not need me to recommend it, but it takes place over centuries, and describes the existence of an entity that is capable of moving in and out of living things—animals, men, and finally a woman—and feeling what they feel. This sort of embodiment was the thing I felt toward the nurturance I mention above, as if it somehow lived on its own. So I appropriated the idea from Bowles and used it in a much different, more subdued form.

I do not see this as a theft, but rather a reward for having read Paul Bowles. I don't delude myself into believing everything I come up with is highly original. Another image I know I borrowed that appears in "Heritage" is that of Joseph's father's words consumed in flame the moment Joseph thinks of them. This idea came from reading Loren Eiseley, who watched his mother burning his father's letters after his father's funeral. I am not saying I'm proud of having used these writers' ideas, metamorphosed as they are in my story. But I am saying such use is unavoidable if one reads and is struck by what one reads. That reaction is no less autobiographical than many things I have lived.

Having taken on this entity, I realized it was necessary to describe its effect on each character. At that point, I began to work with a disembodied narrator, one that could move in and out of the characters' minds and bodies as does the entity. Such a choice presents problems, since I think it is the most difficult point-of-view to contain, even as it is liberating. But the story demanded that perspective, so, in that sense, I did not make a choice. Almost immediately I wrote the first line of the story as it now appears, and the first page or two came relatively easily.

I wrote the story over several months' time, which is not something I prefer, but child-rearing and its accompanying exhaustion would not allow otherwise. The story risked becoming what I call a garbage can story, not only because that's where it may eventually end up, but because the day-to-day refuse of life is thrown in to the point it begins to emit a distinct odor. The one advantage of time in this form is occasionally something happens that can further enlighten a story—a trip, a new friendship, in my case, the growth of my son.

He was eight months old—ten months past the inception of the story, two months since I'd begun writing it—and sitting on a blanket with me in the back yard, his mother out shopping. It was late afternoon in early spring, with all its peculiar light. Having folded towels that had dried on the line, I took them into the house alone, the first time I had left my son by himself outdoors and out of my sight for even a few seconds. The thrill of fear that most parents must face in these days where photographs of children appear on milk cartons consumed me for those moments of absence. And what struck me when I stepped back out the door, and of course he was still there, was the contrast of his expressionless face, his smallness in the immensity of a spring day to which he seemed oblivious, utterly vulnerable yet somehow utterly deathless. This event transformed the writing of the story, gave the unborn child's laughter another dimension for Joseph, underscored its endlessness. These experiences, and far more insignificant ones, are those which I seem almost always ready to distance, to partially but never wholly objectify, when I'm in the *habit* of writing.

The story roared to a finish, as many of mine do. I write, for me, excruciatingly slowly up to the half-way or three-quarters point, and then I finish in an afternoon or two. Small and unrelated details from my own life ran through the mill of the story and appeared on the page: a few words my wife had actually said during her pregnancy, chicory—my mother's favorite summer flower, the porch swing at my grandparents' house when I was young. The juxtaposition of these is intellectually interesting to me, but their appearance was never planned or orchestrated. And there are *more* significant details that I have not mentioned that, I suppose, were at one time autobiographical. But that is the luxury that a fiction writer has: an emotion or idea that was fleeting in his own life can gain permanence for one of his characters.

And yet I think it's important to remember there's a prognosis for every character in a story, at least those that do not die. Doubtless Joseph's child will be born healthy, doubtless he *will* grow to love it, and doubtless he'll tickle it under its chin, teach it to catch, go to its graduation and so on. These things are *normal*. But normalcy does not interest me as a writer other than as a matter of perspective, and if I imagine my characters' lives beyond the end of the story, I would want them to look back on it as the highest revelation of their lives, the one they *might* turn to at the moment of their deaths. This is the nature of epiphany, I suppose, and I have little stake in a story if that is absent.

And my own son was born healthy, and I tickled *his* chin, and have tried to teach him to catch, and he is now four years old, and this story seems immature to me. How does one then judge its legitimacy? I believe one must return to the moment of its completion. Because despite the intellectualization of the material, despite the distancing of the characters and the characters' lives, despite the disclaimers I've made here that this is not *my* life I'm actually writing about, despite the day-to-day frustrations of the effort of writing, and despite the artificiality of giving life form which life it seems to me resists, it may be sentimental and self-indulgent to admit that when I wrote the last line, I wept.

QUESTIONS

Daniel Lowe's story, "Heritage," and its process essay, "'Heritage': Autobiograpical Sources"

1. With regard to the "It" that appears most prevalently at the beginning and end of the story: from what does it arise? What is it supposed to represent? Recall the intimacy and trust that McCafferty describes as implicit in long car rides. Is this a manifestation of that intimacy and trust, or does it come from something else? How does Lowe tie this to the place through which the characters are driving? On long drives with family members, have you ever experienced this sense of security that offered, in Lowe's terms, a sense of certain protection?

2. The family members tied to the place of the story—Indiana, the midwest—are woven thematically throughout. Would the story be changed if it were in another place? How heavily does Lowe depend on your recognition of it? In your own lives, how has the place you've grown up in affected the relationships between members of your own family?

3. In his process essay, Lowe writes, "And remember this is one story and one writer; do not seek instruction or example here." Why does he include this caution? How heavily has your own writing been influenced by the things your teachers and others have said about it? Do you listen to and heed all their advice? Should you? What are the costs if you don't?

4. Lowe speaks of appropriating certain ideas from Paul Bowles and Loren Eiseley. Does Lowe's defense of this seem legitimate to you? Has he stolen material, borrowed it, learned from it, been affected by it? What's the difference? Would it still be fair for him to call his work original, creative?

Possible Writing Topics

1. Write an essay about the place (or places) that you and your family grew up in, and how that place has affected who you and your family members have become. Here you won't focus specifically on, for example, the house you grew up in unless something about your house speaks specifically to the

town and the geographic area you came from. Are there particular ways of speaking and thinking, particular attitudes, ethics, or morals that mark this place, separate it from others? Are there jobs that you and your siblings will pursue that you wouldn't have an interest in if you had grown up somewhere else? How did your family come to live in this place?

2. Lowe writes, "There is a point of inception for every story. That point may occur years before the story is written, years before the writer knows he will write stories or anything else." Part of the inception for this story is Lowe's experience growing up in the Midwest. Consider the essay you've just written, and write a second essay on what you believe were some of the points of inception for the first essay. What did you consider initially? What choices did you make? Which ideas did you eliminate? What was the first image that came to your mind when you read the topic for the first essay? Why that image, do you think, instead of others?

III

PORTRAITS

Karen Swenson

My Aunt Elizabeth

THROUGH the funeral mass, I stood and sat self-consciously at appropriate times feeling as brittle as Sunday-best china. A choir from the local church belted out hymns no Catholic would have given cognizance to fifty years ago, and the priest delivered an all-purpose eulogy that left her bland and complacently good as all our dead. I tried to hold onto the words of the service, but they escaped like bright swarms of fish into the patterns of stained glass. I found myself focusing on the anomaly of a plastic Cool Whip bowl on the altar covered with clear wrap which contained the hosts for communion. Its inappropriateness was a comfort, a proof of reality beyond this production running smoothly along between the officiating hands of priest and funeral director.

If my dead Aunt Elizabeth did not approve the hymns and the characterless eulogy, at least she would approve of my dress, I thought. It was the black silk I had worn for my father's burial out on the prairie six years before. She'd admired it saying, "Will you wear that to my funeral?" She was ninety-three then. "Yes, if you manage to die before I wear it out," I teased. Her longevity had been a joke between us, and now, within a month and a half of being a hundred, she was dead.

Clothes had been one of our connecting links since, with a fifty year gap between us, we did not have a lot of common ground and we came from a family in which you did not reveal your internal life. Self-revelation was reserved for people in elevators, not family members. For eleven years after my mother died, I flew out to Fargo, North Dakota, each Thanksgiving to eat turkey with my aunt either in one of the local restaurants or at her retirement home.

She was my mother's older sister. She had been a dancer on Broadway in the teens and twenties of this century and then earned her living teaching drama, dance and English at private girls' schools. At one point she taught in Mexico at the American School in Monterrey where I lived with her for a year. She had never married and, in a way, I was her only child as well as my mother's.

The five days I spent with her each year developed into a ritual of events repeated unfailingly each Thanksgiving centering about clothes and the shoebox in the second drawer which contained instructions for her funeral.

When I arrived from the airport, she would strafe me with an appraising glance that could sight a loose button at twenty paces and say, "Brown, you wear too much brown—such a drab color. You need a dress in a zesty color."

In those first hours off the airplane I was often hit with a barrage of disapproval.

"Your hair is all wisps, Dear. You look so blowsy. Why don't you go to a really good hairdresser and get a smart cut."

"That blouse doesn't fit you right. I'm sure it's because you don't wear a bra. Why don't you get one with a little stuffing in it. You're so flat."

"Don't make a face, Dear. Ladies don't grimace." "You're beginning to get a little tummy bulge. At your age you should be wearing a girdle."

There had been a time when this bombardment of criticism had hurt terribly since I loved her and wanted to please. But over the years I learned to take her comments less personally as I came to understand that she had grown up to believe that you showed your love by noting and correcting the faults of those you cared for. Over dinner one year she said firmly, "You must notice my manners, Dear. I depend on you. I live so much alone now that I'm likely to become peculiar," as though she expected at any moment to start eating with her hands.

Once I asked, "Liz, what would you like me to look like? I'm not saying I'll do it, mind you, but I'd like to know."

"Well, Dear, I'd like to see you look like one of those women who are really smart, really well turned out, with every hair in place. They have style."

"A lot of people think I have style, " I said, my temper a bit ruffled.

"Oh, you do, Dear," and then in a deprecating tone, "but it's yours."

Clothes, or more generally style, were not to her a means of self-expression but a clever mask behind which to hide any inadequacies or insecurities and present a uniform, unexceptionable front to the world. One's own taste might expose one to criticism, but what was fashionable was acceptable.

Buying clothes allowed us to chat easily in that companionable way women have when they shop together. But to initiate a shopping expedition she first had to disapprove of what I wore, otherwise, what excuse would we have?

Several of the five days were spent making the rounds of the best stores both out at the mall and downtown. A diminutive—her greatest height had been five feet two and age had compacted her to four feet eleven—white-haired monarch in her latest wig, or her own hair elegantly dressed, she sat on a chair, draped in her worn mink, in the middle of the selling floor at Shotwells or Scutts surveying with a critical eye the offerings the saleswomen presented, accepting, "That might be interesting on, Dear," and rejecting, "It's all right, but ordinary."

We would cover all the dress shops in a day or two. Then over lunch and dinner we would discuss those we had liked best.

"I like the line of that blue jersey particularly. It hangs well on you."

"Yes, but it hasn't any pockets."

"If it had pockets you'd pull it out of that line in no time with your fists in them. I know you."

"I liked the black knit with the dropped waistline."

"Yes, but the neck's a bit daring for day wear."

On the third day we would return in triumph to purchase what we had decided on. Although she paid, or we went fifty-fifty, the final decision was always mine.

The summer before she died, I went out to Fargo twice while she was in good health and then a third time after the first in what was to be a series of strokes leading to her death. When I walked into her hospital room after her first stroke she was strapped into a wheelchair. Her familiar reviewing glance went over my new green dress and she said, on a rising note of surprise, "Nice." The glance and summary comment were so much Elizabeth that it was hours before I realized how badly the stroke had impaired her mind and speech. The polite phrases for the ordinary events of life came readily to her tongue, but, for what she deeply wanted to say, the words were gone, the circuits blown.

"People," she said looking at me intently, "People . . . ," but the next word never came. Her closest friend visited her, and Liz could not say her name. I decided I would not put us through that trial and never asked if she knew my name. I knew she knew me.

I brought her back to her room in the retirement home which she had chosen twelve years before to enter, turning down my offer to have her live with me in New York. As the nurses helped me get her into bed she tried to tell me something, but it was garbled. She held her head in her hands and said despairingly, "Oh God, oh God." I rocked her back and forth in my arms feeling her small body, the flesh slack on her little bones. She tried again, rubbing her lips and gums. I gave her her teeth thinking that was what she wanted. She popped them in and again tried to say something pointing to her mouth. I offered her a soda cracker which she nipped from my fingers and stuffed in her mouth. She made a face and said quite distinctly, "Something good."

Feeling guilty for not having understood before, I bustled to her little refrigerator in her room and searched through the eclectic collection of petit fours, a half empty jar of lumpfish caviar, and exotic soups bought from mail order gourmet grocers until I discovered a pint of Haagen-Dazs coffee ice cream in her freezer. She sat up in bed in her pink nightgown, and I spooned it into her mouth.

That first stroke had not just robbed her of speech. It had metamorphosed her back to an earlier existence. She now blew her nose on her nightgown or her sheet, drank her milk from the carton rather than pouring it into a glass first. And she, the most fastidiously modest of women, lost interest in modesty.

Still, the person I had known all my life would suddenly reappear in a gesture, a word, a facial expression.

Later that afternoon when I hugged her good-bye before leaving for New York, I knew she had no idea where I was going and that this was the last time. The next time I would take the shoebox out of the second drawer.

I've no idea how long the shoebox existed but on the lid was a message "For Dorothy in the event of my death." Dorothy was my mother. This message was crossed out and under it was written "For Kay in the event of my death." The box contained, on small scraps of lined paper with ragged edges, endless pieces of information and instructions for her funeral. Each Thanksgiving we went through the box, reviewing the information and instructions.

One Thanksgiving, many years before her death, we'd come home from a sumptuous turkey dinner at one of the hotels. I had stretched out on her bed, and she had stood by the bureau with the second drawer open taking out a tattered slip at a time and reading from it.

"Give my mink to Norma's daughter if you don't want it. Send what furniture you want to New York and the rest to St. Vincent de Paul. This is a list of my insurance companies. This is a list of some of my friends. You should call them so they'll know I'm dead and will come to the funeral. This is the information you should give the *Fargo Forum* for my obituary. And these are the instructions for the funeral." Her voice took on a commanding tone. "One. There are underthings and nylons, all brand new in tissue paper, in the third drawer on the left hand side." She rustled around and held up a nylon bra and garter belt as samples. "You won't be able to see my feet so I don't need shoes. Two. I want to be in my pink coatdress and my ruffled white blouse." She marched over to the closet, took the two garments out and waved them at me. My mouth was beginning to twitch with laughter. "And," she said coming back to the bureau and the shoebox, "be sure they pin this pin," she took out a fake military decoration from her junk jewelry box, "up very high pulling the collar together so my neck wrinkles won't show." As she demonstrated on the blouse she was wearing our eyes met, and we dissolved into helpless cascades of giggles, me rolling on the bed, she clinging for support to the bureau. Were we laughing at her lovely female vanity still irrepressible in her nineties or at her acting our her own funeral? I don't know but it was her last party, and she planned it with great care right down to how much should be paid for flowers.

The bed on which I had rolled with laughter was the center of many of our talks with its hand knit blankets and row of fluffed pillows. A month before the strokes began she called me one day and said, "You'd better come out. I think I'm dying." I came. We went through all her worldly goods and discussed arrangements. Sitting on the bed in her nightgown—she seldom dressed now— she said, "Your mother always said I made a difference in your life by paying for your music and dancing lessons."

"Oh, Liz," I said, breaking the barrier that usually separated us, "it wasn't just those things. You made all the difference, on every level, physical, mental, spiritual. Yes, you gave me my dancing and music lessons, but you also took me to the Ballet Russe de Monte Carlo. I can remember sitting there and listening to the orchestra while the lights dimmed and the audience rustled less and less, the excitement growing. When we lived in Mexico you understood when I read *Gone with the Wind* for two days straight without talking and didn't pay any attention when I burnt out the flashlight batteries falling asleep over it under the covers. You made me memorize the first twenty odd lines of the *Canterbury Tales*. They are the only poetry I can recite at length by heart. You took me to see Hepburn in *As You Like It* and Boris Karloff in *Peter Pan*. You introduced me to Eleanor of Aquitane, making me aware that there were women in history. And, when people sent anonymous letters about the new black deacon in the church, you were the one who had him and his wife over for dinner. No, I haven't turned out Catholic like you, but I have a set of spiritual values that I believe in. You've been a very important, my most important, role model."

She was so overwhelmed by this speech that she retreated into polite phrases, and we went on discussing the charities to be included in the bequests in her will. But it opened up a channel between us. The next day when I came to go through more boxes and drawers with her as she sat propped up on her bed, she said thoughtfully, "When your father died you took some of the money and went some place lovely. Where did you go? I've forgotten."

"I went to Russia and Outer Mongolia. It was lovely."

"When I die, where will you go?"

"I thought I'd go to Tibet."

"Oh good, that's fine. I like that," she said and we went on to talk of other things.

Three weeks later she had her first stroke. Three weeks after that they called me from the nursing home section of her retirement home to ask if they could put a tube down her nose to force feed her. She had refused food and water for forty-eight hours. In among the papers in the shoebox had been a Living Will which asked that she be allowed to die with dignity. I refused to allow the tubes, and in twenty-four hours I received a call from the home to tell me she had died.

After the funeral, I drove behind the hearse to the edge of town where the land runs flat and utterly treeless to meet the sky. The Catholic cemetery is across from an enormous field whose ditches are full of wild flowers in the summer and whose furrows run straight to the edge of the earth smelling warm under the sun. They are all there now, the first generation with their old fashioned sounding names—Julia, Amelia, Olivia, Claire—in one neat row, then my grandparents and their children—my mother, her husband my father, and now my last one, my aunt.

I drove back into town, went to my favorite store, Scutts, and bought a winter coat, by myself. But I thought all the time of what she'd say about the line, conservative but good, and the way the collar stands up. I also thought about how now there is no one in front of me in the line outside death's door.

On Writing the Essay "My Aunt Elizabeth"

I come from a stiff, uptight family who taught me that to cry is weak. Therefore, I had no way to mourn when my aunt who had spent her last years in Fargo, the town my mother's family originally came from, died. I made the arrangements for her funeral, disposed of her furniture and clothes with the help of a friend, picked out the place for her grave among the family headstones and instructed the monument company, all dry eyed. At night I would go back to my hotel room, have dinner alone, listen to music or watch TV and pray for tears. It wasn't that I didn't feel things. I felt intensely, but there were no tears. Therefore, I was exhausted all the time dragging myself from funeral home to her room at the retirement home. Tears would have given me energy, cleansed me, allowed me to collapse into my grief and rise up rejuvenated, a phoenix. My childhood training forbade it.

Exhaustion was followed by rage, not at her for having died and left me, but existential rage that "this is it"; we live, and then we die. It seems outrageous to me that we humans, who live between the bookends of birth and death, and myself in particular, have so little acceptance of the conditions of life. We are enraged by death when it occurs as though it were a new fact we have never encountered before, as though it were an incredible and insulting injustice perpetrated upon us. Again and again, I have seen myself and others go through this period of rage. We can talk of death most philosophically; yet when the reality intrudes into our lives, we react as though we had never encountered it. Rage, however, was preferable to my previous state because it could be expressed. Having returned home to New York City, I lost my temper at my nearest and dearest and at total strangers whose subway etiquette I found wanting. I discovered that I was enmeshed in a masochistic desire to destroy all my most loving relationships as though I were a child having a temper tantrum—"If I can't have my Aunt Liz to love, I won't have anyone." For me, it is when I need people the most that I push them away.

Rage was followed by a period of intense, inexpressible sadness. One day, during this time I found myself, while waiting on the corner of Flatbush and Eighth Avenue in Brooklyn for a bus, overwhelmed by wave after wave of nausea. It had not occurred to me until then that if you cannot cry you may have to throw up. It was as though I was pregnant with her death, as if it were something I had to give birth to and I was, indeed, suffering from mourning sickness. At this point a friend suggested that I write about Liz's death as a method of catharsis. I tried writing poems, my more usual medium. Over the years I had written a number of poems about her, even about her death. I had made notes during the last months of her life, but just looking at them made my emotions rise up like a cresting tidal wave that would overwhelm and crush me. I knew I couldn't either face those emotions in their raw and undifferentiated state or control them sufficiently to write well. So I wrote the essay "My Aunt Elizabeth."

Having known my aunt for fifty years, I had an enormous amount of material available to me and, therefore, many angles of approach. There was her life. She had not liked her mother and had often run away as a child, sometimes inveigling other children into joining her. I have a picture of her at the age of six, grinning quite unrepentantly, beside a rather scared and rabbity looking little boy, whom she had talked into running away with her. Another time, when she was about twelve and living in Wabasha, a town on the Mississippi in Minnesota, she organized a group runaway, luring five girls in her grade to skate down the Mississippi to New Orleans. Liz, never having been south of Chicago, thought it would be frozen all the way. Their alarmed parents did not find them until after dark when they were discovered about three miles downstream, leg weary, shivering and weeping. At twenty, she had to have a hysterectomy which eliminated marriage as a possibility for her because she felt she would have nothing to offer a man. At least, this is what she told me.

In the early years of the century she was a dancer on Broadway, and the high point of her career had been a solo with Al Jolson in a production called *Sinbad*. She always claimed he had picked her out from among the other chorines because she was the smallest and he had to lift her up during the dance. She was also in a couple of Ziegfeld productions, but being five feet high and slightly pigeon-toed she decided there was not a great future awaiting her on Broadway. She did, during this time, get to know some of the names that were part of the early years of the century—Georgia O'Keefe, the Lunts, Eugene O'Neill. She even dated Gershwin a few times and was there when he played *Rhapsody in Blue* for the first time for some friends. She was inordinately proud of these acquaintanceships and enjoyed embroidering on them—not outrageously, just pleasantly. I have never been able to separate in my memory what was truth from what was embroidery.

Like many of us selfish beings, my aunt existed for me mostly in conjunction with myself, and what I wanted to write about was not so much *her* but *us*, our relationship across a breach of fifty years. The year we spent together in Mexico when I was fifteen established our relationship on a foundation of intimacy which it had never had before. Liz had been a frequent visitor to my parents' house; she even had a room of her own filled with highly romantic furniture including a four poster bed with a ruffled canopy. She came to us for a month in the summer and at Christmas mainly, and to me, she felt like a guest. That sense of her quickly evaporated as we traveled by train down to New Orleans. Despite her childhood attempt to get there, this was the first time she had seen the city. In our year together she influenced me in many subtle as well as direct ways. She taught me that the alien is not only acceptable but exciting and to be sought out, thereby laying the foundations for my own later travels. I learned from her the courtesies of travel—not to say "How much is that in real money," and to accept the discomfort, the odd no man's land status of being a tourist. I can remember her scolding me for making some audible and negative comments on the smell of a Mexican second class railway car.

Our intimacy was increased by illness. She nursed me that year through an unexplained fever that made me sleep almost without interruption for two weeks. That must have been as harrowing for her as chaperoning me through the dangers that naturally accompanied being the only green eyed red head in a hundred mile radius in a Latin country. Several times she came home to find that I had locked all the doors and windows because men in cars had followed my bus home from school. Usually if they were still parked outside when she came home, she went out on the terrace and shooed them away as if they were stray dogs hopeful about a bitch in heat.

It was only after her death that I realized that she had been in her mid-sixties when we lived together in Monterrey. Although I was in my teens, and teenagers are notoriously age conscious, I never thought of her as being of retirement age. If I thought of her age at all I thought of her as being in her forties, younger than my mother, although she was my mother's senior by twelve years. At the end of that school year, when I returned to New York, she went off to Guatemala and other countries in Central America. Part of my inheritance from her is a sizable collection of slides which she took at that time and on later trips to other parts of the world. In her seventies she went off to the Near East to visit Jerusalem and take a trip up the Nile. She prepared for the trip by reading everything in the Fargo library on Egypt and all the historical accounts of Christ's era that she could find. Her letters at this time were full of Herod and a romance of his which particularly caught her fancy.

I wanted to get across the reality of our relationship, that it was not all sweetness and light, that she had edges as I have and that we sometimes hurt each other with those edges or ended up in a stand-off of opposing wills. I hoped also to infuse the essay with a sense of her personality and its contradictions, many of which I still don't understand but which I long ago learned to accept.

She was a very gregarious woman with a charming social manner, particularly toward men whom she would, at a gathering, spend a great deal of time setting at ease. But she lived her entire life largely in physical isolation from both family and friends of whom she had many, although only a few who were close, and she was totally uninterested in men as company in all the time I knew her. They were for her another species—puzzling, omnipotently powerful, and frequently unpleasant—who were to be avoided most of the time. She was interested in spending time with women, as long as they were well read and well traveled—she was an unconscious intellectual snob. She was full of praise for women who were not educated but who worked hard and "raised" themselves above the station they had been born to. She just did not want to spend a lot of time with them. Even those friends she was closest to, her most beloved, she could not let near her. The softer emotions held terror for her. It wasn't until she was in her nineties that she could hug me back when I hugged her. Once I told her I loved her, and she went rigid in my embrace, unable to respond at all. Yet she could tell me when I lost my job in 1976, "Oh, Dear, I wish I'd die. Then you wouldn't have to work as much and you would have a little security."

She was a woman capable of great individuality of thought, and she was a great supporter of the underdog. She gave to the NAACP twenty years before most white people even knew what it was. She was vehement in her belief that homosexuals and homosexuality should be accepted by the Catholic Church. At the same time she was capable, particularly when it came to her vision of women, of being simultaneously supportive and reactionary. One of her reactionary areas had to do with the importance of a woman's looks.

Nothing was as important as the way a woman looked. Liz held strongly to the view that only the young were beautiful. After youth was gone one could only hope to look smart, and the looks of youth were very short lived. A year after the birth of my son, when I was twenty-six, she and my mother and I were sitting at the kitchen table in my parents' house. Liz looked me over with that calculating glance of hers, turned to my mother and said, as though I weren't there, "You should have some pictures taken of her now. She'll be nothing in a year or two." I burst into tears on the spot—for injured vanity, in my family, you are allowed tears, but not for death. A few years before her death I had a poem published in an issue of a poetry magazine that featured on its cover the photograph of a middle aged woman poet, handsome but without any makeup to disguise her age. Liz mumbled something general about my poem but ranted on for twenty minutes. "How could she let them publish that photograph of her. She looks like a hag. She must have either no self respect or an insane misconception of her looks to allow such a photograph to become public property." It was not just the looks of others over the age of twenty-six that upset her. Her own appearance was a source of despair to her. "I never was anything spectacular to look at, of course, Dear, but now I'm a positive crone. I try not to look in the glass in the bathroom. What can you expect in your nineties?"

Most of all, I wanted to get across something of her indomitable spirit, particularly as it was represented by the shoebox. For the last ten years of her life we talked freely and frequently of her death. It was never a dirty secret between us, an unmentionable. Part of what we spoke of was her funeral which she planned, switching her ideas from time to time as she came up with improvements on old notions. Her attitude toward it was that of a hostess arranging a party. She had made up a list of those she wished to invite. She changed the location from the church to the retirement home's chapel because she thought it was a friendlier milieu and the home served coffee and sweet rolls after funerals. She knew what she was going to wear, and she at least attempted to control what I, the substitute hostess, would wear. I even received a lecture on the appropriate grave marker. She didn't want one like my father's which she thought was ugly. Making these arrangements were, undoubtedly, her way of making a *rapprochement* with her own death, but I have never known anyone who went about ordering it in such a systematic manner. By the end, although she feared pain, I don't think she had much fear of death. I would like to be like her.

Writing the essay, attempting to get us, two personalities fifty years apart, and our relationship which bridged those years onto blank pages over a period of weeks has taken the place of tears as an outlet for my mourning. It has occurred to me that mourning is a form of cannibalism. In the process of recalling her in Mexico, in my parents' kitchen, of remembering her words, both the kind and the unkind, her letters written on scraps of paper torn out of old half-used notebooks—she scorned stationery as an effete waste of money—all these things have helped to heal me by placing her in my past, in the historical past of Jolson and Ziegfeld, in my familial past so that I can more easily move forward into my future without her physical presence, but having incorporated her, digested her, into my spiritual and mental being.

QUESTIONS

Karen Swenson's essay, "My Aunt Elizabeth," and its process essay, "Sources for 'My Aunt Elizabeth'"

1. What effect does Swenson's focus on her aunt's concern over dress and decorum have on you as you read? What do you learn about Swenson and her aunt in the dialogue Swenson includes over these matters? Why do you think Swenson chose this material rather than conversations she had with Elizabeth over more-weighty subjects?

2. Why did Swenson end her essay with the sentence, "I also thought about how now there is no one in front of me in the line outside death's door"? Did the sentence surprise you? Are there other indications in the essay of her concern over her own death? What effect does this sentence have on your reading of the rest of the essay?

3. Swenson writes in her process essay that because she was having so much trouble grieving the loss of her aunt, she took a friend's suggestion and wrote about her. Can you imagine ways that writing about someone you've lost, regardless of whether that person has died, could be, in Swenson's terms, a "catharsis"? What does writing allow you to do that talking with someone, or simply thinking about that loss, does not?

4. In Swenson's process essay, you learn much more about Elizabeth's biography than you do in the initial essay. Why did Swenson choose not to include this material in the first essay? If she had included it, how would the essay be changed? Do you think it would be stronger or weaker? While reading the first essay, did you feel as if you didn't know Elizabeth well enough?

❧ Possible Writing Topics ☙

1. Write an essay about someone you know well, but try not to focus on the major elements of that person's personality. Instead allow the person's clothing, the person's manners and mannerisms, the person's way of speaking to you and others suggest a personality. Consider what you might focus on to begin this essay, and what you can select to conclude it. Be careful that you allow those beginnings and conclusions to change if, as you work, the writing demands it.

2. Write a second essay where you pull together a minibiography of the person you wrote about in the first essay . Mention important events in that person's life, some of those things that you believe made that person what he or she is today. Give yourself as much room for detail as you can. After completing the essay, ask yourself which you like better, and which reveals the most accurate description of the person you know well.

Barbara Mellix

When They Come

I'M livin' out here on the old Greene place—right where a little piece of the east edge of Lang touch on the woods what rise up out the north end of the Piney Corner swamp. I'm livin' out here raisin' my baby—Solomon, what two—and mindin' my own business. Mind my own business is the thing folks hereabouts wouldn't leave me do in peace whilst I was livin' amongst them— with my mama and daddy and brothers over in the middle of the colored farmin' section of Lang.

From the time word got out I had a baby on the way, look like every place I turned folks was tryin' to dip in my private business. Everybody was wantin' to know who was the daddy, was he a married man why I was keepin' everything so secret. My mama carried on worse than anybody else. Now I think back on it, I reckon it woulda been strange otherwise. Anyhow, my mama wouldn't hardly ever give me any peace. She would beg and cry, tryin' to get me to tell her about the daddy. She would say, "Hester Bell, how you expect me and your daddy and the rest of the family to love the child right when we don't even know who it is?" I would say, "Y'all know it mine, so just love it like it mine." Then she would say, "You got a lot of nerve talkin' like that when me and your daddy feedin' you and your child and keepin' a roof over y'all heads." I would say, "I earn our keep and more. I work hard as anybody else in this family. Harder than some." Mama knowed I was makin' a hint about my youngest brother, Orie— he was sixteen at the time, nigh on three years younger than me—what didn't never hardly lift a finger to do anything in and about the house, and didn't do much out in the fields.

Mama wouldn't never turn me no answer when I said them things about work. She knowed I was right in everything I said about that. Even when I was big with Solomon I worked in the fields and at the house. Sometime I would pick nigh on two hundred pounds of cotton. And I was still workin' a cucumber plot like just about all the womenfolk hereabouts. I would get up first light every other day in pickin' season and pick my bushes clean. Or sometime I would do my pickin' whilst the sun was goin' down. And when Mr. Buddy come by in his pickup truck every third day, I would have my cucumbers all ready for him to take to the pickle factory over in Browning. I had good crops, too. Matter of fact, I still got leftover money from my last two crops—right there in the house in my Bible.

Mama didn't mean them things she was sayin', anyhow. She was just put out with me cause I was bein' close-mouth about my business. She ain't no different from the rest of the folks hereabouts, just can't understand somebody what keep secrets. I reckon it woulda been kinda nice to tell her about James Tolliver. But I knowed if I told her she would tell somebody. Then that somebody would tell somebody else. So I just didn't part my lips at all—not even when I had to stand up in church and ask God and the congregation forgiveness for my sin and Reverend said, "Get it *all* off your chest, girl. Say who the daddy is so we can pray for his soul same as we prayin' for yours." I didn't say a word after I ask for my own forgiveness, just set back down like I didn't notice how everybody was cranin' they necks and gawkin' at me. I was thinkin' to myself how didn't nobody in that church care a thing about prayin' for the daddy soul, how they didn't want nothin' but somethin' else to run they mouths about. And I said to myself they had another think comin' if they thought I was goin' to answer for somebody else sins and mine too.

Wasn't no way James Tolliver was goin' to pay, anyway. Ain't no way he goin' to pay now. James daddy is the principal of the Lang Colored School. And his mama is a teacher in the school. Top of that, James is married now. To some girl he went to college with. That Morris College. Over in Sumter. Her daddy is a big-time professor over there. And James is studyin' to be one, too. Folks hereabouts think a education make a person a saint. They think can't nobody in that Tolliver family do no wrong. So wouldn't a soul believe it if I said how me and James used to have secret meetings in the woods. That's how I got my Solomon, but wouldn't nobody believe it on just my say-so.

Things between me and James got started one day when I was out in the woods gettin' fat lightenin' and he was out there huntin'. We just happen to run across each other. It was Christmas time and he was home from school. I was out of high school going on a year. I reckon what I'm sayin' here is even though James was older than me—nigh on three years—I wasn't no baby at the time. Anyway, he stopped to talk a bit, asked me wasn't I thinking about gettin' married yet—even though me and him and everybody else hereabouts knowed I didn't have no prospects. Then he got to talkin' about that Morris College, how there was people there from all over the United States, how some of the teachers was white, how he was studyin' to be a teacher. Whilst he was talkin', he set on the ground, said how come I didn't set, too. I set. After he got done talkin' about Morris College, he got to talkin' about me, how the single menfolk hereabouts musta been blind to leave a real woman like me to herself. I said he knowed as well as I did how everybody hereabouts called me fat as a sow, ugly as dirt and black as a pit from pole to pole—some foolishness that snotty-nose Joseph Murray from over in Piney Corner got out some schoolbook and put on me when we was way back in the eight grade. Then James Tolliver said, real soft and serious-like, "I mean the fine woman *inside* you."

Now I look back on it, I reckon it wasn't such a earthshakin' thing. But I thought different back then. At the time, them words and the way James said them was like all the dreams I ever had of a man touchin' me and holdin' me like I was a beautiful woman. It was like all them dreams rolled up into one. I shut my eyes to try and hold on to the feelin'. Next thing I knowed, James was touchin' me. Then he was kissin' me, and I was feelin' beautiful and womanlike for the first time and didn't never want to give up that feelin'. And even though I knowed James didn't mean it like I was feelin' it, even though I knowed he didn't mean me no good in the long run, I let him go on with the touchin' and kissin' and what come after.

Me and James went on meetin' in the woods the whole time he was home. Then I didn't see him no more till the end of the next June, when he come home from visitin' some of his people up north. By then, everybody hereabouts knowed I had a baby on the way. I had already been to church and begged and got forgiveness—for everything except not naming the daddy. I knowed in myself all along James wasn't goin' to own up to the baby I was carryin'. Yet and still I let myself wish it. Until he come back to Lang. Then when he was back for a while and didn't speak up, I said to myself, "So be it." And whenever I seen him in uptown Lang, I would say "How you doin'?" and keep on goin' about my business.

Solomon come the end of that September. He was a big, fat, black baby what was healthy and kickin' and squallin' from the minute he come out in this world. Far as looks go, only thing he had in common with his daddy was the fact he was black as a body could be. Everybody said Solomon was the picture of my brothers—after they near about looked a hole in him tryin' to figure out who his daddy was. They said he had the big shoulders and hands and feet of my brothers, and the same clear, smart-looking eyes and the same strong jaws and mouth. If you ask me, that ain't no different from how I look. Ain't no way it *can* be different being as I look just like my brothers. Trouble with that is it make me look too much like a man and not enough like a woman. So folks said Solomon was a good-looking baby cause he looked like a little man. If my baby woulda been a girl what looked like me, folks woulda gone behind my back and called her ugly. And she woulda had a hard row to hoe—same as me. Thank God Solomon wasn't no girl.

But like I was sayin', Solomon was a fine, fine baby. And sweet. Lord, seem like that child sucked love out of me I didn't know I had. He would look at me with them little eyes like I was the only person in the world. Or he would wrap his little hand around my finger and squeeze. And I would feel the love just pourin' out me. That was when I knowed what it mean to be a real woman. That was when I knowed bein' a woman don't have nothin' to do with all the time havin' a man around. And that was when I knowed it wasn't no sad or hard thing for a woman to have a baby to herself. Let the rest of these womenfolk have all the menfolk they want. I myself don't need no man all the time meddlin' in my doin's. I got everything I need in Solomon. Bad and troublesome as he can be sometime, I still got the same feelin's I had for him when he was brand new.

So naturally, when James got married to that girl back in June and went off to live in Sumter, I said to myself, "Hallelujah and Amen and Good Riddance," and went on livin' my life without missin' a beat. Matter of fact, it wasn't long after that—the middle of November—when Mama Greene passed on and left this house empty and I went to see Mr. Otis Greene about movin' in. I was a woman with a baby to raise, and look like I was one woman too many in my mama house. She was all the time tryin' to tell me how to take care of Solomon and I was all the time tellin' her I didn't need no help. Next thing you know, we would be whoopin' and hollerin' at each other and my daddy would be tellin' me how I had to show respect for Mama long as I was livin' under her roof. Then there was Orie and his nastiness. He took to callin' Solomon, "Stranger." Then me and him would fight. Mama wouldn't say much of nothin', just, "Quit that, Orie." I would tell Mama how she wasn't doin' right, how she was standin' by and lettin' Orie mistreat my child cause she was het up about me not namin' the daddy. Me and her would end up fussin' again and Daddy would step in and put it all on me—one more time.

And folks never did stop runnin' they mouths about me. A while back, Orie come home one night from the Come One Come All and said word was out that crazy old Saunamana Dupree from over in Piney Corner was Solomon daddy. He said folks was askin' Saunamana was he the daddy and Saunamana was grinnin' like he had a secret and tellin' folks, "I ain't sayin' nothin'." I got so mad I woulda foamed at the mouth if I was a dog. Wasn't no way I would ever be hard up enough to lay with somebody simpleminded as Saunamana Dupree. He so off in the head he don't hardly know his own name. For a minute there, I had a mind to let on how Solomon daddy is a educated man. Then it come to me how Orie and everybody else was pointin' the finger at Saunamana just to make me mad enough to name the real daddy. So I said to Orie, "I might be ugly, but I ain't no fool." Orie said, "If you ask me, you both." Next thing you know, me and Orie was fightin', and when it end up Mama and Daddy was puttin' the blame on me.

So I'm out here now, stayin' in this old house what Mr. Otis growed up in and what Mama Greene stayed in by herself till the day she drawed her last breath. Mama Greene was out here tryin' to mind her own business, too. She wouldn't move in with Mr. Otis and Sister Ruth and they children after Daddy Greene passed on. Just stayed out here to herself. She quit visitin', quit goin' to hog slaughterin's and cannin' parties and quiltin' bees. She even quit going to wakes and to church. And she quit havin' company outside of Mr. Otis and his family. Other folks would knock on the door and she just wouldn't answer.

Folks near about worried theyselfs to death wonderin' after why Mama Greene stayed to herself like that. Early on, about a month after Daddy Greene was put in his grave, folks took to askin' Mr. Otis was Mama Greene sick or somethin' and if she was sick how come she wouldn't send out word and take shut-in visits like anybody else would do. Mr. Otis would say Mama Greene was plain and simple griefin' after Daddy Greene and was put out with God and everybody else cause Daddy Greene was took from her. Folks would say they could kinda understand that, could see how some people might be strange in they grief—especially a woman what lost her husband when she wasn't nothing but fifty-five years old. Now I look back on it, I can see clear as day why Mama Greene had reason to be put out with everything livin'—whether she *was* or not. If I was her and had a good man—and Daddy Greene was a good man—die on me whilst the both of us was still young, I would be put out, too. That ain't to say I'm pinin' after a man, you understand. Like I said, I don't need no man. I'm takin' care of me and Solomon just fine by myself.

Anyway, folks would say they could understand how Mama Greene might want to be by herself in her grief. They would say this to Mr. Otis face. Behind his back, they said they couldn't understand why Mama Greene was being so stand-offish with her own blood kins. They went on and on about how she wouldn't have nothin' to do with Mr. Otis and Sister Ruth and they children except on Saturdays—when they would bring her supplies and do whatever she needed done—Wednesday nights, every other Sunday afternoon and holidays. If you ask me, that's plenty enough company—even for somebody what ain't tryin' to have some time to theyself.

Anyway, when time went on and Mama Greene went on stayin' to herself, folks took to makin' up what they didn't know. Next thing you know word was goin' around that Mama Greene was more than likely carryin' on with some man. Folks said there wasn't no other sensible reason why she was bein' so stand-offish. They said there wasn't that much griefin' in the world—except for somebody old. They said Mama Greene was a young woman with plenty sap left—too much to lose interest in everything, especially menfolk. They said it musta been a married man or a man too young for a woman her age to be carryin' on with. They said that was more than likely why she quit goin' to church, said she probably couldn't bring herself to set foot in the House of God whilst she was sinnin' so bad. Folks even took to dredgin' up Mama Greene past life, talkin' about how they wouldn't put nothin' past her since she wasn't no angel in her young days.

I can't say where all that talk got started, but Sister Ruth mouth was right in there with the rest. I used to hear my mama tellin' my daddy or one or another of the womenfolk that such and such a one said Sister Ruth said this thing or that thing about Mama Greene. Everything Sister Ruth said always got down to one thing: every time her or Mr. Otis or one of they children went to see Mama Greene, Mama Greene would try to hurry them off—like she was tryin' to hide somethin' or like she was expectin' somebody she didn't want them to see. I ain't sayin' Sister Ruth was the one what started all the talk. All I'm sayin' is she surely did help keep it goin'. And if you ask me, she shoulda kept her mouth shut out of respect for Mr. Otis. If I had a nice husband like Mr. Otis, I surely wouldn't go around badmouthin' his mama. Not that I want a man. I'm just sayin' if you got a nice one you oughta treat him right. That's all I'm sayin'.

But about Mama Greene and this man. Didn't nobody never see any man. But folks sure did try to get sight of him. They took to ridin' out in these woods in they wagons—makin' out they was lookin' for berries, hickory nuts, herbs, pine-straw and moss for they sweet potatoe banks and such, fat lightenin' for they fires. Like this little section of woods was the only place in the world they could find such stuff. They'd ride past the house, cranin' they necks and gawkin' like fools. I come out here a time or two with my mama and brothers, cranin' my neck and gawkin' like the rest. Shameful was what it was. Folks carried on like a little sliver of Mama Greene business was a ticket to Heaven. But that's how folks is hereabouts. They got to know every little bit of everybody business. And if you don't let your business be known, they'll make some up. I hope to God they don't start comin' out here harrassin' me. I been out here nigh on three weeks now and ain't nobody come snoopin' yet. Course that don't mean they won't start. I don't have no doubts about that. They'll start up that foolishness soon. And Lord knows I ain't lookin' forward to it. Not one bit.

But back to Mama Greene. Folks went on ridin' out here harrassin' her for nigh on a year. Then Mama Greene put a stop to it. She took to runnin' out on the front porch with Daddy Greene old huntin' rifle and shootin' bullets up in the air. She didn't do it but three or four times before folks left her be. They was scared somebody was goin' to get hit with a stray bullet, specially after Sister Bernice Keels from over in Piney Corner claimed she was walkin' to her mailbox one day and had to duck out the way of one of them bullets. Didn't nobody stop to wonder how Sister Bernice—or anybody else for that matter—could move so fast as to duck a bullet. Didn't nobody think about how she was so old and stiff till her folks had to go by her place three and four times a day and do everything for her—right down to emptyin' her night pot—and how one of her grandchildren had to stay with her every night in case she got real sick. Didn't nobody wonder neither about how that bullet musta changed direction before it went whizzin' after Sister Bernice clear on the other end of Piney Corner.

Anyway, folks left Mama Greene be after she shot them bullets up in the air. And didn't nobody see hide nor hair of her until she passed on and was laid out in Mr. Otis front room. But folks never did stop runnin' they mouths about her. And when she was laid out, everybody went over to Mr. Otis house to stare at her body and talk some more. Some of the womenfolk said she didn't look like a woman what was without a man all that time—eleven years. They said she had the look of a woman what wasn't never without a man. Far as I could see, she just looked old and dead. And I thought to myself how folks was meddlin' after Mama Greene even when she was gone to her final rest.

Like I said, I'm livin' out here tryin' to mind my own business like Mama Greene done. And I wouldn't leave if the Devil hisself come out here after me or if the Piney Corner bad-luck ghost—Old Woman—come out the swamp and show herself to me every day. I won't leave even after what happened last night. Lord, what a fright that was. I was layin' in my bed, sleepin' away, when somethin' come to me and said, "Wake up, girl. You. Hester Bell Budd." So I did. Just like that. And what you reckon was the matter? There was a great big old snake layin' up next to me in the bed, tryin' to keep warm same as me. I could tell it was a snake, and a big one, by the feel of it next to my skin. It was all dry and crusty-feelin'—like a old person heels look—and there was this heaviness to it.

I jumped out that bed so fast it's a wonder some of me didn't stay behind. I can't recollect ever movin' so fast before in my life—except maybe when I was a little thing runnin' like crazy cause I thought the Hag was flyin' after me. Anyway, I jumped out the bed, bunched up the bedclothes in a ball and set off runnin' through the house with the whole mess. Time I got in the back yard, I seen the shovel lean' up against the side of the house. I went runnin' to where the shovel was, dropped the bedclothes, snatched up the shovel real quick and commenced poundin' the bedclothes with it. The bedclothes loosened up some and I could see somethin' wigglin' around under the sheets. I took to stabbin' real hard with the sharp tip of the shovel. I went on stabbin' till the sheets was all cut up and wasn't nothin' movin' no more. Then I opened up the sheets and seen this great big old king snake. I put the shovel down right away, since I knowed king snakes don't have poison. Whilst I was standin' there lookin' at that snake, it come to me how it coulda been a rattler, how it coulda bit me and left me layin' in my bed to die, how it coulda crawled on over to where Solomon was sleepin' and bit him, too. Them thoughts made me crazy mad. And next thing I knowed I was jumpin' up and down on that dead snake like some kind of fool.

Right when I was up in the air one time, comin' down to stomp that snake again, somethin' come to me and said, "Girl, you need to quit. What you doin' out here in this frost cold night, in nothin' but your nightgown, jumpin' up and down on a dead snake?" I quit jumpin' and thought how simple I musta looked out there. The thought made me break out laughin'. And there I was in the middle of the night in the middle of the woods, laughin' out loud all by myself. Right when I was enjoyin' the laughin' real good, something come to me and said, "What you need to do is get back in that house. Could be a snake in the bed with your baby. Could be it ain't a king. Could be it's a rattler."

Next thing I knowed I was screamin' and runnin' for the house. Time I got to the back porch, it come to me I didn't have nothin' in my hands to kill a snake with. Same time, I knowed wasn't no way I could make myself stop to look for somethin' or go back for the shovel. Another thought said there wasn't no way I could beat a snake to death whilst it was in the bed with my baby, anyhow—not without hurtin' my baby, too. All the time these different things was spinnin' round in my head, I was steady screamin' and runnin'. Across the porch. Through the kitchen. Across the hall. Then I was in the room where me and Solomon sleep, snatchin' the covers off Solomon and jerkin' him out the bed. There wasn't no snake. Just me carryin' on like there was. And Solomon big-eyed and bawlin' cause of my carryin' on. I reckon we musta been a sight—me goin' from screamin' to cryin' to laughin' all loud and squeezin' Solomon till he almost lost his breath and Solomon goin' from bawlin' to lookin' at me like he was scared of me to laughin' cause I was laughin' to bawlin' again cause I was squeezin' him so hard.

Time I got me and Solomon calmed down, I could see little traces of firstlight in the sky over the woods. So I put a fire in the stove and got us some breakfast. Then I got us washed up and bundled up good and warm and we come outside so I could feed the pig and chickens what my folks give me and the mule what my daddy lettin' me use till I can get one of my own. That won't be hard to do. Mr. Otis don't charge but fifteen dollars a month cause he mainly want somebody to stay here so the house won't get run-down. I still got my cucumber patch. My daddy say it mine no matter what. I can make money in cucumber season and then hire myself out workin' tobacco and pickin' cotton. I can buy me a mule and still be set good for takin' care of me and Solomon. Come another year, I might even be able to replace this old wagon what my daddy give me.

So I got the chickens and pig and mule fed. Then I hitched up the mule and wagon and me and Solomon went in the woods and got some moss and pine straw. I took the ax and a sack with me, and whilst we was, me and Solomon got some fat lightenin' and hickory nuts. I reckon we made a mornin' of it. Time we got back, I fixed us somethin' to eat. Then I went through the house real good, lookin' for snakes. After that, I put Solomon down for a nap.

Now I'm out here stuffin' all the cracks and holes I can find with moss and pine straw mixed up with mud. I ain't about to ask nobody for help. Aside from that, I ain't about to go out of these woods till I have to. And I made sure when I come back here that I wouldn't have to leave for nigh on a whole winter. When my folks helped me move out here, I brought plenty supplies. Only reason I'll have to go anywhere is if me or Solomon get sick enough to need doctorin'. Like I said, all I want is to mind my own business. Course I know everybody runnin' they mouths about me and wonderin' after what I'm doin' back here. I can just hear the talk. and I reckon they near about worry my folks to death askin' after why I'm stayin' off to myself like this. I can just see them questionin' my folks after them two times they come back here to visit. I reckon it's much worse than before I come back here. Well, maybe folks was givin' my business a rest a good little spell before I come back here. I can see that now I think on it. But that don't mean nothin'. Like I said before, they'll start comin' out here pretty soon, cranin' they necks and gawkin'—just like they done Mama Greene. They'll start any day now. That's how come I listen for wagon wheels every day. Maybe even a car engine. Not that I'm lookin' forward to it. Lord, no. And when they start comin', I don't have a notion what I might do. I might stay in the house with the door shut. Then again, I might come out and say,

"How do?" I might let it go on a while, just stayin' in the house. Then I might come out and shoot up in the air with this rifle what my daddy give me—in case I need it for bobcats and such. No tellin' what I might do if it anybody but James Tolliver.

If it James Tolliver—if he ever break up with that girl he married and come back here tryin' to see me and my Solomon—I'll get out my gun for sure. I can see it now. James Tolliver drivin' up in this yard. Not in no wagon, but in that car I hear tell he got now. I'll wait good till he get out the car and come walkin' to the front door. Right when he get midway the house and his car, I'll bring Solomon to the door. I'll leave Solomon standin' behind the screen, and I myself will push open the door with the barrel of my gun and ease out on the porch. Then I'll point my gun at James Tolliver heart and say, "What you doin' back here after all this time? Surely there can't be nothin' back in these here woods you want." He'll be so took by surprise and so scared he'll stop dead in his tracks and start sputterin' at the mouth, tryin' to talk. "Speak up," I'll say. I'll say this every time he try to talk. And all the while I'll have my gun pointin' right at his heart. Then I'll motion my head to where Solomon will be standin' behind the screen. And I'll say, "Who the daddy of this child?" I'll wait for a answer, then. And when he answer, when he say, "Me, James Tolliver," I'll say, "Speak up. Say it louder. Say, 'I, James Tolliver, is the daddy of Solomon what is the child of Hester Bell Budd.'" I'll make him holler this till I hear in his voice how he repent of the wrong he done me and Solomon—the same way I long ago repent for my sin—and how he maybe do care about us a little. Then no tellin' what I might do after that.

The Sources of "When They Come"

*W*HEN one of my former teachers invited me to participate in a writing project on the transformation of biographical material in fiction, I instantly and enthusiastically accepted. I had been for some time—from the time I had written my first story, in fact—fascinated with and disturbed by what I saw in much of my work as a hazy, shifting, almost nonexistent line between fact and invention, between biography and fiction. I chose, then, to write about the transformation of biographical material in what I considered my most fact-based story, a story based on someone I once knew. And I set to work, anxious to discover what I had written (fiction or something else), and if indeed I had written fiction, how I had transformed fact into story. Although I approached my project with some anxiety, I was also confident that I would proceed with little difficulty. I would, after all, be writing about my own work.

I did progress fairly smoothly. Over the course of a week, working an hour or two a day and encountering no more (perhaps a little less) than the usual difficulties of writing—the stops and starts, those moments of paralyzing chaos and those of generative insight—I wrote this:

> When I was growing up in pre-nineteen sixties rural South Carolina, there was in my community a woman (I will refer to her here as Jane) who, during her late teens, gave birth to three illegitimate children. All three children were fathered by the same man, an unmarried rake in his early to middle twenties. As there was nothing remarkable about this man's appearance—he was dark, of medium height and build, and had "regular enough" features (which means that his facial features were sufficiently keen or non-Negroid) we thought him neither handsome nor ugly. So whenever his "looks" were appraised—and no one in our community escaped such appraisal—he was judged merely "passable," "nothing to write home about."
>
> Jane was unattractive by conventional standards. She was short (just over four feet), which was acceptable in a woman. But she was also big and muscular and square. Her hair was woolly, her lips large and thick, her nose broad, flat at the bridge and flared at the nostrils. And her skin was very black, inky black with no hint of brown. We considered her looks the epitome of ugliness, and often, one or another of us, either deliberately or inadvertently, expressed this view within her hearing.
>
> Jane was also slightly mentally retarded—at least she seemed and was considered so. In school, she could not keep pace with students her age, and by the time she reached high school, she had repeated one or two (perhaps more) grades. When she was in the ninth grade, she finally dropped out of school. Afterward, she spent most of her time with her immediate family (mother, father, older brother) either at home or working in the fields. And although she was three or four years my senior, it was Jane's custom to play with me and other children my age. In fact, she was a favorite of the younger children in the community. When I was between the ages (approximately) of eight and twelve, I regularly went with one or two of my sisters and other children from nearby farms to play with Jane at her house after Sunday dinner. We played hide-and-seek, pop-the-whip, bull-in-the-ring, dodge-ball, tag—all sorts of rowdy children's games. If we played house that was rowdy, too. There was always some catastrophe imagined by Jane: a family in a wagon being pulled by a runaway mule, for instance.
>
> At some point during the afternoon, Jane would put on a "show" for us. She was a wonderful mimic—at least we thought so at the time. She would climb upon the chopping block in her back yard and imitate the various people of our town: our parents, teachers, principal, minister, the eccentrics of our community (like old Mr. Sink who walked from farmhouse to farmhouse frightening children with stories of ghosts, the Devil, the Hag, and afterward giving them stale and dirty bits of candy and cookies from his pockets); she imitated the affluent whites who lived uptown, the "poor white trash" who lived on the outskirts.

Alone with us children and her immediate family, Jane was boisterous, loud and full of rough energy, bossy, even. In the presence of others, particularly her peers, she was reticent, shy. She seldom spoke to these others and they seldom spoke to her. When one of them did speak to her, Jane's face closed up, turned neutral, and she did not respond for long moments—if she responded at all. When she did respond, her reply was brief, perfunctory, her voice hardly more that a murmur. She was often called "dumb," "simpleminded," "slow," "off in the head." And although I liked Jane, played with her, had fun with her, I grew up with the conviction that I and many others in the community were "better" than her.

My most concrete memory of Jane involves one of her Sunday afternoon shows. Despite the intervening years—more than twenty-five—this memory comes to me with the vividness of the presence, the clarity with which I see my fingers, here and now, pressing the keys of my typewriter. It is a hot summer Sunday afternoon, in late summer, it seems, because the heat is at that high pitch and heaviness which in my town used to come just before sundown in late August and early September. I am sitting with my playmates in Jane's woodyard, woodchips and sawdust sticking to my damp legs, my nose full of the odors of perspiring bodies, cut wood, animal droppings mixed with heat and dirt. Jane is up there on the chopping block mimicking Reverend. She is rolling her eyes, gesturing, moving her body with the rhythm of her speech as she laments our "low-down, dirty lifes" and warns us of the fire and brimstone of Judgement Day. We are laughing, cheering Jane on with imitations of our parents' preaching Sunday behavior: "Amen!" "Preach it!" "Pull it Reveren'!" "Don' hol' back!" Soon we will be on our feet dancing the Holy dance like Mrs. Bembow, then stretching out on the ground, moaning, our bodies twitching in memory of the visit of the Holy Ghost.

Suddenly, Jane stops, stares past us. At first, I think one of her parents has come outside to scold us for "Blaspheming." But when I turn around, I see that some older girls, girls Jane's age (thirteen or fourteen years old), have come out of the woods adjacent to the front of Jane's house and stopped on the front path—which leads to the clay road that cuts through our community—to watch Jane's performance. They giggle and nudge one another.

Jane does not move. She just stands there on the block looking past us, past the big girls and the pasture behind them, toward the railroad crossing beyond. She has that blank look on her face, the one that proves she's not all there. She looks like she thinks she's alone, like she doesn't have a notion that there are other people around.

In this little space of time—so tiny, so quick, like one flutter of a hummingbird's wing—something scary tries to tell itself to me. But I can't quite get it, and I feel like I do when I try to figure out where God came from.

Then the moment was over. Seeing that Jane was determined not to perform for them, the girls turned away and continued along the path toward the clay road. Jane let out a loud "Whoo!" Then she jumped to the ground, yelled, "It-tag," tagged one of us children and took off running. Then we were all screaming and running wildly, the girls forgotten.

Our alienation of Jane stemmed only partly from prejudice against what we saw as ugliness and retardation. She came from what we considered one of the lowest classes of people. Her parents owned no land, but sharecropped and rented. They had no claim to white or otherwise non-black blood, no educated, business-owning or otherwise "notable" relatives. And they were barely literate, unable to read, write or speak ("proper" English) very well.

But since her parents were hard-working, God-fearing, peaceful, clean people (that is, "decent" people), our community awarded them a certain position of prominence, a certain respect—the kind withheld from the shiftless, the promiscuous, the slovenly, the lawless. In our class system, you see, there were the "no-account Negroes" at the bottom, then the "white trash" (better only by virtue of their whiteness), then people like Jane's parents, "decent" people with nothing else to recommend them, and so on to the top of the scale where resided the best class of whites, and parallel to them, but a little lower, the best class of blacks.

This, as I look back through the haze of time, of subsequent experience, is how I remember our shared view of reality, the world, ourselves and others in the world. And I remember something else, another, deeper part of our shared identity where existed something like an opposing view, one which permitted us to entertain the possibility that, ultimately, blacks were superior to whites. Had whites not invented that brutalizing evil, slavery? And had blacks not borne it with a Christ-like patience and come out in the end not brutalized, after all, but miraculously egalitarian in their outlook and behavior? And did this not suggest that, perhaps, whites were essentially evil and blacks essentially good?

But was this, finally, an opposing view? Was it, in the final analysis, different from basic supremacist ideology which has been and still is the root of so much bitterness and brutality and ruin in the world, that stubborn, knotted root which obscures view of a middle ground? How, finally, is this essentially different from those limited and limiting views which define to death—a certain kind of death—women, blacks, Jews, homosexuals, intellectuals, middle and upper-class white men, even?

There is no real difference, finally. As I recall, the blacks of the segregated community of my youth were—in their quest to achieve a sense of worth, a sense of belonging—no less human than whites, no less prone to frailty, no less caught in the root of our culture.

Convention, then, dictated our treatment of Jane and her parents. Because of Jane's "retardation" and her parents' "decency," the people of my community did not censure or ostracize Jane and her parents during Jane's first pregnancy (which most certainly would not have been the case had Jane "had her right mind" and belonged to a higher or lower class of people). I remember my mother and her friends referring to Jane and her parents as "that poor girl" and "those poor people." And I remember my mother making it a point to talk to Jane's parents whenever she saw them. "There come those poor people," she would say when she saw them—a tall, skinny man and a short, plump woman, both very black like Jane—driving their wagon along the clay road toward our house. Then she would hurry out to the road, hail them and talk with them a while.

Although she spoke to them with respect, there was a haughtiness in my mother's manner when she talked with Jane's parents—as if she were speaking from a height. She was, of course, speaking from a height. She was the daughter of a store-owning minister who also owned some property in the city of Sumter. (It did not matter that the store brought little—if any—profit as it catered to poor blacks who generally bought on credit and often did not pay in money, but in services or goods.) And she had married into one of the most prominent black families of our town: her in-laws were among the largest black land owners in the area; her father-in-law was a well-known, much-respected travelling Missionary; her mother-in-law was the daughter of a German whose blood was clearly visible in the skin, hair and features of the family members; and finally, four of her sisters and brothers-in-law had attended college and two of them had earned degrees. (It did not matter that my father had not earned a degree.) So my mother was justifiably condescending in her attitude toward Jane's parents. And Jane's parents, knowing and keeping to their place, responded with proper deference.

The father of Jane's child—whose identity Jane and her parents did not hesitate to divulge (partly because it was understood that people of their class had no right to such privacy)—was treated differently. He was called "that low-down, dirty dog who ought to be put *under* the jailhouse for taking advantage of a girl like Jane." And often, because he was from a "no-account" family, he and his parents were "told off" about Jane's and her parents' predicament. It was, after all, the right and duty of the "better" people to monitor the behavior of the others.

Attitudes changed with Jane's second and third pregnancies. She was no longer pitied, but regarded as something of a slut. After all, she wasn't so slow that she couldn't learn from experience. And her parents were scolded for not "taking Jane in hand." Jane became known as a bad influence and her parents as incompetents. Children were no longer permitted to visit their house. The father of the children was no longer blamed, though he was still considered a "low-down, dirty dog."

The last time I saw Jane, she was riding in the back of her parents' wagon, one child on her lap, one on either side of her. I left the South shortly thereafter, and I have not seen Jane since. The last news I had of her was a story one of my sisters told me years ago. She said that for a brief time, Jane had lived with her children in an old abandoned farmhouse, and had moved back in with her parents after waking up one night and finding a rattlesnake in bed with her.

This marks the end of what I initially wrote, and the place where I encountered a not unexpected difficulty. I had intended to go on to explain how I had used the facts of my experiences with Jane as a basis for "When They Come," how I had transformed those experiences into fiction. But I could not go on because I knew that much of what I had put down as remembered experience was instead fiction. I had known this even as I wrote, but had been incapable—or unwilling—to stop and set things right.

I do not remember Jane's face so clearly as I described it. When I try to visualize her face, I see only a dark blur. I recall only that her skin was very dark, that her features were not what the people of my community considered "regular enough." Nor do I recall going often to Jane's house to play with her. I remember playing in her yard perhaps two or three times, and I vaguely remember Jane standing on some elevated surface in her back yard imitating our minister. What I recall most clearly about that particular occasion is that Jane was doing something "nasty": she was pretending that our minister was speculating about the underwear of the women in the congregation. This, in fact, is my strongest recollection of an actual experience with Jane. And there is one other memory, almost as strong, but detached now from a particular experience. I see Jane, imagine her, feel her (perhaps on the school bus) laughing. Her mouth, though I cannot actually see it, has the shape of stupidity—sort of slack and lopsided. Her laughter is loud, has a desperate ring. That ring, I think, that shrillness, that sharpness, is the knife of Jane—her loneliness and desire—trying to cut into belongingness, that place where, because she is not "good" enough, she is not permitted.

Strangely, my most vivid image of Jane comes to me not from memory of an actual experience with her, but from the story my sister told me years—two, three, maybe four—after I had seen Jane for the last time. I do not recall thinking about this story, mulling it over, but one day it burst into an image which had attached to it a story of it own. I saw a strong, young woman, healthy, willful, but also weak, vulnerable. She was alone for some reason, cut off from fellowship, and intensely, grudgingly lonely. Her name—which came to me with perfect certainty—was Hester Bell. (I would not know her last name, Budd, until a friend told it to me after hearing the partially written story.) And Hester Bell's story was—is—"When They Come."

"When They Come" is the story of a woman who has been ostracized by the people of her community. And she has come far out into the swampy woods to live alone with her illegitimate child. She imagines, and protests in her own way, that she has had it with society, community, the brutalities involved in human connections, social ties, the rituals of civilized existence, declares that she will not go back for fear of Satan, ghosts or snakes. But she is deliberately deepening her alienation in order *to* belong, but more on her own terms. Her terms, however, are finally no different from those of the others. She wants a position of prominence. She wants, in a sense, to dominate. On the one hand, she laments the privileged positions of men over women, the educated over the less educated. On the other hand, she looks down on someone like Saunamana Dupree. She is smarter than Saunamana, therefore she is better. So Hester Bell

Budd is human, whatever else she may be. And in her quest for a different, better kind of prominence, she tries to create an air of secrecy about herself, her life, which, hopefully, will draw the curiosity, the interest of the community, and perhaps even of the father of her child. And she waits, with a Christ-like patience and faith—which is also, in a sense, Satanic—wondering not *if*, but *when*, they will come.

Hester Bell Budd is, then, in a sense, a very real sense, the Jane of my youth, the Jane of the community of my youth, but a Jane distilled—that is, fragmented and then re-formed into an essence—by a changing vision, a Jane seen from a different, calmer, perhaps safer vantage point, a Jane re-called through the gauze of memory which at once obscures and illuminates, shields and reveals.

I am inclined, now, to believe that the first pages of this essay, those which contain so much fiction parading as fact, as actual remembered experience, represent a draft, the next-to-final draft, of "When They Come." In my inner life, my most real life which, paradoxically, is most hidden from me, I molded and re-molded, I think, the fragments which comprise this story. And then something—I do not know what—brought the bits and pieces together into a unity of thought and feeling so precise, so true for me, that in an essay about this unity, this story, my main character took charge, revealed to me the material from which I drew her essence.

This, I think, is the nature and function of memory in storytelling, in life, actually. All a writer has, all anybody has, finally, is memory. Experience passes. Memory—fragile and potent—is all that remains.

◌ QUESTIONS ◌

Barbara Mellix's story, "When They Come," and its process essay, "The Sources of 'When They Come'"

1. Unlike the other stories and essays you've read thus far, this story is written in a dialect. How did this influence your reading as you began the story? Did you struggle more with this reading because of the dialect than with others? When did you find that you were comfortable with it? Did you respect Hester Bell any less than you would have if she had spoken, as Mellix describes it, "proper English"?

2. How aware is Hester Bell of her predicament, her perceptions, her feelings? She speaks in depth about Mama Greene. Did she want others to notice her as Mama Greene was noticed? With whom is she angry? Are her perceptions of people and the way they talk of others accurate? Is she guilty of such talk herself? In her imagined encounter with James Tolliver at the story's end, what has she gained that she hasn't had through the rest of the story?

3. In her process essay, Mellix writes of "basic supremacist ideology" that dictates not only our attitudes toward people of other races, but people of the same race whose attitudes, preferences, ideas, concerns, religion, wealth differ from our own. She goes on to show how Jane and her family were regarded by those in her community. Is Mellix's perception that racism, prejudice, and persecution are "caught in the root of our culture" an accurate one? Can you think of particular examples that support or contradict this contention? Are such attitudes as pervasive a Mellix describes them? Are they more so? Mellix writes toward the end of her essay that her description of Jane is essentially fictitious. Does this undermine the arguments she has made?

4. Mellix writes at the end of her essay, "All a writer has, all anybody has, finally, is memory. Experience passes. Memory—fragile and potent—is all that remains." In what ways does she help you understand this, and how is this supported in her essay and story? If, indeed, "experience passes," what does memory of that experience come to mean, and how is it "fragile and potent"?

Possible Writing Topics

1. Write an essay where you describe a person who, for whatever reason, is regarded differently in your community, a person about whom people talk. It need not be someone poor or rich or exceptionally eccentric; that is for you to choose. Try to include specific conversation you've heard people have about this person, and how this has influenced your perception of him or her. Do you have a perspective on this person that, because of your experience, others don't have? Would you describe the treatment the person receives as fair, to be expected? Or is there something wrong with this treatment?

2. After completing the first essay, write a second one where you describe the accuracy of what you've written. Did you, like Mellix, create a person that is partly fictitious? Of all the things you described, how much do you know to be true? Before you wrote the essay, how much of what you heard about this person did you believe to be true? Has your perception changed as a result of writing the first essay? When you think of your community's perception of this person, how important do you believe truth or accuracy is to the community?

Kathleen A. Coppula

Reason

KAREN bounced down the stairway to the entrance hall, letting her waist-length black hair wave and fall with each bounce. She was in her fourth year of worldly experience: fourth classroom, fourth reader, fourth teacher. She'd begun the experience with eyes wide open, but lately, she felt safer with her head lowered or with her eyelids at half-mast and pupils in shadow— a balance between the state of knowing and the sin of pride.

She took a single deep breath to compose herself and walked cautiously (lady-like), with her brush and hair ties in hand, to the kitchen where her Aunt Sarah sat drinking coffee at the table. Aunt Sarah had her stand for inspection, and though she focused her attention on the sharp knee bumps under her aunt's pink paisley housecoat, she felt the movement of her aunt's eyes gliding like an iron over the roots of her hair to her face and neck, then over the white blouse and plaid skirt to the tops of her white knee socks on her slightly bowed legs (which she tried in vain to squeeze closed), and finally to the polished black and white saddle shoes. She was roughly pivoted for the back view.

"I don't *see* anything out of place," Aunt Sarah said, leaving open, as always, the possibility of an overlooked flaw, a doubt for Karen to carry with her through the day. Aunt Sarah tugged her closer, split her hair down the back with the brush and began the capable braiding that kept her hair restrained from breezes and random motion—solid reins for her baby brother Chucky when she let him ride her horseback after school. Her aunt slipped the brush into her housecoat pocket, scrubbed her hands at the sink and began making the breakfasts, one at a time, starting with eggs for Karen, who was the first one dressed every morning.

She gobbled the breakfast, without which her aunt wouldn't dream of letting her leave the house. Then she hurried back upstairs. She went past her father's room, which her older sister Charlene called the Master Bedroom. Charlene could remember when their mother was alive and shared the room with their father. She often told Karen stories of how lovely their mother had been, and of all the beautiful things once in that room. Since her own memory could not verify all of these stories, Karen often refuted them, telling Charlene, "You don't know that." Charlene only shrugged and walked away. Then Karen would seek out Chucky, who had no memory of any mother. She would make him listen to her own stories, a combination of memory, hearsay, and invention. But Chucky's attention rarely budged from his plastic toy soldiers or his ball.

Her father was in the bathroom combing his hair in front of the mirror, Chucky at his right side. Her father ran the comb through Chucky's hair and they turned together to go down for breakfast. "Morning, Sweets," her father said.

She smiled for him. "Hi, Daddy," she said. She lingered in the hallway to watch him, his hand on Chucky's shoulder as they walked away from her. She listened a moment to Charlene singing along with the radio music in their room.

She brushed her teeth and ran down to the kitchen to kiss her father goodbye, pushing a kiss just in front of his left ear. He said, "Hmm? Leaving? Okay, okay." Then he turned the little attention he had at that time of the morning to his plate of toast and eggs that her Aunt Sarah slid onto the table for him.

She told Chucky, "Be a good boy today," and gave him a hug, but he was grouchy and he pushed her away.

She snatched up her bookbag and coat from the hallway and stood at the picture window in the living room where she watched for the bus to show itself at the top of the hill, giving her enough time to get out to the bus stop in front of her house before it wound its way there finally. Hers was the last bus stop, which meant she could never take a whole seat to herself like the others did. Sometimes she dreamed of empty seats on all sides of her own and, in the dreams, she could put her feet up on the back of the seat in front of her and kick at the air undisturbed. She stood just behind the driver rather than sit with anyone that morning. The driver, Mr. Whittaker, said, "Maybe you should sit down, honey," but knowing he never enforced the suggestion, Karen clung to the metal pole with both hands, her bookbag swinging with the sway of the bus.

In front of her school, she held her breath and marched herself with all her effort down the three tall steps from the bus and through the open doorway to her locker. She took as long as she could to remove her coat and hang it in the locker. Then she took her books out of the bookbag, one by one, and piled them on the floor before hanging the bag next to her coat. She looked over her shoulder, seeing that the other children had already gone into their classrooms. Then she reached into her coat pocket and pulled out the troll doll that she had decided was her lucky charm, because it was her favorite with its rainbow-colored hair. The ugly face grinned up at her from her hand: squinted eyes, flattened nose and a smile that split the face in two. The students were no longer permitted to bring these troll dolls to school. Sister Ada Marie had proclaimed the toy a pagan idol. So she secretly stroked the pointed hair from root to tip, three times slowly, then tickled her cheek with it once before hiding it away.

With the performance of her daily ritual came the hope that no one, meaning Sister Ada Marie, would see her at all that day. When she was ready to go home, Sister might say, "Why you were so good and quiet, I forgot you were even here today." But as usual, that did not happen. Sister Ada Marie came up behind her as she was closing her locker and grabbed her by the collar to turn her around. "You better be through that door before me and in your seat before I have the attendance book open."

Karen scrambled into the classroom, then into her own seat, pencil in hand. She had her legs crossed at the ankles and she jiggled her right foot as hard as she could to generate energy, repeating to herself, "Ready, set, go!"

Sister assigned them a story in the reading book and the corresponding workbook questions. Karen finished first, as usual, and from her seat in the back left corner, she watched the other students at work. She kept her pencil in waiting so that if Sister looked up from her desk she could pretend she was still hard at it. She was often in trouble for not working hard enough.

She remembered the possibility of the overlooked flaw in her appearance and touched the back of her head for the familiar smoothness of her hair, then felt her collar which was still turned down all the way around. She tucked her blouse more firmly into the waistband of her skirt, then inspected the back view of each of her classmates. She noted two untied shoelaces, a smudge on the shoulder of one boy's shirt, tangled hair on two girls, and one set of knee socks that drooped toward the ankles. She reached down to tug at her own socks, and had to be told twice to pass her worksheet forward. She hurried too much and the corner of the page tore when she tried to rip it along the perforated edges. She rubbed the tear, as if somehow she could reseal the flaw, but Bobby Robinson turned in the seat in front of her and grabbed the page from her. The torn corner remained trapped on the desk beneath her index finger. She rolled the scrap into a ball and pushed it inside her desk, back behind the books. But she shifted uneasily, thinking that somehow what she'd hidden would be exposed.

Just before lunch, her row was called to the blackboard. One by one, Sister reached over each student's head and wrote out a sentence to diagram. When she got to Karen, she wrote a sentence that was twice as long as the others: The girl who thinks that she knows all of the answers may find that, in time, some answers can change, that too often answers can be misleading, and that some answers were never actually correct, though other people confirmed them as both right and just.

Karen stared at the jumble of words. She concentrated, squeezing the chalk between her fingers. She told herself, "Just start. Gotta get started to finish." She circled "the girl," told herself, "next," and circled "may find." She was whispering to keep herself going, "Subject. Verb. Object." She slashed the sentence with chalk marks and made checks above the words she had accounted for in the diagram, chiseling the mass into shape piece by piece. She bit her lip.

Though she tried to close out any sounds, she heard Sister telling the others, "Well done. Very good." Sister dismissed the rest of the class for lunch before she could finish. After she finally set her chalk to rest in its tray, she stood alone with her hands crossed behind her back in the waiting position. Sister did not attend to her right away and she stood in silence waiting for Sister to notice her work. Finally, Sister waved her off without getting up from her desk. "It's correct. You may go," she said.

Karen got her lunch tray as most of her classmates were banging through the double metal doors into the first warm day on the playground. When she finished her lunch and dashed out to join them, the bell rang and the children lined up single file to return to the classroom. Karen took her place at the end of the line.

She needed a reason for Sister Ada Marie's meanness. She thought about the time when Charlene had cramps and stayed in bed all Saturday afternoon with a hot water bottle on her belly. Charlene had yelled at her, had made her fetch hot tea with lemon, and had demanded that she stay in the room with her in case she needed something. On her way back to her desk, Karen tried to detect the shape of a hot water bottle beneath Sister's habit. She saw nothing at all beneath the habit, which in its shapelessness was capable of hiding many things.

Sitting, hands folded on top of her desk, she was ashamed to have compared Charlene (common) to her teacher (blessed). She had been taught the difference—Charlene, "sister," the lower case *s*; Sister Ada Marie, "Sister," capitalized, always. She had now erred in thought, word, and deed. She had glanced at Sister's belly—looking, the sinful deed. She kept her eyes on her hands in front of her, in fear of what else she might see.

On the bus ride home, Karen sat in the last seat with a window and stared at the scenery rather than face the other children. That day, her senses aligned with each possibility of danger. Through the narrow opening of her window, she sniffed the smoke from someone burning papers in a metal drum and saw the flames rise and fall with the strength of the wind. She scanned the area around the burning and noted the dry grass in a field across the street and the tree limbs hovering too close to the fire. The bus moved on and she strained for the source of a siren, and later was startled by the screech of brakes and tires. She swallowed, trying to clear the taste of fumes as a truck let out a black cloud which spread over the bus and crept into her window. She rested her feet against the metal hump covering the bus' wheel, and grew uneasy when the metal vibrated her legs in an irregular rhythm, and when the wheel dropped into a pothole or rose over a buckling pavement.

When the children got off at the stop before hers, and she was the sole passenger, she took out the troll doll and squeezed it tight. She pressed it to her chest and fled the bus, running until she was safely on the covered front porch. She'd been sure that one of the satellites had failed its orbit and, burning through the atmosphere, would fall in heavy pieces to crush her.

She went inside the house where only Charlene and Chucky were at home watching TV. "Hey, Squirt," Charlene called to her.

"Shut up," she told her, nearly crying.

"Touchy, touchy." Charlene turned back to the TV and Chucky scowled up at Karen. She ran to her room, slammed the door, and threw herself on the bed. She stared at the ceiling and stroked the troll's bright hair. She brushed the soft hair across her cheek, moved it down along her throat, then gently over her wrists and soft palms, and to the inside of her thigh beneath the skirt until she grew calm and let her hand drop to her side.

Charlene came into the room but Karen did not move or speak. She let only her eyes turn to watch Charlene sit on her own bed, legs crossed. "You gonna tell me what happened today?" Charlene finally asked. "Or you expect me to guess?"

"I hate school. Sister picks on me."

"Oh she does, huh? Only poor little old you."

"It's true," Karen said, sitting up suddenly. "She hates me." She flopped flat on the bed again.

"Buck up, kid," Charlene told her, chipping off her white nail polish. "You think you're the only kid ever got stuck with a bitchy teacher?"

"But why's she do it, Char?"

"She don't need a reason," Charlene told her, shaking her head. "Come on downstairs now. Aunt Sarah made a bunch of those little apple tarts today. We can sneak one while she's at the store."

In the living room with Charlene and Chucky, she nibbled cautiously at the apple tart, finding it difficult to swallow a normal bite. She thought about what Charlene had said, but all she knew was that something in her sister's view was missing. When she heard Aunt Sarah coming in the kitchen door, she ran to help her with the grocery bags. When Aunt Sarah's arms were finally free, Karen nuzzled against her and clung tight, cheek resting on her aunt's high, bony hip.

"Heavens, child," Aunt Sarah said, prying herself loose and holding Karen by the shoulders at arm's length to look into her face. "Whatever did you *do*?"

"Why's everybody think *I* did something?" Karen asked, her hands now fisted against her hips. "Maybe I'm just an innocent victim."

Aunt Sarah raised her eyebrows. Then she pulled out one of the stiff wooden chairs and pointed to it, indicating that Karen should sit. "Out with it," she told Karen. "You must have done *something*, now what was it?" Karen crossed her arms against her chest and visually sealed her lips. "Well then," Aunt Sarah told her. "I suggest you go up to your room and think it over until dinner. Then we'll see what you have to say."

She went to her room determined not to think but to block her mind. She did all of her math problems, then read about Brazil in her Geography book and answered the questions at the end of the chapter. When Aunt Sarah still had not called her from her isolation, she got a clean sheet of paper and practiced writing with her left hand (in case she ever broke the right). She was midway on the sixth repetition of a lumpy-looking alphabet when Charlene came in and told her, "Dad's home and you're supposed to come to dinner."

Aunt Sarah waited to bring up the subject until she carried out the tray of apple tarts, rearranged now to cover the disappearance of three of them. She poured coffee for her brother, then filled her own cup. When she reseated herself to serve dessert and looked at the plate of tarts, she paused a moment. Karen held her breath, hoping that the theft would distract her and that the burden of the adult conversation might be distributed among all three of them.

"Karen seems to be having some sort of trouble in school," Aunt Sarah said, releasing the subject to hover over the table. Karen's breath shot out in a grunt at the sound of her name.

"Oh?" her father said.

She knew she was expected to answer, but instead, she swung her legs under the table and looked across to Charlene, who only stared down at the plate in front of her, no help at all. Chucky, on her right, between herself and her father, stood all the way up and faced her, waiting to hear what would happen next. She glared at him and said, "What are you looking at? Get back in your chair." But a glance at her father told her she could not divert the attention.

"Karen," her father said. "What's this about trouble in school? Is it true?"

She tried to flip her shoulder in the casual way Charlene used when she talked to her friends. "No big deal," she said, trying to make her voice deep. "Don't sweat it. You think I'm the only kid ever got stuck with a bitchy teacher?"

"*What* did you say?" came at her from two directions simultaneously, then Charlene rolled her eyes and smacked the heel of her hand against her forehead. Finally, slightly delayed, Chucky began to wail beside her. She slumped in her seat, put her fists to her cheeks, trying to cover the blush she felt. She rested her buzzing head that way, elbows propped on the table.

"I'll be going to my room," she mumbled. "In a minute or so."

In her room, she got her faithful troll doll, went inside the walk-in closet, turned on the light and closed the door behind her. She sat on the floor with her legs drawn up to her chest, and stroked the troll's hair for comfort. She was taken by the ugliness of the face. She stared, suddenly uneasy. It made her think of the startled faces of her family around the table and she wondered if she too had seemed as ugly to them then as her troll now seemed to her. And perhaps, she had somehow revealed that interior to her family, and to Sister Ada Marie as well.

She heard someone come into her room. Her father's voice called her name. She wished she had stayed in the dark so he wouldn't see the light under the closet door. She waited for him to go away, but he opened the door to her hiding place. She screamed, "Don't look at me!" But he still looked at her. "I don't want you to see me," she said, crying.

He lowered himself awkwardly to sit beside her and looked straight ahead until she wasn't crying so hard. "I know you didn't mean what you said at dinner. But, Sweets, promise to try to get along at school, for me. Okay?"

She nodded and he left her alone. She closed her eyes and tried to picture her mother's pretty, pretty face.

Karen tried to behave herself all week; she wanted no attention directed her way—no one to see her. On Friday, she looked forward to the afternoon which would end with chorus: the integration of all individual voices.

Late afternoon did not come easily. Karen had first to concentrate on the numbers, sitting with hands folded on the desk like the others. Sister paced at the front of the room. She spoke slowly and tapped the wooden pointer on the floor: tip down to emphasize the numbers, drawn up at each function. "Nine plus twenty-seven divided by four times six minus two divided by four plus seven plus seven divided by nine times twenty-five Stephen respond." Sister turned to face him, but he was too slow, and Sister made no allowance for hesitation. "Becky," she said.

Becky squirmed in her seat. "I think . . ."

"Stand to give your answer," Sister said, interrupting her.

Becky stood. "I think it might be fifty-four," she said very quietly.

Sister mocked her in a loud voice, "You *think*? It *might* be?" She spun around. "Karen, stand. Becky, face her. Karen, is Becky correct, *might* the answer be fifty-four?"

"No, Sister."

"And how do you know that? Look at Becky."

Karen forced herself to see Becky in her discomfort. Becky's place was near the front of the room so that now she had to face nearly the entire class, she and Karen both like tall, wind-jostled weeds in a garden of stilled violets. "I know, Sister," Karen said, "because the correct answer is seventy-five."

"And you are *certain* of this? You might not be incorrect as well?"

"Yes, Sister. I'm certain."

"Class? Is Karen correct? Or Becky? Is it seventy-five, or fifty-four?"

After a moment, the voices came: "Seventy-five. Seventy-five. Karen. Yes, seventy-five."

Sister set her pointer in the chalk tray. "The answer is seventy-five," she said. "Girls, you may be seated."

Karen watched Becky, who narrowed her eyes at Karen before taking her seat. Then Karen's knees began to shake and she scrambled into her seat, thinking, "Forgive me. Please."

After lunch, Karen had only dictation to get through. The exercise was similar to the arithmetic one. Karen prepared herself as she always did; she set her foot in motion and thought again, "Ready, set, go!" There was no room for hesitation. Only narrow endurance would do. One error, one pause to catch her breath, and she would not finish the process.

She flexed her fingers and raised her pencil. Sister began to read slowly, a passage on the dangers of vanity, the sin of pride. Karen let the words enter her ear and flow undisturbed to the pencil. The secret was not to hear the words, but simply to translate sound to spelling. Sister increased her speed; Karen reduced word to syllables. Sister went faster. Karen wavered, hearing pencils slam to desks in defeat and the shuffling of feet. Sister went faster; Karen's fingers cramped. Sound: Letter, syllable, word, space, word, space, word, period. Sister stopped. Amen: the praise of silence.

Finally, they all lined up to join the other fourth-grade class in the music room. Karen was last to leave the classroom. When they merged with the other class to climb the tiered wooden platform, Karen was in the front row beside a strange new girl from the other room. The girl was small, with short, curly blond hair. She smiled shyly at Karen for a brief second before she disciplined her attention—eyes forward, watching Sister Ada Marie's every movement.

Sister had them practice the songs for Sunday's folk Mass. As they sang the Communion selection, Sister paced before them, tilting a veiled ear to seek out any stray notes:

Tell me why you're crying my son.
I know you're frightened like everyone.
Is it the thunder in the distance you hear?
Will it help if I stay very near?
I am here.*

Karen thought the song was beautiful, but as she sang the words, her arms always felt heavy and she always got tears in her eyes. She blinked as she sang the chorus:

And if you take my hand my son,
All will be well when the day is done.
And if . . .*

The girl beside her dropped from the platform to the floor. Some of the children continued singing, the disruption only coming in waves of awareness.

---

*"Day is Done" (Peter Yarrow).

The girl's whole body jerked and she wet herself. Sister ran to the door and screamed for help. Karen kept her head down, watching the girl's feet twitch against the floor. Sister Caroline came in to lead them all into the hallway. She had them line up in front of the lockers, one class facing the other. Karen still stared at the floor.

The school nurse finally came from the next school and took Sister Caroline's place in the music room. Sister Caroline sent her own students back to their classroom, leaving instructions for Karen's class to wait for Sister Ada Marie.

Karen was not surprised when Sister came from the music room directly toward her, nearly lifting Karen from the ground by her collar. "You were right next to her," Sister growled at her, loud enough for all to hear. "Why didn't you do something to help her?"

Sister's face was close to her own. Karen stared at the freckles across Sister's cheek until they blurred together. Then she reached back to feel for the cold metal of a locker in order to steady herself.

When she got home that day, she told Aunt Sarah that she was sick. "Here." she explained, resting the back of her hand limply across her forehead. "And here," she added, forearm across her belly. "I don't want any dinner tonight. I better just go to sleep." She went up to her room, changed to her pajamas and climbed under the covers.

When Charlene came in to question her, Karen said, "My stomach's sick. Can't you understand that?" She turned her back on Charlene and faced the blank wall beside her bed. She tried to be more patient with little Chucky, who came into the room on tiptoe and rested his head on her shoulder without saying a word. She told him, "I'm sorry. I don't feel like playing today."

"At's okay," he said. And before slipping quietly out of the room, he slid the troll doll over her shoulder.

She put the doll in the shirt pocket of her pajamas, out of sight. She wished for her beautiful mother, wished she would whisper down from heaven to her: All will be well when the day is done. But there was no such whisper, no sound, not even the crunch of gravel announcing that her father was home from work. Then she slept.

She sat up into the absolute stillness of the night, commanded awake by her own body's signal that she had slept long enough. Charlene snored in the bed beside her. She slid from the bed, and crept into the hallway, pausing at each doorway: Aunt Sarah's, Chucky's, and her father's. She was the only one in the house who was awake. She was certain of it, and she shivered.

She went straight down to the living room and turned on the reading lamp beside her father's chair, keeping the light to its lowest setting. She lifted the *Encyclopedia of Health* from the bookshelf with both hands, and climbed into her father's chair with it. She scanned the index in the back for the strange word Sister had used to explain what had happened to the girl in chorus: Epilepsy.

The word glared up at her and she whispered the sound of it into the room. She meant to be prepared the next time it happened.

When she flipped back through the pages, the book opened to the section on reproduction, the binding cracked at that chapter from Charlene reading it. Karen had once come in while she read, and if Charlene hadn't threatened her, she would never have known the knowledge was forbidden. Now, in the safety of late night, she turned these pages slowly and looked at the drawings.

There was one done full page in color—a fetus curled within the womb. This she studied, tracing the outlines of the creature with her finger. She was certain it was a girl baby, though the drawing itself showed no evidence for this. She thought it very ugly.

Her hand went up to her pocket that still contained the troll doll. She drew it out and placed it next to the drawing, seeing a certain resemblance between the two, what she too must have once actually looked like inside her mother.

She knew then, absolutely, that she had been the cause of the always whispered secret—her mother's cancer of the uterus. She must have done something to her mother from the inside. She had learned, through hints, that Chucky's had been a difficult birth. Now she knew whatever she'd done inside her mother must surely have been responsible for that as well, and she must watch after Chucky because of it all her life.

She went quietly to the kitchen, unchained and unlocked the back door, and stepped out on the back porch. Her bare feet were cold on the damp cement. She put one foot on top of the other for warmth, and balancing that way, wrapped her arms around herself. She meant to look toward heaven, this one time, to ask her mother to pray for her, a shameful sort of daughter in need of prayer. But the sky was clear, almost bright with the full moon. Her attention was caught, even at this distance, by the variety of shades and textures on the moon's surface, staring down at her, like Sister Ada Marie's face.

She hugged herself tighter, as if holding her shame to herself. And, staring back at the moon, she was free.

Sources for the Story, "Reason"

ANY of the material stored in one's memory can support a story by providing the details of refinement, the polish that gives a story its finishing touches. But the single memory which provides the drive to create a story is much more rare. Often, it cannot be sought out so much as captured and held when it intrudes upon the present events in the writer's life. Part of the writer's job, then, is to develop a receptive nature—a way to pause, to focus attention, and to become immersed in the intrusive memory, be it pleasant or painful. To make that single memory useful for a story, the writer must also analyze the pattern expressed in the crossing of past knowledge and current emotion. This intersection can provide the story's meaning, and the intrusive memory can then become a beacon, guiding but not controlling the story, for though it is active in memory, it is also distant enough to be manipulated by the writer to fit the needs of the story form.

This process describes the way I arrived at the story, "Reason." Before writing the story, I was asked to do something that was a difficult task for me. It involved accepting a responsibility because of personal knowledge, but at an emotional cost: I was forced to confront a view of myself as a victim. This is uncomfortable for me because I am a very controlling person, and because I live in a culture that has been bombarded by psychological theory which insists upon the illusion that an adult *should* be in control of the events of his or her life, or be viewed as flawed in nature. Therefore, for fictional purposes, I would not have used this adult situation for the story. Instead, I used the childhood memory that became superimposed upon that situation.

That beacon memory is the scene in which Karen is assigned the responsibility for the girl's seizure. I was in fourth grade when that scene happened to me in nearly the same way as it appears in the story. I remember clearly being on some sort of platform at the front of the classroom. I remember the girl falling and then the seizure. I remember waiting in the hallway, lined up against the lockers. But most of all, I remember the nun, not my own teacher but the principal of the school, who did make me step forward in line and who did ask only me why I hadn't done something to help the other girl. And I can still see the freckles on that nun's face, though I no longer remember what her face looked like beyond that.

This memory became interesting to me as a writer not only for what it taught me about my present life, but also because of the mystery involved. I felt more free to invent around that memory because there are no answers to the questions associated with the scene. The girl who had had the seizure had been new to the school, and did not return after the incident. I never knew much about her, and I still know nothing about why the nun had picked me to blame. In searching associated school memories, there were other incidents involving this same nun that now, looking back, seem very odd. As an adult, I wonder what could have made her behave so strangely. But as a young girl, I would have assumed that the cause was internal, that the nun's behavior was simply a reaction to something within me. These two perspectives allow the story to be told from the point of view of a distant, more experienced narrator, but in sympathy with the psychology of a child.

From that starting point, the story became a matter of balancing various elements so that the end result would be a short story rather than simply becoming a personal diary entry. That balance is the difficult part. In order to use the memory, I needed first to make the child character become clearly someone who was *not* me, yet was enough like me to help me retain the feeling of the events. I knew I would have to create a family for the girl unlike my own family. During graduate school, I took a semester off and spent some of that time listening to any stories people were willing to tell me. The family in this story began as one of those borrowed memories, because I found the family arrangement interesting. There was the father, whose wife had died at a young age, his three daughters, and his three sisters living in the same house. Each of the daughters had her own personal aunt to mother her. But then, to manage the story, I had to start slicing off parts of the borrowed memory. I abandoned one of the aunts and changed a daughter to a son, keeping a three-to-three correspondence of adult caretakers to children. Partway through the story, I found there were still too many characters and relationships. I was stuck at that point because I did not want to get rid of the aunt I liked better, but unfortunately her personality made her someone who would have helped Karen, and there would have been no story at all. Once I removed her from the household, I began to make progress on the story. This is how the beacon memory helped to guide the story. Knowing I was headed toward the scene of the girl's seizure at school helped me mold the borrowed material.

Once the family was established, I had the distance I needed to see Karen with a separate identity from myself as a child. And that allowed me to use a narrative voice that could view Karen as a character at a distance. Then the balancing act had to begin again. For sympathy, I needed to feel close to the character. For this, I used personal, not borrowed, memories.

Karen coming down the steps in the morning, being inspected in her uniform by her aunt, and watching her father with Chucky, were all invented to help me establish the character within *her* family, not in a family like my own. Then, to help me remember what it felt like to go off to school in fourth grade, I used my own material: watching for the bus from the window, the feeling of going from my own expansive home environment to a crowded bus and full classroom, and the troll doll, a popular toy when I was around Karen's age.

That initial mixture of memory and invention was important because it influenced the structure of the rest of the story. In this case, a pattern was established in which I used imagined detail for those scenes of Karen at home, and remembered detail for those of Karen at school. But the demands of a short story make it necessary for the writer to be what can seem disloyal to memory— unfair to the people involved. All of the material used from my own school memories have been augmented through language, or composed from bits of various memories, or purposefully weighted to keep the story focused toward a single conclusion.

I remember going to the blackboard to diagram sentences. I remember having to take dictation and my own stubbornness in completing every exercise. I remember the oral math exercises and the challenges about the certainty of an answer. However, the way the scenes are presented in the story, they serve to isolate and define Karen. The language intensifies the scenes in a way that makes them seem more important than they had been to me at the time. And, in order to keep the story focused in that narrow, single direction, I also had to omit certain associated memories that would have interfered with the fictional purpose of the writing.

I may remember going to the blackboard to diagram sentences, but I used to enjoy doing them, and I never had to attack a sentence like the one Karen receives—a message. I remember dictation, but when I succeeded in the challenge, I always felt good about it. One of my teachers did have a sort of wicked enjoyment of making students stand to give an answer, and then trying to make them doubt what they had said. But everyone in the class was subject to the method, not one individual. I gave all the behaviors that had aggravated me in several teachers to the character Sister Ada Marie. She represents a real person, yet she is a composite, and she has been given details that were simply inventions. But to keep the story focused, there were things I had to ignore from my memories of this woman, which made me feel I was being unfair to her memory—and a bit of a liar. She was capable of many cruel behaviors, yet I was her favorite in many ways. I got to do special things no one else did, and I got away with things no one else could. But I did not use those memories. I purposely tried not to generate any material in my mind that represented the warm side of the person, only the cruel or confusing side, because Karen was not meant to represent me, and I did not want her to be a favored student.

I did not use any specific details or scenes from my present life events. Instead, I tried to use my feelings, reactions, and observations at the time of writing the story by giving them to Karen. In order to do this, I had to let these emotions stay with me long enough to finish the story when normally I would have gotten over it all more quickly. I had to dwell on my anger, uneasiness and loneliness while discouraging myself from any lightheartedness.

"Reason" contains the language of restraint that parallels the restraint of my sarcasm and anger at the time of writing the story. I introduce the character with "Karen bounced down the stairway to the entrance hall, letting her waist-length black hair wave and fall with each bounce." The second paragraph moves to "She took a single deep breath to compose herself and walked cautiously (lady-like), with her brush and hair ties in hand. . . ." Karen is also given my vague, generalized uneasiness. She experiences it on the ride home as "her senses aligned with each possibility of danger," and as the irrational fear that a satellite will fall on her. Because I gave her the feelings that I was having at the time of writing the story, I could better understand how she might react—wanting not to be seen, wanting her voice to blend with the others in chorus.

At the time of writing the story, I felt lonely as well. I'd already established a character whose mother had died, and it was appropriate to this loneliness. It seems like an accident when I think back on it, but I suppose that a good deal of the writing occurs through a less than conscious, or analytical, level. Once established though, I knew that the absence of Karen's mother should be utilized by making her acutely aware of the absence.

Finally, there is the ending of the story, the culmination of its meaning. That, to me, is directed by an accumulation of experience, but is rooted more often for me in the present situation, the present making me emotionally aware of some possibility, and possibility is what I think fiction represents.

At the time I was writing "Reason," I was watching myself as well as others behaving as though we were all quite logical, when it was fairly obvious that all of the individual reasoning processes stemmed from assumptions based on strong personal needs and drives. Karen is given that same behavior. She creates a sense of freedom for herself by creating her own imagined shame rather than accepting an externally assigned blame. For this, I used one of my own childhood memories, transformed somewhat, but still carrying the same air of mystery. One of my aunts died of uterine cancer when she was in her late thirties. I got the information only in pieces from eavesdropping on adult conversations. I thought that whatever it was, it was so horrible that even the doctors were afraid to face it, because I kept hearing that "they opened her up and just closed her back up again." Accepting the blame for this mysterious horror in the story, Karen makes a cognitive leap that may seem illogical, but gives her something to claim, something useful to her psychological needs. This movement is the fictional possibility of the story.

⁂ QUESTIONS ⁂

Kathleen A. Coppula's story, "Reason," and its process essay, "Source for the Story, 'Reason'"

1. In how many ways does Coppula document Karen's isolation? To what degree is it self-imposed? Is it realistic? Do you feel sympathy for Karen as you read the story? How does Coppula communicate those events that take place daily, and those that happened only in the time the story is told? Which are most important?

2. How has Karen changed at the story's end? Would you argue that she *is* free? If so, what is she freed from? How does the title of the story affect your reading of its conclusion?

3. In her process essay, Coppula refers to the girl who has the epileptic seizure as the "beacon memory." She writes, "Knowing I was headed toward the scene of the girl's seizure at school helped me mold the borrowed material." When you are writing, do you have specific material you are working toward? Does it help to have that material, or does it limit you? Can you imagine ways it could help and hinder?

4. Coppula writes, "And, in order to keep the story focused in that narrow, single direction, I also had to omit certain associated memories that would

have interfered with the fictional purpose of the writing." When you are writing about something that happened to you, do other memories surface? What do you do with them? Do you include them, or choose to eliminate them? How do you go about making those decisions? Do some of the memories or ideas that surface seem more interesting than those you've been pursuing? What do you do then?

❧ Possible Writing Topics ❧

1. Write an essay on a memory that you have associated with an experience in grade school, and make it an essential one, a memory that you find yourself returning to on occasion. Discuss how the experience changed you or changed the person you're writing about. Be sure to include background information on this person so we know part of what led to the experience you are describing. As you prepare to write and as you write, jot down memories that occur to you, ideas you have, on a separate sheet of paper. Note the ones you include and the ones you reject.

2. After you've completed the essay, write a second one where you develop more fully a few of the ideas or memories you had in the first essay. As and after you've developed them, write about why you decided they didn't fit into this essay, why they were better left out. What was the crucial factor in this decision? Are there memories or ideas here that you would like to pursue in a different essay? Do some of them seem more interesting than those you worked with in the first essay?

Eleanor Bergholz

Suspending Dread

ON the waiting room table in the radiation-oncology department of West Penn Hospital is a publication of Alcoholics Anonymous. To me it is an odd magazine for cancer patients to leaf through as they wait for radiation treatment.

I am one of them. Like body graffiti, bold lines of dark, red dye have been drawn on me, defining the area to be treated. Mine are drawn around my right breast where a month ago a malignant tumor was removed. A second surgery followed to remove lymph nodes under my arm. My arm is stiff and painful.

My prognosis is good, the doctors say. The cancer has not spread. Still, they tell me, I have a 20 to 30 percent chance of a recurrence.

The magazine makes me think of one of the AA tenets—getting up in front of the group and saying, I am an alcoholic.

I am to get 30 radiation treatments, every weekday for six weeks. Then eight chemotherapy treatments, every three weeks for six months. When I see the magazine, I think it is meant for me because of how hard it is for me to say—I am a cancer patient.

When one is given a diagnosis of cancer the richness and promise of one's life is suddenly emptied out and filled back up with dread and hopelessness.

The lump was a tiny thing, all of 1.4 centimeters. Yet it could have sent out lethal tentacles to other parts of my body. And it has wreaked emotional havoc with my life.

The lump was removed on an outpatient basis with a local anesthetic. The procedure lacked the drama of the diagnosis that was to follow. After the surgery, the doctor talked to my husband and me for a long time. As he explained what was to follow, I found myself more focused on why my husband, who sat about four feet from me, was so far away than on what the doctor was saying. Other than hearing the dreadful news and scheduling more surgery, I don't remember a thing he said.

When I went to change my clothes, a nurse followed me into the dressing room. Without speaking, she took me in her arms and I cried on her shoulder as if she were my mother. Then she said, "I know you are upset and feel it is the end of the world, but many of the ladies who come here do very well."

All I could say was, "How will I ever tell my kids?"

But the nurse planted the idea that this was something I could work with.

ช่ ร/ค

A few weeks after the surgery I had a dream. My husband and I were sitting in a dark, crowded movie theater. In this setting, quite fantastically, I was the victim of a violent rape. Then I was interviewed by a diligent detective. He wanted the physical evidence that a rape had occurred. He sat poised to write down all the sordid details. But it was as if we are playing in different movies. I kept showing him my arm and where the pain from surgery still lingered. He was uncomprehending.

ช่ ร/ค

Cancer has made a most unwelcome and surreptitious entry into my life. It may be gone, it may not. It may come back, it may not. But the emotional impact is here to stay. I am immersed in cancer. As the doctors work on containing it, I am having an emotional metastasis.

I have to keep reminding myself of what the surgeon said, "The tumor is gone, it is likely that all the cancer is gone now."

It is ironical that when the tumor was growing I didn't even know it was there. I went on as if I were in perfect health. Now that it is gone the aftermath has taken over my life. My body betrayed me. My image of myself as a healthy person has crumbled. I am torn between grieving the loss of my good health and fighting to regain it.

ช่ ร/ค

Radiation therapy needs to be worked over by a good public relations person. They tell me radiation will rid the area where the tumor was of cancer cells and not do other harm to me. But in my layman's ignorance radiation therapy sounds like a contradiction of terms—doublespeak. When I think of radiation I think of being herded to the basement of my elementary school for air raid drills. Or of Three-Mile Island and Chernobyl.

But this is not a nuclear holocaust, it is just my holocaust. I try to beat down old images and believe that radiation will make me better.

So for 30 days I submit, with much trepidation, to lying down on a chilly, narrow gurney. After the technicians carefully line me up under the cobalt machine they scurry out of the room before the red warning light goes on. Bare-chested, right arm outstretched, I feel vulnerable. But I try to think of Pac-man gobbling up any cancer cells left in there.

❧ ☙

Radiation kills cells—cancer cells and some healthy ones too, the doctor tells me. So during treatment, she says, I must eat well, especially protein so my body can make new cells. The doctors worry a lot about weight loss during treatment so part of the program is to put each patient on the scale weekly. I keep telling them weight loss isn't going to be my problem.

I have taken to eating breakfast, something I have not done since college. After the early morning treatments I want to immediately replenish myself with warm toast or scrambled eggs. I fortify myself with good meals.

And I planted a garden. One day after radiation treatment, I went to a spring plant sale. The sight of so many thriving flowers and vegetables bursting with growth had a euphoric, dizzying effect on me. I filled with tears at the sight of so much life pouring forth, perfectly formed and vibrant. My impulse was to buy everything in sight.

❧ ☙

I am at a party having an animated conversation with a cheerful young man whom I have just met. My news—that I have breast cancer—sits in my throat, unspoken, like a cat ready to pounce. Out of courtesy I hold back. It would unsettle this young man. Cancer still evokes a gasp, mentioning it is a terrible public gaffe. And men, I am finding, become distraught over breasts that are not doing well. I know that if I said something I would feel more isolated—it would not elicit the sympathy I so desperately need. But this urge to tell all intrudes in every social encounter.

❧ ☙

My father died 20 years ago. The things I remember about him these days are not the grand things he did or said to me. Rather, what I recall with most intensity are the infinitesimal images such as the curve of his shoulders as he read the newspaper at the kitchen counter or leading me by the hand through the crowds at a baseball game.

My son is sitting at the kitchen counter watching me make him a tuna fish sandwich for lunch. I feel the power of the moment as if this mundane chore of motherhood will imprint on him some lasting magic from me.

The present has taken on a vividness it never had before cancer. I used to make plans, talk about the future and hurry a lot. Now I feel severed from what is ahead. Nothing irritates me more than people talking about "someday."

❧ ☙

Years ago, on my son's fourth birthday, he opened a present from his grandmother and told her bluntly, "This is exactly what I always never wanted."

We all laughed at his forthrightness, but now I know how he felt. In addition to feeling I must tell the world of the cancer and my treatments, I also feel a need to reject it totally—shuck it off and go on as if it never happened. Breast cancer is exactly what I always never wanted. But here it is.

Each morning I change into a baggy hospital gown and wait my turn with the other cancer patients who have red lines drawn on various parts of their bodies. We talk. Where is your tumor? Are you tired? Are you eating well? But mostly, we ask each other—How many treatments do you have left? It is a support group of sorts but one none of us ever wanted to belong to.

Lined up in the waiting room, I wonder morbidly—if we had a reunion a year or five years from now, how many of us would be alive to attend?

Some mornings when I finish a treatment I feel a suffocating, claustrophobic dread, imagining the worst that may be ahead. I want to run away and cooperate no more. I daydream of moving to a new city, finding a job and beginning anew. Yet I know wherever I run I will have to take this body with me.

But at other times I find myself dwelling on the difficult things I have had to deal with in the past. I feel as though I am gathering together the strength gained from those experiences to use it to knock this cancer down to size.

In one tearful consultation I am told by a doctor, "I expect that you will do fine. But you need to give yourself time. It will never go away but you will learn to co-exist with it."

Co-existence seemed a magic word, a way to go forward. Unspeakable things can happen, but you find you can work with them.

I can see now that increasingly in the days ahead I will go to work, laugh, cook meals for my family, read a good book.

When it comes up I may say, "I had breast cancer," and be able to leave it at that, feeling confident that it is contained, at least for now, to a quiet, private corner of my life.

Sources for "Suspending Dread"

I work as a journalist for a large metropolitan newspaper. One of the things I like about newspaper work is the opportunity to organize and bring perspective to other people's lives.

Journalists are great simplifiers. Many are slick with words. They enter people's lives at some high, like winning an election, or low, like a murder trial, and they bring into focus, in 10 to 15 inches of column space, events and motives which were extremely complex in the making.

I find much pleasure in bringing order—in words, sentences and paragraphs—to the events and feelings of other people's lives. Rarely have I attempted to write about my own. It has become second nature to hide my voice in the voices of others.

The "Saturday Diary" is a column in the newspaper I write for. It is one of the only places in the paper for first-person accounts. I enjoy reading the "Saturday Diary" and I have even thought of ideas I would like to write about for it. But my own life has never lent itself to easy written discourse.

Then came cancer. It was an event so overwhelming that it had me completely tied up for months, physically and emotionally. I returned to work soon after the surgery, but I realized I wasn't ready to be back. People would ask—how are you—and I found I could not answer with a simple—"fine"—and leave it at that. I wasn't fine. My sense of well-being had unraveled. I decided to take a six-week leave.

For work I keep a small notebook nearby so I can write down thoughts for stories as they occur to me. I have learned to have great respect for these seemingly random phrases which, more often than not, come to mind away from work, such as when I am doing laundry or making dinner.

I have learned to make sure I capture them. Often these thoughts are some new understanding or focus for a story. I may build a simple phrase into a new lead. Suddenly harnessing a phrase or image can mean that all the pieces of the story, which, up until then, seemed to me to be just floating, will finally fall into place.

With the essay on breast cancer, many of the feelings in it were churning about in my mind long before I wrote it. In fact, I had notes on nearly every section even before I decided to write it.

I puzzled over the Alcoholics Anonymous magazine many mornings when I waited for radiation treatments. The dream, or nightmare—an especially vivid one—found its way into the notebook. Old images of radiation such as air raid drills and Three-Mile Island kept coming to mind.

I recalled my son's phrase, "This is exactly what I always never wanted," which he said during an incident I had not remembered in years. The incorrect grammar seemed to give his rejection a force not possible in the confines of proper English. It was a force I found appealing.

Running away was an idea I gave fleeting attention to. Images of my father floated in and out.

Most of the ideas for the essay came to me at night when I could not sleep. At night thoughts are freed to gather vitality and momentum.

I do not believe that writing is therapy. But for me I do feel that struggling to put something into words, and finally finding the words that satisfy, can mean putting some inner struggle to rest. So it was for me with this essay.

My emotional struggle over cancer involved accepting the reality of cancer and at the same time re-establishing hope in my life. I found that my notes had both images of despair—the dream about rape, the holocaust of radiation—and images of hope—planting a garden and eating good food.

But I could not figure out where I was between the two. It was not until I remembered what one of the doctors said to me—"You will learn to co-exist with this"—that I knew I would write the essay. It seemed a way to accept the cancer, yet get on with life.

I wrote the essay the first two days after I returned to work. It became, I think, my way of getting the lid back on my life. It was my transition back into writing about other people's lives.

I felt the idea of "co-existing with cancer" would give the essay coherency yet I knew the feelings and images leading up to it were scattered and seemingly unrelated. So I decided to use asterisks to separate sections so that each part would be a story in itself. Yet, by the end, all would be related to the whole.

Before beginning to write I decided to use the milieu of the radiation treatments as the way to root the essay in time and place. It was, in fact, the period of time when the struggle I wanted to write about was most difficult for me.

But I also wanted to convey some of the realities for the cancer patient—the red lines drawn on your body, the chilly gurney, the huge cobalt machine, the technicians who bolt the room when the red warning light goes on, the sympathetic banter among patients in the waiting room.

I felt strongly that the essay needed this concrete detail of what it is like to be treated for cancer to balance the more abstract thoughts and feelings that run throughout.

As with every story I have ever written, I had most difficulty with the beginning. I still find it awkward. But why shouldn't I—me, a very private person declaring my cancer so publicly.

My journalist's training made me feel I must put all the facts—the who, what, where, why and when—right up front. The waiting room became a useful place to start—where treatment begins. Any my puzzling over the magazine there brought the point of the essay squarely into focus: How to say, I am a cancer patient, and still get on with life?

As in many stories, after I write the beginning, I often find it is not the beginning at all. And so I have to reach further back to anchor the beginning in something of even more significance that happened before.

For every cancer patient, time will always be divided into life before the diagnosis and life after. So I felt the scene with the doctor, when I heard the diagnosis, had to be told.

One area of my life where I have always felt strong and competent is in relation to my children. To them, I have been an invulnerable force. Telling them about the cancer felt like a deep humiliation, a failure, an admission of my weakness, my humanness. Perhaps all of that was too unspeakable to say at the time I wrote the essay so I let the sentence, "How will I ever tell my kids?" stand on its own.

I wondered whether it was tasteless to include the dream about being raped. I decided in favor because it represented for me a kind of bottom-line feeling of terror, pain and victimization.

Next to the beginning, I found the section describing talking with the young man at the party the most difficult to write, perhaps because to this day, six months later, I still have not completely made cancer a "quiet, private corner of my life."

I know initially I felt an almost promiscuous need to soak up the caring of friends and family. I was hurt and angry when people would recoil at the mention of cancer. I wanted to shake them and say—"I am still here! I am still part of this world! Don't abandon me now!" My feelings about it were so strong and jumbled that I am not sure I ever fleshed out that scene to my satisfaction.

More than the physical threat, cancer for me was the terror of being flooded and overwhelmed with feelings I could not control. While the actual writing of the essay only took me a couple of days, the fodder for it was germinating for weeks. Writing it was a way to harness these feelings and "knock this cancer down to size."

∾ QUESTIONS ∾

Eleanor Bergholz's essay, "Suspending Dread," and its process essay, "Sources for 'Suspending Dread'"

1. In her essay, Bergholz writes, "Cancer still evokes a gasp, mentioning it is a terrible public gaffe.... But this urge to tell all intrudes in every social encounter." Why is mentioning cancer such a public gaffe? What does this say about our treatment of those who are severely ill and their subsequent isolation? In your experience, is Bergholz's statement accurate? What comfort would she receive in "telling all"?

2. Doubtless you have read many essays, have seen many television programs, that have treated the topic of cancer with sentimentality. What strategies does Bergholz employ in order to circumvent sentimentality? Is there any point in the essay where you pity her? Look at the structure of the sentences and note the lack of contraction—Bergholz always writes "I am" rather than "I'm," and "it is" rather than "it's." What quality does this lend her writing that it would otherwise lack?

3. About writing—or rather the preparation for writing—Bergholz writes, "I have learned to have great respect for these seemingly random phrases which, more often than not, come to mind away from work, such as when I am doing laundry or making dinner." When you've been preparing to write something, has this happened, too, or does everything come to you when

you first sit down? If such "random phrases" do occur to you, do you write them down? And if you don't, do you forget them, or are they recollected when you actually begin writing?

4. In her process essay, Bergholz says, "Writing [the essay] was a way to harness these feelings and 'knock this cancer down to size.'" You have read several process essays now where writers say that writing helped them deal with and confront something urgent and crucial in their lives. What is it about language, particularly written language, that allows this to happen? And why do you think these writers chose the more formal story or essay as the vehicle for their writing, rather than journal or diary writing?

❧ Possible Writing Topics ❧

1. Write an essay about a time when you or someone you knew well suffered a calamity, whether this was an illness, the death of a loved one, a fire — whatever source is most interesting to you. Try to report the emotion you and others felt honestly, without sentimentality, and work to include the response of those who watched this happen. Did your perspective on this person change over time? What has happened since the calamity passed? Do you respond differently to the memory of what happened than you did to the event at the time it happened? As you prepare to write this essay, and during the writing of it, take notes on *how* you prepared and the environment you've cultivated for writing.

2. After completing the first essay, write a second on the habits you have for writing. When do ideas first occur to you? How do you preserve them? Where are you when you write? Do you eat or drink when you write? How many breaks do you take? If a friend asks you to leave your work, will you? Do you wait until the last minute if the writing has been assigned to you? Why? How many drafts do you write? When you're writing your first one, what attention do you pay to matters of grammar, punctuation, spelling?

Melissa Greene

All the Hours of the Night

FOR thirty years in Hart County, Georgia, all through the Depression, a woman named Pearlie Burton delivered the babies. There were other midwives at the time, licensed by the state, loosely supervised by the county physician, but Pearlie was the favorite.

"I can't stand it anymore," announced a midwife named Lula Hurd at the monthly meeting. "When everybody have a baby, they go to get Pearlie Burton, never do come get me."

"What is your name, please?" asked the nurse instructor.

"Lula Hurd," she said, and stood up.

"Yeah well you *look* like a Lula Hurd," said a voice from the back of the class, and all the young and middle-aged women burst out laughing. They picked up their fans from their laps and began fanning themselves.

"And just how is a Lula Hurd supposed to look?" Lula Hurd demanded to know, and the dressed up ladies on their folding chairs in the basement of the courthouse covered their faces and laughed. "I'll tell *you* all something: I *quit!*" said Lula Hurd. She snatched up her things and stormed out, muttering, "Look like a Lula Hurd," while the ladies rocked back and forth in their laughter. She could still hear the merriment coming through the basement windows from the courthouse lawn outside.

Pearlie Burton predicted the gender of unborn babies with celebrated accuracy. "I look at the way the mother's stomach set," she told her friends. "Most of the time, old boy be laying kind of flat. Girl sits up nice and straight, nice and straight." She was famous for her ability to confirm or deny pregnancy simply by looking at a woman. "No quicker that I lay my eyes on her, I can tell."

"Go get Pearlie," the old ladies whispered when the morals of a young woman came under suspicion.

"Lord please don't let me run into Miss Pearlie today," guilty young women prayed.

Pearlie Burton delivered babies in bedrooms, in fields, and in barns. She delivered a baby whose mother had been hit by lightning and she delivered a baby in a bed while a rooster stood on the headboard and clucked. She delivered over a thousand babies in the 1920s, '30s, and '40s, and was the first black midwife to be sought out by white families, as well. She was one of a new generation of midwives who received a smattering of state-sponsored instruction as supplement to their motherlore. At bi-weekly meetings, they learned about prenatal care, nutrition, labor, delivery, and postpartum problems.

"It was nine of us started all together to be midwives," she said. "We had a meeting twice a month about vitamins, blood pressure, how long to cut the cord, and different things. A lady had a row of sticks, one a little bit longer than the next. They represented some vegetables and some cereals. The longest stick was collard greens—that's the healthiest thing you can eat when you're carrying a baby."

Pearlie Burton had her own prenatal advice to offer as well: "You can mark a child," she told the young women. "Going to have a sweet personality, going to grow up and be something in life, or going to be hateful and cause trouble—that come from the mother. A mother who will sit and read, and think, 'Now what I want my child to be?' and go out and sing and pray, well that child's going to be something in life. But you ever see children some of them just *look* nasty? You know that mama was just a nasty slouching thing when she was carrying that child.

"I know a little child now, nine years old, got the devil all in him, he's hitting on somebody, using bad words. I asked that mother about it the other day. I said, 'When you carried that child, you just as mean and hateful as you could be.' She said, 'I sure was.' She said the man she was staying with would wake up in the morning and say, 'How you feeling this morning, honey?' and she would say, 'You can just go to hell.' That come from the parents, sure."

"Drink a lot of milk," she told the women. "That'll make it be big-boned. Eggs will put that marrow in there."

She urged her new mothers to breastfeed their babies, but most didn't want to. "They said they had to work," said Pearlie. "That's why the babies so mean now, can't do nothing *with* the children. They nursing the bottles now, nursing old cow's milk, old goat's milk, some of everything's milk, can't do nothing with them."

She had her own philosophy of when to cut the cord: "Some people is more hot-natured than others. I'll just come right out and say the plain thing. Some people has more nature than others. Some mens have more nature, some mens don't have very much nature at all, and you know why? Because whomsoever delivered them cut that cord too soon. You've got to wait until that cord quit beating and the nature goes back into you. If you cut that cord before it quit beating, they don't have no nature to amount to nothing. The nature is in the cord."

An ancient black woman named Julie Adams had been the reigning midwife before Pearlie got started. Miss Julie had one tooth in her head, smoked a corncob pipe, and gave her patients liquor. "No, you don't need liquor," Pearlie Burton told her laboring mothers. "God give you that baby and He going to let you bring it." But the women were used to old Julie. Pearlie's second patient protested that a midwife in her thirties was too young for the job. "Pearlie Burton is too young to be a midwife and I *know* she don't know what she's doing," the laboring woman announced to everyone in her bedroom. She yanked up the sheets and glared angrily between her knees at Pearlie: "I *know* you don't know what you're doing."

"You'll be all right in just a few minutes, honey," said Pearlie.

After the baby came, the woman carried on just as loudly, but in a new vein: "Deliver me from those old midwives, Lord! Don't want nobody but Pearlie Burton from now on."

Pearlie Burton had special techniques for relaxing the mother and monitoring the labor. "This is what I would always do when I first go in: I would speak to them, maybe laugh and have a little funny joke. Then I'd put on my little white apron and cap and wash up. I had some rubber gloves, get me some grease, and I'd take this finger and feel around there. You know there's a certain ring inside where they open up? I could tell by how it was open about how long it was going to take them.

"They might say, 'I want something for my pains.' So I give them syrup, cane syrup, homemade. And a hot glass of water. I tell them, 'You help yourself and get down there and get hot.' That cane set them on fire. They get so hot they don't know what to do. And when you get real hot, the pains will come.

"One time I had a lady say,' *I aint gonna take that syrup.*'"

I said, 'Well all right, the pains are real hard, the baby's ready to come, if you don't want the syrup, where's the dirty clothes?' I say, 'Give me a pair of her husband's pants!' I threw them around her neck—Good God Almighty—in about five minutes those pains went to racking her body and that baby jumped out.

"You put the pants around the neck with the open part against the back of the neck. Wrap them around the neck good. That'll get you hot, that'll stimulate you."

"Trouble with these young girls having babies and not married?—you can't get a pair of their husband's old pants."

Pearlie Burton is a sweet-tempered, modest little lady of 82, who hoots with laughter at compliments, waves away the flatterers, and then covers her mouth to keep from laughing her dentures out. Strangers stop her on the sidewalk when she goes into Hartwell or Elberton to shop. "Aint you Miss Pearlie?" a man in a suit and tie will ask. "My mama told me you slapped my behind and I'm going to get you for that!" And she will lean on the man's arm, look up at his face, try to recall his name, give up, and jiggle with laughter. Young women still seek her out for advice. "White girl came up to me not long ago, said, 'Look at me good. What I'm going to have?' I said, 'I don't know what you gonna have and I don't know what position you was in when you got him.'"

Pearlie wears, for special occasions, a shiny black wig and a polyester blouse with a floral pattern. She lives ten miles outside Hartwell, in a wooden cabin painted white and blue, surrounded by miles of corn and cotton fields. Untrimmed tree lengths hold up her porch roof, still notched by hacked-off branches. They, like her shutters and trim, have been painted bright blue. Retired, Pearlie spends most of her time in an armchair in her front room, next to a gas heater she keeps turned up high until midsummer. The shabby room is crammed with beds and sofas. In a crib along one wall lies a six-year-old crippled foster child; his wheelchair is parked between two armchairs. The wood-panelled walls are decorated with doo-dads, a Santa Claus made out of sequins, a pot holder, a decorative paper plate, a fan from church. Clothes wrapped in plastic hang from all the doors because the closets leak. Pearlie stays home most of the time now, except for Sundays, when she teaches Sunday school, and Mondays, when she works as a maid in Hartwell.

"I delivered over a thousand babies but I don't know the over-a-thousand number because my last house burnt up with all my papers," she said. "I know I delivered the nine children of Mr. and Mrs. Cathell Fleming: all are successful, one is a successful teacher in Hartwell. I know I delivered the twelve children of Mr. and Mrs. Jerry Fouck: all are successful, one is a department manager for Millikin Industries. I remember I delivered the fifteen children of Mr. and Mrs. Pete Allen: five are successful teachers. I certainly delivered the fourteen children of Mr. and Mrs. Hollis Rucker. . . ." So she muses, sitting by her heater.

"At first I charged five dollars, then went up to seven, then went to ten. A whole lot of times they pay me in corn or syrup, sometimes they give me chickens. One time old Mac Jones got a girl pregnant and asked me about delivering her. 'I'm going to pay you,' he said.

"'Well all right, I'm looking for you to pay me.'

"'I aint got no money but I got a pig.'

"He give me a pig. I laughed at Mac Jones till he died about that. A lot of them folks owe me till today."

Poor herself, Pearlie one day stood at the front door of a family who owed her. She heard voices, and chairs scooting inside. A little boy opened the door. "Good afternoon," she said. "Is your folks home?"

"No ma'am. They is gone to town."

"They is, is they?" said Pearlie. She could see two pairs of feet side-by-side under the closet curtain. "Will you tell them something for me?"

"Yes ma'am."

"You tell them Pearlie Burton stopped by, and tell them next time they go to town, be sure to take their feet with them."

Pearlie Burton was a farmer and a midwife. For most of her life, the morning found her bent at the waist, a straw hat on her head, hoeing corn beside her husband, Lafayette Burton, in the fields surrounding their cabin; but there was no telling where the night would find her. Many a night she was out under the constellations, aboard a horse- or mule-drawn wagon, sitting erect in her yellow bonnet, rattling down the dirt road past cabins full of snores.

"I have travelled all the hours of the night, all the *hours* of the night," she said. "Sometime it be so cold you couldn't hardly go. Some nights I don't have no way to get back home and it might be two or three hours before time for the baby. I've gotten where I was so tired, didn't know what in the world to do.

"Sometimes I go and deliver the baby in the morning, but the rest of the family be gone to the fields. I have to wait there till dinner time for them to bring me home. That the hottest part of the day. Don't have no umbrella. Once I pulled up a old bush and held it over my head for shade."

She was accustomed to the sound of urgent voices on her doorstep in the small hours of the night: "Miss Pearlie, it's her time!" Husbands whispering, speaking an octave higher than normal. "Pearlie, my wife's sick!"

"Let me get up!" she'd call. "Why, Mr. Wilkins, how you *doing*?" she'd say at the door, a hairnet on her head and grease on her face. She would not be hurried. "You better come quick, Aunt Pearlie," they always said. "I'm coming, I'm coming. Let me get dressed," she said. If it were a first baby, she took all the time she needed to make herself a sandwich and collect a book to take along. Time passed slowly while a woman labored; then it sped up as pains and breaths came quickly; then all time stopped and there was a moment of deafening silence. Then God winked and the world opened to let the baby enter.

In the time it took her to dress, the young husband, holding his horse, would begin to despair. Where else could he ride for help? Just as he resolved to speed on, the door would open and here would come Pearlie Burton down the step, carrying a number of neat parcels and wearing a string of blue beads and a Sunday hat.

"I delivered four sets of twins," said Miss Pearlie. "First ones, I was so surprised I didn't know what to do. I think she was a Gumptry. The baby was born and had a little old short cord. I said that the shortest cord I ever did see. Well I waited till it quit beating and she going on about her stomach was still hurting. Directly she said, 'Oooooh, my stomach's hurting so bad!' I went down there and said, 'Honey, you fixing to have another baby!' It excited all of us so bad. They went in there and telled that daddy and he about had a fit he was so happy.

"Of course, when Ethyl Marie Creek had hers, they didn't want no twins. I said, 'Honey, you ought to be glad, the Lord give you a set of twins.' They kind of calmed down then, but said, 'Lord, what in the world we going to do, can't support no twins.'

"Next time it was Duffy Bank's wife. She was a great big old woman. She had one, then she say, 'There something else wrong with my stomach,' and here come the next one. That's what you call identical twins, one right behind the other."

One night forty years ago, a hammering at the door in the middle of the night disturbed the Burtons. "Let me get up!" called Pearlie. But it was no husband or relation of any of her patients who stood at the door. It was a disheveled thin woman in her twenties, wearing a dress, worn-out high heels, and lipstick. A long car sat in the dirt yard.

"Aunt Pearlie? You Aunt Pearlie Burton? I'm Lorraine, your second cousin, Lorraine from Philadelphia."

"Lorraine? Well I declare! What you say? Lorraine? Geneva's child? Mmm-mmm-mmm. Lorraine, sure enough, come on in."

"I can't stay, Aunt Pearlie. I came to ask can you keep my two little boys? They don't have a home and I aint got none for them. If you can't, do you know of any church aid society that could take them?"

"No, I don't know of a society," said Pearlie carefully. "How old are they?"

"One-and-a-half and three. Can you take them?"

"I just don't know. I'll have to see what my husband say." One little boy watched from the car window. Pearlie closed the door slowly and went to wake up Lafayette. "Fate, listen here. Fate! You want two little boys?" The room was humid with the soft breathing of a dozen sleeping children, none of them born to the Burtons. "Fate, you want two more?"

In a time and a place filled with children, Pearlie and Fate Burton were childless. They had their own house; they raised sweet potatoes, corn, cane syrup, and hogs; they were happy together; and they had waited long years for a baby to come to them. "Go in the field in the morning, work till the bell rang, go to the house and we'd cook," said Pearlie of their life together. "He'd help me cook. Then we'd eat. We used to eat syrup, fatback meat and gravy. You hoe cotton all day till evening time, you gonna sit down and have that fatback meat, syrup and gravy. Now you can't hardly eat fatback anymore, it run up your blood pressure. Then we lay down and go to sleep, get up and go back to the field. Yes, we just come up happy. We wanted a baby so bad, but every month, here come the blood. I decided well, I'm not going to have any children."

Then an unmarried girl named Rita Mae had a baby. "Whyn't you give it to Pearlie?" people asked; and one morning Rita Mae did, walked across the field with a little brown-skinned baby girl named Carrie Lee: "Mama said to ask you do you want her."

The Burtons did want her. They drove to the county courthouse with Carrie Lee and adopted her and people began to notice how Fate and Pearlie loved children.

"Tood tacious alive!" said Pearlie in a high-pitched voice to Carrie Lee. "Is it seepy?"

"Well *suh!*" said Pearlie to outspoken baby boys. She addressed babies and small children as if they were already important individuals temporarily inconvenienced by drooling and lack of language skills. She looked them right in the eye. "You going to be something in life, going to have a lot of friends," she told newborns she delivered. Soon there were others in the rural county asking, "Miss Pearlie, can you take him?" and "Keep her, Pearlie. I don't want to see her." Pearlie was leaving home in the middle of the night to attend a birth and returning at dawn, worn-out, and carrying a fuzzy-headed, frowning newborn to raise. She and Fate adopted the five brothers and sisters of Carrie Lee, all delivered by Pearlie. Neighbors, fellow congregants, and folks from surrounding counties brought the Burtons their unwanted children. In the forties, the county authorities heard about the Burtons and asked them to be foster parents, the first black foster parents in Hart County.

The Burtons raised 69 children over 40 years. Today they write and send gifts from all over America and a dozen have settled down near the Burtons' farm. When Pearlie was widowed after 45 years, she continued to keep children, and has a houseful of teenagers and the six-year-old with cerebral palsy living with her today.

"Clean that refrigerator, now, Sister!" she calls from her armchair.

"Yes, Mama."

But forty years ago, it was: "Fate, can we manage with two more?"

"That's you," he said. "If you want to raise them, that's you. You know it's all right with me."

"We'll take them" she said to Lorraine outside, and watched, almost sick with disapproval, as the young woman unloaded the little boys from the car. "Come to Pearlie, babies," said Miss Pearlie. They started to cry. She turned to their mother. "Now I want you to tell me when we're going to hear from *you* again." Lorraine gushed with promises regarding the money she was going to send and the visits she was going to make, then she hugged the children, got into the car, and drove away. The older brother broke away from Pearlie and ran down the dirt driveway behind the car, crying. Lorraine stopped and leaned out the window: "You better go on back! Aunt Pearlie's going to give you a home! I sure aint got none for you!"

"I can see it right now, clear as day," said Pearlie, in her armchair. "That car driving off and that little fellow running behind it crying. The older one remembers that night. He'd tell me, 'When we was with our mama, she'd fasten us up in the room and go away and big old rats was in the room. She'd give us a chocolate candybar and leave us till the next day.'"

The two brothers graduated from high school and entered the military before they laid eyes on their natural mother again. The morning after their arrival, when all the dark sleepy heads began to bob up in the bedrooms, there were two new boys among them, two of the very few not actually delivered by Mother Pearlie.

"I always knew I wanted to be something in life, but yet and still I got married," said Pearlie Burton. "I come up in a big family, 15 children, but the majority died at birth. We raised our syrup, our corn, our sweet potatoes, and growed our hogs. When picking cotton time come, we get out there and pick cotton. We were working for the white mens and back in that time, they take everything you make, talking about, 'You ate it up.' The kids didn't go to school but seven months a year. I remember the first school I went to was at Shiloh and I learned this poem:

> *Drive the nail right*
> *Hit it on the head*
> *Strike with all your might*
> *While the iron is red.*
>
> *Standing at the foot*
> *Gazing at the sky*
> *You can't get up*
> *If you never try.*

That poem have always followed me.

"Fate was in my class at school and he always like to stand side of me. Now here comes the drama: Mary Ruth Hardy want to stand side of *him*. He was a little old light-skinned man with blue eyes. He had funny-looking eyes. They all would tease me about those eyes, called them 'cat-eyes.' He didn't have no brothers or sisters with eyes like that. But he was always nice.

"We got married at 18, in my mother's house. I had on a white poplin dress, a white veil, white lace shoes, and white silk stockings—silk to the knee and cotton the rest of the way up. I thought I was something. And Fate had on a green suit, I can see it right now, with a little white stripe in it. His uncle had a T-Model Ford car and brought Fate to the wedding in it. People thought that was the grandest thing in the world.

"His mother was a midwife. I went around with her a little while, then I said, 'Well, I reckon I can do this on my own.' The first baby I ever delivered was my brother's baby. They told me to name him and I named him Cleophus.

Cleophus. I thought that was the prettiest name in the world. He's gone now. But I done good. And I thought, 'Now I'm on top of the world.'

"After that, on and on, on and on, every time we turn around, someone coming for me. I went all around. I went every which way to deliver babies. I didn't have to call the doctor in but three times. But I have had some awful times. God has seen me through them. Had one child born with its naval on its leg. Had one born, prettiest face you ever saw, wasn't no girl, wasn't no boy. It lived a little while, then it died.

"I delivered one little girl born with like a veil over her face and I had to clip it. It said eh, eh, eh, trying to cry. It was about a half dog, half person. It lived about a hour and a half. I asked the mother who the father was and she just burst out hollering and crying and she never did tell who the daddy of that baby was. Well that was one of my awful times that I had. The funniest feeling that you ever saw looking at the little thing, a half dog and half person. She aint never had none other. She live in Augusta now. I see her every once in a while, but aint nothing ever mentioned about that little dog.

"The second child I had born that way, well the child was all right but it had a bad long nose and some big ears. That the ugliest thing I ever saw. It lived, though. It's *still* alive, live up in Youngstown, Ohio, right now, yeah, and still ugly. I don't know what in the world that was. I thought, Lord! I wouldn't want this thing. But they kept it and—honey?—they was crazy about that ugly thing. If anybody laughed at it, you had a fight on your hands. All the rest of their children was all right. I asked the mother how come it happened and she said she coming across the field one day and got scared of a mule and that's what done it. The last time I saw it, it was *still* ugly.

"One time I went to deliver a baby down in Rutherfordville. When I got back with the husband, the baby had been born. Woman said she thought her bowels had to move, she squatted down, and the baby been born. It was winter. She took that baby and wrapped him up and stayed down there on her knees. It was so cold, they didn't have no wood or no fire. She wrapped that baby up in a blanket and pushed him up under the bed trying to keep him warm. She was all wet herself. I got there and I made a fire. The baby laying up there just as warm. God took care of him. Curled up just as warm.

"There was some Suttons, stayed way down there in Elber County. They was white; that man had old long hair, he looked scary. He came after me late one evening. My husband said, 'You want me to come back after you in the morning?'

"'No,' I said, 'I want you to come with me and wait there.'

"It was a barn they were living in. Old dogs laying up around there. They had a drainage pipe for a heater. I was scared a snake was coming out from under the bed to bite me on the leg. I heard a noise, scared me something terrible. 'What's that?'

"'Just a old mule.'

"Them the poorest folks I ever saw. I kept hearing something like 'cuk cuk cuk cuk, cuk cuk cuk.' Said 'That sound just like a chicken.'

"'There he is,' they said. Old rooster up there on the head of the woman's bed. I looked up, some more chickens sitting over there. That's the worsest mess I ever been in in my life. The baby come and they didn't have nothing to wrap the baby up with. 'Where's the baby's clothes?'

"'Don't have none.'

"'You aint got nothing like a little undershirt?' They had three or four more children.

"'Nope.'

"I didn't bathe the baby. There was no heat. I put grease on him. Old grandma gave me a old gown. I took it and sewed a little something for him. And it was cold in there that night. Heard 'unh unh unh'—there was hogs in there too. Hogs in one stall, mule in another, all of them in that barn together. I went to Elberton the next day to the Health Department: baby aint got no clothes. Poor little pitiful baby. Little five-year-old boy in britches big enough for a ten-year old. It was a scandal and a shame."

The baby Pearlie Burton is the proudest of delivering is now the Reverend Eddie Thornton of the Norman Grove AME Church, her pastor and pastor of the largest circuit in the Elberton District. The way Pearlie puts it is this: "The most interesting delivery I can recall is the fact that the baby I listen to every Sunday is my pastor, the Rev. Eddie Thornton.

"And he's not ashamed of being delivered by a midwife," she said. "Sometimes we go to different churches and a whole lot of times he have me stand up, say, 'That's Mother Pearlie. That's the first somebody that saw me in this world.' I remember well when he was born. Started to holler, then I held him, and he hushed and started to look around. Said something special about him, one way or another. And oh, that man can preach, Lord have mercy, he can preach. I'm so proud of it I don't know what in the world to do.

"I have found that most everybody is happy about a baby unless it's a young girl pregnant. I delivered a baby for a young girl one time and that baby's grandma cried and cried. I stopped working with the baby and I turned to her. She just having a fit: 'Why did Emma Louise have to have that baby? She know she don't need it. What in the world we going to do?' I laid that baby down and I said, 'It's just one of those things. But I don't *never* want to see nobody cry like that when a baby is born.'

"There are two things I don't like to see: cry and carry on when somebody be married, and cry and carry on when somebody be born, because they aint going to have good luck. Just as sure as someone carries on that way, they going to suffer. And that baby been so mean inside; it been in trouble ever since it been big enough. That marks a child, sure enough."

Pearlie Burton has what she identifies in others as "motherwit." No matter what cropped up, she would manage: "I just don't believe it wasn't nothing much—it might have been—that I didn't know about a mother and the baby." If people are born with pre-ordained gifts—and Pearlie Burton, of all people, certainly would say that they are—then hers has been this: that her heart has reached out to the babies, even as her wise hands have done.

When a baby's arrival has been lamented because the family was poor, the mother was too young, or the baby was a twin, she has reprimanded the family; and if the family has gone on being unhappy about it, she has wrapped the baby up herself, gathered her things, and taken it home with her. At every birth she attended, there has been at least one soul celebrating. She has greeted the arrival of babies emerging from their dark tunnels as she would the arrival of her loved ones stepping off a train.

She says she would live it all again: "Yes, Lord, would go right back, just like I did from the beginning, because I loved it, I sure did." In retirement, she remembers and cherishes the memory of the over-a-thousand times when out of the whole history of the world, the newest, youngest, freshest person on earth squeezed into view, with an eye on Mama Pearlie, and somersaulted into her hands.

Essay on Midwife Story

I first met an old-fashioned midwife, what they called in north Georgia a "granny-woman," six years ago, when I was pregnant with my first child, a daughter. "Stand up and let me look at you," she said. "That's a boy."

"I bet it's a girl," I said.

"Yeah, a boy, and coming in November," she pronounced.

"I'm due in October," I said, but she would have none of it. When I turned up again, in October, with newborn Molly, she remembered. "You got your girl," she said.

"I did."

"If you'd waited till November, it would have been that boy."

No matter how many high-tech procedures the pregnant woman is put through these days; no matter how stylishly coiffed and business-suited she might be as she sits in the O.B.'s waiting room, leafing through the files from her briefcase; no matter with what authority the hospital technicians, manning the ultrasound screen, assert, with their backs turned, "It's a boy," there is still something unknowable about the whole business, something ancient, instinctive, and mysterious. But we live in an age of sonograms, amniocentesis, and fetal monitors. We live at a time when the question most frequently asked of pregnant women is not "What are you hoping for?" but "What sex is it?" We live in an age and country in which vast numbers of women give birth supine on a metal table, feet in stirrups, shaved and enema'd; and where the highest percentage of women in any nation on earth lie half-drugged during childbirth, while the obstetrician makes an incision.

I lived on fresh eggs and whole-wheat bread, garden tomatoes and pitchers of whole milk while pregnant, and walked through the countryside swinging my arms and singing. I did not want this onslaught of technical procedures and medications. Therefore I sought out a midwife, a modern one, to deliver my child, though it meant my husband had to drive me in labor an hour-and-a-half to get to her. She was a skinny, gum-chewing wise-cracking woman of about thirty, with curly blonde hair and graduate degrees, and I liked her very much. In the early morning darkness, when I clung to the side of the bed for dear life and the bed rocked like a boat, she was as blasé as a summer day. When she hauled the wet baby up into the sharp air, she was like a fisherman who had made a great catch. She stroked my hair, and wrapped the baby and me in blankets together, and brought me a breakfast tray. I learned that not so long before, in north Georgia where we lived, midwives had been all around.

For a solid year after my daughter's birth, I dwelled on the event for a few moments every night before sleep: how I'd gotten to understand the rhythm of the contractions; how I'd pushed the baby out; how my husband and the midwife had cheered me on; how the black-haired, black-eyed, rosy-cheeked baby had come wringing through. After a year I still felt, on some deep level, intrigued by the bare facts: that we'd driven to the hospital birthing center with me in the back of the station wagon, the baby inside me, and the overnight bag in the carseat, and driven home the next morning with the suitcase in the back of the station wagon, breakfast inside me, and the baby in the carseat.

I wrote about my daughter's birth and about modern midwives for *Country Journal* in 1982. The article did not wear out my interest in the subject, nor lessen the pressure I felt to tell everyone that there was another way to go about childbearing. Most of the women I spoke with at that time—my mother, and friends, and friends' mothers—seemed skeptical; I was an Amazon, they concluded; I might as well have bragged that I'd discovered you could cook food over a fire and had begun cooking dinner over a campsite on the kitchen floor. It seemed to me a rich subject to write about again.

I suppose, in a way, my constant subject in nonfiction has been people whose stories recall an earlier time. A few years ago, when I lived in coastal Georgia, I wrote a portrait of an old man who'd grown up on Tybee Island (now named Savannah Beach) when a coal-burning little train carried tourists out there, and Guy Lombardo and the Dorsey Brothers performed for Roaring Twenties dance crowds on huge graceful wooden pavilions above the surf. In recent times, Savannah Beach had become a tired little row of chain motels and burger joints and cheap carnivals, but in Mr. Buckley's eyes it was a fine and elegant place. The following year I interviewed elderly people in a rural black community in McIntosh County, on the coast: a man whose childhood memories began with the assassination of President McKinley—"It were a black man caught the killer when he ran, and the people were so proud"; and a woman who'd been raised by her manumitted grandmother, who had slave stories firsthand to repeat—"She said it were the Yankees what freed them. Yeah, the Yankees. You ever seen a Yankee?"

The language of these old people was the most vivid, the most idiosyncratic and personal, and the wittiest I'd ever encountered. Mr. Buckley embarked, one day, on a description of the women's bathing suits of the 1920s, which consisted, I gather, of bloomers and various fasteners. He gave up, finally, and said, "I really knew nothing then about the nomenclature and wherewithal of the female." The stories of Deacon Curry and Mrs. Palmer in McIntosh County were hilarious and truthful and sad. When I interviewed them, I used a tape recorder. I set it down close to them and when I played the tapes back later I played and rewound, played and rewound, sometimes listening to a phrase half a dozen times to get the syntax right, the cadence right, the meaning right, because it was not the kind of language I could recreate myself. I spend a reasonable portion of my research time interviewing younger, college-educated professional people, and though I often use the tape recorder with them, especially if they speak quickly, I don't pore over it when transcribing. The language of my peers is smooth, brisk, and efficient, full of modern references and bland expressions, and easy to simulate if a word is lost in transcription. When I played back Mrs. Palmer's tapes—and she was a very old and hoarse and nearly toothless woman, living with her retarded son in a cabin the dirt roads didn't even go to—I found myself transcribing mere sounds, at times unconnected syllables, because I simply couldn't understand what she was saying. On the tape was my cheerful, high-pitched, well-enunciated little question, then silence, then a deep bass, hoarse, rough and coughing noise, then a pause, then another perky question. I read the rows of transcribed syllables aloud to myself and sometimes, remarkably, I heard sentences. I loved this work. It is a writer's version of archaeology.

Pearlie Burton was easy to understand, but her language had all the unpredictability, invention, and wit that I loved, that you simply won't find—or very, very rarely—in our contemporaries. When not inundated by the flat urban vocabulary of radio, television, and newspapers—when fed, on the contrary, by the holy effusions of rural preachers—talk fills up with fun and daring, and the mind finds its own way to get at a subject.

Pearlie Burton was the mother-in-law of a woman, a former city bus driver, who babysat for my children when we move to Atlanta. I told her a midwife had delivered the children and she told me of Pearlie Burton. I had her call Hartwell to introduce me, then Pearlie and I had a few shouting conversations over the crackly phone lines. "Sure, you come on up!" she yelled. The directions to her house—a drive of several hours—were like those I'd received before when trying to drive to subjects who lived in houses without house numbers on streets with no names: "You come on down, you come on down, then stop at a store and ask somebody."

I took my little son with me. I took him for several reasons. For one, he was a baby and still nursing. For another, there is no better way to break the ice—especially with old people, or with people from a different culture, or with anyone who might find you intimidating or unwelcome—than to show up either pregnant or with a baby. And finally, since Pearlie was a midwife, I thought it would be fine to show up with her favorite topic of conversation. She was warm and gracious, and loved the baby—"He's gonna be something in life," she said, "going to have lots of friends"—and she fed me the worst lunch I have ever eaten. I think she couldn't begin to fathom what a tall white woman from Atlanta might eat, and she presented me with a peanut butter and jelly sandwich on a hamburger bun with a thin-sliced hot-dog covered with ketchup inside. I guess she wanted to cover all the options. The next time I went to visit, I *brought* lunch for both of us.

She was an easy subject and a natural storyteller. (And these, too, are hard to find. Sometimes, even when the speech is colorful, you've got to wait a long, long time for it to meander in the direction of a point being made.) She was happy to have some company. We got along well together, laughed a lot while I flipped the cassette tapes and she rocked my child. She showed me old pictures and introduced me to neighbors and seemed to look forward to my visits. Now, pregnant with my third child, I've wondered a few times whether I'd ask Pearlie Burton to deliver this next baby if she lived in Atlanta. The answer is: I'm not sure. But I wouldn't say unequivocally no. If she lived next door and could deliver me at home, I'm fairly certain I would choose that option over laboring in the back of a Toyota on I-20 West.

As for writing the story, it went pretty quickly. The trick is simply to write down precisely what interests and amuses you and not a word more. No filler. No background unless it sparked an interest in you when you heard it. When you re-read, strike all sections you find yourself skimming. An article should read like good conversation, like the best conversation, and should be full of ups and downs and surprises. I've learned that from the old people. When your subject herself talks like that, the business is twice as easy. When your subject is a college-educated younger person, the actual quotes you use may be fewer, and you'll have to provide the liveliness of language yourself.

In college I attended a lecture given by a prominent visiting feminist. She invoked the matriarchal societies of humanity's primitive past and spoke of the awe and respect surrounding women who magically conceived and fattened and bore. She joked that she liked to imagine the look on the face of the first Stone Age woman who figured out what *actually* was initiating pregnancy, all comets and floods and harvest dances aside. It must have been a look which implied, "You have *got* to be kidding. *That?*" "It was another fifty thousand years," said the speaker, "before the women told the men."

I liked this story and I like it even more today, a dozen years later. I've seen how pregnancy is nothing at all—bears no earthly resemblance to—copulation; how giving birth is, in its turn, nothing at all like pregnancy; and how living with a baby is remarkably unlike the prior three events. There is absolutely no hint at any stage of what lies ahead. There's no logic to it. There is logic in the concept that if you overeat, you'll gain weight. But copulation, pregnancy, birth, and parenthood are four distinct and unique episodes which we, following the lessons of the millennia, have learned to string together like beads and read in sequence. Viewed askance, the sequence makes about as much logical sense as: you go for a jog; when you come home, your hair has turned red; nine months later you swim the English channel; and when you go back home, four cats start living with you.

I was interested in Pearlie Burton's ability to read childbearing events by the light of her own reason and logic, as if a precocious child, or a visitor from another planet, were to observe and try to make sense of things without reference to the authorized version. By the light of Pearlie Burton's wisdom, there are crucial steps along the way to carrying and delivering a healthy baby, but they have less to do with what modern science tells us, and more to do with the magical sense that our primordial minds make of the process. If you pray and sing and wear clean clothes, you're going to have a prettier and smarter baby than if you slouch around cussing. Who can deny that that makes perfect sense and is, moreover, deeply satisfying in a way that the results of an ultrasound cannot be? If there is anything in our lives that should not be antiseptically stripped of the motherlore of a hundred thousand generations, it has to be pregnancy and childbirth.

These days, I'm asked all the time, "Is it a boy or a girl?" though the baby's not due for two months yet. I would not know, for the world. From the first moment I felt yet another of these minuscule, veiny, shrimp-like creatures clamp on inside and commence the long uncurling, I felt it to be full of infinite potential and beauty and secrecy. Who wants to hear that the nameless, silent, unborn wonderchild weighs *x* milligrams and has a penis visible to the sonogram videoscreen?

I loved Pearlie Burton when I met her, and loved her talk, and loved most of all her knowledge about childbearing, which contains the knowledge women always have had about childbearing—knowledge dating, I believe, from the years before they told the men.

QUESTIONS

Melissa Greene's essay, "All the Hours of the Night," and its process essay, "Essay on Midwife Story"

1. Pearlie Burton is uneducated in a traditional sense; she has no college degree and speaks with a dialect. She has perceptions about pregnancy and child-rearing that most doctors of obstetrics would dismiss. How does Greene—obviously educated herself—lend credence to the education Pearlie does have, the intelligence she does possess? How does she give Pearlie's observations and insights legitimacy? Does Greene ever appear condescending toward Pearlie?

2. The essay is not written in the first person. While we know as readers Greene has interviewed Pearlie Burton, Greene's physical presence is not in the essay. Why do you think Greene made that choice? What advantages does this strategy give her? What disadvantages? How would you describe the voice of the narrator when Pearlie Burton or someone else is not speaking? Is it objective or subjective? What does the narrator achieve that a simple transcription of an interview could not achieve?

3. In her process essay Greene writes, "I wrote about my daughter's birth and about modern midwives for *Country Journal* in 1982.... It seemed to me a rich subject to write about again." Are there essays you've written in this or other classes that after finishing them you felt you had more to say or more to offer, that you hadn't exhausted the topic? If you have a copy of such an essay, return to it and reread it. What seems to be missing? What other directions would you pursue? What have you learned since you wrote that essay, both about the topic and about writing?

4. Greene says of writing, "The trick is simply to write down precisely what interests and amuses you and not a word more. No filler. No background unless it sparked an interest in you when you heard it. When you re-read, strike all sections you find yourself skimming." When you're writing, are you conscious of when you're using "filler"? Do parts or all of your writing seem uninteresting? If so, what is the source of the disinterest, and how could you go about changing the way you write or present information in a particular essay in order to make your work more interesting to you?

Possible Writing Topics

1. Consider the people you know or are acquainted with or have access to, and choose one to interview in order to form an essay about that person.

Try to choose someone whose experience is vastly different from your own, someone from whom you would have much to learn. Perhaps this person will be from a different country, or a different part of this country, but this isn't necessary. The key is that you're able to conduct an interview where the information you receive will be rich with material. You may want to prepare questions in advance and bring along a tape recorder. Remember, you're not simply transcribing an interview, but instead writing an essay based on an interview.

2. After you've completed the essay, write a second one on the difficulty you had composing an essay based on an interview. Was your job fairly easy, or was it difficult? Did you find as you wrote that you lacked information you needed for completing the essay? How did you connect parts of the interview you conducted, and which parts did you choose to eliminate and why? Was the interview itself difficult? How? What questions would you ask now that you failed to ask the first time?

Julianne Moore

Vanishing

*I*T was bitter cold, the playground just snatches of coat colors and blowing bright scarves and bobbing hats. The discordant children's voices fused, and the wind-child voice, as with a foreign tongue, seemed to speak one single word to a hidden listener.

Patch, Beverly, Nadine, and Nadine's 6th grade brother Scamper huddled together in a corner of the schoolyard, in a closed circle against the wind. Scamper took a cigarette from his sock and lit it.

"Gimme a hit," said Nadine. Both Scamp and Nadine were gangly, with chaffed greyish skin.

"Yeah," Beverly said. She was a thickset girl, almost squat; her facial skin was darkish yellow, her round fattish cheeks, the color of old butter.

"Gotta inhale," said Scamp and passed the cigarette to Beverly. "I got somethin' to do anyhow."

Nadine said, "You're gonna get your ass caught." Her hair plaits were tight so her eyebrows seemed to arch and give her face a quizzical expression. Scamp brought a spray can from the breast of his jacket and lay on his back on the cold gravel; he painted black squiggles along the bottom of the school wall, as he did most days. He called this his "writin'."

"That don't even say nothing," said Beverly, as she always did, and tossed her scarf over her shoulder, the theatrics of the gesture lost in the scarf itself as it was loosely knitted and blue and cheap. Then she took a drag from the cigarette.

"It say what that I know," said Scamp, and dotted a squiggle as though it were an "I."

"Tell Sidewinder that in the office," said Patch, in such a small voice that the wind swept it off before the others heard. She was a slender child, better dressed than the others, and tentative in all her movements; her careful gloved hands crept about her pockets now, then rapidly balled into fists.

Nadine squinted at Scamp's hieroglyph. "Ain't nobody can read it but you."

Scamp said, "That's right. Nobody gonna read me, but me."

Patch glanced from the wall and looked for, but didn't find, her first grade brother in the schoolyard; she felt a twinge of sadness, of the sort that's perceived only at the moment of its vanishing.

"You gonna get a hit or what?"

Patch turned and took the cigarette from Beverly—from one of her new friends, one of the children whom teachers addressed when they spoke of "personal hygiene," from one of the children to whom teachers gave the canned goods the rest brought from home before holidays.

Patch's former friends—Lisa, Joan, Elizabeth, Susan—passed in an impenetrable line of navy woolen coats, their arms linked, and Lisa, with whom Patch had once been closest friends, held the privileged position in the center of the line. Patch took a drag from the cigarette, imitating the way a television actress might smoke, waving her arm about before she brought the cigarette to her mouth. She tilted her neck backwards as she inhaled and closed one eye.

"Git it down, girl," Scamper said. His lip jutted at an ugly angle, exposing a row of crowded yellowed teeth. "DOWN," he said. "What you tryin' to do?" The school bell rang.

Patch stared at the line of her old friends and exhaled, as if the force of smoke itself might have some effect on their movement. She dropped the cigarette and ground it out in the gravel with the heel of her patent leather shoe, telling herself then, not in words, but with the language of a child's feeling, that she alone understood the seduction of the adult world, a world of smoking and painting and the dim dank apartment houses she visited now with her new friends, a world that was rich, cold, and dark, like earth itself.

"Go on," said Patch. She nodded for the "grits" to leave her. She leaned against the fence, pretending to straighten her thick, starchy leggings. She'd never smoked and she was dizzy. Then she ran, hat in hand, unevenly across the yard, passing swingsets and courts. The gold cross she wore bounced between her chin and her cumbersome scarf. Above, the clouds thickened and obscured her shadow, but the ground beneath her feet felt hard and real. The wind whistled, saying Who? Its one current rushed past her uncovered ears. Who?

The stairwell was dark and windless, enclosed by the building's contours. There, Lisa and the others blocked her way. The girls, as always, said nothing, but only stared as though Patch were the landscape offered by a window often passed. Their little shut up lips held back secret words, but only the vacuous eyes spoke, announcing Patch's invisibility. Cement, so hard and real before, turned to water and splashed soundlessly about Patch's feet. Then the silence spoke; Patch strained to hear the hatred hidden within the unsaid.

Lisa only cleared her throat and spit the secret onto Patch's cold, chapped cheek. Patch forced a smile. Lisa's mouth opened, an emptiness of fogged breath.

Like the laughing wind, WHOOSH, came the frightened excited laughs of the girls. The chatter of their dainty shoes echoed through the school house as they ran.

Patch was in the "smart class" with her old friends. That day, Mrs. Preston continually called upon her. Patch responded always correctly; she couldn't afford to be a poor student. Otherwise, she examined Lisa's fine white-blonde hair and the bold red apples against the pale blue fabric of her dress. How could the usual gamesome bickering have led to these silences which served now to position Patch as an outcast?

Sometimes, between questions, Mrs. Preston's or her own, Patch would think of the words her new friends used: that don't say nothin', ain't nobody can read it but you. Or of Lisa Louisa, who had black hair, and no skin at all, which made her odd, but then she wasn't white or black and she could smite the other Lisa with a look. Lisa Louisa carried a missal throughout the sky, and the sky was small, yet filled with laughter; unlike the wind's, it was not at anyone. Lisa Louisa had no father in such fantasies which, that day, were interrupted by the bell. Patch rose quickly from the hard seat of her desk so that she could leave before the others.

Patch and her brother Herschell, whom Patch called Hero, walked home together under the dim, filmy sky. Lisa's spit still burned on Patch's cheek, an almost welcome exterior locus for her internal mortification. The children studied and watched television until supper. At 6, their mother summoned them. Patch and Hero went down and sat together at the end of the dining table nearest the warm light of the kitchen where Mother transferred their meals from foil tins to earthenware plates. In silence, Mother laid two woven mats to protect the lace of the table cloth, then laid the heavy plates before the children. They felt then, in the removed expression of her eyes, the absence of their father.

"Have everything you need?" she asked, her voice distant.

Yes. The children nodded this response, attuned to their mother's needful silence. Then, their mother disappeared to another region of the house; Patch and Hero positioned their open books between the woven mats and their plates so that the plates pressed the binding and the pages would not turn as they ate. At 8, their bedtime, their father wasn't yet home.

The windowsill was flush with Patch's mattress; her face and pillow felt cool by the window. The cross Patch wore rested in her mouth and she pushed it about with her tongue. Across the street, the last lights in Lisa's house were extinguished, as if to further shun her from that world of blondeness and peace. The rose wallpaper with its barely visible pattern of scattered stars was illuminated by the sweeping beam of a headlight as a car rounded the corner outside, and the crucifix above the headboard, the watching Jesus, gleamed from the rose paper. Patch sat and seeing that it wasn't her father, sank again into the hard cold cotton of the sheets. The beam passed, erasing the star-filled room and Christ; Patch was left in darkness.

It was much later when the car door shut on her father's coat. He tugged at it, slipped on the ice, fell, got up, tugged, slipped on the ice. Then, he shook the coat off, leaving it caught in the door, and came inside. He was thirty, so Patch thought of him as an old man.

"Is that you?" came Patch's mother's voice.

"Well, I don't know. What do you think? Do you think it's me? I'll be; it's me." Her father laughed.

Her mother's voice rose, "You're going to wake my children." Downstairs, the bedroom door slammed.

Simultaneously, Patch prayed and recited her new friend's deviant phrases: Where ya at? Hail Mary full of grace the Lord is with thee. I ain't got nothin' bitch. Pray for us sinners now and at the hour of our death. O Master let me walk with thee in lowly paths of service and tell me thy secret—a favorite hymn.

From downstairs, the secretive murmur rose up, and her mother was saying, "You don't care about anything but yourself." Her father burst into a sloppy song: Many such ere we were born, have befallen here, ere this; May he that was crowned with thorn; Bring all men to His bliss, all men to His bliss.

Only at mass was there order and sweet silence. There—Patch genuflects, led by Lisa Louisa. She breathes frankincense and myrrh from the censor which swings about her, hears the organ's complex voice, gazes towards the figures of the Saints. She enters a pew and sinks into velvet pillows, all as if the scratchy wool of her Sunday dress might bunch, as if the whole vision might vanish, erasing the voices of father and Priest, those men's voices fusing into one voice that echoes the voice of God. *Bring all men to His bliss.* Her mother becomes as the Virgin and Patch is awed by her womanliness—her reserve and grace. Breasts and hips, obscured by pleats of a dress, are not body, but container of spirit. Perfume, incense itself. *Bring all men to His bliss.*

"Please stop."

"Oh," he began saying, "I know so much I can't take it, simply can't. I'm going to sell the house. Sell the house, that's what I'll do." Doors opened, shut. He appeared on the lawn with a "For Sale" sign, which he kept in the cellar.

Hero came to Patch's bedroom, wearing a cotton school shirt; he stood for a moment in a triangle of light cast from behind him in the hallway. He shut the door and lay next to Patch. Neither spoke; it was a ritual visitation, understood and requiring no words. Hero's thin knobby legs pressed against Patch's. Patch smoothed his hair, as if by mothering the boy, she mothered herself.

Hidden in the window, they watched their father pound the sign into the frozen ground with the flat edge of the ax. Their mother came outside and stood at a safe distance, wearing sneakers. Her nightgown hung to the ground beneath her open winter coat. The sign firmly set, their father staggered toward the house, dragging the ax behind him.

Though their father had long vanished within, their mother called out: "Patrick, Patrick, PAT, Patrick, Patrick, Patrick," until the name lost all meaning through its repetition. The last cries of the nameless name "Patrick" weakened in the wind and then the wind took his name to the other houses, announcing him to the ever present ears of the unseen others. A light in Lisa's house came on, a light so bright it leapt through the window, where Patch lay with Hero, just to flood her soul with shame. Outside, their mother released their father's coat from the car door, then leaned on the car. Slowly, she brushed the coat's wool with her tired hands, dusting off dirt and gravel from the drive, smoothing the wrinkles. Later, Patch felt the warmth of Hero's silent body as it slipped away. She reached out to keep him by her, whispering, "Please, Hero, don't go," but the sheet beside her, where he'd been, was cold.

Patch always woke unsure, but that morning too, the sign was gone. The house swelled with the sweet, rich odor of blueberries. Downstairs, her mother turned pancakes, wearing a soft, new robe. Patch's father smiled and continued eating.

Her mother smiled. "How many?"

"Two please," Patch said. "I'm starving."

"One," Hero said. "Please." He wore the same cotton shirt, having slept in it so he would not be late.

After breakfast Hero went to the living room and sat on the sofa and waited. Patch went upstairs for the children's school books. When she returned, her mother leaned her back against the oven, embracing Patch's father. Patch watched from the door frame, transfixed, both repulsed by and yet desirous of such a touch. Her father's hands pressed against her mother's outer thighs and pushed upwards over the roundnesses of her hips, causing the soft hem of the robe to rise. Her father opened his eyes, but only returned Patch's gaze as though such a moment were usual.

"Patch?" Her mother abruptly severed the embrace. Patch turned and went to the living room.

"C'mon," she said to Hero.

The two went to the car, aware of but not seeing the uprooted ground where the sign had been. Across the street, Lisa was leaving, her family car already started and warm, black jets pushing from the exhaust. Sometimes, Patch's father would offer a ride; Lisa's mother declined politely. Today, he cursed and pumped the gas unnecessarily, while attempting to start the car.

"Warming up now?" he asked, guiding the car beneath the whitish winter-bare branches of the tree-lined street.

"Yes, Daddy," the children said. "Yes."

The girls from Patch's class were filing inside, their arms rigid, their brightly gloved hands in warm balled up fists. The car felt suddenly warm.

"Bye, kids," her father said, and leaned over the seat, closing the car door behind the children.

"See ya," said Hero at the first grade door. He tugged at his coat and moved along the green wall, past construction paper crafts and a rigid row of desks with sharpened pencils in their blackened indented slots. He hung his wrap on the wooden peg cloak rack at the back of the room.

At recess, it was too cold to play outdoors. Patch's 3rd grade class filed to the multi-purpose room, boy-girl, boy-girl. A janitor arranged a circle of chairs for Mrs. Preston.

"Half of you sit," she said. Those who remained standing were to be directly behind those sitting down. Patch positioned herself behind Earl Shoemaker. Earl was distant and kind, a bookworm.

The Happiness Game began. The soft song commenced: *Nothing could be better than to be boys and girls, There's nothing finer in life.* Those sitting shut their eyes; the others were to walk the circle's periphery and whisper a kind thought into the ears of the sitting children. Patch bent and whispered to Earl *Nothing could be finer in life.* She moved on, her lips uncomfortably near the warm winter white paleness of others' skins. She listened: What would others say?

But then, the listeners no longer knew her. Her mind began to swell with voices. She whispered, "You are blessed among women. . . . You walk with me in lowly paths of service. . . ." The parental embrace still operative deep within her, she allowed herself to touch the others—the urgent skin of her cheek to graze other pale skins, the round of her shoulder to nudge into curved smalls of backs, damp terrified palms to bear on shoulders—but all so tentatively that the others, perhaps, felt nothing. "May he that was crowned with thorn," she whispered, "Bring all men to His Bliss." When she reached those whose silence tormented her, she held her sealed lips by their ears.

The children reversed positions. The chairs were high. Patch's feet wouldn't touch the floor. Outside the sitting circle, Patch could feel the others, comfortable in their own seeing circle, watch her shut her eyes and fold her hands. A song ended, another began, but no one addressed her; silence weighed within silence, an emptiness in emptiness, the music too, emptiness.

"Nigger lover, Catholic smoker, Patch is an ugly bitch." Hot sour breath lisped and hissed over the soft music, mimicking adult intonations. "Slime, lessy, fuck you." Patch rooted herself in the chair, apprehending then the maliciousness in the hearts of the others. She recognized Earl's voice, "Spring comes soon." It was a fool voice, ineffectual, stupid. Then it was done. She filed to the classroom with the others.

"Would you like to wash the boards?" Mrs. Preston asked at the door. It was a task for privileged students.

Tease, slut. Patch tried, but couldn't imagine girl-words coming from Mrs. Preston's small, inquiring mouth. She felt a fierce overwhelming despair mixed with longing, and reached in her blazer pocket, taking out a small hairbrush. She gave it to Mrs. Preston. "I love you."

Mrs. Preston laughed and said, "I know," as she had to many children. In the hallway, Patch thought that perhaps the voices of the others didn't matter.

God spoke through all. Perhaps He had chosen her, for some Divine reason, to be among the hated.

Later, after the last bell, Patch and Beverly stood on the school steps. Hero crossed with the school guard, his tiny self-possessed figure all bundled up, and so seemingly innocent and easy, that suddenly Patch yelled, "Hero." He turned in the street. She waved. "Be careful." His red hat bobbed in reply.

Scamp and Nadine waved from the school bus, their hands long grey shadows on the sidewalk. "Goodbye," they called from the window. "Goodbye." Their voices merged with those of the other parting friends. "Later. See ya. Til tomorrow. Call ya. After while. Goo-bye."

Patch and Beverly waved. "Goodbye."

Then they walked through the alleyways to Beverly's. Her apartment was a unit in a divided house, the exterior of which was the red color of mud-clay. A heavy door led through another door, then to a hallway which was like a dank canal, narrow and unlit.

Inside, in the main room, which was high ceilinged and cold and sparsely furnished, the girls lay their coats on the floor by the threadbare couch. Through the empty dining room were two doors; Beverly went into one of the rooms, brought back a flannel shirt and tossed it to Patch. "Oughta put something on," she said. The shirt was a man's shirt and soft, ripped in the sleeve. Patch pulled it on over her blouse. Beverly herself put on another sweater; she seemed to already have breasts, though there were only fatty rows of skin, visible beneath the tightness of her sweater. The room smelled of incense that Beverly's mother burned in flat brass censors, the odor of mass.

Beverly knelt by a steam heat register and grunted, trying to turn the knob.

The other bedroom door opened. "Told you not to be turning that thing." Beverly's mother, a thin woman with long grey hair, leaned in her bedroom door jamb, in a nightgown. There was a triangle of light where her legs parted. "You gonna answer me?"

"*She's* here," said Beverly.

Beverly's mother shrugged. "There's cokes if y'all want them." She went back in her room, shutting the door.

"She don't like the steam up," said Beverly. She grunted again, the knob gave, and a gurgle of water, like a brook in the room, sounded from the register. Beverly flicked a radio on, and the two girls sat on the couch. All the songs were of love but the music only served to expose the room's barren poverty. Patch could feel the draft from the windows and glancing behind her saw that towels lay along the windowsills to keep out the wind. She pressed the collar of the flannel shirt to her mouth and breathed; her breath fused with the soft smokey smell of the shirt. The girls swayed and sang the radio songs, tapping their feet in time on the cold, bare floorboards. Unlike Beverly, who knew all the words, Patch only lifted bits of phrases and choruses. The girls' voices returned. "Scuzzy nigger lover bitch." Patch blocked them whispering, *I love ta love ya baby.*

"Get offa me, faggot," came J. T.'s deep voice. He was Beverly's eighth grade brother. He came in, shaking Paul's hand from his shoulder. When he saw the girls, he flashed a wide, strong-toothed smile.

"Lookey here," he said. "Lookey here." He ran his hand through his thick, black, curly hair. Paul was taller than J. T. and very thin, with slouching shoulders and a body that looked bent, like a bow. He threw his jacket in the floor and lay down on it, hands clasped behind his head.

"Who might you be?" J. T. asked, still standing.

"Met you before," Patch lied, attempting to replicate the hard, guttural sounds of Beverly's and J. T.'s speech.

"You never met me before," J. T. said. "You're lyin'."

Patch stared straight into J. T.'s eyes which were wide-set and round and dark. She said, "No way."

"Why don't you just get outta here?" said Beverly.

J. T. took off his jacket and leaned down and shoved a rolled magazine and a notebook into the jacket's sleeve. He tossed his jacket on top of Patch's.

"I wanna watch t.v.," Paul said from the floor. "Don't y'all wanna watch t.v.?"

"Fuck no," J. T. glanced toward the girls as if to gauge their response to his obscenity. Patch, mimicking Beverly, ignored him and rocked to the music. *I know something about love.*

J. T. went to the kitchen and returned with a spoon of peanut butter. He sat on the couch, between Patch and Beverly.

Beverly's heavy upper body stopped shimmying. "I'm gonna tell ma if you don't get outta here."

"Think she cares?" J. T.'s long pointed tongue curled about the spoon. He turned towards Patch. "Listenin' to the radio?" Patch mouthed *Do ya, do ya, do ya wanna dance.* "Go ta school? Whadda ya like ta do? That my shirt?"

"Is it?" Patch's snapping fingers made no sounds.

"Ya want your stupid shirt?" asked Beverly.

"I guess she can wear it," said J. T. He made smacking sounds with his mouth and lay the clean licked spoon on the coffee table. He drummed the table with his hands, and whispered along with the song, watching Patch. *I think we're alone now. There doesn't seem to be anybody around. Look at the way we've gotta hide what we're doin'.*

"Gotta cigarette?" said Paul loudly. The two boys laughed. Patch missed some words of the chorus and half smiled as if she understood their laughter.

"Sure." J. T. tossed a cigarette to Paul, then held two in his mouth, lighting them both. He gave one to Patch.

"What about me?" J. T. tossed another cigarette to Beverly's feet. "Thanks a lot," she said and turned up the radio: *Don't give me no hand-me-down love, I got some already.* Patch inhaled and tried to fight the dizziness.

"So tell me something good," said J. T. Paul burst out laughing. His lip jutted out at an ugly angle and exposed a mouth of crowded yellow teeth. He fell suddenly silent and drew on his cigarette. Patch shut her eyes against her dizziness and the voices: lessy, fuck you, nigger lover. J. T.'s voice was low, deep, and yet soft. "Ain't you gonna say nothin'?"

"She's a mute," said Paul. "Ya know, one of them people who don't never say nothin'."

Patch stubbed her cigarette out. Then, hands empty, she held her cross between a thumb and forefinger and ran it up and down its gold chain. Patch shrugged, glancing around. "Where's your room?"

"Wherever I want," J. T. said. "That right Paul?" Paul nodded.

"Why don't y'all go somewhere?" Beverly said suddenly.

J. T. said, "We went to right here. Why don't y'all girls get us some cokes?"

"Don't wanna." Beverly stood, tugging at her sweater which had risen as she shimmied. "C'mon," she said to Patch. Standing, Patch saw the crumpled magazine in the sleeve of J. T.'s coat. A white lacy garter, a white thigh. She followed Beverly to the kitchen.

"They wanna fool around," Beverly said as she poured the drinks. Her voice was noncommital. Patch shrugged with an equal indifference. The girls re-entered the room, Patch smiling, nervous now, like a hostess, a drink in each hand. She forgot that Beverly was even there; she was so distant from Patch's own beauty, excitement and charm.

Patch sipped her drink and took another cigarette from J. T. when he offered it.

"Aren't you going to drink your coke?" she asked.

"Naw," he said.

Beverly sang loud, *Baby, ba-baby try to find a little time and I'll make you happy, Oh so happy, I'm so happy.*

The cigarette smoke sickened Patch's stomach and burned deep in her throat. Dizzy, she squinted through the smoke, into the dank largeness of the room. Somewhere beyond the love-music was the steam heater and beyond that the gurgling of water. The damp and cold seeped through the floorboards, through shoes and socks; she tapped her feet, no longer in time with the music, on the black dirt of earth itself. And the outer wind was in the room, drifting through the towels along the windowsills. It spoke, "Worm, nothing." *Oh my baby love.*

She said, "I feel dizzy."

"Feel ok?" asked J. T. "Lean on me; you're gonna be all right. Lean on me, my baby love—" his soft sonorous voice weaved itself through the love-music. "It's all all right."

"Leave her alone," said Beverly. "She's my friend."

"Wanna go now and get you some air?"

"Sure," Patch said. They got their coats. Patch walked across that floor feeling as though she were stepping into her soul.

She felt confident following J. T. and Paul through the kitchen door and around the side of the building. In the silence, the songs still played for her: the complex chapel organ sang—O Master let me walk with thee in lowly paths of service. Her protests unheard, Beverly's fat, unattractive figure drifted off towards a hedge and some trashcans. She averted her face and swayed by the cans.

Bring all men to His bliss, all men to His bliss. Patch followed J. T. down the cellar stairs, with Paul behind her. The wind rushed by saying Who? Who? Who are you? but for Patch, for the first time, the wind said nothing, only moved in a comfortable silence. *Tell me thy secret.*

Paul's hand pushed her shoulder, but Patch only felt and heard the wind's silence. At the cellar door, J. T. half turned to Patch in the wind-silence only she could hear. His beautiful round black eyes had many little lights deep inside them and all were lit up. "We'll come in here, it's warmer," he said. "So much warmer."

The cellar door opened. Inside, white cords of clothesline were strung across the room. The clothes, hung wet, were frozen, the arms of blouses, rigid.

"Whatever you want," Patch said. She smiled into the deep black lights of J. T.'s eyes.

Sources of "Vanishing"

COLERIDGE writes that his poem "Kubla Khan" was "conceived in a profound [anodyne] sleep . . . in which all the images rose up as things without any sensation of consciousness of effort. . . ." Drug sleep, visions, mystery, spontaneity, genius, intuition, talent—some part of all writers, amateur like myself or professional, like Coleridge, wants to talk about the craft of writing and its process in such terms; to do otherwise is to sever our privileged connection with God, the muses, the Inspirer. However, I can't rely on Coleridge's earlier language. It seems more useful nowadays for writers to recognize themselves as workers. Our product, our writing, involves planning, thinking, re-working, and long hours of devotion and sore behinds. Intuition alone hardly produces works of fiction.

If a story is a complex form, to turn around again and tell the story of the "sources" of one's story is a task, doubly complex, unless one makes Coleridge's claims. Porter, in a source essay, likens the task to "tapping one's own spinal fluid," and talks about the way in which each new writing project immediately announces a new series of problems. For me, this source essay posed more problems than the story itself. First, do you really wish to tell others how hard you work? Perhaps, if your story's Faulkner's "Barn Burning," and you don't mind severing your connection with spontaneous genius. And then, how accurate is your memory? You know there's no presence of event, that you perceive, then slip, delete, embellish, and finally, you may as well just say, create. Memories mold together in odd ways; time collapses; clocks melt; the contradictory is juxtaposed, umbrellas and spools stand side by side. All surreal paintings tell the story of memory. Then, the story itself has a sly way of displacing memory. This is both a reader's and a writer's problem. When we read stories for the first time, whether the story is our own or another's, we tend to overlook the way in which details "add up to" or fit in with the main ideas of the story. Why does a character have a certain name or live in a particular sort of house? At first, we tend to say, "Well, it just happened that way," forgetting momentarily that the details in the story have been carefully selected by the writer. The author, who makes decisions and selects details, is obscured in story. My own memories feel false; finally, I say of my own stories, "X or y happened because that's the way it really was."

Once I have an image of a character, I can write his story. My character Hero, in "Vanishing," seems, in retrospect, to be a real boy. In my imagination, I see Hero as he is when he crosses the street with the school guard. He's never bundled and warm as he is in the story; he doesn't bother to button his coat; his shirt's wrinkled and awry. At 6, there's a whole world inside him. It's clear already that he's a person who will never much care what he looks like, how he's perceived by others. Is he a conflation of my own brothers? Patch's desire to protect, my own desire? Have I seen that child at some bus stop or grocery? I can't recall. He's just Hero as he crosses the street with a school guard. I once thought that Beverly, Scamp, and Nadine were real, that I had even used their real names, but in yearbooks, I can't find the names or faces that match my mind's pictures.

When you've completely lost, as I have here, a very sure sense of what "really" happened—when fictional characters seem real—you can no longer claim to perform two differing activities, to tell a "fictional" story and to write an essay grounded in fact. Is this essay any less a reconstructing of, or creation of, my experience than the story itself?

Further, I ask as Welty does: How can one make generalizations about process when each story is a specific event with its distinct process, and set of problems and circumstances? "Vanishing" is in its 3rd draft, and it isn't finished. The surrealistic events I'd hoped to include in it never made the page; the wind hasn't said enough, the cement hasn't become water enough.

Patch, as far as I'm concerned, in part anyway, has been raped by language, since she has internalized the violent voices she hears from her schoolmates, mass, and even her parents. Through internalizing and repeating these outside voices, she loses her "real self." A reversal occurs: at the end of the story she reacts not as the person she was at the beginning of the story but as a person who is filled with others' voices. In such an upside-down world, it seems fitting that things should be personified, that the wind should talk more in a new draft. I can't generalize about "process" here. This is only one of, I think, three stories that I've revised. Many of my other stories were actually written like "Kubla Khan" in one sitting, some in anodyne sleep; none were revised. Or, I should say that none were revised in the exact manner of this one.

Other questions arose during the writing of this essay. In speaking of sources, what should you say or not say about your own personal life? Should you focus on textual changes through drafts? Is the mental-emotional state you might write about that state as it's recalled in the memory of event: how I now think I may have felt as a child? Or, state of mind during composition as you recall it: which draft? What about intertextual references? It seems important that I was reading *Their Eyes Were Watching God* and wanted Zora Neale Hurston's voice, and that I wished I could make my character Hero more like Holden Caulfield's sister Phoebe in *The Catcher in the Rye*. The books we read greatly influence the way we write. The mechanical process itself seems a "source" to me; my new willingness to revise has as much to do with the advent of word processing as anything else. Traditional story form itself is surely a source of this story. The form of the story, with its necessary beginning, middle, end, and emphasis on character development and change, gives me a prescribed way to structure and form the chaotic stuff of memory. Also, in a sense, the form creates me. As I said before, I tend to forget actual memories after writing a story; the story *feels* like something that really happened to me. So stories create a new past for me. While writing this essay, I also asked myself: How would this story be different if it hadn't been produced for a class I was taking? I'm sure I asked myself, though not consciously, if the others in the class would find that the story lacked a traditional climax—a change for the "better" in the main character's consciousness. I knew people would say there were point of view transgressions, places where the narrator sees things that the main character doesn't.

Clearly, the creation of the sources of one's story is not a restorative activity, a reconstructing, an activity that intends to explain a story's "real" origins and through doing so explain the story. Once, my students (for lack of a better designation for they do not belong to me) produced story-narratives in reaction to Edvard Munch's painting, "The Scream." A wide variety of interpretations emerged. The painting's main figure was said to be both male and female, for instance. I read Munch's own visionary account, his painting a "scream passing through nature ... clouds as actual blood." The students admitted: either they were wrong or Munch was a bad painter, one unable to produce his intended effects. Was he famous, someone asked. It seems to me that, on the one hand, any writer of a something is finally relegated to the position of reader, like any reader. The students' interpretations of "The Scream" were as valuable as Munch's. It's a difficult position sometimes, as any writer might say, to find that one's "real, translated, relayed" experience, one's deeply felt point, one's words, are interpreted, to find that you don't "own" your own story, to see that your sense of a piece may have next to nothing to do with what makes it make sense for another. On the other hand, a writer is always a special reader of her work. Writings reverberate with the residual, early drafts, the untold material, the material told and cut, the time spent in production, the complex emotions that the writer felt and that asked the piece to be written, and, too, the sense of one's own failures and accomplishments in the story. Having now rid myself of half my project by asking questions, I'll now try to be that "special reader."

This story has a few beginnings. One, though I couldn't say the first, is the last paragraph's image: I see brown snow, patched grass and empty cellar stairs on the kind of bitter day when concrete looks white. The cellar door's green, its paint chipped, its knob, a round ring, and through it I see strings of clothes line, from corner to corner to corner of the cellar, like streamers; it's a macabre, mock-party image; the brightly colored clothes, made white by an ice-dust that covers them, hang upside down, crumpled and wrinkled, in dancer-like positions, sexual and yet completely frozen. In describing the image for this essay, just now, I have transformed it yet again. Initially, the image was not necessarily sexual. It was just one of many mental pictures, like a photograph in quality, which was detached from a specific time or place. I've no idea why it found its way into this particular story or, vice versa, how it may have given rise to other material. Only now does it appear as "sexualized" to me, much more so than in the story. Before now, I didn't see the extent to which the clothes were a necessary part of the mock party I was writing. Indeed, I hadn't described the scene in this particular way, as a "mock, macabre party." The clothes just felt right; I couldn't explain them. Until now, this image was still nearly bare, though it had some unnatural, surreal quality even before; it congealed with other story elements, then re-emerged as more potently sexual. At this moment I am re-writing the story. I see now that the clothes are, in fact, or could be in another draft, dancing. That seems now what I meant to say. This is Patch's situation: she "dances" with J. T. only at the moment when she no longer has being, when she's a locus of others' voices, when she is frozen. She doesn't speak voices. Rather, at the story's end, the voices which she's internalized speak her, causing her to act in a way she wouldn't have before. To me, this seems an almost unreal moment, in which clothes must dance and the wind must speak. Through writing this essay, it has become increasingly clear to me that my story is unfinished. I suddenly want to account for my "scatteredness," like Coleridge, saying that I too was "called out by a person from Porlock and detained by him for above an hour," and thus my "vision" lost.

Another beginning is in the things I wanted to learn about writing. My next story, I had told myself, was to be re-written, to be first person, to be serious, not funny, and to be about childhood—all things I hadn't done before. Some lessons I learned, some I didn't. The first draft began, "When I was eight and in 3rd grade, and my secret name was Lisa Louisa . . ." The narration was straightforward, and thus taught me nothing about the indirection that 1st person affords, about being, as Fitzgerald's character Nick Carraway, "unusually communicative in a reserved sort of way." The first person did offer a tension between past and present, as the piece was centered around an adult narrator's memories of alienation from her peers and her encounter with a former teacher, but the narrative voice emerged as too bland and nostalgic. I'd wanted to write about being shunned from the real Lisa's group when I was a child, to explore the effect that had on me, and the voice that made the page couldn't speak my anger. Doubly so since, as a story about alienation and childhood initiation, I wanted to, in some ways, express my anger at institutions, family, church, and school. I was more interested, then, in some of the material from my own memory that came from that speaker's mouth, material that's all been cut in revision. Much of this now seems to me the "unwritten place" in this story.

I'd remembered the pool where I'd swum as a child. It was a private pool sandwiched between Upper and Lower Donnely Hollows. I shouldn't say sandwiched though because the pool was at the mouth of Lower Donnely, a middle class section; Upper Donnely was separated by a few miles of empty country road; the few poor children from my grade school lived there. Three or so miles from the house where I grew up, it's a place I've only seen once. I'd remembered Upper Donnely kids, sometimes double on stingray bikes, leaning against the small section of the Greenbriar's fence, the part that wasn't hedged in, fingers through the fence. Inside, our mothers seemed oblivious to everything—never sweating, never getting wet; they had large round raccoon whites about their eyes from their huge sunglasses; their husbands, our fathers, had disappeared to their mysterious jobs.

I'd remembered that someone, Norman Lewis, I think, brought a black boy there to swim, and that he wasn't allowed in on some pretext of his swim trunks being not quite right.

I'd remembered a writing prize I'd won in the 6th grade. Annette Greene, a black girl, who lived in Upper Donnely, but who was somehow surviving in the system, not beaten down by hygiene lectures, who produced good work, badly wanted to win the prize, a savings bond. The theme of our essay was "patriotism." I giggled at the back of the classroom with my friend Joan; we made a contest of the assignment to see who could produce the most cliche-ridden essay. (We wouldn't have used the word "cliche"; I don't know how we termed it then.) My essay ended with a country worth "living for, fighting for, dying for," and the joke won. Annette Greene cried in the bathroom.

I'd remembered that in first grade, in punishment for talking in class, I was sent to the 3rd reading group, a small group composed of the children who were bused to school. I'd read more books than anyone in my first grade class and thus had more gold stars beside my name on the chart at the front of the room. I was devastated by my punishment. I wonder now what the others felt.

School days, as I recalled them, were barbaric. The architectural space was terrifying too—rows of toilets, sinks, desks—the "smarter" children seated in front, the poorer in the back, boys and girls separated spatially. My feet never touched the floor, giving me the constant sense of floating, being ungrounded. My grade school was ugliest in its attempt to hide its many ways of separating people. Bulletin boards, doorways, hallways, and stairwells were plastered with brightly colored signs and decorations. These were the things I had remembered.

In the 1st draft, the memories congealed around the themes of race, class, education, but they were childhood memories, and the speaker spoke them as such from a time when I had experienced myself as an insider, secure to some extent in family, church, school, friendships. But things had changed for me. After all it was I who had been transferred from high school to high school, a disciplinary problem; I who had left school and my family, full of rage, at 16. Annette Greene stayed in Charleston, in Upper Donnely, graduating with the others; she won scholarships.

So: I dropped the speaker and memories, though retained some better sense of what the issues of the story were. This, in turn, created another problem: Could I tell the story from a child's point of view and still tell an "adult" story? This is perhaps the greatest of writing problems. I knew I wasn't an accomplished enough writer to even attempt such a "voice," so I chose a more distant narration which might have the possibility of detaching itself from the character; the narration doesn't do this as much as it should, but at several points in the story does see things Patch doesn't. At the end of the story, the wind is speaking; Patch doesn't hear it.

In the period immediately preceding the writing of this story, I'd been sick and hospitalized for a month. It was during this time that a number of disparate elements came together: the Lisa material, the initial image, a story I'd once heard from a man whose alcoholic father kept a For Sale sign in the basement which he put up during fights with his wife. That story came to me here for several reasons. First, because the story as the man told it was not so much about the sign itself, but about his embarrassment and feelings of alienation upon "accidentally" telling the story of the sign to a group of adults from less dysfunctional homes. Second, at that point, I felt I needed a parental scene, to help account for the actions of the child. This man's story moved into that slot. If I were to re-write now, that's something I might change. I'm not sure the story fits with the other material. Why a For Sale sign? The "Happiness Game," which the children play when it's too cold to go outdoors, somehow attached itself. The game is really a self-affirmation therapy exercise which I took part in once. It was much as it's written in the story. About 50 adults were present and were told to whisper to others things they wished their parents had told them as children. I was deeply moved by that experience. This, as well, became grafted onto the sense of a domestic scene that attempts to explore my household, as I recall it, immediately before my parents' separation. Why did these things come together as they did? What causes one memory to gel around another? Try as I might, I really can't say.

There are many other things I could say. The connected memories of untold place that I bring to this story, as its special reader, are incomplete. The questions I raised in the beginning of this paper give some sense of where I would go if I were to continue. I don't understand the terms—mystery, talent, genius,—and much less do I understand a "writer's intuition," which attempts to sever the connection between storytelling and "intellectual thought." This story, finally, exists for me in the heart of an intellectual problem. On the one hand, it bespeaks my distaste for traditional form and my fear of being changed, unaware, by internalizing languages from the outside world. I refuse a traditional climax in this story, as I said before, and thus refuse to admit, through form, that suffering necessarily brings inevitable, positive change. On the other hand, I feel deeply indebted to story form; only stories can give me a way of ordering complex and disparate emotions and events. Only through writing do I feel that I've grown and have some mastery over life and some critical distance from my experience. I feel myself caught in a Patch-like relationship to language; I too continually internalize the world's voices. Yet, the only alternative seems to be the production of Scamp's writin', writing that only the writer herself may read.

QUESTIONS

Julianne Moore's story, "Vanishing", and its process essay, "Sources of 'Vanishing'"

1. What has happened to Patch by the story's conclusion? How does she respond to the voices she hears, her father's, her mother's, the priest's, the children's in the Happiness Game? How does Patch's perception of the wind speaking, the concrete turning to water, affect your perception of the state she is in? How would you describe that state?

2. Patch is isolated in this story just as Karen is in Kathleen Coppula's story, "Reason." How is Patch's isolation different? Whose situation is most dire? For which character do you have the most sympathy? Do you identify more with one than another? Does either's experience seem more "realistic" to you? How are the characters' perceptions of their lives affected by their experience with religion?

3. In her process essay, Moore writes, "It's a difficult position sometimes, as any writer might say ... to see that your sense of a piece may have next to nothing to do with what makes it make sense for another." When you have written an essay that you've given to a teacher or a friend, has your teacher or friend responded to it in ways you'd never intended? How did you respond to that response? What was the source of the misunderstanding?

Whose responsibility was the misunderstanding? Are there ways you could have revised the essay to make it clearer? Did you want to make those revisions, or did you want the essay to stand as it was?

4. Several times in her process essay, Moore says that she feels the story is not finished. But she has turned the story in for publication and you have just read it. When you complete the final draft of an essay, do you feel that it's "finished"? Do you find yourself thinking about it after you've completed it, rearranging certain parts, adding material that you failed to include? When you receive or have received a paper from your teacher with a grade on it, does that mark the time you're "finished" with it? Is there a difference in your response to being finished based on the quality of the grade you were given?

❧ Possible Writing Topics ❧

1. You have read several stories and essays now that have dealt with religion as a central or subsidiary theme. Write an essay where you describe the effect of religion on your life or on the life of someone you know well. The essay will be about a person's experience with religion, how it affected or transformed him or her. The person, of course, may be young or old. How does religion or spirituality affect this person's daily life? When you've visited this person, is there evidence of religion in his or her environment? Does this person speak of his or her religion? What is your assessment of his or her religion's effect on his or her life?

2. After you've completed the essay, exchange it with another student in class. Write a full response to the essay you receive in the margins, offering your impressions, your comments, your criticism, and then make a concluding remark at the essay's end on the effect it had on you. Make sure your comments are explicit and readable; comment on the essay as you would want another to comment on yours. After your own essay has been returned to you, read the comments and write a second essay where you evaluate the comments you've been given. Which seem accurate to you, which inaccurate, and why? Did your reader respond in ways you hadn't intended? What do you make of that response? Are there parts of the essay you'd now want to revise based on your reader's response? What would you change? Did you think the criticism was fair? What is your response to criticism in general? How seriously do you take comments written on your papers?

IV

VIEWS: POSITION AND PERSPECTIVE

Mark L. Shelton

Notes on the Writing of Medical Nonfiction

*I*N 1985, I began research for a nonfiction book about a neurosurgeon, a project larger in scale and scope than anything I had ever attempted before. In the course of that research—library work, interviewing, hanging about a hospital—I of course made many small decisions that affected the form the material would ultimately take, but I also made what I consider to be several larger decisions about the approach I would take in writing the book, a book called *Working in a Very Small Place*. In making these decisions, I have had an opportunity to reflect on the nature of these decisions, and how they compare with the apparent nature of decision-making in the field of nonfiction, in particular nonfiction books about medical subjects.

To try and explain the decisions I made and how I believe they have resulted in a book that goes against the mainstream of what I will call "medical nonfiction" (resisting the impulse to say "medifiction"), it may be helpful for me to try and establish a context for those decisions, beginning with my understanding of what I believe are the basic assumptions that medical journalists often adhere to, and why I believe that those assumptions lead journalists to write a particular *kind* of nonfiction, a kind of nonfiction that fundamentally differs from more traditional definitions of nonfiction; while seldom as flashy as what we often call "New Journalism," it does share some characteristics: the use of the "composite" character, the explicit presence of the journalist as a character in the story—indeed, the very notion of "characters" in nonfiction at all.

This new medical nonfiction is becoming prominent for several reasons. First, medicine, while always a rapidly growing and changing field, more and more regularly appears to be on the brink of discoveries of truly epic proportions. Contemporary medical research has grown at about the same rate in two directions: in the direction of increasingly sophisticated and improved methods of treatment for a wide range of diseases and maladies—"clinical" medicine—and in the direction of "basic science"—approaching an understanding of how, at the cellular and, often, the genetic level, the human organism works, and how it can be made to work better, to last longer, to defeat previously undefeatable diseases. Not only, for example, are specialists in neonatology—care of the newborn—having greater and greater success with the survival of very premature infants, and infants with more and more complex birth defects, their counterparts in the laboratory are beginning to understand what causes those defects in the first place, and developing strategies for preventing them. The same is true of cancer research, research into nervous system diseases such as Alzheimer's Disease, organ-specific specialties that now may rely upon organ transplantation when all else fails, and research into chronic diseases such as diabetes. Medicine is becoming more prominent because it is becoming more successful at more things.

Second, there is a well-established reading audience interested in technology, and books about new and "high-tech" medicine are counted on, I think, to appeal to this audience, even though (as I will discuss later) most medical nonfiction is decidedly non-technical in its conception and execution. Finally, I would hypothesize that an interest in medicine and medical issues is connected to the increasing interest in the self, most obvious perhaps in the runaway success of books and articles about exercise and diet programs, and which might be seen as a natural extension of the "me-ness" that has led to phenomena such as the "yuppie" and the "dink" ("young urban professionals" and "double income, no kids," should these terms already need glossing)—in short, a growing awareness of the body as a piece of machinery for which we are responsible for caring, rather than the ephemeral repository of the human spirit that used to serve as the dominant self-image.

Given that medicine is increasingly becoming a part of our lives and our general awareness, it is not unexpected that journalists will seek to explain and open up this world to the reading public. It should also not be unexpected that those journalists will choose from a wide variety of approaches to their material, as journalists have always done. Finally, it should not be unexpected that journalists who are expert in other fields, or self-described "generalists," would be drawn to write about medicine (again, or that physicians themselves would begin to write about medicine for a general audience), bringing with them certain assumptions, and adopting others as the subject seems to require.

The first of these assumptions dictates that medical nonfiction is best told by telling the story of the patient, rather than the physician, the treated, as it were, rather than the therapist. There are a few good reasons for this, and several that are not so good reasons. Much medical nonfiction is written this way, unfortunately, for the not so good reasons.

The most spurious reason is that the patient's story has the built-in components of sympathy and drama, thus encouraging the reader to "identify" with the patient; after all, most of us are more likely to become patients at some point in our lives, rather than physicians, right?

That may be "right," but it is to me still a poor reason for making a journalistic decision, because of what happens most of the time with such books: the patient becomes not so much a conduit for conveying information as a shortcut to a visceral response. Even physicians, with a few rare exceptions, succumb to this when writing about their craft, and journalists, thrust into the drama of disease and dying, can find that if they are not careful, the book is shaped to a large degree by that drama—the journalist loses distance, and with that, often even the fiction of objectivity goes soon after. The change from observer to soul-sibling with the patient comes next, and the chapters become the chronicle of the struggle for life. We meet the patient, we learn of the affliction, we are as one with the patient (*and* the journalist) as he battles his disease, or the psychological trauma that accompanies the disease, or the side effects of the medication or the long rehabilitation after surgery. Will he win the battle, or lose, dying in the dark watches of the night with no one to mourn him, it seems, but the journalist? This is the high impact, high velocity, "human" side of medicine. And because it resembles nothing in life so much as a TV movie, it sells books, or at least draws tears out of reviewers.

That it is also bad "journalism"—"journalism" isn't quite the right word, but I don't think we have the right word in English—is often beside the point. It is bad journalism because it tries to do the right thing, which is to open up a closed and unfamiliar world for the reader, but for the wrong reasons, or at the expense of the right ones. We know that people get sick, often with horribly painful diseases, and we know that they die. We know that this happens to children, to mothers, to young Ph.D. students, to journalists—disease is largely democratic. We also know that if one spends one's time in close proximity to doctors, who spend a great deal of time with sick people, one will also be in close proximity with sick people, and with sick people who often die. If one is not careful, one can very easily lose the temperament that comes with discovery of one's subjects; one cannot see the forest for the trees, where the trees are the patients, and the forest is the world to which the journalist is ostensibly supplying vicarious access.

But it is *so* seductive to tell a story in this way, despite the fact that what is mostly happening is just that—telling a story, versus reporting on an event or a world. What was the journalist doing there in the first place? It if could be any hospital, any patient, why were these chosen and some others not? What were the criteria for selection? What exactly was the journalist trying to portray? Was he just trying to get us to feel sympathy and sadness for the plight of the patients in his book? If so, do we need—or heed—journalists who take it upon themselves to tell us that such sadness exists? I do not. In fact, I think that the "case history" approach to medical nonfiction has done more damage than any other innovation, in part because it bleeds over as a method for telling even the not-so-dramatic stories. The books become not so much books as a series of chapters in response to the implicit question, "And what did the next guy have?" This does not open up a world vicariously; instead, it reinforces our tendencies toward the voyeuristic; we are permitted by the journalist to feel, in order, that 1) sickness and disease is horrible and sad, and 2) Thank God that hasn't happened to me. The close identification with the patient allows us to exercise *denial*, and hence demeans the patients, robs them of their dignity, because they are not just "cases," or illnesses incarnate, they are people, individuals who have the misfortune to be ill.

Doctors, in the verbal shorthand that often appalls outsiders, will refer to "the perforated bowel in (Room) 221," or "the bypass in ICU." Doctors, however, are allowed, allowed because they don't do this (or very rarely, anyway) when they're talking to the patient; they may dehumanize to save a few words, but I never observed one being actively dehumanizing. That is so often left to the journalists.

It may seem strange that I refer to as "dehumanizing" that which is in fact most often considered as the style of writing that is most humanistic. A distinction that I think should be made, but seldom is, has to do with what I called a bit earlier "the journalist's role." As a professional journalist, I pick and choose my subjects according to two criteria: does the subject, the material, lend itself to fresh treatment, and is there fresh information for readers available about the subject? I sometimes think it ironic that in my month to month duties at *Pittsburgh Magazine*, for which I am an editor and staff writer, I rarely write about medical subjects. The reasons for this are simple; by the time I joined the magazine, the obvious subjects had already been covered, in the obvious ways, generally by freelance writers. I look back at the last two years' worth of issues and see stories about chronic pain, infertility, aging, emergency medicine, cancer, sickle-cell anemia, AIDS and transplant surgery. The only "hot" topic not covered is medical research in the chemistry of the brain.

If, however, I alter my selection criteria slightly, or rather, alter my definitions of "fresh treatment," and "fresh information," I could easily write about all of these subjects, and write about them monthly, because the "standard" framework of medical journalism has become so oriented to the patient story, the case history. AIDS? Find a victim of this debilitating and tragic disease, and write about his suffering. Infertility? Find a childless couple, ideally one that will soon have children. Also, write about the child when it's born. Emergency medicine? Ride around in an ambulance, hoping for something with real drama, but be satisfied if you end up writing about a broken ankle. And so on. The "fresh information" becomes "a different human interest story," and from that will flow a magazine article, or more and more frequently, a book.

Consider one of the most successful books of medical nonfiction ever, the story of a half-dozen patients at a well-regarded hospital for children. The organization is not democratic, in that one patient, an adolescent with cystic fibrosis, becomes the focus of the book, and indeed, of the journalist's day to day life, as she describes his illness, his decline, and finally, his death. Cystic fibrosis is a horrible disease, and one for which, despite massive and energetic research, there is no cure. The story of any child with cystic fibrosis is sad; the experience of watching someone grow sicker and sicker is difficult to watch. I do not mean here to minimize these facts, but I do think that the style of journalism that uses the story of a patient with a debilitating and ultimately terminal disease as a paradigm for human suffering produces what I think is an unintended effect: the effect of "Thank God, it's not me (or my child)." Like the ship in Auden's poem about Brueghel's painting "The Fall of Icarus," we have somewhere to get to, and sail calmly on. Journalism can do more than this, and should.

But how? I, of course, was faced immediately with this question when I began to try and shape my researches and interviews for *Working In A Very Small Place;* after my first two interviews with Dr. Jannetta, I spent a month reading perhaps two hundred articles from medical journals and medical textbooks by and about microvascular decompression, the technique by which Jannetta cures a wide range of neurological disorders. That was an easy decision to make, because I felt that I first must understand the science, the theory, before doing anything else. Soon after, however, I had to make a series of choices as to the methods by which I would open up Jannetta's world to my prospective readers. I've just sketched the obvious approach; can one do otherwise? I believed then, and I believe now, that one can. I began by imagining Jannetta and his work as though it were that of a non-clinical researcher—that is, a medical researcher without patients, which of course he is not (he has operated on perhaps 2000 people with cranial nerve dysfunction, and his colleagues and students have operated on a like number—it is a peculiarly human condition and therapy for a peculiarly human range of diseases, the most prominent being chronic facial pain), but which it was helpful for me to imagine in terms of structuring the story. I emphasized very early in my initial summary and prospectus for the book that this was *not* just the story of people with chronic pain, or disabling dizziness caused by vascular compression of the cranial nerves, but rather, was the story of a medical researcher interested in curing those and other disorders. From that perspective came the outline for the book. "If *Working* were only the story of the people that Dr. Jannetta has treated for chronic facial pain," I wrote in that prospectus, "it would be an enlightening and uplifting book about people from all walks of life who have been released from a prison of pain. But the story is much larger than that; it is the story of a medical discovery...and it is the story of the applications of that discovery, applications that have changed the way physicians think about a wide range of chronic conditions.... It is the story that can serve as a paradigm for contemporary medical treatment."

I of course do tell the stories of several patients within the book; their stories are necessary to the larger story as a route by which the reader can come to understand just what it is that Jannetta does, and why; thus, I do not advocate eliminating the patient's story from medical nonfiction—far from it.

I do advocate, however, a dispassionate—"objective," one used to say about journalism—evaluation of what purpose the story of a particular patient serves, and toward what larger end it is useful in opening up a strange world to a reader.

The "human interest" angle, of course, has a long tradition in journalism, and particularly in medical journalism. The story of a patient often serves as a way of bridging the familiar—our own bodies and how they function—with the often unfamiliar—how and why our bodies malfunction. The key word, here, however, is "bridge"; when the bridge becomes the story, the science often gets short shrift.

Which leads me to the second assumption that I find to be both unwarranted and unfortunate: the question of how much medicine there should be, or can be, in medical nonfiction.

It has been sobering to me in the past few months to be asked what I am working on, and when I respond with, "a nonfiction book about a neurosurgeon," the next question invariably is, "Oh? Like a medical textbook?"

It is a sad fact that most people, even those who would count themselves as well-educated and intelligent, envision that the publishing industry could not be producing a book for the reading public about a medical subject, even as medicine becomes a larger and larger part of the contemporary world. They have been taught this partly, no doubt, by the publishing industry, but the publishing industry learned it to some degree from its writers, perhaps to as great a degree as they think they have learned it from the reading public. Regardless of who has learned what where, there is a suspicion that the reading public has been so ill-taught in "the sciences" that any "technical" or "scientific" language or thought in a book will be so alien as to be incomprehensible. That this assumption feeds directly into the assumption presented earlier is clear; in fact, it would be a toss-up to try and decide which came first—the abandonment of careful explanation in favor of pathos, or pathos setting such a standard as to drive careful explanation from the page. Nor does it matter, particularly.

What does matter is that, with rare exceptions, journalists seem perfectly willing to make the swap, and that often, they are extremely successful in doing so—successful in the sense of producing books that illuminate an unfamiliar world within certain constraints of vocabulary and explication. The largest task I felt I had taken on was to write about a fairly complicated and unfamiliar world in such a way so as to allow entrance for the reading public. In addressing such a task, I had occasion to think at some length about what exactly makes technical subjects "technical," and why I ultimately felt that in spite of the general assessment of the reading public's ability to understand such material, writing clearly and appropriately about a complicated subject was not an impossible task.

A good example is vocabulary. The vocabulary of medicine is highly specific, and thus often unfamiliar, for good reasons. It is crucial for physicians to be able to understand each other at a very high level of specificity and accuracy, and it is crucial for the nomenclature of medicine to be standardized. In casual conversation among laymen, specificity and standardization are not as necessary as they are when one physician is seeking to explain a patient's symptoms, or anatomy, or physiology, to another physician. For example, Peter Jannetta performs surgery for cranial nerve disorders in a region of the brain known as the "cerebellopontine angle," which might be defined as the region bounded by the cerebellum and the pons. If one knows where the cerebellum and the pons are, one can know the cerebellopontine angle. However, if one doesn't know the location of these two structures, the cerebellopontine angle and all its mysteries remain a closed book.

However, I maintain that while "cerebellopontine angle" *sounds* technical, it sounds technical primarily because it is unfamiliar; to explain where it is is not like explaining the physiological process by which the heart beats, or by which we smell coffee—those processes are somewhat complex, rather than simply unfamiliar. If I am able to explain to you where the cerebellum and the pons are, you are able to understand the meaning of "cerebellopontine angle," just as one is able to find the New York Public Library or the distributor cap on an automobile engine.

It is not easy to absorb large additions to one's vocabulary—but it is not impossible, either, and it is, in fact, not even so difficult as it might seem, given that good writers provide context for new terms and analogies to explain them just as good readers take advantage of such devices in understanding them; this is in fact what most reading *is*.

Or, again, what it should be. It is arguably much easier to skip the science when writing about medicine—I think back to the several hours I spent writing the fifty or so words in *Working* that describe the cerebellopontine angle—but the trade-off is a costly one, one that as a writer I am unwilling to make. Which brings me finally to what I call "temperament."

By "temperament," I mean the attitude the writer adopts in making the decisions that go into the writing of a nonfiction book about medicine. Or perhaps instead of "adopts," I should say "portrays," because I have no way of knowing the pressures of the marketplace—agents, editors, publishers—that other journalists are subjected to when making decisions about shaping their material into published form. I may have been lucky in finding an agent and a publisher that agree with me about questions such as those I have raised here, and thus it may seem luxurious for me to say that I would have stuck to my guns and gone elsewhere if asked to make concessions about the form of the book that I could not abide by.

But I view a book, finally, as the culmination not just of a great deal of work and research on my part, but also as an opportunity to do what I believe journalists always aspire to do: open up a strange or unfamiliar world for the reader. To do this, one incurs, I believe, a debt, in my case a debt to Dr. Jannetta, to his colleagues, the residents at Presbyterian-University Hospital, the nurses, the patients, the staff who took the time and the energy to allow me into their worlds. It will be my name on the cover of *Working in a Very Small Place*, but it will be their names inside it, and in many many cases, their words inside it. To them I feel a responsibility to portray as accurately and legitimately as possible the world that they inhabit, which is a world of technical terms and extraordinary pressures, of the exotic and the mundane, a world as palpable and real to them as this one is to us. It seems odd to say that I think more about *their* "reviews"—reviews in the sense of how successful I have been in accurately and legitimately portraying their lives and their world—than the reviews of book editors and critics, but in discovering that this is indeed the case, I find it to be an apt definition of what I mean by "temperament." I would hate to think that those who gave their time and thought and words would feel ill-used by the investment. Such a temperament as this leaves me with little patience for assuming too much—or too little—about the book's readership.

The Usual Constraints

I choose the word "constraints" in the title here, because to me, the writing of an essay is writing within practical, thematic and outside-imposed limits: an essay, then, is a series of compromises between writer and material, between writer and market (that is, the editor who assigns the work in the first place, or reads it and buys it if it comes to him or her complete), and market and material, an unnecessarily complicated way of saying that if you are writing to be read (and paid), you can't do whatever you damn well please, but rather have to figure out how and what you want to do within the limits you discern.

The essay, "Notes on the Writing of Medical Nonfiction," is an excellent case in point. I have for several years talked to anybody who would listen about the distinctions I saw in the way that certain medical writers approached their subjects; these distinctions became more and more apparent as I worked on my book, and as I read more and more work by other writers in the field of medical journalism. In that sense, the opportunity to write "Notes" was an opportunity to organize and codify the many random thoughts I had on the subject. So far, so good.

I threw myself into the project, using the sophisticated strategy of starting at the beginning. Long before I reached the middle, however, I saw several problems with what I was doing. The first problem was that I was, in essence, rewriting my book in the essay, by including long (and, I assure you, highly interesting) sections about how I first encountered the physician about whom the book is written, the importance of the work and how I first perceived it, the work that I did in coming to understand what exactly was going on in the field of contemporary neurosurgery, and so on. All of this was destined to please neither my publisher, nor the publisher of this anthology, nor perhaps very many of the readers of this anthology—you register for a writing class and get pole-axed with 75 pages of neuroanatomy. The balance in that first effort was skewed heavily toward what I wanted to say, but not what the editor or the readers wanted to read.

This is perhaps the single problem I encounter most often. I have the habits of mind that permit me to see vast and intricate interrelationships between almost everything, and the impulse is to write an essay that demonstrates all of these relationships. But the *idea* of essay is antithetical to this; I have to remind myself always of the roots of the word, *exagium,* from the Latin, meaning the act of weighing or analyzing (and from which we get the word "assay," as in determining the composition of a substance, like gold); it is not an all-encompassing act, but rather, an act of selection, of reinforcement, and of linking. The essay should not tell the reader everything about everything, but rather, what the writer knows about some part of something.

"Notes" bears this out: there is finally very little about Peter Jannetta, his work, or my work on *Working in a Very Small Place* in the final version; what there is of this material is used explicitly as examples to illustrate some point that I was making, and implicitly, to establish my credentials to make the observations in the first place.

This last point, about credentials, reminds me of what I saw as the fundamental difficulty in structuring the essay in the first place, a difficulty unique to the subject, rather than the sort of generic difficulties I am experiencing as I write *this* essay (where to begin, how much to include). It would be one thing for a writer of the stature, say, of Berton Roueche, of the *New Yorker* (and probably the best writer about medicine in America today), to point out in his gentle and unintimidating style the problems I see with medical writing; it is quite another for a relatively new writer on the scene, whose first book has yet to appear, and whose impatience with writers who do things he finds annoying comes through loud and clear, to take on several successful and highly popular conceptions about the way that writers write about medicine. In an early draft of "Notes," I spent several pages explaining why I had chosen to use the word "exploitative" in the essay—a word that doesn't even appear in the final version.

It doesn't appear not because I don't think that some writers are exploitative, but rather because describing the complex series of relationships that led me to use the word in the first place would be an essay in itself, and just as importantly, because it would make the essay an exercise in confrontation, not observation—my personality is more confrontational, but my best writing is much more observational, and I had to recognize that I was writing about writing, not about me. In fact, as I think about it now, I was in that early draft doing exactly what I would be seen as condemning others for: writing about writing often borders on the exploitative as often as some writing about medicine does. I still think that there is an essay to be written about what I see as exploitation, but it is emphatically not an essay that tries to illustrate several trends in medical writing, but rather an essay that passes judgment more explicitly about those trends than I felt I had the space, forum, audience and experience to do. I end up writing about two assumptions at some length (using the patient as the vehicle within the book, and skipping over the science), and alluding (at the end of the second paragraph, where I mention New Journalism) to two others (the use of composite characters, and the explicit presence of the journalist within the narrative). Given an infinite number of words and an infinitely patient audience (that sounds like the monkeys and the typewriters), I think that the two assumptions I only mention in passing would make the basis for a fine essay, but an essay that would require extensive quotation, extensive textual analysis, and an extensive examination of the movement from "objective" narration to the participatory techniques of the New Journalists, and beyond.

So, "Notes" became an essay about two readily identifiable and accessible assumptions made in medical writing, with room to discuss briefly some of the reasons why medical writing is worth spending time on in the first place. Given these constraints, I felt that structuring the essay around these two assumptions allowed me enough latitude to make concrete my observations (and annoyances), and again, implicitly, to have these two assumptions be somewhat synecdochical for the field of medical writing, and perhaps even nonfiction writing in general (that is, stories about, say, problems in a housing project that tell the story through the eyes of a resident, or a story about inequities in the income tax code that uses one man's problems to give the picture).

All of this is how I ended up with a straightforward and simple, declarative opening for "Notes." (I find it interesting to mention here that an almost identical process occurred in the writing of this essay; the first draft started out with a marvelous anecdote about fighting for space in the magazine for which I work, but which left me writing about "Writing an Essay," rather than "Writing about a Particular Essay"; as my thinking about "Notes" evolved, so did this essay, to the point where I have here a rather straightforward, simple, declarative opening here as well. I will resist the temptation to analyze every other essay I've written to see if this is a trend, or what my future biographers and *belles lettrists* will call my inimitable style.)

As to making the points I make in "Notes," I recall in rereading the essay all of the places where better judgment won out, and where I used my favorite rhetorical devices at their most scintillating. One of these devices is as old as critical writing itself—what we often casually call "rhetorical questions," but which I call "pointed" questions, as in "finger pointing." When I run up a list such as

> . . . What was the journalist doing there in the first place? If it could be any hospital, any patient, why were these chosen and some others not? What were the criteria for selection? What exactly was the journalist trying to portray? Was he just trying to get us to feel sympathy and sadness for the

plight of the patients in his book? If so, do we need—or heed—journalists who take it upon themselves to tell us that such sadness exists? (paragraph 10)

I can almost see the witness cringing on the stand, sense the jury leaning forward in their chairs, feel the judge's wise old eyes upon me as he nods gravely at my masterful rhetorical garroting of someone who has had the impudence to cross me. This is most certainly a bad habit; criticism by bludgeon is satisfying to write, but runs the risk of being seen as less than temperately reasoned. But I cannot resist some finger-pointing, and I cannot completely abide by Johnson's advice to find one's favorite passages and then excise them. Again, I see that I am illustrating the balances—the tensions—between what one would do if freed from all constraints, and what one reasonably feels he or she can get away with. This is inevitably what happens when one is writing about a subject that one is passionate about.

The most soundly reasoned part of the essay—paragraphs 10, 11 and 12—where I make the rhetorical twist that allows me to say that what are ostensibly the most humanizing aspects of medical writing are in fact dehumanizing, came about from my willingness, in earlier drafts, to be a bit shrill and accusatory. As anyone who has ever been in an argument with me can tell you, when I argue, I *argue*: I talk rapidly, I gesticulate, I pace around the room. When I do this on paper (and therefore, with no one to interrupt me), I find that I can carry the reasoning through to the end: in this case, that the distance and denial we are allowed to practice as readers is dehumanizing and robs patients of their dignity. I still find this argument to be sound, and evocative. Explicitly, it makes a nice point; implicitly, it suggests that some practitioners of the craft are not actively reasoning themselves, but rather are following what it seems that everyone else is doing, which blends well with some of the larger implicit points of the essay as a whole.

Which alas, as I look back over it, is too short by half to contain all of those relationships I alluded to earlier. The example from *Working* that I use in paragraph 22, defining "cerebellopontine angle," was originally almost an essay in itself; the point I wanted to make (and I am transparently slipping it in here) is that we have, as a reading society, developed almost a reflex-like reaction to anything that cannot be immediately understood in the millisecond it takes for the image of a word on a page to move from retina to brain. I argued in a draft of "Notes" that the word "cerebellopontine angle" would have been automatically queried by the editor(s) of this book you're reading now, regardless of context—it is not a word that most encounter in daily life, so it must be suspect. But in fact that attitude belies all that we understand about reading—the idea of context, for example, or the simple device of a schematic of the human brain in the endpapers of the book—I am in the process of reading an interminable book about the Civil War; without the very simple map of the Eastern United States that appears inside the front cover, I wouldn't know if I were reading about Virginia, or Pennsylvania—who knows, really, where Bull Run is, except in context?

Likewise for the ability of the reader to do a little reasoning of his own. I would expect that most readers likely to pick up *Working* would know of the two largest structures of the brain, the cerebrum and the cerebellum. It doesn't take a lexicographer to make "cerebello" into something from "cerebellum," and "pontine" clearly is from "pon" or "pons"—Latin from the same root that we get things like "pontiff," "pontoon," "punt" (as in what one poles along a river)— all bridgelike things. Now, if you knew of the two largest parts of something, and that a third part was something like a bridge, deduction would allow you to draw a picture very like the first pictures I drew when all of this was being explained to me, or for that matter, very like Varoli's own pictures (Varoli being the Italian anatomist who first decided the pons was a discrete structure containing the neural connections between the cerebrum and the cerebellum— the full name for what we call the pons is "pons Varolii," or literally, "Varoli's bridge").

But no one gets to read like that very much anymore, because no one writes like that very much anymore—or edits, for that matter. (For example, is the first occurrence of "cerebellopontine angle" in these essays glossed for you?)

This is only somewhat of a digression. Before you, in the preceding half-dozen paragraphs (if they make it into this book), is the process by which I write, laid bare. What is perhaps more apparent than should be are all of my curses and pleasures within writing: terrier-like tugging at a thread, the preachiness I work hammer and tong to hold down, the wish to lecture, to stand, as Roethke used to, on top of the podium, rather than behind it, the immersion that I believe an essayist should have in the subject he is trying to illuminate. What strikes me now, as what struck me as I worked on "Notes," is the sense that the sort of democratization of writing and writers has changed the rules of the game, and I find that my motivation for writing is in direct response to this democratization, so much so that I find myself wishing I had been able to shoehorn into "Notes" much much more; what I see when I reread "Notes" are all of the places where each sentence could have been the departure for three or four pages of exposition. This, finally, is why to me the constraints to which I refer in the title are, in fact, absolutely usual.

∾ QUESTIONS ∾

Mark L. Shelton's essay, "Notes on the Writing of Medical Nonfiction," and its process essay, "The Usual Constraints"

1. Shelton makes a strong argument against journalists who use the practice of medicine as a way of taking advantage of a patient's suffering. Do you find his argument credible? When you have read the sort of books or magazine

articles he describes, or have seen television shows that deal with the themes, is your response finally a distant one, one that can be summarized by your saying, "Thank God that isn't me"? If you find Shelton's argument credible, how does he establish his credibility? What does he use to convince you of his expertise?

2. Shelton writes, "... good writers provide context for new terms and analogies to explain them just as good readers take advantage of such devices in understanding them; this is in fact what most reading *is*." Shelton is making a statement about the introduction through writing of unfamiliar vocabulary. But the same statement could be made for any writing, particularly writing that is arguing several points. How does Shelton provide a context for his argument? How does he make his argument understandable, and systematic? If he had assumed that you as a reader were familiar with medical nonfiction, how would your response to the essay change?

3. In his process essay, Shelton writes "... if you are writing to be read (and paid), you can't do whatever you damn well please, but rather have to figure out how and what you want to do within the limits you discern." In your own experience with writing, how have you been kept from doing "whatever you damn well please"? What would you write if you were permitted to? How would that writing be different from what you were required to do in this and other classes? Would such writing be more enjoyable or more interesting to you? Would it be more interesting to your readers?

4. Shelton writes, "... I see I am illustrating the balances—the tensions—between what one would do if freed from all constraints, and what one reasonably feels he or she can get away with. This is inevitably what happens when one is writing about a subject that one is passionate about." What does Shelton find that he can "get away with"? As you look through past essays, what do find that you've gotten away with, whether you're using Shelton's definition or your own? Do you feel or have you ever felt passionate about something you're writing? What would passion, as Shelton describes it, lend your writing that it might otherwise lack?

❧ Possible Writing Topics ❧

1. Find a topic to write about for which you think you can pose a strong argument, a topic for which you have more information, more expertise, than many of the others in your classroom. Then write an essay where you "do whatever you damn well please," ignoring for the time being your audience, their knowledge of your topic and the vocabulary you want to use, and the other constraints usually placed on you when you write an essay. Is this sort of writing easier? What do you say here that you usually wouldn't?

2. After you've finished the essay, set it aside for a while and return to it. Reread the essay, and imagine how it would have to change in order for others in class with you to read it, for you to hand it in to your teacher. Write a second essay on what you'd have to cut, what you'd have to explain, what restrictions you'd have to place on the material you used to make your essay manageable for most readers. I may help to quote from your first essay and show what kind of changes must be made by rewriting the portion you quote.

Mark Collins

Reporters Do Have a Heart[1]

*W**HAT* an odd business this is.

I've only been at this job for three months, and I have yet to figure out newspapers. Not the mechanics—which are difficult enough to comprehend—but the concept on "writing the news."

This month, I covered the Port Authority bus accident. It was a "breaking story," where facts seem to change every minute: first the news that a bus hit a building; then the report of injuries; then the word that some injuries may be serious.

I dutifully talked to the right people, tried to ask the right questions, tried to piece together a story from many sources and tried to produce an accurate, coherent account.

But that's not what concerns me.

It seems the first victim in a breaking story isn't the facts but the reporter's sensibilities. Suddenly, it's not a bus accident that's important, but the story itself.

Imagine that.

The article takes on a life of its own. It becomes a separate entity from the event—a living, breathing character that has unique qualities and a personality.

What was written in the article described—accurately, it is hoped—the events surrounding the accident. But did it tell what really happened? The location was given, the people involved were named, yet did it capture the terror of being trapped in a wrecked bus, the awful helplessness the driver must have felt when he realized his steering had locked? Can a news story measure the heroic nature of the passengers who returned to the bus to help the injured?

By definition, good journalism cannot deviate from the facts. "Terror" and "heroism" are subjective words—they have no tangible quality. But dealing strictly with concrete descriptions drastically alters the reporter's perspective: objectivity effectively replaces emotions. This provides a wonderful mental

---

[1] From the *Monroeville Times-Express,* December 16, 1981.

defense. I became so disembodied from what had happened that it wasn't until I was driving home that the impact of what I had written occurred to me: a young woman died in a violent accident.

She was 22. *I'm* 22.

She had a family, a job, a home. I have those things. She was, in most ways, just like you and me. And, at 22, she had the attribute I cherish most: promise. A future.

Did I report that? Did I describe how, in a few bizarre, horrible seconds, it was over? Did I describe the confusion?

No, I didn't. I *couldn't*. News stories do not portray events with emotions.

With more time, I might have provided interviews with the injured, or comments from the woman's family. But could they be any more articulate than myself? Could *they* explain what it felt like to be thrown to the front of the bus, the window collapsing from the force? Or the odd sense of relief in hearing an ambulance siren coming closer?

Journalism is the method of providing information to the public through an objective medium. In its highest form, it captures both the facts and the spirit of the story.

Perhaps my inexperience is showing. With more time on this job, I might learn to wed style and substance. But I wonder if I'll become professional enough to leave my job at work, and not worry about events that—at best—I can merely describe.

I wonder if I even want to.

People Are Too Scared[2]

A few years ago, I was walking near my apartment in Forest Hills. A young girl, maybe 7 or 8 years old, was walking home from school, loaded down with books and a huge poster. The poster was a crayon drawing of a bird's nest, with eggs ready to hatch. It was a science project, I guess.

"Hi," the little girl said. "Could you give me some help?"

I hesitated, then nodded. She handed me her poster. While we walked the half-block to her home, she talked the whole time, but I don't know what she said since I was too busy looking out for the neighbors. Forest Hills was one of the original "Crime Watch" communities. Would someone call the police? What would people say about me?

When we reached her house, the little girl asked if I could bring the poster into the dining room. I set it on the kitchen counter and said, "You really shouldn't ask strangers for help." I stepped outside and shut the door. She stared at me without expression.

---

[2] From the *Pittsburgh Post-Gazette*, Saturday, April 5, 1986.

It was good advice, I suppose, but I also wonder if I planted the first seeds of insecurity in that little girl. She would learn—perhaps as soon as she told her parent what had happened—that you should trust no one except your family and a few select outsiders. Instead, she would learn self-reliance; she'd learn not to ask for help. And when the young girl becomes a young woman, she'll learn that you can't trust certain young men with your heart. She'll learn to be independent, and we'll all call her "mature."

Nowadays, though, our capacity for suspicion lasts our entire lives. On a personal level, the sale of home burglar-alarm-systems is booming. Locking your doors and windows isn't enough; what you need is a fortress. No chance of some out-of-gas motorist coming up to *your* home, asking to use the phone. And "stun guns" are selling well, too, for all those too liberal-minded people who don't want to kill but don't mind maiming.

I'm not suggesting that we blissfully invite trouble. I'm not saying that you should let strangers into your home. What I am saying is that we can only control so much of our lives. Some things are simply arbitrary. An expensive alarm system may protect your house, but can it protect you from all the sharp corners in life, or the uncertain feeling you get when things go bump in the night?

On a national scale, a blue-ribbon panel is now trying to decide whom to blame in the Challenger shuttle disaster. The idea, of course, is to prevent another mistake. A recent commentator on National Public Radio noted that "those memo-writers who covered their tails by shouting warnings" are now safe; those who took the risk are in trouble. And that's the way it should be—with risk comes responsibility. But let's face it: If we want to fly around the heavens risk-free, we don't deserve to go, do we?

What started me on this? The Tylenol deaths. Several families in this country—in Chicago, New York, Tennessee—have had to deal with the unfair, arbitrary nature of life and death. That started a public outcry: No more capsules! No more over-the-counter medications! But to what end? Will that stop those who are murderously deranged enough to commit such a crime?

I'm a cautious person. I wear seat belts. I don't smoke and I don't walk down dark streets alone. I lock my doors and leave a light on at night. And I'm not trying to whitewash the fear of violent crime. I say good for the Crime Watch folks in Forest Hills.

But if common sense can't save me, then I'm doomed, because I sure as hell am not going to live a life preoccupied with death. Sure it's a natural fear, but should it dominate every waking moment? What kind of life is that?

So: If you're throwing away your Tylenol bottles, send them to me instead. I'll save a bundle on aspirin. And if you're not going to Europe because you're afraid of terrorists, send me your tickets. I'll send you a postcard from Paris.

We're like that young girl's science project—with little birds hiding in their shells, afraid of what the outside world might bring. In fact, in terms of a school experiment, we probably deserve to flunk.

Sources for "Reporters Do Have a Heart" and "People Are Too Scared"

*W*HEN I think of writing, I think of my father underneath the hood of a 1969 Oldsmobile Delta 88 Royale—an eight-cylinder dinosaur, the first car I drove. The car was too old to hold together, and it wasn't worth someone else fixing it, so every weekend we brought out bailing wire and rivets and prayed it lasted another week or snuck through inspection.

I hated these car sessions—always on weekends, my body tingling from the near-warmth of Kathy Sutash's kiss the night before, when our breaths fogged the windows of the car and the radio carried hockey scores instead of make-out music. But I'd trudge on out, wearing my oily sweatshirt and last year's jeans, and my father would already be at work: on his back, a mat spread beneath the car and the tools arranged like a clock around him:

"Where's the ratchet?" he would ask.

"Four o'clock, Dad."

"And the three-quarters socket?"

"Ten."

I'd clean the washers with a gasoline rag and grease up the gaskets, but mostly I'd watch—his legs the only visible sign of him, his body rolling and turning as he leaned his awkward weight against the wrench, cursing in rhythm with the cranking ratchet. It always seemed November; it was never warm.

Although I hated it, I helped him—partly because it made my father happy, partly because it gave me a borrowed sense of power, but mostly because I needed the car for Kathy Sutash next Friday night. I helped him because I had to.

And that's how writing is. My editorials, whether assigned topics or ones I feel compelled to write, seem like chores—something I have to do.

I begin each essay the same way: with basic research and lots of groping. Research usually isn't difficult—a matter of confirming the facts of a news story or calling the reference section of Carnegie Library. It's well worth the extra minutes to check the facts—ink lasts a surprisingly long time on newsprint.

The groping is tougher, involving procrastination, pacing and several cups of coffee. Inevitably, my first sentences are tentative, insincere and vague. I strive for a middle-ground posture that's agreeable to everyone—only to find I don't agree. The language is full of modifiers, weak verbs and prepositions ("It *seems* the truth *of* the matter *is we're* all a *little* scared . . . "). I reread my pleasant, bloodless prose, look at the clock, and try to convince myself I'm on the right track.

At this moment I hate myself most. It is also this moment when I truly begin to write. I have this theory: when we love (or hate) with intensity, we are most blind. I want to love my wife and be blind to her faults. I want to walk to my office downtown without seeing bag people. It's human nature to avoid such things—a luxury writers cannot afford.

So there's a point where I turn away from my innocent, polite prose into something angry. Oh, I begin with the same research or observations, but suddenly the sentences sharpen into contentiousness: "We're all scared, lonely, incapable of love." I finish this revision quickly, crossing out prepositions and adjectives from the first draft and replacing the paunchy language with directness. My argument builds into a righteous and triumphant sermon. I *feel* righteous and triumphant, liberating the readership with my bitter, challenging prose.

I go straight to the keyboard and start typing, intent on finishing.* But something feels wrong. I blame it on too much coffee, but that isn't it. I read what I have written, and feel the power of well-honed language, but I cannot feel the passion. Because the fact is I do love my wife, faults and all. And much as I'd like to, I could no more wish away bag people than I could wish away clouds. My world is exactly this cruel, wondrous mixture of love and pain; what I've written is a well-argued lie.

Slowly I begin again, retooling the lead toward compassion instead of sermon. ("How can we try so hard to love each other, yet still feel lonely in a crowded room?") What I mistook for truth in my second draft was really cynicism—distancing myself from the world in order to make fun. I neither deserve nor can afford such arrogance.

Depending on the deadline, I'll either finish the essay as I type, or sit on it awhile and re-gather my thoughts. Sometimes I abandon the argument altogether and start over; other times I'll start on a different subject and leave the first for another day. I've learned—slowly, painfully, and incompletely—to allow enough time to work through all three stages.

It was the same when my father and I fixed the Olds. Just when we seemed conquered, some homemade creation—like a tomato can wired over a hole in the exhaust pipe, or a leaky vacuum tube sealed with a bread wrapper and bathtub

---

*I write out my first drafts longhand, using a legal pad, then type what I think are final drafts onto the computer. I then edit from the printed copy, not from the screen. The computer obviously saves time re-typing, and I've found additional uses: the ability to cut and paste from other sources (notebooks, failed essays, etc.); spellchecking to augment proofreading; loading a standard query letter into memory, so that all I have to change is the name of the publication, the subject and the date; and searching for passive words (is, are, was, were) and replacing them with active verbs.

caulk—would somehow work, against the odds. We'd hoot and backslap each other—my father thinking of the money he'd saved, I marvelling at the versatility of tomato cans and bread wrappers. For that frozen moment when we heard the engine catch, I'd realize that there was more to it than repair. A tomato can mimicking a tail pipe—would I ever look at a tomato can the same way again? What possibilities lie in the concrete world, items prime for re-perception? I'd think about that for awhile, until Dad hollered for the wire cutters.

And that's how I write. The dilemma still haunts me: I write because I have to, but often discover another reason—a reason that lets me restructure the world, with all its greased parts and loosened flanges. It's not pleasant work—it still seems like November—but the rewards come here and there.

Sometimes I'd like to do anything else but write.

That happens, I guess.

❧ QUESTIONS ❧

Mark Collins' essays, "Reporters Do Have a Heart" and "People Are Too Scared," and its process essay, "Sources for 'Reporters Do Have a Heart' and 'People Are Too Scared'"

1. In "Reporters Do Have a Heart," Collins responds to an article he wrote on a bus accident, "What was written in the article described—accurately, it is hoped—the events surrounding the accident. But did it tell what really happened?" Collins laments his situation of reporting an incident without capturing the short-term terror, the long-term loss of those involved in the accident. If you were reading about the accident for the first time, would you prefer Collins' newspaper account, or a more in-depth story of all the emotions involved? Why do newspapers generally limit themselves to the facts of what happened? What advantage is there in this? How do you respond to Collins' concern over those involved in the accident as it contrasts with some of the remarks Mark L. Shelton makes about journalists' writing of patients suffering from disease?

2. In "People Are Too Scared," do you find Collins' argument convincing? In your experience, are people too cautious? How does Collins try to convince you his perspective is accurate? What devices does he use? If you removed his specific references to national events and the events of his life, what would become of the argument? What if you removed those paragraphs in which Collins allows for caution?

3. Collins uses an extended metaphor to describe some of the reasons and the process by which he writes. Does the metaphor work? How is the process Collins and his father go through in fixing the car similar to Collins' writing process? What is his perspective on both? Write a metaphor that describes your own writing process and explain fully why it is applicable.

4. Collins says of writing, "It's not pleasant work . . . but the rewards come here and there." What does it mean for a writer to say this about his life's work? Would you describe your own experience with writing similar? Do you make the stops and starts that Collins makes? Do you throw out material, or do you preserve everything? What effect does a deadline have on your writing?

ೋ Possible Writing Topics ೋ

1. Write an essay where, like Collins, you present a full argument in a specific amount of space (or number of words) in a specific amount of time. Try not to exceed either, but try to make the argument convincing, systematic, and explicit, as you develop it through the sort of verbal illustrations Collins uses in his articles.

2. After you've completed the essay, write another on the effect of the constraints of time and space on your writing. How did these constraints affect the strength of the argument? How did they affect the decisions you made? Is the essay as strong as it would have been if you'd had more time, more space? What would you have changed? What would you have elaborated on? What now would you take out? Do you prefer this sort of writing, when everything must be done quickly and handed in, or do you prefer the luxury of time?

Eve Shelnutt

Questions of Travel[1]

"**SUPPOSE**," said Anna's mother, a shudder running across her chest, "he comes while I'm ironing?"

Irene's right hand would lift from the little pink dress Anna might have worn, for this had happened many times, and she would look, puzzled, at the damp and dry spots—like a leopard's skin, Irene would think—and rub her eyes with her still-warm right hand, as if to erase thoughtlessness.

She would fold up the wooden board with its scorched cover of sheeting, smooth down the dampened clothes bunched in the basket—hands the wings of butterflies, *if* her life would flower: Anna beside her in starched linens, with sailor's collars, and, on her, a rose-bud mouth, willful limbs falling this way and that until, finally, love made her still, to be sipped.

Instead, Anna wore the wrinkled red and navy plaid or red and brown plaid or the dress of muted flowers. These clothes hung limply against Anna's thin legs, and Anna moved as if asleep. A sleep-walker, thought Irene. So there was no need to iron, now was there?

Irene hurried to put the ironing board away, behind the curtain in the hall. "Well!" she exclaimed as she pulled the girl beside her on the couch—the girl who wasn't truly her own yet—a mistake recurring until Anna smiled, claiming her section of—what?—the world? If it unfolded like a warm bolt of cloth, surely it was for Anna.

"Tell me about your day at school."

But they were both listening now, as if he *were* coming. The girl had learned, too, to tilt her head to one side, as if to hear, inconclusively, car tires whipping the wind between stands of trees, then routing the gravel outside. It was, Irene seemed to say, when, like this, she stopped abruptly an activity, simply a matter of sitting properly upright, hands folded in their laps, and allowing

---

[1] Published in *The Musician*, Black Sparrow Press, Santa Rosa, Ca, 1987.

their mouths to form the rounded shapes from which issued the lovely words: *orchestra, oven, ostentatious*—Irene laughing at their game, which had begun, oh, when?

Then, laughing, Irene said as she looked out the window, her fingers sliding over Anna's, "Old, old, old."

You could hear, then, a shoe hitting on a wooden floor.

So Irene laughed again, amending: "Old me," as if a finger burrowed playfully into a furry chest. "I haven't fed you yet, have I?"

Then the two would go into the tiny kitchen where Irene had nonetheless wedged a table, covered in blue chambray with perfect triangles of yellow rickrack decorating the corners. "Sit!" Irene said, "Take a load off your feet," as if Anna were he, the awaited one. And Anna sat as Irene twirled the lazy Susan cupboard beside the stove, saying, "Let's see, let's see."

Soon blue bowls with handles appeared on the table, filled with potato soup, cheese bubbling on top, and Irene smiling as Anna told about her day, which, outside, was moving from dark blue to black.

"A boy?" asked Irene. "Is there always a boy in your stories?" which confused Anna—what did she mean, when it was only Ralph or Jimmie, who sat near her in school?

"Well, eat up," said Irene. "God knows you'll need it," which she'd not meant to say—a muscle loosening. She felt her ribs, *his* touch against them, a finger, as if to separate them—he might enter her there—how he chose the delicate methods of preparing her, until he forgot, his body interceding. Then he was a dozen horses running through a field.

A light hung over the table where it shone brightly on their two dark heads and cast shadows on the checkered linoleum behind them. A wedge of light lit the knotted oak growing close to the tiny room which served as their kitchen. Otherwise the house was dark, even the front porch, where Irene might have left a light burning.

But of course he did not come, not that day nor the next, nor had he been to visit for months. That he *might* come was the habit, like a fish's gills opening, which meant, as if it were the proper environment, saline enough, Irene washed half of their car, ironed a portion of the clothes, let bread rise and harden until she found it cemented to a bowl.

"Old, old, old . . ."

What Irene did when she was taught at school, Anna had no way of knowing. Halfway through a song—"Row, row, row your . . ."—did Irene drift off while the children's mouths drooped and the walls of the music room became discordant? Anna did not take Irene's classes—"No need, Sugar," Irene had said, "when I can teach you myself," as she had intended.

But books were easier, and Anna read, sometimes humming to herself as Irene strummed the autoharp, deciding upon the next day's lessons. So words were accompanied by the chest's throbbing, and they aligned themselves into rhythmical patterns.

As a result of her reading, Anna's eyes were continually pink, a rabbit's eyes, thought Irene, and there was not so much difference between the calligraphy of grass sprouting from the ground and words from the page. *And he'll tell me to get you out into the sun.*

Even there, as if the sun cut holes in the bower of leaves disproportional to her body, Anna swung in half-light. From the perspective of the tree's height, she must have appeared tiny: a miniature swing, a miniature girl swinging on it. She never tanned, even in the hottest months.

And, as it was, Irene stirred herself for school. It came, she acknowledged, with the suits she wore, not his gifts, which were for inside the house, inside their room, but suits picked out by her sister, the disgusted one who had hated him on first sight. Her duty, she said, was to keep Irene looking competent enough to return to the world, should she need to, meaning *when* she needed to, a time coming, was it not, as surely as light from stars?

Irene wore the stiff suits and her children sang on key, loudly, teeth showing, the girls' little sashes riding up around their ribs as they breathed deeply, the boy's pants dropping low. They had no hip bones, so little to cover if the pants fell. Their legs would be as white as the bellies of fish or Anna's forehead.

They loved Irene—these children—knowing nothing of what she asked when she said the words had to be rounded, that their lips should close at once when a note ended. "Not a breath after that, until I lower my arms," Irene would say. They liked her forcefulness, as if something important could issue from them. "O Mary, Mother of Je-sus, O hear, O hear our cry," when this was a public school. And, for that "O beautiful, for spa-cious ski-ies . . . "

While her class sang, Anna was allowed to paint with the fifth graders, below her chronologically by a year and by many in the secret calculations Anna made of Irene's ways, one of which was that Irene was too distracted to wonder why everything Anna painted was yellow and half-finished: suns without middles, flowers without stems, boats without sailors, shoes without feet.

"Ah! The color of music!" said Irene, pantomiming an orchestra leader and tacking Anna's pictures on the refrigerator, when Anna thought of his headlights, moving through Arizona, Montana, all the states which lay hidden under her hand as she pressed it flat against her map.

Or, thought Irene, the color of breasts, mine, when he sucks them, when the stiff suits came off. In the house, she left them freed, wearing the chenille bathrobe and the fluffy slippers, no underclothes. In a dresser drawer were the white batiste nightgowns she wore afterwards, when he'd ridden her. Those she had ironed, a portion of his gifts.

Summer was over, autumn had colored the leaves before they had noticed, with light fading even as the leaves fell to allow more light. Irene called the older sister: "Buy us some of those wonderful apples you have up there. We'll come get them some Sunday." But Irene forgot, and when she wanted in the house the smell of apples, she boiled cider from the grocery, with cloves.

Anna read to the sound of Irene's playing and to the odor of autumn brought down to a kitchen pan—a bubbling of spice, which she could almost taste when she chewed the ends of her braids.

The furnace hummed—Irene ordered the oil while at school, when her other self, the one in reserve, took over. And a boy from school, who worked for Tyson's Grocery, brought the food, the list written on the back of paper printed with octaves and staves during the time Irene's students practiced inventing their own songs in the ruled books.

"I won't let him see you," said Irene one evening when the delivery boy came to the door just after Anna had bathed, her gown wrapped by dampness to her thin body.

"Let him see!" said Anna, "I could care less," because, to her, there was nothing to see.

"Oh no," said Irene, "no one should see you until he is *ready* to see you," which meant *he* had gotten himself ready before opening Irene's suit jacket and pulling down the straps of her slip. And, maybe, even now, he was preparing.

All that he needed stayed with him in California and, when he visited, as if it were not precious, scattered about their room, casually. Then Irene helped him gather it together again, place it carefully back into the leather suitcase. Anna saw from the hall—shapes, the wadded shirts, the belts hung over the chair, and shoes aligned beneath the bureau.

Crossing to the bathroom, he wore a yellow towel, with his initials on it, and another like it around his neck.

Across the street, in mid-October, when all the leaves had fallen and the shack which sat behind Mrs. Rice's house became visible again, they watched a black woman move into the shack, raising the shades, swinging wide open the screen and the wooden door behind it. "Her maid," said Irene.

"*Whose* maid?"

"Mrs. Rice's! Don't you look out? Mrs. Rice used to take the car out herself, and now she has Tercell, from school, do it. She's sick, so the maid's for that."

"Oh," said Anna, and she would have forgotten, but the maid was coal-black and thin and, said Irene, young—you could tell by how she moved across the porch, sweeping it, every day, sweeping. At first, yellow leaves of oaks and red maple leaves flew into the hedges. Then nothing flew, and she swept.

Tercell, the janitor from school ("*Who?*" asked Anna, to which Irene said, "Where *are* you at school? *Tercell,* who washes the blackboards," and then Anna remembered his shape engulfed in yellow dust as he slapped the erasers against the steps outside the cafeteria, face and shoulders haloed in dust.), drove Mrs. Rice home from outings just as Anna and Irene drove up to their driveway after school. Turning from the car, they watched him lift her from the pillows in the back seat and carry her up the back steps, which Irene said Mrs. Rice had never sunk to using before.

Then, just as Anna and Irene had put their books down on the chair by the door, the bell began to clang in Mrs. Rice's back yard, rung by Tercell to call the black girl to her evening chores.

Irene went to the window to watch, so this became the ritual: to observe the girl tilt her head, as if the bell weren't resonating for blocks, lift one leg swung over the arm of the chair she sat on, her black dress sliding high on her thighs as she rose with one hand at the hollow of her back. Then her right arm reached inside the screen door for the white apron, a wedge of white, a suggestion of *apron*. She tied it around her tiny waist, slapped a pocket where, Irene said, she had cigarettes. Then the slow, queenly—said Irene—descent of the steps, her head barely visible over the hedge which ran the length of the ground in front of the porch. When her head became visible to Tercell at the bell, he let the rope go. It grew quiet again, and the last sound they heard was of the back door slamming.

"Ah, so," said Irene, turning from the curtain. But what did she mean?

"Let's make some hot chocolate," Anna suggested. But at the table Irene had nothing to say about what they had watched.

"We could go see," said Anna.

"Us?" said Irene. "Not us."

But Irene watched, watched as the maid came to refuse to keep her black dress on the whole afternoon and began to wear instead black tights and tight pink shorts, with high heels and pink socks over the tights—ankle socks. But Anna was wrong, seeing less than Irene at the window. They were not tights but the girl's very skin.

"Sugar," said Irene, "you're so sweet."

Then, when Tercell rang the bell, the black girl had to enter her shack, remove the shorts and the white tee shirt, step into the black dress. She left buttoning it as she went. The bell clanged longer.

"She'll freeze," said Anna.

"She won't freeze," Irene answered.

On a day off from school, at the Thanksgiving holiday, when Irene and Anna went to buy a turkey in case he should come, they saw Mrs. Rice in the black De Soto, pillows surrounding her as if to hold her upright.

"She's out seeing the world for the last time," said Irene. "A month or two, a year, even, it's still the last time since she knows it."

Where, then, was the black girl? Sitting on the porch in her pink shorts, waiting. Irene saw her in her mind's eyes—it was white lace, she decided, sewn to the cuffs of her socks.

Anna was tired of their watching at the window when they returned from school. The house was cold since the furnace was turned low in their absence. She wanted the warmth of the kitchen, Irene lighting the gas oven and leaving the door open as they ate their soup or chili.

Sometimes Irene brought her robe and slippers into the kitchen and changed there, before the open door of the oven. "Oh!" Irene might say, her nipples warming, standing erect.

He never wrote, had never written, so it was nothing they expected. If Anna thought of it now, it was because the black girl sometimes sat reading a letter on the porch as she waited for the bell to clang.

"What's it like where he is?" Anna asked once.

"Like here," said Irene. "Look around you!" Her right hand flung out to take in the stove, the sink, the table with the two of them sitting across from each other in the circle of light. On one wall was a calendar which her older sister had given Irene, marking the dates she would visit. "What *else*?" asked Irene.

"Why doesn't she"—Anna nodded her head as if the black girl's porch were behind their house—"sit inside, like we do?"

Irene put down her spoon on the blue cloth. She closed her eyes—considering, thought Anna. "Because, I expect," said Irene, "there's nothing *in* the house."

A bed, Irene said to herself, no one's slept in with her.

"Nothing that's hers, Sugar," which objects, Irene thought, annointed, *if* he had touched them, even a match book. *He* smoked Camels, so she could never pass a billboard indifferently.

"*Annointed*," said Irene, taking up their game. "Hear it?"

"Apostrophe," answered Anna, to which Irene rubbed Anna's head, saying, "You're learning something, now aren't you?"

At Thanksgiving, the maid had company, a man in a blue work shirt and two boys Anna's size, going in and out of the tiny house, slamming the screen door, positioning and repositioning the potted geraniums they had brought her. Smoke came from the chimney for the first time and, later, the boys sat on the edge of the porch, dangling their legs off the side. The door behind the screen shut and, later, when the boys began to shoot at birds with sling shots, the man opened the door and hung on a nail beside it his blue work shirt.

At the window, Irene smiled, placed her hands on her ribs, as if her fingers could fill each space. Toward twilight, the man and the two boys got into the Chevy which the man had parked parallel to the porch, even though there was no entrance through the hedges. Wedging through, with Irene thinking she could feel the spines of the hedges brush across the tender parts of the man's skin, the three got into the beige car and drove off.

"You see," asked Irene a week later, "how she leaves the extra chair on the porch?"

"*I* don't watch," said Anna. "It's you. It's not polite."

"So," answered Irene, "you're going to sound like your Aunt Alice now? Well, perhaps you don't need to watch. And I'm through now, if you want to know. I know the rest."

"Like what?" asked Anna. "You don't know."

But now the black girl could sit inside her house; eventually the bell ceased to clang. Though Mrs. Rice's house sat empty, smoke still came from the shack's chimney; and Irene had no lack of imagination.

In California, seen as if tiny strings had held him down, which now he broke, lumbering up so that, from the standing position, he looked normal in size, explicable, he gathered together the clothes he would need, the toiletries, the woven dolls for Anna, and perfumes, boxes of scarves and oranges. He gassed up the black car.

Returning once to the little house set two blocks from the ocean, he kissed once, on the thigh, the girl he was leaving behind—young and modern in her shorts, which made her body seem especially tall. He covered her to her chin with the cotton sheet. He poured bird seed into the cup of the wood cage which hung before the opened window. She was sleeping, the bird was chirping, the sun set as he drove around the corner to the ocean drive.

For miles, far into the night, he would pass the billboards of elongated women pictured dressed in black velvet or the shiny fabric they called *lycra*, which made their legs look especially thin, as cave women look in primitive drawings as they walk toward the fire.

Houses shrank against the backdrop of mountains or hung precariously on the sides of hills, tree limbs dwarfing them, lifting to catch the moon's light. Stars fired the sky or neon pasted a halo against the drape of black.

In Arizona, the radio stations would fade, and silence would engulf the car. Then rain would come, a drumming, and the bodies of cave women transformed on the billboards would waiver as the windshield wipers slashed across the glass. When it let up: another silence, as if all voices had stopped, as if words had not yet been invented, so women in their miniature houses, sitting straight on stools before the open fires, would appear fixed.

He would appear to Irene and Anna as huge, when, at daybreak of the second day, he opened the door, coming upon them surrounded by their objects of love.

Did he think of this?

No. No, of none of it.

The Sources of "Questions of Travel"

"IN going in the direction of meaning, time has to move through a mind," Eudora Welty has written. She is speaking in particular of a character's situation within the tradition of the story which relies on sequence of event and characters' emotional involvement in situation driving characters toward meaning.

For me the statement expresses more of my process as a writer than my characters' motions toward understanding. To write a story is an act of will which requires me to shut the door on memory, including memory of imagined characters, until I make a decision about the story's title, which will in turn suggest point of view. This seems the wrong way around—should I not know the story I want to tell before deciding on its title and point of view?

I have no character's story, in the traditional sense, that I want to tell. There is only memory and my pact with the story form, like a mother's pact with herself to raise a troublesome child no matter its recalcitrance.

I have long been aware of my resistance as a story writer to the efficacy of sequence of scenes in the traditional story if they build upon another only within the logic of plot. It is not that I do not appreciate as a reader many stories within that tradition. I am speaking here as a writer aware of experiences which have shaped my relationship to form.

The story, along with poetry, was my choice of form because it seemed capable of carrying distilled memory and, if manipulated, of undercutting a reader's expectations of explanation as that which literature seeks, propels forward: the mimesis of human action ordered so logically as to produce resolution.

Of course the story *is* a series—we speak of a story's beginning, middle, and end, so weighted by the term *resolution*. And I had chosen deliberately to work within the traditional framework rather than that of anti-story which would have freed me from constraint apart from interior logic. I had made the choice because I knew that the tension between the traditions of the story form and my arguments against them reflected in form would reflect my experiences.

When I began to write I realized that the life my memory had preserved seemed radical, upsetting of unity, an amalgam of experience which had forced change and new recognition. The need to recognize and respond to change *for* the sake of having an identity had been my experience. And as a child I had become aware that change begins in the smallest of increments and includes what happens in one's waking life, including daydreams, and in one's sleeping life. Change was the result of imagination. An imagined action was followed by action usually adjusted by the imaginations of others. Or one awaited the culmination of imaginings, with the act of waiting changing both the self and that which one awaited.

I had learned early about the nature of disappointment—the mind's revenge upon the body as depression and deflation for ignoring the possible disparity between what one imagined and what others imagined. I learned early to make suppositions, to calculate probability, and to leave a large measure to chance.

Everything, then, was dynamic even as the forms of the world appeared, if not stable, striving for stability, which was, it appeared, "good," while instability was "bad." Mine was not a stable family, but we were striving to become one; it was a message undercut by my experience. Semblance was wrought over all things.

To choose as an adult to write within a form which has a firm tradition and the readers' knowledge of tradition while seeking to have that form and the reader's expectations pushed against by language suggestive of mutability and by the silence which surrounds words began to answer what I had experienced as a child. The method I write by and the forms my stories take are deeply autobiographical, more so than any detail or event in my fiction.

It was a typical procedure, then, for me to decide to write a story with no idea of what story I would write. As I often do before beginning a story, I took out Wallace Stevens' *Collected Poems* and Elizabeth Bishop's *The Complete Poems* in order to search for a title, to look for something in language, that is, of interest to me—a sound, an image, a seeming contradiction.

As it turned out, my mood on the day I began "Questions of Travel" was unresponsive to Stevens. When I came across Bishop's "Questions of Travel" I stopped and, for reasons unknown to me since I had many times hovered over that particular poem when beginning to write, I typed the poem's title on the paper.

So this is my proposition, I thought: to explore in form my relationship to the words of the title, their significance for me having been mitigated both by experience and by Miss Bishop's poem. It was a challenge from the part of me which loves form as intricate play more complex than chess but akin to chess in its demands for concentration and memory.

My first simple response to the title was to envision a map of the United States, and it was then that the distance of the story's point of view was determined: somehow the narration would encompass the distance across the country.

Then a memory surfaced, of a house I had lived in at age nine, when my father was away working in, as I found out only much later, radio, television, films. Across the street lived a black woman who had borne twin boys and who worked as a maid for the woman who lived in the big house fronting the adjacent street. In fact, the cabin the maid lived in with her boys belonged to the woman in the mansion. The maid's house faced our own, behind a tall row of hedges. I had watched her, seen the twins at her breasts as she sat on the porch.

My mother had waited in our house, the black woman was waiting still in my imagination, and I had learned, almost as a birthright, that change was always present, both present and bearing itself towards one. But "could Pascal have been entirely right about just sitting quietly in one's room?" For that was how I misread one of the lines in "Questions of Travel," which reads in fact, "Or could Pascal have been *not* entirely right/about just sitting quietly in one's room?"

After I reread the poem and understood that I had misread it, I sat thinking. When I imagine Miss Bishop, I see a woman dressed casually, walking—always—near water, watching. I think of her as two separate people (in my mind she is still living)—the one who observes with her whole body and the one who, remembering her social self, brings forth her personality for the sake of her silent self, to honor it, to give it weight in a world which must have seemed both wonderfully and painfully full. Felicity of language and silence: equal measures. It was then, as I thought of how Miss Bishop's poetry affects me, that I envisioned Irene, a mother ironing her daughter's dress.

I wanted, I think, to acknowledge to myself the fact that I had misread the poem and to ask myself why, in form. As a child, I had been asked by circumstance to choose between my parents, and I had failed. Too late my mother chose stability or its semblances, and my father had never made that choice. Irene of the story is not my mother, but I have often imagined my mother as consistently behaving as she did on occasion—memories which I experience as relief—when her unhappiness at the chaotic life she lived while married to my father fell away and she was at peace with herself and her world. These were moments of invention, of taking what was at hand and finding it delightful or wondrous: Miss Bishop in my mother. I gave Irene a portion of Miss Bishop's love of language—a game to play with Anna; a set of images with which to express her sensuality; and her apprehension of the maid against which to test it.

My interest in story writing is an interest in discovery. I do not know what I think, were I to be forced to judge, about Irene's willingness to wait for the man who may be her husband. I would not wait as she waits, nor do I imagine that many of my female readers would so pinion themselves. I did not know until the last pages that Irene's man (*is* he a husband?) would have a girlfriend in his other home, and I thought for a long time about the judgment a reader might pass on him. And where are Anna's little playmates, a Girl Scout troup, piano lessons, all the things we think a developing girl should have, including a father in the home?

These questions, which I imagined as the reader's questions, did not occur to me immediately but issued naturally from the point of view and later became, in several ways, connoted in form. The specific situation of the characters' pitting themselves against the supposed "norm": it is part of the writer's tension and a method of discovery.

On the first page, having created only a woman ironing and a narrator both watching her and entering her thoughts, I realized that I was choosing not to draw back from Irene in order to tell her history—who, specifically, "he" was, when and why he had left, and why Irene had made the accommodation. Apparently the wide view of the map would have to wait, the waiting having been incorporated into form: is it not possible that one person can so inhabit another that to wait signifies presence?

Although it is an intellectual activity of arrangement and selectivity, writing feels to me to be an almost wholly physical activity—the body sensing what the mind imagines and suggests in language. When I put Irene on the page ironing and thinking of her daughter's incipient sexuality, I understood that Anna was in the room with Irene as Irene ironed, that the house was quiet, and that Irene and Anna were sensitive to each other and to everyone around them.

What was required for me to continue in the point of view of the story was my becoming equally quiet, choosing no word which would violate their presences. I said aloud, softly, the words *oven, ostentatious, orchestra,* and I thought for some time about the word *chambray* because it is not proper material for a tablecloth. The fabric is too soft and slippery for what I imagined was a formica-topped table, except that Irene would have made the cloth herself of leftover material from one of Anna's dresses, found the yellow rick rack in a paper bag of scraps, liked the feel of the cloth and the contrasting scratchiness of rick rack. When Irene says, "Sit!" just as she and Anna enter the kitchen, it is a miniature explosion of sound, coming both from the quiet of the house and from what, in explicit language, I have decided *not* to explain, such as the fact, in my mind, that Irene made the tablecloth herself.

A large part of what interests me about point of view is deciding what to omit. What is not written into a story can act upon a reader as much as what is included even though the reader's primary focus will seem to be on the words themselves. Irene says "Sit!" just after the narrator has told of the tablecloth, with the only word intimating that Irene made it herself appearing in the word *perfect,* during the writing of which I had seen her, head bent over the sewing machine, concentrating on making the rick rack into perfect triangles as if it mattered, and for Irene it does. Since I have "seen" this activity of Irene's as soon as I have them enter the tiny kitchen (which word, *tiny,* made me see the yellow rick rack as miniature and thus more difficult to work with), the choice, then, was to mention that Irene had sewn the cloth or to try to give the sentence containing the cloth a vague suggestion of thought, industry, concentration, and quiet, and to have these suggestions come from words only a few of which mentioned the tablecloth.

If I wanted Irene's words to Anna to be felt by the reader as small explosions issuing from Irene after she has been thinking of "him," as she always is, then to mention the sewing machine, to suggest its humming motor and have it, even in the story's past time, sitting as it must have on the kitchen table, would have added noise to the scene, detracted from the ordinariness of Irene's phrase, "Take a load off your feet" and from the present-time whirr of the lazy Susan cupboard she begins to turn.

I have thought for some time that I am writing partly, in all of my work, a literature of silence, from a need to express a part of my early experience and, in the broadest sense of the word, to make a political statement about noise and its effects. What I was raised without has entered my fiction as silence, an absence of explanation, or as pressure on language: each word sounded, which is possible only when the depths of silence are plumbed.

I was interested as I wrote "Questions of Travel" in recapturing a small part of the ambience I knew in houses without television, radio, daily newspapers, and the ringing of telephones. Later in the story I took away trips to the grocery store and letters from the man Irene and Anna are awaiting. I took away the institution of marriage itself by not clarifying the man's legal relationship to Irene and Anna, and I gave them a car only to get them to school and to travel to see Irene's sister if they chose.

I wrote both to consider the effects of early absences in my own life (absences mitigated by the presence of music, books, and language separated from explanation) and to protest, I think, the self-conscious clutter of objects in contemporary fiction, self-conscious because it seems not, as in Tolstoy, to reflect a social world built upon the supposed solidity of objects but, rather, to signal no social order we can believe in—all objects contested: by ecology, by medical science, by the fact of limits, by the fact of the upper and under classes in disparity, etc. The plethora of objects in contemporary American fiction seems to make a single statement: we have been overwhelmed by the material world. I did not experience poverty but, rather, parental choice which ruled out many objects, and I have come to appreciate what happens between people in the absence of noise that clutter accumulates around itself and the informing substantiality of objects when they are few.

As I circumscribed Irene and Anna's world, I began to love its humility, as a force rising partly out of their imaginations loosened by the absence of clutter and partly from their ability to estimate what they see as they observe with the passion of those for whom observation is sustenance. I felt as I wrote that what Irene and Anna had to say to each other was never extraneous to what they saw or to their needs, which were sensual, and intellectual only if their bodies sought the mind. "You don't know," Anna accuses Irene. But Irene does know, and she chastizes Anna only when she feels that Anna is not paying attention with her whole body.

My imagined reader lives in abundance without question, and it was in recognition of this that I gave Irene a sister who seeks to keep Irene ready to return to the "world": to suggest the demands of a community which would denigrate by finding them pathetic the lives the story tries to honor. After all, Irene is husbandless; Anna, fatherless; and they both are essentially placeless. And I honor them.

This, too, is why the word *lycra* appears near the end of the story: an assault, even visually, on intimacy within a world which crowds out intimacy. It is a fabric of incalculable cost—we do not yet know the real price of chemically-made materials or of our accommodations to the technology such objects require.

My mother owned the kinds of suits Irene wears to teach in—expensive suits bought, in my mother's case, by my father in New York, Los Angeles, San Francisco. They were beautiful and beside the point, representations of a world whose objects could not heal a breech or reconcile to it what had been lost in absence.

Irene's sister, so much of the world, would never find apples "wonderful." Nevertheless, my father had won his case with me through wonder at the world.

But I must specify, since it was years of thought about the tensions between how my parents sought to live that guided me as I tried in the story to balance Irene and Anna between what I imagined would be the reader's impulse toward pity at the expense of understanding.

Neither of my parents ever wavered from their strict codes of ethics or morality or their sense of class; simply, my mother wanted to live within hers in one place and my father within his while seeing America, including its wealth:

could it be gotten within the codes he imposed on himself? It was a difficult proposition for him to contain, but the fact of it was why I toured the country: two big, new cars for the five of us, two trailers behind them holding the Wedgewood china, musical instruments, sheet music in bundles, good clothes in trunks, boxes and boxes of books, the blue velvet wrappers of sterling silver, and the crates of crystal. Our "journeys" lasted for months, sometimes beyond the beginning of school which we children *might* need: we could read, could we not? So we came to know Yosemite National Park years before it filled with tourists, and I learned to ride horses on a bareback, white Arabian on a farm in Wyoming. Where all of this was leading was nothing we had explained to us. The codes by which my parents lived resided with us like extra traveling companions. We were chastized only for not keeping our eyes open, while we were given limitless time for daydreaming and reading.

So Irene became not only Miss Bishop residing in my mother but a coalescense in character of how I felt traveling. It would be good, my mother seemed to say, to get somewhere, and all that my father seemed to say was, *This is good.* But we had maps, we eventually arrived somewhere, we children were dropped into school, tested because it was often mid-year, passed on because we had read so much. And then, before long, we moved on or my father moved on and in time retrieved us. The inside of a car can contain a universe. In schools I wore the equivalent of Irene's suits, adapting to codes of dress in each new place. It was as if we were in a road show, tailoring our play to the community. The world was both large and provincial.

My father, bearing expensive gifts, thought, each time he came to visit, that he knew us. But perhaps not, for the gifts were inappropriate: they could not be incorporated into our lives, into the fantasy of stability my mother wrapped us in when we were not on the road. On the road, in a particular place, they might be useful—one would have to scout the territory and see. My mother's heavy satin robe was gaudy in the morning sunlight as she sat drinking coffee in the kitchen. In the story I leave Irene's gifts in the bedroom.

The implacability of the wider world is what causes Irene to honor the dying woman's last trips in her car, and the body's insistence on its sensuality is what causes Irene to step back from that world in order to feel what she has with the man she awaits, who has caught her in a code of morality or of pure sensuality or a combination of both, which remains unexplained but by its force, as demanding as the world's objects beckoning relentlessly to relieve sensuality through diffusion.

Is Irene right when she tells Anna that where they live is just like the place where the man they await lives? Equal silence, equal sensuality, equal extensions in imagination toward the other?

When the point of view opened to take into account my initial image of the map of the country and the man of the story came on the page, it was a difficult decision to give him a girlfriend, but, in fact, she had been prepared for all along—at least in my mind. When the maid is visited at Thanksgiving, I never thought the visitor's boys were the maid's children but, rather, those of his wife living elsewhere. It was my knowing this, I think, that initially planted the idea of Irene's man having a girlfriend although I was not conscious at that place in the story of the idea lying dormant.

I also think I imagined the girlfriend as a result of the initial tension I felt between my misreading of Elizabeth Bishop's poem and the correct reading: "entirely right"/"not entirely right." I do not like to write within the framework of the imagined ideal except to recognize it as a force which my imagined reader will bring to bear on material. My cavil with the uses to which the humanist tradition has been put is expressed in my writing in small decisions such as this one. I assume that the reader, seeing that Irene is faithful, as we say, will want the man she awaits to be faithful too. Such symmetry parades as order, which is sometimes called stability and deemed "good." But I was never sentimental in this way, and to order my characters' worlds by such symmetry would violate my experiences of the world—would, in fact, violate my view of the uses to which literature can be put. I am interested in having the reader look beyond her definitions of stability, order, right and wrong since our proscribed views often act as violations, on ourselves, including our imaginations, and on others.

I did not want to risk condemning the man in the reader's eyes by giving him a girlfriend and yet I needed the girlfriend because I imagined *his* place and the imprints it held, including those upon the people he sees as he lives his life separate from Irene and Anna. Technically it was most efficient to give him a girlfriend and, having done it, I liked her because I saw that, in terms of form, the questions my title had imposed could now come to fruition: her presence, a discovery, had taught me what some of the questions were because I imagined her, sympathized with her—it helps a writer to feel compassion for all of her characters.

When I put a bird cage with its bird in the man's room, I imagined that he and the girl had chosen it together and, moreover, that he could one day bring Anna and Irene a similar bird and cage, causing them to wonder how he had thought of such a thing. *Is* the girl truly asleep when he kisses her goodbye and, if so, will she know when she awakens, from her knowledge of him, that he has kissed her? At Irene's house, does the man need to be careful in his speech in order not to say the girlfriend's name by accident and, if so, what in his intimacy with Irene is affected? And does the girlfriend want a child such as Anna so that when he sees Anna his view of her has superimposed upon it the girlfriend's desire?

These are questions of travel, for we cannot escape our profligacy, which is ancient—how the cave images came into the story—and often heartbreaking. How to balance the body's aggression as it conceives ways to survive, substantiating presence, on its humble journey toward extinction.

QUESTIONS

Eve Shelnutt's story, "Questions of Travel," and its process essay, "The Sources of 'Questions of Travel'"

1. The story is titled "Questions of Travel," though in a literal sense, the only person traveling is the man Irene feels as absent. How does Shelnutt evoke the passage of time, of scenery, for Irene and Anna? What imagery and situations does she rely on? What effect does Irene and Anna's isolation have on this sense of travel? How do Irene and Anna observe things, and respond to what they observe?

2. What sense do you have of the absent man before the final scene? He is given no name. In what ways is his presence felt throughout the story? Can you sense his presence even when he's not mentioned? How and through what particular scenes? What has the man become by the story's end, and what do you make of the question asked of him and his response: "Did he think of this? No. No, of none of it."

3. In her process essay, Shelnutt writes, "Although it is an intellectual activity of arrangement and selectivity, writing feels to me to be an almost wholly physical activity—the body sensing what the mind imagines and suggests in language." When you are writing and reading, do you sometimes react physically to what is on the page? In what particular writing and reading situations does this happen? How do you respond when you like what you've read or written? When do you dislike it? When are you indifferent?

4. Shelnutt writes, "A large part of what interests me about point of view is deciding what to omit. What is not written into a story can act upon a reader as much as what is included even though the reader's primary focus will seem to be on the words themselves." Can you get a sense of what Shelnutt means by this in your own writing? Are there times when you suggest an idea, an image, an argument rather than mentioning it outright? When you select detail for things you're describing, why do you choose specific details at the expense of others? What do these details evoke that others wouldn't? Go back through essays you've written previously, and remove particular words or images and replace them with others. What is lost? How is meaning changed?

Possible Writing Topics

1. Shelnutt quotes Eudora Welty: "'In going in the direction of meaning, time has to move through a mind.'" Take that direction yourself by trying to recall

a specific piece of clothing—shoes, a shirt, a dress—that you wore and were fond of when you were a young child. As you work to recollect that piece of clothing, jot down on a sheet of paper all the memories that come back in the process of recollection, whether related to that piece of clothing or not. It doesn't matter how insignificant or unrelated they are; simply move as quickly as you can through time and mind to recollect as much as you can. After you've done this, write an essay that works with the article of clothing from the perspective of an adult looking back on a childhood experience, and recall what the article of clothing meant and means to you within the context of experience and memory.

2. After you've completed the essay, write a second one on the process of recollection you went through to claim a subject for your first essay. What, if anything, did you remember that you hadn't in years? What led to this memory? How many of the things you recalled seem directly related to the article of clothing you selected? When writing the first essay, how did you choose which items to include, which memories to omit? Of those you did include, how did you refine the sense of detail that actually appeared on the page in words?

Daniel Lowe

Elie Wiesel: A Response to Some of the Autobiographical Works

I am not capable of writing a critical essay on Elie Wiesel's work, at least not as we conventionally define criticism. What can we say about a writer whose experience of the Nazi concentration camps informs the majority of his writing? What school of criticism do we consult? Do we say that *Night*, Wiesel's testimonial on the death camps, is a better book than *One Generation After* because it has greater narrative unity? Do we compare Wiesel stylistically to Hemingway, or say that he isn't the novelist that Nadine Gordimer is? Do we examine his books purely as texts?

To do so is to fail to confront the issue of the Holocaust in Wiesel's writing, or to diminish it as an issue altogether. And this is what Wiesel has worked so desperately against in his books. If we intellectualize the Holocaust then we begin to rationalize it. If we examine Wiesel's work as literature only, we relegate to ashes the memory of the millions of men, women, and children that Wiesel struggles to preserve. We can make critical assessments, but only to the extent to which they comment on Wiesel's articulation of the issue. We *can* say that the comparative simplicity of Wiesel's style, particularly in the autobiographical works, is the most provocative means to communicate that which defies telling. But we must listen to that telling: at the end of *Night*, after Wiesel has seen his mother and sister fail to survive a Nazi "selection," after he's seen infants thrown living into the crematoria in order to save on the gas used for executing adults and children, after he's seen a young boy hanged in public and has been made to march by and stare him full in the face while the boy yet lived and his tongue was still red, after he has watched his father slowly slip into death as a result of starvation, dysentery, and human brutality, after he has barely survived a bout with food poisoning following his liberation, he stumbles out of bed to look at himself in the mirror for the first time in over a year. Wiesel writes:

> From the depths of the mirror, a corpse gazed back at me. The look in his eyes, as they stared into mine, has never left me. *(Night, 109)*

The sentences are short, uncomplicated, because in all of his work, Wiesel wants us as directly as possible to try to understand those eyes. It is important that I use the word *try* here because Wiesel believes that anyone who did not experience the death camps cannot realize their horror. (I am thirty years old, this is 1987, and I am not Jewish.) And it's equally important that I use the word *understand* because Wiesel does not invite us to see "his eyes"; he does not describe them. Seeing them is an intensely private act; what they reflect is unspeakable. But it can be no accident that the corpse and his eyes are not entirely Wiesel's, since Wiesel writes of them in the third person. With all the power of *individual* recognition in that final moment of the testimonial, Wiesel still gives the corpse its own being. I have to believe that in a book like *Night*, a closely personal narrative, that Wiesel asks us to look through the eyes of one fifteen year old boy's experience in order to recognize and remember the eyes of the six million Jews who were killed.

But we must return to the question of how we, writers and readers born or coming of age long after the liberation, respond to the work of Wiesel and others, like Jersey Kazinski, who use their experience of the Holocaust as material in their writing. To regard this work as somehow historical, or at least as merely historical, reduces the horror of the writing to a matter of time and time passed. Within this construct, we confirm Wiesel's dark prediction that "the ghosts will have to accept the inevitable. Soon there will be no one left to speak of them, no one left to listen" (*One Generation After,* 11). The dead become objects and artifacts of history that we may sift through in reconstructing a war.

So how do we respond, how do we remember that which preceded our memories? How do we keep alive an event, an era where torture, starvation, death and its manufacture were as commonplace as children playing ball in the street? There's no pleasantry in any kind of response. We may bow and shake our heads. We may feel some shame. We may take a fleeting glimpse at that dark pit of our souls that would allow us, under certain circumstances, to act as the Nazis did. But we cannot live day-to-day with that recognition, as the victims who survived the death camps must certainly do. If we did, we would have responded more readily to the deaths of three million Southeast Asians under the Khmer Rouge during the 1970s. If we did, we would respond to oppression in South Africa, to death squads in Central America. But we don't, because we cannot afford to be consumed by such horror, sadness, and sorrow when we must make our daily trip to the supermarket, when we must greet friends, attend to our jobs and studies, when we must do our housecleaning.

So how do we measure a response, critically or otherwise? How can the Holocaust inspire us toward action? I am a writer. Do I use imagery of the Holocaust in my fiction; do I have that audacity which would allow me to assume such experience? William Styron writes a novel titled *Sophie's Choice,* where the protagonist, a mother in a concentration camp, is forced by a Nazi to choose life for one of her two children. A network broadcasts a mini-series entitled *The Holocaust;* millions watch. And Elie Wiesel writes, "No one has the right to speak for the dead, no one has the power to make them speak. No image is sufficiently demented, no cry sufficiently blasphemous to illuminate the plight of a single victim, resigned or rebellious, walking silently toward death, beyond anger, beyond regret" (10). And further: "'The Holocaust as Literary Inspiration' is a contradiction in terms. . . . how can one convince himself without feeling guilty that he may use such events for literary purposes? Wouldn't that mean, then, that Treblinka and Belzac, Ponar and Babi Yar [concentration camps] all ended in fantasy, in words, in beauty, that it was simply a matter of literature?" (*Dimensions of the Holocaust*, 7).

Wiesel leaves us no true response. To be moved to use imagery of the Holocaust is to blaspheme the dead. To be moved by reading of the Holocaust is at best a restricted emotion that is an inadequate response to the power of human brutality, the power of human suffering. To be moved intellectually or self-righteously, as more recently many have been, to ask questions such as, "Why didn't more Jews revolt, why wasn't there some organization of Civil Disobedience," is to become irreverent and irrelevant. (How can we attach blame to so many murdered?) Even to be moved to educate, which would seem the healthiest response, is not without danger if we keep in mind that many of those behind the extermination of the Jews were doctors, lawyers, philosophers, and theologians.

So if we can have no genuine response, if we cannot justly assess and criticize work that articulates such immensity of human brutality, if we are not capable of recognizing darkest instinct in ourselves, perhaps our only response, in reading and writing of the Holocaust, is responsibility. Americans have a sharp sense of that. We have erected a wall in our Capitol that lists and commemorates the names of the fifty thousand men and women who died in the Vietnam War. We stood in outrage and dismay when 52 Americans were held hostage for two years in Iran. But as Americans, we sometimes fail to recognize that it would take 120 such walls to commemorate all those executed in the concentration camps, those whose names disappeared in the smoke of the crematoria. We do not recognize that while 52 suffered physical and psychological trauma in Iran, *three million* Southeast Asians died by execution or starvation in Cambodia. While we cannot measure the value of human life arithmetically, we cannot ignore the arithmetic of human suffering. And we must be responsible.

Criticism and theory are, or can be, expressions of that responsibility, but criticism evaluates and theory slows; neither is foremost in action. And while we cannot act to save the slaughtered Jews, when Wiesel describes photographs taken by German officers of naked women holding their children as they wait in line before the gas chamber, we must realize that in every sense they are still waiting for deliverance. You can see them waiting in Wiesel's novels, in Gordimer's, in V. S. Naipaul's, in Joan Didion's *Salvador*. Under differing times and circumstances, under different political regimes, they wait. And only in our accepting immediate responsibility for them, even if that expression is no more than a letter to a congressman, can the waiting end.

If, as Wiesel suggests, the Holocaust killed not only the Jews, but also language since no words could express abysmal horror, we can at least use words to honor and remember those who walked wordless to their deaths. We can read. Think. Write. Act.

REFERENCES

Wiesel, Elie. *Dimensions of the Holocaust: Lectures at Northwestern University.* Evanston, Ill: The University Press, 1977.
Wiesel, Elie. *Night.* New York: Bantam Books, 1986.
Wiesel, Elie. *One Generation After.* New York: Random House, 1970.

The Wiesel Commentary: Sources

*W*HEN a clergyman in town asked me to teach an adult education class on Elie Wiesel, the Holocaust, and human suffering, I accepted hesitantly. I had, of course, heard of Wiesel, his Nobel Prize, his status as spokesman for the Jewish people, particularly those who survived and didn't survive the Holocaust. I remembered his criticism of Ronald Reagan's visit to Bitburg, Germany, when Reagan placed a wreath at the head of a graveyard where many Nazi soldiers were buried. But I had read none of his work, and felt ill-prepared to lead a discussion, much less to articulate on the nature of human suffering for six million men, women, and children so long dead.

I drove down to a local bookstore and picked up *Night,* the only Wiesel book available there, and read it in a long afternoon I spent in a park as I lay on a hill in the spring sun. I had not read more than ten pages when I was struck by the immensity of my ignorance: I had a Master of Fine Arts degree and a B.A. from two major universities, I had a complete high school education, I had read more books and seen more films than many do, and yet in none of the classes I took, in none of the books I had read, in none of the films I had seen had I ever studied or considered the Holocaust. I had a historical sense of it—I knew the numbers—and a distant sense of its horror, but no educated or visceral reaction.

My initiation through Wiesel was swift and painful. (The book itself is very slim, the writing almost plain.) There was no enjoying the sun that afternoon, the sweet smell of the grass and flowers that Wiesel remembered, too, as he stood in Auschwitz the night after his arrival, the night he'd seen two children thrown into the furnaces, the night when he'd been separated from his mother and sister forever (the book is dedicated, along with his father, to both of them), the night that stripped him of faith, God, and the will to live. The irony of my own comfort struck me then as I paused between pages, paragraphs (Wiesel provides no breaks in despair), and looked out from the hill to see a young man and woman having a picnic under a tree, a child kicking a ball to his mother, their laughter reaching me as it rose on the wind. I was not angry with my comfort, nor was I ashamed. But the stark contrast between Wiesel's experience and my own grieved me, even while I mourned for the first time all those who had died in ways Wiesel describes so powerfully. There was no shared ground. I could not understand utter despair. I could not understand a depth of physical hunger that would cause a son to kill his father over a piece of bread. I could not recognize in myself, in all those I love, a capacity for brutality that defies language.

After finishing the book, I plunged myself into further study: I read Wiesel's *One Generation After,* I looked through two of his novels, I read a series of lectures delivered by Wiesel and others on the Holocaust, I rented movies that documented what had happened, I ordered *Night* for all of my freshman composition classes. In the midst of all this I was asked to write a critical essay for possible publication on the writer of my choice. I asked to work with Wiesel. I had months before the essay was due and all the time I would need to collect and read the material, to gather responses from students at the university and in the Adult Education class.

There is no joy in such reading. There's even less in seeing the films, the photographs. In his books and lectures, Wiesel speaks of a five year old girl undressing her one year old brother before they both walk into the gas chamber. He speaks of countless concentration camp prisoners writing diaries, notes, anything they can at the risk of their lives, burying them beneath the crematoria in order that the terror be documented, that the deaths might be avenged. (Many of us have read Wiesel and Anne Frank, but few have read the work of these dead.) In the films, most taken by American or Russian liberators, Jews are shown too starved to eat, their eyes empty or too full, even those comparatively strong joyless in liberation, their families dead, their homes and communities destroyed. Liberators—thirty years hence—break down crying when they speak of the conditions, of the emaciated bodies they threw like logs onto wagons, of the young, speechless woman who sat down at the battered piano among the starving and half-dead, and played Beethoven beautifully. In the photographs, a girl no more than twelve, stunning, but not pretty, looks out of the picture, her eyes dark and drawn under her brow, a yellow star plain on her gray dress. I looked at so many of these things that it drew me into depression. I asked myself how I could respond. I did not start the critical essay.

In the classes I taught, *Night* was as successful as anything I had ever presented. Students who confessed to never having read an entire book said they finished this one in one sitting. They wrote eloquently in their papers and journals on how the book had impressed them, had hurt them. Some said they hated reading it, had never wanted to know that these things happened, had never wanted to feel the Holocaust's intrusion on their lives. Others said it was absolutely necessary that we read about it in order that such a thing will never happen again. Some spoke of how the book had drastically altered their perceptions of God and religion, and were angry as was Wiesel over God's silence in the death camps. Others spoke in outrage, near tears, over the prisoners' 42 mile run through the snow between concentration camps, so many people slipping under the snow into death. I asked them what our responsibility was to these people. A few gave half-hearted answers. I did not start the critical essay.

Thanksgiving and Christmas were approaching, as was my deadline. I spent six weeks writing a piece of fiction into which I poured many of my questions, much of my anger, anxiety, and despair over the readings and discussions, always careful that I use no imagery of the Holocaust for fear of diminishing its magnitude. I wrote letters to a close friend as a means of trying to outline the effect the work had on me and my response to it. When I went to the grocery store or the mall, I threw coins into every Salvation Army pot I passed; I gave money I did not have to Children's Hospital; I contributed food, toys, time. I did not start the critical essay.

Five days before the deadline, I knew I had to write something. I sat at the typewriter trying to decide a first sentence, a first half-paragraph. For any approach I took I felt embarrassment, something close to shame. And I knew I could not write a critical essay about material that had somehow consumed me. I could not evaluate a writer whose experiences could not be evaluated, at least not conventionally, at least not intellectually. I could not separate the text from its existence as articulated memory. I felt the presence of too many eyes, too many voices saying, "How dare you presume." I do not think I felt guilt. I do think I felt responsibility.

So, finally, that is what the essay is about, though I think it's rather feeble and probably reactionary. There is a danger, I believe, in taking on an issue of such magnitude. Wiesel says that the great writers—Faulkner, Mann, Camus, and many others—did not write of the Holocaust because they were "admitting their inability to cope with themes where imagination weighed less than experience" (*Dimensions of the Holocaust*, 9). I felt some of the same things when writing the essay, or trying to write it, though it wasn't fiction. It was as if I had walked into an arena to fight and represent a people I did not know, had never seen, and, when confronted with an enormity of shadow, took a few weak swings and cowered in the corner.

But despite that danger, and the ease with which it can be avoided, I believe as responsible readers and writers we must take it on, if not through fiction, then through nonfiction, if not through criticism, then through consideration and commentary. I do not expect that most readers' reactions to material on the Holocaust would be as compulsive as my own, nor, perhaps, as naive. But it does demand a reaction and a response; it does demand that we remember. Language is one of the few vehicles of memory we have, perhaps the only one. Those who can't comprehend because they were not there must still speak and write. We need not bury again the Jews who died by using time as a rationalization.

I was born twelve years after the liberation. I cannot speak for the dead, I cannot grasp their suffering, but I can honor them with my own reflected sense of horror. I can try to be compassionate to others in my lifetime who, on some similar or smaller scale, themselves suffer. These few words are no more than pennies thrown into the pot at Christmastime. They ultimately will have very little effect. But they are my expression of duty and my contribution.

That, it seems to me, is an appropriate response for each of us.

∽ QUESTIONS ∾

Daniel Lowe's essay, "Elie Wiesel: A Response to Some of the Autobiographical Works," and its process essay, "The Wiesel Commentary: Sources"

1. Do you agree with Lowe when he says that it is not right to use standard criticism on a text that addresses a writer's experience of unspeakable horror, in this case the Holocaust? Should the source of the writing to some degree make us as critics humble? What ramifications does this have for writing? Elie Wiesel is a professional writer, but if you were to evaluate a writer who wasn't professional and whose work you thought was poor, even though the sources were heart-wrenching and honest and spoke of immense human suffering, what would you say?

2. Is it fair for Lowe to make comparisons between what happens in other countries and what happens in yours? When you recall national tragedies—the deaths of the crew members of the space shuttle Challenger, for example—are we right to mourn these deaths more openly and more profusely than the deaths of those in an airliner that has crashed in Japan? Why? What leads to our different reactions?

3. In his process essay, Lowe writes, "Language is one of the few vehicles of memory we have, perhaps the only one." Do you agree with him? How is language a "vehicle of memory"? What wouldn't you be able to remember without language? To what degree are memory and experience dependent on language?

4. Lowe writes that his essay will amount to "no more than pennies thrown into the pot at Christmastime" and "ultimately will have very little effect," even as he says it is "my expression of duty and my contribution." Can writing as a

response to something that has disturbed you in and of itself be worthwhile, even if what you've written has very little effect? If you write a letter to the president of the United States, there is small chance he will actually read it. Is it still worthwhile to make the effort? What can that effort do for you as a writer?

Possible Writing Topics

1. Write a letter where you respond to a particular policy, whether it is governmental, educational, or cultural. It need not be of national or statewide concern, but may be a local matter. You need not be criticizing the policy; you may praise it or simply offer your perspectives. Try to resist simply stating your support or your objection, and instead reveal the perspectives from which you've considered the policy and the thinking that has led you to your opinions. Retain a copy of the letter and address and mail it.

2. After you've mailed the letter, write an essay on the response that you anticipate, and how waiting for this response differs from waiting for a grade or comments from your teacher. How does your position as a letter writer making a comment differ from your position as a student writer in a class? Did you feel more authoritative as you wrote the letter, or less? As you compare the language, voice, and style of the letter you wrote, how do these differ from essays you've handed in for your teacher's response?

Sally Flecker

Feminine and Masculine Voices: The Beauty of the Countryside

O*NE* of the issues for feminist literary critics, particularly those whose project is film criticism, is a discussion of the narrative as a form that has arisen from patriarchal structures. The narrative is a form so natural and commonplace to story-tellers that, in many ways, we imagine it *is* the story; there can be no story without narrative structure; narrative and story are one and the same. But just as we are coming to see language as a deep structure that is *not* neutral, that is *not* merely the conductor of thought, and that *does* organize the way we perceive, so are feminist literary critics turning their attention to the way that the presence and inevitability of the narrative structure is assumed.

Teresa de Lauretis, in her book on film criticism *Alice Doesn't*, defines the narrative impulse as the location of desire and a mirroring of the Oedipal struggle. In the narrative a character encounters a difficult or un-ordinary situation and embarks on a journey during which something happens that changes him or causes him to change. To translate this into terms that I work with as a writer, I have as my agenda that in the short story a critical moment occurs after which nothing for that character can ever be the same. The reason for the telling of the story—the occasion—is located in a change of consciousness which often has an objective correlative in an act, but which may live, in complex stories, purely in the character's psychology. The occasion may be a subtle, may be almost ineffable even, but must *be* in order to have a story.

Feminists, however, are beginning to point to the danger of the narrative, or, perhaps, the danger in assuming that a narrative can relate the story. The narrative is, after all, a linear movement. It connects two points, at the expense of other relationships. It does not suggest the dialectic, that there are other stories whose telling will change what you see in each.

To not suggest the move to look in other places and other ways for relationships (stories) is to encourage the building of hierarchical, monolithic, and ultimate ideas. (History, feminists as well as other theorists argue, is an artificial construction—the story of the powerful, the dominant—that passes falsely as a complete story.) It is with the complacency of this that feminists, in pointing to the implications of the narrative, are concerned.

As I read Jamaica Kincaid's collection, *At the Bottom of the River*, the criterion of occasion was one that kept insisting itself. Her very short story (a three page, single paragraph story), "Girl," is a list, the mother's harping to her daughter as she tries to mold the girl into a miniature of herself, into the model young woman who is prepared for a domestic life as wife and mother. The tension between mother and daughter is sutured into the flesh of the chant cleanly and with incredible subtlety.

> ... soak salt fish overnight before you cook it; isn't it true that you sing benna in Sunday school?; always eat your food in such a way that it won't turn someone else's stomach; on Sundays try to walk like a lady and not like the slut you are so bent on becoming; don't sing benna in Sunday school; you mustn't speak to wharf-rat boys, not even to give directions; don't eat fruits on the street—flies will follow you; *but I don't sing benna on Sundays at all and never in Sunday school*. This is how to sew on a button; this is how to make a buttonhole for the button you have just sewed on; ... *(pp. 3–4)*

Whose story is this? Although they are the mother's words that dominate the page and it is her personality that is attempting to bend the daughter's, I would argue that it is the daughter's story, that the real tension is hers as she struggles to assimilate what her mother would have her learn and yet give voice to the unfairness ("*but I don't sing benna at all ...*") and the inadequacy of the instructions to guide her realistically through all situations. Her only other line in the story is the second to the last. ("... *but what if the baker won't let me feel the bread?*") (p. 5). There is such tentativeness to her voice. The mother's flat response is the final line. "You mean to say after all you are really going to be the kind of woman who the baker won't let near the bread?" (p. 5). In this final exchange, the girl's complexity (she knows already that the world in which she lives, or wishes to live, cannot be mastered through the axioms that her mother can articulate in sentences of ten words or less) makes itself felt in contrast to the mother's unrelenting and dogmatic presence.

But is this a story or a portrait? For the characters, there does not seem to be a shift in consciousness, nor a denial, in the face of event or act, of consciousness. They are balancing themselves on a timeless tightrope. There is an occasion, but it is one for the readers rather than for the characters. It lies outside the text, within the context of the world that the reader brings to the text. By virtue of its primitivism, perhaps, the story reveals to the reader the complicated theme of opportunity, missed opportunity, and desire in the relationship of daughter to mother.

Rather than the listing of do's and don'ts in "Girl," the first-person narrator tersely states a long sequence of actions in "What I Have Been Doing Lately."

The voice is reportorial, emotionless, and as readers, we find ourselves inside a state of mind that feels like despair and existential angst despite the fantastical abilities of the narrator.

> Still I fell, for I don't know how long. As I fell I began to see that I didn't like the way falling made me feel. Falling made me feel sick and I missed all the people I had loved. I said, I don't want to fall anymore, and I reversed myself. I was standing again on the edge of the deep hole and I said, You can close up now, and it did. *(p. 42)*

The narrator can reverse herself, she can order her world, but there is a sense in which it does not do her any good because she is stuck in a circle that feeds itself. Her journey doesn't take her anywhere but right back to the start.

> What I have been doing lately. I was lying in bed and the doorbell rang. I ran downstairs. Quick. I opened the door. There was no one there. I stepped outside. *(p. 40; 43)*

The narrator finally breaks out of the circle into circularity when she realizes that nothing she can stand on can make her tall enough to touch the sky. She gives up the illusion of the sky's availability to her for the reality of its distance. But along with that knowledge comes sadness and yearning—the realization that she can't have what she wants and that she cannot break out of the repetition. The story ends where it began.

> I said I don't like this. I don't want to do this anymore. And I went back to lying in bed, just before the doorbell rang. *(p. 45)*

Again, the reader is left with that sense of timelessness, that this state of mind is one that goes on and on and on.

There is texture to Kincaid's writing that makes a story *felt* more than seen. Her words sometimes seem to be soft carvings in bas-relief that clarify vision through sensuality.

> In the night, way into the middle of the night, when the night isn't divided like a sweet drink into little sips, when there is no just before midnight, midnight, or just after midnight, when the night is round in some places, flat in some places, and in some places like a deep hole, blue at the edge, black inside, the night-soil men come. *("In the Night," p. 6)*

> I saw the cat open its jaw wide and I saw the roof of its mouth, which was pink with black shading, and its teeth looked white and sharp and dangerous. I had no shells from the sea, which was minutes away. This beautifully carved shelf: you can touch it now. Why did I not let you eat with your bare hands when you wanted to? *("At Last," p. 14)*

The marvel of Kincaid's stories lies in the accumulation, the piling up of detail and act. Because of this richness, the story does not insist on a one on one, linear connection between points. The occasion for the story belongs to the reader by virtue of this multitude of relationships that the reader may construct.

It is interesting to read Kincaid's short novel, *Annie John*, alongside her collection of stories. The focus of the novel is on the problematic relationship between daughter and mother. When reading the two volumes together, it becomes obvious that it is the exploration of this issue that pushes her material in the collection as well. As an aside, I would like to note that her novel ends at the moment at which Annie sets out on her journey, that her relationship with her mother is unresolved; it is still one of great paradox and complex yearnings and angers. If there is to be a point after which nothing can ever be the same, where the character is irrevocably changed, it has not yet occurred.

If Jamaica Kincaid's are stories of the daughter and mother, Peter Taylor's belong to the son and father. Taylor's is the voice of a tradition. His material is informed by the struggle through which the boy comes to own a place in the patriarchy and his stories fit the familiar structure of narrativity.

I am interested in looking at how Taylor looks in light of Kincaid not because I want to dismiss Taylor (one of my concerns with much of feminist literary criticism is the cavalier way that it sometimes privileges the feminine through the simplistically false opposition of masculine and feminine) but because I want to see what there is to see and I do not want to have to buy into one perspective at the expense of another.

Taylor's stories are lovely in their subtlety. They are beautifully and intricately crafted. The stories that I found myself most welcomed into and drawn in by were those with first-person narration. Given that many of these stories are told by an older and wiser narrator looking back, they seem to be about the narrator's coming to see his place in the traditional order. In "Two Pilgrims" when the young narrator makes a remark about how unattractive he finds the countryside through which he, his uncle, and his uncle's lawyer are traveling, his uncle responds:

> "To someone *your* age, it just depends on what kind of country—if any— you happen to be used to.". . . There was a brief pause, and then my uncle fired away again. "Every countryside has its own kind of beauty. It's up to you to learn to see it, that's all." Then Mr. Lowder: "And if you don't see it, it's just your loss. Because it's there . . ."*(p. 229)*

There is, in this story, the sense of new generation meets old. Rather than the construction of a generation gap, however, in which both sides are so angry over what they see as the position of the other that they have to completely devalue and disregard the other, what we see is the older generation's suspicion, but ultimate kindness to the younger and the younger's respectfulness; what we see are two generations communicating, making that dialectical movement which encourages an informed point of view.

"Dean of Men" is a story which begins with a note of not so thinly veiled hostility and remorse.

> I am not unsympathetic, Jack, to your views on the war. I am not unsympathetic to your views on the state of the world in general. From the way you wear your hair and from the way you dress I do find it difficult to decide whether you or that young girl you say you are about to marry is going to play the male role in your marriage—or the female role. But even that I don't find offensive. And I am not trying to make crude jokes at your expense. You must pardon me, though, if my remarks seem too personal. I confess I don't know you as well as a father *ought* to know his son, and I may seem to take liberties. *(p. 3)*

"Dean of Men" takes as its material the story of how the narrator's grandfather and father, in turn, became defeated, embittered men, and how the narrator has narrowly escaped that same fate. But the occasion for the story is the narrator's desire to pass his realization on to his son, and despite the tone of the opening, the final moment of the story is one of generosity, graciousness, and humility.

> A man must somehow go on living among men, Jack. A part of him must. It is important to broaden one's humanity, but it is important to remain a mere man, too. But it is a strange world, Jack, in which an old man must tell a young man this. *(p. 38)*

Not surprisingly, it is the older generation's impulse, in this traditional order, to teach the younger generation the rules and responsibilities of this tradition. Taylor's stories taken together could read as the list of do's and don'ts in Kincaid's "Girl." Men in this culture aren't self-congratulatory or intrusive. They don't discuss their fears and worries. They do enter burning houses, endanger their lives to rescue a stranger's junk. In Taylor's stories, the narrator does embark upon a narrative journey which he comes through changed. Interestingly, though, the boy is never quite erased. He retains his ability to see with his old consciousness as well as with his new consciousness. Rather than simply to undergo assimilation, he undergoes a change in complexity—one that implies resolution, possibly even resignation. His becoming the father is as inevitable, then, as the weight of the sadness.

If I began this discussion by insinuating a similarity between the daughter and the son in Kincaid and Taylor, I would like to conclude with a look at the mother and father. The daughters in Kincaid cannot change into the mothers. The mothers are fixed as well. They cannot acknowledge to themselves or their daughters what the fathers in Taylor, on the other hand, seem to profoundly respectful of—power. The men are so aware of their responsibilities as protectors, while the mothers are aware that they are not big enough to protect in any real sense. They construct blinders, then, and this is what gets in the way of the mother–daughter relationship. For the fathers and sons of the patriarchy, it is their humility in the face of their responsibility that strengthens their bond. And it seems to me that there is an exhilarating and terrible beauty to the countrysides of both.

The Odd Couple

A year and a half has passed since I paired the work of two very different writers, Jamaica Kincaid and Peter Taylor, in the attempt to develop a critical perspective both on their individual works and on the whole issue of what it is that feminist criticism does or can do. Feminism had been so linked to politics for me that it was difficult to imagine it standing independently as an intellectual activity. Compounding matters was that fact that in some of the feminist literary criticism that I was coming across, the critic did not seem to question her own assumptions or see that, in the long run, privileging the feminine can be as problematic as privileging the masculine. What I was after, then, was to see if I could *use* feminist literary criticism as a tool, but not a platform.

There is a small part of me that wants to disown this particular piece of writing. I cringe when I read it because I see "graduate student" written all over it. It's there in the rhythm of the language—short, choppy, declarative sentences with lots of "it's" and "there's" referring loosely to half-stated ideas. It's there in the terms that are used but not defined. It's there in the thoughts that are connected because they follow one another in the text rather than because the writer clearly tells the reader what the nature of their connection is. What I see is lack of control, not enough muscle yet to sustain the attempt.

There is another small part of me that wants to congratulate myself on the brilliance of the idea. Kincaid and Taylor—such an odd couple. And yet, once seen, the connection between the two seems inevitable and enlightening. It's the same kind of "Aha!" and "Of course" that accompany the moment in learning a sport when intellectual knowledge and physical knowledge, mind and body, join forces for the first time.

Mostly, though, the angle from which I look at this piece of writing picks up neither ineptness nor brilliance, but something else altogether. What it picks up is evidence of energy and desire, a willingness to *start* that I think is the most critical habit of mind that a writer can equip herself with. What I finally came to see, and what makes me finally willing to own this essay with all of its flaws, is that writing is not about absolute, forever and for all time, *answers*. It is about questions, about learning to ask the good questions, the questions that open up a stimulating conversation. My attempt to use the tool of feminist literary criticism is, without a doubt, fledgling. But the idea of history as being suspect, the idea that the history we are told is not necessarily the whole story nor even the most interesting story, is a remarkable idea to me. It is also a generative idea.

A generative idea is the idea that not only compels you, like newly-found love, but the idea that suggests where to look if you want to see more. It's the kind of idea that encourages a multiplicity of vision, that calls for a multitude of connections, that insists on complexity. But there are layers to the idea of a generative idea.

A writer, sooner or later, learns to recognize the *seeds* of generative ideas and trusts her instincts in planting them. True, there are always those ideas that sprout on their own so firmly that the writer cannot ignore them. But you're limited as a writer if all you are able to do is watch the ground for signs of new life, to be chosen by an idea rather than to do the choosing. The implications of this for the activity of writing are several. You have to know which soil is fertile. I believe this is writer-specific. My issues, what is fertile to my imagination, what compels me, have very much to do with that intersection in life—the where I have been and the where I am right now. Writing, then, becomes where I am going, where I have not yet been. This does not mean, however, that the seeds should rightfully blow around in the wind and land where they may. If writing is "the where I am going, the where I have not yet been," it is still connected to the intersection. It is not a trip that takes place outside of context. A writer might still have an abundant harvest whether she plants the seeds or only cultivates what sprouts. However, it is useful to raise the question of how many harvests she might expect to reap.

I may be pretentious if I attempt to speak for all writers here. On the other hand, I may undermine the strength of my position if I do not. So what the heck. *All* writers get hooked into this business because they experience the thrill of following an idea through and discovering new territory. We have *all*, at some point, finished a piece of writing and said "I didn't know I thought this until I wrote it" or "I didn't see this until I wrote it." The strength of that excitement is why we begin to imagine ourselves as writers. When I wrote the critical essay on Jamaica Kincaid and Peter Taylor, the energy that I had initially brought to writing was fading. I spent some amount of time worrying that I was using all of my "good" stories or "good" ideas up before I had the skill to do them justice. I was cultivating what I was lucky enough to have had sprout at my feet. What I discovered when I wrote that essay, perhaps because I made the connection between two unlikely people, was that it was I who made the connections, an absolutely empowering moment. I could see clearly the signposts of my intersection. The "Where I had been" was a world in which I had the doubled consciousness characteristic of a person who is a member of a marginalized group in society, in my case being female in a male-dominated culture. The "Where I am right now" was in the worlds that Kincaid and Taylor both create and recreate as well as new worlds suggested by the ideas, those of revisionist historians and feminists, to which I was exposing myself. The "Where I am going, Where I have not yet been" is something I glimpse, but cannot see whole. It is what makes me sure that writing will always be something I do, not something I have done.

⁂ QUESTIONS ⁂

Sally Flecker's essay, "Feminine and Masculine Voices: The Beauty of the Countryside," and its process essay, "The Odd Couple"

1. In her essay, Flecker writes, "History, [some will] argue, is an artificial construction—the story of the powerful, the dominant—that passes falsely as a complete story. It is with the complacency of this that feminists, in pointing to the implications of the narrative, are concerned." Consider this perspective on history and history's presentation to you in this essay and other readings and in classes you've encountered elsewhere. Does this perspective seem accurate? When you think of your education in history and literature, to what degree was it dominated by male figures? Is this a fair way to present or represent history?

2. Flecker writes, "Taylor's stories taken together could read as the list of do's and don'ts in Kincaid's "Girl." Men in this culture aren't self-congratulatory or intrusive. They don't discuss their fears and worries. They do enter burning houses, endanger their lives to rescue a stranger's junk." Is the culture Flecker, Kincaid, and Taylor are writing of an accurate description of the one you're living in? Do the descriptions of these women and men exist there? How and in what manifestations?

3. In her process essay, Flecker writes, "There is a small part of me that wants to disown this particular piece of writing. I cringe when I read it because I see 'graduate student' written all over it." Look back over an essay you wrote in this or another class with which you were particularly pleased. Upon rereading it, are there things now that make you cringe? Why? What would you eliminate? What do you still admire about the essay? What now would you change?

4. Flecker writes, "... writing is not about absolute, forever and for all time, *answers*. It is about questions, about learning to ask the good questions, the questions that open up a stimulating conversation." When you write, are you trying to answer a question, solve an assignment, so as to be "absolutely and forever" done with it? Do you anticipate an audience who will be asking questions of your writing, testing the strengths of its arguments, its logic? Do you see writing as a way of opening up an issue or settling an issue?

Possible Writing Topics

1. Look through the essays and stories you've read thus far and select two of those that for whatever reasons approach writing from different perspectives. Write an essay where you compare the arguments made and what, based on your own experience, are the weaker arguments and the stronger ones. Be willing to quote from each essay or story, and establish a position on the kind of writing discussed in each of the essays. If you agree with one writer or the other, or disagree with both, don't be afraid to say so. Remember to make your reasoning clear.

2. After you've finished the essay, write a second one where you compare this writing project to others you've done in the class that were based more on your own experience of the world. How did your writing process change? How did you make a beginning for this essay as opposed to other essays you've written? Was this essay easier or more difficult to write? What specifically made it so? Considering what you've worked on up to this point in this and other writing classes, what sort of writing do you prefer? Why this sort over others?

Kathleen A. Coppula

Not for Literary Reasons: The Fiction of Grace Paley[1]

AFTER the publication of her second collection of stories (*Enormous Changes at the Last Minute*, 1975), Grace Paley's fiction was described as reconciling "the demands of avant-garde or postmodern form for structural openness and the primacy of surface with the seemingly incompatible demands of traditional realist material for orchestrated meaning and cathartic emotion" (DeKoven, *Partisan Review*, 1981, 48(2)). This description makes Paley seem a hybrid, self-consciously balanced between the demands of two audiences. Although Paley's work may be viewed as a bridge between two opposing literary forces, it seems that the "reconciliation" may come from less critically self-conscious motivation. Paley writes from her own unique personality and social perspective. The movement in her fiction seems to arise from an attempt to unite story and form with writer and culture.

Paley's early stories (*The Little Disturbances of Man*, 1959) are more traditional than her later work. The power of these first stories depends on the voices of her characters—loud, energetic, quirky voices full of Paley's humor. The characters take charge of their own stories.

In "Goodbye and Goodluck," Aunt Rose tells the story of her life to her niece Lillie, establishing herself as a woman with worldly knowledge: "If there was more life in my little sister, she would know my heart is a regular college of feelings and there is such information between my corset and me that her whole married life is a kindergarten." Like any old-fashioned story, Rose begins it with her own "Once upon a time . . ."

> And my reason, Lillie, is a long time ago I said to the forelady, "Missus, if I can't sit by the window, I can't sit." "If you can't sit, girlie,"

---

[1] Originally published in *Mid-American Review*, Vol. VII, No. 1, Bowling Green State University, 1987.

she says politely, "go stand on the street corner." And that's how I got unemployed in novelty wear.

This is a tale to be retold, and there is a sense of living happily ever after, slightly tongue in cheek.

> So now, darling Lillie, tell this story to your mama from your young mouth. She don't listen to a word from me. She only screams, "I'll faint, I'll faint." Tell her after all I'll have a husband, which, as everybody knows, a woman should have at least one before the end of the story.

These voices are important to Paley's early stories. They represent the writer looking beyond herself to people and the world. In her interview with Joan Lidoff (*Shenandoah*, 1981, 32(3)), Ms. Paley sees the use of these voices as a true beginning in her writing.

> Until I was able to use other people's voices, until I was able to hear other people's voices, that I'd been hearing all my life, you know, I was just talking me-me-me. While I was doing that, I couldn't write these stories. And when I was able to get into other voices consciously, or use what I was hearing, and become the story hearer—when I could do that, I just suddenly wrote them. It was a true breakthrough.

In the early stories, Paley seems limited in this role of "story hearer," much like a transcriber of stories that other people might tell. Other than a pattern of eccentricity and energy in her style, Paley is nearly absent. But her first collection contains her tentative departure from tradition—traces of what her later work would develop.

In *The Little Disturbances of Man*, Paley moves toward a more open-ended story. In "Two Short Sad Stories From a Long and Happy Life," Faith (a character who stays with Paley through her second and third collections) gets more than a single story to represent her life. While both "The Used-Boy Raisers" and "A Subject of Childhood" have a resolution or sense of closure, the endings are more like the end of a visit or the end of a day. If, as readers, we are left with a heaviness or a desire to sigh at the end of these two episodes, Paley offers release in the knowledge that for the character Faith, this is but a small portion of her "long and happy life."

Possibility becomes more important in Paley's second collection of stories (*Enormous Changes At the Last Minute*, 1975). It incorporates Paley's personal and political philosophies and becomes an element within the story itself in "A Conversation With My Father." The narrator speaks for Paley the writer visiting her father who is ill and who "offers last-minute advice and makes a request."

> "I would like you to write a simple story, just once more," he says, "the kind de Maupassant wrote, or Chekhov, the kind you used to write. Just recognizable people and then write down what happened to them next."

Her response is a compromise to her father's physical condition, "to please him."

> I *would* like to try to tell such a story, if he means the kind that begins: "There was a woman . . ." followed by plot, the absolute line between two points which I've always despised. Not for literary reasons but because it takes all hope away. Everyone, real or invented, deserves the open destiny of life.

This view of human rights is a central philosophy in many of Paley's stories, but here, the idealism of the philosophy is exposed. It becomes Paley reflecting on herself. In her interview with Lidoff, Paley gives her definition of a story.

> I think it's two events or two characters or two winds or two different weathers or two ideas or whatever, bumping into each other, and what you hear, that's a story.

What bumps into her philosophy that "everyone deserves the open destiny of life" is her father's view, based both on literary tradition and his own life's experience.

> "Jokes," he said. "As a writer that's your main trouble. You don't want to recognize it. Tragedy! Plain tragedy! Historical tragedy! No hope. The end."

Paley acknowledges the validity of the father's view by following his speech with a need for nitroglycerin and a higher flow of oxygen from the tank. His physical condition speaks for his view: "No hope. The end." Life becomes the absolute line between two points—birth to death, the facts of experience. And so the fiction that incorporates Paley's belief in possibility becomes even more essential. The story then reflects on culture versus individuals—what happens in the middle of lives. We can't change the absolute end; we must make changes in the middles, grant, as a culture, the possibility of "the open destiny of life." And the narrator, despite her father's condition, or because of it, insists on that possibility to the end of the story.

Throughout her second collection, Paley's stories do not proceed linearly beginning to end. The form of her stories reflects important moments during the essential middles of her characters' lives. Yet, even though her philosophy has an effect on the open-endedness of her story telling, it does not create a narrative pattern or style. Paley says that form depends on the story itself, not on the writer's manipulation.

> So you try to tell certain stories, but you need the form, that's what it is. You look for the form and until you have the form, you can't tell the story. And the form, I don't know how it's gotten; I consider it received, like grace. . . . I don't think of that as "new." I just think of it as trying to tell a certain kind of story and not having the means. As far as I am concerned,

> the means did not exist in my literary education or in my experience so I had to wait until I had enough writing experience to be able to tell that story. (*Shenandoah*, 1981, 32(3)).

Paley's statement rejects both traditional form and avant-garde trends. Paley believes that the story itself has the power. This gives her the flexibility to tell various kinds of stories, and to be independent from both traditional and postmodern expectations.

Two stories, "Wants" and "Samuel," both fit Paley's definition of story, but they are very different stories told in different ways. Together these two stories show Paley as a writer "bumping into" the expectations of readers for a Paley story form.

"Wants" is a short story barely covering three printed pages. Yet the collision that Paley describes is there in all its force between the narrator's view of herself as fluid, capable of change, and her ex-husband's view that characterizes her in the past. At the beginning of the story, she is returning library books, overdue for eighteen years with a $32 fine. The issue of this story is described through the librarian's interaction with the narrator after she pays the fine: "Immediately she trusted me, put my past behind her, wiped the record clean, which is just what most other municipal and/or state bureaucracies will *not* do." And this is what the ex-husband will not do as well. He tells her, "But as for you, it's too late. You'll always want nothing." The statement stops her cold. No hope. The end.

> He had a habit throughout the twenty-seven years of making a narrow remark which, like a plumber's snake, could work its way through the ear down the throat, halfway to my heart. He would then disappear, leaving me choking with equipment. What I mean is, I sat down on the library steps and he went away.

She recovers herself by composing a list of her wants to combat the accusation. The list includes wanting to be a person who returns library books, ends wars, is an "effective citizen" and has been "married forever to one person, my ex-husband or my present one." This list turns the clash of the two characters in the story into a reflection of culture. These aren't the wants we normally think of, or what the ex-husband wants, which is a sailboat and more money. Culture isn't prepared to recognize her wants because they aren't tangible, and she wants the recognition. But she settles for the satisfaction that she restored the hope her ex-husband tried to take away.

> Well! I decided to bring those two books back to the library. Which proves that when a person or an event comes along to jolt or appraise me I *can* take some appropriate action, although I am better known for my hospitable remarks.

"Wants" is a story of internal reflection and characters with knowledge of one another. It demands that the audience be close to the character. It ends almost where it began—the narrator getting back to the feeling of hope involved in returning library books after her ex-husband drags her away from that emotional spot.

The effect of "Samuel" depends on quite a different form. This story needs the distance created by an uninvolved narrator witnessing and reporting events. The movement in this story is from one beginning to a totally different beginning at the end. The characters who come together in the story are dispersed or lost to the reader. The first part of the story occurs on the subway. The characters, even Samuel, could be anyone.

> Four boys are jiggling on the swaying platform. Their names are Alfred, Calvin, Samuel, and Tom. They men and women in the cars on either side watch them. They don't like them to jiggle or jump but don't want to interfere.

The story continues in this same distant style. One woman yells at them to stop the behavior. They laugh; the lady blushes. It could be any woman. A man, whose distinction is that his "boyhood had been more watchful than brave," pulls the emergency cord because the boy's behavior angered him. Samuel happens to be the one who is killed because he "let go his hold on the chain so he could pound Tom as well as Alfred."

The events are tragic, but the cause is simple: the adults want the children to behave so they don't get hurt. The paradox is the end of the first part of the story, but it begins the second part—a mother must deal with the loss of her son.

> She did not know how she could ever find another boy like that one. However, she was a young woman and she became pregnant. Then for a few months she was hopeful. The child born to her was a boy. They brought him to be seen and nursed. She smiled. But immediately she saw that this baby wasn't Samuel. She and her husband together have had other children, but never again will a boy exactly like Samuel be known.

For Paley, a story may be told, but it doesn't necessarily end. The consequence of the events of the story continue past the printing on the page, refusing to let the reader dismiss the story as finished, set in the past.

In her third collection (*Later the Same Day*, 1985), Paley adds to the forces of tension that appear in her previous work. She incorporates the idea of stories, language, and the writer within stories of ordinary life with ordinary characters.

"In the Garden" is about hearing stories, not literary stories, but in this case stories about neighbors. The story begins, "An elderly lady wasted and stiff, sat in a garden beside a beautiful young woman whose two children, aged eight and nine, had been kidnapped eight months earlier." The mother continues to speak of what will happen when the children come home. The father appears, tough and shouting, speaking to a man who is vacationing in the area. The father describes the neighborhood as if he personally were in control of it in every respect. This new man speaks to other neighbors during his stay and from them he learns more about the parents of the kidnapped children and the details of the kidnapping. He also hears the interpretations of events that these neighbors make. One man interprets the story of the kidnapping as a lesson in accepting powerlessness and limitations.

> But aha! Something went wrong. I'm not afraid to tell you this. *Everyone* knows it. Clearly. The money did not go out quickly enough. Why? Let me tell you why. Because our friend is vain and foolish and believed himself too powerful and lucky to suffer tragic loss.

The elderly woman who appeared at the beginning of the story appears again at the end. "In the Garden" ends with what she's learned from hearing the story of the kidnapping. The vacationing man stops to say goodbye to the couple. The husband reads an article quoting the father of the kidnapped children. The husband responds angrily to the article.

> ... What is in his mind? He thinks because he was once a poor boy in a poor country and he became very rich with a beautiful wife he can bend steel with his teeth.

But the elderly woman, who has a degenerative muscle disease, has learned something from the story of the kidnapping.

> She had been told that this paralysis would soon become much worse. In order to understand that future and practice the little life it would have, she followed the stranger without moving her head—with her eyes alone. She watched, from left to right, his gait, his clothes, his hair, his swinging arms. Sadly she had to admit that the eyes' movement even if minutely savored was not such an adventurous journey.
> But she had become interested in her own courage.

While many other contemporary writers address the inadequacies of language and communication in their fiction, Paley asserts her belief in the power of language to make important changes in our lives. "Anxiety" is about that belief. The narrator watches two fathers picking up their children after school. Both fathers let the children ride on their shoulders. The little girl, Rosie, wiggles too much and her father says, "Stop it this minute," to which Rosie replies, "Oink, oink." The father sets her down hard on the pavement and the narrator intercedes, questioning his reason for doing this.

> Have you ever said oink oink? Think carefully. Years ago perhaps?
> No. Well maybe. Maybe.
> Whom did you refer to in this way?

> He laughed. He called to his friend, Hey Ken, this old person's got something. The cops. In a demonstration. Oink oink, he said, remembering, laughing.
> The little girl smiled and said, Oink oink.
> Shut up, he said.
> What do you deduce from this?
> That I was angry at Rosie because she was dealing with me as though I was a figure of authority, and it's not my thing, never has been, never will be.

The awareness of language and the renewal of historical meaning associated with words, even one as simple as "oink," lead to understanding and change. Of course, it is a Paley story, so after the fathers go off merrily with their children, the narrator worries about their safety beyond her sight and concern.

The writer, as a character, enters the story in "The Story Hearer." This is the writer as a person aware of stories and language in everyday life, and who pauses not only to notice words in the world but to interpret them. Even though this sounds similar to the trends in postmodern fiction, Paley sees her work differently.

> ... First of all, for me the story exists really off the page in a way that for them [the French], it's all lying around there on the table. And for a lot of Americans too it does. And I don't think that's the direction for literature to go. I see it getting deeper and deeper into the page, until it disappears out the back end of the book. So that's the direction it's going to take. It's not that I don't love the page. I mean I love the books. But we really have to think of the throat it comes out of. I feel it's too great a movement away from the people, if you want to put it that way, and certainly away from female life. *(Shenandoah, 1981, 32(3))*

In "The Story Hearer," the narrator relates elements of form to life as a way of speaking about the differences between men and women.

> I said, Shall we begin at the beginning?
> Yes, he said, I've always loved beginnings.
> Men do, I replied. No one knows if they will ever get over this. Hundreds of thousands of words have been written, some freelance and some commissioned. Still no one knows.

The explanation for men's preference for beginnings shows up in another of Paley's stories, "Lavinia: An Old Story," when the narrator tells her views of conception.

> My opinion: What men got to do on earth don't take more time than sneezing. Now a woman walk away from a man, she just know she loaded

down in her body for nine months. She got that responsibility on her soul
forever.

The story hearer goes on to tell the stories of her day. Language and its interpretation is a natural part of that day.

> At this point the butcher said, What'll you have, young lady?
> I refused to tell him.
> Jack, to whom, if you remember, I was telling this story, muttered, oh God, no! You didn't do that again.
> I did, I said. It's an insult. You do not say to a woman of my age, who looks my age, what'll you have, young lady? I did not answer him. If you say that to someone like me, it really means, What do you want, you pathetic old hag?

She encounters an old acquaintance and badgers him about his former use of language for propaganda.

> ... thought up any good euphemisms lately? I asked.
> Ha, ha, he said. He still feels bad about his life in the Language Division of the Defense Department.

While the government's use of language is criticized, so is the literary use of language. One of these euphemisms is picked up and used in a "poetic article." At the end of the story, the end of the day, the narrator has her own desire for beginnings, telling Jack she wants to have a baby. Jack tells her, "You can't. Too late. A couple years too late. . . ." (No hope. The end.) So the narrator turns to the Old Testament for an old story. She is dissatisfied with the ending of that story as well, "with those three monotheistic horsemen of perpetual bossdom and war: Christianity, Judaism, and Islam." Still, she reflects on the hope of beginnings.

> Just the same, I said to softly snoring Jack, before all that popular badness wedged its way into the world, there *was first* the little baby Isaac. You know what I mean: looking at Sarah like all our own old babies—remember the way they practiced their five little senses.

Many contemporary writers and critics turn away from traditional stories because traditional methods are supposed to have lost meaning. Their job is to challenge and tear down those old meanings in order to shake readers from their dullness, from the routine of finding what is expected or already known. But the process of dismantling can only go so far—until there is only empty space remaining. Grace Paley attempts the difficult work, that of rebuilding. If Paley's fiction has elements that seem to meet the demands of both "avant-garde or postmodern form" and "traditional realist material," it is because her work is to renew traditional meaning, not to make that meaning suspect. She sees those meanings as essential to life, in her words from "The Story Hearer":

> In fact, I am stuck here among my own ripples and tides. Don't you wish you could rise powerfully above your time and name? I'm sure we all try, but here we are, always slipping and falling down into them, speaking their narrow language, though the subject, which is how to save the world—and quickly—is immense.

REFERENCES

DeKoven, Marianne, "Mrs. Hegel-Shtein's Tears," *Partisan Review*, 1981, 48(2).
Lidoff, Joan, "Clearing Her Throat: An Interview With Grace Paley," *Shenandoah*, 1981, 32(3).
Paley, Grace, *Enormous Changes at the Last Minute*, Farrar Straus Giroux, New York, 1975.
Paley, Grace, *Later the Same Day*, Farrar Straus Giroux, New York, 1985.
Paley, Grace, *The Little Disturbances of Man*, Viking Penguin Inc., New York, 1959.

Being Heard

I had been given an assignment: Write a publishable literary article. That certainly was not an unusual request for a graduate student in an English Department. What was unusual was my *response* to the assignment. I discovered that I had something which I felt was important to say, and that I wanted to be heard by others involved in literature.

Through my experience as both a student and teacher of writing, I learned that writing only appears to be an isolated act. I see my own writing as resulting from my position or role in relation to others. This can be in the form of direct contact, imagined interactions, or exposure to someone else's written words. By taking account of these influences, a writer can assess and deal with his or her own authority (including the limitations of that authority) in relation to other forces. This assessment can contribute as much to a piece of writing as the research or the arrangement of words on the page. The value of any piece of writing depends on its authority. This does not mean that every reader will believe or applaud the writer's opinion. It means that the writer can be taken seriously enough to generate an active response in the reader, even if the response is in opposition to the opinion of the writer. This is what made the difference for me when I came to write my article on Grace Paley's fiction. I was at a point in my education where I could examine the power or authority both around me and within myself as it related to the subject of the essay.

Because I've said that I had responded to an assignment, the roles of a student and of a teacher immediately come to mind. There is an implied imbalance of power involved. But the relationship between an individual student and an individual teacher requires interpretation. In this case, the message in the wording of the assignment (Write a publishable literary article.) is clear. The flexibility of the assignment tells me that this instructor recognizes a degree of knowledge and ability (authority) within the student. The choices were all mine—which author I wanted to study, what I wanted to say about the work of that author. The student role became less significant. The actual work for me that semester became a question of how to use what expertise I had, how to move toward approaching an essay more as a professional writer.

During that semester, the forces I spoke of in terms of direct contact, imagined interactions, and exposure to the written words of others formed a pattern that became recognizable to me when I came across the phrase which I quoted in the opening paragraph of the essay: "the demands of avant-garde or postmodern form for structural openness and the primacy of surface with the seemingly incompatible demands of traditional realist material for orchestrated meaning and cathartic emotion." Even to a reader without the slightest interest in such literary attitudes, the language of the phrase gives a good indication of the forces involved around the subject I would address in the essay.

When I read those words, my true reaction was something like, "Gawd, them's fightin' words!" I bristled, I growled, I bared my teeth and copied the words into my notebook with a thick black felt-tipped marker and boxed it off in quick black lines bordered with asterisks and exclamation marks. It was the kind of gut reaction that I'd always told my own students would alert them to the fact that they had found a *starting* point for their writing. The author of those words had inadvertently applied a dentist's drill to the sensitive spot of my personal beliefs. Of course, to my peers and my instructors, I might have described my reaction by pointing to the quotation and saying something like "This seems to require a response from a fiction writer's perspective." If I had gone on that gut reaction alone, I would have expected a response of head shaking accompanied by "My, my, aren't we a bit irrational today." After all, simply because I hold a certain set of beliefs doesn't mean that they are automatically valid. I would have to locate, identify, and dissect the elements of my reaction in order to see what strength they possessed. There is the risk that the structure of my beliefs—all that guides me—might crumble to dust, and then what would I have but confusion.

Because I was a student, I was in the fortunate position to have plenty of opportunities for direct contact with others who would be quick to challenge my ideas. Teachers and other students gave me an immediate chance to expand and strengthen my thoughts, or to back off and revise them a bit. At the beginning, I didn't know what to expect from this direct testing of my authority. But the classroom is a fairly safe testing ground. Expressing my views made me an active student, which is what is expected from a student in a discussion format class. If my views were too shaky to stand up to the verbal challenges, I had the chance to revise as I went along, without risk to my position as a student. It would only help my final garde. This was not true when it came to writing the essay. My assignment was to put forward a *finished* product, an end result of the thinking that came before my own conclusions. In writing, revision goes only so far. Eventually, a writer must decide what he or she wants to say, and the printed word is a fairly firm structure.

What I discovered as the semester progressed was that I could influence the opinion of others, or at least keep them listening to me—the enactment of a degree of authority. I also learned to identify and clarify the issues implied both in the quotation I used to open the essay, and in my response to those written words.

Here are those words again: "the demands of avant-garde or postmodern form for structural openness and the primacy of surface with the seemingly incompatible demands of traditional realist material for orchestrated meaning and cathartic emotion." The arrogance of the sound of those words bothers me because it tells me I'm about to be verbally bullied by someone who holds what they see as absolute truths over my head. The stance here is elitist: "If you aren't tuned in to the jargon, your reaction to the ideas which follow aren't worthy of consideration." But these are only elements of the style of one author, which is not what I would address in an essay. That style contributed to my original harsh reaction, but it was one part of the reaction that I had to learn to ignore in order to move forward from my starting point and to write an essay addressing broader and I believe essentially important issues in contemporary fiction.

My reaction to this writer's style, however, does point toward the beliefs I hold about reading, writing, and critical theories. I identify myself not as a literary critic, but as a fiction writer (novice). My fiction is an extension of my own personality and experience, and I'd prefer to claim responsibility for any value within my words as well as for any failures embedded there. I write about what I see as important without asking myself if the structure is open enough or the emotion cathartic enough as I go along. And finally, I believe that stories, still, are about people, no matter what type of story form is involved. These are the beliefs which held up for me throughout my discussions during the semester, as I read Grace Paley's fiction and articles about her fiction, and the whole time I wrote the essay addressed to an audience which I imagined might use the language of that opening quotation.

The language used in that quotation eliminates *people* from the act of reading and of writing. It eliminates the people (characters) within stories. The structure says there is a binary opposition in contemporary fiction. It states that fictional form (a set of abstract constructs) has the ability to demand something when, really, the people involved with literary criticism and the people involved in fiction writing are the ones who created and use words like "avant-garde," "postmodern," and "traditional." As a fiction writer, I wanted to fight the trend to ignore the writer from his or her own writing. I wanted to put Grace

Paley, a real person, up front in terms of her writing. In the essay, I responded to the quotation by moving the language from a structure which implies that "form demands" to one that puts the "demands" where they belong—coming from the mouths of two audiences, two groups of people. And to remind my own I concluded the opening paragraph (which to me gives the essay its form) with "Paley writes from her own unique personality and social perspective. The movement of her fiction seems to arise from an attempt to unite story and form with writer and culture."

I don't think there is any need to cover the process involved in writing the rest of the Paley article. Once I've found the starting point for a piece of writing, it is really only a matter of making practiced choices paragraph by paragraph. I might pause over the wording of a sentence, or over which example would be best to use to make my point. These are editing, not writing choices. The work in writing comes before I pick up a pencil. If I don't have a structure before I start to write, there's generally no point in my trying to form sentences. I know I'll be staring at a blank piece of paper. I'll become restless and wander away from my writing table to empty the dishwasher or to start a load of laundry.

In order to find that structure, I talked about testing my own authority in terms of knowledge and beliefs. But I also had to account for the limitations of my authority. I didn't elect to write a critical essay but did it in response to an assignment. I had to see myself in a different role than just that of student and of novice fiction writer. But the novice in both the student and the fiction writer roles was still important in the voice and method I used in writing the essay. It was a realistic assessment, placing me midway between the uninformed and the expert. Once I discovered what I wanted to say and that I wanted to be heard (published and read by others), I still had to find a way to say it and be viewed as credible. For the assignment, I would be writing about an author who already had a credible reputation in contemporary literature. Because of the assignment, I found that I could say more by joining my voice to Grace Paley's.

At first, I didn't like the idea. It seemed cowardly, as though I were hiding behind the words of someone else. But perhaps what I really didn't like was confronting the realistic limitations of my credibility. If I had written a less formally structured essay discussing my personal views of what contemporary fiction should be, then sent it with a note to an editor of a literary magazine— "Hi! I'm Kathie Coppula, you never heard of me but I'm a student and I've had a single story published so far and here's what I think. . . ."—then I'd expect that essay to bounce back to me quickly with a "ha-ha" rejection note attached.

Grace Paley has earned the right to make strong direct statements about contemporary fiction. She has earned the right to say things such as ". . . the subject, which is how to save the world—and quickly—is immense." I agree with many of Paley's ideas. As a writer, I can express my views, adding strength to my opinion by using Paley's words. I think that accepting the limitations of my authority was the final step in the movement of my role from that of a student toward that of a professional writer, and in the movement of my essay from an exercise in response to an assignment to a published article.

QUESTIONS

Kathleen A. Coppula's essay, "Not For Literary Reasons: The Fiction of Grace Paley," and its process essay, "Being Heard"

1. In her essay, Coppula quotes Paley: "'So you try to tell certain stories, but you need the form, that's what it is. You look for the form and until you have the form, you can't tell the story. And the form, I don't know it's gotten; I consider it received, like grace.'" Is Paley's sense of story form and its origins applicable to the essays you've written? What exactly does she mean by form and what leads to it? When you write, do you feel in control of the form of your essays? Is form something you can plan through an outline or other writing strategies? When you've finished an essay, has it taken a form you expected, or are you surprised by it?

2. What is your response to the quotation that Coppula employs in the first paragraph of her essay: ". . . Grace Paley's fiction was described as reconciling 'the demands of avant-garde or postmodern form for structural openness and the primacy of surface with the seemingly incompatible demands of traditional realist material for orchestrated meaning and cathartic emotion.'" What purpose does such writing serve? For what audience was the sentence written? Do you feel excluded from that audience? If so, what is your reaction to your exclusion?

3. In her process essay, Coppula writes, "The value of any piece of writing depends on its authority. This does not mean that every reader will believe or applaud the writer's opinion. It means that the writer can be taken seriously enough to generate an active response in the reader, even if the response is in opposition to the opinion of the writer." In your own writing, do you sense the authority of which Coppula speaks? Is the authority as important as Coppula makes it out to be? If you don't sense this authority, then to whom does it belong? your teacher? your audience? What power does a writer possess when you are reading his or her work?

4. Coppula discusses the importance of finding a sense of structure before she sits down to write—remember Paley's comments on form—then goes on to say, "In order to find that structure, I talked about testing my own authority in terms of knowledge and beliefs. But I also had to account for the limitations of my authority. I didn't elect to write a critical essay but did it in response to an assignment. I had to see myself in a different role than just that of student and of novice fiction writer." How is your authority as a writer affected by writing in response to an assignment? When you regard yourself as "just a student and a novice," where does this place you when you are writing? How do you go about "finding a different role" in order to become something more than "just a student"?

❧ Possible Writing Topics ☙

1. In this collection, there are several writers who have written four or more essays and stories: Kathleen A. Coppula, Sally Ann Flecker, Garnett Kilberg, Daniel Lowe, Barbara Mellix, Mark Shelton, Kevin Stemmler. Choose one of them and write an essay where you develop your sense of this writer's perspective on what writing means. Does the writer ever make contradictory statements? Does the writer's voice differ from essay to essay, story to essay? What might be some of the reasons for the differences? Do you respond to one voice the writer uses more than another? Is your perspective on writing different from the writer you selected? Can you articulate that difference in the essay you write?

2. After you've completed the essay, write a second one on the sense of authority you felt as you wrote this essay, what sort of power, if any, that you possessed. Did you feel confident as you wrote, or at a loss? Did you feel you had enough information? What was the difference between the authority you had when writing this essay and the authority you had when writing essays on personal experience? Can you account for the differences?

V

CULTURE IN EXPERIENCE

Linda Mizejewski

The Erotic Stripped Bare[1]

*L*ATE one night, as I danced with a handsome young Romanian, he stopped and kissed me. We were standing on the balcony of an apartment in Iasi, a city twelve miles from the Soviet border. The blacked-out streetlights of the city below suggested something other than wartime desolation only because of the candlelight inside, the several glasses of wine we had drunk, and the Willie Nelson cassette playing softly in the background. Everyone else at the party had wandered away. Both of our cultures had taught us that this is the scenario for romance, the moment to stop during a slow dance for a soft kiss that might get deeper and deeper. But when it happened, I was as shocked as if he had suddenly picked my pocket. Then, beyond shock, pleasure. And then, beyond pleasure, I peeled away the wrappings of romance and thought: No, this is Romania, this man a Romanian, this moment imaginary.

The eight months I had spent in Romania had conditioned me to think of romance as a Western luxury, as unofficially disapproved as punk rock or Levi's. Sexuality is officially invisible in Romania, much as it was in the early years of American television on programs like *The Donna Reed Show*. Indeed, if there is an approved image of the individual on black and white Romanian television and in the black and white photographs in Romanian magazines, it is this chaste, happily married icon, dressed modestly and "becomingly," if I may use a word from my parochial school days. The lovely women who sing folk

---

[1] Copyright © 1987 by *Harper's Magazine*. All rights reserved. Reprinted from the March issue by special permission.

songs on Sunday afternoon television in Romania are straight out of Lawrence Welk. Their hairstyles, gestures, and costumes suggest nothing so much as the virtuousness of young motherhood. These are serious madonnas in a country where madonnahood is a state obligation. Childless couples are punished with extra taxes. Birth control devices are banned; abortion is illegal except when the life of the mother is endangered. Even then, there must be a Communist Party official present during the procedure.

The birth control ban was imposed in the late 1960s in an effort to increase the rate of population growth. But living conditions in Romania are wretched and austere enough to discourage family expansion. In cities throughout the country, most families live in two-bedroom flats like the one assigned to me and my husband in Iasi. Ours was in a dirty concrete building where rats, dogs, children, and Gypsies played and grazed around the huge, open garbage pit near the entrance; where the state-controlled thermostat kept our living room temperature at a crisp fifty degrees during the coldest winter since World War II; and where the electricity and the plumbing were equally unreliable.

Feeding even a small family is time-consuming and frustrating, what with long lines for milk and butter that start to form at dawn, winter markets virtually without fresh vegetables or fruit, and ration tickets that will usually buy only the fattiest cuts of pork. And the mother of the "ideal," state-sanctioned, four-child Romanian family unit has likely risked her life four times in hospitals where there is no guarantee that sheets will be changed, and where doctors and nurses often set priorities for care on the basis of bribes: a dressing changed, for instance, in return for an unopened pack of Kents, an underground currency unique to Romania.

There were many questions we were unable to ask even those Romanians we trusted. Where is the microphone in our apartment? Are our desks "checked" occasionally? Is mail sent to us through the university "safe"? The matter of birth control was another such question. All our friends had only one or two children. These couples were roughly our age, in their thirties or early forties. Were they able to obtain black-market devices, perhaps from Greek or Arabic students? Had they had abortions? (The state spot-checks working women for pregnancy in order to prevent them from having abortions.) Or did they simply resort to long stretches of celibacy? My friends told me that the rhythm method was widely known, but they didn't want to talk about what happens when it fails. In crossing the border into Romania, my husband and I also passed beyond a series of spiritual borders: borders of secrecy and distrust. And if a young Romanian's kissing me on a balcony seemed to open a gap in one of those borders, then it closed again as soon as we opened our eyes and remembered where we were.

I went to Romania in 1984 as a Fulbright lecturer in American literature. It was a problematic position, for while university people in Romania are eager to have American faculty, the government is not particularly happy to harbor Westerners, with their nylon parkas, rock music, magazines, and strong opinions. Since I was there with my husband, I was protected from one all too common version of Romanian sexual politics: constant courtship by men eager to marry a passport out of the country. Occasionally such marriages do take place, and the American Embassy tends to be cynical about them, often with good cause. And single men who go to Romania to teach are warned by the embassy that the birth control ban makes them potential victims of seduction and politically sensitive paternity claims.

All relationships between Romanians and *strainii*, the lovely word for foreigners, take place in the nervous ambiguity of an unsettling, badly remembered dream. My husband and I walked on thick pilings of hidden agendas. When we were there, Romanians were required by law to report any conversations they had with *strainii* to the secret police—Securitate—within twenty-four hours. (A more recent decree prohibits all conversations with foreigners without prior permission from the state.) Citizens score valuable points for reporting the unreported conversations of other citizens. A tip about a foreigner might result in opportunities for travel out of the country or access to scarce goods. There are officially trusted university people who are permitted to befriend visiting lecturers, but there were others who took by no means negligible risks to keep company with us, and they asked that in our apartment we never mention their names.

While the birth control *diktat* implicitly puts Securitate in every Romanian bedroom, an American diplomat warned us that they might be more literally present in ours. It seemed to us that any country that can't get its plumbing to work couldn't possibly have a sophisticated surveillance system. Still, there were times when sex itself seemed as covert to my husband and me as our secret friendships, and we gradually came to see this as fundamental to any system that aims to generate such a permeating distrust—a distrust that would certainly prevent conspiracy, a distrust that begins with the senses, with the body, with intimacy. According to the embassy, one of every three Romanians is involved in Securitate, and though we doubted that this was true, we understood that it didn't need to be true. The rumor itself is powerful and valuable, certainly as powerful as our suspicion that we were constantly being overheard.

We will never know if there was in fact a microphone in our apartment. Some of our Romanian friends led us to believe that we were always being monitored, while others seemed certain that the only bug was in the phone. Still, I would go to sleep each night wondering if the words we'd spoken that day had been swept up and saved. Were they now being transcribed, made solid, black and white? Were they being translated into a history of which we could have no interpretation? We'll never know, just as we'll never know how carefully planned and contrived our lives were that year. Once, bending far out over our balcony, where, presumably, the microphone would not pick up our voices, a Romanian friend whispered, "You Americans don't know half of what's happening around you. And it's better you don't know."

Because we knew so little of what was "really" happening around us, because we lived with the possibility that even our bedroom had invisible listeners, our sensibilities became tuned to a coarse materiality, an obsession with details of the physical world. We found this particularly strange, since so little of the urban physical world in Romania is pleasing. I remember my first impressions of Bucharest: the sour smell of market apples left too long in the sun; the grainy imitation coffee in smoky hotels. And then the drive to Iasi: entire villages the color of mud, cities the color of concrete. And then nights without streetlights, without shop lights, with only an occasional lit window.

What I am describing was not poverty. It was not bucolic, other-century quaintness, or Amish simplicity. It was a stripping down, an unnatural diminishment. We inevitably responded most strongly to what we perceived through our senses, and in so doing were plunged into an odd, deprived, deliberately starved material world. Eventually we realized the insidious nature of the oddness: this was a world constructed to be asexual, carefully designed to extinguish any hint of the human capacity for eroticism.

In the West, city scenes keep us in a state of sensory arousal that is implicitly sexual. The emphasis is on contrast, curiosity, surprise; the appeal is to the physical. The new supermarket in my Pittsburgh neighborhood has soft neon signs you would expect to find in a cozy bar. Pasta displays erupt in Rubenesque sumptuousness. The young women behind the deli counters resemble the doll-faced saleswomen posed behind cosmetic counters in department stores. There is a conspiracy to avoid the impression that one goes there to buy bread and milk. One goes, rather, to indulge, perhaps even to sin.

While this sexual appeal to buy groceries is obviously absurd, equally absurd is a world which deliberately suggests that we have no sexuality or sensuality at all. In Romania, the lack of attention to color, texture, and light is only part of a larger pattern of repressed sensuality, a conviction that the senses don't matter, that nothing needs to be beautiful, nothing needs to charm. And while charm and sensuality are often yoked unhealthily to consumerism in the West, their absence creates a great emptiness at the heart of things. At the heart? I am being euphemistic. The emptiness fosters an absence of sexual energy, an absence that was apparent in the pale, passive faces, as well as the florid alcoholic ones, I saw every day on the overcrowded trams.

Today, when I leaf through magazines at the supermarket checkout counter, I find an obsession with fitness and health that almost parodies itself: quizzes to determine if your workout is really working; elaborate charts mapping out the fiber, fat, and carbohydrate content of foods found at the dinner table; ads showing how we should look in aerobics class; interviews with famous fit people. It would seem that our souls and psyches do indeed have a shape: our physical shape. Imagine, then, an anti-world to this, a place where most families feel lucky to have a dinner of fatty sausage and potatoes; where a jogger would surely be mistaken for someone running from the secret police; where one hesitates to work up an aerobic sweat because there is rarely any hot water for a shower afterward. When I realized I no longer cared that I wasn't exercising or eating well, I began to understand the dull indifference to the body that thrives in an environment where little is physically pleasing. I had for so long resisted the Western lie that *only* the physical matters that I was unprepared for the dismantling of that lie and the substitution of another one.

Romanian authorities accuse the West of a decadent material "sexiness," a consumer product they don't want to import. But there is a deliberate misreading here, a confusion between Western definitions of "sexiness" and the energies of human sexuality. And in attempting to control or at least quiet the latter, the most heavy-handed kind of materialism is brought to bear. The Marxist truth was cruelly borne out to us that winter: the roots of the spiritual are to be found in the material. Because we were able to get some canned goods through the embassy, we spent less time in food lines than our friends. But we were constantly preoccupied with planning baths and meals, rationing precious onions, getting chores done before the power and water went off, keeping an eye out for lines that might mean eggs or potatoes. And after spending all day in a classroom where it was too cold for students to take off their gloves, in a building where there was no clean public toilet, let alone one with a toilet seat and toilet paper; after the smelly crowd of the tram, or, on days when the tram had broken down, a forty-five-minute walk home in snow and ice through unshoveled streets—on those days I wanted nothing except to go to bed with a glass of wine and a not very taxing book.

And so, I was dancing on that balcony in Iasi after having lived through such a winter. It was spring, and there were lilacs, yet my husband and I were most excited to have hot water for a few hours every day. Little wonder, then, that the moment with my friend astonished me—and admonished me, reminding me that under the muddy concrete and smoky gray, there was still human desire.

What happens to one's sensibilities in a world where there is a concerted effort to erase all hints of passion, sensuality, sexuality? The word "obsenity" spins out of control when the absence of pornography is part of a wholesale censorship of individualism, eroticism, dissonance. My husband and I were occasionally given American magazines by embassy families, and we came to realize that in Romania, *Mademoiselle* and *Seventeen* could be seen as girlie magazines, what with underwear ads designed for an audience not desperate for a glimpse of such things. The absence of pornography there is no feminist victory. It is a sign of control, not respect. The same is true of prostitution, which exists solely in the hotels designated for foreigners. These services are part of the government's scheme to bring in Western currency, much like the German beers also available in the major Bucharest hotels for dollars only. Though officially illegal, prostitution is overlooked as long as it eases the troublesome national debt. Indeed, it might be a patriotic obligation, like motherhood.

We could only guess what goes on in the luxurious mountain villas built for members of the upper political echelons. Since everything from beef to color television is mysteriously available to a select few, it seemed likely to us that erotic materials might be available as well. But this is only speculation. The upper echelons are invisible in Romania. Only if you drive past those hidden Carpathian resorts (something most Romanians cannot do, since few have cars and gas is rationed) can you glimpse a hint that another kind of life is possible for some, a life that affords more exotic pleasures than scotch and Kents.

And what of the sexual attitudes of the visible majority? We witnessed a telling incident one evening in a movie theater in Iasi. Very few American films are permitted into Romania, although videotapes of some films do manage to enter the country from Greece. These, usually mindless adventure films, are shown at "videoteques," auditoriums where one or two VCRs and monitors have been set up and a Romanian translation is boomed over the sound track. As the name suggests, videoteques are frequented mostly by young people. They are, in fact, among the few places young people can frequent, since there are no discos, no other forms of "night life"—a term that does ironic somersaults in a country where most streetlights are never turned on.

One week a theater in downtown Iasi showed the Christopher Reeve film *Somewhere in Time,* doubtless permitted because it portrays so little of contemporary American life. Toward the end of the film there is a brief bedroom scene of the tactful PG variety. I was surprised that even so modest a scene had gotten past the censors. But the real surprise was the audience's response: an eruption of snickers, hoots, giggles, and catcalls, the likes of which I don't think I've heard since kiddy matinees when the cowboy kissed the girl instead of the horse.

To be fair, such a reaction might not have occurred with a more sophisticated audience in Bucharest. The Romanian friends who accompanied us were plainly embarrassed by it. Yet the outburst still suggests that when the entire spectrum of sexuality is hushed, hidden, and denied, sexuality itself becomes fetishistic, its definition narrowed to things and acts. Thus the Romanian fixation on American film stars and other symbols of sexuality on the other side of the border: sports cars, certain brands of scotch and cigarettes, dyed blond hair. The government's attempt to make sexuality unimaginable has popularized the most reductive, superficial sexual models of the West. It is a collision of the worst of both worlds.

One day our neighborhood Securitate contact, a young man with very uncertain English, appeared at our door to prove his good will by solemnly reciting everything he knew about the United States: Farrah Fawcett, Victoria Principal, Michael Jackson, *Dallas,* Ford Mustang, Ronald Reagan. Reagan's popularity in Romania is enormous, and our friends were always puzzled by our coolness toward the present administration. I realize now that Reagan's appeal arises not only from his stands against their great, feared neighbor to the north but also from his standing in the tinselly pantheon described by our visitor. If the West is sexuality, how fitting that the American president be a ruggedly handsome movie star often photographed in boots and cowboy hat.

Few foreigners in Romania live outside of Bucharest, although in university towns such as Iasi there are a number of students from Greece, Africa, and the Middle East willing to pay hard currency for a degree in engineering or medicine. Most of them are men, and their Mediterranean macho and easy access to birth control combine to violently disrupt the tense and narrow lives of Romanian women, who are suddenly confronted with sexual temptation—and a possible ticket out of the country.

At Romanian universities, men are usually tracked into the physical sciences. The women I taught, the English majors, were generally very bright, very serious, slightly older than most American undergraduates, and eager for English conversation and clues about American life. So eventually I befriended some of them in somewhat safer, outside-the-classroom settings. Their stories were uniformly depressing. The pressure to marry during their university years is great. Unmarried, they would likely be assigned to teach in remote villages; only the top student or two would get an assignment in Iasi. "Shepherds and pig farmers will be my prospective husbands," one told me. As for the married students, their sex lives are acted out on the other side of a thin wall from one set of parents or the other, since young couples generally do not get their own apartments for years.

Once, during class, the word "menopause" came up in a story, and I stopped to make certain it was familiar. Oh, yes, my students said proudly, they knew all about menopause and andropause. Andropause? Yes—when a man "can't do it anymore." I tried to explain that this was not as inevitable as menopause, but they were quick to provide me with a biology lesson: it happens at sixty-five, or at least a man can last that long if he "does it" twice a week. They were too polite to contradict my arguments, but they stared at me with alarm, no doubt imagining that in my ignorance I might be driving my husband to an early andropause. This, too, shows the Romanian attitude toward sexuality, that it is not really a part of us, but something that can be used up and worn out.

The Romanian student-dating scene is limited to videoteques, parties, long walks in the park, and (if dorm roommates are cooperative) the odd hour or so of privacy. Since the double standard still thrives in Romania, the birth control *diktat* makes relations between men and women all the more strained. My women students, terrified of pregnancy, talked about dating as a grim process of fending off advances. These same women told me breathlessly that when foreign students were first admitted a few years ago there was an "explosion" of sexuality. It wasn't hard for me to imagine the effect on my students of these sleek young men from the south, who congregated in the university halls, jeweled hands on hips, insolently smoking their Kents. They brought to Romania their good cigarettes, Western music, and decent cassette decks. They also brought powerful symbols of privacy: cars. In their imported Mercedes-Benzes, they would speed past the dumpy, four-cylinder Romanian Dacias, terrifying pedestrians and reinforcing the general feeling that masculinity—*real* masculinity—is big horsepower, reckless acceleration, fast wheels. No ordinary Romanian student can dream of owning a car, or of doing this kind of dating.

At the senior class graduation party, several Romanian women showed up with Middle Eastern boyfriends, and these couples socialized as a group, never mingling with the Romanian couples. Across the room, the latter talked about their Kent-smoking colleagues with a mixture of envy and contempt. It was suddenly junior high school in the sixties: the world was divided into Good Girls and Bad Girls, who glared at each other across the dance floor with equal pangs of resentment and loss.

As I watched this scene, I understood how sexual stereotyping meshes with the politics of oppression. In order to keep the oppressive machinery working and maintain an environment in which one student is willing to report on another student's comments in class, in which a neighbor is willing to report on a neighbor, a colleague on a colleague, the prevailing mentality must be one of alienation. And the most powerful way to foster this alienation is by subverting sexuality.

Securitate's regulations have the effect of alienating all foreigners from all Romanians, a situation that was exaggerated by our exotic status as Americans. When my husband and I strapped on our backpacks and went out in warm, quilted parkas to wait for a tram, we were a dangerous, fascinating, alien species, scrutinized by the locals like Technicolor inhabitants of Oz mistakenly landed back in Kansas. Whenever we went to the gas station, bypassing the miles-long line of Dacias to go to the single pump designated for *strainii,* our modest Renault would quickly be surrounded by young boys and grown men who stared at the dashboard, the tires, the side-view mirror.

As aliens contained within a special orbit, we literally had our own spaces: the hotels, restaurants, and shops that are for foreigners only. Romanians are forbidden entrance to Dollar shops, those tiny meccas where one can get scotch, cosmetics, cassette players, car accessories, and other select Western goods for convertible currency. Romanians would gather sometimes at the shop windows to stare at the forbidden names: RCA, Marlboro, Revlon.

I remember the patriotic chatter at the embassy about being proud to be an American, proud to be free. But most Romanians perceived our freedom in very particular ways. We were free to enter the sacred rooms containing Gilbey's gin and Shell motor oil; we were free to walk into the Intercontinental, the only hotel in Bucharest that could guarantee a heated room in January 1985, and pay a dollar for a German beer; we were free to order (and actually be served) a green salad in the hotel restaurant.

My husband and I had previously traveled to underdeveloped countries, had felt other lustful eyes on our backpacks and boots. What we had never before encountered was a scarcity and a backwardness that were manipulated, artificial, ideological. No one starves in Romania; no American charity teaches us how to feel about people who want not milk and grain, but an orange in winter, real coffee, real chocolate. Nor do we learn how to understand a cultural, historical tradition that has never resisted, never revolted. We were not prepared for the silent shrug, the lack of anger, the hopeless shaking of the head in the face of each absurd new shortage.

During the winter fuel emergency, when we had little heat and no hot water for months, an ordinance was issued prohibiting the use of kitchen ovens for heating. Our first impulse was to laugh; we imagined the Oven Police checking up on us to see if we were baking a cake or committing a crime. But the resignation of our Romanian friends turned our laughter into anger. Why such passivity? Why weren't they irate? Of course these are simplistic questions; any enlightened person knows that. And months later, privileged with historical and intellectual distance in a heated room of our own, we knew it too. But sitting in our kitchen with the door closed and the oven illegally blazing, we were not in a historical, theoretical mood. Cold and uncomfortable and without a bath or a shower, we were learning contempt.

One January day, on a trip to Bucharest, we sat at a window table at the restaurant in the Intercontinental enjoying a lunch of forbidden foods: roast beef sandwiches, fresh fruit, a green salad. We could see outside, just a few feet away, Romanians shuffling by in their bulky, mud-colored coats, carrying their plastic bags of dirty turnips and potatoes. We were separated by the sheet of glass, by the accident of birth, and, worse, by our impatience, our growing irritation. How can they take it, how can they put up with it? we were thinking. They know this hotel has beef, fresh vegetables, heat; they know certain people get meat and butter; they know their best products are exported. Damn it, what's the matter with them?

In his novel *This Way for the Gas, Ladies and Gentlemen*, Tadeusz Borowski describes the life of a prisoner-overseer at Auschwitz, the life of a privileged prisoner who begins to hate the less fortunate ones. Sitting at the window eating oranges and lettuce, I remembered Borowski's narrator sitting with his looted sausage and cheese as other prisoners are marched past. And then I remembered what was most striking in Borowski's book: the strange, distorted sexuality. Without flinching, the guards would lead a lovely young woman to the gas chamber or flaming pit, and their reward for good behavior might be a visit to the camp brothel for an hour with a woman who might resemble her. At last the marching prisoners, like the Romanians walking by the Intercontinental in their thin boots and tight head scarfs, seemed incapable of intimacy, incapable of any relationship that could link them to the oppressor. In fact, they seemed to have only themselves to blame.

Horrified at the comparison, I quickly thought of our Romanian friends, people I loved. Some of them are my best friends, I thought, there are exceptions, there are exceptional people, they're not all alike—and realized I was using the language of bigotry. *But some of them are my best friends. Just another Romanian.*

The Romanian authorities would be happy to keep visiting foreigners forever behind the windows of the Intercontinental, making friendships with Romanians, thoughtful relationships, impossible. My husband and I were dangerous because we did not stay behind those windows and barriers, but neither did we pretend they were not there.

We returned to the United States the following summer, to Dr. Ruth, aerobics classes, and a restless sense of exile. Our Romanian friends are lost to us; there are only cautious letters in the language one uses when there are invisible listeners. I am still trying to name what authentic sexuality might be, and remain troubled by what I saw on the far side of the border—and by what I could not see, because of the authority of the secret police and the authority of the Western vision that I brought with me to Romania. There is no center to a world so estranged, and the kiss I imagine at its center is as imaginary as it became a moment after it happened. I have not lost my sense of being a privileged prisoner, very fortunate and still enchained.

Sources of "The Erotic Stripped Bare"

*T*ODAY in some office in Bucharest, in a file with my name on it, there is a letter I wrote while living in Romania. It was confiscated at the international airport in the last days of 1984, as my husband and I tried to leave for a holiday in Vienna. The letter was neither political nor inflammatory. A chatty Christmas greeting to American friends, it bordered on travelogue cheerfulness, deliberately underplaying the shortages and hardships that had been the gridwork of our lives there the previous four months. But the heavily armed customs guards had no sense of humor, only orders. The confiscation was meant to silence me, I suppose, to frighten me about turning my experience there into prose, no matter how understated, no matter who the audience.

It did frighten me. Never before had my writing been taken from me. On the other hand, never before had my writing been taken so seriously. One consequence of the act that should have been silencing was a much more public text, an essay about oppression in Romania that I wrote for *Harper's* two years later. Certainly a copy of this, too, has been included in my Securitate file. The secret police must believe I'm a slow learner. But the opposite is true. They were effective teachers.

The power and riskiness of writing in a totalitarian state is almost a cliche in the West, commonly understood as *their* problem, unimaginable in our own media-glutted culture. Now, though, safely across the ocean, I find another map superimposed on where I am, and where writing no longer seems luxurious and safe. My most pragmatic concern, as I write this, is literally what borders this text can cross in some mail pouch or suitcase. My concern is what could happen to real people once this is published and read. Yet the issues here—the intersections of writing, responsibility, and risk—are not contained within specific political borders, even though Romania poses unique problems for any writer.

In an effort toward a comprehensive policing of words, Romanian law requires that all typewriters in the country be state-registered, the print checked and re-licensed every year. Words are likewise dangerous baggage at border crossings; certain book titles, the Bible, pornography, and letters are searched for along with weapons and drugs. Smuggled letters are particularly hot items because any visitor is a potential messenger on behalf of defected, blacklisted, or Westward-looking relatives hoping to evade the censored mail system.

I had naively thought my own letter was innocuous, and so was stunned when it was held up, translated, and read aloud by three frowning military customs officers, their fingers poking at my phrases—"What's *this*? . . . And this?"—just as their fingers had poked through the opened suitcases with the sinister assertion that nothing is wholly private.

My husband and I had already learned to live with that assertion; we had learned that our lightest chatter in our Romanian apartment had to be calculated in the assumption that someone might be listening and gauging our comments for seriousness. When the words were too risky, we wrote them down and flushed them away the next time the water in the building came on.

Yet we were not the ones at risk. When my letter was confiscated, I was furious that Securitate now owned a personal document; but more than that, I was alarmed because I had casually mentioned in it Romanian friends, people who could not leave the country as I could, and who now had extra material in the police files under their own names. The politics of turning people and experience into prose are not very obvious in this country, where our cult of True Confession thrives—the biography business, the personality industry, the personal detail as headline. But they stand out in sharp relief once we imagine a different map, with real boundaries and border guards.

In the states a year later, when I was too angry about what I had seen in Romania to keep my anger private, a powerful, invisible checkpoint arose each time I considered public prose. Looking over my heaps of notes, journals, and letters from that year, I shut them quickly away into my desk, where they beat like the tell-tale, guilty heart. The guilt was crossed with conflicting obligations and loyalties. I imagined those border policemen in their offices scowling at my published sentences, shaking their heads at my Romanian friends who sit across the desk and cannot afford the irreverent shrug. What's *this*? And this? And did you know she was writing *this*?

They didn't. They are guilty only of being my friends. Or rather, I am guilty of being theirs, and a writer.

For the ten years before I went to Romania, I had been a teacher of that odd university subgenre which is the easiest and safest writing of all, what we call Composition, the frozen-entree form of the personal essay: Definition, Comparison–Contrast, and so on, served in distinguishable parts (thesis, body, conclusion) as if on a divided, heatproof tray. Composition does not exist in Romania. Like psychology and sociology, it is a non-subject in the universities, and my students' writing problems there made me curious about this connection.

My Romanian college students were rather good, but as writers of reports and exams rather poor, because they had never been encouraged to practice. Looking for some exercises for them one day, I came across a textbook I'd brought from home called *From Experience to Expression*. And it occurred to me what a radical text that would be in the hands of these students, young people whose experience was the extinction of expression.

I knew that in my classrooms, one student was assigned to report to the authorities what I and other students said; that students' non-classroom conversations with me were supposed to be reported to the police. On my part, one of the worst things I could do—from the official Romanian viewpoint—was to share with students my copies of *Time* and *Newsweek*. In this milieu, even the title of that text, a cause-and-effect linking of personal perception and public expression, suggested dangerous and heady possibilities.

Meanwhile, trying to convert my own Romanian experience into writing, I realized that for ten years I had taught a genre I myself had never written. Every night I sat at one of the country's few unregistered typewriters—my luxury as a visiting lecturer—and tried to compose, make sense of where I was. I wanted the experience there to "mean" something, but all the convenient and conventional meanings and explanations—in fact, the structures that make bad student Compositions bad—had been stripped away.

I was in a byzantine culture dense with its own elusive fictions, and complicated by levels of political fictions ranging in impact from the ironic to the horrifying. Often, what I was seeing—for example, a market display of unusually healthy-looking vegetables—was not what I was really seeing. Or the subject of conversation—about what I was teaching or reading—might not be the real subject of conversation. Like the bewildered Sebastian of *Twelfth Night*, I found myself in a place where "nothing that is so is so."

Writing was not easy, and it certainly was not safe. After the airport incident, my husband and I never left our letters and journals in the apartment unattended. Traveling through the country, we preferred trains to planes because it reduced the risk of our backpacks being searched, although any search without cause was possible by any streetcorner militia, those omnipresent soldier-policemen. At times, carrying explicit journal entries in my pack, I worried that the face I composed on the street was not indifferent or casual enough.

Our writings—the papers themselves, their safety—took on profound physical substantiality. Their location in our apartment, in our backpacks, or later en route to the American embassy mailroom, became one level of preoccupation for us, as constant as listening for the water to come on in the apartment building, or watching for the beginnings of street queues that might mean scarce onions or eggs. Every month or so, we made the journey to Bucharest, and finally arrived at the embassy post room where our writings were deposited into safe Western mail. A hundred yards beyond that room, outside the gates, any militia could have opened my bag, confiscated every letter. Here, inside the embassy, in envelopes with American postage on them, they magically became private property. And we could go back to the street not entirely free, but free of the evidence, technically innocent.

However, no one in Romania with an unregistered typewriter is innocent. At the Fulbright midterm conference in Bucharest that year, the American ambassador addressed the grantees and charged all of us with responsibility far beyond being the good cultural liaisons. We had the right—indeed, he said, the obligation—to return to the States and tell "the truth" about our months in Romania, the obligation to counterbalance the Romanian propaganda image of the free-thinking East Bloc "maverick." Just six months before, we had heard the world cheer as Romanian athletes entered the Los Angeles Coliseum for the Olympics parade, surely a bold flouting of Soviet influence. We were no longer as naive about that kind of gesture and what it masks.

All of us gathered to hear this speech were wearing several layers of clothing because the heat in the embassy buildings had been cut in the nationwide power cuts that January. It was the most severe Romanian winter since World War II. To keep the state factories operating, all non-industrial sectors had their already-rationed power and fuel reduced by fifty percent. This included hospitals, and the embassy had received reports of incubators being shut off, patients assigned two and three to a bed for warmth, hospital deaths tripling. Most of us had been without hot water for weeks, wore gloves in our apartments where the radiators were barely tepid, and were accustomed to daily power outages. Clerks in stores and waitresses in restaurants wore hats and coats. At one Bucharest hotel, foreigners paying Western cash could get a semi-heated room for $90 a night. But for most Romanians, there was literally nowhere to go in the country to get warm.

Listening to the ambassador, I thought how a published exposé of "the truth" would quickly be picked up by right-wing causes at home, gleeful to hear yet another liberal disillusioned by what she saw on the other side. But I was also shivering and becoming more fondly inclined toward the memory of private property—a thermostat, for instance, turned up by a friendly human hand.

American diplomats, frustrated with the slowness of progress against Romania's wretched human rights record and witnessing yearly deterioration of living conditions, had good reason to hope some of "us" would go home and publicize what we'd seen. Yet thinking of my accumulated journal notes and attempts to write about my experience there, I realized I had neither an exposé nor "the truth." For those of us living among Romanians in cities far from the embassy, the definitions and distinctions quickly broke down: private and public, us and them.

In the most official and public relationships, people representing "them" — government institutions and agencies — invariably were vulnerable individuals who had a lot to lose, and who hoped the visiting Americans would simply cooperate and make their own lives a little less tense.

Often, there hovered about them a quaint, old-European sense of etiquette: as the proper hosts, they would pretend insofar as possible that the daily facts of my life there were not outrageous. In turn, as the polite guest, surely I would not be so rude as to point to the unmentionables: censorship, confiscation, shortages, rations, the secret police, the hidden microphones in the apartment, the tapped phone — and certainly such matters would not be discussed in a public way when I returned home. When I did refer to an unmentionable subject, I met embarrassment but also fear. Behind every ideological officiousness lurked a note of anxiety if you listened carefully enough: "Please, don't do this, I have family . . . "

Private relationships were even more entangled. Wary of the dangers of Westernization, Romanian law required that citizens report all their conversations with foreigners to the police within 24 hours. Understandably, our friends sought to avoid this, so the very fact of friendship or contact often involved bizarre aspects of illegality. Our friends conspired to help us survive, guiding us through the labyrinthian technicalities and impossibilities that structure everyday life there. In turn, skirting strange Romanian laws, we tried to help them with access to scarce Western goods, but also, with access to Western books, magazines, ideas. Officially, the latter was the reason I was there at all, as a resource for American culture. But in other equally official ways, this access was the reason most Romanians had to be protected from me: the American with her risky books and opinions.

Our families in the States worried about us while we were in Romania, and it was difficult to convince them we were not the ones in danger. We *were* the danger. We were blatant, walking representatives of dangerous concepts: *Time* and *Newsweek*, the embassy route to uncensored mail, texts like *Experience to Expression*. In retrospect, I think some Romanians risked friendship with us because we were more symbols than individuals. No matter how much we told them about American social problems — racism, poverty, corporate tyrannies — it was all undercut by the fact of our magic blue passports. We could leave. They could not. And here was another danger: I could depart with my unregistered typewriter and access to a free press, while my subject matter remained hostage.

Visiting foreigners are menacing witnesses in Romania, the more so if they are drawn into people's lives and observe the machineries of oppression first-hand. But the hostage effect is powerful. What the ambassador was asking that day was not much different from what many of us heard from Romanians themselves—not from our friends, not from officially-approved connections, but from the connections made more fleetingly and safely on train rides or in the markets—ah, you are from the West, you can go back and tell about all this. Generally, Romanians were aware of and bitter about their misrepresentation to the Western press. But "all this"—the generally miserable, real situation—was tied specifically, for us, to individual stories and lives.

The catch is that with police surveillance so comprehensive, it would be easy to track down those stories and lives. Pseudonyms and composite characters would not help much, since the number of Americans living in the provinces is so few, and the police files so extensive. The syllogism of constraint was simple: the stronger our ties to individual Romanians, the deeper our anger and concern about them, and—the brilliant last term—the more reason we had to go back to the States and remain absolutely silent about what they suffered.

"But look," an American writer friend told me a year later, "if you don't write about it, then their censorship really works, all the way across the ocean." Of course it works. "I wouldn't publish so much as a letter to the editor," one returning lecturer said. This is not senseless paranoia. Anxious to keep its favored-trade status with the United States—which in fact was renewed in the summer of 1987— Romania is obsessed with its image in the West. It employs a finely-tuned scanning service for all Western media. A few years ago, a Fulbright lecturer published an article about Romania in what he thought was a safe, regional magazine in Tennessee. It was quickly reported, and he was accused by Romanian officials of being a secret, illegal journalist. Another colleague of mine was stopped and warned explicitly at the border: "Do not write ill of us if you ever want to come back." Few of us want to go back. That would be a simpler problem.

Long after we left Romania for the last time, my husband and I remained wary about putting things into words if it concerned that country. All over Western Europe, we interrupted our conversations to look over our shoulders in the cafe, glance up at the light fixture in the hotel room. At the least-threatening customs gate, I felt nervously implicated when asked what I had to declare, as if anyone in any uniform could guess I'd memorized and carried our stories.

It was dizzying, then, to return to the States and walk through air pulsing with radio and television waves full of opinion, protest, criticism, gossip. It was dizzying to know I could carry my suitcase full of papers and not be questioned about them at airports and highway police stations. I can even wear messages across my chest, anything from the political to the suggestive. So much is published that most of it seems to dissolve into thin air, or generate not much more than editorial debate, more paper and ink. It should have been easy to write about Romania from here.

Instead, each time I sat at the typewriter, the guard was there, the uniform and M-16. Looking at poetry and literary criticism I'd published before my Romanian year, I thought at first that those genres are safer, the boundaries between experience and interpretation, writer and subject, more stable and reassuring. But that is not true of the best poetry, I realized, or the most powerful scholarship. Writing is innately risky, if it's worth doing at all. It creates a way of seeing, an activity not easily divisible into the private and the public, or traceable to final consequences. It takes on the eyes of Sebastian, the warning that nothing that is so is so.

My Romanian friends understood this in a passionate way. They were also experts about the other end of the spectrum: silence, which is also safety, which is also tyranny. Silence implicates no one at all.

Romanian censorship works because it depends on paranoia and compassion of would-be writers. It also depends on a reliable way of making judgements: as Definition, as Comparison–Contrast. I remembered the way I used to teach Composition, the facts lined up in two rows on opposite sides of the page. In the concluding paragraphs, students argued for the most reasonably superior army of facts. Dividing up American sympathy or interest, for example, it would be difficult to find much left over for Romania. When I returned to the States, almost everything conspired to make me forget it, or write it off as one odd year, connected to nothing else. The politics of Comparison–Contrast tucks experience into discernible blocs of its own.

I started to write. I pressed details to their leanest, to make individual people invisible. I let phrases soften to blur the faces and come down hard on the ordinary, horrifying fact. Still, I was at the checkpoint each time I sat at the typewriter—tense, slightly nauseated—as I am now, wondering if I want to make this crossing after all.

I learned later that as soon as the essay was published, each of my Romanian friends was brought in for interrogation by the secret police. There was official anger and denouncement, private astonishment and fear. Police surveillance of my Fulbright successor increased. The text of the essay itself became a hot underground item. But because few copies are available anywhere in the country, rumors proliferated about its contents. This enabled Securitate to make especially effective interrogations: aha, you tell *us* what she would write about.

Eventually a copy got through to the people I knew there. They can no longer write to me at all, but some careful responses have trickled back in roundabout ways. As I suspected and risked, they are not sorry. However, there are silences, too, which I try to read like the cautious archeologist, handling the delicate past and guessing at pressures.

I would not want to return to the innocence of never having lived in Romania, or never having written about it. Occasionally, I still teach writing, though I no longer have students organize the opposing armies for attack and blame. But it's difficult to make them imagine a border over which every word is important, and come to believe the border is the empty page.

❧ QUESTIONS ☙

Linda Mizejewski's essay, "The Erotic Stripped Bare," and its process essay, "The Sources of 'The Erotic Stripped Bare'"

1. In her essay, Mizejewski writes of her preoccupation with acquiring food, heat, water, and privacy, things that as an American visiting Romania she had greater access to than the Romanians. She writes, "The Marxist truth was cruelly borne out to us that winter: the roots of the spiritual are to be found in the material." In how many ways is this "truth" developed in the essay, especially in terms of sexuality? Does the "truth" seem applicable to your culture? If your material possessions were stripped away, what would you rely on for spirituality? Can you imagine how you would respond in a culture similar to the one Mizejewski describes?

2. Toward the end of her essay, Mizejewski is horrified to find herself feeling some contempt for the Romanians—their complacency, their inability to revolt, their incapacity for intimacy—and finds herself "using the language of bigotry." As you read through the essay, what has led her to these feelings? In your own experience, have you seen others express contempt for those less fortunate? What was the situation? Where does that contempt come from? Can we simply relegate it to "human nature"?

3. In her process essay, Mizejewski writes, "The power and riskiness of writing in a totalitarian state is almost a cliche in the West, commonly understood as *their* problem, unimaginable in our own media-glutted culture." Is Mizejewski's description of "the West" an accurate one? Recollect Daniel Lowe's essays on Elie Wiesel and the Holocaust. Is the reaction Mizejewski describes a fair one? Should we consider "their" problem "our" problem? Is this even possible for us, since most of us, unlike Mizejewski, have befriended no one who lives in a totalitarian state?

4. Mizejewski writes, "Writing is innately risky, if it's worth doing at all. It creates a way of seeing, an activity not easily divisible into the private and the public, or traceable to final consequences." Do you find writing "risky"? What makes it so, or perhaps more importantly, what sort of writing is risky, and what sort isn't? What does Mizejewski mean when she says writing "creates a way of seeing"? Who is doing the seeing? What allows for it? What about writing is private, what public?

❧ Possible Writing Topics ☙

1. Write an essay about one aspect of the culture you live in that you feel you can evaluate and criticize. Mizejewski says that in our culture, "city scenes

keep us in a state of sensory arousal that is implicitly sexual." She describes our culture as "media-glutted." These are aspects of our culture that you may want to pick up on, but your own experience of culture—not one handed to you by another writer or teacher—will probably be the most interesting for you to work with here. Remember, you're not taking on all of culture or society here. Mizejewski's essay is strong because its focus is sexuality. Find a similar focus for your own essay. What led you to this choice? What led to the conclusions you make in this essay? How did your perspective develop through time, and through what sort of experiences?

2. Mizejewski says writing "creates a way of seeing, an activity not easily divisible into the private and the public." After you've completed your first essay, write a second one where you address the subject of how writing your essay allowed you to see what you hadn't seen previously. Did your perspectives on the aspect of culture you selected change as you wrote? Were your opinions and arguments stronger or weaker after completing the writing? What, if anything, did you consider that you hadn't considered before? Are there aspects of the first essay that seem private rather than public? Of the things you considered in the essay, how many would you speak of to friends? in front of a group? When writing in a class such as this one, is writing for you a public or a private act?

Cynthia Kadohata

South Springs

My father's name was in the newspaper once. He and some of his friends had been part of what my mother called a gambling ring, though my father said the so-called gambling ring was really "just a few guys with a bookie." One day the police arrested the bookie and some of his clients, and the newspaper named my father as among those arrested. The police also arrested four of my father's closest friends: Max Kitano, Collie Morita, Nori Watanabe, and Hugh Tanaka. That happened not long after the war. I was too young to remember, but my mother once showed me the clipping. The story, only three paragraphs long, said that the bookie had been arrested every year for the past seven years. "It's sort of a tradition," said the chief of police. They arrested twelve people. The whole affair caused quite a stir among my father and his friends. They thought they would be run out of town. When I was older and listened to them discuss the arrests, I could still hear in their voices something of the distress they'd felt, and once in a while I felt it, too. I doubt, though, that anyone else besides us really cared or remembered.

There were only a few Japanese families in our town—South Springs, Arkansas—plus a handful of Japanese in each of the towns on either side of us. We were bound to them in the same way that my mother, father, three brothers, and I were bound to each other, and in the same way that our relatives in California saw us as bound to a small southern town, bound to something they saw as inescapable. When I left to go to college, it was my parents' friends that we invited to the going-away party. We had the party in August, the night before I left for school.

My parents and I waited outside for their friends. My father was small; my mother was tall. Hills in the distance blocked out the sky. They were pure black, the way the sun is pure light. To the side a restaurant sign rose off the highway. I could view the sign from my bedroom; sometimes it was the last thing I saw before I fell asleep. There were only two other houses on our stretch of road. One, across the street, was empty. Down the street lived the Stemmlers. They had no children, and I didn't know much about them, though on holidays they exchanged pastries with my family.

I always think of my going-away party not as the night before I left for school, but as the night my brother Ben disappeared, or at least as the night we thought he disappeared. I had three brothers: Ben, thirteen; Walker, twelve; and Peter, seven. Walker and Ben spent most of their time together. Ben was the leader. He was also the household terror and practical joker. Peter had always been my special charge. He'd helped me decorate the house with colored paper, and I helped him hang a ten-foot good-bye sign that he had made himself. We placed plates of fruit on all the tables. As we sliced the fruit, he looked up at me after each slice, to see whether he'd done it right. I kept nodding in approval and smiling. Sometimes my brothers seemed perfect to me.

Ben and Walker ran through the front yard.

"No one's coming," Ben yelled, to tease me.

"No one's coming," Walker yelled. He liked to copy what Ben said—he was a master at mimicking even the smallest gesture of each of us.

"Anyway," said my father, "read some good books for me. I never have time." He paused, and I could tell he was searching his mind. My parents were full of advice for me lately. "Read Charles Dickens," he finally added, triumphantly.

"Do you think?" said my mother. "If she reads too much she'll hurt her eyes and get headaches and ruin her good nature." She turned to me. "Just read what you have to."

"Stop copying me," said Ben.

"Stop copying me," said Walker.

"Ahhh, I can't stand this."

Ben tore off down the road. Walker chased him, shouting, "Ahhh, I can't stand this."

My dress rustled every time the wind blew. It was a sky blue cotton dress with an ivory lace collar and an ivory ribbon belt. It wasn't formal, though it was too nice for school or even for the sort of parties I had been invited to that year, and this was the first time I'd worn it, except in my room. It was the first dress I'd ever bought with my own money.

I had a secret boyfriend who was coming to the party. His name was David Takahashi, and he was a secret because he was twenty-nine. I had met him a year-and-a-half earlier at the only other party we'd ever had, for New Year's. We'd lined our windowsills with tangerines and pounded-rice cakes, the way my mother said her family had when she was little. So tangerines always reminded me of David.

Actually, I didn't talk much to him at the party. I felt shy with my parents around, and with a new dress on.

After a while Walker said that Ben had gone down to the vending machine at the gas station a mile away to get drinks, but he'd never returned. That, Walker said, had been more than an hour ago. Everybody searched all over and couldn't find Ben, and when my mother called the gas station, the attendant said he hadn't seen anyone.

Hugh Tanaka raised his beer bottle and stood up and said, "Charge! Let's go find him!"

"Honey," said his wife. "Calm down."

Peter had come into the living room and was listening intently, one ear inclined toward the conversation as if to help him hear better.

"I hope nobody did anything to him!" said Hugh.

I turned to my father. He had a cool, almost calculating look on his face.

I thought Ben was just playing, but we decided to go searching for him. I accompanied David, my father, and another man in one direction, and Hugh and a few people went the opposite way. Hugh, who'd had quite a bit to drink, was loudly giving orders. When I looked back, I saw that he and a couple of others had found large sticks somewhere. The Stemmlers' curtain moved. They must have been watching from inside their dark house. Perhaps they were scared. I felt a sudden fear that they would call the police, and my father would get arrested again. I reached out for him, but he was already way ahead.

We walked through a field. You could see the hills from where we walked. Two flashlights made splinters of light in the blackness. Far off, it was thundering, but it hadn't started to rain. The night seemed unusually quiet, as if all the crickets who made a racket most evenings had deserted South Springs. I started to think that Ben wouldn't have gone out right now, even for a joke. All my brothers could be reckless, but only during the day, and only with someone else to show off for. I picked up a rock. I noticed that my father had found a thick piece of wood somewhere. My father looked tiny against the fields stretched out around us. He and the other man walked ahead, with David and me following. It had started to rain, the drops like static over the fields. There was something strangely erotic in the fear in the air; it drew me to David. For a moment I rested my hand on his back, ostensibly to keep my balance. It was like when you put your hand to a window, and your hand can feel how it is on the other side, whether it's windy or still. I could feel inside of him: he felt something in the air, too. My father turned suddenly to wait. He hesitated, then said brusquely that we ought to hurry.

"This field goes on until the highway curves through it," I said.

"Do the boys ever come out this far?"

"I doubt Ben would come out here tonight. But if someone did something to him . . . " I started to cry. I hadn't even known that I wanted to cry.

We continued to the highway, stopping sometimes to look through bushes, and then we headed back to the house. Several women were huddled in the front yard under umbrellas. My father, the other man, and David left again immediately, and my mother and I went in.

Peter had fallen asleep in the living room. A baseball bat leaned against him as he slept—he'd been scared, too. I sat on the floor and laid my head on the couch. The rain fell in a sudden spurt on the front porch. I noticed I was still carrying a rock. I felt sleepy and alert at the same time.

The couch shook and I looked up and saw Walker smirking.

"What's with you?" I said.

"What's with *you*?" he answered, smirking again.

When the phone rang, he jumped up and laughed, and I knew the call would be about Ben. In a moment my mother was calling out, "He's with Bill and Susan. He's with Bill and Susan." Bill and Susan Tanizaki. I went into the kitchen. My mother said Ben had hidden in their car when they'd left, for a joke, and then he'd stayed awhile, because he thought that this would make the joke better.

Back in the living room, Peter was still sleeping. I took his bat and set it aside. The Tanizakis didn't live far. When they brought Ben back he looked proud of himself, and he didn't understand why everyone was so mad at him. My mother's sister, who was visiting, said she had half a mind to box his ears, but my mother didn't scold him at all.

"Well, you get to go away," he said to me. "So why couldn't I, just for a while?"

"I wish you and Walker would please go to bed now," I said. Ben's face fell, but I couldn't help turning my back. I felt jealous of him. He and my other brothers were allowed to be reckless—sometimes even expected to be reckless—in a way that I, just a few years closer to some of the things that had happened to my parents during the war, had never felt free to be.

I waited at the front window for my father and David to get back. The hills were black again; everyone must have been searching the other side. My mother came up and put her arm around me and said, "Ben's too old for nonsense like this, but in a way I'm glad at least he wasn't around tonight." Later, I decided she'd meant she was glad that at least Ben had not had to be scared like the rest of us.

When my father returned and saw Ben, his face took on a singular expression, confused and overwhelmingly relieved. It was as if at that moment the expression got etched permanently onto his face, because even today when he hasn't seen one of us for a long time, I still see remnants of that confusion and relief.

Some of the men went to work getting drunk right away. Hugh passed out, lying half on my father's favorite chair and half on the floor. Now and then he came to life and took a swig from his bottle.

My mother had said that my brothers could stay up as late as they wanted. Peter went to sleep right away. And when some of the men began getting drunk, Walker and even Ben hid in the hallway and peeked into the living room, just as if they weren't allowed to be awake. Hugh started rousing himself every so often and saying, "Long live college!"

His wife looked embarrassed. "Hugh, you're upsetting the children," she said, meaning me. Hugh was my father's best friend. They had lived next door to each other in Little Tokyo in Los Angeles before the war, but were separated when they were sent to different internment camps. They'd resumed their friendship afterwards. Hugh had come to Arkansas before us. He opened a garage, and later we came, and my father bought a half-interest in the garage.

My mother had noticed that the Stemmlers had turned their lights on, so she gave me some food to take to them. When I knocked, their curtains moved first, and then they opened the door. I told them how Ben had been lost earlier and we'd gone to search for him. They said that that was nice, and asked me how I was. I told them that I was going away to school the next day, and they said that that was nice, too. And then, though we'd lived near each other for years, we said "Good night." Maybe we would have liked to say more, but we couldn't thing of anything.

Back at home, I decided to take one last walk through the grove of trees behind our house. I used to play out there all the time a few years earlier. I would test myself. From the direction of my house, I could enter the grove at any point, and with my eyes closed find my way to a certain tree in the center. I stepped into the trees and stood very still. The air conditioner from the Stemmlers' house whirred barely audibly. David and I had made love here once, and I felt as if I could still feel something of our presence among the trees. I remember our love as a love of rests—sometimes, when his hand rested against me, it was almost as if he were feeling for a pulse. The first time we'd made love his hand had lain momentarily against my throat before moving over my breasts. I stood in the trees and I remembered his mouth, resting, momentarily, on my breasts, on my shoulders, against my face.

Later, when the party was over, everyone shook my hand and kissed my cheek and left. David did just like everyone else. But then he leaned in again and whispered, "Soon." I watched out the window after him. He lived a few hours' drive away. The only time he came to town was to visit relatives or to see me. We would lie in bed after making love and talk for a long while. He would tell me who in his life he had cared about and why, and who he had not cared about and why not. I thought at the time that he had known many people, and many different kinds of people. At the time, everything he said was interesting to me. "A lot of excitement, but I guess that doesn't change anything for you," my father was saying. "I guess you're still leaving later."

My father and I couldn't sleep, so we cleaned up and then decided to go down to the restaurant at the highway. The sky was getting light. There was something almost violet, something lovely and pale, in the sky and the street. It seemed ridiculous to me that just a few hours earlier we'd been not only worried, but very scared. And of what? It had even crossed my mind that the Stemmlers had done something to Ben. Now, even the fluorescent lights of the restaurant seemed softer, paler than usual. The few other customers watched us with blank faces, but, feeling suddenly lighthearted, I smiled at them. I *was* leaving later.

We took a booth. My father picked up a packet of sugar and turned it over in his hands. His hands were thick and dark, but I knew they were deceptively agile. The blue veins stood out like welts.

The waitress, Sandra, came over. She had a blonde beehive set on top of her red hair. "Long time no see," she said.

"She's going away to college today," said my father.

She nodded seriously. "So you have a brain after all. I always thought you might."

"Thank you," I said, feeling pleased with myself.

I had never ordered coffee at a restaurant, so that's what I asked for, part of the new sophisticated me. She scribbled that down. "No, make that orange juice." I didn't even like coffee. She erased. "Oh, no, I want to stay awake. I have lots to do. Coffee, please."

Sandra sighed as she scribbled, erased, scribbled. She had a thick southern drawl. "Like I always tell my husband," she said, "Sweetpea, you put me through too many changes." She went to get our order.

My father knocked his thick knuckles against his lips. The restaurant shook as a truck drove by. "I made a mistake," he said. "We should have called Susan and Bill as soon as we couldn't find Ben."

"We had no reason to think he would be with them."

"See, I try to get through every day without making any mistakes."

"What?"

"You probably wouldn't understand." Another singular expression passed over his face, not of hate, really—at least, not of hate toward me. But, maybe, of resentment. I had never noticed him looking that way before, and it made me feel defensive, and then sad for just a few of the things that bound my family together: fears, resentments, necessities.

He leaned forward. "Take the garage for an example. I try to be exact. I don't want to use any more movement than I have to to get a car fixed. I look at it and make my decisions as quickly as possible, and then do everything I have to do—get my tools and so forth—with the least possible movement. I want to be perfect. Don't you ever want to be perfect?" His voice sounded monotonous, automatic. I realized he had probably been very drunk earlier. "When we were searching for Ben I didn't feel anything. In the same way, all day my whole mind is focused just on what I'm doing. I think about this all the time, and here's the way I see it. When I'm fixing a car, or, say, working in the garden for hours, my hands become what most people's hearts are. They feel for me. That's a trick I learned during the war, how to let my hands feel for me. So *I* don't have to feel anything."

Sandra, sensing a change at our table, brought our coffee quietly and left. I looked at my father's ugly hands and had a feeling almost of awe at the weight they had carried.

"In case you ever wondered what I do all day," said my father.

My family lived in a home built especially for us. It had a neatly trimmed lawn in front and a swing set in the large back yard. During the summers, I used to pull the centers out of honeysuckle flowers and suck the sweetness, or else chew lambsleaves, those tangy sour plants that grew wild and looked like clover. The first summer we'd moved to South Springs, I'd played alone a lot. I caught bumblebees in my mother's gold-plated cigarette case or collected caterpillars in coffee cans. Evenings, we might take quilts into our back yard. Sometimes we talked but usually we were quiet. On those quiet nights, we would sit within a few feet of each other, but would be so far away in mind that we each felt free to dream as we pleased.

That's what I thought about later as we drove to the next town so I could catch the bus. Waiting at the station was a young couple with a baby, and two men who looked in their twenties. One had a crew cut and the other wore his hair slicked back.

My father eyed both of them suspiciously. I knew what he was thinking: I hope she has the good sense to sit near the front of the bus.

Ben was swinging a neck chain in his hand. At the end of the chain hung what looked like a clear white shell.

"Where did you get that shell?" said my father absently.

"Don't you remember? That's from last year when I tripped on a hoe and ripped off the nail from my big toe."

My father started, as if someone had just splashed water on him.

My mother began to sob. "Don't get fat," she said. "Men don't like that."

I got on the bus and smelled exhaust, air conditioning, cigarette smoke, and the unfamiliar scents of people I had never met. I was glad to leave my parents. That was one of the things they didn't know about me. My parents had taught me many things that they had not meant to teach me, and that I had not meant to learn. One of those things was fear. Their first big fear—during the war; their fear when my father was arrested; their fear when Ben was missing; their fear that I would be all right in the future; and a hundred other fears I'd seen in them over the years and that we shared with our family friends—all those fears were connected. That was what I wanted to leave. As I looked out at my parents' faces, full of hope for me, I realized they didn't know that a part of me I had to fight against already believed that what I wanted in life far exceeded what I thought I could get. They didn't know many of the things I believed, some of which I later found to be true, and some false, things that I wanted to tell them about but did not because I did not think they would want to know. I had a future. Theirs had been taken away.

Sources of "South Springs"

I work in cycles. The cycle starts when I've just finished a story. Then, I try to read more fiction than usual, some of it similar to what I'm planning to write next, some of it different, depending on what my needs seem to be. For a few weeks, I take frequent notes, scratching down details and bits of dialogue and ideas for scenes that all revolve around the fictional idea I've chosen for my next story. So I always have a center point. But often the details and dialogue with which I surround the center are so loosely constructed that the story fails. One of the technical goals I've set for myself since I wrote "South Springs" is to concentrate more on making my stories cohesive, without letting go of the illusion of looseness that I like to have.

Memory comes most into play during this early phase of the cycle. As a child, I lived in Arkansas, and I remember going to parties some nights with my parents. There would be all Japanese families at the parties, and a lot of beer — usually Budweiser — and a lot of cigarette smoke. I remember that sometimes there would be rice crackers and pastel-colored mints that I loved. I'm not saying that this is the way it happened, just that this is the way I remember it. I was always on the outside of these parties — my world was the world of rice crackers and pastel-colored mints, while the beer-drinking men were in another world. In "South Springs," the narrator is growing up, is halfway between those two worlds.

The story involves the same narrator I'd used in other stories. Since the major characters were familiar to me, I was to some extent advanced into the story before I'd started. I knew what I wanted to write a story about — fear and ethnicity — but I needed a narrative. I decided to make that narrative what happened when one of the protagonist's brothers is missing for a while on the night of her going-away party.

When I've decided on the narrative and when I have enough notes to feel "full," I begin to arrange the notes on paper, the way I've already been arranging them in my mind. By arrange I mean I try to weave the pieces into the narrative. This is something fairly new to me — a couple of years ago, I would just create scenes and arrange them on paper in a way that pleased me. I would type everything up at once, in a rush, then clean it up for several drafts. Now I proceed more slowly. I want to have some control from the start. The first few pages have to satisfy me before I can go on. I want to make the last word of a story related to the first. Even those inevitable parts of a story that surprise me as I'm writing need to be related to the narrative. Before, it didn't matter to me if they were related so long as I had connected everything on paper, even if the connections were arbitrary.

When I start arranging, and, eventually, typing, I think I become more alert in my daily life—I listen in a different way to what people say on the phone, at parties, on the street. For instance, one line in "South Springs," where the waitress Sandra says, "You put me through too many changes," is something I obtained from my roommate. My roommate happened to mention that this line was something her brother-in-law had said to her sister. Any other time, I might not even have taken note of this. But because I was alert for things to fit into my story, I *heard* it differently. I'm not alert for anything, only for pieces that seem to fit naturally and properly into a story.

Whenever I write a story, there are a series of obstacles that I have to try to coax the story over. I try listening to music, reading, smelling old perfume bottles, reciting poetry. With this story, I felt quite lost at one point and decided one night to leave New York, where I live. So I took a train and spent the night in a small town in West Virginia. While there, I saw an image that struck me—the darkest, blackest hills I had seen in a long time. Somehow, that image was a crucial one for me, and I used it in my story, which then seemed to me to coalesce.

When I'm done with the first few drafts, I try to think about places in the story where I may have been too baldly truthful, using too much experience and memory and not enough imagination. In a way, once experience becomes memory, it becomes a type of imagination. Memory brings forward feelings that will always be with me, while imagination creates feelings that pass, that have to be replenished with more imagination. But on the page, they have the same authority—the page equalizes memory and imagination. I always feel that telling factual lies keeps me from betraying real-life people. In any case, I fabricate facts and situations to try to create an effect. I worry about the morality of writing, and about the way it seems to separate me from the people and experiences on which I might base a story. I don't want to betray anyone; I want to write for the people I know, not about them. Yet I wonder whether there is also a cold writerly part of me that does exploit people, even people I love. Sometimes I try to think up excuses and rationalizations and justifications for this, but I think this exploitation just represents a bad side of me.

Often, the factual truths in my stories have to do with setting. In "South Springs," one paragraph about chasing bumblebees and sitting on quilts in the back yard is a paragraph I took almost verbatim from an essay I wrote during college. Several other things are true: my father's family was interned during the war, and my father did have a bookie in Arkansas, and the bookie did get arrested, though none of his clients did. (I wonder whether even in this essay I'm exploiting my father, a private man.)

I think many stories contain both their apparent meaning and the meaning's opposite. When I read other people's work, it always says more to me than the author most likely intended, and also reveals a lot about the author. I'm not objective enough to see what my own work says about me. When I think about this story, it seems pessimistic. The author seems to believe that life breaks people in ways that can be imperceptible, and that this family—and maybe everyone in the story—has lived the type of life that breaks you in this way. Yet despite the narrator's need to escape her parents and despite the fear the parents' past has created for everyone, the narrator wants to redeem her parents' lives with her own life, and the parents badly want her to be safe and happy. So in this way, the family has escaped its problems. At least, that's what I wanted the story to say. The author of this story is, I think, mostly an optimist. I think all writers are optimists. No matter how dispiriting a story is that I read, and no matter what I may know about the desolation of a particular author's life, I think every act of writing is an act of optimism—it says that the author believes there will be someone out there to talk to, someone who will listen and maybe talk back or tell a story too; so that writing becomes different people from different decades telling each other stories, having conversations across generations. The struggle to be a good writer (or editor) becomes the struggle to be in conversation with as many different people, from as many different times, as possible.

QUESTIONS

Cynthia Kadohata's story, "South Springs," and its process essay, "Sources of South Springs"

1. In the story, the narrator says of the Japanese families in the town she grew up in, "We were bound to them in the same way that my mother, father, three brothers, and I were bound to each other, and in the same way that our relatives in California saw us as bound to a small southern town, bound to something they saw as inescapable." How did you respond to the ethnicity of this story? Was it pronounced? Where did it appear, and in what ways? If you stripped away the ethnicity, what would become of the story?

2. The story takes place the day before the narrator leaves for school, though it is clear that the narrator is looking back on this experience years later. How does Kadohata evoke the sense of parting, and through what devices? Is this parting mitigated only by the fact of her leaving for school? How is this story different from others you have read about or seen on television where children have left home and gone to school? What, if anything, lends the story its resonance?

3. Kadohata says in her process essay that she took a piece of dialogue from a conversation with her roommate and used it in the story. Of this, she writes, "Any other time, I might not even have taken note of this. But because I

was alert for things to fit into my story, I *heard* it differently." When you are preparing to write or are in the habit of writing, do you "hear" things differently? When you're struggling for a topic, are you more attuned to conversations friends may be having over their own struggles with writing? Have you used ideas you came up with as a result of a chance conversation? an offhand remark? Did you like the essay you wrote based on these ideas?

4. Kadohata writes, "I worry about the morality of writing, and about the way it seems to separate me from the people and experiences on which I might base a story. I don't want to betray anyone; I want to write for the people I know, not about them." In your own writing in this and other classes, have you withheld or altered information in order to protect those whose private lives you didn't want to reveal? Do you believe your essay would have been better if you had revealed the information? When you decide to disclose something you are uncertain about, on what, finally, do you base your decision?

Possible Writing Topics

1. Write an essay where you describe the kind of bond that developed among the people you grew up with. This need not be a matter of ethnicity, but it may be. Perhaps in the community you grew up in, many people worked the same jobs, held the same religious affiliations, or enjoyed the same recreations. What you're describing here is the manner in which people you grew up with came to rely on each other, depend on each other in ways that led to a sense of security, community, and protectiveness.

2. After you've completed the first essay, write a second one on the people and past times you mention in the first where you deal with the issue of the disclosures you made. Of those you mention in the essay, whom would you allow to read it? Why would you allow some to read it and not allow others? If you worked in information that might embarrass certain people in your community, how did you decide that it was better to write it than exclude it? If your essay were published and distributed to the people in your community, how would they respond?

Catherine D. Miller

The Use of Contemporary Culture in American Fiction: A Question of Mystery

IN her 1957 essay, "Writing Short Stories," Flannery O'Connor writes: "There are two qualities that make fiction. One is the sense of mystery and the other is the sense of manners. You get the manners from the texture of existence that surrounds you." For O'Connor, this meant unveiling the details of her experience of life in rural Georgia—girls with wooden legs, tattooed men, "good country people"—against the obsessions of Bible Belt preachers, the pull of religion, the question of free will. While O'Connor wrote well about the details of everyday life, she was also interested in the mystery that elevated these details into a different realm, in other words, what worked to make these details distinctive and meaningful. In *her* case, because she happened to be a converted Catholic living in the midst of a predominantly fundamentalist environment, the mysteries consisted of questions about religion, free will, obsession. But for each writer, the mysteries are different.

Given the way O'Connor juxtaposed "the manners" of her details against her sense of mystery, chances are that she would not have recognized what contemporary writers consider "the texture of existence that surrounds" us today, nor their use—or, actually, abandonment—of "mystery." I'm speaking of the kind of writing that has become popular, where exact details about contemporary culture abound. Such writing is exhibited in the works of Raymond Carver, Ann Beattie, Bobbie Ann Mason, and a host of others.

Writing about Raymond Carver's 1977 collection of short stories, *Will You Please Be Quiet, Please?*, one reviewer praised Carver by saying: "Remarkably few writers have been able, in the short story form at least, to say much about the way in which we live now." In 1977, what Carver did was startling and new. In the 25 stories in the collection, Carver portrayed in minute detail the "texture of existence that surrounds" us. His characters shopped, ate, watched a great deal of television, and housesat. They were engaged in everyday activities that had never much interested other fiction writers. The stories are undercut by language almost bereft of metaphor or simile, creating a style uniquely Carver's own. It is an almost textureless style that seems to suggest by the *absence* of many of the typical traditions of fiction writing that O'Connor probably would have understood, that something is lacking in his charaters' lives and—since their lives are so "Every-Man-ish"—that something is lacking in the lives of all Americans.

When Carver combined common everyday experiences with flatness of tone and spare language, the result was the creation of characters who are revealed almost exclusively through their ties to the material world. In this kind of world, since little of what is put before the reader is "mysterious," what happens in such a story?

"Put Yourself in My Shoes," originally published in 1976 as a chapbook, is about a man named Myers who recently has quit his job to write a novel. He spends the first third of the story vacuuming his house, because he can't think of anything to write. A physical description of Myers is never given, but because the title serves as an invitation, the reader unwittingly places himself in the position of the main character and evokes his own machinations over how horrible (or dull at least) life must truly be. Because this is a clean, well-crafted, tightly woven story, we assume that there must be more to it than meets the eye. So we make the vacuum cleaner a symbol or metaphor for Myers' life: He's giving his life a clean sweep, isn't he? His isolation reflects his unwillingness to attack the problem, doesn't it? In a story thus unfettered by language or rhythm, such references to our "existence" must take on a heavier meaning and become symbolic. Whatever "happens" seems to depend as much on the reader as the writer.

Ten years later, applauding the mundane aspects of daily life is still Carver's trademark. His contemporary Ann Beattie and newer writers such as Bobbie Ann Mason and Jay McInerney have taken Carver's technique one step further: they come right out and *name* the products that reveal their characters' immersion in materiality. Ann Beattie's stories, dotted with references to "Saturday Night Live," John Belushi, and the Grateful Dead, reveal the lives of the grown-up post-hippie generation. Bobbie Ann Mason has taken on the working class; Jay McInerney, the New Yorker or would-be New Yorker, or anyone interested in reading about a young man who tries to destroy himself with drugs, sex, and rock 'n roll. All of these writers are good at one thing: telling us *exactly* how "we live now" in minute detail, peppering their stories with brand names, products, and the names of popular entertainers or best sellers.

But, while K-Mart, Tammy Wynette, and McDonald's have become steady presences in American culture and may continue to affect more than one generation, some writers make erroneous assumptions about using contemporary culture *in toto*. They forget that *all* such references are *not* timeless but rather are effective only so long as readers respond to the images. For instance, in the novel *Love, Always* Ann Beattie uses the common contemporary device of comparing a character's physical or emotional characteristics to those of an actor or television personality. She writes that a character "had about as much class as John Belushi doing Samurai Swordsman." Similarly, Bobbie Ann Mason introduces her main character, Norma Jean, in the opening of "Shiloh," by writing: "With her legs spread apart, she reminds Leroy of Wonder Woman."

These images work as a sort of shorthand or telegraphy that sends the image or message across to the reader immediately. It would seem that in the kind of literature that counts so heavily on detail as a shortcut to experience and emotionality that the writer has to make sure that his reader has the *right* image in her mind.

What does a writer have to do to assure that the reader receives the right message? It seems that the writer must make a number of assumptions about his reader. First, he assumes that the reader immediately understands the reference. (Easy to do if the reference is to K-Mart or Tammy Wynette or McDonald's; not so simple if the reference is to a television show that lasted only one season or a popular song that turned out to be a flash-in-the-pan success.) Second, the writer assumes that once the reader makes the identification, she will immediately carry the identification several steps further. If another character reminds the narrator of John Belushi, and the reader knows who John Belushi is, the reader must have to be able to summon up everything she knows about John Belushi to fill in the blanks and see clearly the manner in which the writer intends the character to be seen. She says to herself: "I've seen John Belushi on 'Saturday Night Live.' He has dark hair, bushy eyebrows, a crooked mouth, a puzzled look, and a big stomach. When he played the Samurai Swordsman, he wore a costume that looked like a big white diaper..." and so on. In essence, when a statement (or images) is telegraphed in this manner to the reader, she must identify the statements and put them together piece by piece, like a puzzle to get an entire picture.

The reader must also assess her emotional paraphernalia and biases and ask herself, "Did I like John Belushi? Did I like him as the Samurai Swordsman? How did I feel when I was watching him? Was he funny? If so, *this* character must be funny."

Assuming the reader knows exactly who John Belushi (or any reference) is and what he represented to American society, this all works fine. Does the story change in any way by our new knowledge that Belushi died of a drug overdose three years after the story was written? And what if the reference is more vague? In the same novel, Beattie makes a similar reference to a comedian named Jack Carpenter. Jack Carpenter appeared on the Ed Sullivan and Jack Paar shows during the 1960's; any reader over the age of 30 may remember him; if the reader is younger, then she probably doesn't.

And what if the reader has been in the Peace Corps in Uganda for the last five years, or is 60 years old and has heard of "Saturday Night Live," but has never seen it and hasn't the slightest notion who Belushi is? Or the reader is a South African writer who has never been to America? If the reader falls into any of these categories, she would not be able to understand the frame of reference from the context of the sentence because these kinds of references rarely have "contexts." They usually stand alone.

In the case of the Belushi and Jack Carpenter references, it would be interesting to find out just what the reader does see when she reads these names on the page. Does she see the character about which the author is writing? Or, once the contemporary image is put before her, does the character become shadowy or disappear altogether, to be replaced by John Belushi himself?

Does it *matter* what the reader sees or that some readers simply will not be able to understand the reference? It does if the reader wants to understand the story and what the writer is attempting to say. Along with making assumptions about what his audience *knows*, the writer is also, then, assuming who his audience *is*. By fully accepting and promulgating the kind of writing that tells us about "the way in which we live now," are we saying that it is acceptable for Americans to write only for themselves within this very narrow time period? Are we then saying that the converse is also true—that since our stories are accessible only to us, stories from other countries are accessible only to *those* readers and that we should, therefore, not bother to read them?

Actually, many readers might contend that a certain kind of universality or timelessness may really exist, but that we are too bound by our own views of the world to see it. For instance, they could say that the way in which some contemporary writers protray our culture in their fiction is no different from how Chekhov portrayed a world of snow and ice and carriages in "The Lap Dog." Some people would also say that just as Bobbie Ann Mason's, Ray Carver's, and Ann Beattie's worlds can be none other than the United States in the 1970's and 1980's, Chekhov's world was none other than 19th-century Russia. He used, they might say, *his* own symbols just as we use *ours*.

One way to question the issues of timelessness and universality is to think about the reader of the future. Will the readers of 1995 and beyond be able to understand this new kind of fiction in a world in which our cultural artifacts are gone, replaced by new ones? Will they still be able to *see* the character exactly as contemporary readers see him and as the writer originally intended to portray him? Or has timelessness become an altogether unimportant or unnecessary consideration?

To go one step further, is it possible that now, as a number of critics have posited, all art should be disposable in a world threatened by nuclear war?

When Katherine Anne Porter described her main character in her 1944 short story, "Maria Concepcion," she wrote: "Her grand manner sometimes reminded him of royalty in exile." Here, the writer has made many associations for the reader, by placing the character in a context, a frame of reference that relies heavily on language. The reader sees "grand," "manner," "exile." He knows these words in a different way from words such as "K-Mart," "Tammy Wynette," and "McDonald's." The last three are words that gain much of their strength, are embued, as symbols, through their relationship to and place in American culture. "Grand," "manner," and "exile" are of a more universal language. Because they are not grounded in any specific culture (they are neither American—the author's nationality—nor Mexican—the place of the story), they transcend time and place. The way they are placed against one another and the way association is built upon association makes them full of the "texture of existence," if the texture of which Flannery O'Connor speaks also implies the character's inherent mystery. Although the *place* of the story could be none other than Mexico, and the *narrator* of the story sees the incidents through an American sensibility, the play of texture and mystery works together to create a universal, timeless story, the kind that often seems absent in current fiction.

It could be that writers who use the icons of American culture in their fiction *mean* to be universal by choosing images that are so deeply engrained in our culture and, therefore, so identifiable or, in computer jargon, easily accessed. The book blurb on Bobbie Ann Mason's collection of short stories, *Shiloh and Other Stories*, reads: "Like Type-O blood, Bobbie Ann Mason's fiction can be given to almost anyone." The title story in Mason's book is similar in premise to Katherine Anne Porter's "Maria Concepcion." In both stories, a child has died and the parents grieve in their own ways, unable to communicate. Most shocking is how the death is handled in each of the stories.

In "Maria Concepcion," these are the lines that portray the immediate occasion of the death itself:

> Maria Concepcion did not weep when Juan left her; and when the baby was born, and died within four days, she did not weep. "She is mere stone," said old Lupe, who went over and offered charms to preserve the baby.

Porter begins and ends the sentence with "[she] did not weep," which strengthens the portrayal of pain. Then she uses a simile, "She is mere stone," to both undercut and heighten the experience of grief. In a moment as powerful as the death of a child, it seems appropriate that an organic image such as stone be used.

In "Shiloh," Mason describes her couple's discovery of their dead child:

> Norma Jean and Leroy were at the drive-in, watching a double feature ("Dr. Strangelove" and "Lover, Come Back"), and the baby was sleeping in the back seat. When the first movie ended, the baby was dead. It was the sudden infant death syndrome. Leroy remembers handing Randy to a nurse at the emergency room, *as though he were offering her a large doll as a present. A dead baby feels like a sack of flour.* (Italics mine)

In a consumer-oriented era such as ours, the young couple's grief is aptly revealed through a material object. But a doll and a sack of flour have associations in our own world which are comical. This choice of images, coupled with the contemporary allusions to the movies, gives the scene an almost slapstick quality that detracts from the emotionalism of the death.

In another instance, both sets of characters begin to discover that there are problems in their marriages. Maria Concepcion accidentally espies a young village girl and her own husband together:

> Juan and Maria Rosa! She burned all over now, as if a layer of tiny fig-cactus bristles, as cruel as spun glass, had crawled under her skin. She wished to sit down quietly and wait for her death.

In "Shiloh," the husband, Leroy, busies himself with a familiar product after his wife tells him she wants to leave. He, too, thinks of death, but it could be because they are sitting in a cemetery at the time.

> Leroy remembers to drink from his Coke. Then he says, "Yes, you are *crazy*. You and me could start all over again . . . "
>
> The cemetery, a green slope dotted with white markers, looks like a subdivision site. Leroy is trying to comprehend that his marriage is breaking up, but for some reason he is wondering about white slabs in a graveyard.

Of course, we could say that Maria Concepcion's association with "tiny fig-cactus bristles" are the same kinds of associations that Leroy makes when he sips his Coke or sits in the cemetery. They are both "artifacts" from these characters' cultures. Porter, however, draws out the association with the simile that the fig-cactus bristles are "as cruel as spun glass." What does it mean that the cemetery "looks like a subdivision site"? Most American readers probably have a general idea of what a subdivision looks like, but how is a reference to a "subdivision site" supposed to make us feel? If you grew up in one, you may feel one way. If you aspire to live in one, another; if you disdain them, a third. And do any of these associations make you feel as you feel when you are in a cemetery? The problem here is that Mason, like many other contemporary writers, has simply substituted one image from our culture for another, without making a translation for us, or letting us see how she sees the relationship. The reader has to make the association by thinking about all that the word "subdivision" means in America.

The idea of depicting *exactly* how we live *is* different from Kafka's idea that literature is meant to break "the frozen sea within us." Or Eudora Welty's notion that stories are celebrations of life, with "the mysteries rushing through them unsubmissively by the minute."

It is doubtful that we are, as some critics think, embarking on a new kind of fiction, one that simply celebrates the artifacts of its culture. What is probable is that, in the very near future, we will have to begin to examine a literature that makes large-scale assumptions about all of its readers and operates as if traditions such as timelessness and universality no longer matter. Both readers and writers will begin to ask questions. One question should predominate: Is there mystery in a world that is given back to us, as if we are looking in mirrors at our own reflections?

Getting Rid of the Audience: What I Have to Do Before I Can Write

ONE evening several years ago, I found out that my friend and housemate, Monette, prepared for writing in the same way that I do. It was an odd discovery to make, given, first, that I wasn't quite sure what it was that I did just seconds before being able to come up with that "first perfect sentence." The first perfect sentence, which I will talk more about later, is the sentence that would enable me to go further, to write the entire piece I had been struggling with in my mind for days. And, second, because neither one of us have ever met anyone else who goes through the same exact ritual.

She had just completed an article of literary criticism; I had just finished a short story. And, as we often did, we emerged from hours in our respective rooms and came together over cups of tea, in our cold, gray lineoleum-floored kitchen. That kitchen, we agreed, was a fitting room to sit in because of the torture that we had to put ourselves through each time we wrote.

We already knew that we indulged in the kinds of procrastinations that only writers can partake in. Saturday afternoons were the worst. Other people we knew were relaxing or doing errands, cross country skiing, or reading books they *wanted* to read, while *we* knew what lay in store for us: a day of misery and guilt over not being able to write, not even being able to *begin*—and then, a Sunday of more of the same, or, if we were very very lucky, a Sunday of writing—the prize for having tortured ourselves mercilessly until we got hold of that elusive first perfect sentence.

And so, in lieu of working, all Saturday long, we procrastinated: with a ritual of Scrabble games, Mexican pizzas (delivered to our door), and *Wild, Wild West* re-runs. The re-runs were a particularly odd touch because we hated the show immensely and had both hated it as children. The ground rules seemed to be: no matter what else, we could not leave the house and we could not have real fun. By five o'clock, we either gave up altogether or began serious work. By Sunday morning we usually felt so guilty we had a prolific day. For me, a prolific Sunday sometimes carried over to a Monday, when I would take a vacation day or call in to work sick.

I was working full-time, as I am now, as a writer/editor for a large corporation, going to graduate school for my M.F.A., and trying to write stories in the evening and on weekends. Monette was preparing for her Ph.D. and writing articles she hoped to submit for publication. A third woman lived with us. She worked at my company and was a poet. She had a wonderful social life. We envied her. We saw her getting ready to go out while we sat in the livingroom watching horrible television shows as if we were waiting outside a doctor's office for some good news. She dashed in and dashed out, always going to dinner with a friend or to attend an art opening. Sometimes one of us would whisper to the other as soon as she closed the door and we heard her footsteps on the porch, "She must never get any writing done." To us, that was the unkindest cut of all. But, alas, she, too, must have been carrying out her own private writing ritual because, since we all left that house and went our separate ways, she has given poetry reading upon poetry reading and has had a number of other successes.

So it was late one Monday night, then, after a day of procrastination and two days of real work, that we talked about creativity and what we had to produce and of the rituals we always had to go through, like two Catholic priests lamenting that we could not give up the old ways. We also talked about those strange, infrequent moments when the writing went really well and seemed as if it were *everything*.

We talked, as we had in the past, about finally getting the first perfect sentence. We both knew that the first perfect sentence was not really perfect at all. But it came out, whole, organic, a thing that seemed complete, the starting point for all the writing that was going to come after it. That first perfect sentence was like a well-made, but unpainted, door. Once constructed, the door could be opened to an entire world— Monette's article, my short story. It didn't matter that the door was unpainted. It could be painted later. The door was the beginning. All of the trips to the refrigerator, the pacing, the contemplating, the act of putting the cat out and letting him in again were behind us, once we went through that door.

And before that? We pondered. Monette puffed on her cigarette.

"Oh, I *know*," I said. "Just before I begin to write I imagine Room 526 [the room at the university where critics and fiction writers alike read their work]. It's full of people, and I'm standing at the podium as if I'm giving a reading. I'm about to read the story I'm working on as if it's already finished."

Monette's face took on a look of recognition.

"And then," I said, almost gleefully, "I make them disappear, one by one."

"Yes!" she said, nodding her head.

"Until," I continued, "until the room is completely empty. They're whisked off somewhere. The chairs are empty. *Then* I can begin."

"Well, *I* kill them," she said frankly, putting her pack of cigarettes on the table with a thump. "I imagine them all dead."

"Are they there in the room dead?" I asked. We began to laugh, thinking of faculty with their arms and legs strewn about the chairs as if they were at some horrible faculty party where there had been a massacre.

The macabreness of our little ritual struck us at that point and we laughed until we were almost sick.

Monette finally said, "Good God, no. They're not in the room. They're just gone—that's all."

"Well," I said. "I suppose that's what I do, too. I didn't know I was *killing* them."

And we began to laugh again at the thought of our own personal *deux ex machinas* in reverse—whisking the worrisome, possibly judgmental, audience away.

That, I discovered, is how I begin to create.

To "kill" our audience seems, of course, diametrically opposed to that age-old bit of English professor wisdom which tells us to "know our audience." It is by knowing our audience, imagining what they are like, envisioning their perspective, that we will know how to treat our subject and thereby strengthen our work.

Of course, I realize that you can't know your audience by killing them. Or, at least, you won't know your audience for very long. So, if I reveal my ritual of "killing" my audience, or if I at least tell you what my audience looks like and what they always do that makes it necessary to kill them, then, this may make better sense.

First, whenever I envision the audience, I am in that Room 526 that I mentioned before. It is aptly named, that room, with a number. It may have had a name at one time, but if so the name is no longer used. Room 526 is located on the fifth floor of the gothic Cathedral of Learning built in the 1940's in Pittsburgh. The room is comfortable to me because I have had many classes there, given a few readings, attended many readings. If I am to stand back from it, I remember that even though Room 526 is paneled in oak, it is in dire need of a new paint job for the existing plaster, could enjoy several new sets of draperies and a pair of window washers so that a person could see out of the windows. It has radiators that clang ominously in the winter. On a dismal winter day it reminds me of an apartment I had once, where the teenaged son of a friend announced, "It looks like a murder's been committed in here." Room 526 is sometimes like that when you have to read there.

When I am just about to begin a short story, Room 526 is more than half full and it doesn't look as much as if a murder has been committed there. The chairs are occupied by friends, faculty members, and many anonymous but friendly faces. I assume these anonymous faces to be those of the "anonymous" public who, never having met me, might pick up a literary magazine and read my work. Strangely enough, the many editors of the literary magazines to which

I send my work never appear in this imaginary meeting. I always assume they are off somewhere looking for some other hapless soul's lost manuscript. And now that I've really consciously thought about it, I may not be able to keep the editors from coming to my reading.

Just as I am about to begin to write, I look out at the faces. I compose myself. I take three deep breaths just as I do before I actually read. And then I try to concentrate. At this point, it is a contest of wills between me and this audience. I stand firm. I'm saying nothing, of course, just staring them down. One or two of the people begin to smile at me, expressing, I believe, their confidence in me in real life. But questions gather as if they are being sent telepathically from that rotten audience which is stirring in its seats. I see them shifting around like so many hens setting on eggs. The questions are sort of a low mumble and portend to get worse, but I continue to concentrate, to pull further inside of myself, to summon up the strength to begin the first perfect sentence. This drowns them out before their voices become a roar. The questions, if I ever really listen to them, hear them out, run something like this: "What are you going to tell us that's new?" someone mumbles. Another snickers under his breath: "Try to entertain me, just try." And still another: "I'll bet you *write* well, but you can't make me *feel* anything. And besides, there are thousands of others just like you. Young writers who haven't made it." An older woman with an umbrella says nothing but her face hardens; I can just tell that she has recently finished a Barbara Pym novel and will like nothing I have to say. Even the one or two professors who gave me encouraging smiles are beginning to get doubting looks on their faces, just for the sake of joining the crowd and being critical. But before the mumbles surface to a low roar, I get control of the situation. I stare them down. I have confidence because I have been down this road before. And whether it is just an image that I have been carrying around with me for days or a full-blown story that has surfaced from some aspect of my memory or my creation of memory, I *just know* that I have the floor, that I am about to open the door, to let in that first perfect sentence from which everything else will flow. From where I stand, I eject them from their seats—*deux ex machina* in reverse. I focus in on them, hear their tiny complaint, and then dismiss it in my own mind, for in this place *I* am the creator, the one in control, and, like so many characters, I can do with them what I like.

One, two, three, the troublesome ones in the first row are gone. The ones who seemed to smile encouragingly and then turned at the last minute, they're gone. The scowling ones with their arms folded are gone too. After the first two or three groups, it is easy. The rest I dispose of one by one. The Barbara Pym woman is the last to go. Just by virtue of the sheer weight of her, she has been difficult to dislodge from her position. I close the door behind them. And then, I'm ready to begin.

Unfortunately, when writing the essay, "The Use of Contemporary Culture in American Fiction," *I could not kill the audience.* The essay was to be an examination of a new stylistic trend in fiction, that of using contemporary culture (particularly brand names) to denote emotion or character. The room for this imaginary audience was the same—Room 526. But now, in fact, it seemed even more ominous, unfriendly, as if perhaps a murder *had* been committed there. Before I began the first draft of the essay, in my mind, I stood as usual in front of the audience. I was surprised that they were not the same audience as the ones who had come to hear me previously. Before, the room was only half full, but this time the room was crammed to capacity. There were the usual faces— the friends, the professors, the anonymous public of fiction lovers. But there were new faces as well. They had cold, hard stares, and I realized that they were comprised of two groups: literate people who had opinions, too, and—horrors— critics. This startled me. Upon closer inspection (I put on my glasses) I realized that many of the literate people with opinions were the former lovers of fiction who came, this time, not to be entertained but to stand up for their favorite authors. They liked, it seemed, some of the people I was about to criticize, and they weren't going to let me get away with it. The critics were a wild bunch, older men in tweed with pipes and nasty expressions. There were a few editors in there, to boot. I looked at my friends and professors for support. They surprised me by not looking back. They looked off to the side or down at their laps. Some of them were reading. I heard one whisper to another, "It's too bad. She isn't used to this sort of thing. She's going to be annihilated." I could see that no one, this time, was going to stand up for me, or even give me an encouraging nod.

Until now, I thought that writing the essay would be easy. I was writing about a topic that I felt strongly about. Suddenly, I realized that I wasn't prepared. But, it was too late; I had made them wait so long already. If I was ever going to get rid of them and get myself through that door to the first perfect sentence I had to begin. At the top of the page I wrote:

THE CHANGING METAPHOR IN CONTEMPORARY AMERICAN FICTION

That got their attention. The room went silent. It was not the kind of silence that a writer likes to hear. The readers stopped reading and looked up. The pipes were taken out of clenched teeth and held in their owners' hands for a moment. One of the critics even gave me this, "Now, *that* is interesting." The man on his left said, "Yes, but what is she going to do with it? *I* heard she was going to talk to us about brand names. Now *that's* something I'd like to hear about."

A woman behind him sat with her knitting on her lap. She had a K-Mart bag by her side and had a very round face. She leaned forward and tapped the first critic on the shoulder. Interestingly, even though it seemed she would be the kind of person to agree with him, he ignored her until she began to practically shake him by the shoulder. "Did you say *brand names?*" she kept repeating, until he answered her.

Haughtily, he said, "Yes, my good woman, I did. Brand names it is—or it was until she finally started speaking up there."

"Does she like brand names or doesn't she?" the woman asked. I tried waving my hands to get their attention so I could put the reading back on track, but by now no one was looking at me. The audience was on its own.

"*Doesn't* like them," the first critic said.

"Hrmmmph!" the woman said, picking up her knitting again. "Knocking brand names! If I'd *known* that this was all about brand names I would'nt have come. I *like* brand names in fiction. It gives me something to relate to. I like writers who write like that."

This caught the second critic's attention. "Yes, madam," he said, swiveling around to talk to her. "*Many* readers—and writers—like the current trend in fiction. It reflects the needs and passions of our society." He gave me a dirty look, as if I didn't already know that.

Thankfully, when the word "passion" was mentioned, the woman picked up her knitting and moved to another seat. I thought that now I would be able to get some control over these people. But at this point, a free-for-all started and questions were hurled at me: "What are your credentials?" "Aren't you just a fiction writer?" "A not-very-published fiction writer," someone else added, unkindly.

I *must* show them, I thought. I have thought about this topic. This is important. I am going to change their minds. Hurriedly, I began:

> No one can deny that the United States is seeing the greatest surge of interest in the short story since the Forties, when more than 40 commercial magazines published quality fiction and paid well for it. Suddenly, America has rediscovered the short story and Americans are buying short story collections and novels the way they used to await the next installment of radio theatre. Why this sudden interest in fiction? Has American story telling changed to make it perhaps more accessible or palatable to the American reader?

A few people laughed out loud. Many, by now, were smiling as if to themselves. The woman with the knitting leaned forward again: "What's she talking about? She's not telling *me* anything I don't already know."

"My sentiments exactly," the critics said in unison.

As the essay went on, people began talking over me, proffering their opinions and offering to restructure my essay for me. Two professors said, simultaneously, "*Here's* what you need to do." They proceeded to give me directly opposite advice. I decided to structure the first draft as I would a short story (attempting to write *to* the ending); I begged them to hang on until I got to the end.

Needless to say, the audience was a hostile one. I could not get them to leave the room so that I could write decently. And, what was worse, I kept imploring one of the professors with the facts of the situation: This was just too hard. "There are," she telegraphed to me with her knowing eyes, "*no* excuses in writing—what do you plan to do, send a cassette with your work explaining why you couldn't do it properly?" That wasn't a bad idea, I tried to joke.

When I was finished, there were no accolades, just that silence again. A few friends smiled as if they were thanking God that the muse didn't visit upon them in this way.

The title of my second draft was a little more to the point: "The Use of Brand Names in Contemporary Fiction." This at least was said with conviction. The first perfect sentence was still a problem. The same audience was there: the friends, the professors, the critics, the editors. The woman with the knitting had finished the first piece she made during my talk and was working now in blue wool. (*She*, at least, I told myself when I saw her, had created something.)

Between the first draft and the second, I was determined that I would not let the audience get the better of me. I was going to be prepared. I spent almost two months reading and re-reading. First, I read the "old guard" writers: Katherine Anne Porter, Eudora Welty, Flannery O'Connor, J. F. Powers, Philip O'Connor, and others. I read the "new guard," particularly the writers who I felt were using the new style that I wanted to write about in my essay: Raymond Carver, Anne Beattie, Bobbie Ann Mason, Jay McInerney, Tama Janowitz, Peter Cameron. I took my perverted interpretation of someone's advice and threw long quotes from all of these people into my essay, like a kind of stewpot of language. One thing I'd learned from my audience was that they were, to a person, much more intelligent than I. By my skillful manipulation of laying certain quotes side by side, I reasoned, the intelligent reader could draw his own conclusions.

I went on in similar manners—each time with a different set of problems—through two more drafts. By the third draft I had a catchy sub-title: "Attention All K-Mart Shoppers, There's a Special on Metaphors in Aisle 2." This got me a laugh from the audience but little else.

After the third imaginary reading, however, I asked a professor and a friend who teaches for advice. The professor was the same professor who had told me I can't send my essay out with a cassette tape of excuses; the friend is the woman at the beginning of this essay, the one with whom I made the discovery about the imaginary audience. They pulled me out of Room 526 and into the hallway of real life and said: "Before you do another draft, ask yourself—just what is it you are trying to say." They said other things as well, mostly about the structure of the piece, how one idea lead to another or didn't. But their blunt statement that I was simply making no sense whatsoever was the unkindest cut of all—and the truest one. I could see now that my imaginary audience, which had always been such a big help in the past, were really the characters that I myself had created because of my own lack of self-confidence in the area of essay writing. They had driven me mad and made it impossible for me to really *say* anything at all.

How did I get from draft three to draft four (a finally acceptable position that lacked some transitions)? By putting two of my best critics—the professor and the friend—in the front row seats and giving them the loudest voices. And by writing with the knowledge I had gained by going through all of the little failures. After that, the voices of the imaginary audience drowned out, I was able to eject them from the room and to get hold of that first perfect sentence.

At the end, I gave the professor a confession of sorts, hoping that such an act would absolve me from ever going through such a painful writing experience again. I said, "*That*, I believe, was the hardest process I'd ever gone through to get a piece written." She looked at me and smiled, surprised, and said, "Well, yes. That's what writing is."

QUESTIONS

Catherine D. Miller's essay, "The Use of Contemporary Culture in American Fiction: A Question of Mystery," and its process essay, "Getting Rid of the Audience: What I Have to Do before I Can Write"

1. Do you agree with Miller's argument that the use of contemporary culture is finally an exclusive form of writing, writing that may be inaccessible to readers of future generations? How important is it that we write for readers in the future, that we have, in Cynthia Kadohata's terms, "conversations across generations"? What value might the writing you've done in this class have for future generations? What would a great-great-granddaughter think if she found 100 years from now essays you've written during the last months?

2. In her essay, Miller mentions many names of writers and quotes from others with whom you may be unfamiliar. What is your response when you read those names? Do you feel uninformed, uneducated, excluded? Does it matter to you? When you encounter names with which you're unfamiliar, how does this affect the interest you have in the essay or story you're reading?

3. In several process essays, including Miller's, writers mention their techniques for preparing to write, many of which include procrastination. Why is it so easy to put off writing? Why does Miller "torture" herself in order to work up the energy and the disposition to write that first sentence? Is your greatest trouble with writing finding the frame of mind to do it, coming up with the first sentence that allows you to close off the rest of the world that wants to invite you to do anything other than writing?

4. Miller writes of the conflicting advice she received for writing her essay and her inability to ignore the voices of her peers and teachers as she struggled with her writing. When your teachers and peers have given you advice while you were in the middle of the writing process, what effect did it have on

your work? Did you take the advice offered? Is there a difference in the way you respond to the advice of teachers rather than fellow students? Has such advice ever frozen you, made you unable to write? How much advice in your writing is too much? How much, finally, should you listen to those who speak to you about your writing while you're writing?

❧ Possible Writing Topics ❧

1. Write a letter to a relative of yours who will find the essays you've written in this class and read them long after you've died. This should be a cover letter where you are finding ways to explain to your reader what you wrote, why you wrote what you did, and who you were when you wrote these essays. You may need to provide a context for some of the things you have said in your essays that will need explanation. And this will require that you closely read the essays you've written thus far in order to get a sense of what you have or haven't accomplished in this class.

2. When you've completed the letter, write an essay on the imagery, the ideas, the sensibilities that appear in your essays that you think might be accessible and inaccessible to readers of another generation. Be sure to quote from your essays. To what degree have you relied on contemporary culture? To what degree are you and others even capable of stepping outside it? To what degree is it necessary that you try? If you had to make that which seems inaccessible accessible, how would you change it? Do you like the changes you'd make, or is the writing weaker with them?

Elwin Green

Quest

*T*HE hole was back.
Devon Jackson was waiting for the light at 7th and Center to change when he noticed it—the black hole that came on certain nights around 3 A.M., when only ghosts and hookers were left on the streets. It would quietly blossom in his gut, draining away life and light, leaving him with something not quite sadness, something he had never named.

He rummaged the pile of cassettes beside him in the front seat of the cab, felt the ragged label of the Vivaldi tape, put it into the portable stereo. Music helped. Not that it completely stopped the hole from feeding; but as long as he could enjoy Vivaldi (or the Modern Jazz Quartet, or whatever), he knew it had not sucked him entirely away.

Turning left to head toward the garage as the music began, he noticed the figure standing uncertainly at the curb in front of Mick's. A skinny little white guy, maybe a few inches taller than Devon's five-four, weaving.

Maybe he won't—

The man began waving a bill in the air.

Too late.

"Taxi!" the man shouted, in a high-pitched voice.

I hope he ain't no faggot.

He didn't feel like dealing with one of them tonight. That was not what he spent his time in the gym for.

In fact, if I stay in this lane—

He started to accelerate.

"TAXI!"

He was in the air. The damn fool was in the air, leaping over the remnants of that afternoon's winter rain, waving both his arms, and a second later he landed, sprawling across the right headlight of the cab as Devon slammed the brakes.

"FOOL! GET THE FUCK OFFA MY CAB!!"

He had barely completed his outburst before the fool was scrambling into the back seat. In the shadows of the entrance to Mick's a couple of sisters had their hands to their mouths.

"Hi! How the hell are ya?"

Devon lowered the volume of the tape as he turned to face him.

"Man, are you crazy?"

Up close, the man looked even worse than he had from a distance. Then he had only looked drunk. Now he looked weird. Goofy, lopsided grin. Thick horn-rimmed glasses. Pale blue marbles for eyes. He reached forward, patted Devon's shoulder.

"'s okay, brother. Be cool."

Devon whipped back around, away from the touch. If there was one thing he could not stand, it was some drunk white guy trying to talk black. Especially when they made "cool" a two-syllable word.

"So what's your name?" the man said, squinting at the operator's card. "Devonn?"

"Devon. Where to?"

"But it looks like Devonn."

"They spelled it wrong, okay? Now where to?"

"Oh. 'scuse me. Devon."

"Where you wanna go, fella?"

"Oh, yeah. Wait a minute." The man rolled down the window, leaned out. "Okay girls, let's roll." And the sisters came out from the shadows, one tall and voluptuous, the other petite as a teenager (which, for all Devon knew, she might have been). Both clad in short, tight, low-cut.

Great, just great. Another white idiot with a hangup on black women.

He turned up the volume of the tape slightly.

They pranced around puddles and noisily entered the cab, chattering, baby this, sweetie that, as the man said, "Come right on in, girls. Make yourselves comfy. My man here's even got some nice music to get you in a romantic mood. Classy, hunh?"

"I don't want to be romantic, baby," the short one said as she slid across the man's lap, putting him in the middle. "I just want to be funky."

"Where to, mister?"

"Barclay Hotel, my man. And make it snappy." He snapped his fingers. "Snap-snap!"

"Sure thing, my man," Devon muttered, looking into the rearview mirror, watching the women. They must have told the guy to take them to the Barclay; he wouldn't know about it otherwise. Not him.

"Make it snappy, 'cause I'm feeling happy!"

Why the hell do I put myself through this?
The tall one ran a finger across the john's thin, pale lips.
"You think you're happy now, just wait til we get through with you."
"I'm waiting, sweeetheart. Been waiting all my life for this. And it's finally going to happen. I'm finally gonna get me a taste of brown sugar. Brown sugar, brown sugar baby, all night long!" He nuzzled the short one's neck.
"You wanna go all night, baby?" the tall one said as she began rubbing his chest. "You wanna be nasty all night, Irrviiing?"
Irving. It fits.
"You know it, doll. An all-night feast—"
You won't last twenty minutes, fool.
"—I've always heard that dark meat is the juiciest meat of all."
Man, why don't you just shut up?
"Melts in your mouth, baby," the short one said. "You'll never be satisfied with white meat again."
"You're gonna love it. Just wait and see."

"And they just went on and on, y'know? All the way to the hotel."
Downtown again, he was telling the story to the waitress at Burger Castle whose nametag said Diane, but whom he had always known as Deedee—except for a few months two years ago, when he knew her as Wonder Woman, Main Squeeze, Hot Mama, and on one particular night (he had never told her) as simply a nameless and terrifying miracle, too good to take. He was more relived than hurt when she insisted that they go back to being just friends, although he had never figured out just how he should feel about having lost out to Jesus. He supposed that having been Deedee's last lover before she got saved should make him feel good. But he often wondered if she would not always be trying, maybe even without thinking about it, to get him saved too, to draw him into her new world. Less often, he wondered if he were secretly trying to draw her back into her old one, into his. The tension, once painful, was rarely so now; it made their conversations shimmer. She was still, pound for pound, the best woman he knew.
He sat hunched at the counter, his hands loosely cupped over his coffee to preserve its fading heat.
"Bunch of goddam silly shit, y'know?"
Deedee tilted her head at him, and he remembered.
"I'm sorry, baby. I know you don't like to hear that—"
"That's okay—"
"—but it just made me so—mad! I swear, Deedee, I just wanted to reach back there and rip that sucker's tongue out," he said, lifting his hands from his coffee, shaping them into claws.
She placed her hand atop one of his, stroked lightly.

"Can I ask you something?"
"Yeah, baby, what is it?"
"You've seen this before, right?"
"You know I have."
"And you usually don't let it get to you like this. So why now?"

He shrugged, shook his head. "I don't know, baby. It's just that, sometimes—sometimes it's like I never did see it before. Like I'm seeing it for the very first time, y'know? And it just tears me up inside, Deedee.

"I swear to God, it just tears me up."

As usual, talking with Deedee calmed him somewhat; but he still lay awake in bed until nearly five o'clock, wrestling with the memory. And when he had plummeted into a seamless concrete sleep, he wrestled still.

He's driving them to the Barclay, this Irving guy and the two sisters. Only the sisters are different somehow, exaggerated—larger breasts and buttocks, more revealing clothes, behaving even more flamboyantly. Shoving their breasts into their john's face and he going on and on about brown sugar and dark meat, and finally: my grandaddy said the best loving he ever got was from a nigger woman. And he never once did it with Granma without wishing that she was Lulabelle. And he, Devon, stops driving, but the car keeps moving, steering itself, and he dives into the back seat with a roar that comes right up from the very bottom of his gut, and the women back away as he grabs Irving by his lapels and yells YOU'RE GONNA DIE YOU'RE GONNA DIE and starts banging the guy's head against the back of the seat. Only now the rear of the car has expanded and the sisters, one on each side, are twenty or thirty feet away, in opposite corners of—yeah, a wrestling ring, and the john isn't sitting upright, he's flat on his back, and Devon is crouching over him, slamming his head against the mat in unison with his yelling DIE, DIE, DIE. But Irving isn't dying, he's just staring back real glassy-eyed, with that goofy grin of his, until he finally says, real quiet and weird, Okay girls, and Devon looks up and sees that the women, one in each corner, are lady wrestlers, now, and the tall one, who's over to his right, comes flying toward him with a banshee screech. He rolls with her impact, and they struggle, and she is STRONG, but he manages to get her on her back, straddling her, and he knows that for the very first time in his twenty-seven years he's going to hit a woman, and he wants to make it good and he summons all the energy in his body and all the rage in his soul to drive his fist into her jaw. But instead of meeting her jaw with a satisfying crack of bone, his fist goes through her jaw, through her entire head, which then simply withers, collapsing upon itself, and her body beneath him deflates as his fist plunges deep into the mat, his entire arm sinking up to the shoulder into a soft mallowy substance which is studded with what feels like tiny stones. The substance begins to contract rhythmically around his arm and the pebblelike things, which he now knows are teeth, begin grinding, sparking lightning bolts of pain. He wants to call the other sister to help, but she's disappeared. And the john, Irrviiing, comes and drops to one knee beside him and says in that same weird and quiet voice, You're no match for me, nigger. You never were and you never will be. And do you know why? And he gets back up, standing over Devon, and pats his crotch. Because you're not half the man that I am. Not half. And his crotch swells out, bulging improbably, impossibly, it keeps swelling until his fly rips open and there springs forth from the front of his pants a river, a flood, of coins, so many that they start to cover Devon, to suffocate him. And Irrviiing is laughing, laughing, laughing. And Devon, with his free hand, grabs the john by one ankle. The man staggers, raises his other foot high and comes down HARD with it, right into Devon's groin so that he jerks upright by reflex, gasping—

He jerked upright, gasping, flinging the covers aside with one hand, body taut, mouth dry, his vision filled with meaningless shapes that bounced, BOOM-boom, BOOMboom, while somewhere an alarm was going off, LOUD.

A moment later, fully conscious, he recognized his bedroom, glowing with midday sunlight; recognized the unsettled thrumming of his heart and the ringing of the telephone; realized that he did not remember the dream that had tuned him to such a high pitch; and in the same moment realized that he didn't want to.

He bounded into the living room, snatched up the handset.

"Yeah."

"Turn on your TV, right now. Channel 7."

"Deedee?" She sounded strange.

"Turn it on, Devon, quick."

"Okay, okay."

Noon news. The anchorman's voice became distinct before his image did, so there were two pairs of lips reciting as two pairs of eyes read.

"The suspect has been described as a white male, five-six to five-eight, one hundred forty pounds, with blue eyes, dark hair and glasses."

"Is that him? The guy you had last night?" Deedee asked, as the newscaster's image was replaced by a police artist's sketch. Not a perfect likeness, but—

"That's him. What happened? What'd he do?"

"They found two women this morning at the Barclay. Somebody had stripped 'em, tied 'em up, stabbed 'em a bunch of times—"

"Jesus Christ!" Devon backed away from the set, paced the room. "I knew he was weird! Didn't I tell you he was weird? Jesus! And nobody saw nothing, nobody heard nothing?"

"At the Barclay?"

"Oh, yeah—what am I sayin—"

"Besides, he cut their throats."

"Oh, man!" Devon shivered with disgust. "And to think that I was with him. I mean, he touched me, Deedee!" He remembered the hand on his shoulder: 's okay, brother. Be cool. With two syllables. He shivered again. "Oh man, oh man, oh man—"

He was beginning to remember the dream.

"Well, I don't know how much good that did," he said to Deedee as they left police headquarters, "but at least it's done."

"Well, like the man said—" she replied, and left it hanging. She was good at not forcing conversation. She had offered to drive him down to the station, and it had been a quiet ride all the way, he scowling out the window, occasionally shaking his head, while she drove.

The police had been courteous and appreciative. In the end, it seemed that he added little to what others had already reported. But he did help, they said, to corroborate some things, and that was important. They told him to contact them again if he remembered anything else about the suspect, anything at all.

"You know, I just keep running over it in my mind," he said as they were getting into her car, "Wondering if somehow I should have been able to tell. I mean, I *did* think he was weird, but I just thought he was goofy weird, not psycho weird. I mean, it just didn't occur to me that I had Norman Bates in my cab, y'know?"

"I know."

He had not told her the dream. He hated the nakedness of it; was angry that his mind was saying those things to him.

"I just wish I could do something. It's bad enough that I didn't see what was happening last night, that I didn't do anything then. But now—now those two sisters are dead, and the nut who did it is out loose somewhere, probably getting ready to do the same damn thing tonight, and I know who it is—I mean, I could spot him from a mile away, Deedee—and I still can't do a thing about it.

"Not a single solitary thing."

༄ ༄

He did do one thing, as time went by. He remembered. Remembered the glassy eyes, the high-pitched voice, the lewd intimations. Remembered so vividly on certain nights, nights of ghosts and hookers, that he ignored potential fares, choosing to cruise in solitude as he nursed the hatred that flowered darkly where once the hole had been.

He also remembered while sleeping, remembered in dreams that took him inside the Barclay to behold, impotently, such gore that he woke up vomiting.

Winter passed into spring, and during the following summer, the Barclay, its business having wilted in the glare of publicity, began to regain its obscurity and therefore its popularity—until Halloween, when pranksters suspended a pair of grotesquely painted mannequins from the window of the room where the murders had taken place. By then Devon had given up listening for the "Barclay Hotel murders" on the news. But he had not given up scanning crowds for Irving's eyes, Irving's lopsided grin.

Winter again; the anniversary. He didn't want to be alone, arranged to visit Deedee. But the evening went wrong. She didn't stroke, wouldn't listen. It's not that you can't forget, she said, it's that you don't want to forget. Why should I, he said. Because it's killing you, she said. Killing you just as much as it killed them.

She had suggested before that he try keeping a journal, an idea which he had thought useless. That night, he made his first entry:

> She thinks I want revenge for what he did to those two hookers, but there's more to it than that. I mean, I didn't even know them, and hookers aren't exactly my favorite people to begin with. No, it's not just what he did to them. It's what he did to me. He made me a part of it. He practically killed them right in front of my face. I know he was thinking about it all the time.
> *And I let him.*
> I wish I could see him again, if only for five min—no, for one minute. That's all the time I would need. God, if you're real, then please let me see him just one more time.

He was surprised by the intensity with which he felt that last line as he wrote it, by how much he meant it. Images from the Sunday School days of his childhood, of a thundering bearded deity, combined with those of aged saints stretching their souls out to God, and with the sense of smallness that had come upon him two or three times before in his life, when viewing a mountain or an ocean, to form a single coherent understanding that drew him toward itself.

He wrote again:

> O GOD, PLEASE LET ME MEET WITH HIM AGAIN.

and after a moment's consideration added:

> And please help me to be *ready*.

He read the prayer aloud, several times, before going to bed. Each time it felt more perfect. He decided to recite it upon awakening, and found that doing so triggered the sense, not quite an articulated thought, that today might be the day. He prayed it again a second night, a second morning, with a deepening of the first results.

The prayer began to enter the empty spaces of his day and to fill them with expectancy. After a week or so, it struck him that the fulfilment of the first clause might hinge upon his own fulfilment of the second clause, and the pursuit of readiness began to govern his life.

His workouts at the gym, previously a cosmetic exercise, gained a new fervor. He gave up chips and soft drinks, and began collecting his change in jars until he could find something else to do with it, something which matched his purpose.

In the spring, the Barclay changed hands, underwent renovation, changed names: Hotel Avalon. There was a brief mention on the 11 o'clock news: "The murderer was never found," He dreamt of construction workers finding corpses between floors, inside walls. He thought of calling Deedee, but thought better of it. She would try to soften him.

That summer, he enrolled in karate classes, and gave up fried foods, then meat. One day he went without eating, simply as a result of busyness, and enjoyed the consequent feeling of lightness; he began fasting, once a week, twice a week, three days a week.

He continued to pray the prayer, with the devotion of a monk; conversations which he once would have enjoyed became increasingly offensive to him as he saw that people spoke as they lived, without purpose and without judgment.

Another year had passed, and the anniversary was drawing near. He had decided to commemorate in solitude and had a reservation for that night, at the Avalon (a use for the spare change). It would be a night of recommitment, of fasting and of prayer. For forgiveness of shortcomings in his readiness. For greater discernment, greater purity, for the consummation of a meeting.

When he got home the night three days prior to the anniversary, the phone was ringing. Assuming it to be either a wrong number or an obscene call, he took his time answering.

"Hello."

"Hello, is this Mr. Devonn Jackson?" An unfamiliar voice, young man, white, talking fast.

"The name is Devon Jackson, and if you're selling something, I don't want any."

"Oh, no sir, I'm not selling anything. I'm just an intern at the University Medical Center. We have a guy here who came in on emergency last night who keeps saying he wants to talk to you."

"Who is it?"

"I don't know. He won't give us his name. He just keeps saying that he's gotta talk to Devonn Jackson."

"Wait a minute, wait a minute—how did he get checked in without giving his name?"

"He was unconscious. Some other guy checked him in, I don't know who, I wasn't here. Whoever it was didn't know him, either; he just found him on the street and brought him in."

"Whoa—are you saying this is some bum off the street?"

The voice on the other end dropped, became more intense.

"You can call him a bum if you like, Mr. Jackson. All I know is that it was nine degrees last night, not counting the wind-chill factor, and this guy was found lying unconscious on a grate by somebody who had enough heart to bring him in. I also know that the past year or so of his life has been hell—he has some fractures that were never set properly and some lacerations that were never properly treated and a bleeding ulcer that should have killed him six months ago. And right now he's about to lose at least one limb to either frostbite or gangrene, whichever comes first—if he survives at all, which, frankly, he doesn't seem inclined to do.

"Now, I don't know what the story is between the two of you, and I don't care. But I am trying to learn to save lives. And if you don't want to talk to this guy—"

"Okay, okay. I'll talk to him."

Rustling and creaking, then a raspy voice which he didn't recognize.

"Devonn. I need your forgiveness."

For what—mispronouncing my name?

The memory popped up like a jack-in-the-box: But it looks like Devonn. They spelled it wrong, okay? Oh, 'scuse me.

Holy hell.

It wasn't supposed to be this way. He was ready to spot him on the street, in an elevator—in almost any circumstance except this one. Into his stunned silence, Irving continued.

"I'm dying. I've been dying ever since it happened, but I'm really dying now. I need forgiveness. You're the only one who can give it to me. You're the only one who knows."

"Forgive me, Devonn."

Devon exploded.

"Forgive you? *Forgive* you? Man, I wish I could get to you! Man, do you know what you *did*? You're a butcher, man! A beast! You don't deserve to live, man!" Slamming his forearm against the wall. "You do not deserve to live! Do you hear me, man? Do you hear what I'm saying?"

A single long, deep, wheezing cough. Then the younger voice again, telling him what he didn't need to hear.

He didn't replace the handset; he flung the entire phone across the room. It's not fair! It's not fair!

He smashed a lamp, kicked in the television screen, swept books and papers onto the floor.

WHAT ARE YOU DOING TO ME, GOD?

Banged both fists against the wall until his energy was gone, collapsed on the couch, stared at the ceiling and wept. First for his lost opportunity; then for the man he had become.

I can't forgive. It's too late to pay him back, and I can't forgive.

He picked up the phone, slowly started to dial as he brought Deedee's number back to mind.

In Quest of "Quest" (or "How Martin Scorsese Changed Devon Jackson's Life when the Two of them Never Met, I'm Sure")

"*Q*UEST" was written as an assignment for a writing seminar taught by Eve Shelnutt at the University of Pittsburgh during the winter semester of 1987. It was my first story with a black man as the protagonist, and I began it shortly after completing my first story featuring black characters, period, centering on a 10-year-old name Freddie.

Part of my reason for not having written any recognizably black fiction before Freddie's story was that I had seriously doubted by ability to write about black people. Mind you, I had grown up black, in a black neighborhood, attending primarily black schools—but from my 50's childhood through my 60's adolescence, my literary sensibility had been shaped by Jules Verne and Edgar Allan Poe, by Hawthorne and Melville and Donne, so that as I reached adulthood, I was, as a writer, anything but black, with scarcely a notion of how to render black speech, black life.

("Mind you?" How white can you get?)

Freddie's story had turned out better than I expected, giving me the courage to attempt a more adult story in black. This desire, to do a recognizably black story, was all that I knew when I wrote the original opening line of "Quest": "I'm so tired of white folks."

That line seemed to establish well enough that the speaker was probably, if not definitely, black. But I felt a greater emotional weight attached to it than a reader would be likely to realize from the words on the page. In itself, that opening line might express anything from mild exasperation to anger to playfulness (a black person can really mess with a white person's mind by saying stuff like that). It just so happened that when I read those newly written words for the first time, they suggested to me a deep tiredness of both body and spirit, and the image of the speaker as a black cabdriver, sitting in a diner during the coldest part of a winter night, began to emerge.

Why a cabdriver? The most obvious answer is because I drove a cab myself for awhile some years ago. But I think a better answer is that of all the jobs I know about by virtue of having done them, cabdriving is most likely to produce the deep tiredness, the world-weariness, that this man was feeling.

So it was that the initial draft of this story opened, not with the encounter between Devon Jackson and his customer with the two prostitutes, but with Devon at the Burger Castle, preparing to tell the story of that encounter:

"I'm so tired of white folks."

Devon Jackson hunched at the counter of the downtown Burger Castle, his hands cupped over the hot coffee which he had not begun drinking yet, letting the chill ease its way out of his bones. He didn't need the small plastic clock with the crack in its face, perched on the pop dispenser, to let him know that it was a couple of minutes shy of 3 a.m. He would have known without the clock, without his watch, without the notation on his trip sheet that said he had dropped off his last fare at 2:51 at the Barclay Hotel. His body told him, and something inside him that wasn't his body, some kind of black hole that blossomed in his gut and was slowly but surely sucking the life out of him. It didn't come often, but when it did come, it was always around three o'clock in the morning. His eyes were tired.

I thought this opening did a pretty good job of establishing that Devon Jackson was a black male, that he drove a cab, and that he was feeling especially frustrated with white folks as the story begins.

One thing which it did not establish was Devon's age, which I first understood to be somewhere between forty and forty-five. The eventual decision to make him nearly a generation younger was based on two factors. The second factor, which I'll explain later, was a deference to Martin Scorsese. The first was the physicality of this man, for whom a world-weariness which someone else might experience intellectually was felt as a "black hole that blossomed in his gut."

This physicality brought to mind a young man I knew a few years ago, a fledgling boxer named Reese. Reese lived from one troublesome situation to another, largely (I suspected) because his sheer physical energy and appetite for physical pleasure drove him to behave in ways that his intelligence would have warned him to avoid (had he listened).

I began to model Devon after Reese, trying to invest him with the kind of action-oriented persona that made Reese as dangerous as he was interesting. Along the way, I remembered that Reese's physicality expressed itself not only in the choices he made and the ways his body moved, but in his speech; and I knew that it had to be so with Devon—that a large part of my task was to capture his voice, a voice which in itself would be an expression of physicality, of intense energy. For that reason as much as for any other, the two pages which I wrote in my first session with this story consisted, other than the paragraph about the hole, almost entirely of dialogue between Devon and Deedee.

(At the start, Devon and Deedee were not ex-lovers; I simply wanted to capture a sense of the kind of relationship which often grows between a waitress and a regular customer at a diner— casual, sympathetic, undemanding.)

Although physicality was the single characteristic of Devon's which I strove most to convey, I found that when I sat down for my second session with this story, the black hole bit made me nervous—I had no sense that that particular image would be an important part of the story as a whole (ouch!), and felt that the first full paragraph of the story ought not to be devoted to something which might turn out to be irrelevant.

Which left me with the problem of establishing physicality and mood without employing that troublesome metaphor (however much I liked it). I responded by rewriting the opening to show more of Devon's physical person, sooner:

"I'm so tired of white folks."
Devon Jackson hunched at the counter of the downtown Burger Castle, *a cigarette perched at his lips*, his hands cupped over the hot coffee which he had not begun drinking yet, letting the chill ease its way out of his *short, muscular frame*. The small plastic clock with the crack in its face, perched on the pop dispenser, read 2:57. He had dropped off his last fare at 2:51, and as far as he was concerned, that was it for the night.

That felt better, and the story began to unwind smoothly, as Devon told his tale of picking up "another white idiot with a hangup on black women." It went smoothly, that is, until I saw that in my desire to capture Devon's voice, I was employing him to tell the reader, by telling Deedee, material which deserved to be shown; that he was describing the true opening scene of the story.

I began anew, starting this time with the scene itself rather than with Devon's description of it; and the black hole returned as the primary metaphor for his mood at the time of the encounter. Since it was being so insistent, I promoted it (still not knowing how it would prove relevant), letting it have the first line all to itself: "The hole was back."

By this time I wanted to detach Devon somewhat from Reese, and gave some of my taste for Vivaldi—a detail intended simply to deliver him from stereotype or caricature.

I was not nearly so kind to Irving, who in this first appearance was much more caricature than character. In fact, he was not even Irving. He was nameless, and was too fascinated with his playmates to find out Devon's name, either. Devon's attention was also focused more strongly, and warily, on the prostitutes (in my experience, hookers were bad news for cabbies), so the interaction between the two men was minimal.

As I came back to the scene at the Burger Castle, Devon's relationship with Deedee had subtly changed under my fingers; they were not yet ex-lovers, but they were good friends beyond the confines of the diner. Which made it natural for her to call him with the news of the murders.

In my first attempt at moving into that phone conversation, I sought to capture the physical sense of being awakened by the telephone from an intense and troubling dream, without describing the dream itself:

> Talking with Deedee calmed him somewhat, as usual, but when he got in and went to bed, he still lay awake until nearly five o'clock before plummeting to a seamless concrete sleep.
> WHAT??!
> He jerked upright, gasping, flinging the covers aside with one hand, body taut, mouth dry, his vision filled with meaningless colored shapes that bounced, BOOMboom, BOOMboom, while somewhere an alarm was going off, LOUD.
> A moment later, fully conscious, he recognized his room, glowing with midday sunlight; recognized the unsettled thrumming of his heart and the ringing of the telephone in the living room; realized that he did not remember the dream that had him tuned to such a high pitch; and in the same moment realized that he didn't want to.
> He bounded into the living room, snatched up the handset.

The dream sequence then came as a flashback triggered by the news from Deedee. (Considering my original treatment of the opening scene, it seems I was unconsciously resisting a chronologically straightforward narrative. Who knows why.)

At the end of that sequence, I locked myself into a closet and banged my head against the wall in the dark.

At least that's what it felt like. I had worked rather hard to create a believable and interesting character, a character less accustomed to thought than to action. I had placed him in a situation of inherent tension—indeed, of crisis—with two major shocks to his psyche, the news of the murders and the memory of the dream. And now, suddenly, I was brought to a dead stop. I had no idea what was to happen next. Deedee was asking Devon what he was going to do. I was asking Devon what he was going to do. Devon wasn't telling.

With nothing to go on other than an intuition that Devon's course of action would be rather dark and grim, it occurred to me that if he were in his early 40's, he could well be a Vietnam veteran. Hmmm. That had possibilities.

Enter Martin Scorsese.

I had scarcely begun to explore those possibilities when I remembered Scorsese's film, "Taxi Driver," and realized, first, that any story with a cabdriving Vietnam veteran on a vendetta would seem like an imitation; and second, that in this instance, it would be a poor imitation, since I knew nothing about being a Vietnam vet. To preclude such a blunder entirely, I changed Devon's age, as given in the dream sequence, from "forty-two" to "twenty-seven"—far too young to have fought in Vietnam.

As it turned out, that miniature change brought air and light into my closet, for my dark ignorance of what should happen next had resulted from simply not knowing Devon well enough to say what he would do. Making him twenty-seven re-introduced me to him, and forced me to fresh thought concerning his entire history prior to page one.

Science-fiction and fantasy author Roger Zelazny, in his essay, "The Parts that Are Only Glimpsed," notes that "any story we tell is as much an exercise in omission as inclusion." As I developed a personal history for this younger Devon, I learned, among other things, that his relationship with Deedee was an extremely important part of his life, here only glimpsed; that Deedee's concern was not that of a casual friend, but of an ex-lover who still loves; and that she was now a Christian—a reasonable explanation of her "ex-" status, and a chance to take a stab at presenting a believable Christian in a work of fiction (as a Christian myself, this became important to me).

However, the reconstruction of Devon's history and the deepening of Deedee's character were not enough to see the story through. It seemed inevitable that Devon would meet the john again, and that inevitability hung over the narrative of his self-directed spiritual journey (I resisted the temptation to make him some sort of inner-city Zen master by remembering often that reflection and study were foreign to him). In order for that encounter to work, I knew I had to make the john more real, to apprehend his realness much more fully, than I had yet done.

So far, I have learned two ways of apprehending a character's realness. The first is to base that character on someone (or several someones) I have known, as I did with Devon (and, to a lesser extent, with Deedee). The second is to talk to the character, to empathize, to get inside his or her skin.

The second thing is what I did with the john. For starters, I went back and gave him a name, Irving, and a certain taste for Vivaldi. That gave more substance to the opening scene, and seemed like a good detail to use when he and Devon met again.

But I still needed more, and so I began to explore the effects of that night at the Barclay on Irving's life. In doing so, I discovered that this story was essentially as much his as Devon's. In the end, the dual murder itself was transformed in my mind, from a mere event injected into the plot to stimulate my protagonist, to the action of a personality. Irving became real to me, not as a psychotic, but as a man whose capacity for violence—which he shares with us all—was unleashed by the unique set of circumstances prevailing that night, extreme drunkenness being chief among them. I could not merely despise him, nor leave him merely despicable; and thus the knowledge of Irving's story finally provided the conclusion for this one.

(That conclusion, in turn, generated a bit of dialogue for the opening scene, when I decided to have Devon recognize Irving by the mispronounced

"Devonn," rather than by some reference to Vivaldi, which now seemed elaborate and forced.)

I say "finally" because for a time it seemed that this "Quest" would never end. I had been accustomed to writing a story as a description of a pre-fabricated plot. To start from word one every time I sat down, without knowing where the next new word might take me, scared me. To arrive at a satisfactory conclusion was not merely a relief, but a wonder.

But a greater wonder is to see the wholeness of the story now, built up from so many little pieces. A person might honestly think from reading it that I knew what I was doing all along.

ॡ QUESTIONS ॡ

Elwin Green's story, "Quest," and its process essay, "In Quest of 'Quest'"

1. Before the story actually begins on the page, Devon Jackson is an unhappy man. What are you invited to believe is the source of that unhappiness as the story unfolds? Are there several sources? The first time we see Devon we're told, "The hole was back." The last time, he is calling Deedee. Given all that transpired between these events, what is the significance of both, and how has Devon changed?

2. How would this story have been changed if Devon weren't black? Would there be a story? How pronounced is the theme of race in the story? What about the theme of Christianity? As a character, how does Devon interest you beyond theme? Is his response to the murders legitimate? What is the source of his rage, his vengeance?

3. In his process essay, Green writes, " . . . I had grown up black, in a black neighborhood, attending primarily black schools—but from my 50's childhood through my 60's adolescence, my literary sensibility had been shaped by Jules Verne and Edgar Allan Poe . . . so that as I reached adulthood, I was, as a writer, anything but black. . . . " In your own writing, have the subjects of your essays been more determined by your experience or your reading? If by experience, has your reading affected your writing at all? Have the essays you've read in this class affected the way you approach your writing? Doubtless you've heard that you can't be a good writer without being a good reader. Do you believe this is true, or has your experience shown otherwise?

4. Of his central character, Green writes, "And now, suddenly, I was brought to a dead stop. I had no idea what was to happen next. Deedee was asking Devon what he was going to do. I was asking Devon what he was going to do. Devon wasn't telling." What does it mean for Green to ask his character

what he is going to do? Has Green relinquished control over his story at this point? Do you ever reach a place in your essay where all you've written has determined that you must work in a particular direction, and yet that direction eluded you? How do writing and the writing process demand their own direction that you as the writer may seem to have little control over?

Possible Writing Topics

1. Underlying the story there is a perspective on the relationship between blacks and whites that is never actually pronounced. Write an essay where you discuss your perspective on this issue based on your experience; the books, stories, and essays you've read; the television programs and movies you've seen; and the opinions expressed by other people you've known. You need not mention each of these, but each has probably contributed to your perspective. To what degree have you previously thought through this issue? Can you trace the sources of your perspectives? Have many of your opinions been given to you by others? Do you question those you respect who offer their opinions on this and other issues?

   As you write this essay, keep track of the places you stop, get stuck, and then proceed. What do you do when you get stuck— leave the essay or persevere? Make notes on the ideas that occur to you when you stop, the ones you reject and the ones you use.

2. After you've completed the essay, write a second one on how you overcame the problems of the first essay, particularly those moments when you didn't know how you would proceed. How many ideas or first sentences did you reject before you settled on one? What did you do when you became stuck at some point in the writing? Did you leave the essay? If you did, was it easier to pick up where you'd left off when you returned, or more difficult? Did ideas occur to you while you were away from the essay? When and under what circumstances? When you were working, did you write a full draft in one sitting? How many sittings did it take to finish a final draft, and what decisions did you make with regard to the material you included? Did you observe the same writing habits for this essay as you had for others? What would happen if you changed those habits?

James McCommons

Michigan's "Peace Invasion"

OGOTZ was trying to thumb a ride out of Ironwood when he saw J.J. coming toward him from a corner bar wearing only blue jean cut-offs, a sleeveless jacket, a medicine bag necklace and a bandana around his head—a solitary black man in a country of white faces. Although they had never met, they recognized each other.

"Hey man, you going to the Rainbow gathering?" asked J.J. Oogotz nodded.

Three hours later, they were bouncing along in a pickup on a dusty, tree-lined road in Ottawa National Forest. J.J. told Oogotz, in a jive Cincinnati drawl, that he had been at the gathering for more than three weeks.

"I know this place like my back yard," J.J. hissed. "Each day I walk through the forest. I *scan*. I pick up rocks and see what's underneath. I look inside hollow trees. I *see* everything."

Oogotz said he was hitchhiking from California to Seattle when he was told of the gathering. From his backpack he unfolded a soiled handbill and map given to him by another hitchhiker.

He said he hopped a freight in Seattle and hung on desperately to the wheels of a piggy-back semi-trailer for two days as the train screamed 100-miles-an-hour across the prairies of Montana and North Dakota to Minneapolis.

Someone interrupted his story to say they had some pot. The contingent pulled over on the deserted road, passed a joint, and rubbed on insect repellent.

J.J. pointed to a run-down, unoccupied hunting camp back in the trees.

"See that, man? Somebody lives there." After a pause, "They'll blow you away."

No one who came to the Rainbow Family Gathering got blown away, but some people in nearby Watersmeet, Mich. kept their shotguns handy.

The "invasion," as some called it, began in late June when Watersmeet first heard that the Rainbow Family—a conglomeration of counterculture advocates, religious zealots, jugglers, musicians, garbologists, peace advocates or, as the New York Times called them, "shaggy barefoot hippies"—had chosen the abandoned 19th-century logging townsite of Interior in the Upper Peninsula for its national gathering.

They came in beat-up busses, flatbed trucks and cars painted with flowers and rainbows, but most hitchhiked to Watersmeet—a one-main-street town of 800 residents whose largest employer is the U.S. Forest Service.

The gathering was 10 miles from Watersmeet, but the Rainbows needed rides, food and a Welcoming Center, so they came to town.

Signs began appearing on telephone poles: "This way for love" and "Home."

Rainbows played Frisbee in the town square, and each night the Family sent a bus into town to round up the strays and bring them home.

The Forest Service closed off all roads to the gathering to the satisfaction of the Rainbows, who kept all vehicles nearly two miles away. This was a nature gathering. No machines allowed.

The parking lot was filled with bumper stickers: "No Nukes," "Deadheads," "Save the Planet," "Smoke Pot," "Stop Continental Drift," and "U.S. out of El Salvador." License plates read like an atlas of the country.

Past the cars, a stream of people marched along in the heat like an army of ants, burdened with backpacks, guitars and other assorted baggage.

On the day Oogotz arrived, a man and woman—both nude but wearing shoes on the sharp gravel—smiled at those who passed. "Welcome home, brother," said the woman, her long hair falling over her breasts.

Her balding companion was in his late 30s; what remnants of hair still there were long and bouncing off his shoulders. He had the look of a literature teacher from a Midwestern college. Secured to his remaining hair was a two-foot-long fern, held in place with bobby pins.

"Hey man, put a fern on your head; it really works," he said.

Fifty yards ahead were two young men, also nude, trying in vain to ward off the mosquitoes and deerflies landing on the tenderer parts of their bodies. A swarthy, bearded man, his head wrapped in a turban, passed by leading another man by a plastic chain of peace symbols. The "slave" had a subservient, fearful look in his eyes as his "master" jerked him forward like a disobedient dog.

The road wound down a hill, and a river valley opened below. Drums beat out a rhythm that became louder with each step. Welcome home, brother.

At the height of the event, which culminated on July 4 with a world peace prayer vigil, more than 5,000 had trudged or floated down the road.

By the fourth of July, the city of the Rainbow Nation had been hewn out of the forest.

The overwhelming question to the people of Watersmeet was, "What's the Rainbow Nation?"

"We are the pure white light that, like a rainbow, is made up of all colors, all creed, all religions and all races," explained one Rainbow.

Family members used only first names or pseudonyms like Badger, Bear, Feather, and Interstate Mike.

Michael John was a leader among a leaderless people. He rode a fat-tired, secondhand bicycle around the gathering and, in a soft but authoritive voice, gave suggestions to the kitchen help, the blanket traders and the shanta-sheena, the Family's peace police.

A serious man of 30 with wispy hair, a sparse beard, intense eyes and a direct stare, he publishes *The Rainbow Nation Directory or The People's Guide to the Liberation of Earth*. It lists members who provide healing services, shelter, food, good vibes, or other cosmic services.

Several nuances of belief exist within the Family, depending on whom you speak to, but most Rainbows continually refer to a general manifesto which states that the New Age of Aquarius has dawned and the Family is part of that birth.

Since its beginning, the Family has looked for signs. Of the first gathering, held near Granby, Colo., a man named Don with a long ponytail and a bead on his forehead recalled:

"The silent vigil was interrupted when people started to point and shout — a rainbow appeared over the gathering. The 30,000 had set off a vibration."

Michael John said the silent vigil for world peace, held at noon each July 4, is "to give respect to all of those who have aided the positive evolution of the earth and humankind. We are calling upon the masters to impart knowledge."

The Family has met in a remote area of national forests around the country to limit outside contact and to practice their religion of sharing and ecology.

"We come here to Michigan, the center of the continent, where our prayers will go in every direction," Don explained. "We come to feel the earth under our feet, sit around the open fire, and get away from the cities. The only way to concentrate on healing the planet is to get away from the machinery and return to Mother Earth."

All decisions concerning the Family are made by groups sitting in a circle. Anyone may speak. Agreement is not reached until there is total consensus. Circles discuss latrine construction, food distributions, and the location of the 1984 gathering — Shasta, Calif.

Feeding the 5,000 people was a main concern, since there were no loaves-and-fishes miracles.

Members of the Rainbow Nation are called twice a day to meals prepared in rustic kitchens with donated food or food purchased with funds collected by passing a "magic" hat.

In the meantime, people meandered through the encampment on the "Rainbow Highway" (a dirt path) with tin cups, plates and forks dangling from their belts.

The camp itself was spotless. All garbage was sorted and recycled by a woman named "Swamme Mommee"—the guru of garbage. She also ran an establishment where tea was boiled in converted 10-gallon cans.

A banner draped across a bridge leading over the Ontonagon River read "Welcome Home."

"Are you coming in, brother? Well, relax. You're home."

Love—sincere or not—was thick in the air, as was sharing your space, food, cigarets and anything else you had. Tolerence of each other was an unspoken absolute; any form of nonviolent behavior was acceptable.

For the past four years, Pilgrim has constructed Madam Frog's Tea Garden and World Peace Station #2 out of plastic tarps stretched over a wooden frame.

Inside, he and "Mother Nature" discussed peace with those who sat cross-legged around a "put-take" bowl.

Pilgrim, a 40-year-old former humanistic psychologist, left a wife, children, and a big house in the San Francisco suburbs to bring peace to the world.

"The bowl is like life. You have to put something into it before you can take something out." he explained.

Its contents included joints, cigarets, razor blades, replacement parts for a backpack, and a map of British Palestine ripped from an encyclopedia.

On July 4 and other days during the gathering, Pilgrim went on "word fasts" and spoke only in sign language. But most days, he talked incessantly about peace to the crowd at Madam Frog's.

"I come to the gathering to touch base with those few who are working more than just intellectually for peace," he preached. "Here, I find those relationships that I could never find on the outside. Here it's quickened."

Pilgrim wasn't always thrilled by being among the Rainbow Family. He did not consider himself a "Rainbow."

"Many of these people here are like children, looking for love, for someone to tell them where their place in the world is," he scoffed. "They come here to have the group do for them what they haven't been able to do themselves. Who knows? It may heal them. Perhaps the music, the woods, the psychedelics, taken in the proper therapeutic environment, will give them insights."

Others were at the gathering for less profound purposes.

John, walking around naked, came from Washington, D.C.

"I did some Owsely acid in Berkely in 1965; that really opened my eyes. This is a chance to be free again. It's part of my lifestyle," he explained.

Two things everyone agreed on about the Rainbows: They were weird, but they were friendly. Watersmeet resigned itself to their temporary presence, since the Family brought a booming business to a town hard hit by an ailing tourist season.

Nordine's Grocery Store sold beansprouts and took in more food stamps in a week than it usually does in a year.

Clem's Cafe, which normally caters to canoeists and fishermen coming off the Sylvania Tract wilderness, filled its tables with wet Rainbows one night during a rain and wind storm.

While waitresses rushed to take orders, a table in the corner did the *Ommm* chant; others took turns using the phone to reverse long distance calls as the chants reverberated through the restaurant. The locals didn't bother to look up, but two khaki-clad fishermen hurriedly finished their sandwiches, glancing furtively behind them.

George Peterson, township supervisor and owner of the Standard gas station and grocery store, had as much contact with the Rainbows as anyone.

More than once they ate him out of Snickers bars, which George had been advised to stock up on by the shanta-sheena. "They sure like them Snickers bars," he said.

When the first Rainbow contingent arrived, George received calls from residents demanding to know what he was going to do about the "hippies" urinating behind the big tree in the town park.

A few days later Peterson, with a Detroit Tigers cap on his head, was obviously enjoying himself as he rushed to pump gas into the vans and buses lined up at his pumps.

"I know a lot of them by name now. They ride by yelling, 'Hey George, when you going to come out and see us?'"

He told of one woman who came to the station barefoot in a flowing skirt, with a baby in a sling about her neck. She wanted a used tire for her car, which had broken down a few miles away on US-2.

"I only have $1.70," she said as they looked over tires in the parts graveyard behind the station.

"Well, that's exactly what these tires cost," said Peterson.

Inside the station, George's family decorated his jeep for the town's Fourth of July parade. On the hood, they fashioned a crude dove grasping a live branch. In red, white, and blue tissue paper on the window was the slogan: "America wants world peace."

"Some of these people are just the nicest people to talk to, and you just have to agree with what they are saying about peace and taking care of the earth," Peterson said.

Although Peterson never made it to the gathering, a lot of other locals did.

Farmers with cowboy boots and soiled John Deere hats and retirees wearing doubleknit pants, carrying lawn chairs and steel thermoses full of Kool-

Aid, threaded their way through the crowd. Everyone was welcomed home and hugged.

State Police Post Commander Peter J. Buda, whose officers were hugged by a naked man when they first toured the site, said the gathering had been less trouble than a high school keg party.

"There were no B&E's, no rapes, no murders, no anything," he said, sitting under a map of the county and spitting tobacco juice into a plastic cup. "It's been surprising."

Watersmeet Chief of Police Jeff Zylinski didn't like the idea of hippies traipsing through his town.

"They're like a mosquito biting you on the ass. By the time you know about it, it's too late. They've already bitten you on the ass," he said.

Zylinski and the state police, whose token presence was hardly enough to deter any violence had it occurred, relegated their patrols to cruising the forest roads.

Two or three dusty police cars were parked in front of the post daily. When Buda was asked what precautions had been taken for July 4, he declined to comment, saying only "We don't want to show our strength."

The attitude was more aptly expressed by another state police officer. "What goes on out at the gathering is the Rainbow Family's business," he said. "Look, we don't want to load up our jails with these people. Then we got to get them lawyers and feed them. This is already costing money. We just want them to get the hell out of here."

Buda said his officers had seen little evidence of drugs in town, but at gatherings, drugs were everywhere.

A spacey, nude girl carrying only a small leather sack about her neck asked, "When was the last time you tripped? Would you like to trip in 1983 at the Rainbow Gathering?"

In Coyote Kitchen, the long-haired, bearded men manning the stoves solicited dollar bills to stuff in a jar: "It's not for food, man; it's for drugs."

Nightly LSD, peyote and or mushroom ceremonies were held in the basement of Madam Frog's. A trench had been dug for an east entrance to let the rising sun's light enter. Many spoke of hallucinating as a religious experience, but for most, it was simply a way to get high.

There was talk of manipulation of stoned Rainbows. The Forest Service reported that people tripping on acid were used as slaves to dig latrines.

Pot was the favorite drug and easily obtained through bartering, especially with camping items such as plastic tarps, canteens and insect repellent — what the locals called "bug dope."

Alcohol was forbidden inside the camp. But in the parking lot, winos from Chicago and New York hung out in knots with bottles sticking out of their hip pockets.

Alcohol makes people violent; the Rainbows were nonviolent. The perception is that you're not as likely to get rowdy if you're just plain stoned.

Fourth of July morning dawned overcast. In Watersmeet, the annual parade went on as usual with a float of a six-foot-tall Woodsy Owl, the high school band, and George Peterson's peace jeep.

A motorcyclist on his way to the gathering ended up being the first vehicle down the street after the parade. Dressed in a tie-dyed shirt and pants, with mirrored sunglasses and a World War II helmut, the cyclist moved down mainstreet between onlookers.

"And the winner!" yelled out a townie.

The celebration at the gathering was profoundly different. The silent vigil began at noon. While not everyone joined in, more than 3,000 sat on a grassy hillside in meditative poses or reached their hands up to the sky in prayers.

After an hour, a parade of children, their faces brightly painted, marched into the circle followed by jugglers and musicians singing, "Love, love, love is beautiful."

In a matter of minutes, the entire crowd was on its feet. Runners took turns carrying through the crowd a modified United States flag, its red and white stripes replaced with rainbow colors.

Bob Burton, information officer from the Ottawa National Forest Supervisor's Office, stood out in his drab, green uniform as he took photographs.

A woman wearing only a skirt, her face painted with a crescent moon and her breast adorned with a rainbow, asked Burton, "Isn't it wonderful how we're all here to care for the planet?" Burton assured her that it was.

"It's strange, but you get used to the nudity and all," he said, waving his hand at the scene.

"But I just don't think this is going to bring peace or heal the earth. When we heard they were coming, I thought this would be something substantial, but it's really superficial."

"But on the other side of the coin, it's amazing they were able to feed all these people, keep the place clean, the water pure, and not kill one another. It's an unusual type of gathering, that's for sure."

Burton took a few more pictures to send on to the Shasta National Forest next year as part of the Rainbow Family's traveling file.

Late that afternoon the rains fell, and many people who came for the weekend trudged the road back to the parking lot.

At the gathering's east entrance, Forest Service officers sat inside their truck out of the downpour as they counted Rainbows and manned the roadblocks.

The cardboard sign wired to the stop sign sagged in the dampness. "Road Closed," it read. "Rainbows Ahead."

Sources for "Michigan's 'Peace Invasion'"

I sat crosslegged on the dirt floor of Madam Frog's Tea Garden watching Pilgrim fingerpaint pictures of whales on the clear plastic walls.

Outside, campfires illuminated the crowns of the surrounding hills. Coyotes yipped and howled in a nearby swamp. Shouts of "I love you" occasionally relayed through the camp.

I put my notebook back into my pack and accepted a cup of tea from a woman named "Mother Nature." Pilgrim was on a "wordfast." I wasn't going to get a quote from a man who would not speak.

So went my first night with the Rainbow Family.

Three months before, I'd heard a rumor that "scouts" from a group called the Rainbow Family were searching the national forest for a place to hold their gathering.

I was a reporter for the Daily Press in Escanaba, Mich. The Hiawatha Forest was my beat, and a potential convention would be good news for the depressed tourist economy.

But after a visit with the communications officer at forest service headquarters, I knew this gathering was not what local businesses had in mind.

A few days later, I saw a man on a street corner playing an accordion. Colorfully dressed, he resembled a gypsy or a pirate. Passing senior citizens threw change into a hat. Since Escanaba didn't have street musicians, I surmised that this was a "scout."

"Gypsy Michael" played all afternoon for gas money to get back to his farm-commune in southern Michigan. But before he left, we spent an hour in a local park discussing the Rainbow Family. He said that he'd been partly responsible for bringing the gathering to the Upper Peninsula, what he called the "heart of the continent."

Later that day, I telephoned a forest ranger in Idaho who'd been the forest service liaison to the Rainbows at the previous year's gathering. He characterized the gathering as an "invasion of hippies" and gave me plenty of good anecdotes.

Using these sources, I wrote my first and only Rainbow story for the Daily Press. My interest was piqued. Five thousand hippies descending on an Upper Peninsula village made a compelling image.

To my chagrin, the Rainbows chose a site 156 miles away, far outside the Daily Press' readership area. The editor decided we wouldn't cover it. I decided to "string" the story to another publication. Although I'd never freelanced before, I was convinced that I had a jump on a good story.

I called the major wire services and a few metropolitan dailies that print Upper Peninsula news. The Milwaukee Journal and United Press International (UPI) were enthusiastic.

A week before the gathering's official start, I drove to Watersmeet where about 500 Rainbows already had assembled. I spoke with local citizens and the police chief who was plainly disgusted with "all these freaks." I located the town supervisor at his service station. While I sat on a stack of tires and took notes, he finished a brake job on a pickup truck.

I needed directions to the site several miles from town. The Rainbow "Welcoming Center," staffed by people named Feather, G-Man, and Om, was a table set up in the town square. There, I met J.J. and Oogotz. Our experience of getting lost in the woods became the opening of the magazine piece.

The following days I lived in the Rainbow camp, wandering about by day, writing notes in my tent at night. One evening Gypsy Michael and I toured the campsite, riding tandem on a white horse that had a Unicorn horn attached to its head.

My first stories to the Journal and UPI showed a citizenry ambivalent to the "hippies" streaming into their village from across North America and Europe. But by the July Fourth weekend, Watersmeet residents either loathed the Rainbows or were enjoying the spectacle.

I shuttled between the campsite, where I tracked down and interviewed the Rainbow's leaders, and town, where I spoke with citizens and law enforcement authorities.

Sitting in the town square, I'd organize my notes and write the story in longhand. There was no time for revision; sometimes I had just half-an-hour to write. I called the stories in from a phone booth. The deadline pressure was intense. But it was worth it to read my stories in the next day's paper.

The news stories, like the later magazine piece, were filled with my own observations. Confusing and bizarre, the Rainbow gathering couldn't be summed up by quotes from participants or onlookers. It needed a reporter's eye for selected detail. Specific and well-placed description enriches a news story. Reporters too often purge their observations from their stories in a quest for objectivity.

Some days it was difficult to find a lead, or a news hook, that epitomized each day's occurrences. That wasn't true on the Fourth of July, however. Watersmeet held its annual parade, complete with patriotic music and prancing horses, while in the woods, the Rainbows prayed in silence and danced naked to tom-tom drums. The contrast was striking.

A few weeks later, back in Escanaba, I spread the wire and newspaper clippings on the kitchen table. Notes and scribblings filled two notebooks. A photographer friend and I had taken scores of pictures.

After looking over all the material, I decided to write a magazine article. There is a profound difference between newspaper and magazine journalism. With a magazine-length piece, I could interpret and analyze the gathering in a way that had been impossible in the newspaper stories. I could ignore the restraints of space and objectivity.

The writing had to mimic the sheer craziness of the Rainbow Gathering. Told in a straightforward journalistic fashion, the piece probably would have failed. I wanted to get across my own amusement; to write a tongue-in-cheek portrait of these flower children of the 80s. But I didn't want to poke fun or ridicule the Rainbows.

I admired the sharing, organization, and resourcefulness that fed 5,000 people for a week. And I'd met several intelligent people who were earnest about their pursuit of world peace. But so many others were shallow and self-righteous, content to spout tired bromides about peace, love, and understanding.

My aim was to craft a fair and accurate article that gave the color and flavor of the gathering.

I let the Rainbow leaders explain themselves in their own words. Also, I quoted the state police commander, who begrudgingly gave respect to the group's nonviolent behavior.

My encounter with J.J. and Oogotz provided a natural opening for the piece. J.J.'s apprehension about the local people illustrated the clash of cultures and lifestyles. Oogotz's journey from the West Coast epitomized the distances the Rainbows were traveling. I reconstructed J.J. and Oogotz's first meeting from their conversations with me.

I wrote about two hours an evening for about three weeks. There was so much material that the hardest part was deciding what to leave out.

Although the Detroit News covered the gathering, I decided to send the article to "Michigan Magazine," the News' Sunday supplement.

I received a swift response. The editor said she loved the story and paid me $500.

Three months later, she bought a profile piece from me, and then assigned me another article based on my previous work. She has since moved to another publication, but I continue to do work for her. Also, she's a reference on my resume.

The Rainbow piece became an extremely important clip in my portfolio. Along with later freelance pieces, it helped me jump from a small-town daily to the city beat at the Times-Union, a metropolitan daily in Rochester, N.Y.

In 1986, when the Rainbows gathered in a national forest in Pennsylvania, my editors at the Times-Union urged me to cover it.

Watersmeet had been replaced by Tidoute, Pa., and the hardwood forest was distinctly different from the Michigan pine woods. But there was another long hike down a muddy trail that ended at the main campfire in "Boggie Meadow."

It wasn't until the second day that I found what I was looking for. Back on a hill was a rustic geodesic dome of bent sticks and plastic: Madam Frog's Tea Garden.

I went inside. There sat Pilgrim behind the put–take bowl, but this time he was talking incessantly about peace.

I took out my notebook . . .

☙ QUESTIONS ☙

James McCommons' essay, "Michigan's 'Peace Invasion,'" and its process essay, "Sources for 'Michigan's 'Peace Invasion'"

1. After you completed the essay, what was your response to "the Rainbows"? Were you sympathetic towards them? Would you, like some of the townspeople, have felt threatened by them and their beliefs? Did you take their cause seriously? Did you laugh at them? What led to this reaction?

2. McCommons never appears in the essay as a person making the observations he records. How does he communicate his perspective? Do you find his perspective an objective one? Do you feel that he is attempting to elicit a certain kind of response from his readers? Suppose someone who was more sympathetic—or completely unsympathetic—to the Rainbows' cause had written the article. What details might that person have selected in order to offer a different perspective, and how might they have been presented?

3. In his process essay, McCommons discusses at some length the research he conducted in order to get background information on the Rainbows for the newspaper articles he wrote. As you read the first essay, did you ever stop and think, "Hey, he must have had to do a lot of leg work for this essay." What may have happened to McCommons' essay had he not done this advance work? In any piece of writing, should you as a reader be able to stop and appreciate all the work that went into it? Or does that undermine the purpose of reading? To what degree do you research writing projects you undertake, particularly those that aren't based on past experience or previous knowledge?

4. Of his essay, which in each of its forms was printed in a newspaper, McCommons writes, "It needed a reporter's eye for selected detail. Specific and well-placed description enriches a news story. Reporters too often purge their observations from their stories in a quest for objectivity." Of what importance is objectivity in writing, and to what degree can it be achieved? Obviously, in a personal essay, a writer need not be objective. But even then if the essay is emotionally overloaded with subjective detail, do you find it more difficult to

trust the writer's observations? Are the details recorded in a research report or a science project objective? What about newspaper and magazine articles? Finally, can the relative objectivity of a piece of writing be determined?

∽ Possible Writing Topics ∾

1. Write an essay where you go out into a community or an area of a city, or meet with a small group of people whom you regard as interesting, and write an essay on your experience with them. For the essay, you will probably have to interview these people, record their reactions to the questions you ask them, observe the way they interact with each other, and try to determine what makes them slightly different from other communities or groups of people. In the essay, try to stay out of the first person, as McCommons did, and allow your observations and your documentation of dialogue to shape the essay, to give it voice and direction.

2. After you've completed the essay, write a second one on what level of objectivity you retained while writing the first. Did you bring certain prejudices to your subject before you researched it? What were they? Did the prejudices change or disappear as you worked? Was it an effort to get past them? Are they apparent in any of the drafts of your essay? Did you choose a subject with which you were already quite familiar? How did this affect your perception of your material and the objectivity with which you recorded it? On what basis did you make the decisions on the material to include? How would you describe the voice of your essay? Is the essay finally informative, funny, serious, dramatic, all of these?

VI

LANGUAGE AS THE SHAPER OF IDENTITY

Barbara Mellix

From Outside, In[1]

TWO years ago, when I started writing this paper, trying to bring order out of chaos, my ten-year-old daughter was suffering from an acute attack of boredom. She drifted in and out of the room complaining that she had nothing to do, no one to "be with" because none of her friends were at home. Patiently I explained that I was working on something special and needed peace and quiet, and I suggested that she paint, read, or work with her computer. None of these interested her. Finally, she pulled up a chair to my desk and watched me, now and then heaving long, loud sighs. After two or three minutes (nine or ten sighs), I lost my patience. "Looka here, Allie," I said, "you too old for this kinda carryin' on. I done told you this is important. You wronger than dirt to be in here haggin' me like this and you know it. Now git on outta here and leave me off before I put my foot all the way down."

I was at home, alone with my family, and my daughter understood that this way of speaking was appropriate in that context. She knew, as a matter of fact, that it was almost inevitable; when I get angry at home, I speak some of my finest, most cherished black English. Had I been speaking to my daughter in this manner in certain other environments, she would have been shocked and probably worried that I had taken leave of my sense of propriety.

---

[1] Originally published in *The Georgia Review*, University of Georgia, 1988.

Like my children, I grew up speaking what I considered two distinctly different languages—black English and standard English (or as I thought of them then, the ordinary everyday speech of "country" coloreds and "proper" English)—and in the process of acquiring these languages, I developed an understanding of when, where, and how to use them. But unlike my children, I grew up in a world that was primarily black. My friends, neighbors, minister, teachers—almost everybody I associated with every day—were black. And we spoke to one another in our own special language: *That sho is a pretty dress you got on. If she don' soon leave me off I'm gon tell her head a mess. I was so mad I could'a pissed a blue nail. He all the time trying to low-rate somebody. Ain't that just about the nastiest thing you ever set ears on?*

Then there were the "others," the "proper" blacks, transplanted relatives and one-time friends who came home from the city for weddings, funerals, and vacations. And the whites. To these we spoke standard English. "Ain't?" my mother would yell at me when I used the term in the presence of "others." "You *know* better than that." And I would hang my head in shame and say the "proper" word.

I remember one summer sitting in my grandmother's house in Greeleyville, South Carolina, when it was full of the chatter of city relatives who were home on vacation. My parents sat quietly, only now and then volunteering a comment or answering a question. My mother's face took on a strained expression when she spoke. I could see that she was being careful to say just the right words in just the right way. Her voice sounded thick, muffled. And when she finished speaking, she would lapse into silence, her proper smile on her face. My father was more articulate, more aggressive. He spoke quickly, his words sharp and clear. But he held his proud head higher, a signal that he, too, was uncomfortable. My sisters and brothers and I stared at our aunts, uncles, and cousins, speaking only when prompted. Even then, we hesitated, formed our sentences in our minds, then spoke softly, shyly.

My parents looked small and anxious during those occasions, and I waited impatiently for our leave-taking when we would mock our relatives the moment we were out of their hearing. "Reeely," we would say to one another, flexing our wrists and rolling our eyes. "how dooo you stan' this heat? Chile, it just too hy*ooo*-mid for words." Our relatives had made us feel "country," and this was our way of regaining pride in ourselves while getting a little revenge in the bargain. The words bubbled in our throats and rolled across our tongues, a balming.

As a child I felt this same doubleness in uptown Greeleyville where the whites lives. "Ain't that a pretty dress you're wearing!" Toby, the town policeman, said to me one day when I was fifteen. "Thank you very much," I replied, my voice barely audible in my own ears. The words felt wrong in my mouth, rigid, foreign. It was not that I had never spoken that phrase before—it was common in black English, too—but I was extremely conscious that this was an occasion for proper English. I had taken out my English and put it on as I did my church clothes, and I felt as if I were wearing my Sunday best in the middle of the week. It did not matter that Toby had not spoken grammatically correct English. He was white and could speak as he wished. I had something to prove. Toby did not.

Speaking standard English to whites was our way of demonstrating that we knew their language and could use it. Speaking it to standard-English-speaking blacks was our way of showing them that we, as well as they, could "put on airs." But when we spoke standard English, we acknowledged (to ourselves and to others—but primarily to ourselves) that our customary way of speaking was inferior. We felt foolish, embarrassed, somehow diminished because we were ashamed to be our real selves. We were reserved, shy in the presence of those who owned and/or spoke *the* language.

My parents never set aside time to drill us in standard English. Their forms of instruction were less formal. When my father was feeling particularly expansive, he would regale us with tales of his exploits in the outside world. In almost flawless English, complete with dialogue and flavored with gestures and embellishment, he told us about his attempt to get a haircut at a white barbershop; his refusal to acknowledge one of the town merchants until the man addressed him as "Mister"; the time he refused to step off the sidewalk uptown to let some whites pass; his airplane trip to New York City (to visit a sick relative) during which the stewardesses and porters—recognizing that he was a "gentleman"—addressed him as "Sir." I did not realize then—nor, I think, did my father—that he was teaching us, among other things, standard English and the relationship between language and power.

My mother's approach was different. Often, when one of us said, "I'm gon wash off my feet," she would say, "And what will you walk on if you wash them off?" Everyone would laugh at the victim of my mother's "proper" mood. But it was different when one of us children was in a proper mood. "You think you are so superior," I said to my oldest sister one day when we were arguing and she was winning. "Superior!" my sister mocked. "You mean I'm acting 'biggidy'?" My sisters and brothers sniggered, then joined in teasing me. Finally, my mother said, "Leave your sister alone. There's nothing wrong with using proper English." There was a half-smile on her face. I had gotten "uppity," had "put on airs" for no good reason. I was at home, alone with the family, and I hadn't been prompted by one of my mother's proper moods. But there was also a proud light in my mother's eyes; her children were learning English very well.

Not until years later, as a college student, did I begin to understand our ambivalence toward English, our scorn of it, our need to master it, to own and be owned by it—an ambivalence that extended to the public-school classroom. In our school, where there were no whites, my teachers taught standard English but used black English to do it. When my grammar-school teachers wanted us to write, for example, they usually said something like, "I want y'all to write five sentences that make a statement. Anybody git done before the rest can color." It was probably almost those exact words that led me to write these sentences in 1953 when I was in the second grade:

> The white clouds are pretty.
> There are only 15 people in our room.
> We will go to gym.
> We have a new poster.
> We may go out doors.

Second grade came after "Little First" and "Big First," so by then I knew the implied rules that accompanied all writing assignments. Writing was an occasion for proper English. I was not to write in the way we spoke to one another: The white clouds pretty; There ain't but 15 people in our room; We going to gym; We got a new poster; We can go out in the yard. Rather I was to use the language of "other": clouds *are*, there *are*, we *will*, we *have*, we *may*.

My sentences were short, rigid, perfunctory, like the letters my mother wrote to relatives:

> Dear Papa,
> How are you? How is Mattie? Fine I hope. We are fine. We will come to see you Sunday. Cousin Ned will give us a ride.
> > Love,
> > Daughter

The language was not ours. It was something from outside us, something we used for special occasions.

But my coloring on the other side of that second-grade paper is different. I drew three hearts and a sun. The sun has a smiling face that radiates and envelops everything it touches. And although the sun and its world are enclosed in a circle, the colors I used—red, blue, green, purple, orange, yellow, black—indicate that I was less restricted with drawing and coloring than I was with writing standard English. My valentines were not just red. My sun was not just a yellow ball in the sky.

By the time I reached the twelfth grade, speaking and writing standard English had taken on new importance. Each year, about half of the newly graduated seniors of our school moved to large cities—particularly in the North—to live with relatives and find work. Our English teacher constantly corrected our grammar: "Not 'ain't,' but 'isn't.'" We seldom wrote papers, and even those few were usually plot summaries of short stories. When our teacher returned the papers, she usually lectured on the importance of using standard English: "I *am*, you *are*, he, she, or it *is*," she would say, writing on the chalkboard as she spoke. "How you gon git a job talking about 'I is,' or 'I isn't' or 'I ain't?'"

In Pittsburgh, where I moved after graduation, I watched my aunt and uncle—who had always spoken standard English when in Greeleyville—switch from black English to standard English to a mixture of the two, according to where they were or who they were with. At home and with certain close relatives, friends, and neighbors, they spoke black English. With those less close, they spoke a mixture. In public and with strangers, they generally spoke standard English.

In time, I learned to speak standard English with ease and to switch smoothly from black to standard or a mixture, and back again. But no matter where I was, no matter what the situation or occasion, I continued to write as I had in school:

> Dear Mommie,
> How are you? How is everybody else? Fine I hope. I am fine. So are Aunt and Uncle. Tell everyone I said hello. I will write again soon.
> Love,
> Barbara

At work, at a health insurance company, I learned to write letters to customers. I studied form letters and letters written by co-workers, memorizing the phrases and the ways in which they were used. I dictated:

> Thank you for your letter of January 5. We have made the changes in your coverage you requested. Your new premium will be $150 every three months. We are pleased to have been of service to you.

In a sense, I was proud of the letters I wrote for the company: they were proof of my ability to survive in the city, the outside world—an indication of my growing mastery of English. But they also indicate that writing was still mechanical for me, something that didn't require much thought.

Reading also became a more significant part of my life during those early years in Pittsburgh. I had always liked reading, but now I devoted more and more of my spare time to it. I read romances, mysteries, popular novels. Looking back, I realize that the books I liked best were simple, unambiguous: good versus bad and right versus wrong with right rewarded and wrong punished, mysteries unraveled and all set right in the end. It was how I remembered life in Greeleyville.

Of course I was romanticizing. Life in Greeleyville had not been so very uncomplicated. Back there I had been—first as a child, then as a young woman with limited experience in the outside world—living in a relatively closed-in society. But there were implicit and explicit principles that guided our way of life and shaped our relationships with one another and the people outside— principles that a newcomer would find elusive and baffling. In Pittsburgh, I had matured, become more experienced: I had worked at three different jobs, associated with a wider range of people, married, had children. This new environment with different prescripts for living required that I speak standard English much of the time, and slowly, imperceptibly, I had ceased seeing a sharp distinction between myself and "others." Reading romances and mysteries, characterized by dichotomy, was a way of shying away from change, from the person I was becoming.

But that other part of me—that part which took great pride in my ability to hold a job writing business letters—was increasingly drawn to the new developments in my life and the attending possibilities, opportunities for even greater change. If I could write letters for a nationally known business, could I not also do something better, more challenging, more important? Could I not, perhaps, go to college and become a school teacher? For years, afraid and a little embarrassed, I did no more than imagine this different me, this possible me. But sixteen years after coming north, when my youngest daughter entered kindergarten, I found myself unable—or unwilling—to resist the lure of possibility. I enrolled in my first college course: Basic Writing, at the University of Pittsburgh.

For the first time in my life, I was required to write extensively about myself. Using the most formal English at my command, I wrote these sentences near the beginning of the term:

> One of my duties as a homemaker is simply picking up after others. A day seldom passes that I don't search for a mislaid toy, book, or gym shoe, etc. I change the Ty-D-Bol, fight "ring around the collar," and keep our laundry smelling "April fresh." Occasionally, I settle arguments between my children and suggest things to do when they're bored. Taking telephone messages for my oldest daughter is my newest (and sometimes most aggravating) chore. Hanging the toilet paper roll is my most insignificant.

My concern was to use "appropriate" language, to sound as if I belonged in a college classroom. But I felt separate from the language—as if it did not and could not belong to me. I couldn't think and feel genuinely in that language, couldn't make it express what I thought and felt about being a housewife. A part of me resented, among other things, being judged by such things as the appearance of my family's laundry and toilet bowl, but in that language I could only imagine and write about a conventional housewife.

For the most part, the remainder of the term was a period of adjustment, a time of trying to find my bearings as a student in a college composition class, to learn to shut out my black English whenever I composed, and to prevent it from creeping into my formulations; a time for trying to grasp the language of the classroom and reproduce it in my prose; for trying to talk about myself in that language, reach others through it. Each experience of writing was like standing naked and revealing my imperfection, my "otherness." And each new assignment was another chance to make myself over in language, reshape myself, make myself "better" in my rapidly changing image of a student in a college composition class.

But writing became increasingly unmanageable as the term progressed, and by the end of the semester, my sentences sounded like this:

> My excitement was soon dampened, however, by what seemed like a small voice in the back of my head saying that I should be careful with my long awaited opportunity. I felt frustrated and this seemed to make it difficult to concentrate.

There is a poverty of language in these sentences. By this point, I knew that the clichéd language of my Housewife essay was unacceptable, and I generally recognized trite expressions. At the same time, I hadn't yet mastered the language of the classroom, hadn't yet come to see it as belonging to me. Most notable is the lifelessness of the prose, the apparent absence of a person behind the words. I wanted those sentences—and the rest of the essay—to convey the anguish of yearning to, at once, become something more and yet remain the same. I had the sensation of being split in two, part of me going into a future the other part didn't believe possible. As that person, the student writer at that moment, I was essentially mute. I could not—in the process of composing—use the language of the old me, yet I couldn't imagine myself in the language of "others."

I found this particularly discouraging because at midsemester I had been writing in a much different way. Note the language of this introduction to an essay I had written then, near the middle of the term:

> Pain is a constant companion to the people in "Footwork." Their jobs are physically damaging. Employers are insensitive to their feelings and in many cases add to their problems. The general public wounds them further by treating them with disgrace because of what they do for a living. Although the workers are as diverse as they are similar, there is a definite link between them. They suffer a great deal of abuse.

The voice here is stronger, more confident, appropriating terms like "physically damaging," "wounds them further," "insensitive," "diverse"—terms I couldn't have imagined using when writing about my own experience—and shaping them into sentences like "Although the workers are as diverse as they are similar, there is a definite link between them." And there is the sense of a personality behind the prose, someone who sympathizes with the workers: "The general public wounds them further by treating them with disgrace because of what they do for a living."

What caused these differences? I was, I believed, explaining other people's thoughts and feelings, and I was free to move about in the language of "others" so long as I was speaking *of* others. I was unaware that I was transforming into my best classroom language my own thoughts and feelings about people whose experiences and ways of speaking were in many ways similar to mine.

The following year, unable to turn back or to let go of what had become something of an obsession with language (and hoping to catch and hold the sense of control that had eluded me in Basic Writing), I enrolled in a research writing course. I spent most of the term learning how to prepare for and write a research paper. I chose sex education as my subject and spent hours in libraries, searching for information, reading, taking notes. Then (not without messiness and often-demoralizing frustration) I organized my information into categories, wrote a thesis statement, and composed my paper—a series of paraphrases and quotations spaced between carefully constructed transitions. The process and results felt artificial, but as I would later come to realize I was passing through a necessary stage. My sentences sounded like this:

> This reserve becomes understandable with examination of who the abusers are. In an overwhelming number of cases, they are people the victims know and trust. Family members, relatives, neighbors and close family friends commit seventy-five percent of all reported sex crimes against children, and parents, parent substitutes and relatives are the offenders in thirty to eighty percent of all reported cases. While assault by strangers does occur, it is less common, and is usually a single episode. But abuse by family members, relatives and acquaintances may continue for an extended period of time. In cases of incest, for example, children are abused repeatedly for an average of eight years. In such cases, "the use of physical force is rarely necessary because of the child's trusting, dependent relationship with the offender. The child's cooperation is often facilitated by the adult's position of dominance, an offer of material goods, a threat of physical violence, or a misrepresentation of moral standards.

The completed paper gave me a sense of profound satisfaction, and I read it often after my professor returned it. I know now that what I was pleased with was the language I used and the professional voice it helped me maintain. "Use better words," my teacher had snapped at me one day after reading the notes I'd begun accumulating from my research, and slowly I began taking on the language of my sources. In my next set of notes, I used the word "vacillating"; my professor applauded. And by the time I composed the final draft, I felt at ease with terms like "overwhelming number of cases," "single episode," and "reserve," and I shaped them into sentences similar to those of my "expert" sources.

If I were writing the paper today, I would of course do some things differently. Rather than open with an anecdote—as my teacher suggested—I would begin simply with a quotation that caught my interest as I was researching my paper (and which I scribbled, without its source, in the margin of my notebook): "Truth does not do so much good in the world as the semblance of truth does evil." The quotation felt right because it captured what was for me the central idea of my essay—an idea that emerged gradually during the making of my paper—and expressed it in a way I would like to have said it. The anecdote, a hypothetical situation I invented to conform to the information in the paper, felt forced and insincere because it represented—to a great degree—my teacher's understanding of the essay, *her* idea of what in it was most significant. Improving upon my previous experiences with writing, I was beginning to think and feel in the language I used, to find my own voices in it, to sense that how one speaks influences how one means. But I was not yet secure enough, comfortable enough with the language to trust my intuition.

Now that I know that to seek knowledge, freedom, and autonomy means always to be in the concentrated process of becoming— always to be venturing into new territory, feeling one's way at first, then getting one's balance, negotiating, accommodating, discovering one's self in ways that previously defined "others"—I sometimes get tired. And I ask myself why I keep on participating in this highbrow form of violence, this slamming against perplexity. But there is no real futility in the question, no hint of that part of the old me who stood outside standard English, hugging to herself a disabling mistrust of a language she thought could not represent a person with her history and experience. Rather, the question represents a person who feels the consequence of her education, the weight of her possibilities as a teacher and writer and human being, a voice in society. And I would not change that person, would not give back the good burden that accompanies my growing expertise, my increasing power to shape myself in language and share that self with "others."

"To speak," says Frantz Fanon, "means to be in a position to use a certain syntax, to grasp the morphology of this or that language, but it means above all to assume a culture, to support the weight of a civilization."* To write means to do the same, but in a more profound sense. However, Fanon also says that to achieve mastery means to "get" in a position of power, to "grasp," to "assume." This, I have learned—both as a student and subsequently as a teacher—can involve tremendous emotional and psychological conflict for those attempting to master academic discourse. Although as a beginning student writer I had a fairly good grasp of ordinary spoken English and was proficient at what Labov calls "code-switching" (and what John Baugh in *Black Street Speech* terms "style shifting"), when I came face to face with the demands of academic writing, I grew increasingly self-conscious, constantly aware of my status as a black and a speaker of one of the many black English vernaculars—a traditional outsider. For the first time, I experienced my sense of doubleness as something menacing, a built-in enemy. Whenever I turned inward for salvation, the balm so available during my childhood, I found instead this new fragmentation which spoke to me in many voices. It was the voice of my desire to prosper, but at the same time

---

* *Black Skin, White Masks* (1952; rpt. New York: Grove Press, 1967), pp. 17–18.

it spoke of what I had relinquished and could not regain: a safe way of being, a state of powerlessness which exempted me from responsibility for who I was and might be. And it accused me of betrayal, of turning away from blackness. To recover balance, I had to take on the language of the academy, the language of "others." And to do that, I had to learn to imagine myself a part of the culture of that language, and therefore someone free to manage that language, to take liberties with it. Writing and rewriting, practicing, experimenting, I came to comprehend more fully the generative power of language. I discovered—with the help of some especially sensitive teachers—that through writing one can continually bring new selves into being, each with new responsibilities and difficulties, but also with new possibilities. Remarkable power, indeed. I write and continually give birth to myself.

Sources for "From Outside, In"

"*From* Outside, In" began as a writing assignment for a graduate seminar in the teaching of English composition. The assignment directed that, as my final project for the course, I compose an essay explaining how I had learned to write.

Because—at the outset—I was working primarily in response to an assignment rather than from my own initiative, my process of composing commenced with the process of interpreting the assignment, the process of "figuring out" what my teacher expected as a final product. To determine *what* my teacher wanted, I asked myself *why* he would want me to put into written discourse my experience of learning to write. And to answer my question, I reflected on the overall purpose of the course and how the final project fit into that purpose.

During the term, my colleagues and I (teaching fellows and assistants) had acted as both students and teachers (of English, of language), but primarily as students. Under the guidance of our teacher, we had studied and responded to (both verbally and in writing) the diverse ideas of experts, the works of experienced teachers and scholars. Early in the term, for example, we had studied the course descriptions of experienced teachers and then developed with the assistance of our teacher course descriptions for our own students. We had performed individually in our respective classrooms. However, the assignments that we gave to our students were prepared by the heads of our department—though we were given considerable latitude for interpreting and teaching from the assignments. We had responded individually to our students' work, but we had also evaluated student writing in seminar under the guidance of our teacher.

And, likewise, we had evaluated one another's work. In short, we had been functioning as apprentices in a course whose purpose was to help the beginning teacher of English discover and refine her theoretical and practical understanding of language and transform that understanding into an effective pedagogy.

I concluded, then, that the assignment addressed me primarily as a student, an apprentice, and that my teacher expected me to use the assignment as a learning strategy, a way of continuing to refine both my understanding of language and my pedagogy. That is, I concluded that I was to use my experience as "learner" (my experience of learning to write) to define myself as "teacher." This meant that my final product, my written account of how I had learned to write, should represent or show a developing language-user and teacher, a scholar and writer and teacher coming to be.

I concluded also that the assignment demanded more of me as a teacher than had previous assignments for the course. An obvious reason was that my response to the assignment would be my final work for the course, my "last word," so to speak, as a developing teacher. Certainly my teacher would want my essay to evidence a teacher who had grown increasingly capable through study and practice. I also saw and heard the demand for my most teacherly self in what the assignment directed me to do and in the voice speaking through the assignment. For the first time in the course, my teacher was asking me to write about *having learned to write*. He was, then, recognizing me as someone who *knew* how to write and therefore *knew* the distinction between "good" and "bad" writing, someone qualified to evaluate the written work of others. In this, I saw my teacher's recognition of me as an equal—at least for the purposes of the assignment. And I interpreted this as an invitation, indeed, a command to enter into the ongoing and informed dialogue and work of the experts. Further, the tone of assignment was less paternal than that of previous assignments; that is, it was less gentle, less instructive, less helpful, more distant. I imagined my teacher stepping back and saying, "You've had a term of instruction, guidance, and practice. Now speak to me as one expert to another. Show me your expertise, what you have learned. Show me the teacher you have become thus far."

My process of interpreting the assignment was not as lonely and methodical and calm as this account of it implies, however. I worried over the assignment for a while and discussed it many times with a more experienced beginning teacher before finally deciding that my finished essay should represent both a learner learning and a teacher teaching. My interpretation, then, was partly the result of collaboration, something I recently learned to recognize and value as part of my process of composing.

After determining what my teacher expected as a final product, I turned my attention to my process of learning to write. I began by trying to pinpoint *when* I had begun learning to write, *when* I had begun learning to talk on paper. I immediately thought about my first college composition course—Basic Writing. It was not until after I had worked my way—with what I remembered as much difficulty—through that course that I began expressing myself through written discourse with a degree of effectiveness and consistency. I decided, then, that my experience in Basic Writing marked the beginning of my process of learning to write. And since I had saved all of the papers I had written as an undergraduate, I decided that I would use those papers, beginning with those from Basic Writing, to explore and explain my development as a writer.

As I studied my Basic Writing essays, I recalled the difficulty with which I had produced them. I remembered my inability to get inside the language, my feelings of separateness from it, and I remembered my fear and frustration. These recollections—or the emotions they aroused in me—triggered another memory: the memory of my parents in my grandmother's house, uncomfortable, reticent, almost apologetic in the presence of talkative, "proper-speaking" city relatives. This connection of two experiences brought about by the recollection of emotion or feeling led to my decision or realization that my process of learning to write directly related to my process of getting inside English. I was certain that I could not talk about one without talking about the other.

My essay began taking shape the moment I recognized that my process of becoming a writer was bound up in my process of becoming intimate with English. I immediately recalled several childhood and adolescent experiences that illustrated my relationship with English. I recorded these and put them aside until I could clear my project plans with my teacher. My teacher approved my plans within a day or two, and I immediately began writing. After many false starts, each commencing with a description of my parents in my grandmother's house, I decided to begin naturally, as if I were telling a story. "When I was growing up in Greeleyville, South Carolina," I began, and found my way into my experience of learning to write. I wrote five pages with relative ease, the words and structure coming readily. It was as if the experience—already formed—had been waiting a long time to be let out.

With some struggle, I wrote seven additional pages. There were times when the language and structure I wanted would not come, times when the emotion I had been transforming into thought disappeared. Such times, I began retyping the essay, beginning with the last passage that I considered both emotionally and intellectually true. This strategy often helped me find direction again.

I revised "From Outside, In" many times and received editorial advice from many people—from graduate students to Stanley Lindberg of the *Georgia Review*—before it was finally accepted for publication. Most of the revision was done on the second half of the essay, where I discuss more recent experiences. These experiences were more difficult to explore and articulate, I think, because I was not as distanced from them as I was from my childhood, adolescent, and young-adult experiences. It was more difficult, then, for me to make sense of these relatively fresh experiences that had changed me in ways that still made me uneasy and doubtful and fearful.

My seminar teacher guided me through the major revision (long after I had completed his seminar). He read and commented—in writing—on several versions of the essay. I sometimes did not like his suggestions (which were frequently couched in questions) because they asked me to look too squarely at the changed and changing me. When I wrote in the first version, for example, that my difficulty as a beginning writer issued from my fear that I was not college material, his reply was blunt: "I don't believe this." His response angered me, probably because he was right. I had gone to college because deep down I believed that I *was* college material, someone who could succeed in college if she worked diligently. But I said just the opposite in my essay partly because—not having thought it through—I believed it at the time and partly because I had not yet come to terms with the real reasons for my difficulties. Two or three revisions later, however, I had discovered and faced the root of the difficulties: the fear of change.

As I look back at my experience of writing "From Outside, In," I am reminded how much writing is the result of collaboration. And I am set firmer in my belief that language, the resurrector of ever-passing experience, does not breathe life unless fueled by passion. I say this because my best work results when I am engaged in my project, when what I am writing matters to me or when (if necessary—as is often the case with writing assignments) I find ways to make it matter.

QUESTIONS

Barbara Mellix's essay, "From Outside, In," and its process essay, "Sources of 'From Outside, In'"

1. Mellix writes of growing up speaking black English while believing that standard English spoken by blacks was the superior language. She writes, "... when we spoke standard English, we acknowledged (to ourselves and to others—but primarily to ourselves) that our customary way of speaking was inferior. We felt foolish, embarrassed, somehow diminished because we were ashamed to be our real selves. We were reserved, shy in the presence of those who owned and/or spoke *the* language." In your own experience, would you describe the language you use as "standard English"? How does your experience with language differ from Mellix's? How does the language itself differ? In your writing class and other classes you've taken, do you believe you possess the language of higher education? If you don't, does this make you feel inferior?

2. Mellix writes of the "generative power of language" and her discovery "that through writing one can continually bring new selves into being, each with new responsibilities and difficulties, but also with new possibilities." Is this contention supported by all she has written in the essay? Do you find her statement convincing? How is writing a way to "give birth" to one's self? Has this been your experience with writing? Do you believe that, in order

to develop Mellix's sense of writing, you would need much more experience with writing? Why?

3. Of the assignment that led to the essay "From Outside, In," Mellix writes, "...I saw my teacher's recognition of me as an equal—at least for the purposes of the assignment. And I interpreted this as an invitation, indeed, a command to enter into the ongoing and informed dialogue and work of the experts." In this comment, Mellix suggests that in previous assignments, she was not recognized as an equal by her teacher. What effect would such recognition have on your own writing? If your teacher regarded you or regards you as an equal, what sense do you have of his or her ability to teach you to write? Would the recognition destroy the "teacher–student" relationship, and would this then mean that you had learned all you can from this particular teacher?

4. Mellix writes, "...I am set firmer in my belief that language, the resurrector of ever-passing experience, does not breathe life unless fueled by passion." Several writers in this book have made similar statements. What does it mean to write with passion? Would you say that most of the writers you've read in this book write with passion? Have you sustained passion in your own writing through this course? Which essays that you've written do you feel the most passionate about? Is there a marked difference between these and other essays you've written?

∾ Possible Writing Topics ∾

1. Write an essay where you describe a particular time when you felt your own language—written or spoken—was inadequate or inferior. How did this inadequacy manifest itself? How did others respond to you? What were you thinking as it happened? What did you think afterward? What do you think now? Could the situation arise again? How would you attempt to change your response to it? Was it language itself that gave others this power over you, or were there other factors as well?

2. After you've completed the first essay, write a second one where you describe the techniques of a teacher of writing or reading that are particularly memorable, regardless of whether you thought the teacher was a good one. How did the teacher and his or her techniques make an impression? What power over language did that teacher possess that affected your own writing and reading? How did he or she present writing and reading as things to learn? Did the teacher's use of language cause you to feel inadequate or inferior? Was there the sense of invitation that Mellix speaks of in her process essay?

Laura Lynn Brown

Praying with a Pencil:
The Writer's Journal as Religious Quest

I'VE been daydreaming about the apartment I'm about to move into. My new bedroom will be a wonderful room to wake up in. The light will shine through bamboo blinds every morning, and I'll wake early, before the alarm goes off. I will face east, and smile as if I were not alone in the room. My bare feet will praise the holiness of hardwood floors, and I will breathe the incense of coffee steaming in a stoneware mug that reminds me of the ocean, and I will worship the morning, not knowing whether to write or to pray. I will probably go to my desk, near a window, and open my journal, and do both.

I've been thinking over the past few months about the kind of writing I like to do and want to do, and the different reasons I feel compelled and impelled to write in a journal. I've also been thinking over the past few months about religion and spirituality. I've been looking for places I feel comfortable in—for the right genre, for the right church—and I'm struck by how much these two quests resemble each other. It's become almost impossible for me to discuss one without the other popping up in the conversation. So I'm going to talk about this spiritual quest I've begun and probably will be on for the rest of my days. I hope something about my attitude towards keeping a journal gets said between the lines.

I had an abscessed tooth once. I was twenty years old, and it was spring, and dogwoods and redbuds were blooming all over the Arkansas university campus I was living on, and I was taking a British literature course that would turn out to be one of the best classes I ever had, and I couldn't enjoy any of this because my jaw felt like it was on fire. I wasn't able to eat, or even to talk very much, because the exposure to food and moving air made the pain worse. When I drank, the liquid soothed the pain for a second, but then the fire would start again, even hotter. I took a paper cup of water into the literature class one day and set it on the floor beside my seat in case I needed a sip now and then.

The water ran out before the class was over, and I remember sitting there with the pain spreading through my jaw, taking control of my head so that I couldn't even hear what was being said. Involuntary tears were running down my face from the pain; I thought I might have to leave the room.

I had forgotten about that abscessed tooth until a student's discussion of Thomas Merton's *The Seven Storey Mountain* in a class on writers' journals. The student seemed disappointed that Merton had had no revelatory conversion experience that prompted him to become a Catholic and a monk; he apparently drifted into the decision because there was a war on and he had a toothache. The class hooted at that; I laughed too, but mine was a laugh of recognition. I remembered that burning pain that kept me awake nights, the worst pain I've ever had, and I remember thinking that was as close to hell as I ever wanted to get.

I would like to remember that I started praying more after that toothache, or that I paid closer attention to Sunday sermons, but all I remember is thinking, "If hell hurts worse than this, I don't want to go there." People are moved toward faith by any number of reasons, and fear of pain is one of those reasons. It certainly wasn't enough to sustain my faith, or even to move me past contemplation to action, but now I have some touchstone against which I can gauge hell: hell is worse than an eternal abscessed tooth.

I wanted to see what Thomas Merton had to say about toothaches and faith, so I read *The Seven Storey Mountain*. His experiences with tooth problems were not exactly like mine, but we did have other things in common. I, too, had a flirtation with Communism—I got in trouble in seventh grade for writing "Long Live Chairman Mao" on my homeroom teacher's blackboard— but I found more relevant comparisons than that. Right now, I'm at about the same age Merton was when he was baptized into the Catholic Church and began to think he might have a vocation as a priest. I've probably been asking myself some of the same questions he asked himself at that stage in his life.

I got thinking about my own baptism while I was reading that book. I woke early the other morning to the sound of water. Rain was spattering outside, but water was running inside the apartment, too. Our heating system has water (or some kind of fluid) running through it, and several times a day I can hear water running just above the ceiling, running as if it were a stream on its way to some larger body of water. I can hear water running other times, too; any time the neighbors in the apartment next to ours or the two above ours take a shower or use the dishwasher, I can hear water running somewhere. I like the background music of water. It's comforting in the same way that the flame in our old gas oven is comforting; when it's turned on, the flame flares on and off, perhaps blown by some internal draft, and it makes a sound as vital as a heartbeat, as regular as breathing. I think I'm meant to live by water; I've always said I want to have a house on the beach.

I lay in bed that morning, waiting for the alarm clock to go off, hearing but not really listening to the water. I thought about the way a morning shower or a romp in the cold ocean can purify me: secular baptisms. I was baptized in a lake at a Christian youth camp when I was fourteen years old. I wore denim cut-offs and a yellow T-shirt. I didn't think to wear a bra; I seldom wore one at that age—I didn't need it then and hardly do now— and I didn't think about how sheer a wet T-shirt would be. Someone wrapped me in a blanket quickly after it was over; I thought it was to protect me from a chill, but I realized later it may also have been for reasons of modesty. The whole camp had come down to the lake that day. A lot of people hugged me. They had sung some hymn as I and Bob Henry, the minister who baptized me, were wading out into the water. It was a song I didn't know then and wouldn't recognize now.

I just realized that I hadn't ever seen anyone baptized before that day. The camp had been, for several summers, my only connection with the church. We had stopped going to church when I was five or six, and my memories of the church services were sitting in that hot little building where the stained-glass windows were thrown open in the summer, fanning myself with the colorful fans that were stuck in the pew racks with the hymnals and Bibles and had Bible scenes on one side and the names of funeral homes on the other, looking out the window now and then to watch a barge heavy with coal moving slowly down the Ohio River, and wondering why I couldn't drink the grape juice that the adults passed over my head in silver trays.

I never even thought about baptism much until I heard that another camper had been baptized one night. Her name was Michelle something—Watson? Watkins?—and, coming from a Catholic family, she had made what I recognized even then as a difficult, courageous decision to forsake the church of her parents and choose what she thought was right. Hearing about her put the idea in my head. One night, just before lights out, I told one of the counselors what I was thinking about. (We called her Mother Nature, for vague reasons having to do with some practical joke.) "Well, put your pants on," she said, which scared me; I thought I could at least wait until the next day.

During the girls' swimming period that day, Bob Henry came down to the lake. He sat chatting with Mother Nature. "Bob's over there," my cabin mates kept pointing out. "Why don't you go talk to Bob?" That would have been a logical time to do it—we were already at the lake—but between my friends' prodding and the furtive, hopeful looks I could feel shooting from the direction of Bob and Mother Nature, I was afraid to move. Bob came to Mother Nature's cabin that night; we discussed what I was contemplating, and he asked me a few questions to make sure I understood what I was doing. He smiled at my simple but satisfactory answers, and he asked me whether I wanted to go that night or to wait until the next morning. The next morning, I said, thinking about how cold and dark the lake would be at night. I'm embarrassed now to think about how I hesitated, putting it off three times. What if the world had ended that night? But the inevitability of nuclear war didn't loom in my imagination then the way it does these days. So I was baptized on July 11, 1975, the day some people refer to as their spiritual birthday.

I'll have a lot of friends celebrating birthdays in July; I'll be ten years old myself, spiritually, that is. Will anyone celebrate with me? How do you celebrate something like that? I'd like to call Michelle, wherever she is, and tell her she'll never know what a difference her influence has made in my life. If I hadn't been spurred by her example, I might never have made that decision. The lake was closed off to swimmers the following summer because cows had gotten into it and fouled the water; Bob Henry, whom I had always looked up to as an almost pontifical figure, stopped coming to the camp a year or two later, and there were strange rumors about his being seduced by some cultish offshoot of the church and being fired from the congregation where he preached.

But maybe a few more summers at the camp would have brought me to the same decision. That camp was the first place I ever felt the presence of God. I felt it in the park itself, in the crescendo of wind through the trees and in the slats of light that showed through the clouds, rays I thought of as the fingers of God when I was a child. I felt it in our singing around the campfire at night, and I felt it during our prayer circles just before we went to our cabins. We would form two or three large circles—one near the basketball court, one or two on the softball field—and we would hold hands, and bow our heads, and pray. When you were finished, or if you didn't want to pray aloud, you squeezed the hand of the person next to you with a hard, firm squeeze. There was another kind of squeeze, a quick, almost self-conscious squeeze, that you used when your heart swelled inside you and you wanted to communicate to the friend next to you an emotion too mystical for words. The friend would squeeze back, understanding perfectly, and you would listen as the sound of one voice talking to God moved around the circle, and you would listen to the blank spaces, imagining those hand squeezes moving like electricity around the chain. I first learned to pray in those circles. When the leader of each prayer group was done, he or she would turn on a flashlight and shine it at the sky. When a light was shining from each circle, Bob Henry's voice would sweep across the open field, saying, "Good night, and God go with you." You would squeeze the hands on both sides of you, and then the circles would break, and you would pick up your own flashlight from the now-damp grass at your feet and light your way to your cabin. Once, when the circle I was in was waiting for another to finish, some of us who happened to be looking at the right spot in the sky saw a falling star. I imagine a lot of hands were squeezed then.

I saw God in that star. I suppose I was a pantheist then; I saw Him in every wildflower, in a grove of trees swaying in the wind, in sunlight in any form and especially the dazzling flash of light across water. I ran across a book of Thomas Merton's photographs, and I think he must have had the same tendency. The photos are of simple subjects: driftwood, a snowfall, water and rock meeting on a beach, grass sprouting from a crack in a boulder—the kind of pictures anyone with a borrowed camera and a penchant for nature might make. But they're full of light; of one hundred photos in the book I counted the play of light—not simply light, but the meaningful play of light and shadow—in seventy-four of them.

The universe is filled with light—the power play of holy fire, as Annie Dillard says in her book *Holy the Firm*—and I think it's as necessary in writing as in photography. Merton reached a point at which the spiritual world seemed more real to him than the material world; that's a thought I had long before I ever heard of Thomas Merton. If I were pressed at this moment for a definition of God (a definition always subject to change), I would say He is Spirit, infinite in both space and time, and we and this earth are products of His imagination. In other words, creation is God's fiction. It's an autobiographical fiction, full of metaphors, and we are all students, expected to explicate the symbols. Laura, what does the sun represent? It is pure light, burning and bright, the life source of every living thing. Stare at it too long and you'll burn your retinas blind; yet in our own fantasy fiction we would journey to the sun, like moths, sacrificing ourselves against a naked bulb. "No one may see me and live," God said when Moses asked to see His glory; so He stuck Moses in the cleft of a rock, covered his eyes and passed by. Moses was allowed to see God's back, which was enough to make his face glow so radiantly that the people were afraid to come near him. Enoch walked with God, the Bible says, and never died because God took him. Translated him, they say sometimes. Did he see God's face? The Arabs had a legend that Enoch invented writing.

There's something else in those photos besides the play of light; there's a simplicity, almost an austerity, that conveys peace. I see it in the photos of doors and windows and straight-backed chairs set against whitewashed walls. When Merton finally did decide to enter a monastery, he chose the Trappists, nearly the most ascetic of Catholic orders. There have been times when asceticism appealed very much to me. (I confess that a life unencumbered by material possessions looks good now that I'm about to pack up the accumulations of the past few years and move them from one apartment to another.)

For some reason, the Quakers have always vaguely struck me as an appealingly simple and austere group. (I always associate the Shaker hymn "'Tis a gift to be simple, 'tis a gift to be free" with the Quakers.) When I was eleven or so, about the same time I decided I'd be a writer when I grew up, I thought I might like to be a Quaker. (I also contemplated vegetarianism, during my humane, be-kind-to-animals kick, but my mother said to be sincere about it I would also have to give up the shoulder bag and moccasins I had gotten so fond of. I could give up meat, but I couldn't give up leather, so I lost that argument.) I finally went to a Quaker meeting this year. It was a freezing Sunday in January, and I was afraid my car wouldn't start, so I thought about the churches within walking distance: the big Presbyterian church on Fifth Avenue, or Mass at St. Paul's Cathedral, or the Friends meeting house. I wanted to wear pants, and I wanted to go somewhere where I would feel comfortable in my corduroys, so I chose the meeting house. When I walked in, the foyer was full of people chatting. They seemed—well, friendly. They gave me a name tag to pin onto my sweater, and a few people, noticing a new face, talked to me. One animated little woman who told me her husband was a birthright Quaker (meaning his parents had both been Quakers) asked me if I was a member. No, I said; I was just visiting some different churches, trying to get a broader view of how other people worshipped God. She said something about all of us worshipping in our own individual ways; before I mentioned God, she had called Him "God, or that Great Spirit, or whatever it is up there." I suppose she didn't want to offend me in case I believed in Him only as some vague cosmic intelligence.

A big black and white sign on the wall in a simple Roman typeface told new worshippers how to conduct themselves and what to expect during meeting. Go in when you are ready, it said; put aside your earthly concerns; meditate; seek that calm center within you. The Quakers believe each of us has something of God within us, and that worship is a very personal relationship between the believer and God.

I went in when I was ready. The meeting room was a calculatedly austere room with a pine floor, high white ceiling, brown walls, and, on three sides of the room, large, plain windows which let in a lot of light. The seating arrangement was split down the middle, with each half of the rows of chairs facing the other half. It was so quiet you could hear a stomach growl across the room; you could hear a noise whenever someone shifted in a chair. Some people looked straight ahead; some closed their eyes. Most sat absolutely still. I was afraid my mind would wander, but I was surprised later at how easy it had been to keep my mind focused on things spiritual. I prayed, and then asked myself questions and tried to articulate (mentally, not aloud) answers that tested and stretched what I already knew about myself. Then one young woman was moved to speak. "Last night a woman came to me," she began, and her story sounded almost like a dream. The woman was searching for a more spiritual life, and she wanted advice on prayer and meditation. "Sometimes," this woman said, choosing her words carefully, "sometimes we get to a point where we're stagnant in our own spiritual lives; we've ceased to grow. I wondered whether *I* should have gone to *her* and said, 'What should I do?'" She sat down. About ten minutes later, an older woman with wavy silver hair stood up. She had typed out a quotation from George Fox, the founding father of the Quakers. I don't remember it very well; it was something about walking peaceably among all men and showing the same human kindnesses to everyone. She commented on it, and as she was about to sit down, another woman asked, "Read it again," so she read it again. I had read on another sign in the foyer that a worshipper could harm the worship in two ways; by going into meeting having already resolved to speak, or by going in having already resolved to keep silent. Wasn't this woman breaking that principle? Maybe she had been carrying that typed card around in her purse for weeks, waiting for the Spirit to move her to speak.

After about ten more minutes, a short, middle-aged man with graying hair and beard stood up and started talking about the convention of scientists he had attended a week earlier. Some of the discussions there, he said, turned to religion. He talked about scientific evidences of a supreme being, and then he started to talk very technically about particle physics, and I couldn't make sense of any of it. I looked at the man sitting in front of him. The man had had his eyes closed tightly during most of the meeting. When he did open his eyes, and they met mine for an instant, I had to look away because his was the kind of gaze that can pierce your eyes and look down deep into your soul. The physicist stopped and sat down. After a few minutes, the man with the eyes reached out and shook hands with the young woman sitting a few chairs away from him, and then a sort of tension was broken, and we all shook hands with the people around us. After a few announcements, the group broke up, many staying for coffee in the foyer. I stayed and talked with a few people. The *Pittsburgh Press* carried a big article on the Friends that day, and from that article I learned that the man with the eyes was the clerk of the meeting, a sort of elder. One of the people I talked with was the woman whom the clerk had first shaken hands with. She was a student at a local women's college. She and I and a friend of hers, another graduate student, ended up talking about libraries.

The people I met and listened to seemed sincere and earnest; for some reason I felt there might be less hypocrisy there than I had run across in some of the churches of Christ I had attended. I said this to my friend Bill, who had a party a few weeks later at which I ran into this woman again. She recognized my face and asked whether she had seen me on campus. "I met you at the Friends meeting house," I said, and she got a funny look on her face and quickly excused herself from the conversation. "Sincere, huh? No hypocrites, huh?" Bill said to me later, and then he said, "Do you know where she went tonight?" She and one of his roommates had been at the meeting house, which they regularly used as a trysting place, he told me.

I liked the simplicity of Quaker worship. One of the women quoted in the *Press* article said, "I speak when I can no longer keep silent." I liked the idea of being so sensitive to the Spirit in oneself. And the people I had met seemed like a group of people I would fit in with socially. But I wasn't looking for a social club, and I don't think I could sustain my faith for very long without singing and communion. I told my friend Liz that I was not comfortable with the congregation I was meeting with and that I wanted to understand how other people approached Christianity. "You should come to my church," she said. So I did, the next Sunday.

She goes to St. Luke's, a tiny Episcopal church with about fifteen people attending on a good Sunday. We were the youngest people there. The building itself induced a kind of spiritual feeling—stained glass windows, ornate woodwork at the front of the building, the gold pipes of the organ. I liked some parts of the service, enough to visit the church again, but other parts would take a lifetime to get used to, I think. It feels very right to spend a lot of time over communion, to stand when we sing, to kneel when we pray, to go up to the altar rail to take communion rather than having it passed down the pews, and to drink the wine out of the same cup as everyone else. But I'm used to singing a cappella. I realize an organ seems like a necessity to cover up the weak spots in a small group's singing. But I think the singing of fifteen voices unadorned is still pleasing to God; I like to think the singing of one voice in the shower is pleasing to Him. And no matter how eloquent and thoughtful the preacher's sermons are, or how well he enunciates, a man in a clerical robe still looks silly to me.

A few Sundays later I went to Mass at St. Paul's Cathedral. I had never been inside it before, so of course I was impressed by the newly remodeled interior. But I made the mistake of sitting too far back to be able to participate in worship. When it was time for the service to start, a man in what looked like a red sweatshirt stepped up to the pulpit and started speaking. There were at least a half dozen tall columns between me and the front of the building, and each column had a speaker on it, so by the time his amplified voice reached me, it was so thick and distorted that I could pick out only a few words. Not only was I too far from the front, I was too close to the thundering pipe organ in the balcony. I tried to sing the unfamiliar hymns, but none of the people around me were singing; even if they had been, the jumble of the organ was so close that I could barely pick out the melody. The people around me mouthed the liturgy so mechanically I wondered whether they felt it at all. Maybe their mothers made them go to church.

As some of the throng filed forward to take communion, I saw that the red sweatshirt wasn't a sweatshirt at all, but some kind of clerical vestment. How can you ever approach God, I wondered, when there's always a priest in the way? Is it a relief to confess your sins to a man, so you don't have to face God with them? I don't mean I'm basing my opinion of Catholicism on one visit to a Catholic Mass at a huge cathedral. And, as they say, some of my favorite writers are Catholics—Flannery O'Connor, for example. But I have never felt further from God during a worship service than I did then.

I ran into a friend on the way out. "I didn't know you were Catholic," he said.

"I'm not," I said.

"Then why are you here?"

"On a whim."

"Did you feel holy?" he said, a tad mockingly. I couldn't tell whether he meant, "Were you in a holy mood and decided to go to church?" or "Did you feel holy, having been in *the* church and not the one you usually sit in on Sundays?"

"I've felt holier," I said, figuring that would answer either question.

I was visiting my family for Easter, so I went to the church I used to go to when I lived there. I don't feel right using the word "refreshing" to describe a church service, but that's what it was—to see men wearing regular clothes, to sing with the strength of 300 voices and no accompaniment, to look at the simple beige walls and plain translucent glass windows and boomerang-shaped support beams that I've seen in so many church buildings. Maybe I was simply able to appreciate this familiar service more after having sat through such unfamiliar ritual and lack of ritual; but it was, in a sense, coming home. Next to St. Paul's, that building could be described as austere. It felt right to me.

I don't mean that we should respond to God according to what feels right, that we should choose a "high" or "low" church based on what we like to wear or what kind of building we like to sit in on a Sunday morning. Annie Dillard, in her book *Holy the Firm*, says this about high and low churches:

> The higher Christian churches... come at God with an unwarranted air of professionalism, with authority and pomp, as though they knew what they were doing, as though people in themselves were an appropriate set of creatures to have dealings with God. I often think of the set pieces of liturgy as certain words which people have successfully addressed to God without their getting killed. In the high churches they saunter through the liturgy like Mohawks along a strand of scaffolding who have long since forgotten their danger. If God were to blast such a service to bits, the congregation would be, I believe, genuinely shocked. But in the low churches you expect it any minute. This is the beginning of wisdom.

Of course, it's possible to make a religion of anything, to allow habit to become ritual to the point that one day's omission seems like a transgression, and you feel as guilty as though you had sinned. I could be accused of making a religion of my morning routine. I plead guilty. My faith and my writing are mutually dependent on each other, and I didn't know that until I started discussing it with my journal these past few months. I say discussing—that's exactly what I do. The journal has become personified for me. I feel guilty and shy about facing it if I've neglected it for a few days; I look forward some nights to coming home and opening it up and putting the day's stories into it, the same way I look forward to talking with my roommate at night. I tell it what I'm thinking about, and worrying about; together we analyze the situation and plan for the future in what little way we can. I've had to decide recently whether to concentrate on my fiction or my nonfiction. I was agonizing over the decision, putting it out of my mind as much as possible. Finally I opened my journal and let the fiction writer in me talk face to face with the nonfiction writer. I think it was a fairly natural conversation. I didn't control them; I just listened to them and wrote down what they said. The nonfiction voice was the confident one, the one in control, the one who appeared to be thinking about what was best for both of them. The fiction voice sounded scared at times, and selfish. I wrote out that dialogue, and the decision was made. I'm discovering that I'm a better storyteller in my journal than I've been so far in my fiction, and that the records I keep there could be material for all kinds of writing. I feel no shame in saying that I practice writing in my journal; I practice style; I sweat over the rhythm of a sentence. There was a time when I wanted to be a symphony flutist. I practiced several hours a day, and often when I had finished practicing the "serious" music I would put some jazz albums on the stereo and practice improvising, just for the fun of it. I'm starting to feel the same devotion for writing that I used to feel for my music.

But the process is slow. Thomas Merton didn't wake up one morning suddenly knowing he wanted to be a Trappist monk, or even that he wanted to be a Catholic. I doubt that it works that way for anyone. There are days when the work flows well, and I don't ever want to do anything else. And then there are days when the words won't come and I wonder what I'm going to do next and if I'm just fooling myself to think writing is my true vocation.

I *do* think it's my vocation, and keeping a journal helps me to remember that, just as prayer and song and communion keep me looking in another right direction. In the middle of her meditations on the nature of God, Annie Dillard mentions her students: "How many of you, I asked the people in my class, which of you want to be writers? . . . All hands rose to the question. (You, Nick? Will you? Margaret? Randy? Why do I want them to mean it?) And then I tried to tell them what the choice must mean: you can't be anything else. You must go at your life with a broadax."

Writing in my journal—which has the potential to become a much bigger project, as this essay is proof of—is one of the few pursuits I would stay up all night for, either by choice or by force. There are nights like that; like the Quaker woman, I write when I can no longer keep silent, and I lose all sense of time, so that my writing and I are as fused as two lovers, and I'm startled by the sounds of birds waking up. I would like to think that anyone walking into the room at that point would be frightened by my radiant face.

I watched the sun come up today. First I heard the birds, so I opened the blinds. The day was still a pink and lavender streak on the horizon. Then the lavender faded to blue and to white, and the sun was on the rim of the earth. I stared it down for only a second, but that made its impression; when I tried to write, I couldn't see the words unless I looked slightly to one side of them.

I know it doesn't matter that my bedroom windows will have bamboo blinds, which remind me of the Orient and of meditative Eastern religions. I know I don't need a hardwood floor under my feet. I suppose I wouldn't write much differently if I didn't always have the security blanket of tea or coffee near me, and there's probably nothing inherently magic about drinking it from one of the variously patterned blue and bone-colored mugs I've collected from potters and on visits to the east coast. I'm still convinced I need either a yellow legal pad or a black and white speckled composition book and a medium point pen with black ink, although that's probably mere superstition. But I do demand as much light as I can get close to. Direct sunlight was my main criterion when I was looking for a new apartment. And the light of early morning, I've noticed, is like no other light in the day. The slant rays are discriminating; they don't wash out everything, like the light of midday, but the places they do strike are pierced with such brightness that it's a sin not to notice.

The light passed through a vase of flowers between six and seven this morning and cast a circle of rainbow colors onto the seat of a chair nearby. I laid a piece of typing paper on the chair so I could see the colors better. I slid a finger between the vase and the light to see just what part of the glass was acting as a prism. It wasn't the base, or the rim, as I would have guessed, but the surface of the water in the vase. I turned the vase slowly. The light sharpened and focused into three multi-colored spots forming the points of a triangle, then fanned out into a long stripe of smaller rainbow-colored stripes. I went back to my writing, but I glanced at the light now and then. It had taken a different pattern, like a kaleidoscope, every time I looked. Finally, like a rainbow, it faded away.

I'm glad I was awake to see it. I'm seldom awake at that hour of the morning, but when I am, something happens. I want to pray and I want to write, and the two impulses become one. My journal is my prayer, and I'm going to start praying earlier. I don't want to miss a thing.

Towards the Mirage of Truth

*W*HEN I wrote in the essay "Praying with a Pencil" about what I thought waking up in my new apartment would be like, I lied. There was a hardwood floor in that apartment, but only in the entry hall; the bedrooms were carpeted. And there were bamboo blinds in one bedroom, but it was my roommate's; the windows in my room had Venetian blinds. Getting up in the morning, my feet would not praise the holiness of hardwood floors, but would merely acknowledge the stain-speckled tan carpet, with a warmer but less spiritual touch under my soles. And, until my roommate decided to chuck the bamboo blinds (which I then appropriated) in favor of curtains fashioned from bedsheets, I would look to the east through dusty aluminum slats.

I didn't know this when I wrote the piece; I didn't know it until I moved into the apartment a few weeks later. But I did not change the essay to make it factually correct because preserving the accuracy of my memory was more important to me than acurately describing the scene. I tell you this now because I believe in being scrupulously truthful in my essays. I also believe trying to define what constitutes "truth" in nonfiction could engender discussions that never reach a consensus. Like my definition of God, my definition of truth is always subject to change. But I do have some specific notions of the truth contained in the writing I did, both fiction and nonfiction, when I wrote "Praying with a Pencil," so I want to talk about that.

A few years ago I was keeping a journal. I've kept journals since childhood, but this one was different: I was keeping it as a class requirement for a course on writers' journals. At the end of the term, I was going to have to write a long essay on my theory of the journal, using examples from this journal I was keeping.

"Praying with a Pencil" is that essay. I reread that journal recently, and one of the most interesting things in it was not a journal entry but a marginal note I made, commenting on an entry. It was scolding, written in all capital letters, and it said: "YOU'RE WRITING THIS AS IF IT WERE THE JOURNALS CLASS TERM PAPER RATHER THAN A JOURNAL ENTRY. AT THIS POINT YOU HAVE NO AUDIENCE BUT YOURSELF."

In my journal, this is often untrue. Sometimes my journal acts as an exercise book for rough drafts, scenes I want to write and need to practice on. I imagine someone reading those entries; in fact I write to an audience, to that general literate audience which essays are said to be addressed to—which is often like writing for a certain professor I had in college. He taught advanced composition, and he shocked me into the knowledge that writing was work by giving me a C+ on the first paper I wrote for him. (Everything I had ever written in my life up to that point had received an A.) I craved A's from him after that, and I began to write—in his courses and in others—with him in mind as my discriminating audience.

But there is another audience I imagine; I don't write to this audience, but in fear of it. It is like writing in a journal when you know someone—a little brother, a roommate—is going to sneak a peek and read your secrets. I would not practice when I wrote these entries, would not play with word choices or think about the cadence of my language. I would write quickly; my handwriting would be smaller or messier, and I would be more likely to abbreviate, as if to encode my language and make the writing as difficult to read as possible. I would not name people but give them fictitious names or initials. I would write as if I expected someone over my shoulder any minute.

This is an exaggeration; but now, going back and reading a journal I kept nearly three years ago, that is how it looks to me: odd that even in my journal, my most private writing, I would be cryptic about events that I might later openly discuss. This vast difference is voice in my private writing, that confident voice that enjoyed an audience alternating with the timid one that feared an audience, paralleled what was happening in my public writing—that is, what I was turning in in my classes. It had to do with the way I handled autobiographical material; it also had to do with what I have, with some reservation, chosen to call truth. I will eventually look at some more technical questions about the writing of "Praying with a Pencil," but this is the main issue I want to address.

As I said, I went back and read the journal I kept that semester. I wanted to see how much of the essay came out of the journal, and how much work those sections needed to transform them from unshaped journal entries to a well-woven essay passage. And I wanted to get some sense of how I had rearranged chronology. I considered the essay to be, besides a discussion of the similarities between the discipline of writing and my quest for spirituality, a distillation of my experiences that term, and so I also read the jouranl to see if I was right about that.

As in the essay, two themes dominated my journal that semester. As a graduate student beginning work on a master of fine arts, I was writing fiction, but having serious doubts about whether I was any good at it. And, having grown up in an evangelical Christian church and done my undergraduate work at a church- related university, I was beginning to question some assumptions I had grown up with; I was questioning the church and looking to other churches for at least some answers. Both of these running discussions in my journal became quests. I was searching for answers I needed to find. In the case of writing, I needed to make a decision, one which would have some bearing on my future as a graduate student. In the case of faith, I did not expect to find quick or permanent answers, to find God by the end of the semester; but, having come to the big city and having stopped observing rituals (like going to church) that I had observed for years, I felt I had gotten derailed from some track that I wanted to be back on. So there was a sense of urgency to both quests. And I believe they had origins in the same place in me—a driven place, never quite satisfied with itself, conscious of an ideal but never working hard enough to reach it.

If you were to read that journal, besides following these themes, you would see what you see in the essay—a perhaps inordinate interest in the places I lived, especially the apartment I was about to move into; a questioning of religious values; descriptions of the places I ventured into to test those values; the impulse to pray, and the belief that it is important; a love of waking early.

But you would also see recurring themes that are not in the essay, themes that perhaps contradict what I do say and make me out to be a different person. There is discussion of my infrequent prayers, or at times an inability to pray. There is a shockingly large amount of space given to (and amount of guilt over) all the times I slept in and wasted those mystical morning hours. There is a huge struggle to be a fiction writer (which is not the same as a struggle to write fiction well), and a lot of secret doubt over whether I was or would ever be one. The essay mentions my decision to switch to nonfiction, but does not convey the continual doubt and soul-searching that came before that decision.

One of the short stories I wrote for my fiction workshop that semester came back from the professor with the note, "You have to search deeper within yourself for material." I can't remember that note without thinking of the other hot topic of that semester's journal: I was trying to get over the first love of my life. It was a very complicated situation, that relationship; it was also full of "good stories." In fact, after it was over, my ex and I joked grimly that our story, written down without any changes, would make great fiction. I was trying to deal with this relationship in almost all the fiction I wrote that year, but I was squeamish about writing autobiographical fiction; I thought that to be literature it had to be made up. I *believed* those disclaimers in the fronts of novels, saying they were works of fiction and any resemblance to anything living or dead was purely coincidental. And so I was trying to get my imagination to tell good stories, and trying at the same time to sift through the detritus of that relationship and to make sense of what had happened (and to make permanent in writing what would never be permanent in life). And although it was good advice, at the time I was offended by that marginal note. I thought that material had come from the deepest place within me. It did come from a certain depth; the problem was, I wanted to keep it there.

"Praying with a Pencil" is the most successful piece I wrote that semester. I was able to accomplish something in that essay that I had not accomplished in any of my short stories. At the time, I might have attributed the difference to a failure of the imagination: I was able to see metaphor in my life and in my surroundings, but not able to make it. Now, however, I would use the word truth, which is not to say that essays are truer than fiction in general; I mean my essays were truer than my fiction. The fiction came from those journal passages written in cramped handwriting, those stories I was cryptic about even with myself; the essay came from the confident passages which wanted an audience.

I have to tell you at this point that I have spent several years, in college and in the real world, studying and practicing journalism. No matter how disreputable the profession may be viewed these days, I and the journalists I know feel a serious obligation to write truthfully and accurately. We forget the compliments and fan letters we might have received, but we remember the mistakes, the time we misspelled a source's name, the statistic we got wrong, the corrections that had to be made for our stories. And just as my religious background, so ingrained in me, makes me see the world a certain way, that early training as a journalist has instilled me with a stubborn insistence on truth.

But I began by telling you that I lied. And if I made errors of fact when writing in April about an apartment I had seen in March, how accurate was I when writing about events that happened ten or twenty years ago? I had no notes, no photographs, no journal entries from church camp, no material to jog my memory. Or perhaps material like that would only verify, substantiate my memory; perhaps the journalist in me would like such documentation to back up my story. But when the essayist in me began to write, I called on memory and found that the more I wrote, the more I remembered. I worked very hard to describe what it was like to pray out there under the stars, and what it was like to be a little girl passing time in church. I would stand by those passages as being as true as I could make them.

I can't let the thought of description pass without pointing out another difference between that essay and the fiction I wrote that semester. The professor who taught me that writing is work liked to say that the aim of all writing is to serve. And I remember that statement finally taking root in me, and the idea dawning on me—or, rather, striking like lightning—that what I say is more important than how I say it. I knew instinctively that description enlivens writing, but I suddenly realized that at times I wrote description for the sake of description. Or, to be more truthful, I fight a continual battle when I write, a battle between writing about something so you will admire the way I string words together or writing about something because I want you to see it or understand it.

This is a matter of perspective and focus, and it is a matter I bring up in my journalism classes, being a teacher who believes that it can be mutually useful to hash over the problems I face in writing with my students. We discuss it using the metaphor of a camera. Imagine, I tell them, that you are filming this scene for the reader, and think about what you want to focus the lens of your camera on. Do you want them to see it as if they are viewing it firsthand, or do you want them to watch you in the scene? We decide that it is better to shift emphasis off of ourselves and onto what we are writing about.

The other idea that fascinates these beginning journalism students is the discovery that there is no such thing as absolute objectivity. The words we choose, the quotations we decide to use and the ones we leave out, the order in which we arrange our material, the things we juxtapose—all of these are conscious choices, and convey ideas to the reader. We talk about explicit and implicit statements, about connotative and denotative meanings. We talk about the responsibility of using words, and the need to identify and understand these choices we make.

I left the newspaper business because I did not have the time to examine such choices, and I seldom had the time I would have liked to polish a story. Such throwaway writing, day after day, frustrated me; writing for editors who were hesitant to let reporters take creative risks, I was afraid that my creativity would atrophy. So I left it and came to grad school to write fiction.

After floundering through nearly two semesters of fiction workshops, feeling for the first time that my credentials as a writer were tenuous and believing I was bluffing my way through these courses, I began to think of switching to an emphasis in nonfiction. There were purely financial reasons for making the change: I would be more likely to receive a teaching assistantship if I defected from the competitive ranks of the fiction writers to the smaller knot of nonfiction writers. But there were other reasons for putting my short stories aside for a while. I wanted my writing to be truthful and honest. I could go back to writing news stories, where I wrote just the facts and let the reader try to conjure those nine tenths of the iceberg hidden under the surface; or I could choose to work with the essay form.

I've said I'm big on truth, and yet I have confessed to standing by a factual error. I have said a writer should keep the focus on the topic at hand; yet you might say all I write about in "Praying with a Pencil" is myself. I might answer that by saying that I wanted the essay to evoke the intimate, conversational tone of my journal, and by saying that I wanted to take readers to church with me, and to take them back to the scene of my baptism, and to places they couldn't go without having me there. I might also answer that by saying that truth is a mirage when you're writing. It shifts and changes shape and becomes obscured now and then. If you want to survive, out there alone in the desert, you will have to write your way out of it. You know that palm tree you see might not really be there. But you see it—you see it—and you do your best to tell me what it looks like.

❧ QUESTIONS ☙

Laura Lynn Brown's essay, "Praying with a Pencil: The Writer's Journal as Religious Quest," and its process essay, "Towards the Mirage of Truth"

1. Brown creates an elaborate metaphor where she compares her pursuit of spirituality and her recognition of God with writing, especially in her journal. Did you find the metaphor believable? What did or didn't make it so? How would you compare Brown's radiance when she completes a night of journal writing with Barbara Mellix's statement in "From Outside, In" that as a writer she continually gives birth to herself? Are the experiences similar?

2. Brown writes, " . . . I write when I can no longer keep silent, and I lose all sense of time, so that my writing and I are as fused as two lovers. . . . " What sense do you have of Brown's need to write when she "can no longer keep silent"? Are there times when you, too, can no longer keep silent? What form does your response to that take? What are other possible responses? Why, for Brown, does writing seem the best response?

3. In her process essay, Brown writes, "The professor who taught me that writing is work liked to say that the aim of all writing is to serve. And I remember that statement finally taking root in me, and the idea dawning on me—or, rather, striking like lightning—that what I say is more important than how I say it." Do you agree with this perspective on writing, that its aim is to serve? Whom do you serve when you write in this class? Whom do you serve when you write on your own? Consider the sort of reading that you do. Do you feel served when you read? What is the difference between what you may say in your writing and how you may choose to say it?

4. Brown writes of the difference in the voice of her personal journals and what she calls her "public writing," and how the voice in both changed over time. How does the voice in your own personal writing—diaries, journals, letters—differ from the voice you use when you write papers for classes? What would happen if you used your private voice in essays for this or other classes? Would you or your teacher consider this appropriate? Should there be a difference between the writing voices we use in private and those we use in public? From what source do the demands for private and public voices come?

❧ Possible Writing Topics ☙

1. If you have kept a journal in this or other classes, or you have written diaries or journals on your own, go back to those now and work to assess some meaning you have gotten from them. What do they say about you and the time at which you wrote them? How and in what ways have things changed for you since you wrote them? Why did you keep a journal in the first place, or what were the reasons your teacher gave you? Will you keep it? Why? What does the journal provide that memory in and of itself cannot? Are you willing to quote from the journal? How difficult will it be to write this essay if you do not? You may want to note that Brown never quotes from hers.

2. After you've completed the first essay, write a second one where you describe the voice you used when writing the journals, and the degree to which that voice changes as you move from entry to entry. On what occasions were you most elaborate in the journals? Did you always work with what Brown describes as the truth? Were there times when your writing seemed more public than private? If the journal was written for a class, did you find yourself working to employ a voice that your teacher would find acceptable? How would the voice have changed if you hadn't had that concern? Were you secretive, worried, as was Brown, over the unknown audience that may someday dig up your journal and read it? Whom were you writing for when you wrote the journal? Whom, if anyone, did it serve?

Min-zhan Lu

From Silence to Words: Writing as Struggle[1]

> Imagine that you enter a parlor. You come late. When you arrive, others have long preceded you, and they are engaged in a heated discussion.... You listen for a while, until you decide that you have caught the tenor of the argument; then you put in your oar. Someone answers; you answer him; another comes to your defense; another aligns himself against you, to either the embarrassment or gratification of your opponent, depending upon the quality of your ally's assistance. However, the discussion is interminable. The hour grows late, you must depart. And you do depart, with the discussion still vigorously in progress. —*Kenneth Burke, The Philosophy of Literary Form*

> Men are not built in silence, but in word, in work, in action-reflection.
> —*Paulo Freire, Pedagogy of the Oppressed*

My mother withdrew into silence two months before she died. A few nights before she fell silent, she told me she regretted the way she had raised me and my sisters. I knew she was referring to the way we had been brought up in the midst of two conflicting worlds—the world of home, dominated by the ideology of the Western humanistic tradition, and the world of a society dominated by Mao Tse-tung's Marxism. My mother had devoted her life to our education, an education she knew had made us suffer political persecution during the Cultural Revolution. I wanted to find a way to convince her that, in spite of the persecution, I had benefited from the education she

---

[1] Copyright © 1987 by the *National Council of Teachers of English*. Reprinted with permission.

had worked so hard to give me. But I was silent. My understanding of my education was so dominated by memories of confusion and frustration that I was unable to reflect on what I could have gained from it.

This paper is my attempt to fill up that silence with words, words I didn't have then, words that I have since come to by reflecting on my earlier experience as a student in China and on my recent experience as a composition teacher in the United States. For in spite of the frustration and confusion I experienced growing up caught between two conflicting worlds, the conflict ultimately helped me to grow as a reader and writer. Constantly having to switch back and forth between the discourse of home and that of school made me sensitive and self-conscious about the struggle I experienced every time I tried to read, write, or think in either discourse. Eventually, it led me to search for constructive uses for such struggle.

From early childhood, I had identified the differences between home and the outside world by the different languages I used in each. My parents had wanted my sisters and me to get the best education they could conceive of—Cambridge. They had hired a live-in tutor, a Scot, to make us bilingual. I learned to speak English with my parents, my tutor, and my sisters. I was allowed to speak Shanghai dialect only with the servants. When I was four (the year after the Communist Revolution of 1949), my parents sent me to a local private school where I learned to speak, read, and write in a new language—Standard Chinese, the official written language of New China.

In those days I moved from home to school, from English to Standard Chinese to Shanghai dialect, with no apparent friction. I spoke each language with those who spoke the language. All seemed quite "natural"—servants spoke only Shanghai dialect because they were servants; teachers spoke Standard Chinese because they were teachers; languages had different words because they were different languages. I thought of English as my family language, comparable to the many strange dialects I didn't speak but had often heard some of my classmates speak with their families. While I was happy to have a special family language, until second grade I didn't feel that my family language was any different than some of my classmates' family dialects.

My second grade homeroom teacher was a young graduate from a missionary school. When she found out I spoke English, she began to practice her English on me. One day she used English when asking me to run an errand for her. As I turned to close the door behind me, I noticed the puzzled faces of my classmates. I had the same sensation I had often experienced when some stranger in a crowd would turn on hearing me speak English. I was more intensely pleased on this occasion, however, because suddenly I felt that my family language had been singled out from the family languages of my classmates. Since we were not allowed to speak any dialect other than Standard Chinese in the classroom, having my teacher speak English to me in class made English an official language of the classroom. I began to take pride in my ability to speak it.

This incident confirmed in my mind what my parents had always told me about the importance of English to one's life. Time and again they had told me of how my paternal grandfather, who was well versed in classic Chinese, kept losing good-paying jobs because he couldn't speak English. My grandmother reminisced constantly about how she had slaved and saved to send my father to a first-rate missionary school. And we were made to understand that it was my father's fluent English that had opened the door to his success. Even though my family had always stressed the importance of English for my future, I used to complain bitterly about the extra English lessons we had to take after school. It was only after my homeroom teacher had "sanctified" English that I began to connect English with my education. I became a much more eager student in my tutorials.

What I learned from my tutorials seemed to enhance and reinforce what I was learning in my classroom. In those days each word had one meaning. One day I would be making a sentence at school: "The national flag of China is red." The next day I would recite at home, "My love is like a red, red rose." There seemed to be an agreement between the Chinese "red" and the English "red," and both corresponded to the patch of color printed next to the word. "Love" was my love for my mother at home and my love for my "motherland" at school; both "loves" meant how I felt about my mother. Having two loads of homework forced me to develop a quick memory for words and a sensitivity to form and style. What I learned in one language carried over to the other. I made sentences such as, "I saw a red, red rose among the green leaves," with both the English lyric and the classic Chinese lyric—red flower among green leaves—running through my mind, and I was praised by both teacher and tutor for being a good student.

Although my elementary schooling took place during the fifties, I was almost oblivious to the great political and social changes happening around me. Years later, I read in my history and political philosophy textbooks that the fifties were a time when "China was making a transition from a semi-feudal, semi-capitalist, and semi-colonial country into a socialist country," a period in which "the Proletarians were breaking into the educational territory dominated by Bourgeois Intellectuals." While people all over the country were being officially classified into Proletarians, Petty-bourgeois, National-bourgeois, Poor-peasants, and Intellectuals, and were trying to adjust to their new social identities, my parents were allowed to continue the upper middle-class life they had established before the 1949 Revolution because of my father's affiliation with British firms. I had always felt that my family was different from the families of my classmates, but I didn't perceive society's view of my family until the summer vacation before I entered high school.

First, my aunt was caught by her colleagues talking to her husband over the phone in English. Because of it, she was criticized and almost labeled a Rightist. (This was the year of the Anti-Rightest movement, a movement in which the Intellectuals became the target of the "socialist class-struggle.") I had heard others telling my mother that she was foolish to teach us English when Russian had replaced English as the "official" foreign language. I had also learned at school that the American and British Imperialists were the arch-enemies of New China. Yet I had made no connection between the arch-enemies and the English our family spoke. What happened to my aunt forced the connection on me. I began to see my parents' choice of a family language as an anti-Revolutionary act and was alarmed that I had participated in such an act. From then on, I took care not to use English outside home and to conceal my knowledge of English from my new classmates.

Certain words began to play important roles in my new life at the junior high. On the first day of school, we were handed forms to fill out with our parents' class, job, and income. Being one of the few people not employed by the government, my father had never been officially classified. Since he was a medical doctor, he told me to put him down as an Intellectual. My homeroom teacher called me into the office a couple of days afterwards and told me that my father couldn't be an Intellectual if his income far exceeded that of a Capitalist. He also told me that since my father worked for Foreign Imperialists, my father should be classified as an Imperialist Lackey. The teacher looked nonplussed when I told him that my father couldn't be an Imperialist Lackey because he was a medical doctor. But I could tell from the way he took notes on my form that my father's job had put me in an unfavorable position in his eyes.

The Standard Chinese term "class" was not a new word for me. Since first grade, I had been taught sentences such as, "The Working class are the masters of New China." I had always known that it was good to be a worker, but until then, I had never felt threatened for not being one. That fall, "class" began to take on a new meaning for me. I noticed a group of Working-class students and teachers at school. I was made to understand that because of my class background, I was excluded from that group.

Another word that became important was "consciousness." One of the slogans posted in the school building read, "Turn our students into future Proletarians with socialist consciousness and education!" For several weeks we studied this slogan in our political philosophy course, a subject I had never had in elementary school. I still remember the definition of "socialist consciousness" that we were repeatedly tested on through the years: "Socialist consciousness is a person's political soul. It is the consciousness of the Proletarians represented by Marxist Mao Tse-tung thought. It takes expression in one's action, language, and lifestyle. It is the task of every Chinese student to grow up into a Proletarian with a socialist consciousness so that he can serve the people and the motherland." To make the abstract concept accessible to us, our teacher pointed out that the immediate task for students from Working-class families was to strengthen their socialist consciousnesses. For those of us who were from other class backgrounds, the task was to turn ourselves into Workers with socialist consciousnesses. The teacher never explained exactly how we were supposed to "turn" into Workers. Instead, we were given samples of the ritualistic annual plans we had to write at the beginning of each term. In these plans, we performed "self-criticism" on our consciousnesses and made vows to turn ourselves into Workers with socialist consciousnesses. The teacher's division between those who did and those who didn't have a socialist consciousness led me to reify the notion of "consciousness" into a thing one possesses. I equated this intangible "thing" with a concrete way of dressing, speaking, and writing. For instance, I never doubted that my political philosophy teacher had a socialist consciousness because she was from a steelworker's family (she announced this the first day of class) and was a Party member who wore grey cadre suits and talked like a philosophy textbook. I noticed other things about her. She had beautiful eyes and spoke Standard Chinese with such a pure accent that I thought she should be a film star. But I was embarrassed that I had noticed things that ought not to have been associated with her. I blamed my observation on my Bourgeois consciousness.

At the same time, the way reading and writing were taught through memorization and imitation also encouraged me to reduce concepts and ideas to simple definitions. In literature and political philosophy classes, we were taught a large number of quotations from Marx, Lenin, and Mao Tse-tung. Each concept that appeared in these quotations came with a definition. We were required to memorize the definitions of the words along with the quotations. Every time I memorized a definition, I felt I had learned a word: "The national red flag symbolizes the blood shed by Revolutionary ancestors for our socialist cause"; "New China rises like a red sun over the eastern horizon." As I memorized these sentences, I reduced their metaphors to dictionary meanings: "red" meant "Revolution" and "red sun" meant "New China" in the "language" of the Working class. I learned mechanically but eagerly. I soon became quite fluent in this new language.

As school began to define me as a political subject, my parents tried to build up my resistance to the "communist poisoning" by exposing me to the "great books"—novels by Charles Dickens, Nathaniel Hawthorne, Emily Brontë, Jane Austen, and writers from around the turn of the century. My parents implied that these writers represented how I, their child, should read and write. My parents replaced the word "Bourgeois" with the word "cultured." They reminded me that I was in school only to learn math and science. I needed to pass the other courses to stay in school, but I was not to let the "Red doctrines" corrupt my mind. Gone were the days when I could innocently write, "I saw the red, red rose among the green leaves," collapsing, as I did, English and Chinese cultural traditions. "Red" came to mean Revolution at school, "the Commies" at home, and adultery in *The Scarlet Letter*. Since I took these symbols and metaphors as meanings natural to people of the same class, I abandoned my earlier definitions of English and Standard Chinese as the language of home and the language of school. I now defined English as the language of the Bourgeois and Standard Chinese as the language of the Working class. I thought of the language of the Working class as someone else's language and the language of the Bourgeois as my language. But I also believed that, although the language of the Bourgeois was my real language, I could and would adopt the language of the Working class when I was at school. I began to put on and take off my Working class language in the same way I put on and took off my school clothes to avoid being criticized for wearing Bourgeois clothes.

In my literature classes, I learned the Working-class formula for reading. Each work in the textbook had a short "Author's Biography": "X X X, born in 19— in the province of X X, is from a Worker's family. He joined the Revolution in 19—. He is a Revolutionary realist with a passionate love for the Party and Chinese Revolution. His work expresses the thoughts and emotions of the masses and sings praise to the prosperous socialist construction on all fronts of China." The teacher used the "Author's Biography" as a yardstick to measure the texts. We were taught to locate details in the texts that illustrated these summaries, such as words that expressed Workers' thoughts and emotions or events that illustrated the Workers' lives.

I learned a formula for Working-class writing in the composition classes. We were given sample essays and told to imitate them. The theme was always about how the collective taught the individual a lesson. I would write papers about labor-learning experiences or school-cleaning days, depending on the occasion of the collective activity closest to the assignment. To make each paper look different, I dressed it up with details about the date, the weather, the environment, or the appearance of the Master-worker who had taught me "the lesson." But as I became more and more fluent in the generic voice of the Working-class Student, I also became more and more self-conscious about the language we used at home.

For instance, in senior high we began to have English classes ("to study English for the Revolution," as the slogan on the cover of the textbook said), and I was given my first Chinese- English dictionary. There I discovered the English version of the term "class-struggle." (The Chinese characters for a school "class" and for a social "class" are different.) I had often used the English word "class" at home in sentences such as, "So and so has class," but I had not connected this sense of "class" with "class-struggle." Once the connection was made, I heard a second layer of meaning every time someone at home said a person had "class." The expression began to mean the person had the style and sophistication characteristic of the Bourgeoisie. The word lost its innocence. I was uneasy about hearing that second layer of meaning because I was sure my parents did not hear the word that way. I felt that therefore I should not be haering it that way either. Hearing the second layer of meaning made me wonder if I was losing my English.

My suspicion deepened when I noticed myself unconsciously merging and switching between the "reading" of home and the "reading" of school. Once I had to write a report on *The Revolutionary Family*, a book about an illiterate woman's awakening and growth as a Revolutionary through the deaths of her husband and all her children for the cause of the Revolution. In one scene the woman deliberated over whether or not she should encourage her youngest son to join the Revolution. Her memory of her husband's death made her afraid to encourage her son. Yet she also remembered her earlier married life and the first time her husband tried to explain the meaning of the Revolution to her. These memories made her feel she should encourage her son to continue the cause his father had begun.

I was moved by this scene. "Moved" was a word my mother and sisters used a lot when we discussed books. Our favorite moments in novels were moments of what I would now call internal conflict, moments which we said "moved" us. I remember that we were "moved" by Jane Eyre when she was torn between her sense of ethics, which compelled her to leave the man she loved, and her impulse to stay with the only man who had ever loved her. We were also moved by Agnes in *David Copperfield* because of the way she restrained her love for David so that he could live happily with the woman he loved. My standard method of doing a book report was to model it on the review by the Publishing Bureau and to dress it up with detailed quotations from the book. The review of *The Revolutionary Family* emphasized the woman's Revolutionary spirit. I decided to use the scene that had moved me to illustrate this point. I wrote the report the night before it was due. When I had finished, I realized I couldn't possibly hand it in. Instead of illustrating her Revolutionary spirit, I had dwelled on her internal conflict, which could be seen as a moment of weak sentimentality that I should never have emphasized in a Revolutionary heroine. I wrote another report, taking care to illustrate the grandeur of her Revolutionary spirit by expanding on a quotation in which she decided that if the life of her son could change the lives of millions of sons, she should not begrudge his life for the cause of Revolution. I handed in my second version but kept the first in my desk.

I never showed it to anyone. I could never show it to people outside my family, because it had deviated so much from the reading enacted by the jacket review. Neither could I show it to my mother or sisters, because I was ashamed to have been so moved by such a "Revolutionary" book. My parents would have been shocked to learn that I could like such a book in the same way they liked Dickens. Writing this book report increased my fear that I was losing the command over both the "language of home" and the "language of school" that I had worked so hard to gain. I tried to remind myself that, if I could still tell when my reading or writing sounded incorrect, then I had retained my command over both languages. Yet I could no longer be confident of my command over either language because I had discovered that when I was not careful—or even when I was—my reading and writing often surprised me with its impurity. To prevent such impurtiy, I became very suspicious of my thoughts when I read or wrote. I was always asking myself why I was using this word, how I was using it, always afraid that I wasn't reading or writing correctly. What confused and frustrated me most was that I could not figure out why I was no longer able to read or write correctly without such painful deliberation.

I continued to read only because reading allowed me to keep my thoughts and confusion private. I hoped that somehow, if I watched myself carefully, I would figure out from the way I read whether I had really mastered the "languages." But writing became a dreadful chore. When I tried to keep a diary, I was so afraid that the voice of school might slip in that I could only list my daily activities. When I wrote for school, I worried that my Bourgeois sensibilities would betray me.

The more suspicious I became about the way I read and wrote, the more guilty I felt for losing the spontaneity with which I had learned to "use" these "languages." Writing the book report made me feel that my reading and writing in the "language" of either home or school could not be free of the interference of the other. But I was unable to acknowledge, grasp, or grapple with what I was experiencing, for both my parents and my teachers had suggested that, if I were a good student, such interference would and should not take place. I assumed that once I had "acquired" a discourse, I could simply switch it on and off every time I read and wrote as I would some electronic tool. Furthermore, I expected my readings and writings to come out in their correct forms whenever I switched the proper discourse on. I still regarded the discourse of home as natural and the discourse of school alien, but I never had doubted before that I could acquire both and switch them on and off according to the occasion.

When my experience in writing conflicted with what I thought should happen when I used each discourse, I rejected my experience because it contradicted what my parents and teachers had taught me. I shied away from writing to avoid what I assumed I should not experience. But trying to avoid what should not happen did not keep it from recurring whenever I had to write. Eventually my confusion and frustration over these recurring experiences compelled me to search for an explanation: how and why had I failed to learn what my parents and teachers had worked so hard to teach me?

I now think of the internal scene for my reading and writing about *The Revolutionary Family* as a heated discussion between myself, the voices of home, and those of school. The review on the back of the book, the sample student papers I came across in my composition classes, my philosophy teacher—these I heard as voices of one group. My parents and my home readings were the voices of an opposing group. But the conversation between these opposing voices in the internal scene of my writing was not as polite and respectful as the parlor scene Kenneth Burke has portrayed (see epigraph). Rather, these voices struggled to dominate the discussion, constantly incorporating, dismissing, or suppressing the arguments of each other, like the battles between the hegemonic and counter-hegemonic forces described in Raymond Williams' *Marxism and Literature* (108–14).

When I read *The Revolutionary Family* and wrote the first version of my report, I began with a quotation from the review. The voices of both home and school answered, clamoring to be heard. I tried to listen to one group and turn a deaf ear to the other. Both persisted. I negotiated my way through these conflicting voices, now agreeing with one, now agreeing with the other. I formed a reading out of my interaction with both. Yet I was afraid to have done so because both home and school had implied that I should speak in unison with only one of these groups and stand away from the discussion rather than participate in it.

My teachers and parents had persistently called my attention to the intensity of the discussion taking place on the external social scene. The story of my grandfather's failure and my father's success had from my early childhood made me aware of the conflict between Western and traditional Chinese cultures. My political education at school added another dimension to the conflict: the war of Marxist-Maoism against them both. Yet when my parents and teachers called my attention to the conflict, they stressed the anxiety of having to live through China's transformation from a semi-feudal, semi-capitalist, and semi-colonial society to a socialist one. Acquiring the discourse of the dominant group was, to them, a means of seeking alliance with that group and thus of surviving the whirlpool of cultural currents around them. As a result, they modeled their pedagogical practices on this utilitarian view of language. Being the eager student, I adopted this view of language as a tool for survival. It came to dominate my understanding of the discussion on the social and historical scene and to restrict my ability to participate in that discussion.

To begin with, the metaphor of language as a tool for survival led me to be passive in my use of discourse, to be a bystander in the discussion. In Burke's "parlor," everyone is involved in the discussion. As it goes on through history, what we call "communal discourses"—arguments specific to particular political, social, economic, ethnic, sexual, and family groups— form, re-form and transform. To use a discourse in such a scene is to participate in the argument and to contribute to the formation of the discourse. But when I was growing up, I could not take on the burden of such an active role in the discussion. For both home and school presented the existent conventions of the discourse each taught me as absolute laws for my action. They turned verbal action into a tool, a set of conventions produced and shaped prior to and outside of my own verbal acts. Because I saw language as a tool, I separated the process of producing the tool from the process of using it. The tool was made by someone else and was then acquired and used by me. How the others made it before I acquired it determined and guaranteed what it produced when I used it. I imagined that the more experienced and powerful members of the community were the ones responsible for making the tool. They were the ones who participated in the discussion and fought with opponents. When I used what they made, their labor and accomplishments would ensure the quality of my reading and writing. By using it, I could survive the heated discussion. When my immediate experience in writing the book report suggested that knowing the conventions of school did not guarantee the form and content of my report, when it suggested that I had to write the report with the work and responsibility I had assigned to those who wrote book reviews in the Publishing Bureau, I thought I had lost the tool I had earlier acquired.

Another reason I could not take up an active role in the argument was that my parents and teachers contrived to provide a scene free of conflict for practicing my various languages. It was as if their experience had made them aware of the conflict between their discourse and other discourses and of the struggle involved in reproducing the conventions of any discourse on a scene where more than one discourse exists. They seemed convinced that such conflict and struggle would overwhelm someone still learning the discourse. Home and school each contrived a purified space where only one discourse was spoken and heard. In their choice of textbooks, in the way they spoke, and in the way they required me to speak, each jealously silenced any voice that threatened to break the unison of the scene. The homogeneity of home and of school implied that only one discourse could and should be relevant in each place. It led me to believe I should leave behind, turn a deaf ear to, or forget the discourse of the other when I crossed the boundary dividing them. I expected myself to set down one discourse whenever I took up another just as I would take off or put on a particular set of clothes for school or home.

Despite my parents' and teachers' attempts to keep home and school discrete, the internal conflict between the two discourses continued whenever I read or wrote. Although I tried to suppress the voice of one discourse in the name of the other, having to speak aloud in the voice I had just silenced each time I crossed the boundary kept both voices active in my mind. Every "I think . . ." from the voice of home or school brought forth a "However . . ." or a "But . . ." from the voice of the opponents. To identify with the voice of home or school, I had to negotiate through the conflicting voices of both by restating, taking back, qualifying my thoughts. I was unconsciously doing so when I did my book report. But I could not use the interaction comfortably and constructively. Both my parents and my teachers had implied that my job was to prevent that interaction from happening. My sense of having failed to accomplish what they had taught silenced me.

To use the interaction between the discourses of home and school constructively, I would have to have seen reading or writing as a process in which I worked my way towards a stance through a dialectical process of identification and division. To identify with an ally, I would have to have grasped the distance between where he or she stood and where I was positioning myself. In taking a stance against an opponent, I would have to have grasped where my stance identified with the stance of my allies. Teetering along the "wavering line of pressure and counter-pressure" from both allies and opponents, I might have worked my way towards a stance of my own (Burke, *A Rhetoric of Motives*, 23). Moreover, I would have to have understood that the voices in my mind, like the participants in the parlor scene, were in constant flux. As I came into contact with new and different groups of people or read different books, voices entered and left. Each time I read or wrote, the stance I negotiated out of these voices would always be at some distance from the stances I worked out in my previous and my later readings or writings.

I could not conceive such a form of action for myself because I saw reading and writing as an expression of an established stance. In delineating the conventions of a discourse, my parents and teachers had synthesized the stance they saw as typical for a representative member of the community. Burke calls this the stance of a "god" or the "prototype"; Williams calls it the "official" or "possible" stance of the community. Through the metaphor of the survival tool, my parents and teachers had led me to assume I could automatically reproduce the official stance of the discourse I used. Therefore, when I did my book report on *The Revolutionary Family*, I expected my knowledge of the official stance set by the book review to ensure the actual stance of my report. As it happened, I began by trying to take the official stance of the review. Other voices interrupted. I answered back. In the process, I worked out a stance approximate but not identical to the official stance I began with. Yet the experience of having to labor to realize my knowledge of the official stance or to prevent myself from wandering away from it frustrated and confused me. For even though I had been actually reading and writing in a Burkean scene, I was afraid to participate actively in the discussion. I assumed it was my role to survive by staying out of it.

Not long ago, my daughter told me that it bothered her to hear her friend "talk wrong." Having come to the United States from China with little English, my daughter has become sensitive to the way English, as spoken by her teachers, operates. As a result, she has amazed her teachers with her success in picking up the language and in adapting to life at school. Her concern to speak the English taught in the classroom "correctly" makes her uncomfortable when she hears people using "ain't" or double negatives, which her teacher considers "improper." I see in her the me that had eagerly learned and used the discourse of the Working class at school. Yet while I was torn between the two conflicting worlds of school and home, she moves with seeming ease from the conversations she hears over the dinner table to her teacher's words in the classroom. My husband and I are proud of the good work she does at school. We are glad she is spared the kinds of conflict between home and school I experienced at her age. Yet as we watch her becoming more and more fluent in the language of the classroom, we wonder if, by enabling her to "survive" school, her very fluency will silence her when the scene of her reading and writing expands beyond that of the composition classroom.

For when I listen to my daughter, to students, and to some composition teachers talking about the teaching and learning of writing, I am often alarmed by the degree to which the metaphor of a survival tool dominates their understanding of language as it once dominated my own. I am especially concerned with the way some composition classes focus on turning the classroom into a monological scene for the students' reading and writing. Most of our students live in a world similar to my daughter's, somewhere between the purified world of the classroom and the complex world of my adolescence. When composition classes encourage these students to ignore those voices that seem irrelevant to the purified world of the classroom, most students are often able to do so without much struggle. Some of them are so adept at doing it that the whole process has for them become automatic.

However, beyond the classroom and beyond the limited range of these students' immediate lives lies a much more complex and dynamic social and historical scene. To help these students become actors in such a scene, perhaps we need to call their attention to voices that may seem irrelevent to the discourse we teach rather than encourage them to shut them out. For example, we might intentionally complicate the classroom scene by bringing into it discourses that stand at varying distances from the one we teach. We might encourage students to explore ways of practicing the conventions of the discourse they are learning by negotiating through these conflicting voices. We could also encourage them to see themselves as responsible for forming or transforming as well as preserving the discourse they are learning.

As I think about what we might do to complicate the external and internal scenes of our students' writing, I hear my parents and teachers saying: "Not now. Keep them from the wrangle of the marketplace until they have acquired the discourse and are skilled at using it." And I answer: "Don't teach them to 'survive' the whirlpool of crosscurrents by avoiding it. Use the classroom to moderate the currents. Moderate the currents, but teach them from the beginning to struggle." When I think of the ways in which the teaching of reading and writing as classroom activities can frustrate the development of students, I am almost grateful for the overwhelming complexity of the circumstances in which I grew up. For it was this complexity that kept me from losing sight of the effort and choice involved in reading or writing with and through a discourse.

REFERENCES

Burke, Kenneth. *The Philosophy of Literary Form: Studies in Symbolic Action.* 2nd ed. Baton Rouge: Louisiana State UP, 1967.

———. *A Rhetoric of Motives.* Berkeley: U of California P, 1969.

Freire, Paulo. *Pedagogy of the Oppressed.* Trans. M. B. Ramos. New York: Continuum, 1970.

Williams, Raymond. *Marxism and Literature.* New York: Oxford UP, 1977.

"Writing as Struggle" : Conversions and Conversations

"*WRITING* as Struggle" began as a nine-page paper to fulfill an assignment for a teaching seminar I took with David Bartholomae in the Fall of 1984. The assignment asked us, a group of graduate students teaching freshman composition for the first time, to use our own experiences as writers to reflect on how one learns to write and what one does when one writes. The assignment intrigued me from the beginning because it is an assignment which, through a series of questions, can start a writer on a project that inevitably gets bigger and more complicated. By the end of the Fall term, the paper had grown to a thirty-five page seminar project. In the following two years, I prepared for my dissertation while teaching a series of composition classes. My schedule was tight, but I found myself tinkering with the essay every bit of time I could take away from my other projects. It bothered me that I was spending so much time and energy on that project while the practical conditions of my life as a graduate student suggested that I should have been focusing my energy on completing my doctoral degree requirements as soon as possible. Looking back, however, my fascination with the project seems to make sense. The project gave me an occasion to puzzle over and respond to a series of questions concerning the teaching and learning of writing which preoccupied me as a writer, a teacher, and a parent.

I began "Writing as Struggle" at a point in my life when teaching at the University of Pittsburgh Composition Program and reading the writings of post-structuralists and post-Marxists had opened up a whole new way for me to think about the nature of writing. My exposure to these composition and critical theories was beginning to make clear to me that some of my traumatic experiences as a writing student were related to the way writing is represented and taught as a tool for survival and the way my teachers and parents tried to make what they saw as the "choice" way of writing my "natural" way of using language. Comparing the composition classroom in which I learned to write with the classroom I was learning to build as a new composition teacher further reinforced my conversion to my new theoretical stance. When I started "Writing as Struggle," I knew that some of the most frustrating and confusing moments in my growth as a writer, moments which I felt eventually led to a writing block when I left high school, could serve as powerful examples to illustrate how and why the pedagogical practice of my home and school was detrimental to a writing student's development. I began with the conviction that I had a point to make. In trying to make that point, however, I found myself skipping through my past for obvious examples and packaging them into an argument. Yet, thinking about one incident brought back other incidents. The voices of my parents and teachers began to talk back, reminding me of their concern, love, and commitment to their teacherly responsibilities and of my own desire to be the good student they expected.

These memories complicated the point I was making, for they suggested that much more was going on in those classrooms than the relationship between the theoretically naive parents/teachers and the victimized writing student. Yet, I felt unable to tackle my vague sense that "more was going on." I "finished" the paper to meet the deadline for the teaching seminar, and showed it to my two chief readers, David Bartholomae and Bruce Horner. They were generous and warm in their support but ruthless in their comments. They spotted the center of the problem I faced at that stage and encouraged me to find a way of "letting my story tell itself." This launched a whole series of revisions, a series which lasted two years. I have since often wondered if, in making such comments, Dave and Bruce had anticipated the bulk of work their comments would eventually bring them. For both ended up reading and responding to every page of my manuscript through its seven major revisions. I myself certainly began the first stage of my revision with very little sense of how far and long my project would take me. I made three major revisions between the Winter of 1984 and the Spring of 1986. This stage of my revisions might be characterized as my fight against the urge to appropriate my earlier experiences with my commitments to particular critical and composition theories. I began to pay attention to the positive as well as negative forces operating in the classroom of my adolescence. Reflecting on my parents' and teachers' commitment to my education and my own hunger for knowledge, I began to find some links between my past and several situations in my present life with which I had been preoccupied for some time.

The first of these situations was the resistance I encountered in my writing students. I found my students irritated by my effort to teach writing as a form of strenuous and constant work. It concerned me that all they seemed to want was for me to fix their papers and to give them some quick steps to good writing. These students reminded me of myself as a student, my anxiety to quickly become a good writer, and my belief that writing should come easily and naturally to me when I left the classroom. I saw a parallel situation in David Bartholomae's teaching seminar as I listened to myself and other graduate students turning to him for tips on good teaching. Dave is the kind of teacher who is aware that although good teaching and learning inevitably involves a process of imitation, it must not stop with that process. Therefore, although he speaks strongly and persistently about his notion of what is involved in the teaching of writing and about what he does as a teacher, he also self-consciously forces his students to contest his position as a teacher by actively locating themselves in relation to that position. While most of us understood and admired his teaching in theory and tried to enact such a method in our own teaching, our anxiety to become good teachers often made us wish he would "ease up" by giving us some tips on good teaching.

A third situation was the concern of my husband and myself with my daughter's education. Although we are both composition teachers committed to teaching writing as a form of critical thinking, we found ourselves caught between our conflicting desire to make life smooth and pleasant for her and our desire for her to explore what is involved in living. Our tendency to present what we think is best for her as the right way of thinking and acting reminded me of how my parents and my teachers educated me. In theory, our concern as parents has been how to teach our daughter to share the beliefs and values about which we feel strongly without taking away from her the ability to reflect on and qualify these beliefs. In practice, our concern to protect and guide her makes problematic what we see as central to good teaching—the teaching of critical thinking. My preoccupation with these situations added a further dimension to how I approached my past in my essay. "Writing as Struggle" gradually became a reflection on not only why and how the teaching method of my home and school were bad but also why such a bad method could speak so powerfully to good teachers, parents, and students committed to the teaching and learning of writing.

By 1986, I had thirty-some pages of what most people would call an autobiographical account of how I learned to write, and I felt it was ready to reach a wider range of readers. I submitted the essay to *College English* and started to read sections of it at national conferences. Two types of recurring responses to the manuscript defined for me both the strength and weakness of the piece. Most readers found the "personal narrative" evocative. There was a split, however, in their reaction to the absence of explicit theoretical references in the essay. One group of readers found the essay lacking in scholarly or theoretical perspective. Another group of readers treated it as an illustration of their own individual theoretical perspectives, including the very perspectives on language and writing which my essay critiqued. I myself felt that the choices I made in how I selected incidents from my past and in how I approached these incidents in the "narrative" were choices which grew out of my commitment to specific critical and composition theories. The power of my "narrative" resided in the way these theories helped me to make sense of and order the story of my past. Therefore, I imagined that the way I "narrated" my past would function as the kind of theoretical reference which usually took the form of citations or footnotes. It bothered me, however, that most of my readers found such references to be either "absent" or "open." It bothered me even more that the few readers who did recognize the theoretical framework of my "narrative" seemed to be people who already shared my stance as a teacher and critic. For my sense of how composition is taught in a large number of American classrooms made me feel an urgent need to talk to those who did not share my theoretical stance. I realized that bringing out in more explicit terms the critical and composition theories which had informed my writing would be one way of enabling them to hear my critique of their theoretical stance which my "narrative" seemed to allow them to ignore.

I began the second stage of my revision thinking I could make these references by adding a few paragraphs to the essay. The essay underwent three major revisions from the Spring to the Winter of 1986 because, not surprisingly, the paragraphs I added on to the essay sounded exactly like paragraphs merely added on. They read like a footnote by another writer "explicating" for the reader the theoretical framework of the essay. My habitual way of discussing critical and composition theory in what most people would call critical essays jarred with the way I used theory to make sense of my past in "Writing as Struggle." My revision became a search for a way of bridging the separation between the "narrative" and the theoretical references I was adding to it. Both the compliments on the evocative power of my personal story and the criticism of its unscholarly form provoked me to look for an "unscholarly" way of providing my theoretical references. I experimented with ways of "narrating" rather than "explicating" the theory of language and writing which informed my work through a set of metaphors. My first breakthrough came when I found in Burke's parlor scene a "narrative" which gave me the language to highlight both what I saw as most vital in the understanding of writing in post-structuralist and post-Marxist theories and what I saw as most regrettably missing in my parents' and teachers' understanding of language. At the same time, I felt that since the organizing force for this writing was the act of reaching to the past in search of a new way of understanding, the theoretical discussion should enact such a movement. I looked for a way of taking my reader through my earlier experience twice, first on a more "narrative" level and then on a more "theoretical" level. Gradually, my experience in writing a book report on *The Revolutionary Family* came to strike me as the ideal point of return for my "theoretical" discussion.

Looking back, it seems all very "obvious" why "Writing as Struggle" took the final shape it did. My work as a writer, a teacher, and a mother brought me into contact with a group of writers, students, teachers, colleagues, editors, and, most importantly, their words and actions. In the solitude of my study, I labored in front of my computer through many long and agonizing hours. But my "silent" collaborators made their presence known, forcing me through one revision after another with both their contentions and their support. They taught me to be persistent when the argument became fuzzy and muddled and to be suspicious when it became too obvious and final. "Writing as Struggle," once "finished," became a voice which now lives a life of its own. It visits me as I work on my other writings. In giving that voice life, I experienced the excitement of talking back to voices with power enough to dominate the conversation. "Writing as Struggle" has itself become one of those voices with which I am learning to converse.

❧ QUESTIONS ☙

Min-zhan Lu's essay, "From Silence to Words: Writing as Struggle," and its process essay, "'Writing as Struggle': Conversions and Conversations"

1. As does Barbara Mellix, Min-zhan Lu writes of languages she learned that served different purposes in different places, though her situation might be seen as more severe since she learned a political language during the Cultural Revolution in China. To what degree in this country were you taught a political language through which you view your culture and other cultures? What are some of the components of that language? Are the "languages" you use in school, in reference to your country, and in your conversations at home as distinctly different as Min-zhan Lu's? Does this make the political language you learned any less influential?

2. Min-zhan Lu writes that when she could no longer keep the language of school from the language of home, she fell silent. Doubtless you have fallen silent yourself in certain situations, or seen friends and fellow students fall silent as well in the classroom. How does this silence differ from the one Min-zhan Lu describes? What is *its* source? Is the silence borne of the lack of skill the student has acquired, as Min-zahn Lu suggests, in the discourse of the classroom? Would this problem be less severe if students were encouraged to use in class the discourses they have learned outside the classroom?

3. Min-zhan Lu writes in her process essay of having worked on her article for two years. What would it mean to have that much time to work with an essay? Would you ever choose to spend that much time on one essay, one story? What would be some of the advantages of writing over so much time? What about the disadvantages? What would make it worth so much struggle, so much effort? What would it require of you as a writer? When you read, how do you think of the essay or story that you're reading? Do you assume that it was written in one sitting? Does it change the way you read and write to know otherwise?

4. At the end of her process essay, Min-zhan Lu writes, "'Writing as Struggle,' once 'finished,' became a voice which now lives a life of its own. It visits me as I work on my other writings." How can the voice of a particular essay "live a life of its own"? Have you ever finished a particularly successful paper and wanted to return to its voice, its sensibilities, for other essays and papers you write? What is the value of that? And what might that successful voice impede?

≈ Possible Writing Topics ≈

1. Write an essay where you work to define the effect that the language or discourse of your education or your culture has had in shaping your opinions, perspectives, ways of thinking, ways of believing, ways of seeking meaning. You may want to think in terms of the rituals you observed in grade school, the ways you were taught, and the language that was used to teach you. You may want to consider the language used in television programs, in television commercials, in newscasts, in magazines and books that you've read. How do these media work to influence you, to form a perspective? Do you find them deliberately manipulative, or no more so than language used by friends and family?

2. After you've finished the first essay, write a second one where you discuss whether we need to use language as "a survival tool" against the kind of discourses you have written about in your first essay. Should we fear the discourse of the media? of education? Do we need to fight it in order to claim our own ground as free-thinking individuals? *Is* there such a thing as a free-thinking individual? Are there ways of approaching these discourses so that we might use them rather than fight them? use language as a way of understanding them rather than as a tool for surviving them?

Kevin Stemmler

Boo, Boot, Boots: Building Language

RECENTLY, a student in my Basic English class asked me why I ended up being an English teacher. At first I thought his comment was intended as an insult and I became at once defensive. Pausing a moment, I looked at him and realized that his question was sincere, that because he was not interested in writing he was trying to figure out why someone else would be. Since this is the very same question I have been known to ask math teachers, I knew that he was wrestling with a question that was trying to figure out human nature and individual interests. Knowing his question was fair and sincere, I answered, "Because I'm fascinated with words." This answer brought mixed reactions of bewilderment and smirks from the students in the class, so I went on to explain my point.

As children, one of the first basic skills we learn is how to recite the alphabet. This was not only true when I was a child but I see it still holds true today as I hear my cousin's youngest son sing: "A-B-C-D-E-F-G . . . " anytime I am around him. While both children and parents are proud and delighted that the alphabet has been memorized, and they are eager to share the recitation of it with any audience, I think that somewhere along the way many people lose their pride and delight with letters.

Perhaps I am an exception to the rule, but I cannot really remember a time in my life when the alphabet did not hold an element of mystery for me. Not only was I proud to have learned that series of letters but I was eager to learn how to use them. Being the youngest of four children, I was jealous of the fact that everyone in my family knew how to write and I anticipated the day when I, too, would learn to put letters together to form words.

Words. That's what this all leads up to. My interest in writing is a result of my fascination with words, both their spelling and their sounds. When I was in the hospital with an eye injury at the age of four, a neighbor brought me two books, one about a cowboy, the name of which I cannot remember, and one whose name I cannot ever forget: *The Boy Who Fooled the Giant*. The book about the giant was of special interest to me since I wanted to identify with the boy in the story who reaches into his bag of tricks to slay the giant and save the town. I had everyone who came to visit me in the hospital read that book to me until I finally reached a point where I had memorized all the words of the story. After my recovery, my parents would ask me to recite the story anytime relatives came to visit. I, too, was proud of my accomplishment and I remember quite clearly one recitation in front of a group of my uncles gathered in my one uncle's basement where I drew back my shoulders, raised my chin and proudly spouted: "Long ago and far away there was a boy. His name was Billy. He was nine years old." My father stood grinning throughout the entire, long recitation, even though he had heard the story for the umpteenth time. It was such approval that kept my interest in words and stories alive.

Although I had mastered the art of memorizing words, I was still unable to read them for myself. When I was five I was the only child left at home during the day, so while my father was at work and my brother and sisters were at school, my mother would read to me to pass the time. My godparents had given me a large book that Christmas called *365 Bedtime Stories* which alloted me one story for each day of the year. The stories took place on What-A-Jolly-Street and the children who lived there spent many an afternoon at the home of Mrs. Apricot who entertained them with stories of her own. I do not remember the circumstances surrounding this event, but one morning, while my mother was downstairs doing laundry, I was left unattended with my book. Again, I do not remember what caused me to do this or even how I figured out how to do this, but I selected a large, purple crayon from my crayon box and turned to a page that illustrated Mrs. Apricot surrounded by the children of What-A-Jolly-Street. Taking crayon in hand, I touched the purple tip to the page and wrote, slowly and thoughtfully, the word: BOO. I remember staring at the word for a while, then sounding it out. Boo. Boo. Then somehow I made some sort of association and picked up my crayon again. In the middle of the page I recopied the word, only this time I added the letter *T*. I stopped to survey the results of my effort and sounded out my second word: BOOT. Quickly I picked my crayon up again and this time I added another letter, an *S*. Scrawled across the top of Mrs. Apricot's living room wall was a list of my first words: BOO, BOOT, BOOTS. It was the stringing together of these words, the discovery that adding a letter or taking a letter off created a new word, that began my fascination with the written word and my relationship with language.

When I finally started first grade, I was disappointed to find that the curriculum involved more than just reading and writing. While I had hoped to pursue the interest I had in discovering language and learning how it worked, I found myself having to share my time with other, less important subjects like arithmetic and geography. Although I never lost my interest in reading and writing, I had to put my narrow pursuit of it on the back burner for a while as I gave into learning how to add and subtract and locating Pennsylvania on the map. It wasn't until the fourth grade that I reopened the door to discovering the sounds of language and the feeling of words.

When I was in the fourth grade I had difficulty breathing. I don't know how *real* my symptoms were, but at the time they were real enough. Although

I can recall a certain tightness in my chest, a difficulty getting air into my lungs, I also remember that I envied, at the time, a girl named Denise. Denise had asthma and had to get shots to treat it and take pills to control it. I thought the ailment made her special because it allowed her to be pampered. Denise was, as I wanted to be, excluded from gym class. Asthma, I thought—what a wonderful solution.

As I said, it was also in the fourth grade when I rediscovered my interest in language and words. Since my first daily class was reading, I found that the sound of a particular word could keep me silently occupied all through my math and geography classes. I grew up, then, sacrificing mathematical skills and geographical knowledge for the sake of language. My breathing problem, too, was a sacrifice I made for my discovery of words.

Asthma. Just the sound of it was something exotic, the way it hissed across the tongue and lips. Asthma. I wanted to own the word. "I have asthma," I wanted to say. But I couldn't take the risk of simply blurting out to my parents: "I have asthma." I needed, first, for them to suggest it. Quite simply, their suggestion, "Maybe you have asthma," would have given me custody of the word.

"I can't breathe," I said on a Sunday evening when my parents were watching the tail-end of a late football game.

"It's from jumping on your bed," my father said, always the voice of logic.

"It's all in your head," my mother said, always the voice of wisdom.

"No, really," I protested, "I can't breathe!"

"Then go to bed. It's close to your bedtime anyway. And don't think you're staying home from school tomorrow," my mother said. Stay home from school? Me? And miss gym class?

While my parents' failure to diagnose asthma, thereby refusing me custody of that lovely sounding word, came as a disappointment, I learned to live with the word in private. And my breathing problem never really went away, either, for I found if I concentrated hard enough I could make it appear on cue. All it took was a little focus, a little fine tuning of my senses and—wham—I couldn't get air into my chest. Instantly my lungs were sacks of wet sand.

One day, after school, I was standing in the backyard trying to decide whether or not I really wanted to have asthma. I had been watching my father plow the remnants of the garden under ground—tilling the soil, he called it. I had recently risen from my seat in the wheelbarrow where I had been watching him for a long time. I was soon spinning around in circles, watching my father, the rotatiller, the house and yard spin dizzingly by. The whole world blurred. I stumbled out of my spin and stood for a moment on uneasy ground. When I regained control of movement, I stood very still. My heart pounded out a rhythm that matched the awkward grind of the rotatiller. My heart, too, was tilling, breaking new ground inside of me, overturning a sorrowful soil that would never be plowed under again. For a new word was taking shape inside of me. Exotic? Yes, in a dull, mournful way, it was exotic. But I could sense from the start that this was a word I did not want to own, for even from the very start I felt a sense of dread taking shape with that word, so real that, to this day, I suffer from the sound.

I took my seat in the wheelbarrow again and stared at the evening sky. The sun, somewhere in my spinning daze, had set and the day had quickly turned dark, like a typical autumn evening, and cold. The metal of the wheelbarrow was ice against my skin. The sky was suddenly the darkness of winter—black, heavy, and threatening somehow. The short distance between where I sat and where my father plowed seemed to expand. He grew further away from me in the darkness, became fuzzy in the sudden grey light. My father's figure growing faint before my eyes may have brought the word to my mouth. Or perhaps it was the message my heart was pounding to my brain, for my heart had plowed a serious soil, a soil of hard earth that could not be seeded. My heart sent death to my mouth and I could taste and feel it all at the same time. It was exotic in its heavy dumbness, graceful in its clumsy sound. Death. It was an easy word to say, requiring only that the tip of my tongue meet the roof of my mouth, then force air over my teeth and lips. And there it was, in the grey twilight, looming across the sky, evident in my father's vague shadow. Although I wanted to run to the shelter of the well lit house where my mother, I knew, would be saying her rosary, I felt I couldn't leave my father there, unattended in the dark.

When he finished his last, long row he brought the tiller over to where I stood and motioned, with one hand, that I should follow. I grabbed the handles of the wheelbarrow, and slowly pushed it in the path of my father's shadow.

Death, I realized, was something Denise could not claim to own—"I have death" was not a possibility. That she could die from her asthma was a possibility, however remote. Logically, that anyone could die, at any moment, was a fact, not just a possibility.

My mother was working at my uncle's turkey farm that autumn, late into the evening hours, and had been working since long before Thanksgiving. The turkey season ran clear through December, forcing my mother to begin her Christmas shopping early. To save time, she wrapped each present as she bought them, putting name tags on each gift that warned us not to open them until Christmas Day. Coming home from school each day with my sister, we'd take the housekey from the metal milkbox on the backporch and let ourselves into the house, making a beeline for my parents' bedroom. Early in December we started shaking presents with our names on them, venturing guesses on what was inside based on what sounds we heard. One day my sister exclaimed, "Look at all the presents Mom and Dad bought us," and it dawned on me that there was not a Santa Claus. I wasn't really upset—at least if I was, I hid it to avoid my sister's taunting remarks—I was mostly disappointed that the words *Santa*

Clause no longer had meaning. They were empty, hollow, dull. They were words that had lied to me for years.

One day my sister ventured to peel the tape from the corner of a bulky package. "I got a doll," she screamed, "I got a doll!" She was happy because my mother had explained that she was getting too old to play with dolls. This discovery, however, erased any previous disappointment that my sister suffered. And so, at my sister's encouragement, we unwrapped, each day, a different gift until shortly before Christmas we had a careful inventory of every single gift we were to get. Then disappointment settled in: we would not have any surprises on Christmas Day. But that wasn't entirely true.

On Christmas Eve my mother grew sick and by the end of the day had been admitted to the hospital. When my father came home from the hospital without her, I felt a heaviness swell up inside my mouth. I suddenly realized that opening my presents early resulted in my mother's death. I was being punished for trespassing in my parents' room. There, on the gifts surrounding the tree, the "do not open" gift tags taunted me. Just as I was about to perform a teary confession, my father spoke up: "She'll be fine. It's just a virus, but she's very sick." I felt my asthma creeping back. I couldn't breathe from suppressing tears.

"Since we have to have Christmas without her, you may as well open your presents now," my father said. But there was no joy in opening our gifts, despite the fact my sister and I tried to feign surprise as we opened each package. Each gift I opened served as a reminder to me that my curiosity had almost killed my mother. There was, at the end of our unwrapping, one final surprise. My father presented us with small, heavy packages. Opened, we compared our finds. My sister held a purple transistor radio in her hands and I held a blue one in mine. "A transistor radio?" I questioned, "I didn't even ask for one."

"At least you got one surprise," my father said. And I felt warm as I tried to deny the accusation that we would look at our presents early. It wasn't bad enough that my mother couldn't be with us for the holiday, now I felt obligated to develop a sense of language that I had never really used with my family before. The language of deception is a painful system of words where one lie leads to another. Discovering the word death seemed to have opened a Pandora's box of painful, hurtful words.

My mother did not die in the hospital. On Christmas Day we called her on the telephone in my grandparents' kitchen. When I heard her voice my heart began to race and my throat tightened. I wanted to cry when I heard her but because my relatives were standing there I would not give in to tears. I said meekly, softly to prevent the tears, "Merry Christmas, Mom." But my voice went up at the end of the line because it wasn't a merry Christmas in the least.

"Don't be upset because I'm not there. I'm going to be fine," she said on the other end of the phone.

"Mmmhmm," I said, because I had lost my ability to use words.

"I have something for you here," she added. "I'll send it home with Dad tonight."

"Mmm." And regardless of my relatives' close eyes and wide ears, I made an attempt at speaking. "It's not the same . . . " I started, but I could not say "without you." Those words wedged sideways in my throat.

Even though she was sick, my mother maintained her wisdom. "Put your sister on," she said, then "Merry Christmas."

When my father came home from the hospital that night he handed me the present my mother had sent. "Here you go," he said, placing in my hands a homemade gift. It was two pill cups filled with pink and green mints, covered over with a fine red mesh. Inverted, it was a pair of Christmas bells, and I found it beautiful. That night I took it to my bed with me and placed it on the nightstand so I could lie on my side and stare at it. While I cried, finally, the smell of peppermint came to me in short bursts, curing my asthma and calming my fear of death.

Later that week my mother was discharged from the hospital. She came into the house steadied on my father's arm. I looked at them and felt a new sound being sent from my heart to my mouth. The taste of love was full and round, and I enjoyed the sound so much that I refused to let it leave my lips.

Such refusal to allow words to leave my mouth, perhaps because I am too embarrassed or shy to say them, is one of the reasons I write. I have found that words are sometimes difficult to say no matter how exotic or beautiful they may be. Those same words, however, easily find their way into my writing. What I did not explain to my student who asked why I write was that everytime I commit a word to a piece of paper I am taking custody of that word. This word becomes another thing I own. As much as this sounds materialistic in a way, I mean it in the most positive way. What I should have told that student was the story of the boy who fooled the giant and won power over him. It is through language, through the manner in which Billy phrases his dares, that he gains control and power over the giant. Billy's words, as much as any action, are what finally destroy the giant.

In a way, the story of Billy parallels my writing life, for each word I discover or celebrate becomes part of my bag of tricks so that, like Billy, I can reach in at any time to choose the appropriate word to get the job done. Even better, each time I reach into the bag I can pull out the same word but it never has to be used in the exact same way. What continues to fascinate me is the simple fact that at the very heart of the matter one thing is true: all the words we own are formed out of the arrangement of only twenty-six letters. As much as I hate math, I must admit that I am drawn to the mystery of the infinite in a finite set.

Finding the Root

*T*HE most difficult part of any writing assignment is figuring out where or how to start. This is a problem I am constantly forced to solve, whether I am writing a letter, a short story, or an essay. Because this is a problem, I force myself to start with the first idea that comes to me, knowing I can always go back and begin again.

For "Boo, Boot, Boots: Building Language," I knew from the start what my general purpose was because I had a topic controlling what I wrote. I had given an assignment to my Freshman English class on finding voice by writing about a family memory. As a challenge, I decided to try addressing the same assignment I had given my students. But from the moment I wrote the first sentence I felt I was veering in a direction that the assignment was not asking.

The essay originally started with the line, "When I was in the fourth grade I had difficulty breathing," and was meant to tell the story of my bout with asthma. As I wrote, I suddenly realized that I wanted to write about my response to first hearing the word "asthma" since the memory has come to represent my fall from innocence with language. From the moment of that discovery I knew I wanted the essay to be about language and my experiences with learning the meaning of words. After writing that sentence—which is now the start of the second paragraph on page 439—I went on to tell the stories I remembered that were significant moments in my learning the relationship between words and their meanings. The essay's first draft ended with my mother's homecoming from the hospital—now the bottom of page 443. When I finished, I reread my essay from start to finish.

The first thing that struck me was that the essay was too personal and, therefore, not traditional. It did not resemble any essay I had ever written. Thus, I was faced with a new problem: how to make my essay seem more traditional.

While I had envisioned my final product as an essay from the very start, I realized I had ended up with the outline of a short story. The fine line separating my essay from story was the fact that the essay was entirely true. While I always use autobiographical information to inform or influence my fiction, I do not record pure autobiography in story form. When I'm working on a story I always disguise the truth by altering it somehow. This piece of writing, however, made no effort to avoid or conceal the truths of my life. It was, pure and simple, an accurate presentation of details from my life. Although I was tempted to turn the essay into a story, I resisted the urge (a decision I'm still not convinced was proper) and pursued the essay genre. After all, a personal essay should deliver what the title promises: a record of a circumscribed personal experience.

I read the essay once again, this time with a voice in the back of my head reminding me that it was to be read *as* an essay. But it seemed too vague somehow. It was obvious that something was missing, that my point was not as clear as I envisioned it. Although in teaching pedagogy the issue of audience has become passé, I found myself asking what audience I intended for my essay. While I could not place or see an audience, I at least became aware of the needs of one and realized the essay was actually opening in the middle of the action. While this technique was effective for the Greeks, today's audience has come to expect that a beginning will precede the middle.

If I were to look at the shape or structure of my essay as a word, my first draft would be the root. What I needed was a prefix that would alter the meaning of the original essay. As it turned out, what I am calling the prefix of the essay changed the root a little, shifting the focus of the essay as well as my purpose.

The prefix of the essay is what makes it more traditional. Here I begin by presenting the point that will lead the reader into an understanding of the latter part of the essay. The example I begin with is a thinly disguised introductory paragraph of the traditional five paragraph essay that our English teachers have warned us about, implying that if we dare touch it our essay may fall off or we'll go blind. Since all writers must make decisions and take risks, I decided that I could at least try to get by with the basic introduction that says: "Here is the purpose of this piece of writing." While part of me felt like I was committing the crime I am always warning my students to avoid—introducing a paper with a phrase like "It was October of 1967"—the other part of me felt like it was the easiest solution to the where-to-begin problem and a logical way to get started.

Perhaps my other reason for beginning the essay in this manner is due to the experiences I've had in taking fiction writing workshops where I've been exposed to a different approach to writing. Learning that a good story makes evident its occasion, I found myself sensing that, again, the essay had much in common with a story. As in fictional stories, I needed to have a reason for telling the story in the first place. Since the essay is dealing with learning in a loose way, it seemed logical that I would begin with the example that came from one of my classes and allow it to serve as the occasion for the essay being written. It was ironic and convenient that I had recently been asked the question by the student and that my answer so easily fit into the issue I was addressing in the essay. This seems, in fact, too good to be true, as though I had stretched the truth and created a device. But like the rest of the essay, the incident is entirely true.

The second paragraph of the essay, in fact, is a rehashing of the example I gave to the student in the classroom who asked me why I teach. Because the example made sense at the time and seemed to satisfy my students as an adequate answer, I decided it would make sense in relation to the essay's purpose. Notice that from the very first paragraph through the second I am making a move from a more abstract idea to a more personal idea. This progression was, I suppose, planned, although I do not recall a conscious decision to structure the essay this way. Unconsciously I knew I had to get back into the personal frame of mind so that when I came to the material about having asthma the reader would not feel this as a change in the essay.

In a way, the structure of the essay parallels the content of the essay. While I begin by talking about letters forming words, I finally get to a point where the attention is focused purely on words. If I go back to the example that the original start of the essay is the root and the first few pages are the prefix, I can see that adding letters onto the root word is like the reverse of the Boo, Boot, Boots example. Because of the essay's content, though, the reader sees the essay's structure lining up more with the Boo, Boot, Boots discovery of adding another letter onto the root word. This is because I start with the basic alphabet, then move into memorizing words, then into the act of printing my first series of words.

The rest of the essay is then given to providing examples from one particular year in my life when I started to realize that words were more than several letters arranged in a particular way. Suddenly words had relationships with objects, and words I had always known, heard, and used suddenly had meanings attached to them.

Upon reading that version of the essay, I realized that the prefix had solved the problem I had created for myself, that the root of the essay now had a reason for existing. But now I felt that the essay was out of balance. While I must admit that I was tempted to end with the material about my mother's discharge from the hospital and the discovery of the word "love," I knew instinctively that it was too personal a note on which to end the essay. Also, I felt it seemed too much like an attempt to manipulate the reader's emotions. Had the essay ended there, I would have been using a shortcut that I always reprimand my students for taking when, for example, they end a descriptive paper on a person with the event of the person's death. This is asking the reader to feel sorry for the writer and to forgive the paper for not really coming to any conclusions about the person it is meant to describe. If successful, the emotional ending can make the reader forget to be critical of the writer's work. Considering my objection to this "trick" of writing and due to the addition of the prefix, I felt obligated to add a suffix to the essay's root.

Reshaping the essay again turned out to be a larger problem than I had anticipated. How could I bridge the gap from the personal to the less personal? How could I guide the reader from an emotional moment to a more abstract moment without losing the reader's attention or breaking the train of thought? I don't know how deliberate my decision was, but I see now that the end of the essay is like a reverse of the beginning. After writing several pages working strictly with personal experience, I felt the need to move back into the abstract. I can't say that it made sense at the time, but I do remember that as I wrote the ending it seemed to feel right.

First I reintroduce Billy and the Giant into the essay and use it as an illustration for my overall purpose. This is then broken down to be a comment on the power of the single word and from there I am asking the reader to go back to the very beginning: the idea that the alphabet is the start, our foundation for language, in the same way the alphabet is the foundation that the essay is built upon. After this comment, I go back to the point about mathematics that I introduced in the essay's first paragraph. In short, I have built up, then torn down, the structure of my essay.

Examining the structure of the essay in the way I have seems to reduce it to a piece of work that is more simplistic than it really is. But there is a more complicated way of looking at the process involved in writing the essay.

What I could have done was to take the time to explain what decisions were made in terms of having to weed out examples that illustrated my point or offered feelings concerning my attitude toward writing. I could have included other examples from my past, how reading my first two real books—Helen Keller's autobiography and a biography of Sam Houston—made me want to be a blind, Texan writer when I grew up. I mean this in all seriousness for I realized, without being able to verbalize it then, that even a subject like Helen Keller's disabilities could be romanticized by words. The fact, too, that I was moved by her story taught me something about the power of language and reading.

The essay could also have been very cynical in its tone and approach because of the kinds of issues I was working with in relation to my life's circumstances at the time I wrote it. For instance, I could have reported that on the day the student asked my why I taught English I had roughly seventeen cents in my pocket and a smaller balance in my checkbook. I had just spent seventy five cents mailing out a story I knew would be rejected, and I spent my lunch hour envying my old high school friends who skipped the college scene and got jobs and spouses and children and nice homes in the country. In short, I could have focused on all the sacrifices I have made and continue to make in pursuing a teaching career and a career in writing.

Perhaps the essay I wrote and the need I felt as an impulse for writing it is a result of the omitted material. Perhaps this essay was a way of convincing myself that I had no choice in life but to pursue that which has always meant something to me. Maybe all along I knew that on those days when I have only seventeen cents to my name, I also know that there are things that I can claim as my own: mainly words or memories. The irony, I suppose, is that language can enrich my life but cannot make me rich. For a moment I almost suggested that at least language does not cost anything but in a way words aren't free either, which is, I guess, the overall point of my essay. Sometimes the price we pay to own a word is very high because of the pain or difficulty we have come to associate with the memory involved with taking custody of the word. For me the main focus of this feeling is the experience of my fourth grade year. You might say that having all of these events take place in such a short period of time in one specific year of my life seems a little too convenient to believe. But I swear it's true. And after all, you don't really have any choice but to take my word for it.

ଊଓ QUESTIONS ରୁଅ

Kevin Stemmler's essay, "Boo, Boot, Boots: Building Language," and its process essay, "Finding the Root"

1. Several times in the essay Stemmler writes of parental approval as motivation for keeping his interest in words alive, particularly when reciting the story from memory and his parents' power to give him custody of words such as "asthma." In your experience in your own development as a writer and reader as well as those you've watched develop as writers, how important is the approval from authority figures in developing an interest in language, and what power do those in authority have over developing such an interest? Had you been encouraged, would you enjoy writing more? Do you know of those who didn't receive such encouragement and still became interested in writing (or any other aspect of education)?

2. Stemmler makes much of the sound of words, the feel of them in his mouth as he pronounced them, as if when he came to own a word he could feel its presence in his body. Of what significance is this in Stemmler's developing love of language? Can you appreciate his experience of the sound of words? Have any words struck you the same way? Of what importance is a love of the sound of language in becoming interested in language?

3. In his process essay, Stemmler says that the most difficult part of writing is knowing where to start. He writes, "Because this is a problem, I force myself to start with the first idea that comes to me, knowing I can always go back and begin again." Do you use a similar procedure when you write? If not, does it seem a wise one? How often when you begin writing—and finally end up throwing out the opening you initially intended to use—do you find the information or the ideas turning up later in the essay? And what does this say about writing and the writing process?

4. Stemmler writes, "Sometimes the price we pay to own a word is very high because of the pain or difficulty we have come to associate with the memory involved with taking custody of the word." How is memory, pleasant or painful, triggered by language? To what degree do we rely on language to

call forth memory? Have you found, as does Stemmler, that the mentioning of a certain word can recall your first real experience of it?

❧ Possible Writing Topics ☙

1. Remember a time when you learned the meaning of a word or series of words or when those words took on new meaning, and write an essay about that experience. This essay need not take on a sad or profound topic; the words don't necessarily have to be so heavy. What meaning did the words have for you prior to your new recognition of them? What happened that changed their meaning? As you look back now, has the meaning of the words changed again? And what does this say about language and its relationship to experience and the acquisition of memory?

2. As with many writers in this book, Stemmler struggles with truth, the fact that truth takes on a different meaning in an essay rather than a story. Read through the essays you've written in this class, and write an essay where you discuss how truthful, in the sense that these writers have described, your writing has been. Is there a difference between being truthful and being honest in writing? Can you tell the truth even while inventing some of what happened? Have you developed a new definition of the word "truth"—as Stemmler does for "death" and "love"—as you've read and written for this class? How has that definition developed? How important is honesty when writing an essay that supposedly "really happened"?

Ingrid Mundari

Language as Image Maker

THE West Indies is a multi-lingual, multi-ethnic cluster of islands and Trinidad, my home for the first fifteen years of my life, is a prime example of this "melting pot." It is a melting pot, however, with subtle delineations and demarcations which enforce a class system based upon language. The system of education is based upon traditionally British lines and the common language is English—it is the shared language of public intercourse and the one which defines the island's public life. Patois, the Creole dialect and one of the island's secondary languages, is used mainly in the home and in the market-place.

As a child, I would accompany my mother on her shopping trips to the big, open-air market which stood at one end of the city. Amidst the cacophony of sounds and the constantly shifting swirls of people and colors—brightly dressed vendors hovering over deep red mangoes, yellow guavas and green coconuts—the farmers would call to each other and to the shoppers in Patois, splicing their dialogues with announcements about their wares, and a sentence or two of English. With my hand tightly clasped in my mother's, I would walk with her from stall to stall, tiptoeing to peer at the array of produce displayed on the slabs of waist-high sandstone. I would stare fascinatedly at the deft movement of the fisherman's knife as he eviscerated a huge mackerel or swordfish, while he kept up a running commentary in Patois to my mother. I was able to understand a phrase or two here and there, but Patois was a language of secrets and great mystery to me, made more so by the fact that it was a language of my elders. None of my friends spoke it, but their parents and grandparents did.

English was spoken everywhere else, but in the marketplace and the home Patois held sway. Of course when visitors dropped by everyone spoke English, and in the commercial districts of the city where the men dressed in suits and the women wore their hair piled on top of their heads, it was the same.

As a child, Patois seemed to me to be a language of exclusion. If the adults were having a conversation and there were children present, they would speak Patois when the topic was something we were not allowed to hear. This was generally the case with my mother and my aunts. They would be having a normal conversation and one of them would suddenly throw a significant look in our direction which would then cause them to switch to "their" language. When, at the market with my mother, I was able to respond in the few sentences of Patois I knew to queries about my age and my preference for either mangoes or guavas, I was petted and praised. However, when I tried to demonstrate this knowledge at home it produced different results. When I would unexpectedly break into one of my mother's Patois conversations, she would look at me as though seeing me for the first time and send me off to the garden to play with my cousins. I couldn't understand this. I felt proud of the fact that I was able to grasp enough of what was being said to participate in the conversation, but conversely, it seemed that my very understanding of their language shut me out even more.

At school it was altogether different. There, I entered another world, the boundaries of which were delineated by English and religion. Apart from Patois, and to a lesser extent, French, Portuguese and Spanish, there were two "types" of English spoken on the island": "the King's English" as the nuns at my school labelled it, and the sing-song dialect spoken by many islanders. This dialect dispensed with the phonemic sounds of many English words so that the "th" and "g" sounds disappeared, and the substitution of the verb "done" for various forms of the verb "to be" comprised a large part of its structure. In response to a query regarding someone's whereabouts the answer might be: "He done gone a long time now." In addition, there were word substitutions and portmanteau words which conveyed entirely different areas of meaning from the original English. Then, too, a shift in the tone or cadance of an islander's voice could do the same.

By the time I was ten, I was quite used to speaking Patois with some degree of fluency at the market, speaking "Island English" with my friends at home, and speaking school English in the classroom. There were several prep schools run by nuns of different orders on the island, and these schools were considered special. They were where young girls went not only to be made into ladies, but to receive a sound education in the process. A convent girl was always immediately recognizable, from the spotless white shirt and neatly pleated skirt of her uniform, to the way in which she carried herself. But the real test of a convent girl, as we were reminded time and again, was the way in which she spoke. "Even if she's out of uniform, from the time a convent girl opens her mouth, you know who she is."

The way in which a convent girl spoke, of course, had everything to do with the way she was taught to speak in school. Throughout my early school years, it seemed that part of each day was given over to a reading and recitation period during which our teacher would read a story, poem, or passage aloud, and we would recite it back to her line by line, while following along in our Readers. She would have us repeat certain words and phrases over and over until she was sure we had mastered the pronunciation. Those of us who allowed the island-lilt to creep into our voices were made to go over each syllable again and again, until she was satisfied with the result. In the beginning we saw it as nothing more than learning to read; curling our tongues around words with a lot of letters and stringing them together.

Our Reader in the second grade was a long, thin book with a red cover which contained rhymes such as:

> *There was a naughty boy*
> *And a naughty boy was he*
> *He ran away to Scotland*
> *The people there to see*
> *And he found that the ground was hard*
> *That a yard was long*
> *That a song was merry*
> *That a cherry was red*
> *As a berry . . .*

We enjoyed reciting these, and the tendency was to run all the words together. They seemed to have a momentum that rushed your tongue along and allowed you to swallow half of the words as you progressed. But that was precisely it — you weren't supposed to swallow any part of the word, or drop any part of its sound. We would be made to repeat the rhyme until the "d" could be clearly heard, and the tendency to say "foun" and "groun" was given over to the desire to enunciate clearly.

There were Speech Days for which the entire school was assembled and prizes were given to the best elocutor for her rendition of a poem, or a piece of prose. The accent was on pronunciation, inflection and cadence. You didn't allow your voice to rise at the end of the line unless you were asking a question; you pronounced your "g's" and "th's" clearly, and you certainly didn't offer your delivery in a sing-song tone of voice.

I was being initiated into the mysteries of language through these techniques, realizing that if a certain word were said a certain way it could have a whole new meaning. And nowhere was this clearer than at choral rehearsals. Sister Columba, the music mistress, had a habit of walking through our ranks during choir practice and putting her ear to our mouths. Ostensibly, this was to ascertain pitch and make sure we were in the right key, but it was a technique that served other purposes as well. On one occasion as she stood in front of a classmate, she motioned the rest of us into silence and listened intently as the unhappy culprit was made to sing the same line over and over. The line was "As we bathe in your blood, cleanse us O Lord," and the word "bathe" was being sung as "bade." She told us that the entire meaning of the line had been changed, assured us that the two words had nothing in common, and assigned us the task of looking up both words in the dictionary and formulating several sentences to demonstrate the correct usage of each word. My days were filled with many such incidental lessons, stemming not only from my music teacher, but from anyone in whose presence/hearing we had violated the rules of pronunciation.

As I grew older, it became increasingly difficult to shift my use of language as I had been accustomed to doing. The ease with which I had once moved from Patois to "Island English" to school English was rapidly evaporating. At home, when my playmates made verbal mistakes, I couldn't help correcting them. Of course I was teased for being one of those convent girls, who thought she knew everything. At the same time, my visits to the market were becoming more and more infrequent, as was my use of Patois. The fascination of Saturday morning trips to the market was beginning to fade, although the fascination with words and the rich and varied levels of meaning they could create was growing.

Interestingly enough, Latin and French were the languages which had begun to replace my interest in Patois. The Mass, as well as many of our school prayers, was said in Latin, and most of us had memorized whole sections of the Liturgy long before we fully knew what the words meant. It was enough to repeat them phonetically and take pleasure in the heavy, full syllables which rolled off our tongues.

"Do-mi-nus For-bis-cum."

"E-cum-spi-ri-tuo."

By the time we were eleven we had already begun a formal study of Latin, and although the text of the Mass had already begun its changeover into English, the learning of Latin was still stressed. It was the language next to "school English" which quickly came to shape my world. We attended Mass every morning in the school chapel and twice on Holy Feast Days. We were constantly surrounded by or participating in some form of prayer, and we learned hymns in Latin and English and sang both versions.

Latin, like Patois, was also shrouded in a mystery I had difficulty penetrating. The difference, however, was that with Latin I did not seem to mind as much. I didn't feel as shut out as I had in my earlier interactions with Patois. Whatever secrets the priests held as they intoned the words of the Mass, they gave me a chance to share, and though I could not fully comprehend, I could participate. When I responded during the service, whether in Church or in school, I was included because my response, my words, and the knowledge I was attaining of the language I was using allowed me entrance into the world which this language had created.

A similar pattern had begun to develop with my study of French. Even though my knowledge of Patois made the transition to French easier, I was conscious of the fact that I was being taught the "proper" words and the "correct" pronunciation, two things which created whole new levels of meaning and opened up entirely new doors for me. The Patois equivalents to the words, phrases, sentences, with which I was becoming daily more familiar, seemed to be different not only in tone and cadence, but in purpose as well. And in the same way I corrected my friends when they spoke "Island English," I now corrected my mother when she spoke Patois, adjuring her to use the "right" French word for its Patois counterpart. Along with the inevitable teasing that this engendered, I was conscious of the fact that my older brother seemed to have little difficulty in moving in and out of the various language systems. He seemed easily able to cross the boundaries between Patois, Island English and "proper English."

For me, however, there existed a gap where none had been. As much as I tried, I couldn't move myself back into a speech pattern with which I had once felt so comfortable. I began to second guess myself, carrying on monologues and pretended snatches of dialogue in my head in my "Island voice" and in my school voice, trying to navigate myself through the differences. The school voice seemed more pronounced, more powerful, and bit by bit, the Island voice seemed to be fading. I found myself listening to people's pronunciation in a way I never had before. This made me even more irritated with myself, not only because I would lose track of what was being said to me during a conversation, but also because of the very intrusiveness of the act in which I was engaged.

At Mass on Sundays when we responded in English, my ears picked up the sounds of swallowed "t's" and bowdlerized "h's," whereas in the school chapel, my voice blended in with a sea of others, all strong, all self-assured. Here, no one faltered at the syllabic stress on the "w" in "hallowed." I imagined our tongues caught firmly between our teeth when we enunciated the "th" sounds, just as I envisioned the sing-song cadences evaporating away when we recited the Pater Noster. We seemed to send forth each word as though they were perfectly round, hard pebbles, making clean arcs through the air before returning to land in the sea of our voices, without eliciting so much as a splash.

The division between who I had been, the person who the combination of "Island English," Patois and school English had shaped, began to separate me from whom I was becoming, the person who had recreated her world in terms of the latter. And, along with this came the realization that the ways in which I used language seemed to have a great bearing on who I was.

On Assembly Days when Mother Superior spoke before the school, her voice stayed with me throughout the rest of my day. What she said seemed as important as the way in which she said it, and one of the things she said repeatedly was "to speak well is to write well." Creating myself through language, through the words I spoke, seemed inextricably meshed with creating myself through the words I wrote. For when I did write I was conscious that sounds like the "wh" in the word "what" had as much significance on the page as when it was pronounced "what" instead of "wat." I was conscious of the fact that the word "witch" had nothing in common with "which" and that the double level of meaning they involved was just as significant on paper as it was when verbalized.

Language and its use came to denote many things for me, not the least of which was the recognition of its shaping power and its ability to structure a world and a world view for its user. The circle of friends and acquaintances with whom I now spent most of my time was comprised of people that made me feel at ease, that didn't shut me out, and didn't tease me about the way I spoke. More importantly, to me at least, I didn't find myself involuntarily correcting anyone's speech, or having to go through a composing process in my head before I spoke. I didn't have to worry about *how* I spoke, because the person I was and the person I had spoken into being were now one and the same.

Essay on "Language as Image Maker": The Shaper and the Shaped

*W*HEN I began writing the essay "Language as Image Maker" I had one clear idea, or theme if you will, that I wished to explore: the way(s) in which language could be used as a shaping device, and the process by which this was accomplished. As I wrote, the question I seemed to be addressing was whether we shaped language or it shaped us. Like the old conundrum of the chicken and the egg, language and its user (and in turn, the ways in which it was used) appeared to operate as two sides of the same coin. That one could use language as a tool in much the same way that a sculptor employs a knife to carve out an object, to give shape, texture, dimension, to what was formerly a block of wood, stone or clay was a concept which not only fascinated me, but which seemed to be one of the main threads in the fabric of my essay. The thing about this, though, is that language is a tool which shapes and defines its user as much as it is used to give shape and definition to that person's world. This was something I had known intellectually, something with which I was academically familiar, but which did not become fully actualized for me until the writing of my essay.

Exclusion and inclusion are terms which play important roles in the lives of children, and though they may now know the meaning of these words, they care even at an early age about fitting in, acceptance, and not being left behind or closed out. A child who "has a way with words," who can exercise a certain command of language, possesses a degree of power that she soon learns to use. That child can not only name the world, and in so doing give shape and definition to her understanding of it, but she can also use this verbal passport to the worlds of others like her playmates. A shy child is one who does not use language easily and who all too often feels, or is made to feel, left out from the circle which other children create through their use of language. I was not a shy child, but I still found myself subject to a form of exclusion because of the different worlds which certain uses of language created. In order to gain admittance and to become a part of these worlds I had to master the use of the tools which built them.

The earliest memory of my realization of the power of language and my ability to tap into that power is of my Saturday morning visits to the marketplace with my mother. I chose to begin my essay by writing about this because, even today, the remembrance of the special way I felt, the special way I was made to feel each time I demonstrated my ability not only to understand the words of Patois being addressed to me, but to reply in kind, is still a vivid and potent recollection. I was allowed to feel, if only for a short time, that I could share in a significant occasion, participate in a different and important world, and this meant a great deal. I knew that what I wanted to do at that point of my essay was describe how and why I felt the way I did. I didn't yet know that the theme of language use as an inclusionary and exclusionary medium would assume the importance it did in light of the overall essay, for my main concern then was to show the power that this memory of my first brush with a different use of language had on me.

I had many friends my own age, but that wasn't enough, for I wanted to be a part of the grown-up world. I wanted to know what they talked about, whispered about, laughed about. I wanted to be in on the joke. I can recall the times when my mother or father would make a comment about something and I would join in the general laughter which ensued, only to have my brother tease: "What are you laughing at? You don't even know what we were talking about." And that, for me, was the secret they shared. If I knew the words they were using, the sentences they were speaking, I could be just like them. I too could talk and laugh with them on their level. At the movies, I wanted to sit with my sister and her friends up in the balcony where the "big girls" sat, not downstairs with my parents. I wanted to know what they whispered and giggled about, and my sister's response of "you wouldn't understand" seemed unfair. What it all seemed to boil down to was that there was a dividing line created by language, and I was determined to bridge the gap.

There were several problems in bridging this gap, however. It was not only a matter of mastering "their" language, which seemed difficult enough, but as I was also beginning to realize, *what* they said seemed at times as important as *how* they said it. The nuances and inflections their voices took on when they said certain things seemed to provide a whole new area of meaning for them, while I was left still trying to figure out the original import of what I'd heard. One family story in particular dealt with an episode from my aunt Christine's girlhood, in which she'd apparently said something awkward to the priest during Confession. At the time, since I did not fully understand what an "Act of Confession" meant, I was even more at a loss when my mother's voice would change significantly during her retellings of the story, and a word which she'd used previously and no one had laughed at was now being said in such a way that everyone around her, including my aunt, would dissolve into paroxysms of mirth.

Another problem that I faced in terms of bridging this prohibitive gap was that of having to deal with different languages. In my essay, when writing about the differences in meaning which speech inflections and nuances conveyed, I began to realize that these were just as exclusory as the speaking of Patois could be. But Patois wasn't enough, it seemed, for I also had to navigate my way through Island English and School English which provided a whole new set of complexities for me to figure out. This, then, was the next route my essay took, charting my course through the two forms of spoken English with which I had to contend. In recollecting this part of my life, calling up my school experiences in order to put them on paper, something else became clear: the world I had created through language with my childhood friends outside of school, the world shaped by Island English, had been impinged upon from two sides. One was my own dissatisfaction with my outsider status which my elders' use of language conferred on me, whether in English or Patois, and the other was the new world which the use of School English had begun to construct. I decided to explore, in even greater depth than I had first intended, the specific kinds of things I had been required to do in school, in that part of the essay. I had hit upon something, but I wasn't as yet quite sure of where it was leading or what it might turn out to be. I knew I needed to discuss the impact that School English had on me, and writing about the rhymes I had to learn, the recitation classes with the accent on pronunciation, the exhortations to speak clearly all came together for me on the page in two ways. These things had combined to play a pivotal role in what already seemed like a confusing melange of the types of signals I was both giving and receiving in my use of language, but also, the shape that my essay was now taking was enabling me to make sense of the confusion.

If my desire had been to be part of the world of my elders by attaining mastery over what seemed so easily accessible to them, "their" language, I now found myself in a place, both in terms of writing the essay and in recalling this memory, where for the first time it seemed I had been given a choice. The recognition of this choice was not something I had fully comprehended even as I was faced with it. In writing about it now, in ordering up these memories to create the essay "Language as Image Maker," many things became clear, even as to how this choice was made and why. I chose to use a language which did not make me feel excluded. I chose to master this tool and use it to shape a world in which I felt I belonged, and more importantly, which belonged to me. I no longer had to stand outside the door which I perceived my elders' use of language as erecting, waiting to gain admittance. The skill I attained in this usage gave me an importance which at first began to make up for, and then replace, that which I felt had been lacking in my unwieldy application of my elders' tools.

My years in Convent School, my participation and interaction in a community of girls who were being taught to perceive themselves, the world, and ultimately, its relation to them through the implementation of a certain type of language use, engendered political and social ramifications which came into full realization for me in the writing of my essay. Looking back over those years I have come to understand something which I then grasped only dimly, and which began to work itself through in writing "Language as Image Maker." Not only is the ability to use the spoken and written word the employment of a powerful tool, but in using that tool to shape, carve, define and build, there is as much of a process of shutting out as there is closing in, taking place. In my essay, as I wrote about the feeling of acceptance and importance which School English conferred on me, what became clear was that I was also moving away from the circle of belonging which Island English had allowed me to enter. Even as I was being included in a group whose demarcations were forged by a particular use of language, I was exluding, and in a sense, being excluded from the group whose language I hardly spoke anymore. The phrase which I had heard innumerable times throughout my school years was true in many more ways than I had first imagined. You did know a Convent girl from the moment she opened her mouth. Because the way in which she spoke, had been taught to speak, signified her mastery of the tool of language, her use of which indicated several levels of meaning to her audience, not the least of which was the statement she was making about herself. She had used a particular kind of language to shape her world, and it in turn had given just as much shape and definition to who she was, to what she had become.

QUESTIONS

Ingrid Mundari's essay, "Language as Image Maker," and its process essay, "Essay on 'Language as Image Maker': The Shaper and the Shaped"

1. As Kevin Stemmler does in "Boo, Boot, Boots: Building Language," Mundari describes the pleasure that came from the pronunciation of certain words and certain verses, and how she was taught that a mispronunciation changed the meaning of all that was said. In your own experience, when you have mispronounced words or heard others mispronounce them, what has been your reaction? When you were corrected, did you feel inferior to or less educated than the person who pronounced the words correctly? How is Mundari's experience similar to Barbara Mellix's in "From Outside, In"?

2. What would you describe as the equivalent in writing of mispronunciation, of learning different ways to write based on the expectations placed on you by those who read your work? When you read, how do you respond to a misspelling? What about a sentence that is poorly punctuated? How is your assessment of that writing changed by these errors? Do you skip over them? Do they confuse your reading? Are you able to read through them? How does your response to these questions affect the "correctness" of your own work?

3. In her process essay, Mundari writes, "A child who 'has a way with words,' who can exercise a certain command of language, possesses a degree of power that she soon learns to use. That child cannot only name the world, and in so doing give shape and definition to her understanding of it, but she can also use this verbal passport to the worlds of others like her playmates." Here again, a writer is dealing with the issue of language and power, that a facility with language gives power to its user. Of those you know personally and publicly, who has garnered power and authority because of his or her facility with language? How does language allow him or her to reach others? Certainly there are those who gain power through other means than linguistic facility. In your own experience, what has led to the authority and power others have over you, and does language affect that power?

4. Mundari writes, "In writing about it now, in ordering up these memories to create the essay 'Language as Image Maker,' many things became clear, even as to how this choice was made and why. I chose to use a language which did not make me feel excluded." Here Mundari discusses writing as other writers have throughout this book: Ideas and memories that were only half-shaped in her mind were made vivid by the writing process. After having written and read many essays about the process of writing, what argument would you make about the shaping power of writing, its ability to clarify ideas and perceptions that remain muddled when left in your head? In what ways does writing differ from speaking? Do you believe you know more about your ideas, your memories, your perspectives having written about them in this class?

∾ Possible Writing Topics ∾

1. Write an essay where you assess what you've learned about writing from this book and the work you've done in this class. Many ideas have been presented to you by many writers, some of which have been contradictory. You have written and read a number of essays and stories in this class; you have gained memory, experience, and authority from the work you've done. You are in a position as a writer and reader to present your perspectives on what you think writing is and what it does. You should answer the question "What have you learned?" but more important are the answers to the questions "What do you know, how have you come to know it, and how have you been affected by this knowledge?" Will the knowledge affect the way you approach writing in other classes? What about any writing you do outside the university? Will you read differently? And do your knowledge of and perspectives on writing and reading affect the way you view your world, your culture?

2. When you've completed the first essay, write a second one where you discuss what power you have gained, if any, from writing this and other essays in this class. Have the reading and writing of these stories and essays given you any sort of power, whether it is of the generative kind that Barbara Mellix describes or the power of inclusion that Mundari and others have described? What does it mean to have this power? How is it exercised? Does it seem genuine? Is the word "power" appropriate for what you and other writers should do with language? Can you think of a term that is less threatening? Is that term more accurate?

Notes on Contributors

ELEANOR BERGHOLZ has worked as a reporter for the *Pittsburg Post-Gazette* where for five years she wrote news and feature stories. In preparation for a journalism career, she studied in the undergraduate writing program at The University of Pittsburgh and gained practical experience as a stringer for the *Post-Gazette* before assuming a full-time position. Her article reprinted in the text won the 1987 feature writing award from The American Cancer Society. She is 44 years old.

LAURA LYNN BROWN is a graduate of the Masters of Fine Arts Writing Program of The University of Pittsburgh where she taught journalism as a teaching assistant. Prior to studying in the MFA program, she worked as a newspaper reporter in eastern Ohio. About her writing, Laura has said, "A continued questioning of spiritual belief, the power of memory (and the notion that what is not remembered can be as powerful as what is), a sense of place—these are the ideas that inform my essays.

MARK COLLINS has worked as a newspaper reporter, public relations specialist, and currently as director of marketing for a consulting firm. A 1986 graduate of the Master of Fine Arts Program in Writing at The University of Pittsburgh, he continues to write essays, profiles, and, currently, a novel.

KATHLEEN A. COPPULA was born in Export, Pennsylvania in 1954. She graduated from Mercy Hospital School of Nursing in 1974 and worked as a registered nurse for six years, mainly in Intensive Care and Psychiatry. During her psychiatric nursing experience she became "interested in the stories of peoples' lives as well as in the interpretation of the language with which they expressed themselves." She left nursing to take writing courses at The University of Pittsburgh where she received a Masters of Fine Arts in Writing in 1987. Her stories have been published in *Four Quarters* and *Cream City Review*. The essay reprinted here appeared in *Mid-American Review*.

ଊ ୨୧

MELISSA GREENE, a native of Georgia, graduated from Oberlin College in 1975 with a B.A. in English. She has written feature articles and criticism for *The Atlantic; The Washington Post; Country Journal; Ohio Magazine; Southern Exposure; The Georgia Review; The Iowa Review*, among other publications. She is 36 years old and lives in Atlanta with her three children. The essay reprinted in the text was nominated for a national magazine Award in the Feature Writing Category.

ଊ ୨୧

ELWIN GREEN was born in Louisville, Kentucky in 1952 and educated at the Simmons Bible College in Louisville, at Michigan State University, and The University of Pittsburgh where he studied in the undergraduate writing program. He has been a cab driver, a keypunch operator, a television studio assistant, a radio broadcaster, and, between 1972 and 1975, a soldier in the U.S. Army. An ordained minister, he is Associate Minister at the Bethany Baptist Church in Pittsburgh where he lives with his wife Janet, a librarian.

ଊ ୨୧

SALLY FLECKER studied in the Masters of Fine Arts Writing Program at The University of Pittsburgh where she also teaches composition. Also a freelance writer, her magazine articles have ranged from writing about the Guardian Angels to forensic odontology. She is currently involved in the production of a video documentary on single-mothers-by-choice. She has said, "I'm not sure that I believe in the "little woman" theory of history, that one person can make a difference, but I think that it is important to *act* as though what I can do matters. In a sense, this takes the same act of faith that good writing takes, with the emphasis on doing rather than having, imagining that my primary goal is to have learned something by the end."

ଊ ୨୧

KATHLEEN GEORGE, born and raised in Johnstown, Pennsylvania, received her B.A. and Ph.D. degrees at The University of Pittsburgh where she is an Associate Professor in the Theater Department. She is the author of *Rhythm in Drama* and has directed numerous plays. She has recently completed the Masters of Fine Arts Program at The University of Pittsburgh, completing a collection of short stories.

ଊ ୨୧

BARBARA H. HUDSON was born in 1956 in El Paso, Texas. After studying biology at Vanderbilt University, she studied nursing in Vanderbuilt's School of

Nursing before realizing that her primary interest was in literature and writing. In 1984 she received a B.A. degree from Belmont College in Nashville and her Masters of Fine Arts degree in writing at The University of Pittsburgh in 1989. She has said, "In the process of reading and living and listening to others read, I grew to value written words and to discover the struggle and delight of using them myself."

CYNTHIA KADOHATA was born in Chicago in 1956 and has lived in Georgia, Arkansas, Michigan, California, and New York City where, after a year in The Masters of Fine Arts Program at The University of Pittsburgh, she studied writing at Columbia University. Her stories have appeared in *The New Yorker* and *Grand Street*. Her novel *The Floating World* was published in 1989 by Viking Press. She has said, "I really don't know whether I can say how I came to write fiction. Choices are laid out in front of you, and there's one that you *desire*. It becomes an obsession, so you do it."

GARNETT KILBERG began writing as a newspaper reporter while attending college on a part-time basis. In 1981 she returned to college on a full-time basis and graduated in 1982 from The University of Cincinnati. In 1985 she graduated from the Masters of Fine Arts Program in Writing at The University of Pittsburgh. Her fiction has appeared in *Chicago Magazine, Pittsburgh Magazine,* and *The Literary Review*. She is currently teaching world literature and computer-assisted composition at Columbia College in Chicago and creative writing at Harper College, also in Chicago.

DANIEL LOWE was born in Bloomington, Indiana in 1957. After receiving a B.A. degree from Western Michigan University in Kalamazoo, he entered the Masters of Fine Arts Program at The University of Pittsburgh, receiving the MFA in 1983. He has taught freshman composition for five years at Indiana University in Indiana, Pennsylvania. Among his publications are stories, poetry, and essays in *The Wisconsin Review; The Rhode Island Review Quarterly; The Montana Review; The Long Pond Review; Spitball;* and *Notes on Teaching English*.

JAMES MCCOMMONS has studied photography in Boston and creative writing in the undergraduate writing program at The University of Pittsburgh. He has worked as a reporter in Wyoming, Michigan, Minnesota, and Rochester, New York. He currently lives in Syracuse, New York. He has said, "I'd recommend newspaper writing to recent college graduates who need to write every day. I didn't earn much money, but journalism allowed me to earn a living as a writer, and the people I met and the experiences I had are finding their way into my fiction." McCommons was born in 1957.

JANE MCCAFFERTY was born in Wilmington, Delaware in 1960 and graduated from The University of Delaware in 1983. She received her Masters of Fine Arts in Writing in 1989 from The University of Pittsburgh. One of her stories won the *Mademoiselle* Fiction Award in 1986 and other stories have been published in *The New England Review*.

BARBARA MELLIX, an Assistant to the undergraduate dean at The University of Pittsburgh, was born in 1945 in Greeleyville, South Carolina, where she lived on a cotton and tobacco farm with her parents and ten sisters and brothers until 1964 when she moved to Pittsburgh, Pennsylvania. She currently lives in Pittsburgh with her husband (whom she married in 1968) and their two children. She received her B.A. in 1984 and her masters of Fine Arts in Writing in 1986, both from The University of Pittsburgh.

DAVID MARTIN was born in Kalamazoo, Michigan in 1955. He received his BA in English from Western Michigan University in 1979 and his Masters of Fine Arts in Writing in 1983 from The University of Pittsburgh. He has published fiction and poetry in a number of literary journals. He is an academic advisor for the University of Wisconsin at Milwaukee, where he also teaches writing.

CATHERINE D. MILLER, a graduate of the Masters of Fine Arts Writing Program at The University of Pittsburgh, has published fiction in *The Apalachee Quarterly; Confrontation; North Dakota Quarterly;* and *Sinister Wisdom*. Of her essay, she has said, "I wrote it as a self-examination of why *I* want to follow the traditional mode in my own story writing."

JULIANNE MOORE was born in Charleston, West Virginia in 1959, and is the oldest of three children. When she was sixteen, she moved, and lived with another family in Orlando, Florida, where she completed her high school education. As an undergraduate, she attended both Marshall University and West Virginia State College, and she recently received her MFA in creative writing from the University of Pittsburgh. She has worked in restaurants, in office supplies, and hair salons.

LINDA MIZEJEWSKI was born in 1952 in a small mill town near Pittsburgh. She has said, "My father drove a truck for a paper company and he often brought home ruler-lined yellow tablets that had been damaged in shipment. As I was learning to read, these wonderful tablets in the house seemed like a specific reason to write, too. I can't remember a time when doing both wasn't the best entertainment." She holds a Ph.D degree in literature and a Masters in creative writing. She has published articles on women writers, modernism, and film theory as well as essays on her travels. She has published several dozen poems and a poetry chapbook.

INGRID MUNDARI was born in Trinidad in 1955 and educated first in a convent school and later at The University of Pittsburgh where she is currently writing her doctoral dissertation in English literature. She has published stories in a number of journals, including *The Bridge; Riverrun;* and *The Brooklyn Review*. She has said, "My years in Convent School were especially valuable, for my teachers, believing as they did that the way in which one spoke influenced the way in which one wrote, enabled me to perceive the symbiosis between the way I was being taught to speak, my reading, and my writing."

KATHRYN M. MONAHAN was born in West Germany in 1956. As a child, she traveled extensively, due to her father's career in the Army. Her family relocated in West Virginia when she was thirteen, and she remained there until her graduation from college. Currently, she resides in Pittsburgh, Pennsylvania, where she works as an operating room nurse and studies writing and literature at the University of Pittsburgh. She attributes her interest in writing to her mother's influence and her stay in West Virginia.

MIN-ZHAN LU was born in Shanghai, the People's Republic of China. She came to Pittsburgh in 1981 for graduate work in literature at The University of Pittsburgh and received her Ph.D. in 1989. She teaches literature at Drake University while also writing fiction.

MARK L. SHELTON was born in 1958 in Chicago and received his BA in English from Western Michigan University and the Masters of Fine Arts in Writing from The University of Pittsburgh. After receiving the degree, he worked in public relations at Presbyterian University Hospital where he met Dr. Peter Jannetta and became interested in Dr. Jannetta's work. Leaving public relations work, he concentrated on researching and writing a book on Dr. Jannetta, *Working in a Very Small Place,* which was published in 1989 by W. W. Norton. Along the way, he turned a freelance writing assignment at *Pittsburgh Magazine* into a full-time job as Associate Editor. Currently he resides in Athens, Ohio and edits and writes for *Ohio Magazine.*

ଔ ໖

KEVIN STEMMLER was born in Latrobe, Pennsylvania in 1959 and received his BA and Masters in Literature from Indiana University of Pennsylvania. He is currently enrolled in the Ph.D. program in literature at The University of Pittsburgh, where he has also taken courses in fiction writing and taught both literature and composition.

ଔ ໖

KAREN SWENSON was born in New York in 1936 and raised in Westchester County. She attended Barnard College and received her MA from New York University. She has taught at City College of New York for 20 years, except during a five year period during which she taught across the country, at Clark University, Skidmore College, The University of Idaho, Denver University, and Scripps College. She has been published in *The New Yorker; The New York Times; The Nation; Saturday Review.* She has published two volumes of poetry, *An Attic of Ideals* and *East-West.* A third volume is forthcoming..